Occult Bibliography:

An Annotated List of Books Published in English, 1971 through 1975

by

THOMAS C. CLARIE

The Scarecrow Press, Inc.
Metuchen, N.J. & London
1978

Library of Congress Cataloging in Publication Data

Clarie, Thomas C 1943-
Occult bibliography.

Includes indexes.
1. Occult sciences--Bibliography. 2. Psychical research--Bibliography. I. Title. [DNLM: 1. Occultism--Abstracts. Z6876 C591o 1971-75]
Z6876.C56 [BF1411] 016.133 78-17156
ISBN 0-8108-1152-9

Manufactured in the United States of America

Dedicated to

JOSEPH W. OGLE

of Wallingford, Conn.

ACKNOWLEDGMENTS

The author would like to thank: William Coulombe, whose casual interest and enthusiastic questioning led to an unintentional arousal of the author's desire to work; friends Michael DelSole, Timothy Horan, and Edward Moore for their support; my parents, T. Emmet and Gertrude Clarie, who always treated me with loving care on my weekends home, while I plagued them with my file cards, eraser flakes, and leaking pens; and, finally, Joseph W. Ogle, to whom this book is dedicated--for his faith and friendship.

TABLE OF CONTENTS

GENERAL PURPOSE
OF THIS WORK

This book has been designed to fulfill five major functions:

(1) to control (make retrievable) published information on the occult by the three classic approaches of author, title, and subject;

(2) through providing all possible bibliographic information for each item listed, to give numerous leads to researchers where all other research tools fail;

(3) to allow browsing and discovering in the occult field by means of the rich body of work here listed;

(4) through annotations, to give the researcher enough information on a book to know if he wishes or needs to read the work itself; and

(5) to serve as a buying guide for libraries, associations, institutions, and individuals, by means of asterisks, first-line comments in each annotation, and the Most Important Occult Books section.

NEED FOR THIS WORK

The aim of this work is to attempt some control of the great volume of occult literature that has been published over the last few years. Access to such material is important not just to occult fanatics, but to scientific researchers, social scientists, writers, and all other inquiring souls. Except for this bibliography, many of the items listed here might be forever lost.

OTHER OCCULT BIBLIOGRAPHIES

At present, there are two fine bibliographies available that touch on the occult field: White and Dale's Parapsychology: Sources of Information (Scarecrow Press, 1973) and Robert Ashby's Guide Book for the Study of Psychical Research (Samuel Weiser, 1972).

However, the main coverage of both is in the area of parapsychology--only one aspect of the occult.

Furthermore, both works discuss relatively few books. White and Dale mention 282 works, all annotated. Ashby discusses 269 works, only 82 annotated. The Clarie bibliography covers about 1,850 books, of which 68 per cent are annotated.

White and Dale's cut-off date is basically 1971; only 10 titles are listed that were published in 1972. Ashby's cut-off date is 1970. The Clarie bibliography covers books published or reissued from 1971 through 1975. As for true occult bibliographies, there is really nothing. Phillips's Occult Bibliography (Gordon Press, 1975) could not be found for reviewing. It seens impossible to order from jobbers or the publisher. Popenoe's Books for Inner Development (Random House, 1976) is essentially a bookstore catalog for the Yes! Bookshop in Washington, D. C., and emphasizes Eastern religion and health books more than the occult. Its concept and scope thus severely limit its use as an occult bibliography. However, the Popenoe work is exceptionally well-done.

For all the above reasons, this work will definitely fill a vast gap in the field of occult research.

GENERAL LIBRARY CUMULATIVES

There are several vast cumulations which attempt to list all books published in certain time periods for certain countries. However these general cumulatives are very expensive, from $100 for the most awkward to $2000 for the most useful. Because these works cover all published books, one cannot browse from cover-to-cover. These general works usually cover only American or British books; the Clarie bibliography covers both, and even includes a few Canadian, Australian, and Indian items.

Subject headings are average to very poor in the general cumulatives. Some occult works are not picked up by them. The present work does not stop with ordinary library tools, but includes the results of searching through occult journals and bookstores. The best of the general cumulations has no title index. The Clarie bibliography not only adds a title index, but provides coverage by joint editor, editor, compiler, pseudonym, illustrator, photographer, translator, and writer of preface or introduction.

The Clarie bibliography is annotated. This is especially valuable in the occult field, because many books are not reviewed in regular library sources. For some books, it is literally impossible to find a review anywhere. Without this work, the reader would have to buy most of the less popular works to find what is in them. With all information in one volume, the reader will find opened up to him or her the whole body of occult literature to study carefully and at leisure. The indexes and annotations will lead the researcher to hundreds of books he or she would perhaps otherwise never have noticed.

HOW TO USE THIS WORK

MAIN SECTION

The main section of the work is arranged alphabetically by author (or by title if there is no author) and the entries are serially numbered. These numbers are cited in the indexes.

AUTHOR INDEX

The first index is arranged by author, joint author, editor, composer, translator, illustrator, photographer, and introduction-, preface-, or postscript-writer. One will be given entry numbers in this index that refer to all books that a person has had any part in, even if he or she is not the main author of that book.

TITLE INDEX

The second index is by title. If a work has been reissued under a new title, the reader is sent to the correct entry by looking under either title. If a work first appeared in a foreign language, the original title will be found in this index, which sends one to the English translated title entry. If the title was only a part of a book, the index sends one to the main book. All initial articles (the, a, an) have been dropped from this index.

SUBJECT INDEX

The subject index is placed last for ease of access. It is a major part of this work and is intended to be of great use to libraries and researchers who fail to find occult books through other sources.

No subject index this writer has ever used is truly adequate, let alone perfect. The choice of subject headings causes the problem. Standard library subject headings are often so unbending and formal that they are useless (one humorous one: OCEANS--CURIOSA instead of BERMUDA TRIANGLE). Also, they become convenient catch-alls; how many thousands of occult works have as their only official library heading, "Occult Sciences" or "Psychical Research." Such headings do not exactly unlock the content of a book to potential readers!

However, overuse of informal headings can make a subject index so spread out and miscellaneous as to fail to bring materials together for the researcher.

In this work, a shaky compromise has been employed, with both formal headings and more convenient ones used. "Voice Phenomenon" may be forbidden in library use, but it is essential in occult research, for example.

ANNOTATIONS POLICY

To attempt a scientific criticism of the facts in each book of an occult bibliography is a fatal error. The very reason all these books fall into the "occult" field is that their reality is a mystery to us. To review a book about ghosts or alchemy and call the book ignorant trash because the reviewer is sure both fields are fake is the height of conceit and stupidity.

Therefore, although no criticism will be found in this bibliography concerning the nature of the contents of any book, criticism <u>has</u> been made on the depth of research, the author's credentials, the arrangement of the work, and the style of writing.

The content of a book is of major importance. Researchers want to know exactly what is in a work before they then determine for themselves what they can accept as valid. Therefore, a strong attempt has been made to indicate clearly what a book discusses. If possible, some or all of the chapter headings will be listed. If a chapter heading keys on a person's name, and the chapter is of significant length, that chapter topic has in most cases been listed in the subject index.

Any specific information on what general group of readers a book was written for will be mentioned--for example, juveniles; adepts in the field; or laypersons.

The order of comments within an annotation will be roughly as follows. The first line is set aside for the key statement about the book. If it is an excellent work, it will contain the sentence, "This work is a major new contribution to occult literature" (reprints would not qualify for this remark). The first line may indicate a book that is very good in a narrower sense (excellent graphically, for younger children, a classic in the field, or a good survey of the literature). Or, the first line may be a simple summary of the book's scope and aim. The author's credentials and background, if known, are then given, followed by the contents of the work. Any criticism the book has attracted in reviews or among readers or users in the field, or this reviewer's criticism, follows. A note about any specific readership for which the book was intended is placed last.

CRITERIA FOR EXCELLENCE

("Excellence" here means: annotated with the introductory phrase, "major new contribution to occult literature"; and/or preceded with an asterisk or asterisks; and/or listed in the Most Important Occult Books. In decreasing order of importance, the criteria are (1) the number of major book-reviewing journals which discuss the work; (2) the number of major occult periodicals which review the work; (3) the lengths of the reviews; (4) the depth of the work itself, and the care with which it is written; (5) the credentials of the author; and (6) the credentials of the publisher.

USE OF THIS BIBLIOGRAPHY AS A SELECTION AID

There are three devices (excluding the Subject Index) that can be used as selection aids:

(1) Those books introduced by the words "major new contribution ..." have three asterisks (***) immediately below their entry numbers. This is to make it easy to spot them without having

to skim the whole work looking for that phrase in the first line of each annotation. Libraries and collectors should definitely try to stock most of these *** books; 104 works (6 per cent) are so marked. Those books that are, as indicated by the annotation, strongly recommended have one asterisk (*) immediately below their entry numbers; 360 works (20 per cent) are so marked.

(2) The Most Important Occult Books lists, by year, those books considered most important for that year. All of these books should definitely be stocked.

(3) One can skim the first lines of the annotations to focus on exactly what is the value of a book. Further, one can read the entire annotation if it is deemed necessary.

SCOPE OF THIS BIBLIOGRAPHY

Basic coverage: any work newly published or reissued during the five years, 1971 through 1975. An attempt was made to list all American and British books published during that period, with some coverage of other English-language books (Canadian, Australian, and Indian). There were some exclusions: if a work failed to meet any of the "criteria for excellence," and was not reviewed by any magazine, and was not found in any bookstore, it was purposely excluded. This is dangerous in a bibliography that seeks to be comprehensive; however, it seemed essential in order to avoid works that may indeed have been pure science fiction.

There were two works included that did not fall within the 1971-1975 time frame. The encyclopedia Man, Myth and Magic (item 1070) came out in 1970. Yet, because it is so important, and is still being marketed in 1978, it is listed. The Catalogue of the Library of the [British] Society for Psychical Research (item 215) came out in 1976. However, it, too, is so important a work that it is listed here.

FEATURES OF THE SUBJECT INDEX

Certain headings in the subject index do not denote subjects, but rather types of literature. The major ones are Reference,

Juvenile, Autobiography, Biography, Theses, and Bibliography (citing entry numbers of all books with bibliographies over two pages long).

MOST IMPORTANT OCCULT BOOKS

For a book to appear on this list in a given year, it must be newly published as an original work in English for that year, except that the first list gives the most important books issued 1971-1975 that were originally published before 1971.

MISCELLANEOUS

Different editions of a work are listed together under one annotation. Horoscope publications with twelve parts (one for each birth sign) are listed as one set, with twelve volumes contained within that one work. Annuals are listed as one work, unless they are significantly different each year.

The reliability of the bibliographic information is only as good as the sources used. Although "official" and supposedly trustworthy sources were used, numerous errors occurred in these tools. This writer caught many of them. He apologizes for any he failed to spot, and especially for any he has created himself!

Some libraries balk at purchasing bibliographies such as this work, since they lack most of the books it lists, and fear it will only anger patrons when they find they cannot put their hands on the books they want in 30 seconds. This reasoning is faulty. It is precisely those libraries with small collections that should emphasize bibliographies, so that their patrons are aware of what exists nationally. Then, through interlibrary loan, a book may very likely be obtainable from another library. Waiting time is usually two to six weeks. If the local library is not large enough to handle all the requests the patron has, the patron can perhaps find a friend to get them from a college library. Used in conjunction with interlibrary loan services, bibliographies such as the present one literally open up the libraries of the United States to the delighted patron's use.

Some readers of this bibliography may be angered at the inclusion of works on psychical research (parapsychology). They will argue that the occult and parapsychology are totally foreign to each other, one being, say, an art, and the other, a science. We could not disagree more. Parapsychologists have made the fundamental error of ignoring occult/spiritualist phenomena that is actually parallel, even identical, to their own work. The last few years have seen a gradual merging of the two areas. UFO's have now become "other reality levels"; witches on brooms are now said to have experienced astral projection or out-of-the-body experiences; mediums' communications from the beyond are now called "super-ESP," while the trance used to get the messages is called an "altered state of consciousness." We do not attempt to discredit parapsychology by joining it to the occult. We merely seek to reflect reality--especially where it will be in twenty years.

INTRODUCTION

Working in the field of the occult is definitely not for the weak of heart. The unknown is frightening to the most confirmed cynic--and there is so much that is unknown, now and perhaps forever. A simple bibliographer is no more immune to unusual phenomena than a researcher deeply immersed in work at the front lines. The skimming of hundreds of books can transform keen insight into visions, and make lazy dreams joltingly close to astral projection.

Nor is this field one for the easily discouraged. The literature of the occult is extremely diverse and unwieldy. A potential researcher sees a body of knowledge seemingly inaccessible to the grasp. The field remains a true bibliographic wasteland.

This is due in large part to the difficulty in defining the term "occult." This writer would define it as an event or series of events supernatural or extra-natural to man, the sources or reasons for which can be determined by any human gifted or sensitive enough, and particularly, by any person willing to devote the necessary patience to fathoming the system of the universe that is behind all events.

Nearly all areas of knowledge could be placed in this field. Theology falls into it easily, as do such areas as physics and mathematics. Psychology, sociology, and anthropology are obvious companions. The study of such phenomena as the existence of auras keeps shifting almost yearly between the occult and scientific worlds. It is a state of mind more than a study of a particular subject area. Some contact with the Universal Power itself--not with some long-standing religious doctrine, historical principle or scientific school--is the key ingredient here. The most meaningful way to study the occult is to approach it as a whole, attempting both to discover the universe's unifying system and to apply it to one's life.

This is what is so fascinating about the occult field. In it, people put together theology, philosophy, science, history, scholarly research, personal experience and intellect. Out of this mixture they can evolve a highly personal method for coping confidently with the universe in their daily lives.

Unfortunately, such individualism has left us with a bibliographic nightmare in the field of the occult. No two books have quite the same depth, level, and area of coverage. Each writer tells his own highly personal tale and evolves his own philosophical system. The researcher in the occult field has often been left with a large, musty pile of autobiographies and personal diaries--and little else.

At times, occult works have seemed to fall into two areas. First, there were works written by deranged maniacs who apparently did their "research" in graveyards under full moons, or between table changes at an afternoon bridge club meeting. Secondly, there were the books done by journalists who were either too gullible or too cynical to write sensibly. Between these two extremes--the sick autobiographical tome and the slick, yellow-paged "pot-boiler"--there had been little.

Recently, however, we have seen a change in occult literature. Many journalists are now daring to do extensive research. Psychic researchers are writing deep, scholarly works. Scientists from other disciplines are today crossing over into the occult field and offering creative, exciting new views of life in the universe. Enough fine material is being published that a comprehensive bibliography in the field is warranted and necessary.

As this bibliography commences, however, it is wise that both bibliographer and researcher keep one thought in mind. The final aim of all true occult research throughout the ages, from alchemist to physicist, has been for personal illumination and inspiration. Salvation, and not publication, is the final goal. Thus, the occult, contrary to fervent wishes and volumes of words, will remain esoteric--and eternally enticing to researchers and bibliographers.

SURVEY OF OCCULT BOOKS, 1971-1975

(A brief discussion of the big stories in the occult field over the last five years, in descending order of importance)

GELLER

It may seem inappropriate to select a person as the most important story instead of an exciting concept. However, Uri Geller has had a greater impact on the media and the scientific community than anyone else in the last five years. This former Israeli magician has done it all: bent spoons over British airwaves, subjected himself to strict tests at Stanford Research Institute, and even won over such conservative scientific journals as Nature. The cry of "Hoax" follows him everywhere. Yet he and his agent Puharich have still kept the respect of many--even more remarkable when one remembers Geller's statements that he is controlled by extraterrestrial intelligences.

BERMUDA TRIANGLE

This area of ocean off the United States has sold books and movies carrying its theme. (This writer even has an "I Traveled the Triangle" shirt from Bermuda.) Actually, the only truly frightening disappearances involved two airplane incidents over 20 years ago. Authors of the Triangle books, however, toss into their writings any ship or plane that vanished in the entire Atlantic over the last thousand years! Still, the topic makes for exciting reading. There well may be some natural phenomenon there and at selected ocean spots around the world that causes time warps or funnels.

EXORCISM

The movie (and novel) entitled The Exorcist has encouraged the publication of numerous books on demonology, possession, and exorcism. The topic has had some quiet interest in England for years, but in the United States it seems terrifyingly new. More than any other topic, it points up the philosophy of the occult field: it makes little difference whether you call possession the work of the Devil (religion), Evil (philosophy), schizophrenia (psychology), or glandular imbalance (physiology). The occult field simply knows it as a phenomenon--who cares what it is called. It exists, and the occult sciences try and "package" it in a symbolic form the human mind can understand.

EXTRATERRESTRIAL VISITATIONS IN THE PAST (Von Däniken)

Von Däniken has been the prime mover in getting across this point of view to the public. Many of these theories have been assimilated from Kolosimo, Bergier, Fort, Le Poer Trench, and many others. The basic thought is that much of our history has been directly influenced by visits of spaceships from other stars. Evidence used in these discussions comes from the Bible and other scriptures, and archaeological research at sites in the Holy Land, Egypt, and South America. As of 1978, some severe criticism of Von Däniken has been raised. One writer viewed his research as not partially, but "totally fabricated from inaccurate sources." No matter how the argument comes out, no one can doubt the impact Von Däniken has had. Mistaken or not, he has attempted to find a unified theory, and deserves credit for the attempt.

PSYCHIC SURGERY

Here is yet another occult category filled with controversy and cries of "Fraud!" The field is not new. Puharich was investigating the most famous such surgeon, Arigo, back in the 1960's. However, only with the publication of Arigo in 1973 by Fuller did the storm break. For all of 1973, England's Psychic News repeatedly splashed pictures of "operations" across its front page. As of 1978, the furor has died a bit. Many claims that psychic surgeons faked cutting, and used animal tissue to show what they supposedly cut out, dampened their credibility.

BIORHYTHMS

The books discussing this topic propose that there are mental, physical, and emotional high and low points to a person's months. These can be charted accurately and far in advance of events, allowing an individual to do important things on his best days. Charts have been done on golfers and football players explaining why they lost or won the big one. The theory is now so well accepted that sports commentators mention it regularly.

ACUPUNCTURE

This field has gone from an occult one to a scientific one in the last five years. The thawing of Chinese-American relations has allowed doctors in the West to get a true idea of what has been going on these thousands of years in Chinese medicine. Already in the United States, there are many acupuncture clinics with a thriving business. However, the field still has important occult ramifications, since the medicine is practiced on the basis of psychic energy points surfacing at various areas on the human body. (Biofeedback is another area that has moved almost entirely into the scientific area; that is why it is not discussed here.)

PYRAMID POWER

In the most recent publications, the topic refers to small pyramids that can be manufactured to scale in accordance with the Great Pyramid of Egypt. Done in this scale, the models seem to create forces inside the structure that keep razor blades sharp and vegetables fresh. The hope is that sleeping or working under such a structure will enhance life. In its broader implications, pyramid power also refers to the real-size structures in Egypt, especially the Great Pyramid. Chief attention is paid to the dimensions of the structure, and the use to which it may have been put.

ASTRAL PROJECTION (Out-of-the-Body Experience)

Of all the fields listed in this survey, this is growing perhaps most quickly as of 1978. The phenomenon is one that perhaps all humans can accomplish. It is simple, yet has important ramifications in many fields. Some scientists call it merely a dream or an hallucination. Whatever it is, the phenomenon of leaving your body and being able to look down at it, then travel far away and later return is an exciting one.

MOMENT OF DEATH

This area is allied to astral projection at times. Yet its philosophical and religious nature demands that it be considered separately. More and more research, particularly of the case study type, is being done in this field. Attempts are being made to find similar phenomena occurring at the moment of death, and then codify them. Stories of views of the "other side," or visits from the hereafter, are the only real evidence we have of a life after this. Hence, one can understand the deep satisfaction felt by researchers in this area.

VOICE PHENOMENON

The experience of picking up the voices of dead spirits on tape recordings dates back at least to the mid-sixties. Only in the last several years, however, has word of it reached the English-speaking public. It requires careful technique, the proper apparatus, and a very keen ear (not to mention patience).

ALTERED STATES OF CONSCIOUSNESS/ TRANSPERSONAL PSYCHOLOGY

Obviously, moment of death and astral projection have a place here. What is mainly meant in this category, however, is the unified study of all the possibilities for human consciousness. Such studies have mainly been personal quests by scientists to experience all states of consciousness and perhaps reach a final supreme state from which they can properly view the others. Often, the search has been strongly aided by drugs (Timothy Leary and Carlos Castaneda). It can take strange twists (witness the life of dolphin researcher John Lilly). It can even result in a fine scholarly journal, the Journal of Transpersonal Psychology. The personal quest is always, however, long, very dangerous, and offering no promises or guarantees.

BIGFOOT

Theory has it that a creature comparable to the yeti of the Himalayas exists in the great Northwest of the United States. At times, attempts are made to tie in the creature's existence to flying saucer landings, with their occasional reports of hairy creatures. As yet, there seems no truly hard evidence to support the theory. As for loose evidence--there is lots of it.

KIRLIAN PHOTOGRAPHY

This area is trying hard to gain total scientific acceptance, but still has not accomplished it. By now, it is obvious that, with the proper apparatus, a leaf or human hand can be photographed so as to show an aura around the object. This aura seems to vary according to the emotional state of the object (perhaps similar to mood rings). Supposedly, people such as Matthew Manning can focus their energies so as to make the photo show a pinpoint aura. Criticism has been leveled a bit at the Kirlian method. Just because a photographic procedure results in a certain phenomenon, that does not show that it means anything. Nevertheless, it is an important phenomenon, and does appear to be steadily gaining scientific acceptance, however limited.

DREAM RESEARCH

Research has been going on for years on the purpose and significance of dreams. At places such as the Maimonides Dream Laboratory, a new twist has been added. As reported by such books as Ullman, Krippner and Vaughan's Dream Telepathy, research is progressing on whether dreams form a means of subconscious communication.

U.S.S.R.

Chiefly through Ostrander and Schroeder's works, it is becoming obvious that the Soviet Union and other Communist nations are devoting quite a bit of time and money in studying psychic and even occult phenomena.

PLANTS

Tompkins and Bird's Secret Life of Plants has been perhaps the most talked-about occult work of the last five years. The authors presented evidence that plant life can receive telepathic messages from humans, and also pick up vibrations and moods. Some critics pointed out that when researchers tried to duplicate Backster's lie detector results (evidence Tompkins and Bird relied heavily on), they failed. However, try telling that to the residents of the Findhorn Community in Scotland. Supposedly, through maintaining proper mental outlook toward plants, the residents have been able to obtain mammoth-size vegetables in worthless, sandy soil. The debate thus goes on.

MOST IMPORTANT OCCULT BOOKS

Published Before 1971 and Reprinted 1971-1975

1. Man, Myth and Magic (1070)
2. Fodor. Encyclopaedia of Psychic Science (522)
3. Von Däniken. Chariots of the Gods? (363)
4. Ostrander and Schroeder. Psychic Discoveries behind the Iron Curtain (1214)
5. Michell. View over Atlantis (1117)
6. Hansen. Witchcraft at Salem (677)
7. Sanderson. Invisible Residents (1456)
8. Godwin. This Baffling World (586)
9. Pauwels and Bergier. Morning of the Magicians (1249)
10. Fort. The Complete Books of Charles Fort (527)

Published in 1971

1. Wilson. The Occult (1820)
2. Raudive. Breakthrough (1334)
3. Thomas. Religion and the Decline of Magic (1670)
4. Castenada. A Separate Reality (212)
5. Pearce. The Crack in the Cosmic Egg (1251)
6. Bayless. The Other Side of Death (76)
7. Brown. Unfinished Symphonies (157)
8. Ellwood. Psychic Visits to the Past (469)
9. Russell. Design for Destiny (1421)
10. Montgomery. The World Beyond (1134)

Published in 1972

1. Tenhaeff. Telepathy and Clairvoyance (1665)
2. Roll. The Poltergeist (1398)

3. Shumaker. Occult Sciences in the Renaissance (1500)
4. Koestler. The Roots of Coincidence (901)
5. Sanderson. Investigating the Unexplained (1455)
6. UFO's--A Scientific Debate, ed. by Sagan and Page (1712)
7. Ashby. Guide Book for the Study of Psychical Research (40)
8. Michell. City of Revelation (1115)
9. Napier. Bigfoot (1157)
10. Pearsall. Table-Rappers (1255)

Published in 1973

1. Tompkins and Bird. The Secret Life of Plants (1686)
2. White and Dale. Parapsychology: Sources of Information (1807)
3. Ullman, Krippner, and Vaughan. Dream Telepathy (1713)
4. Vaughan. Patterns of Prophecy (1742)
5. Gauquelin. Cosmic Influences on Human Behavior (566)
6. Jacobson. Life without Death? (810)
7. Sargant. Mind Possessed (1458)
8. Pratt. ESP Research Today (1298)
9. Brier. Precognition and the Philosophy of Science (143)
10. Holiday. The Dragon and the Disc (729)

Published in 1974

1. Psychic Exploration (Mitchell), ed. by White (1313)
2. Fuller. Arigo (548)
3. Berlitz and Valentine. The Bermuda Triangle (99)
4. Klass. UFO's Explained (888)
5. LeShan. The Medium, the Mystic, and the Physicist (988)
6. Rogo. The Experience of Phantoms (1392)
7. Talamonti. Forbidden Universe (1652)
8. MacKenzie. The Riddle of the Future (1047)
9. Manning. Link: Mathew Manning's Own Story ... (1076)
10. Moss. The Probability of the Impossible (1143)

Published in 1975

1. Geller. Uri Geller; My Story (568)
2. Krippner. The Song of the Siren (907)
3. Kusche. The Bermuda Triangle Mystery--Solved (923)
4. Rhine. Psi, What Is It? (1364)
5. Christopher. Mediums, Mystics and the Occult (247)
6. Swann. To Kiss Earth Good-bye (1643)
7. Hynek and Vallee. The Edge of Reality (797)
8. Rogo. Parapsychology: A Century of Inquiry (1395)
9. Black. Ekstasy (104)
10. Green and McCreery. Apparitions (621)

THE BIBLIOGRAPHY

1 Abayakoon, Cyrus D. F. Astro-palmistry: Signs and Seals of the Hand. Illus. by Dorothy Abayakoon. New York: ASI Publishers, 1975. $15 LC 75-7187 ISBN 0-88231-012-7

2 Abd-Ru-Shin. In the Light of Truth: The Grail Message. 2nd ed. 3 vols. Vomperberg: Alexander Bernhardt Pub. Co.; London: Grail Foundation, 1971-1975 (previous ed. of this translation, 1954-1959). (Translation of "Im Lichte der Wahrheit." Munich: Verlag der Ruf, 1931) Vol. 1, 236p. £1.75 ISBN 0-902307-06-1; vol. 3, 512p. £4 ISBN 3-87860-069-0

3 ________. Questions and Answers, 1924-1937. Vomperberg: Alexander Bernhardt Pub. Co.; London: Grail Foundation, 1972. 232p. Index (Translation of "Fragenbeantwortungen." Vomperberg: Bernhardt, 1953) £1.20 ISBN 0-902307-08-8

4 Abraham ben Simeon, of Worms, 15th cent. The Book of the Sacred Magic of Abramelin the Mage, as Delivered by Abraham the Jew unto His Son Lamech, A.D. 1458. Trans. from the original Hebrew into the French, and now rendered into English by S. L. MacGregor Mathers. New York: Dover Publications, 1975 (also, New York: Causeway Books, 1975; reprint of the 2nd ed., London: J. M. Watkins, 1900). xlviii, 268p. Illus. $3.50 pa. LC 75-12248 ISBN 0-486-23211-5

This work is supposedly the authentic magic manual of a Jewish magician of the Middle Ages, translated from a rare manuscript in the Bibliothèque de l'Arsenal in Paris. It has the reputation of being a genuine and powerful magical manual. The first part, "Advice and Autobiography," is addressed by the author to his son. The second section discusses the means of obtaining magical powers (preparation before practice, time, place, how to address spirits). The third part covers the application of these powers to produce magical results. It consists mostly of word square diagrams ("symbolic pentacles"). The book has a very complete list of names of spirits to be contacted.

5 Académie Nationale de Médecine, Paris. Report of the Experiments on Animal Magnetism. Ed. by J. C. Colquhoun. New York: Arno Press, 1975 (reprint of the orig. ed., Edinburgh: R. Cadell, 1833). (Perspectives in Psychical Research) $15 LC 75-7371 ISBN 0-405-07022-5

This book discusses the mental phenomena occurring during somnambulism (which they called animal magnetism at that time). It is the work of the Medical Section of the French Royal Academy of Sciences. The committee was appointed in 1825, and read its final report at the meetings of the 21st and 28th of June, 1831. The work studies clairvoyance, and attempts to diagnose conditions in people psychically while in sleep state. Their conclusion was that the phenomena were real, and of possible future medical use. This reprint adds an historical and explanatory introduction, and an appendix. This book is not an important acquisition, except as a document.

6 Adam, B. Astrology: The Ancient Conspiracy. Bethany Fellowship, 1973. $.95 pa.

7 Adam, C. G. M. Occult Astrology. London: L. N. Fowler, 1971 (orig. pub., London: Modern Astrology, 1939). 225p. Illus. £1 ISBN 0-85243-214-3

8 Adams, Evangeline Smith, 1872?-1932. Astrology; Your Place Among the Stars. New York: Dell, 1972 (orig. pub., 1930). x, 478p. $1.25 pa.

9 ________. Astrology: Your Place in the Sun. London: Muller, 1971 (orig. pub., New York: Dodd, Mead and Co., 1928). xxiii, 343p. Illus. 2 ISBN 0-584-10015-9

10 Adams, William Henry Davenport, 1828-1891. Witch, Warlock and Magician; Historical Sketches of Magic and Witchcraft in England and Scotland. Detroit: Gale Research Co., 1973 (reprint of orig. ed., New York: J. W. Bouton, 1899). $17.50 LC 70-141746

This is a good historical survey of magic and witchcraft in England and Scotland, with major concentration on the 17th century. Discussions include the following as subjects: Roger Bacon, Dr. John Dee, William Lilly, English Rosicrucians, Janet Wishart, James I, Matthew Hopkins, witches of Taunton, witches of Aberdeen, Dr. Lambe, Edward Kelly, decline of witchcraft in England, the literature of witchcraft.

11 Addey, John M. Astrology Reborn. The 2nd C. E. O. Carter Memorial Lecture delivered at the Astrological Association Conference, Fitzwilliam College, Cambridge, England, September, 1971. Bournemouth, England: Astrological Association, 1973. 23p. Illus. (Carter Memorial Lectures) £0.35 ISBN 0-9502658-2-9

12 Adleman, Robert H., 1919- . Black Box; An Excursion into Inner Sensory Perception. Los Angeles: Nash Pub., 1973. 170p. Bibliog.

The title of this book comes from a term some neurosurgeons

and psychiatrists give to the part of the brain that still remains a mystery to them. The author does not feel that the occult has anything to do with the mystery. He believes more in ISP (inner sensory perception) than in ESP. He notes that the Russians study ESP in relation to physics and biochemistry, not in terms of psychology. He believes that no real progress will come in understanding the mind's mysteries until the West forgets fields such as reincarnation, apparitions, precognition, and faith healing. The work is loosely structured, short, and reads like a theoretical essay.

13 Agrippa von Nettesheim, Heinrich Cornelius, 1486?-1535. Philosophy of Natural Magic. New foreword by Leslie Shepard. Secaucus, N.J.: University Books, 1974 (reprint of orig. ed., Chicago: De Laurence, Scott, 1913). 307p. Illus. (Translation of Book I of "De Occulta Philosophia." Köln, 1533) $8.95 LC 74-196072 ISBN 0-8216-0218-7

This handbook discusses natural magic, white magic, black magic, spells, divination, sorcery, unctions, and love medicines.

14 ________. Three Books of Occult Philosophy or Magic. Ed. in part by Willis F. Whitehead. New York: S. Weiser, 1971 (also, Chicago: Hahn and Whitehead, 1898). 288p. Illus. (Translation of Book I of "De Occulta Philosophia"; the 2nd and 3rd books were not published) $7.95 LC 70-166413

Part of the work covers natural magic, which Agrippa discusses in 74 chapters. His early life is also touched upon. Another part of the book is a message to mystics concerning full instructions on construction and use of the magic mirror.

15 Albertus, Frater. The Alchemist's Handbook: Manual for Practical Laboratory Alchemy. Rev. ed. New York: S. Weiser, 1974. 124p. Illus. $7.95 LC 74-187902 ISBN 0-87728-181-5

16 Albertus Magnus, Saint. The Book of Secrets of Albertus Magnus; Also, a Book of the Marvels of the World. Ed. in part by Michael R. Best and Frank H. Brightman. Oxford, England: Clarendon Press, 1973 (orig. pub., ca. 1550). xlviii, 128p. Illus. Bibliog. (Translation of "Liber Aggregationis")

This work is less a handbook of magic than an anthology of lore that had been written of in various sources the author read. It was compiled in Latin toward the end of the 13th century and translated into all major European languages. The first English translation was in 1550, with many reprintings over the next 90 years. Following a long introduction by the editors come chapters on herbs, beasts, astrology, stones, plants, and marvels of the world. The accuracy of these wonders was not checked by the author. However, the book presents valuable folklore of the time.

17 Ald, Roy. The Man Who Took Trips; A True Experience in Another Dimension. New York: Delacorte, 1971. 245p. $6.95 LC 79-126381

This book is a highly personal account of astral projection adventures which will make some readers cringe in disbelief. The man was Paul Lerner, an English professor who quit teaching, began taking LSD, and moved to Bohemian quarters. While on LSD, he had a psychosexual experience with an extraterrestrial, Alotha. Her race gave Paul their philosophy, called psychosynergic determinism (PSD), the answer to all man's problems. Ald writes as an interviewer of Lerner. Needless to say, this work is rather hard to believe!

18 Alderman, Clifford Lindsey. Cauldron of Witches: The Story
* of Witchcraft. New York: Pocket Books, 1973 (also Folkestone, England: Bailey and Swinfen, 1973; orig. pub., New York: Messner, 1971). 182p. Bibliog. $.75 pa. LC for orig. ed., 70-160311

This is a fine juvenile survey of the subject. The first half of the work discusses the hysteria, huntings, persecutions, and trials surrounding 16th- and 17th-century witchcraft in Scotland, England, France, Germany, and colonial Massachusetts. It is as much concerned with the killing of innocents as with actual witchcraft, and describes in detail the tortures used to extract confessions. The second half of the book becomes more anecdotal, discussing African witchcraft, werewolves, voodoo, obeah, leopard men, Sect Rouge, and witches today. This work is recommended for grades 7-10.

19 _______. Witchcraft in America. New York: J. Messner, 1974. Bibliog. $5.95 LC 74-7586 ISBN 0-671-32685-6

This juvenile work traces the history of witchcraft in the United States from its practice in the colonies to the present. It compares New England, Southern, and New Mexico witchcraft. Also discussed are American Indians, sorcery, Pennsylvania hexes, and New Orleans voodoo. Contemporary witchcraft is likewise covered. Much of the author's material is from publications of historical societies and folklore societies. Included are records of the trials and eyewitnesses. This work is recommended for grades 8-12.

20 Alexander, Marc. Haunted Castles. London: Frederick Muller, 1974 (dist. by Transatlantic Arts, Inc.). 352p. Plates Index $12.50 ISBN 0-584-10112-0

21 _______. Haunted Inns. Illus. by Sandra Biggs. London: Frederick Muller, 1973. 279p. Illus. Index £3.20

22 _______. Phantom Britain: This Spectre'd Isle. London: Frederick Muller, 1975. 256p. Illus. 32p. of plates Index £5.75 ISBN 0-584-10210-0

23 Allen, Paul M., ed. Christian Rosenkreutz Anthology. Blauvelt, N.Y.: Steinerbooks, 1974. 702p. $12.95 pa.

This large, nicely illustrated book gives the major Rosicrucian writings throughout history. Included are writings by Rudolf Steiner, Thomas Vaughan, Robert Flood, and others. The Fama and Confessio were the first Rosicrucian documents to appear in Europe. They are here in the 1690 translation of Thomas Vaughan. Chymical Wedding, the primary example of alchemical allegory, is here in Foxcraft's 1690 translation. Also included are many of Steiner's works (Steiner is the founder of the modern Rosicrucian movement). The book is very useful in that it also reproduces many original texts and their allegorical illustrations.

24 Allison, Paul D. The Social Aspects of Scientific Innovation: The Case of Parapsychology. Master's thesis, University of Wisconsin, 1973. (available from University Microfilms, Ann Arbor, Mich.) 223p. $15 (Xerox)

This work studies the social pressures facing psychical researchers and how well they have coped with them. The author studies the structure of the field and its scientific accomplishments and history. Allison views parapsychologists as a "coherent social group" specializing in an innovative field. As such, most research is done in only a few centers, with general isolation from other scientists and world events. Historically, three main periods are covered: Early (1882-1920); Middle (1920-1947--discussing Rhine and the almost authoritarian influence he had); Late (1947-1972--emergence of new centers). The author uses two sources. One is the parapsychological literature, especially the Journal of Parapsychology and other Rhine material. The other is a mail survey of North American membership of the Parapsychological Association. This work is a serious study of a rather narrow topic--social pressures.

25 Alvery, Robert. Out of the Body Experiences. Foreword by Harry Edwards. London, Regency Press, 1975. 118p. £1.80 ISBN 0-7212-0414-7

26 Anderson, Jean, 1913- . The Haunting of America: Ghost Stories from Our Past. Illus. by Eric von Schmidt. Boston: Houghton Mifflin, 1973. xiii, 171p. Illus. $4.95 LC 73-5864

This is a loosely constructed collection of 24 stories about ghosts, hauntings, and poltergeists from throughout the U.S. and from various periods of history. Also presented is discussion of a mysterious fireball and a chapter on Bigfoot. The stories are random cases the author has heard of over the years. The cases are not documented. As a whole, the book serves as a popular, breezy introduction to the subject.

27 Anderson, Mary, 1921- . Palmistry--Your Destiny in Your
* Hands. Wellingborough, England: Aquarian Press, 1973. 64p. Illus. (Paths to Inner Power) £0.35 ISBN 0-85030-110-6

This book is a good short introduction to the subject. Chapters include the following topics: hand; fingers; thumb and mount of Venus; mounts and their meanings; major lines (life, head, heart, fate, sun, health); marriage and children; travel; palm markings; luck. This is perhaps the best book to start with for beginners.

28 Anderson, Nancy E. Astrology According to Shakespeare: Antique Astrology Revised. Ashland, Ore: Aquarius Press, 1974. 129p. Illus. Bibliog. $2.95 LC 74-79035

29 Anderson, Peter. Talk About the Devil. London: Word Books, 1973. 108p. £0.45 pa.

30 Andreae, Christine. Seances and Spiritualists. Philadelphia:
* Lippincott, 1974. Illus. (The Weird and Horrible Library) $5.15 ($1.95 pa.) LC 74-8044 ISBN 0-397-31555-4

This juvenile survey discusses the various aspects of spiritualism and some of its more famous mediums, such as Eileen Garrett, the Fox sisters, Daniel Home, and Arthur Ford. Also covered are Mesmer, Edgar Cayce, astral projection, automatic writing, auras, plants, Kirlian photography, and Findhorn. The final chapter concerns the author's visit to a medium in Washington, D. C. Also mentioned is how to test a medium's worth. The work is illustrated with black and white photos. Recommended for grades 7-10.

31 Andrews, George, ed. Drugs and Magic. St. Albans, England: Panther, 1975. 591p. Illus. Index £1.50pa. ISBN 0-586-03931-7

32 Andrews, Sheila. In the Beginning Was the World. London: Regency Press, 1974. 158p. £1.80 ISBN 0-7212-0343-4

33 Angebert, Jean Michel [pseud.]. Occult and the Third Reich.
* Trans. by Lewis A. M. Sumberg. New York: Macmillan, 1974 (also, New York: McGraw-Hill, 1975). 306p. Illus. Bibliog. (Translation of "Hitler et la tradition Cathare") $7.95 LC 73-2748 ISBN 0-02-502150-8

This work is concerned with the mystical origins of Nazism and the search for the Holy Grail. The author's name is actually the joint signature of Michel Bertrand and Jean Angelini. The authors feel there is evidence that Hitler was possessed and also possessed others. They believe that his life and death were only episodes in a vast struggle between neo-Paganism and Christianity. Attempts are made to trace Nazism back to the traditions of the Cathars of France, and traditions of Zoroaster, Mani, the Holy Grail, and Atlantis. Much of the book is on Gnosticism, which the authors feel is an excellent doctrine, but was misunderstood by the Germans. They condemn Wagner, Nietzsche, Rahn and Haushofer. The authors feel that past writers have only studied Nazism from a rational point of view, and have thus failed to understand it. The work was based on supposedly secret society archives in Europe, but there is no real documentation for views expressed.

34 Angoff, Allan. Eileen Garrett and the World Beyond the Senses.
*** New York: Morrow, 1974. xi, 241p. Bibliog. $6.95 LC 73-21500 ISBN 0-688-00250-1

This work is a major new contribution to occult literature. The author went to work for Eileen Garrett after World War II, and stayed in close touch with her right until she died in 1970 at the age of 76. The work is an excellent biography on Garrett's childhood, marriages, and careers as book writer, magazine publisher, medium, and founder of the Parapsychology Foundation. It mentions her abilities in clairvoyant diagnosis, healing, mediumship, astral projection and precognition. The book is honest, even in showing her in some of her worst moments. It is revealed that she never could decide the worth of her mediumship, and for years, hired psychics and scientists to try and determine what the nature of it was. She became more and more doubtful of the worth of the occult field, but could not resist staying part of it. The last chapter gives excerpts from various opinions written about her, given by Ira Progoff, J. B. Rhine, William Brown, Jay Ehrenwald, Robert Laidlaw, and Lawrence LeShan. The book is mostly on her work, and does not cover her personal life as much as some might wish. In sum, though, it is an excellent biography about an important figure.

35 Annual Summary of Information on Natural Disasters, 1973
* [vol. 8]. Paris: Unesco Press, 1975 (dist. by Unipub, New York). $4.65 ISBN 92-3-001269-6

This fine reference book, published annually since 1966, gives complete coverage of the year's unusual natural phenomena. There are chapters on earthquakes, tsunamis, volcanic eruptions, landslides, avalanches. Each section has two columns of print per page--one in English and the other in French. The earthquake section is the longest in the book. It starts with a short introduction, and then goes region by region. It includes a fold-out map on earthquakes. The other sections are arranged either region by region, or else chronologically. This is an important annual on unusual phenomena.

36 Arkle, William. The Geography of Consciousness. London: Neville Spearman, 1974. £2.75

This is a very personal exploration of consciousness by a mystic. The work discusses religion, astrology, fields and levels of consciousness, bodies of communication, the self and will. The book is a difficult one to read and follow.

37 Arroyo, Stephen. Astrology, Psychology, and the Four Elements: An Energy Approach to Astrology and Its Use in the Counseling Arts. Davis, Calif.: CRCS Publications, 1975. xvi, 191p. Bibliog. $5.95 LC 75-27828 ISBN 0-916360-01-6

This work discusses the usual houses and signs, but tries to distill the major astrological principles, especially the four elements, into psychological terms. It concentrates on individual and interpersonal relationships, and discusses healing processes.

38 Artemidorus Daldianus. The Interpretation of Dreams. Trans. and commentary by Robert J. White. Park Ridge, N. J. : Noyes Press, 1975. Bibliog. Index (Translation of "Oneirocritica") (Noyes Classical Studies) $12.50 LC 74-81537 ISBN 0-8155-5029-4

This classic work of the A.D. 100's is here translated with notes by the classicist R. J. White. There are extensive commentaries by White, but they have a classical, and not a dream interpretation slant. Artemidorus, who wrote five books on dream interpretation, made his personal experience an important part of this book. His symbolic interpretations of the dreams are quite surprising in their insights.

39 Arundale, George Sydney. You. New rev. and abridged ed. Wheaton & London: Theosophical Pub. House, 1973 (previous ed., Adyar, Theosophical Pub. House, 1935). vii, 176p. Index. £1.00 pa. ISBN 0-8356-0434-9

Basically, this is an outline of principles of theosophy applied to the author's life. There are sections on parents, family, education, business, world in peace and war, decision-making, love, death, the quest of beauty, theosophy and society. The work is presented to the reader as a highly personal example that the reader need not follow at all. The author only suggests that a person construct his own guidelines to life using theosophical principles as a basis.

40 Ashby, Robert H. Guide Book for the Study of Psychical Research. New York: Samuel Weiser, 1972. 190p. $2.95 pa. LC 72-78575 ISBN 0-87728-188-2
***

This work is a major new contribution to occult literature. It is an important reference tool, functioning as a bibliography and handbook. There are chapters on the nature of psychical research, procedures for sitting with a medium, a list of resources (libraries, organizations, publications), important figures in psychical research, and a glossary of terms. The bibliography sections list 269 books, with 82 of these annotated. The annotations are excellent. It is unfortunate more of the 269 works were not so treated. The books are listed by degree of difficulty. This excellent reference book belongs in every English-speaking library in the world.

41 Ashton, John, 1834-?. The Devil in Britain and America. Detroit, Gale Research Co., 1974 (also, Ann Arbor, Mich.:

Gryphon Books, 1971; orig. pub., London: Ward and Downey, 1896). x, 363p. Illus. Bibliog. $18.50 LC 73-18391

This work discusses witchcraft persecutions of the 17th and 18th centuries, using contemporary accounts as a basis. It is illustrated with many woodcuts from the period.

42 Association for Research and Enlightenment. A. R. E. Library
* Book List; February, 1975. Virginia Beach, Va.: The Association, 1975. 36p. free.

This periodically revised catalog is a selected list of holdings of the A. R. E. Library, now housed in a beautifully designed new building overlooking the ocean. Approximately 1,700 titles are listed alphabetically by author under 15 subject headings. These headings are astrology, Bible, biography and autobiography, dreams, health (physical, mental and spiritual), metaphysics and philosophy, prayer and meditation, prophecy and earth changes, psychic phenomena, psychology, reincarnation and survival, religious thought, theosophy and anthroposophy, yoga, miscellaneous. Since this association was formed to publicize and carry on Edgar Cayce's work, library acquisition policy is slanted towards the areas Cayce's gifts suggested. Even the smallest libraries specializing in these fields should send for this free catalog, since the A. R. E. Library is a major collection. Non-members are welcome to use the library there.

43 Austin, Mary. Textbook of Acupuncture Therapy. New York: ASI Publishers, 1972. 276p. $12.50 LC 72-78147 ISBN 0-88231-000-3

The author, a British osteopath and acupuncturist, has written a basic textbook to the field. It covers the philosophy, theory and techniques of acupuncture. There is an especially detailed discussion of the acupuncture points. It is illustrated with many diagrams, but lacks footnotes and a bibliography. The work is recommended for graduate students and above, as it contains fairly technical discussions of anatomy and physiology.

44 Automobile Association [of Great Britain]. Haunts and Hauntings. Written and produced by the Publications Division of the Association; Illus. by Outline Art Services. Basingstoke, England: AA, 1974. 65p. Illus. Map Bibliog. £0.20 ISBN 0-901088-57-9

45 Aylesworth, Thomas G. Alchemists: Magic into Science. Read-
* ing, Mass.: Addison-Wesley, 1973. 128p. Illus. $4.75 LC 72-7495

This is a fine juvenile survey of the subject. It tells the

stories of Merlin, Albertus Magnus, Thomas Aquinas, Paracelsus, and Cagliostro, describes the beginnings of alchemy, and also includes some frauds. Concentration is on those serious alchemists who were the forerunners of modern science, and who were usually under the protection of their kings or rulers. The author presents the purposes of these men in trying to convert base metals into gold, lengthen life, and cure disease. The work has excellent illustrations, with numerous engravings, woodcuts, paintings, and book illustrations from the periods discussed. This book is reccommended for grades 6-9.

46 ________. Astrology and Foretelling the Future. Illus. by
* J. H. Breslow. New York: Franklin Watts, 1973 (also, London: Franklin Watts, 1974). 63p. Illus. Index (A Concise Guide) $3.95 LC 72-8797

The author has written a fine juvenile survey concerning divination and astrology. His information came from conversations with people who practice divination, or from books (although no sources are mentioned). The first half of the work discusses astrology, covering the influence of the planets, zodiac signs, and defining such terms as cusp and decans. Other sections mention aeromancy (reading the skies), tasseography (reading tea leaves), cartomancy (fortune-telling with cards), and dominoes. The last chapter discusses the author's theory of man's attempts to learn the future. Some may object to the author's views on experimenting with divination for fun: "this book can at least help you to have a good time." The drawings accompanying the text are clever and amusing. This book is recommended for grades 6-10.

47 ________. ESP. Illus. by Ric Estrada. New York: Franklin
* Watts, 1975. 63p. Illus. Bibliog. Index (A First Book) $3.90 LC 74-26797 ISBN 0-531-00826-6

This juvenile survey treats three areas: telepathy, clairvoyance, and precognition. The discussions include history, research, and case studies. Research in the United States is covered, including Mitchell, Geller, and mice precognition experiments (now discredited). There is also a chapter on psychical research in the U. S. S. R., and a glossary. The writing is largely uncritical, and the written text actually covers only 35 pages. The rest of the work consists of black and white illustrations. This book is reccommended for grades 6-9.

48 ________. Vampires and Other Ghosts. Reading, Mass.: Ad-
* dison-Wesley, 1972. 127p. Illus. $4.50 LC 76-39296 ISBN 0-201-00157-8

This juvenile work discusses vampires, animal ghosts, voodoo, and zombies. There are many quotes from firsthand reports and studies. The author states that there may or may not be reasonable explanations. His theory that these legends have spread largely through fictionalized versions in literature is questionable. The work is illustrated with many woodcuts, motion picture stills, and engravings. The book is recommended for grades 7-10.

49 _______. Werewolves and Other Monsters. Boston: G. K. Hall,
* 1973 (c1971). vii, 131p. Illus. (Large print ed.) $5.95 LC 72-12885 ISBN 0-816-6071-6

This juvenile book discusses stories and legends about werewolves, trials of supposed werewolves in the 16th and 17th centuries, and medical/psychological explanations for werewolf belief. It also covers other legendary land and sea monsters. (The author won the PIA Graphic Arts Award competition in 1971 for another work, Servants of the Devil). This werewolf book is illustrated with woodcuts and prints. It is recommended for grades 7-10.

50 Bailey, Alice Ann. The Consciousness of the Atom. New York: Lucis Pub. Co.; London: Lucis Press, 1973 (orig. pub., New York: Lucifer Pub. Co., 1922). 163p. Index £0.80 pa. ISBN 0-85330-101-8

51 _______. A Treatise on Cosmic Fire. New York: Lucis Pub. Co.; London: Lucis Press, 1973 (orig. pub., New York: Lucis Pub. Co., 1925). xxvi, 1367p. Illus. Index £3.90 pa. ISBN 0-85330-117-4

This classic work provides a compact outline of a scheme of cosmology, philosophy and psychology. It is designed as both a textbook and reference. The work has a fivefold purpose: an outline; an explanation of the relationship of spirit and matter; a demonstration of the coherent system of everything in universe; practical information about focal points of energy; a discussion of the Hierarchies of Existence who form out of their substance all seen and unseen. The author wrote the book in close contact with her spirit guide, the Tibetan. With this information, he gave her supposedly the key to cosmic creation. As an example of the continued reading of this 1925 work, rock singer Todd Rundgren's recent album, Initiation, is based on this text. Alice Bailey's work is still being publicized by Lucis Trust and their World Goodwill Publications.

52 _______. The Unfinished Autobiography of Alice A. Bailey. New York: Lucis Pub. Co.; London: Lucis Press, 1973 (orig. pub., 1951). iii-xi, 304p. £1.20 pa. ISBN 0-85330-124-7

53 Baker, Roger, 1934- . Binding the Devil: Exorcism Past and Present. New York: Hawthorn Books, 1975 (c1974). viii, 187p. Bibliog. Index $7.95 LC 74-22920 ISBN 0-8015-0640-9

This book presents viewpoints of psychiatrists, priests, exorcists, and victims who have been exorcized. There is a great deal of emphasis on sex, paranoia, and trickery.

54 Baldwin, Gordon Cortis, 1908- . Schemers, Dreamers, and
* Medicine Men; Witchcraft and Magic Among Primitive People. New York: Four Winds, 1971 (c1970). 176p. Illus. Bibliog. $4.88 LC 76-124188 ISBN 0-7163-1001-5

This juvenile survey discusses occult beliefs among primitive people throughout the world. It covers anthropology in general, then primitive religion. Next, there are chapters on magic, fortunetelling, lucky numbers, ghosts, witches, medicine men and witch doctors, primitive medicine and magic, rituals, and modern magic. The author connects primitive beliefs to our superstitions today. The work includes the customs of Indians of North and South America, African blacks, Siberians, Eskimos, and Australian aborigines. There are black and white photos of ritual items (especially masks), and of medicine men. The work has an eight-page glossary. This fine work is recommended for grades 7-9.

55 Ballantyne, Ned, and Stella Coeli. Your Horoscope and Your
* Dreams; 25,000 Interpretations of the Predictions of the Sun, Moon, and Stars and of the Messages Received in Sleep. Rev. ed. New York: Franconia Pub. Co., 1973 [work is now in 16th printing, 9th ed., 1976]. 768p. Illus. $5.95 LC 73-173486

This work is actually two books in one. The first part is on astrology, and includes the usual discussion on houses, planets, and signs. Other sections include the moon in various signs, love, romance, marriage; what to expect of your mate, astrological guide for parents, business, friendship, career, bad points, money, attracting love, moods, the meaning of terms. The second half of the work is a dictionary of dream symbolism (over 500 pages long). There is a short discussion at the end on how to find a number to correspond to your dreams.

56 Bander, Peter. Voices from the Tapes; Recordings from the
*** Other World. New York: Drake Publishers, 1973 (first pub. as "Carry on Talking," Gerrards Cross, England, 1972). 167p. Illus. $6.95 LC 73-181609

This work is a major new contribution to occult literature. Since 1959, many scientists and electronics experts have been recording the "voice phenomenon"--unaccountable voices on recording tape. Konstantin Raudive, following the experiments of Friedrich Jurgenson, recorded voices of the dead, and then published a book reporting his findings (see entry 1334). Peter Bander wrote the introduction to Raudive's book (Breakthrough). In Voices from the Tapes, Bander discusses what it was like working with Raudive, and summarizes his attempts to tape the voices and verify Raudive's claims. Also discussed are the reactions of scientists, religious, and spiritualists (who attack the book) to Breakthrough, which was the first major work to report the phenomenon. Bander reports eventual success in recording the voices, and mentions other investigators who have tried to obtain similar recordings.

57 Banerjee, H. N., and William Charles Oursler, 1913- . Lives Unlimited; Reincarnation East and West. Garden City, N. Y.: Doubleday, 1974. 187p. Includes bibliog. refs. $5.95 LC 73-9171 ISBN 0-385-03912-3

This work is based in part on case studies taken from Banerjee's files at the Indian Institute of Parapsychology in Jaipur. Also, the authors quote Annie Besant, Rudolf Steiner, and others. They call reincarnation "extracerebral memory." The work also contains a small glossary.

58 Bangs, John Kendrick. Ghosts I Have Met, and Some Others. Illus. by Newell, Frost, and Richards. Hollywood, Calif.: Newcastle Pub. Co., 1971. 190p. Illus. $2.45 pa. ISBN 0-87877-005-4

59 Banta, Martha. Henry James and the Occult: The Great Extension. Bloomington: Indiana University Press, 1972. 273p. $9.50 LC 72-75386

This work is a revision of the author's Ph. D. dissertation in American literature. It nicely complements Kerr's work, Mediums and Spirit-Rappers and Roaring Radicals (entry 862), which covers 1850-1900. Chapters 1, 2, and 3 deal with the background of James's choices on whether or not to use supernatural material. His brother William figures in this section prominently. Chapters 4, 5, 6, and 7 examine his application of supernatural traditions to his own individualized fictional style. Chapter 8 discusses James's unique contribution, with his views of consciousness living at "the pitch of passion." The author mentions that James deplored contemporary psychical research and the Society for Psychical Research, who he felt took the drama out of events by unduly laboring to record them. Banta feels that James used ghosts to coerce people to move from innocence to a self-understanding that might ultimately save an individual.

60 Barbanell, Maurice. This Is Spiritualism. Spiritualist Press, 1975 (c1959). £2

The author of this work is also editor of the monthly English spiritualist magazine, Two Worlds. A good deal of the book is devoted to survival evidence produced by Edgar Wallace after his death. Most of Barbanell's contact with Wallace came through sittings with the famous medium, Estelle Roberts.

61 Barbault, Armand. Gold of a Thousand Mornings. Trans. by Robin Campbell. London: Spearman, 1975. xvii, 130p. Illus. Plates (Translation of: "L'Or du millième matin." Paris: Editions Publications Premières, 1969). £2.50 ISBN 0-85435 052-7

The author, a practicing French alchemist, feels that alchemy is not only a spiritual quest, but the real science of hyperchemistry. He calls alchemy "celestial agriculture." Its goals are to produce potable gold, to be used in a process of changing matter and curing disease. The first step is the collection of first matter ("philosopher's peat"), and combining it with plants and dew. This combination produces "major leaven," a powder containing the salts of all life forms. This part took over 14 years. The procedure is vague and confusing. The author states that it is only his personal alchemy. It may not work for the reader.

62 Barber, Dulan Friar. The Horrific World of Monsters. London: Marshall Cavendish, 1974. 121p. Chiefly illus. (some color) Index. (A Golden Hands Book) £1.95 ISBN 0-85685-070-5

63 Barborka, Geoffrey Avery. Mahatmas and Their Letters. Madras; London: Theosophical Pub. House, 1973. 422p. Illus. Plates Bibliog. Index £3

64 Barclay, Glen. Mind Over Matter; Beyond the Bounds of Nature. Indianapolis: Bobbs-Merrill Co., 1973 (also, London: Pan Books, 1975; orig. pub., London: Barker, 1973). 142p. Bibliog. $5.95 LC 73-3908 ISBN 0-672-51867-8

The author theorizes that psychokinesis may be involved in the martial arts of the East. He gives a history of self-defense arts in the West, and says they are totally devoid of occultism. He then covers judo, karate, kiai-jutsu, shorinj kempo, aikido, and Chinese boxing, each of which has more and more occult aspects. These arts seem to generate great forceful blows with little effort. The author, a history professor at the University of Queensland in Australia, feels that our science is redefining the wisdom of the East, and not really breaking new ground.

65 Bardens, Dennis. Ghosts and Hauntings. New York: Ace Books, 1973 (c1965). 253p. $.95 pa.

This work includes the classic cases of hauntings, such as Borley Rectory, and also some little-known but interesting hauntings--Winchcombe ghost, nun of Coventry Hall, Wynyard apparition, and dog of Peel Castle.

66 Barham, Tony. Witchcraft in the Thames Valley: Traditional Witchcraft Tales of the Thames Valley. Bourne End, England: Spurbooks, 1973. 63p. Illus. £0.60 pa.

67 Barkun, Michael. Disaster and the Millennium. New Haven,
* Conn.: Yale University Press, 1974. 246p. Bibliog. Index $10 LC 73-86884

The author, a political scientist at Syracuse University, treats "millenarianism" as a phenomenon of modern life. This field really opened up with Norman Cohn's The Pursuit of the Millennium. Barkun's work is a synthesis, and a good assessment of the current state of the field. Moreover, he presents a new view: millenarian movements follow in the wake of social disasters. He suggests that the root of such movements is in local disasters. This very scholarly work is not designed as an occult book, but has implications for the field.

68 Bartell, Jan Bryant. Spindrift: Spray from a Psychic Sea. New York: Hawthorn Books, 1974. 245p. $7.95 LC 73-10648

This autobiographical account by an actress and poet concerns the haunting of her Greenwich Village townhouse on Tenth Street. The phenomena began very mildly, and may almost seem imagined to the reader. Later, the phenomena became stronger. She began to study the occult, and became convinced the building had a curse. She fled, but came back after three non-haunted years. Nine families living in the building were hit by death over several years. The author moved away, and began writing this book. A month after she delivered the manuscript to a publisher, she died of a heart attack. The author had had several psychic experiences as a child, and at other times. Also, at one period of illness, when taking valium, there were no psychic impressions. Bartell felt many occurrences demonstrated the concept of synchronicity; she mentions this throughout the book. With discussions of the last 16 years of her life, the work is a useful case study.

69 Basham, Don Wilson. Deliver Us from Evil. London: Hodder and Stoughton, 1973 (orig. pub. in U.S. by Chosen Books, 1972; dist. by Fleming H. Revell, Old Tappan, N.J.). 221p. £2 ISBN 0-340-16931-1

70 Bashir, Mir. Your Past, Your Present, and Your Future Through the Art of Hand Analysis. Garden City, N.Y.: Doubleday, 1974 (c1973). $8.95 LC 74-5523 ISBN 0-385-02632-3

This survey discusses the lines of the palm, the shape of the fingers, and explains the various meanings to every possible aspect of the hand. The text is rather complex, but the illustrations are easy to understand.

71 Baskin, Wade. Dictionary of Satanism. New York: Philosophical Library, 1972. 351p. Illus. $12.50 LC 75-155971 ISBN 0-8022-2056-8

This is a very useful dictionary of about 2,500 terms connected with satanism. Dictionaries published by the Philosophical Library have the reputation of being mediocre. These are their usual traits: short information under entries; no documentation or list of sources used; many entries having nothing whatever to do with the title of the book. Fortunately, this Dictionary of Satanism does not in general share the entry problem. Most are pertaining to satanism, although there is an occasional inexplicable entry, such as one for "Murphy, Bridey." However, there is no list of sources used, and most entries are very short. In spite of critics' comments however, the work is very useful. Most of the entries are of proper names.

72 ______. The Sorcerer's Handbook. New York: Philosophical
* Library, 1974 (also, London: Owen, 1974). 635p. Illus. $15 LC 73-77399 ISBN 0-8022-2112-2

This dictionary has over 2,000 entries, some over one page long. Terms were chosen on the basis of their relating to the art of manipulating the forces that control the universe. There are biographies of occultists and philosophers, magical terms, occult terms, and entries for numbers (the number seven has three and a half pages). Sprinkled throughout are actual incantations, charms, potions, curses, and magical operations. There are many very small line drawings. The same criticisms can be voiced about this dictionary as were stated in entry 71. However, the work is a very useful reference tool, in spite of its faults.

73 Bates, Emily Katharine. Seen and Unseen. Folcroft, Pa.: Folcroft Library Editions, 1975 (reprint of the orig. ed., London: Greening and Co., 1908). 323p. $20 LC 75-32535 ISBN 0-8414-3234-1

74 Baumann, Elwood D. Bigfoot: America's Abominable Snow-
* man. New York: Watts, 1975. 107p. Illus. Bibliog. $5.95 LC 74-11407 ISBN 0-531-02793-7

This juvenile book is primarily a collection of stories and anecdotes about Bigfoot. The writing style is very lively, and the work covers a lot of ground in its case studies. The book is recommended for grades 6-12.

75 ______. The Loch Ness Monster. New York: F. Watts,
* 1972. 153p. Illus. $4.95 LC 72-182896 ISBN 0-531-02031-2

This juvenile book reviews sightings and searches for the Loch Ness Monster, and emphasizes 20th-century sightings. The author discusses different theories for the origin of the monster, and covers the many searches, as well as hoaxes. This anecdotal work is pro-monster. Baumann in a member of the Loch Ness Phenomena Investigation Bureau. Some phrases such as "naughty" fisherman, or "a man monster and a lady monster" may not appeal to this age group. The book is recommended for grades 5-9.

76 Bayless, Raymond. The Other Side of Death. New Hyde Park,
* N.Y.: University Books, 1971. 191p. $5.95

This work attempts a synthesis of ideas and lore about death gained from the mutterings of mediums and astral projectors. The author discusses the first waking moment after death, opportunities for spiritual development, and spheres around the earth. He feels that the ridiculous things in the ideas come from the medium, while the similarities of ideas come from actual other-side testimony.

He finds these similarities occurring over and over: the existence of several planes; spiritual development determines which plane one goes to; individuality gradually disappears; the truth of group souls; the survival of animals. Bayless feels survival is a fact, and chastises modern parapsychologists for being so colorless and conservative. However, Bayless's theory that agreement among mediums means something is true does not necessarily follow.

77 ______. Voices from Beyond. Foreword by D. Scott Rogo.
* Secaucus, N. J.: University Books, 1975. $7.95 LC 74-28542 ISBN 0-8216-0252-7

Twenty years ago, Bayless first experimented with taping spirit voices with psychic Attila von Szalay. This work discusses these experiments, and many other similar phenomena. The work is mostly on mediums of the late 19th and early 20th century. It surveys trumpet or direct voice mediums of the past: Emily French, Margery Crandon, George Valiantine, H. Dennis Bradley, John Campbell Sloan, the Moore sisters, Etta Wriedt, Elizabeth Blake. There are some he considers frauds: the Koonses, the Davenport brothers, William Cartheuser (it seems a bit dangerous to pick frauds and good mediums based on contemporary accounts, as does Bayless). There are two chapters contributed by Robin Saunders-Clark, former member of the British College of Psychic Science, on sittings with Scottish mediums and on setting up a circle. Bayless is against schizophrenia and multiple personality theories in any attempt to explain the strange voices coming from the mouths of mediums.

78 Bazak, Jacob. Judaism and Psychical Phenomena. New York: Garrett-Helix Publications, 1972 (dist. by Taplinger). 144p. Bibliog. $6.50 LC 71-184295 ISBN 0-912326-27-1

This work is a study of extrasensory perception in Biblical, Talmudic, and Rabbinical literature in the light of contemporary parapsychological research. The first half of the book is on psychic phenomena in general, with some mention of Jewish writings. The second half gets to the sources themselves. Most were considered magic at the time they were written, and were usually condemned. The author is a judge in the magistrate's court in Jerusalem, who took up the study to gain perspective in witchcraft and magic cases before him. Later, he went much more deeply into it, resulting in this work. He concludes that Jewish condemnation of magic is correct, because it crushes initiative. However, he thinks it is good to study such phenomena because it helps one to understand things better. The book is mostly a loosely organized collection, with not too much attempt at interpretation.

79 Beard, Charles Relly, 1891-1958. Lucks and Talismans; A Chapter of Popular Superstition. New York: B. Blom, 1972 (reprint of 1934 ed.). xix, 258p. Bibliog. $12.75 LC 72-80494

80 Beard, George Miller, 1839-1883. The Psychology of the Salem Witchcraft Excitement of 1692, and Its Practical Application to Our Own Time. Stratford, Conn. : J. E. Edwards, 1971 (orig. pub., New York: G. P. Putnam's Sons, 1882). xx, 112p. Limited ed. 500 copies. $10 LC 11-8994

This work is largely a comparison of the Salem witchcraft trials with those of Cadet Whittaker and Charles Guiteau.

81 Beard, Paul. The James-John Experiment. London: College of Psychic Studies; Bexhill on Sea, England: Survival Joint Research Committee, 1973. 43p. (College of Psychic Studies Papers, no. 6) £0.36 ISBN 0-903336-05-7

This work was an experiment in cross-correspondences (trying to get the same survival evidence from different mediums). The sittings took place in autumn 1966 and were arranged by Brigadier Firebrace. Sitters were John's widow; Firebrace (a friend of James); and Mr. Beard (as a proxy sitter). Attempts were made to get cross-correspondences from two dead communicators, James and John. There were 24 sittings, using eight mediums, all well-known. No cross-correspondences resulted. No evidence was provided which went beyond the evidence of Brigadier Firebrace's mind. James had died a long time before the experiment, and this may have affected results, according to the author. John, however, had only died two years before, and many facts were given about him in the sittings.

82 ________. Survival of Death: For and Against. London: Psychic Press, 1972 (orig. pub., London: Hodder and Stoughton, 1966). xi, 177p. Bibliog. Index £1.50 ISBN 0-85384-035-0

83 Beer, Constance Margaret. Towards an Understanding of the Life Spiritual. Sherborne, England: C. M. Beer, 1975 (dist. by Abbey Press). 44p. £1 ISBN 0-9504169-0-8

84 Behrend, Michael. The Landscape Geometry of Southern Britain. Preface by Anthony Roberts. Foreword by Nigel Pennick. Cambridge, England: Institute of Geomantic Research, 1975. 29p. Illus. Bibliog. (Institute of Geomantic Research. Occasional Papers, no. 1) £0.75 pa. ISBN 0-905376-01-3

85 Bell, Charles Bailey, 1869- . A Mysterious Spirit; and, Bell Witch of Tennessee, by Harriet Parks Miller. Nashville, Tenn. : C. Elder, 1972 (facsim. reprod. of "Bell Witch; A Mysterious Spirit," first pub. in 1934, and of "Bell Witch of Middle Tennessee," first pub. in 1930). 228p. $5 LC 72-190904

86 Beloff, John, ed. New Directions in Parapsychology. Metuchen,
* N. J. : Scarecrow Press, 1975 (also, London: Paul Elek, 1974). $8.50

This work is a fine survey of research done in the field. In the introduction, Beloff gives a general view of parapsychology. Most of the book is on experiments, especially ones that can be repeated in orderly fashion. Some of the papers are Charles Honorton's "ESP and Altered States of Consciousness," Hans Bender's "Modern Poltergeist Research," Helmut Schmidt's "Instrumentation in the Parapsychology Laboratory," K. R. Rao's "Psi and Personality," J. G. Pratt's "In Search of the Consistent Scorer." John Randall's "Biological Aspects of Psi" (on animal experiments) was written before the Levy scandal on fudging results, but is still good. Roll's paper, "New Look at the Survival Problem" (on out-of-the-body experiences and transpersonal consciousness) views both as partial death experiences. There is a glossary of general terms, including major organizations, used in the book.

87 ______. Parapsychology; The Way Ahead. (Based on a lecture delivered by Dr. Beloff at Imperial College, London, under aegis of Institute for Cultural Research, May 24, 1974.) Tunbridge Wells, England: Institute for Cultural Research, 1974. 14 leaves. (Institute for Cultural Research. Monographs, no. 13) £0.45 ISBN 0-904674-02-9

88 Bendit, Laurence John, 1898- . Mysteries Today, and Other Essays. London and Wheaton, Ill.: Theosophical Pub. House, 1973. 154p. £1.50 LC 73-177693 ISBN 0-7229-5024-1

89 Bennett, Ernest Nathaniel, 1868-1947. Apparitions and Haunted Houses; A Survey of Evidence. Foreword by the Dean of St. Paul's. Ann Arbor, Mich.: Gryphon Books, 1971 (dist. by Gale; also, London: Faber & Faber, reprint of 1939 ed.). xix, 396p. $15 LC 76-164100

90 Bennett, John Godolphin, 1897- . Gurdjieff, a Very Great Enigma; Three Lectures. (Given at Denison House, summer, 1963.) New York: S. Weiser, 1973 (c1969). 100p. $2.50 LC 72-91951

Lecture two discusses the sources of his ideas. Lecture three discusses his teaching and methods used over the period 1889-1949.

91 ______. Gurdjieff: Making a New World. New York: Harper and Row, 1974 (c1973). 320p. Illus. Maps Includes bibliog. refs. $8.95 LC 73-18675 ISBN 0-06-060778-5

This work gives a fine portrait of Gurdjieff's personality, his strange disciples, and the period from 1920-1940. The author was a former pupil of his. Bennett attempts to explain the many seeming contradictions in Gurdjieff's thought, seeing them as a continuation of ancient schools of wisdom in Central Asia. He discusses Gurdjieff's message, and outlines the methods he used to transmit the message to his followers. The author's knowledge of Turkish language and customs is a great help to him in writing about this Armenian mystic and teacher.

92 _______. Witness: The Autobiography of John G. Bennett. New ed. London: Turnstone Books, 1975 (new ed. orig. pub., Tucson, Ariz.: Omen Press, 1974; previous ed., London: Hodder and Stoughton, 1962). ix, 380p. Illus. Plates £2.75 pa. ISBN 0-85500-043-0

93 Bergier, Jacques, 1912- , and the Editors of Info Journal, comps. Extraterrestrial Intervention: The Evidence. Chicago: Regnery, 1974. 240p. Illus. $7.95 LC 74-6884 ISBN 0-8092-8369-7

Nearly all of the book consists of articles on mysteries reprinted from the International Fortean Organization's Info Journal. Bergier wrote the preface and four articles. There are four sections in the book: vanished civilizations, extraterrestrial beings among us, strange creatures, and Fortean phenomena. The work discusses, among other things, UFO's, Bigfoot, half-million-year-old spark plug, dinosaurs, poltergeists, and vampires. There are many good photos and drawings.

94 _______. Extraterrestrial Visitations from Prehistoric Times to the Present. Chicago: Regnery, 1973. xi, 207p. $5.95 LC 73-6451

This book presents nine cases the author claims represent possible extraterrestrial intervention in our history. He mentions an ancient map; large stone blocks at Baalbek in Lebanon; strange visits recorded in the Middle Ages; Kaspar Hauser; Sir Henry Cavendish. He includes discussions on 18th-century esoteric knowledge, and theorizes that this extraterrestrial knowledge was kept alive by mystic groups in the Middle Ages. Also, he gives examples from modern times. Some may criticize the book for taking almost any mysterious event (such as the Hauser case), and calling it extraterrestrial interference.

95 _______. Mysteries of the Earth: The Hidden World of the Extra-Terrestrials. Trans. by Lorraine O'Grady Freeman. London: Futura Publications, 1975 (this translation orig. pub. in 2 vols. as "Extra-Terrestrial Visitations from Prehistoric Times to the Present," Chicago: Regnery, 1973; and as "Mysteries of the Earth," London: Sidgwick and Jackson, 1974). viii, 207p. Index (Mysteries of Time and Space) (Translation of "Extraterrestres dans l'histoire." Paris: Editions J'ai Lu, 1970). £0.60 pa. ISBN 0-86007-152-9

96 _______. Secret Doors of the Earth. Trans. by Nicole Taghert. Chicago: H. Regnery Co., 1975. 159p. Illus. (Translation of "Visa pour une autre terre." Paris: Editions Albin Michel, 1974). $7.95 LC 75-17763 ISBN 0-8092-8208-9

This author has a reputation similar to von Däniken's--loose with the facts. Bergier says, "I will not talk about things I know to be false--healers, mediums, water diviners, flying saucers."

Instead, he discusses secret societies possessing superior knowledge, what knowledge they might have and how they initiate new members, and a belief that some members of these societies may be immortal. Even the publisher's blurb calls it "an interpretation of improbable facts." Chapters include: "Secret Doors," "They Are Among Us," "Secret Societies and Centers of Energy," "One Remains on Earth and Gathers the Chosen Together." In spite of the seemingly wild theories, Bergier makes some good points, and the book makes for fascinating reading. The author's basic premise--that secret doors have always existed which open up to unknown areas of the earth and universe--is a very interesting one.

97 Bergrun, Norman R. Tomorrow's Technology Today. Campbell, Calif.: Academy Press, 1972. 65p. Illus. LC 73-152747

98 Berlitz, Charles Frambach, 1913- . Mysteries from Forgotten Worlds. With contributions of photographs, drawings and
* field archeology reports by J. Manson Valentine. New York: Dell Pub. Co., 1973 (c1972). 225p. Illus. Bibliog. $1.25 pa. LC card no. for orig. ed.: 79-175360

The author theorizes the existence of technologically and culturally advanced prehistoric civilizations in the Americas which were in contact with both Atlantis and the Far East. For evidence, he examines similarities in legends and languages of unrelated peoples, artifacts and huge ruins, evidence of ancient knowledge such as accurate maps of supposedly unexplored lands, past catastrophes of the earth, and race memory. He is a diffusionist, rejecting the possibility of independent cultural development. The book contains 48 pages of photographs, and also drawings and maps.

99 ________, and J. Manson Valentine. The Bermuda Triangle.
*** Garden City, N.Y.: Doubleday, 1974 (also, New York: Avon, 1975). 226p. Illus. Bibliog. $7.95 LC 74-3691

This work is a major new contribution to occult literature. It was on the New York Times Best Seller List two months of 1974 and most of 1975, for a total of over 40 weeks. It is hard to determine exactly why it and not the several books that had already come out before it on the Triangle became a best-seller. Berlitz and Valentine's work seems better researched, organized, and written than those that preceded it. Also, it received national promotion. Berlitz discusses mostly others' opinions, and clearly points up all sorts of explanations and possibilities. He offers no answers, however. Chapters include "Triangle of Disappearing Planes," "Sea of Lost Ships," "Some Who Escaped," "Time-Space Warps," "Suggestion from the Ocean's Past," "Surprises of Prehistory," "Watchers--Protectors, Raiders, or Indifferent Observers?" In spite of the many books out as of 1978 on the Triangle, the Berlitz and Valentine work has established itself as the classic on this topic.

100 The Bermuda Triangle; An Annotated Bibliography. Buffalo,
* N.Y.: Buffalo and Erie County Public Library Librarians Association and Buffalo and Erie County Library, 1975. 39p. $1

This work is one of several Bermuda Triangle bibliographies that have been produced by local libraries. It lists 64 books which have at least a small section in them on the Triangle. The periodical section lists 37 magazine articles on this topic. The newspaper articles section lists 226 news columns from the London Times and the New York Times from 1840 to 1975. The last part is a 12-page subject index, with 61 subject headings. Most of the headings are names of ships or planes. Under each heading are listed any whole articles or books on that topic, saving one from having to turn back to earlier parts of the work. The book and periodical sections have brief annotations under each item listed. A well-done bibliography on this narrow topic.

101 Beskow, Katja, and Stig Ericson. Spooks. Glasgow: Blackie, 1975. 32p. Illus. Index (Find Out About Series) (Translation of "Här far du Veta Nagonting om Spökevier." Stockholm: Bonnier, 1971) £1.75. ISBN 0-216-90096-4

102 Beyond Reason; Playboy's Book of Psychic Phenomena. Chicago: Playboy Press, 1973. 189p. Col. Illus. $1.25 pa.

103 Biteaux, Armand. The New Consciousness. Willits, Calif.: Oliver Press, 1975 (dist. by Scribner's, New York). vii, 168p. Advertisements Illus. Index (Finder's Guide, no. 5) $3.95 pa. LC 75-326244 ISBN 0-914400-04-5

This reference work gives a one-paragraph to one-page discription for 128 groups dealing with spiritual awareness. Over 60 of the groups are located in California. The description for each gives address, information on founder, philosophy of the organization, a list of its journals and publications.

104 Black, David, 1945- . Ekstasy: Out-of-the-body Experiences. Indianapolis: Bobbs-Merrill Co., 1975. 243p. Bibliog. Index $7.95 LC 74-17679 ISBN 0-672-51972-0
***

This work is a major new contribution to occult literature. It is very well-written and researched, with a bibliography of over 20 pages. The book has four sections: introduction, with many personal anecdotes from modern times; laboratory experiments; theories; and conclusion. People discussed are Blue Harary, Robert Monroe, Ingo Swann, Karlis Osis, Andrija Puharich, Edgar Mitchell, Robert Morris, Stanley Krippner, Pat Price, Russell Targ, D. Scott Rogo. The author has traveled around the country interviewing people and visiting major research centers. He finds the out-of-the-body experience universal in most times and cultures. However, he feels that the phenomenon has yet to be conclusively proven as an objective reality.

105 Blacker, Thetis. Pilgrimage of Dreams. London: Turnstone Books, 1973. xviii, 164p. £2.50 ISBN 0-85500-020-1

106 Blair, Lawrence. Rhythms of Vision: The Changing Patterns of Belief. Foreword by Lyall Watson. London: Croom Helm, 1975. 244p. Illus. Index £4.50 ISBN 0-85664-261-4

The author discusses Eastern religions, science fiction, the occult, biofeedback, acupuncture, and astrology. He has a Ph.D. from Lancaster University, and is a lecturer in mysticism. He feels that our times are seeing a joining of modern science and old wisdom. A mystical experience of his own changed his way of looking at things, and he began to notice basic forms and cosmic patterns behind everything. He sees energy and vibrations as the key to outside reality and man's mind. Blair emphasizes the importance of sex, drugs, and the occult for spiritual realization today. This may turn off some readers.

107 Blakeley, John Dyson. The Mystical Tower of the Tarot. London: Robinson and Watkins, 1974. xiv, 193p. Illus. Bibliog. Index. £4.50 pa. ISBN 0-7224-0135-3

108 Blankenship, Roberta. Escape from Witchcraft. Grand Rapids, Mich.: Zondervan Pub. House, 1972 114p. $.95 pa. LC 72-85565

109 Blatty, William Peter. I'll Tell Them I Remember You. New York: W. W. Norton, 1973. 114p. $5.95

This book is an autobiography by the author of The Exorcist. Most of the work discusses his youth in Manhattan and his Lebanese mother in often humorous words. The last part of the book mentions occult phenomena that took place in 1969, two years after his mother's death. There was ouija board action, things falling to the floor, and a broken-down music box working twice while he was thinking about his mother. Blatty advises people not to grieve over the past, since he believes we all live forever. The book is interesting mainly because of his Exorcist connection.

110 Blavatsky, Helene Petrovna, 1831-1891. Dynamics of the Psychic World. Comp. with notes by Lina Psaltis. Wheaton, Ill.: Theosophical Pub. House, 1972. xv, 132p. Bibliog. (Quest Book Original) $1.95 LC 72-78193 ISBN 0-8356-0429-2

This work includes comments by Blavatsky on psychism, mediumship, magic, and the power of the spirit.

111 ______. Isis Unveiled. Wheaton, Ill.: Theosophical Pub. House, 1972 (orig. pub., 1877). 2 vols. 650p. and 848p. $20

Volume 1, on science, discusses the history of science, cyclic phenomena, paranormal phenomena, mysteries of nature, Egyptian and Indian wisdom. It supposedly foreshadows radioactivity and the atom. Volume 2, on religion, discusses ancient sources of Christianity, pagan rites, mysteries of the Orient and Occident, alchemy, Egyptian, Hindu, Chinese, Tibetan, Mexican, Hebrew, Greek, and Rosicrucian mystery teaching.

112 ______. The Key to Theosophy. Abridged ed. by Joy Mills. Wheaton, Ill., and London: Theosophical Pub. House, 1972 (orig. pub., 1889). xv, 176p. Index (Theosophical Classic Series) (A Quest Book) £1.95 pa. ISBN 0-8356-0427-6

113 ______. Studies in Occultism. Foreword by Dennis Wheatley. London: White Lion Publishers, 1975 (orig. pub., London: Sphere, 1974). 191p. (Dennis Wheatley Library of the Occult) £4.50 ISBN 0-7274-0001-0

These articles originally appeared in H. P. Blavatsky's magazine Lucifer in the years 1887-1891.

114 ______. The Theosophical Glossary. Detroit: Gale, 1974 (orig. pub., London: Theosophical Society, 1892). 389p. $15 LC 74-142546

115 Bloom, Ursula. The Great Tomorrow. London: Hale, 1971. 175p. £1.80 ISBN 0-7091-2245-4

This book discusses spiritualist viewpoints of the life after death.

116 Blum, Ralph, and Judy Blum. Beyond Earth: Man's Contact with UFO's. London: Corgi, 1974 (orig. pub., New York: Bantam, 1974). 248p. Illus. Plates Bibliog. Index £0.50 pa. ISBN 0-552-09686-5

This work mainly covers the many UFO sightings of 1973, but also mentions some earlier ones. The authors' main concern is with the witnesses, and they discuss how the experience alters the witnesses' lives. One interesting discussion centers on two men who saw a spacecraft in the Mississippi River on October 11, 1973.

117 Blumrich, Josef F. Spaceships of Ezekiel. New York: Ban-
* tam, 1974 (also, London: Corgi, 1974). 179p. Illus. Bibliog. Index (Translation of: "Da Tat sich der Himmel auf." Düsseldorf: Econ-Verlag, 1974) $1.95

This excellent work has not been listed as a major occult contribution only because its subject is narrow and the book is rather short. However, the subject matter is of major interest. Having read von Däniken's claim that Ezekiel's visions in the Bible really describe a spaceship encounter, Blumrich originally set out to prove von Däniken wrong. This NASA engineer and co-designer of the Saturn V rocket soon changed his mind, and came to agree with von Däniken. Blumrich became convinced that Ezekiel had seen several beings from another planet, at least two spacecraft, and flown on different times from one spot on earth to another. Blumrich comes up with a design which he feels is only 50 years ahead of present technology. Most of the book goes line-by-line through Ezekiel, and then comments and interprets that section. In this way, it is much like a traditional Bible commentary book. Other chapters pull themes together: the mission, the spaceship, technical discussion of the design (in the appendix). Because of the author's credentials (he began a career in aircraft design in 1934), this work is a fascinating book.

118 Boguet, Henri, ca. 1619-?. Examen of Witches. New York: Barnes and Noble, 1971 (facsim. of 1929 ed.). liii, 328p. (Translation of "Discours des sorciers") $11.50 LC 71-27506 ISBN 0-389-04142-4

119 Bok, Bart Jan, 1906- , and Lawrence E. Jerome. Objections
* to Astrology. Buffalo, N.Y.: Prometheus Books, 1975. 62p. Illus. (Impact Series) (Reprinted from The Humanist, 35, no. 5 September/October 1975) $2.95 pa. LC 75-29798 ISBN 0-87975-059-6

This work is a harsh criticism of astrology. The first main section, "Objections to Astrology," has a basic statement of condemnation followed by the names of 192 scientists who signed it. Of the signers, 19 are Nobel Prize winners. The basic statement says that "... there is no verified scientific basis for their beliefs and indeed that there is strong evidence to the contrary." The second section is a "Critical Look at Astrology," raising such questions as why the moment of birth has to be considered as the crucial moment. The third section is titled, "Astrology--Magic or Science." This chapter criticizes astrology's trying to use evidence for biological clocks as proof of astrology's claims. Also criticized there is statistical astrology. Bok states that Gauquelin's research is all right, but that he made a mistake based on the very statistical method he bases everything on. The section also criticizes "humanist astrology" (Rudhyar), which seeks a holistic approach to man using archetypes very similar to Jung's. It is often hard to find critical comments on astrology. This book provides the case for the other side.

120 Bonewits, Philip Emmons Isaac. Real Magic: An Introductory Treatise on the Basic Principles of Yellow Magic. New York: Coward, 1971. xix, 236p. Illus. Bibliog. $6.95 LC 70-146087

This book covers occultism, witchcraft, magic rituals, and also parapsychology. The author got the University of California at Berkeley to give him a B.A. degree with a major in magic (the diploma appears on the back of the jacket). Yellow magic is defined as the magic of the mind and nervous system. The author discusses how anthropology, mythology, psychology, and theology form the basis for magic. The writing contains a lot of jargon, such as "clairolfaction" and "psychopyresis." The book contains a glossary.

121 Booth, Sally Smith. Witches of Early America. New York: Hastings House, 1975. 238p. $9.95

The book is mostly on New England witchcraft. The author discusses the confessions and accusations from the viewpoint of sociology and psychology. Also, there are chapters on legal aspects and the punishment of witches. The last chapter is on Salem.

122 Bord, Janet. Ghosts. Newton Abbot, England: David and Charles, 1974 (dist. in U. S. by David and Charles, North Pomfret, Vt.). 80p. Illus. Index £1.95/$4.95 ISBN 0-7153-6632-7

This work mentions phantom armies, and some not well-known contemporary hauntings. It covers many of the same cases as in Aidan Chambers's Book of Ghosts (entry 227).

123 ________, and Colin Bord. Mysterious Britain. Garden City,
* N. Y.: Doubleday, 1973. $14.95

This book discusses leys (straight lines connecting churches and old sites in Britain), and old astronomical sites made of stones in lines and circles. There are 14 sections. Eight are on monuments, such as the stone circles. The other six are on themes the author considers important to studying Britain's ancient sites. Topics mentioned are Stonehenge, why we make wishes at old wells, hill figures as possible signals to the gods; dragon symbols on church carvings, old manuscripts, and landscape formations; huge mounds all over England, and why ghosts are so selective in choosing their haunting spots. The numerous photos are of fairly good quality. Some may be bothered by the themes of outer space visitors and psychic abilities of early man.

124 Borgia, Anthony. Life in the World Unseen. Foreword by Sir John Anderson. London: Corgi, 1975. (orig. pub., London: Odhams, 1954). 220p. (Corgi Library of Psychic Exploration) £0.50 pa. ISBN 0-552-09940-6

A Monsignor Robert Hugh Benson supposedly communicated with Anthony Borgia, and this book is a result of that communication.

125 Bosman, Leonard. The Meaning and Philosophy of Numbers. London: Rider, 1974 (facsim. reprint of 1st ed., orig. pub. in 1932). 156p. £2.25 ISBN 0-09-119270-6

126 Boss, Judy. In Silence They Return: A Message of Spiritual Assurance. St. Paul, Minn.: Llewellyn Pubns., 1972. 216p. Illus. $5.95 ISBN 0-87542-080-X

127 Bourguignon, Erika, 1924- . Trance Dance. New York: Johnson Reprint Corp., 1973 (reprint of the 1968 ed., which was issued as no. 35 of Dance Perspectives). Includes bibliog. ref. $6 pa. LC 73-774

128 Bovet, Richard. Pandaemonium. Introd. and notes by Montague Summers. Wakefield, England: EP Publishing, 1975 (orig. pub., London: J. Walthoe, 1684). xxvii, 191p. Illus. Facsims. £3.75 ISBN 0-7158-1136-3

129 Bowen, Mollie. Space--Fact and Fiction. Illus. by Gerry Wood. Ed. by Dan Lloyd. Glasgow: Collins, 1972 (orig. pub. as "Flying Saucers and Outer Space," London: Tyndall, 1969). 46p. Illus. (color) (Treasure Trove Series) £0.35 ISBN 0-00-138004-4

130 Bowness, Charles. Romany Magic. Wellingborough, England: Aquarian Press, 1973. 96p. Index £1.50 ISBN 0-85030-106-8

This is a collection of many facts and legends about gypsies. They migrated from India centuries ago. The race is decreasing, with no more than 10,000 in Britain. Bowness has been friends with the Romanies, and is bound by promises not to divulge certain secrets. Chapters include: development of Romany magic; family lore; lore concerning animals; plants and objects; evil eye; protective and healing magic; fortune telling; glossary of Romany terms. There are many sub-sections within each topic. With about one page under each boldfaced heading, the work really functions as a sort of encyclopedia.

131 Boyd, Helen M. The True Horoscope of the United States of America. New York: ASI Publishers, 1975. iii, 171p. Illus. Index $7.25 pa. LC 75-7188 ISBN 0-88231-007-0

132 Boyer, Paul, and Stephen Nissenbaum. Salem Possessed: The
*** Social Origins of Witchcraft. Cambridge, Mass.: Harvard University Press, 1974. 229p. Illus. Maps Index $10 LC 73-84399

This work is a major new contribution to occult literature. It explores everyday life in the Salem of 1692. The authors are both history professors at the University of Massachusetts. They have made use of a previously neglected body of documents, by studying archives at the First Church of Danvers, Mass., location of the 1692 parish. They studied voting records, wills, lawsuits, and so forth, to understand divisions inside the community. They believe that studying the daily lives of ordinary people is the best view of a culture. Similar outbreaks at Northampton in 1735 were regarded as divinely inspired, and led to revivals. However, the Salem phenomena were interpreted as demonic. Targets in Salem were self-made successes, who caused the jealousy of other people. Three main issues are brought into focus: Salem village's independence from Salem; Samuel Parris's ministry; and church membership. The accused witches and their defenders lived in the east part of the village; the accusers lived in the west part. This fine work is one of quantitative history and rural sociology.

133 Boyle, John P. The Psionic Generator Pattern Book. Englewood Cliffs, N.J.: Prentice-Hall, 1975. 89p. Illus. $4.95 pa.

This book includes patterns for building a pyramid, an "occult illuminator," and 10 other devices to be used in connection with ESP. Included are instructions on how to use the devices.

134 Bramwell, James. Lost Atlantis. Hollywood, Calif.: Newcastle Pub. Co., 1974. 288p. $3.45 pa.

This book studies opinions on Atlantis by Plato, Lewis Spence, Ignatius Donnelly, and others.

135 Branley, Franklyn Mansfield, 1915- . The Book of Flying
* Saucers for You. Illus. by Leonard Kessler. New York: Crowell, 1973. 72p. Illus. (part color) $4.50 LC 72-78278 ISBN 0-690-15188-8

This is a good juvenile survey on the subject. The author is the astronomer of the Hayden Planetarium. He feels that most UFO's sighted have rational, although unusual, explanations. The physical possibilities of life beyond earth are discussed, as well as hoaxes, the will to believe, Ezekiel, and St. Elmo's fire. There are simple wash drawings on each page. This book is recommended for grades 5-6.

136 Branston, Brian, 1914- . Beyond Belief: True Tales of Psychic Phenomena. New York: Walker, 1974. 200p. Illus. Plates Includes bibliog. refs. $7.95 LC 74-82166 ISBN 0-8027-0472-7

The author, a BBC radio and television producer, discusses hauntings, poltergeists, possession, precognition and clairvoyance. He was involved in some of these cases, especially 1965 and 1966 happenings in a former London church hall then used as a photographic studio. The owner often went into trance, and phenomena such as table-turning occurred. A program based on this was shown on BBC-2 in May 1967. A sceptic, Prof. Eysenck, part of the television show, concluded that a group of people under great emotion believed that the hall was haunted, and that this could have influenced results. Branston also discusses Gerard Croiset, and work done in producing a documentary on him. The author believes the pineal gland may be responsible for psychic ability, and admits much ESP is not yet proved.

137 Brennan, James Herbert. Astral Doorways. London: Aquarian Press, 1971. viii, 115p. Illus. Plate £1 ISBN 0-85030-075-4

138 ______. Beyond the Fourth Dimension. London: Futura Publications, 1975. 164p. £0.40 pa. ISBN 0-86007-116-2

139 ______. Five Keys to Past Lives. New York: Weiser,
* 1971 (also, London: Aquarian, 1971). 63p. (Paths to Inner Power). $1.25 ISBN 0-87728-163-7

This work is a practical, not a theoretical, guide to reincarnation. The author attempts to explain how to gain information about the possible past lives of the reader, and then help the reader check out this information. He cites two main problems when investigating past lives: death trauma and self-deception. Chapters include "Ouija," "Hypnosis," "Symbol Contemplation," "Depth Meditation," "The Akashic Record," "Astral Travel," "Notes for Serious Students," "Case Histories." This entire "Paths to Inner Power" series is remarkably well-done. Each volume in the series offers a short, seriously written introduction to its topic. They are all strongly recommended.

140 ______. Occult Reich. London: Futura Publications, 1974 (also, New York: Signet/New American Library, 1974). 188p. Bibliog. £0.40/$1.50 ISBN 0-86007-012-3

This work discusses Hitler's practice of magic. The author's thesis is of a black magic, anti-Semitic, Germanic occult organization seeking world control. He makes Prof. Karl Haushofer the chief villian. The book is not well researched.

141/2 Brent, Peter. Fortune Telling. Hicksville, N. Y.: Marshall Cavendish, 1974. 64p. $1.95 pa. [Also pub. as How to Tell Your Fortune London: Marshall Cavendish, 1975. 64p. Illus. (chiefly color) (Golden Hands Books) £1.60 ISBN 0-85685-104-3]

This well-illustrated work discusses divination by cards, palmistry, I Ching, dice, dominoes, tea leaves, and numbers.

143 Brier, Robert. Precognition and the Philosophy of Science;
*** An Essay on Backward Causation. New York: Humanities Press, 1973. 105p. Bibliog. $5 LC 73-12754 ISBN 0-391-00325-9

This work is a major new contribution to occult literature. The book analyzes a special problem in considering causality: is backward causation (where effect precedes cause) possible? The first chapter is titled, "Gale on Backward Causation." Gale discusses the example of someone in the present warning someone in the past--"retrowarning." Chapter 2, "Dummett and His Critics," is the longest chapter in the book. Dummett gives the example of the dancing tribal chief who dances to make Indians brave even after the event is over. Is his dancing the last two days still important? Chapter 4, entitled "Scriven and Flew," discusses Whately Carington's experiments in precognitive drawing. All of these papers discussed by Brier were written in the last 20 years. His conclusion is that there is no logical objection to precognition. In fact, there is no adequate proof that precognition involves backward causation anyway. He feels one of the problems is defining the term "effect." Demands that it come after cause could be a mere terminological difficulty. A change in the definition could erase the problem.

144 Briggs, Harold William. Group Psychology, Linguistics and Precognition. Reading, England: H. W. Briggs, 1973. 32p. Illus. £0.15 pa. ISBN 0-9501812-3-4

145 ______. Mind Is Not Conserved. Reading, England: H. W. Briggs, 1971. 17p. Illus. £0.10 ISBN 0-9501812-0-X

146 British Unidentified Flying Object Research Association. Guide to the UFO Phenomenon. London: The Association, 1972. 17p. Illus. £0.42 pa. ISBN 0-903649-00-4

147 Broekman, Marcel. The Complete Encyclopaedia of Practical
* Palmistry. St. Albans, England: Mayflower, 1975 (also, London: Souvenir Press, 1974; orig. pub., Englewood Cliffs, N.J.: Prentice-Hall, 1972). 223p. Illus. £0.75 pa. ISBN 0-583-12511-5

This work is designed to allow the reader to start at page 1 and read directly through the book, learning in depth as he goes along. Part 1 includes all lines and markings dealing with events (life line, head line, heart line, fate line, sun line, health line, areas). Part 2 includes lines that indicate character and potential (thumb, fingers, nails, hand shape, markings, mounts). Part 3 discusses special questions such as love, marriage and success, and their location on the palm. Part 4 gives six sample readings complete with palmprint for each. The book gives 200 detailed line drawings used to illustrate the text. This work is very well-organized and complete.

148 Brother Philip. The Secret of the Andes. London: Corgi, 1973 (orig. pub., London: Spearman, 1961). 126p. £0.30 pa. ISBN 0-552-09232-0

149 Brown, Barbara. New Mind, New Body; Biofeedback: New
* Directions for the Mind. Foreword by Hugh Downs. New York: Harper and Row, 1974. 464p. Illus. Bibliog. $9.95 LC 73-14249 ISBN 0-06-010159-6

This work attempts a synthesis of all literature on the subject. The author is one of the pioneers in the field. She has worked at UCLA, and directs a lab at a veterans' hospital in Sepulveda, Calif. She discusses oscillographs and alpha brain waves, and the self-regulation of sweat glands, heart rate, blood pressure, temperature, muscles, and brain activity. Biofeedback has helped patients control hypertension and migraine. The author represents her thoughts on current research, but there is some controversy in the field. The reader should be aware that Brown's views are not the total output of opinion. However, it is wonderful to have a book on biofeedback written by a Ph.D. in physiology.

150 Brown, Christopher. Haunted Sherborne: A Tour of Ghostly Places. Sherborne, England: Abbey Bookshop, 1975. 32p. Illus. £0.50 pa. ISBN 0-905233-00-X

151 Brown, Raymond Lamont. The Book of Witchcraft. Illus. by Ernest Petts. New York: Taplinger, 1971 (also, Newton Abbot, England: David and Charles, 1971). 116p. Illus. $4.50 LC 71-143222 ISBN 0-8008-0940-8

152 ______. Casebook of Military Mystery. Cambridge, England: Stephens, 1974. 184p. Illus. Bibliog. Index £3.95 ISBN 0-85059-152-X
*

This work is a blend of military fact and fantasy. The author discusses ghosts from the Stone Age to the present day, and also describes occult practices and superstitions of the world's armies. Many of the sources are from legend and folklore. Brown feels that, in wartime, the main source of superstition is the armed forces. As examples of contents: one study showed that the most common amulets carried into battle by Americans were Bibles, crosses, rabbits' feet, clovers, and dice; another study states that in World War I, novels by Sir Henry Rider Haggard were found to be unlucky by gunners at Ypres.

153 ______. Magic Oracles of Japan: How to Divine Your Future with These Thousand Year Old Systems. London: L. N. Fowler, 1974. 141p. Illus. Bibliog. Index £1.95 ISBN 0-85243-330-1

154 ______. Phantom Soldiers. New York: Drake Publishers, 1975. 184p. Illus. Bibliog. Index $9.95 LC 74-22585 ISBN 0- 87749-777-X
*

This work is a real treasury of military ghost stories, most of them European. Also included are essays on the paranormal origins of martial music, insignia, and medals. The book contains very good illustrations. It is an excellent collection, saving many stories otherwise lost.

155 ______. Phantoms of the Sea: Legends, Customs, and Superstitions. New York: Taplinger Pub. Co., 1973 (c1972). 192p. Illus. Bibliog. $6.50 LC 72-11939
*

This work is an excellent anthology on the subject. The author discusses ghost ships (such as the Mary Celeste); submarines (especially the U-65); haunted islands and shores; voices from the deep; phantoms plaguing cruise ships (particularly the Llanstephan Castle, where several passengers leaped to their deaths); and submerged church bells foretelling disaster. There is an excellent section called "The Occult Way of the Sea," which discusses sailors' superstitions, amulets and talismans, figureheads, and launchings.

156 Brown, Rosemary. Immortals by My Side. Chicago: H. Regnery Co., 1975 (orig. pub. as "Immortals at My Elbow," London: Bachman and Turner, 1974). 239p. $8.95 LC 75-13248 ISBN 0-8092-8173-2

This sequel to Unfinished Symphonies (next entry) tries to deal with the spiritual implications of her work with the deceased composers. She writes that she has received very favorable testimony from many British musicologists that the music seems to be genuine. There are also non-musical items. In the appendix is the message she supposedly got from Bertrand Russell. In another chapter, she claims messages from Jung.

157 ________. Unfinished Symphonies: Voices from the Beyond.
* Foreword by the Bishop of Southwark. London: Pan Books, 1973 (also, New York: Morrow, 1971; orig. pub., London: Souvenir Press, 1971). 175p. Illus. Music £0.35 pa.

This book probably deserves the *, but it is the kind of work that makes one feel uneasy. The author, a widowed London housewife, claims that she is visited regularly by the ghosts of Beethoven, Liszt, Chopin, Debussy, Schumann, Bach, Rachmaninov, and Brahms. These spirits help her play and write music far beyond her abilities. She states that she is even given their new compositions which they have written on the other side. She has had no academic musical training, but experts are amazed at the level of her works. She has supposedly convinced parapsychologists at the State University of Utrecht in the Netherlands. She relates her life of poverty, and other psychical happenings. She discusses each composer and her views on him. Unfortunately, there is no list in her book of the over 400 pieces she has received. (See also entry 156.)

158 Brown, Slater, 1896- . The Heyday of Spiritualism. New
*** York: Pocket Books, 1972 (orig. pub., New York: Hawthorn Books, 1971). 296p. Illus. Bibliog. Index $1.25 pa. ISBN 0-671-78153-7

This work is a major new contribution to occult literature. It discusses the spiritualist cults of 19th-century America. The book discusses animal magnetism work; traveling clairvoyance--that is, the faculty of seeing remote or hidden things; influence of Swedenborg; evocation of the dead; the Shakers; Andrew Jackson Davis; the Fox sisters; Phelps family poltergeist disturbances in Stratford, Conn.; spirit communications; Davenport brothers; trance stereotypes (only famous people communicating, and so forth); D. D. Home. The book has an excellent bibliography, and is very well-researched. This fine over-view is strongly recommended to all readers, believers or not.

159 Brown, Wenzell. How to Tell Fortunes with Cards. Folkestone, England: Bailey Bros. and Swinfen, 1971 (orig. pub., New York: Sterling Pub.; London: Oak Tree Press, 1963). 128p. Illus. £1.40 ISBN 0-561-00095-6

160 Browning, Norma Lee. The Psychic World of Peter Hurkos.
* New York: New American Library, 1973 (c1970). 237p. Illus. $1.25 pa. LC 76-114751

A confirmed skeptic at the beginning of her research on this book, the author became convinced that Hurkos has psychic powers rivaling Cayce himself. This biography discusses the accident that began it all; the beginnings of Hurkos's psychic detective work; the odic force; the Boston Strangler case; the Jim Thompson case; Hurkos in Hollywood; the Ann Arbor murders; the Sharon Tate case. The work includes speculation based on research into the medical nature of Hurkos's powers.

161 Bruteau, Beatrice. Evolution Toward Divinity. Wheaton, Ill.: Theosophical Pub. House, 1974. 270p. $10

This work relates the writings of Teilhard de Chardin to Hindu traditions (in spite of Teilhard's negative feelings toward Hinduism). The four main chapters take themes in his writings and quote any Hindu documents that agree with them. The author feels Teilhard should have appreciated the Hindu traditions.

162 Bryan, Lola Inez. Astrology's Looking Glass. Baton Rouge, La.: Woodale Pub. Co., 1972. 100p. $2.50

163 Bucke, Richard Maurice, 1837-1902. Cosmic Consciousness:
* A Study in the Evolution of the Human Mind. New York: Causeway Books, 1974 (reprint of 1901 ed., pub. by Innes, Philadelphia, with a new introd.). xvii, 326p. Includes bibliog. ref. $8.95 LC 73-92548 ISBN 0-88356-033-X

This book is definitely one of the all-time classics of occult literature. The first three parts are: introduction; discussion of evolution; discussion of the transition from self to cosmic consciousness. The fourth section presents instances of cosmic consciousness (Buddha, Christ, Paul, Mohammed, Dante, Blake, Whitman). The fifth part discusses some of the lesser, imperfect, and doubtful instances--Moses, Socrates, Pascal, Swedenborg, Thoreau). The work is on those who have had the power of transcendent realization or illumination. Bucke felt that this illumination is more and more on the increase.

164 Buckland, Raymond, and Hereward Carrington. The Amazing Secrets of the Psychic World. West Nyack, N.Y.: Parker Pub. Co., 1975. Bibliog. $7.95 LC 74-22327 ISBN 0-13-024042-7

This book presents case histories collected by Carrington in the early 1900's, as edited by a modern writer. There is added information on controlling your future.

165 ________. Here Is the Occult. New York: House of Collectibles, 1974. 143p. $1.25 pa.

This book contains chapters on voodoo; satanism; witchcraft. Also, it includes a dictionary of occult terms.

166 ________. Tree: The Complete Book of Saxon Witchcraft. New York: S. Weiser, 1974. 158p. Illus. Bibliog. $2.95 pa. LC 74-79397 ISBN 0-87728-258-7

This book is presented as the Seax-Wica "Book of Shadows," with annotations and additional material by Buckland. However, in the work, it is stated that this book is not a reconstruction of the original Saxon religion, but a new tradition hung on an old peg. It discusses history, structure, rites, magic, herbal lore, songs, recipes, and divination.

167 ________. Witchcraft from the Inside. St Paul: Llewellyn, 1971. xiii, 141p. Illus. (Llewellyn Occult Manual) $2 pa. LC 70-24986 ISBN 0-87542-049-4

The author has a Ph. D. in anthropology, and is founder and director of the Museum of Witchcraft and Magick in the U. S. The book discusses definition of witchcraft, history of witchcraft, Christianity, popes and Middle Ages persecution, the 18th and 19th centuries, today's rites, working naked, fairies, commanding spirits, voodoo, Crowley, poems, and witches' recipes. The author is of the Gardnerian school.

168 Buckley, Doris Heather. Conversations with the Beyond. Los Angeles: Sherbourne Press, 1971. 163p. (For the Millions Series) $2.50 pa. LC 71-162389 ISBN 0-8202-0014-X

The author and members of her group are called from the beyond to do rescue work, help foundering spirits leave their recently deceased bodies, and comfort those in the agonies of death. Teachers from the beyond guide her.

169 ________. Spirit Communication. New York: Award, 1971 (c1967). 154p. (Orig. Title, "Spirit Communication for the Millions") $.95 pa.

170 Budapest, Z. Feminist Book of Lights and Shadows. Venice, Calif.: FBLS Collective, 1975. 123p. $4 pa.

This book discusses rituals for sabbats and esbats, curses, spells, cures, methods of forming Dianic groves and covens, how to use natural ways of birth control. The author claims that the book will be worthless to males, since its very soul is that of a woman.

171 Budge, Ernest Alfred Thompson Wallis, 1857-1934. Egyptian Heaven and Hell. LaSalle, Ill.: Open Court Pub. Co., 1974. 200p. $3.45 pa. reprint

172 ________. Egyptian Magic. Magnolia, Mass.: Peter Smith,
* 1972 (New York: B. Blom, 1971; reprint of 1901 ed., issued as v. 2 of Books on Egypt and Chaldaea--Dover Book, rebound). xv, 234p. Bibliog. refs. $4.50

The introduction of this classic work is on the role of magic to control the gods. The book discusses use of amulets to ward off evil, scarabs, use of wax images, magic pictures, formulas, use of secret words and names, rituals and curses. Many magic formulas are fully given, in Egyptian sounds and English. There are many excerpts from papyri and tomb paintings.

173 Buess, Lynn M. Tarot and Transformation. Illus. of Tarot
* cards by Roxana R. Donegan. Lakemont, Ga.: Tarnhelm Press, 1973. 256p. Illus. $2.95 pa. LC 73-77608

The author has written an intelligent, well-organized introduction to the Tarot for modern-day practitioners. This was the author's master's thesis at West Georgia College. Chapters include "Involution and Evolution--Man's Inner Growth," "Tarot on the Plane of Self-Consciousness" (22 major cards discussed), "Tarot on the Path to Cosmic, God-consciousness" (22 major cards discussed on this higher level), "Tarot and Self-growth," "Tarot in Divination." The rest of the work gives the meaning of each minor card, for use in divination. Especially interesting are the author's own personal thoughts and experiences.

174 Dunn, I., and M. Burgess. Haunted Lowestoft: The Most Easterly Ghosts in England. Illus. by I. Bunn. Lowestoft, England: B.S.I.G., 1975. 18p. Illus. £0.30 pa. ISBN 0-9504602-0-6

175 Buranelli, Vincent. The Wizard from Vienna. New York:
* Coward, McCann and Geoghegan, 1975. 256p. $8.95

This is a fine biography of Mesmer. His earliest training was in law and religion. He proposed a universal fluid too fragile to be measured scientifically but which had influence on the human physical body. This led to his theory of animal magnetism, a force he claimed could cure illness. He was ridiculed. Part of it was his own fault--he dressed often in robes while waving about a wand. Mesmer later wrote that animal magnetism could explain paranormal phenomena. This caused him to be remembered as an occultist, and not as the father of abnormal psychology. The book discusses Mesmer in relation to the history of psychology, the Society of Harmony, and the occult. Buranelli stresses that Mesmer had the right facts, but the wrong theory. Also mentioned is Mesmer's effect on men such as Poe and Mozart.

176 Burden, Virginia. The Process of Intuition. Wheaton, Ill.: Theosophical Pub. House, 1975. xv, 83p. (A Quest Book). $2.50 pa. LC 75-4170 ISBN 0-8356-0466-7

177 Burland, Cottie Arthur, 1905- . Beyond Science; A Journey into the Supernatural. New York: Grosset and Dunlap, 1973 (c1972). 128p. Illus. $9.95 LC 72-83611 ISBN 0-448-02157-9

This veteran writer shows how the old rituals of Christianity are related to earlier rites which have survived as an orgiastic underground religion. The author discusses the rise of magic and witchcraft throughout history. He emphasizes how church religion and witchcraft have coexisted as two approaches to the supernatural. Modern occult practices are really signs of a trend back to the magic of nature. The book reads like a long, rather disorganized essay. The excellent illustrations, some in color, give this work the appearance and style of a coffee-table book.

178 ______. Echoes of Magic: A Study of Seasonal Festivals through the Ages. London: P. Davies, 1972. 234p. Illus. Bibliog. Index £3.50 ISBN 0-432-01963-4

Much of this book is on the sexual content of early festivals. He investigates British festivals and their continuity over the centuries. There is also a chapter on the element of chance. The author favors a return to the fairy tale quality of the nature festival, instead of our over-intellectualized rituals of today. The appendix is a "Calendar of Saints' Days and Festivals." The writing is anecdotal and relaxed.

179 ______. Secrets of the Occult. London: Ebury Press, 1972. 128p. Illus. (some color) Index £3.15 ISBN 0-85223-023-0

180 Burr, George Lincoln, 1857-1938. New England's Place in the History of Witchcraft. Freeport, N.Y.: Books for Libraries, 1971 (reprint of the 1911 ed.). 35p. Bibliog. refs. $6.50 LC 71-164592 ISBN 0-8369-5876-4

181 Burroughs, Melba. Astrology Reveals Life and Love. St. Paul, Minn.: Llewellyn Pubns., 1973. xx, 231p. $2.95 pa.

This book discusses how a person's love-needs are influenced by three factors--Mars, Venus, and the sun. Charts allow one to find the positions of Mars and Venus at one's birth. The significance of the various positions is explained.

182 Burt, Cyril Lodowic, 1883-1971. ESP and Psychology. Ed. by Anita Gregory. New York: Halsted Press, 1975 (also, London: Weidenfeld and Nicolson, 1975). 179p. Bibliog. Index $11.50 LC 75-16165 ISBN 0-470-12531-4

After a short biography in chapter 1, essays written by Burt appear in the chronological order in which they were written. Most of them were written after Burt was 80 years of age. His younger years were spent in the fields of theoretical and applied psychology. The second chapter is Burt's review of Gardner Murphy's book, Challenge of Psychical Research. The third chapter is on Jung, and the fourth on soul. The fifth is a history of parapsychology. Chapter 7 is on a control experiment for cross-correspondences. There are other chapters on: the Lethe case and the statistics of probability; a review of Alister Hardy's lectures; and the longest chapter in the book, one on evolution and parapsychology. The last chapter contains Burt's suggestions for future psychical research. He stresses the need for publicity, and gives areas for further study. His conclusions are that the human mind is such that psychical phenomena are possible.

183 Burton, Maurice. The Sixth Sense of Animals. New York: Ballantine Books, 1974. 244p. $1.65 pa.

The author states that animals can detect the passage of time, temperatures, and directions. The work does not really discuss paranormal abilities, since all these are peculiar physical abilities, mostly using the five regular senses. This book is a good discussion of normal abilities, and should alert psychical researchers about abilities that should not be considered paranormal. Much of the information is not referenced.

184 Busteed, Marilyn; Richard Tiffany; and Dorothy Wergin. Phases of the Moon: A Guide to Evolving Human Nature. Berkeley, Calif.: Shambhala, 1974 (dist. in U.S. by Random House; also London: Routledge and Kegan Paul, 1975). 223p. Illus. Bibliog. $7.95 LC 74-10249 ISBN 0-87773-056-3

This work is based on a synthesis of humanistic astrology and the schemata of Yeat's "A Vision." It introduces a new interpretation for the phases of the moon. Part 1, an introduction of about 50 pages, discusses cycles, the lunar mandala, and time. Part 2 discusses the pattern of 28 lunar phases as a tool for understanding natal astrology; it is the major section in the book. Part 3, the appendices, presents well-known people's phases, symbols used in the book, and a glossary.

185 Butler, Bill. Definitive Tarot. London: Rider, 1975. 254p. Illus. Bibliog. £4.50 ISBN 0-09-121010-0

186 ______. Dictionary of the Tarot. New York: Schocken
*** Books, 1975. 253p. Illus. Bibliog. $7.95 LC 74-9230

This work is a major new contribution to occult literature. With all the varying interpretations given to each Tarot card, it is a great pleasure to see a book come along that seeks to give all these interpretations. The reader can make exciting comparisons between the views of various authors and Tarot experts. For the minor arcana, this book gives for each card the following interpretations for "design": Marseille, Waite, Aquarian, Crowley, New (c1969, by John Starr Cooke). For the minor arcana, Butler then gives these "interpretations": Case, Crowley, Douglas, G. Dawn, Gray, Grimaud, Huson, Kahn, Kaplan, Mathers, Papus, Thierens,

Waite, suggested. For the major arcana, Butler gives for each card these "designs": Gringonneur, Bembo, Swiss, Insight, Marseille, Italian, Wirth, Waite, B. O. T. A., Aquarian, Crowley, New. For the major arcana, he then gives these "interpretations": Case, Christian, Crowley, Douglas, Gray, G. Dawn, Grimaud, Huson, Kahn, Kaplan, Knight, Lind, Mathers, Mayananda, Papus, Sadhu, Thierens, Ussher, Waite, suggested. Butler also includes a short history of the Tarot, and an excellent glossary of about 500 terms. This well-done work is an essential reference tool for work with the Tarot.

187 Butler, Eliza Barian, 1885- . Ritual Magic. Hollywood, Calif.: Newcastle Pub., 1971 (c1949). 328p. Illus. Bibliog. (Occult Book) $3.45 pa. ISBN 0-87877-001-1

188 Butler, Walter Ernest. How to Develop Psychometry. New
* York: S. Weiser, 1971 (also, London: Aquarian Pub., 1971). 63p. (Paths to Inner Power) $1.25 ISBN 0-87728-088-6

This book is an excellent survey concerning the ability to divine information about a person or event by touching an object connected with that person or happening. This work discusses: a psychometrist at work; astral light; reflecting ether; psychic gifts; preliminary training; ability to observe; actual steps involved with doing a reading; charged objects; rules of conduct. The book is another excellent survey in the "Paths to Inner Power" series.

189 _______. How to Read the Aura. London: Aquarian Press 1971. 64p. (Paths to Inner Power) £0.35 pa. ISBN 0-85030-069-X

190 _______. An Introduction to Telepathy. New York: S. Weiser,
* 1975 (also, Wellingborough, England: Aquarian Press, 1975). 64p. (Paths to Inner Power) $1.25 ISBN 0-87728-350-8

This work is a fine, short introduction to telepathy. The discussions include: what is telepathy; physical conditions for successful experiments; psychical and psychological conditions; training for telepathy; hypnotic and Mesmeric telepathy; telepathy and superphysical healing; telepathic thought-forms. There have been so many books written about telepathy; yet it seems impossible to find one good survey. Look no further, for this is it.

191 Buttlar, Johannes von. Journey into Infinity: Travels in Time. Trans. by Olga Sieveking. London: Spearman, 1975. 208p. Illus. Plates Bibliog. Index (Translation of "Reisen in die Eurigkeit." Vienna: Econ, 1973) £3.25 ISBN 0-85435-302-X

This work discusses, among other things, voices from the other side and reincarnation, especially that manifested by hypnotic regression.

192 Byfield, Barbara Ninde. The Book of the Weird. Garden City, N.Y.: Doubleday, 1973 (c1967). 160p. Illus. $3.95 pa.

This book is a humorous collection of definitions for such creatures as werewolves, vampires, trolls, elves, gnomes, knaves, and other mystical, fantastic subjects.

193 Byrd, Elizabeth. Strange and Seeing Time. London: Hale, 1971. 190p. Illus. Plates £1.80 ISBN 0-7091-2081-8

This book is advertised as a discussion of times in the author's life when she became a wanderer in another dimension, and when other wanderers have entered her world. Actually, it is a breezy autobiography of her and her husband Barry, and experiences they had in a rented house in Scotland. She saw many ghosts, and also had occurrences where she saw colored film in her head of various incidents. Apparently, her first unusual experience occurred in 1961, when she had a sudden mystical vision of oneness with the universe.

194 Byrne, Peter, 1925- . Search for Big Foot: Monster, Myth or Man. Foreword by Robert Rines. Washington: Acropolis Books, 1975. Index $8.95 LC 75-13943 ISBN 0-87491-159-1

The author, a former big-game hunter, is associated with the Bigfoot Information Center in Oregon. He discusses his attempts to collect evidence on Bigfoot to determine precisely its identity. He discusses eyewitnesses, his own unsuccessful searches, and a 1967 movie supposedly of Bigfoot. He believes it exists.

195 Campbell, Elizabeth Montgomery, and David Solomon. Search
* for Morag. New York: Walker, 1973 (also, London: Tom Stacey, 1972). 192p. Illus. Bibliog. $6.95 LC 72-95804 ISBN 0-8027-0422-0

This is a balanced, complete study of the subject. In 1969, a creature was seen in Loch Morar in Scotland for the first time. The authors point out that similar sightings have come from at least nine Scottish lochs. They state that Loch Ness and Loch Morar each contain more than one creature. In 1970 and 1971, a Loch Morar survey was conducted. The conclusion was that the lake was capable of supporting such animals. Two chapters are devoted to over 30 eyewitness accounts between 1900 and 1971. One of the best chapters is "Problem of Credulity." The work has illustrations and tables, and offers possibilities for future research.

196 Campbell, John Gregorson, 1836-1891. Witchcraft and Second Sight in the Highlands and Islands of Scotland. Detroit: Singing Treee Press, 1970 (also, Wakefield, England: EP Publishing, 1974; orig. pub., 1902). 314p. $15 LC 78-137356

This collection of tales and traditions is taken entirely from oral sources.

197 Campione, Michael J. Anit-"Black" Magic. Cinnaminson, N. J.: The Author, 1973. 136p. Bibliog. $3 pa.

198 ______. UFO Manual. Cinnaminson, N. J.: The Author, 1973. 31p. Illus. $1 pa.

This book summarizes 25 years of the author's research into recognition factors, sizes and shapes, colors, sounds, speeds, and flight formations of UFO's. Two pages of drawings are included.

199 Canning, John, ed. Fifty Strange Stories of the Supernatural.
* London: Souvenir Press, 1974. 483p. Illus. Index £ 2.95 ISBN 0-285-62146-7

This is a very good collection of true stories. Chapters include the following: Orient, witches, ghosts of Britain, strange hauntings, spectres of the sea, they came back, of saints and a church, war and the supernatural, ghosts benevolent, ju-ju and voodoo, messages from another world, curses, spirit healing and psychic surgery, and practitioners and prophets.

200 Carrington, Hereward, 1880- . Laboratory Investigations
* into Psychic Phenomena. New York: Arno, 1975. (orig. pub., Philadelphia, 1939). (Perspectives in Psychical Research Series) $14 LC 75-7370 ISBN 0-405-07021-7

This work gives detailed descriptions and photos of many devices Carrington and others used to detect any unusual phenomena present at the time of his investigations. Most of his research is on mediumship and out-of-the-body experiences.

201 ______. The World of Psychical Research. New ed. South
* Brunswick: A. S. Barnes, 1973 (also London: Yoseloff, 1973; orig. pub. as "Invisible World," New York: Beechhurst Press, 1946). 190p. $5.95 LC 72-6371

The author spent 45 years in the field of psychical research, many of them as Director of the American Psychical Institute. Chapters include: "New Spiritual Awakening," "Haunted Houses," "Palladino," "Mrs. Piper," "Trumpet Mediums," "Poltergeists," "How Spirit Photographs Are Faked," "Psychic Photography," "Visions of Jeanne d'Arc," "Free Will and Determinism in the Light of Psychic Phenomena," and "Yoga and Magic." The author hoped that psychical research would lead us to understand that "mankind is indeed one great spiritual brotherhood, encompassed by One Great Mind." As with most books by Carrington, this one is a classic.

202 ______. Your Psychic Powers and How to Develop Them. San Bernardino, Calif.: Newcastle Pub. Co., 1975 (reprint of earlier ed., orig. pub., New York: American Universities Pub. Co., 1920, as part of Occult and Psychical Sciences Series). $3.95 pa. LC 75-22483 ISBN 0-87877-033-X

203 Carroll, David, 1942- . Magic Makers; Magic and Sorcery
* through the Ages. New York: Arbor House, 1974 (dist. by McKay, New York). 286p. Illus. $8.95 LC 73-91503 ISBN 0-87795-080-6

The first chapter argues against magic as presented by skeptics, and then presents the author's view of true magic as a state of being natural to man's psychic make-up. He feels true magic is very rare today, because of the march of technology. The work discusses Egyptians, Hebrews, Greeks, Romans, Appollonius of Tyana, Edward Kelley, Cornelius Agrippa, Faust, Count de Saint Germain, Cagliostro, John Dee. The last chapter is written by a modern magician, unnamed. The work is illustrated with rare woodcuts and engravings.

204 Carter, Charles Ernest Owen. Astrological Aspects. Rev. and enlarged ed. London: L. N. Fowler, 1975. 160p. (Previous ed., 12th, 1972). £0.90 pa.

205 _______. Principles of Astrology. Wheaton, Ill.: Theosophical Pub. House, 1971. xi, 188p. (Quest Book) $2.45 pa. LC 79-154829 ISBN 0-8356-0423-3

206 _______. Zodiac and the Soul. 4th ed. London: Theosophical Pub. House, 1972 (orig. pub., 1968). 120p. Illus. Index £1 ISBN 0-7229-5098-5

207 Carter, Mary Ellen. My Years with Edgar Cayce; The Personal Story of Gladys Davis Turner. New York: Harper, 1972. xiv, 140p. $4.95 LC 78-175159

This is the story of Cayce's secretary for over 20 years, who was present at most of his trances. She recorded nearly 14,000 readings he gave up to the time he died in 1945. She lived and traveled with the Cayce family. Most of what she has to say, though, has been said before by the many fine biographies out on Cayce.

208 Carus, Paul, 1852-1919. Chinese Astrology. LaSalle, Ill.: Open Court, 1974 (c1907). (Abridged version of author's "Chinese Thought"). $2.95 pa. LC 73-20411 ISBN 0-87548-155-8

209 _______. History of the Devil and the Idea of Evil; from the
* Earliest Times to the Present Day. LaSalle, Ill.: Open Court Pub. Co., 1974 (also, Land's End Press, 1969; New York: Bell Pub. Co., 1974; orig. pub., 1900). 496p. Illus. Index $5.95 pa. ISBN 0-87548-307-0

This classic work is a fine historical survey of the idea of evil. The 350 illustrations (old woodcuts and engravings) take up one fourth of the book, and further enhance its value. Chapters include: good and evil as religious ideas, devil worship, Egypt, Persia,

Israel, Buddhism, Christianity, Greece and Italy, demonology of Northern Europe, Inquisition, Reformation, verse and fable, philosophical problem of good and evil. The book is a world view of theories of demonology and evil. It is a very scholarly book with great detail, and many references to rare sources.

210 Casanova's Book of Numbers and the Daily Horoscope. Trans. and ed. by Jerzy Laskowski. Seattle: Vulcan Books, 1975. 146p. $2.95 pa. LC 74-78608 ISBN 0-914350-05-6

This book discusses astrology and numerology as conceived by Giacomo Girolamo Casanova de Seingalt, born 1725, died 1798.

211 Castaneda, Carlos. Journey to Ixtlan: The Lessons of Don
*** Juan. London: Bodley Head, 1973 (orig. pub., New York: Simon & Schuster, 1972). 315p. £2.25 ISBN 0-370-10482-X

This work is a major new contribution to occult literature. It is the third book of a series, the first two works of which are The Teachings of Don Juan and A Separate Reality. The first two were mainly concerned with the use of hallucinogens by Don Juan, a Yaqui sorcerer. This is a quite different book. Here, Castaneda announces the sorcerer must be taken seriously on his own terms and reality. He states that his earlier assumption that hallucinogens were necessary to gain proper perception was wrong. Also, he now states that the Western view of reality is not the only valid one. This is a change, for in the first books, he felt that his experiences could be understood in terms of Western reality. The present work discusses experiences in relation to hills, valleys, plants, animals, and Don Juan. It describes the lessons--exercises of will and body--by which one is prepared to see things as they really are. Grueling desert marches, apparitions, and magic tricks are among the topics discussed.

212 ________. A Separate Reality. New York: Simon & Schuster,
*** 1972 (c1971). 317p. $2.95 pa.

This work is a major new contribution to occult literature. In this book, Don Juan teaches Castaneda how to "see." "Seeing" is a complex process by which a man of knowledge perceives the essence of the things of the world. It is done by smoking peyote. With the aid of Don Juan, he meets various "supernatural" entities. He sees a friend of Don Juan's standing on a hill 100 miles away. He sees a leaf fall to the ground, and replays it over and over again in his mind. The book is an expression of the development of the spirit.

213 ________. Tales of Power. New York: Simon & Schuster,
*** 1974. 287p. $7.95 LC 74-10601 ISBN 0-671-21858-1

This work is a major new contribution to occult literature. From January to December 1975, it appeared 19 times on the New York Times weekly Top 10 Best Seller List for Non-Fiction. This book is the fourth in the series. It makes a distinction between "tonal" (everything in the physical world), and "nagual" (non-physical, or unknown). Through heightened perception, one can reach the "nagual." When he does this, Don Juan disappears, and Carlos faces the unknown. The author discusses the process for becoming a "warrior." He urges us to experience the world without interpretation, to stop our internal dialog.

214 ______. The Teachings of Don Juan: A Yaqui Way of
* Knowledge. New York: Pocket Books, 1974 (orig. pub., University of California Press, 1968). 256p. $1.95 pa. LC 68-17303 ISBN 0-671-80498-7

This work is not given a *** only because it was originally published in 1968. It has already become a classic, and could still be considered the most important of the four Don Juan books, of which it is the first. The author describes the use of peyote, datura, and hallucinogenic mushrooms under the watchful eye of a North Mexican Indian witch/sorcerer. These are taken as "allies" to help one become a "man of knowledge." There are many memorable events in the book. One occurs after Castaneda takes peyote. He sees the "god" Mescalito, whose head looks exactly like the surface of the peyote plant. At one point, Castaneda looks into a hole on the back of Mescalito's hand, and sees himself as an old, feeble man with bright sparks flying about him. Another has Castaneda use datura paste on his temple with a lizard perched on his shoulder to actually see past events. A third shows Castaneda taking datura paste and then "flying" at extraordinary speed over mountains and through clouds. Of the many quotable comments, this bibliographer enjoys most: "The particular thing to learn is how to get to the crack between the worlds.... There is a place where the two worlds overlap. The crack is there. It opens and closes like a door in the wind." Castaneda is a young anthropologist, and, actually, all the Don Juan books could more accurately be called anthropology than occult writings. All his books have been reviewed in important journals of anthropology, sociology, and ideas. Some critics have even seen them as literature (fiction). A few even dare classify them as science fiction. However, it seems two of the books were accepted for a master's degree and a Ph. D. degree. This book has had a tremendous influence in the U. S. these last 10 years, especially among high school and college students. The writing style is ingenious, and built on a question and answer format. The style seems to literally strip the reader of his normal view of reality, and stand him right next to Castaneda as he undergoes his "ordeals." All four books are absolutely essential reading for any educated reader, and a must for all libraries.

215 Catalogue of the Library of the [British] Society for Psychical
*** Research. Boston: G. K. Hall, 1976. 341p. $50 ISBN 0-8161-0008-X

This work is a major new contribution to occult literature.

It did not make our cut-off date of 1975, but is of such importance that it is included here. This library catalog contains a title arrangement with 3,514 cards, and then an author arrangement with 3,627 cards. Earlier catalogs of the Society's holdings were published in 1883 (400 volumes), and 1929 (6,400 volumes). In 1957, when the Society moved from Tavistock Square to Adam and Eve Mews, the number of books was about 8,000. In 1973-74, the Society reorganized the library and reduced the numbers of nonessential books. This library is generally acknowledged to be the greatest psychical research library in the world, and this volume is therefore an important reference tool. There are many French and German works listed. The catalogue itself is printed on permanent, durable acid-free paper.

216 Cathie, Bruce L., and A. W. Reed. Harmonic 33. Wellington, N. Z.: Reed, 1973, c1968 (dist. by Charles E. Tuttle, Rutland, Vt.). $8.95

The author, a New Zealand airlines pilot, has been a believer since 1952, when he and six companions saw a saucer. Since then, he has seen five more. He believes that once, a worldwide grid system existed buried deep underground. This system was built by earlier humans for extraterrestrial visitors. From it, the UFO's got their power, and used the grid also for navigational purposes. He feels the saucers are today rebuilding the grid. Much of his evidence consists of photos taken by the U. S. ship Eltanin at a depth of 13,500 feet, showing an antenna-like object (many feel it is only a live creature of some kind).

217 ________, and P. N. Temm. Harmonic 695: The UFO and Anti-gravity. Wellington, N. Z.: A. H. and A. W. Reed, 1971 (dist. in U. S. by Charles E. Tuttle, Rutland, Vt.). 201p. $9.25

218 Cavendish, Richard, 1930- . Encyclopedia of the Unexplained: Magic, Occultism, and Parapsychology. Special scientific consultant, J. B. Rhine. New York: McGraw-Hill, 1974 (also, London: Routledge and Kegan Paul, 1974). 304p. Illus. (some color). Bibliog. Index $17.95 LC 73-7991 ISBN 0-07-010295-3
***

This work is a major new contribution to occult literature. It was picked as one of the American Library Association's Reference and Adult Services Section "Notable Books of 1974." Coverage is mainly of psychic phenomena in the Western world since 1800. Emphasis is more on the occult and magic, and less on parapsychology. The book covers parapsychology, magic, astrology, ESP, spiritualism, Eastern beliefs, divination. Long articles are signed. J. B. Rhine wrote a long introduction, "How to Cope with a Mystery." His wife wrote an article on apparitions. Roll wrote on mediums and poltergeists, Gauld on spiritualism. There are also articles by Benjamin Walker and Francis King. Cavendish tries to adopt an editorial attitude of "sympathetic neutrality." The preface states, "All the territory we cover is disputed." The 200 illustrations contain many photos, drawings, and engravings, plus 18 color plates. There is a bibliography of 521 entries. Also appearing are indexes of persons and book titles.

219 ______. Powers of Evil in Western Religion, Magic and
* Folk Belief. London: Routledge and Kegan Paul, 1975 (also, New York: G. P. Putnam's Sons, 1975). ix, 299p. Bibliog. Index £5.95 ISBN 0-7100-8117-0

This work discusses vampires, witches, dragons, demons, ghosts, and other forces, such as sex, death, and evil. This popular survey serves as a source book for cases and anecdotes from the ancient world, old religions, and daily life. Cavendish says he was more interested in the ideas themselves than in their validity. He often tries to explain causes in psychological or socioeconomic terms. He does not consider the phenomena as truly objective, or as possibly originating outside of the psyche.

220 ______. Tarot. New York: Harper and Row, 1975 (also,
* London: Joseph, 1975). 191p. Illus. (some color) Bibliog. Index $19.95 LC 75-868 ISBN 0-06-010688-3

This survey covers the history, evolution, and meaning of the cards. There are also sections on the relationship to the Cabala, and methods for using the Tarot in divination. Cavendish states that the authors of Tarot books mostly invented its history. The book is very attractive, with color plates and diagrams.

221 Cayce, Edgar Evans, 1877-1945, and Hugh Lynn Cayce. The
* Outer Limits of Edgar Cayce's Power. New York and London: Harper and Row, 1973 (c1971). 170p. Illus. $4.95

After establishing their dad's 43-year record of accuracy, Edgar Cayce's two sons examine the readings of Cayce which were failures, the aim being to better understand the nature and limits of his powers. Chapters include: "Locating Missing Persons" (including the inaccurate reading on the identity of the Lindbergh baby kidnapper); "Readings for the Dead," "The Elusive Treasure of White Hill," "The Lost Dutchman Mine," "Oil Wells," and "Indian Gold in Arkansas."

222 Cayce, Hugh Lynn. Venture Inward. New York: Harper and
* Row, 1972 (also, Toronto: Fitzhenry and Whiteside, 1972; orig. pub., New York: Harper and Row, 1964). 207p. $.95 pa. ISBN 0-06-087021-4

This attempt at writing a survey of psychic phenomena by Edgar Cayce's son uses his father's cases and views throughout. There are many long quotes from the case studies. The book discusses hypnosis, mediumship, automatic writing, Ouija boards, possession, dianetics and Scientology, peyote, mushrooms, and LSD, telepathy, dreams, meditation, and place of the small group in the spiritual search. The book makes for fascinating reading, and its small print packs in a vast amount of information.

223 A Century of Psychical Research: The Continuing Doubts and
* Affirmations. Proceedings of an international conference held at Le Piol, St. Paul de Vence, France, September 2, 3, 4, 1970. Ed. by Allan Angoff and Betty Shapin. New York: Parapsychology Foundation, 1971. xii, 212p. Illus. Bibliog. refs. $6 LC 73-153407 ISBN 0-912328-19-3

The "doubts" were expressed by Eric Dingwall, John Cutten, Daniel Cohen, D. J. West, and C. E. M. Hansel. The following papers are also presented: Alister Hardy's "Parapsychology in Relation to Religion," W. G. Roll's "Critical Examination of the Survival Hypothesis," Walter Pahnke's "Use of Psychedelic Drugs in Parapsychology," Herbert Weiner's "Mystical Phenomena of Our Day and the Kabalah." Benson Herbert presents a discussion of psychic phenomena and lower temperatures accompanying poltergeist activity and levitation. James Hillman discusses psychic research and Jungian psychology.

224 Cerullo, Morris. The Back Side of Satan. Carol Stream, Ill.: Creation House, 1973. xii, 224p. Illus. Bibliog. $4.95 LC 72-94922

225 Cerutti, Edwina. Olga Worrall: Mystic with a Healing Hand. New York: Harper & Row, 1975. $7.95 LC 75-9317 ISBN 0-06-061358-0

Warrall has spent a lifetime in healing, had researchers test her, and had articles written about her in medical journals. One chapter is on her lab work. Most of her efforts are centered at New Life Clinic at the Mount Washington Methodist Church in Baltimore. She does laying-on of hands after religious services, and also healing from a distance. She sees her mission as twofold: spiritual healing and preaching the gospel of survival. Survival she tries to prove through spirit communication. She can also do astral projection, including projection to the other side. The book has a great deal in it about life on the other side. Worrall keeps notes of all communications, and this book has excerpts from them. The author is an enthusiastic supporter of Worrall's, and thus, the book is uncritical. The Worralls published 10 years ago a summary of their careers called Gift of Healing. This present book seems to add little new to that.

226 Chaij, Fernando. Exploring the World of Psychic Powers: How Hypnotism and Spiritualism Can Affect Your Life. Nashville: Southern Pub., 1971. 223p. Bibliog. $2.50 pa. LC 71-152849

227 Chambers, Aidan. Aidan Chambers's Book of Ghosts and
* Hauntings. Illus. by Antony Maitland. Harmondsworth, England: Puffin Books, 1973 (also, Harmondsworth: Longman Young Books, 1973; Baltimore: Penguin, 1973). viii, 144p. Illus. Map Bibliog. Index £0.50 pa.

This juvenile book is a fine contribution to occult literature. The author has gone to the records of the [British] Society for Psychical Research to make the research authoritative. It includes the famous Morton apparition, and the Enniscorthy poltergeist of 1910. Renée Haynes of the Society for Psychical Research adds a chapter called "Investigating Hauntings" and tells how to submit an account of one to the Society. Also included is a map of haunted places in Britain, with some sketches of the most famous sites. In a chapter on spirit photography, the author concludes that such pictures are totally fraudulent. Spiritualists have criticized this chapter, especially concerning the Mrs. Deane case of 1924. There are many excellent illustrations throughout the book, with photos interspersed. This fine work is recommended for grades 7-10.

228 _______. Great British Ghosts. Illus. by Barry Wilkinson. London: Pan Books, 1974. 125p. Illus. Plans (Piccolo True Adventures) (A Piccolo Original) £0.30 pa. ISBN 0-330-24070-6

This book gives obscure stories culled from 19th-century psychic research reports and also more familiar ones, such as the Angel of Mons. It also covers modern tales, such as the haunting of a bowling alley, and phantom sailors who appeared in Sefton, Lancashire, England, in early 1973.

229 _______. Great Ghosts of the World. Illus. on cover by David Roe; illus. in text by Peter Edwards. London: Pan Books, 1974. 138p. Illus. (Piccolo True Adventures) (A Piccolo Original) £0.30 pa. ISBN 0-330-24058-7

230 _______. Haunted Houses. Illus. by John Cameron Jarvies. London: Pan Books, 1971. 123p. Illus. (Piccolo True Adventures). (A Piccolo Original) £0.20 pa. ISBN 0-330-02820-0

231 _______. More Haunted Houses. Illus. by Chris Bradbury. London: Pan Books, 1973. 124p. Illus. (Piccolo True Adventures) (A Piccolo Original) £0.25 pa. ISBN 0-330-23470-6

232 Chambers, Howard V. Occult Dictionary for the Millions.
* New York: Award Books, 1971 (orig. pub., Los Angeles: Sherbourne Press, 1966). 160p. $.75 pa.

This small dictionary gives short definitions for approximately 750 terms of the occult, including areas of magic, astrology, divination, religion, plants and drugs, numerology, stones and woods, symbolism, spiritualism, mythology. The definitions themselves show a strong attempt by Chambers to give an accurate, thorough description. All reference collections should definitely stock this and all other occult dictionaries, since each book contributes additional material often not found in the others.

233 Chaney, Earlyne. Remembering; The Autobiography of a Mystic. Los Angeles: Astara's Library of Mystical Classics, 1974. 382p. $8.95

This book is an autobiography of the leader of Astara and her husband, Robert Chaney. She used to be known as Early Cantrell, a steadily rising young actress. Her husband-to-be died. She began to search for a pair of eyes that appeared to her in dreams and visions. At Camp Chesterfield, Ind., she met Robert Chaney, a Spiritualist medium. The eyes were his. They married, and she developed her mediumship. At the age of 12, she was contacted by a life force that was to guide her through life. She called the force "Father Teacher" and later learned its name was Kut-Hu-Mi, the master who had helped organize the Theosophical Society. He later aided her in writing the Astara Book of Life.

234 Chaney, Robert. Adventures in ESP. Los Angeles, Calif.: Astara's Library of Mystical Classics, 1975. 137p. $3.95 pa.

The author is co-leader of Astara. He has worked over 35 years in the psychic field. The exercises he discusses are ones a person can easily do in daily routine. These lessons aid people in developing their clairvoyance, psychometric powers, and intuition.

235 Chaney, Robert Galen, 1913- . Mediums and the Development of Mediumship. Freeport, N.Y.: Books for Libraries, 1972 (c1946). 215p. (Essay Index Reprint Series) $11 LC 70-156628 ISBN 0-8369-2761-3

236 Chappell, Helen. The Waxing Moon; A Gentle Guide to Magick. New York: Links, 1974. 214p. Illus. Bibliog. $3.95 pa. LC 73-89670 ISBN 0-8256-3032-0

This work is a survey on magic practice and religion. Discussed are: magic; demonology; amulets and talismans; voodoo; herbalism. There is also a directory of magic supplies.

237 Charles, A.N.S. New Dimensions of Healing. Madras, India: Centre for Telergic Research, 1975. 14p.

This work discusses the author's use of dowsing and radiesthesia for healing.

238 Charroux, Robert. Lost Worlds: Scientific Secrets of the Ancients. Trans. by Lowell Blair. London: Fontana, 1974 (orig. pub., New York: Walker; London: Souvenir Press, 1973). 288p. Illus. Plates Index (1973 ed. entitled "Forgotten Worlds; Scientific Secrets of the Ancients and Their Warning for Our Time") (Translation of, "Livre des mondes oubliés." Paris: Laffont, 1971) £0.60 pa. ISBN 0-00-613435-1

The author theorizes that extraterrestrial beings brought about man and his civilizations. Discussions include the pyramids, Easter Island, and UFO's. The book comes out strongly against Christianity and Jesus.

239 _______. The Mysterious Past. London: Futura Publications Ltd., 1974. 316p. (Translation of "Livre du passe mystérieux." Paris: Laffont, 1973) £0.50 pa. ISBN 0-86007-044-1

240 _______. The Mysterious Unknown. Trans. by Olga Sieve-
* king. London: Corgi, 1973 (orig. pub., London: Spearman, 1972). 319p. Illus. (Translation of "Le Livre du mystérieux inconnu." Paris: Laffont, 1969). £0.50 pa.

This work sold 250,000 copies in France. It is a good survey and gathering of incidents. Each chapter has many subdivisions. Topics include unsolved enigmas, ancient science, megaliths, vanished civilizations, Celtic civilizations, words, apes, and dolphins, water, sorcery. The final chapter is a theoretical discussion of universal laws and cosmologies.

241 Chase, Lorienne, and Clifton W. King. Human Miracle: Transcendent Psychology. New York: Hawthorn Books, 1974. 206p. $8.95

This work discusses how to bring the body, mind, and spirit into balance. Chase sees five basic urges: self-preservation; self-expression; sex; gregariousness; and thirst for knowledge. The five evil aspects in man to crush are hostility, greed, lust, vanity, and attachment. Thought is the most powerful energy man has, and thought shapes destiny. There are case histories of improvements in illnesses at the two Chase-King Personal Development Centers in southern California.

242 Chase, Warren, 1813-1891. Life-line of the Lone One: or, Autobiography of the World's Child. 3rd ed. New York: AMS Press, 1974 (reprint of 1865 ed. pub. by B. Marsh, Boston). (Communal Societies in America) $16 LC 72-2950 ISBN 0-404-10715-X

243 Chaudhuri, Haridas. Being, Evolution and Immortality. Wheaton, Ill.: Theosophical Pub. House, 1974. 204p. (A Quest Book) $2.75 pa.

This book is an attempt to join man's intellectual knowledge with the spiritual world underlying that knowledge.

244 _______. Mastering the Problems of Living. Foreword by R. Gordon Agnew. Wheaton, Ill.: Theosophical Pub. House, 1975 (orig. pub., New York: Citadel Press, 1968). 222p. (A Quest Book) £1.75 pa. ISBN 0-8356-0463-2

245 Chetwynd, Thomas. How to Interpret Your Own Dreams (in One Minute or Less); An Encyclopedic Dictionary. New York: P. H. Wyden, 1972. xiv, 239p. Bibliog. $6.95 LC 72-189523

This work is supposedly based on Jungian archetypes and psychology. The author uses major categories, either images dreamed or key psychological concepts (conflict, archetypes, and so on). There are many sub-categories under most entries. The book was a Literary Guild alternate, and excerpts from it appeared in Family Circle.

246 Chicago Psychic Guide. Rev. ed. Chicago: Elinora Jaksto, 1975 (dist. by Astro-Occult Bookshoppe). $1

This work lists psychic organizations, bookstores, publications, spiritual groups, astrologers, and readers.

247 Christopher, Milbourne. Mediums, Mystics and the Occult.
*** New York: Crowell, 1975. 288p. Illus. Bibliog. Index $6.95

This work is a major new contribution to occult literature. The author is past president of the American Society of Magicians. He debunks Geller, Hurkos, Arigo, and others. Also, he is critical of scientists who have been fooled by these men. His thesis is that all abnormal events can be explained by the word "deception." Illustrations demonstrate these methods. Christopher states that he has managed to fool onlookers with Geller-type spoon-bending. Historical parts of the book are excellent. There are chapters on Mina Crandon of Boston (Margery) and Anna Fry. Chapters on modern persons include the following: Geller, psychic surgery, eyeless vision (faking blindfold tests), psychic feats of yogis, ESP in outer space, Ted Serios, Arthur Ford, mystics from the East. The Hurkos chapter is particularly interesting. Puharich (who has also "managed" the careers of Geller and von Däniken) brought Hurkos to the U. S. in 1956 to be tested in his Maine lab. The author brings out details about Hurkos never seen in other books. Psychic researchers and others have criticized Christopher's basic thesis that any event that theoretically could be duplicated by deception is a fraud. This sounds sadly like Condon's premise is his UFO report. However, this excellent work provides a needed balance to the wilder occult books.

248 ______. Seers, Psychics and ESP. London: Cassell, 1971
* (orig. pub. as "ESP, Seers and Psychics," New York: Crowell, 1970). x, 268p. Illus. Bibliog. Index £2.25 ISBN 0-304-93760-6

This work relates anecdotes and stories on mind readers, mediums, table-tilting, live burials, fire-walking, astrologers, and fortune tellers. He explains for each how a magician could duplicate them. He shows how Indian fakirs and Houdini could endure burials. Christopher studies parapsychological occurrences of today and the past in the U.S., Japan, India, Europe, and the Caribbean. He also discusses ESP in animals and people, Jeane Dixon, and others. He is critical of accounts of poltergeists. The author uses some previously unpublished papers of Houdini.

249 Church of Scientology of California. Scientology--The Other Case. East Grinstead, England: Church of Scientology World Wide, 1972. 23p. £0.50 pa. ISBN 0-9501803-5-1

250 _______. Scientology: Twentieth Century Religion. East Grinstead, England: Church of Scientology World Wide, 1972. 122p. Bibliog. £0.75 pa. ISBN 0-9501803-4-3

This is a manual of the formal viewpoint of L. Ron Hubbard's church. Chapters include religious nature of Scientology, re-discovery of ethics, education, environment, marriage and the family, race relations, co-operation of all churches, Commission on Human Rights, psychiatric violations; Narconon Drug Rehabilitation Program, action in social reform, mental health industry, Dianetics Information Group, new civilization.

251 Churchward, James. The Lost Continent of Mu. London:
* Futura Publications, 1974 (orig. pub., New York: Rudge, 1926; also, London: Spearman, 1959). 286p. Illus. Maps £0.45 pa. ISBN 0-86007-029-8

This work is considered a classic, although some consider it science fiction.

252 Clark, Adrian V. Psycho-Kinesis; Moving Matter with the Mind. West Nyack, N.Y.: Parker Pub. Co., 1973. 218p. Includes bibliog. refs. $6.95 LC 73-9782

253 Clark, Jerome, and Loren Coleman. Unidentified. New York: Warner Paperback, 1975.

The author's main thesis is that UFO's are a manifestation of the collective unconscious (an idea that originated with Jung). The evidence Clark uses at times includes modern frauds and older cases of questioned worth. One interesting point is a mention of the similarities between contactee stories and fairy tales and legends.

254 Clark, Linda A. The Ancient Art of Color Therapy. Old Greenwich, Conn.: Devin-Adair, 1975. 145p. $6.95

This work discusses the psychological and physical effects of light and color on man, including gem therapy, auras, and amulets. The early chapters are on light and its effects on man, animals, and plants. Then, the author gives excerpts from case studies, and discusses the healing impact of colors (colors of food, light, water, gems). There is a chapter on auras, and also one on color breathing (in yoga). Many out-of-print sources are used by the author in writing her work.

255 Clarke, Ida Clyde (Gallagher), 1878-1956. True Tales of the Occult; Men Who Wouldn't Stay Dead. Illus. by Dorothea Braby. South Brunswick: A. S. Barnes, 1973 (first pub. in 1945 as "Men Who Wouldn't Stay Dead"). 288p. Illus. $6.95 LC 72-6370

This is a collection of 28 ghost stories, all supposedly true. Many of them are based on family traditions among famous people, including Napoleon, the Hapsburgs, Walt Whitman, and Andrew Jackson.

256 Clements, Jonathan. Lucky for You! Illus. by Roger Smith. London: Armada Books, 1975. 127p. Illus. £0.40 pa. ISBN 0-00-690963-9

257 Coates, Austin. Numerology. London: Muller, 1974. 126p. Illus. Index £2.95 ISBN 0-584-10167-8

258 Coates, James. Photographing the Invisible; Practical Studies in Spirit Photography, Spirit Portraiture, and Other Rare but Allied Phenomena. New York: Arno Press, 1973 (c1911). xxi, 394p. Illus. $23 LC 72-9189

259 Cobb, Stanwood. The Scientific Study of the Hand. Washington, D.C.: Avalon Press, 1974. 142p. $3.90 pa.

This book is illustrated with 36 case studies of palm prints.

260 Coblentz, Flora. For All Who Seek. San Jose, Calif.: Redwood Press, 1973. xxiii, 184p. $5.95 LC 73-75413

261 Cohen, Daniel. Curses, Hexes and Spells. Philadelphia: Lip-
* pincott, 1974. Bibliog. (Weird and Horrible Library) $5.50 LC 74-6425 ISBN 0-397-31493-0

This juvenile book is a good survey even for adults. It discusses the following: old family curses, accursed creatures, accursed places, curses of wanderers and ghosts, everyday curses, black magic, amulets and talismans, Bermuda Triangle, curse on Mary Celeste (ship), and the legend of the Wandering Jew. As is usual with Cohen, he discredits supernatural explanations. The book is recommended for grade 7 and up.

262 ________. ESP: The Search Beyond the Senses. New York:
* Harcourt Brace Jovanovich, 1973. 187p. Illus. Bibliog. $5.95 LC 73-5238 ISBN 0-15-226250-4

The author discusses first the Hebrew prophets, Greek oracles and Roman sibyls, then moves through Darwin and the [British] Society for Psychical Research. He discredits the Society's

ESP work, as well as card tests by Rhine, Soal, and others. He looks at current dream work at Maimonides Hospital with mild approval, but advises caution even there. Also mentioned are Jeane Dixon, Pike, out-of-the-body experiences, and poltergeists. At the book's conclusion, he remains skeptical about the subject, even when confronted with cases of spontaneous ESP. A review in the Journal of Parapsychology criticized Cohen's selection of material, saying he presents the most questionable cases he can find. The Journal goes on to criticize his works as "pseudo-objective critical books." The complaint about his selection of material is often accurate with Cohen, and a good point to watch with this author. This juvenile book is recommended for grades 7 and up.

263 ______. The Far Side of Consciousness. New York: Dodd,
* Mead, 1975 (c1974). x, 214p. Illus. Plates Bibliog. Index $6.95 LC 74-11797 ISBN 0-396-07002-7

The author, former managing editor of Science Digest, has written a good introduction to the U.S. psychic scene. The book covers dream telepathy, altered states of consciousness (out-of-the-body experiences and drugs), mind control, Kirlian photography, auras, meditation, biofeedback, faith healing, plant consciousness, brainwashing, hypnosis, and psychosurgery. As usual, he is a skeptic. He has "grudging respect" for psychic investigators. The purpose of this work is not to ridicule, he says, but to balance the wilder claims of the psychic world.

264 ______. Greatest Monsters in the World. Illus. New York:
* Dodd, Mead, 1975. Index $4.95 LC 75-11433 ISBN 0-396-07188-0

This juvenile survey covers the history and existence of the Loch Ness monster, the yeti, Bigfoot, sea monsters, and dragons. Cohen is skeptical (the Kraken, beached at Thimble Tickle in Newfoundland, turned out to be a giant squid). The book is recommended for grades 5-8.

265 ______. How the World Will End. New York: McGraw-Hill,
* 1973. 256p. $5.95

This fine juvenile survey discusses the scientific view of the world's end through comets, meteorites, radiation, war, climatic change, or the death of the sun. It also discusses various religious sects who have forecast the end of the world. Cohen states that man has always believed that the world will come to a cataclysmic end. He studies the Millerites of the 19th century, led by William Miller, who predicted the end in 1843. Cohen does not agree with Velikovsky's theories. Also, he does not feel that the 1908 Siberian explosion was due to a spaceship.

266 ______. In Search of Ghosts. New York: Dodd, Mead,
* 1972. 182p. Illus. Bibliog. $4.95 LC 70-175312 ISBN 0-396-06485-X

This fine juvenile book discusses ghosts, spirit photography, and poltergeists. Nearly one third of the work is a history of spiritualism. He presents eight classic stories of all ages and mentions the Fox sisters, mediums, the Society for Psychical Research, haunted houses. There is a chapter titled "Secrets of the Seance," describing an imaginary seance with almost every fraudulent device possible. Another interesting discussion is on Eusapia Palladino, who was discovered to be a fraud at Cambridge sittings in 1895. This author is highly critical of the field. He does not believe in ghosts, but says he is afraid of them. The book is recommended for grades 6-9.

267 ______. The Magic of Foreseeing the Future. New York:
* Dodd, Mead, 1973. 192p. Illus. Bibliog. $4.95 LC 72-6882

This juvenile book discusses fortune-telling, Tarot, Cayce, Evangeline Adams, and other famous people in the field. Cohen questions some old occult beliefs, and thinks little of Nostradamus or Swedenborg. He also attacks Mother Shipton, Dunne's famous study of dreams, and Jeane Dixon, and considers laboratory evidence for clairvoyance and psychokinesis unconvincing. The book is recommended for grades 6-9.

268 ______. Magic of the Little People. New York: Julian
* Messner, 1974. 96p. Illus. $6.25 LC 73-19236 ISBN 0-671-32637-6

This good juvenile book debates the possible existence of the little people--fairies and so forth. He sees four main classes: fairies, dwarfs, hobgoblins, and elves. He examines theories that try to account for the universal belief in them. He mentions the theory that they have evolved from pagan gods whose strength was weakened by Christianity, or from tales of heroes from magic stories. He discusses the theories that fairies are UFO visitors, or the descendants of an ancient pygmy race. The famous Cottingley photographs are mentioned in their own chapter. Cohen seems to believe their authenticity. The book is recommended for grades 4-6.

269 ______. Magicians, Wizards, and Sorcerers. Philadelphia:
* Lippincott, 1973. 159p. Illus. Bibliog. (Weird and Horrible Library) $4.95 LC 72-12520

This well-done juvenile book has discussions on ancient magicians (goddesses, Pythagoreans, Simon Magus, agnostics); medieval magic (Bacon, Agrippa, John Dee); alchemists (Hermetic tradition, Rosicrucians, Nicolas Flanal, Paracelsus); magic in the Age of Reason (Saint-Germain, Cagliostro, Mesmer); new world of magic (Levi, Mathers, Crowley, Blavatsky); today's magicians. The author states, "There is indeed no solid evidence that magical secrets of any kind really exist." However, Cohen does state that magic is not to be scoffed at, and that it has appeared almost as a necessity to man in every culture. This fine juvenile work is recommended for grades 7 and up. Adults will enjoy it as much as juveniles.

270 ______. Masters of the Occult. New York: Dodd, Mead,
* 1971. x, 234p. Illus. Bibliog. $5.95 LC 74-165669
ISBN 0-396-06407-8

This book presents biographical information on various occult practitioners, and is highly critical of them. The work discusses Rosicrucians, Hermes Trismegistus, Agrippa, John Dee, St. Germain, Swedenborg, Mesmer, D. D. Home, Blavatsky, Eileen Garrett, Faust, Hubbard.

271 ______. Monsters, Giants, and Little Men from Mars; An
* Unnatural History of the Americas. Garden City, N.Y.: Doubleday, 1975. 242p. Illus. Bibliog. $5.95 LC 74-4534 ISBN 0-385-03267-6

This juvenile book discusses the Abominable Snowman, the Abominable Chicken Man of Oklahoma, the Hodag (man-eating creature of the swamps of Wisconsin), giant people, sea monsters, UFO's, tripodero, giddyfish, the White River Monster, Indian legends that supposedly support mammoths in Alaska, and the Cardiff Giant. This book is recommended for grades 6-8.

272 ______. Mysteries of Reincarnation. New York: Dodd,
* Mead, and Co., 1975. 172p. $5.50

This juvenile work discusses transmigration, Theodore Flournoy, Edgar Cayce, Bridey Murphy, Ian Stevenson. He also discusses the supposed reincarnations of Helene Smith, Madame Blavatsky, and Joan Grant. He feels Cayce had many limitations on his powers and abilities. The work surveys the acceptance of belief in reincarnation throughout Western history. It is recommended for grades 10-12.

273 ______. Voodoo, Devils, and the New Invisible World.
* New York: Dodd, Mead, 1972. xii, 204p. Illus. Bibliog. $5.95 LC 72-2346 ISBN 0-396-06638-0

This book has chapters on witchcraft, satanism, voodoo, creatures beneath the sea and under the earth and aliens from outer space. Also, there is a well-done chapter on secret societies (Masons, Rosicrucians, and the like). The society chapter gives history and present status. Cohen believes that the widespread belief in occult areas shows great disenchantment with the modern view of the world.

274 Cohn, Norman. Europe's Inner Demons; An Enquiry Inspired
*** by the Great Witchhunt. New York: Basic Books, 1975. 302p. Illus. Bibliog. notes Index (Columbus Centre Series: Studies in the Dynamics of Persecution and Extermination) $12.50 LC 74-79498 ISBN 0-465-02131-X

This work is a major new contribution to occult literature. The author tries to find causes for the Great Witchhunt of the 16th and 17th centuries, mainly through study of the Classical/Middle Ages background. He shows how flimsy most of the evidence is of witchhunting prior to 1500. He finds no evidence that a society of medieval witches ever existed (this contradicts Jeffrey Russell's Witchcraft in the Middle Ages [entry 1424]). He feels the causes of persecution were a combination of peasant beliefs that evil-doers were using magic to harm others, with a belief by the educated that those using magic were coworkers with the devil. The stereotype of the witch also developed from the second century, with some Christian sects accused of orgies. Monks later copied details of these. Thus, evidence of witchcraft is really a literary tradition. Cohn considers this work complementary to his famous study on millenarianism.

275 Colby, Carroll Burleigh. The Weirdest People in the World. New York: Sterling; London: dist. by Ward Lock, 1973. 192p. Illus. £1.25 ISBN 0-7061-2397-2

This is a good sequel to the author's previous collection about ghosts. These brief stories cover inexplicable or supernatural happenings; the collection as a whole is written for juveniles. Stories include: "Tales of the Strangled Figurehead," "The Man They Couldn't Bury," "A Plague of Worms"; "The Skeleton in the Pasture," and "The Waterford Ghost's Revenge." This book is recommended for grades 5-9.

276 Cole, Norah. This Is the Truth. Andover, England: Norah Cole, 1975. 32p. Illus. Bibliog. £1 pa. ISBN 0-9503554-2-9

277 Collins, Mabel. Light on the Path. London: Theosophical Pub. House, 1972 (orig. pub., London: Reeves and Turner, 1885). 67p. £0.75 pa. ISBN 0-7229-5006-3

This work was written for those who are ignorant of the Eastern wisdom, and who desire to enter within its influence. It includes an essay on karma.

278 Collyns, Robin. Did Spacemen Colonise the Earth? St. Al-
* bans, England: Mayflower, 1975 (orig. pub., London: Pelham, 1974). 256p. Illus. Plates Bibliog. £0.75 pa. ISBN 0-583-12499-2

The author, a New Zealander, has added a new twist to the large amount written on this. He has researched Maori legends for any references to spacemen. He also discusses Australia, and theorizes that the Garden of Eden was there. The book discusses man's space ancestors; beginnings of ancient and plant life; message of Atlantis; first space settlers in India; dinosaurs and the nuclear holocaust; New Zealand and extraterrestrials; Near Eastern evidence; evidence from Classical mythology; evidence from the Americas;

evidence from Great Britain; UFO evidence in literature; contact with extraterrestrials in the modern era; audio contact with extraterrestrials; scientific proof of extraterrestrials. The author translates some little-publicized writings.

279 Colquhoun, Ithell, 1906- . The Sword of Wisdom: MacGregor Mathers and the Golden Dawn. New York: Putnam, 1975. 307p. Illus. Plates Index $8.95 LC 76-351557

The Golden Dawn did not last long and had few members, but it had a great influence. Much of the book is on S. L. MacGregor Mathers, who married Moina Bergson, sister of philosopher Henri Bergson. The marriage was childless (and probably sexless), but together they produced lots of material. After he died, she took over the organization. The book also mentions A. E. Waite and William Yeats, Maud Gonne, Aleister Crowley. It adds chapters on alchemy, Tantra, Enochian magic. The author studied the society in her early days.

280 Colton, Ann Ree. Watch Your Dreams; A Master Key and Reference Book for All Initiates of the Soul, the Mind, and the Heart. Glendale, Calif.: Arc Pub. Co., 1973. 414p. $1 pa. LC 72-90911

281 Compatibility Guide. Ed. by the astrologers of Super Horoscopes. London: Coronet Books, 1975 (orig. pub. as "Super Horoscopes' Compatibility Guide," New York: Grosset and Dunlap, 1071; London: Cassell, 1973). 412p. £1.50 pa. ISBN 0-340-19857-5

282 Complete Horoscope for All Those Whose Birthdays Fall Between.... Annual. London: Pan Books. 12 vols, each 143p. Illus. £0.30 pa.

283/4 Complete Planetary Ephemeris, 1950-2000 A. D. Gloucester, Mass.: Para Research, 1975. 600p. $25

285 Constant, Alphonse Louis, 1810-1875. The Book of Splendours, by Eliphas Levi [pseud.]. Appendix by Papus. Foreword by W. N. Schors. Wellingborough, England: Aquarian Press, 1973 (New York: S. Weiser, 1973). 191p. (Translation of "Le Livre des splendeurs") £2.50

Part 1 deals with the Great Synod, with a discussion of the Siphra Dzeniuta by Simeon Ben-Joachai in which Levi points out the similarities of Kabalism and Freemasonry. Part 2 is a collection of legends about Krishna from the Bhagavadam. Part 3 discusses lessons on the Kabalah taken from Levi's letters and one of his students. The work contains: "Judaic Sun," "Christian Glory," and "Flaming Star"--all studies on the origins of the Kabalah.

286 _______. The Great Secret; or, Occultism Unveiled. Wellingborough, England: Thorsons, 1975 (orig. pub. as "Le Grand

Arcane," Paris, 1898). 188p. (Studies in Hermetic Tradition, vol. 3) £3.75 ISBN 0-7225-0293-1

287 ______. The Magical Ritual of the Sanctum Regnum Interpreted by the Tarot Trumps. Trans. and ed. by W. Wynn Westcott. New York: S. Weiser, 1971 (c1970; orig. pub., 1896). x, 108 p. Illus. Color plates $7.50 LC 79-27709 ISBN 0-87728-034-7

288 ______. Mysteries of Magic: A Digest of the Writings of Eliphas Levi. With an essay by Arthur Edward Waite. Foreword by Leslie Shepard. 2nd ed., rev. and enl. Secaucus, N.J.: University Books, 1974. xvi, 523p. Index $10 LC 74-75174 ISBN 0-8216-0217-9

289 Conway, David. Magic: An Occult Primer. St. Albans,
* England: Mayflower, 1974 (London: Cape, 1972; orig. pub., New York: Dutton, 1972). 334p. Illus. Bibliog. £0.75 pa.

This well-written survey duscusses magic as a science, and shows how it conforms to the natural law. He prefers white magic, but does mention sexual magic and curses. Much of the book's basis is the Kabbala and Egyptian rituals, presented in totality in the original language. These rituals are not given in English. Then, it gives the correct colors and incenses. The book also discusses astral projection; talismans; spiritualism; magical techniques for finding lovers; rejuvenation.

290 Cooke, Grace, and Ivan Cooke. Light in Britain. Liss, England: White Eagle Pub. Trust, 1971. 118p. Illus. Map £1.50 ISBN 0-85487-006-7

291 ______. Sun-men of the Americas. Liss, England: White Eagle Pub. Trust, 1975. x, 104p. £2 ISBN 0-85487-035-0

This book discusses the beliefs of American Indians based on knowledge brought to man by god-men at the beginning of the current life cycle.

292 Cooke, Ivan, ed. The Return of Arthur Conan Doyle. 2nd ed. Liss, England: White Eagle Pub. Trust, 1975 (2nd ed. orig. pub., 1963). ix, 204p. Illus. Facsims. Index £2.25 pa. ISBN 0-85487-037-7

The book is supposedly a collection of messages received from Doyle, who died in 1930. Several years later, material from him began coming in, and did so over a period of two years. Reportedly, Doyle is under the direction of the Wise Ones to carry their message to the ends of the earth. The first part of the book contains the basic story. Part 2 contains Doyle's message: harmony of heaven life; spirits and angels; free will and destiny (both exist); good and evil; healing of all disease; healing of the nations. This work is a republication with revisions of a book published before World War II titled, Thy Kingdom Come.

293 ______. Temple Angel. Liss, England: White Eagle Pub. Trust, 1974. 33p. Illus. £0.50 pa. ISBN 0-85487-034-2

294 Cookes, H. St. L. The Eyes, Brain and Nervous System in Relation to the Earth's Magnetism. Bideford, England: Devon Rustics, 1974. $6.90

This book tries to give a physical explanation to dowsing, not a psychical explanation.

295 Cooper, John Charles. Religion in the Age of Aquarius. Philadelphia: Westminster, 1971. 175p. $2.45 LC 77-133618 ISBN 0-664-24905-1

This work contains insights gained by the author while teaching at a university and serving at a university church. He feels the occult fascination reflects a need for reassurance in an age of anxiety, and a search for steady guidance in a quickly changing world. He gives firsthand accounts of dangers.

296 Cooper, Michael, 1943- , and Andrew Weaver. An Astrological Index to the World's Famous People. Garden City, N.Y.: Doubleday, 1975. $8.95 LC 74-3545 ISBN 0-385-00507-5

This book gives in two lists over 4,800 names, with profession, birthdate, and sun sign for each. One list goes A to Z, the other day-by-day. Both living and dead persons are included. The work gives moon ephemerides from 1890-1950.

297 Coover, John Edgar, 1872-1938. Experiments in Psychical Research. New York: Arno Press, 1975 (reprint of 1917 ed., pub. by Stanford University, Calif.). Bibliog. Indexes (Issued as "Psychical Research Monograph no. 1," Leland Stanford Junior University Publications). (Perspectives in Psychical Research) $37 LC 75-7372 ISBN 0-405-07023-3

T.W. Stanford in 1911 gave a large amount of money to Stanford University to conduct tests in the psychical field. Dr. Coover headed the research. This volume is the first and last report of the investigations. The overall conclusion was negative, although redoing the experiments later gave some positive indications.

298 Cope, Lloyd. Your Stars Are Numbered. Introd. by Linda Goodman. Garden City, N.Y.: Doubleday, 1971. xiii, 335p. $6.95 LC 75-123685

This book is mostly a numerological discussion of the 12 sun signs. It is a do-it-yourself guide. Cope calls numerology "the shorthand of the cosmic plan."

299 Copen, Bruce. Dowsing for You. Haywards Heath, England:

Academic Publications, 1975. 71p. Illus. Bibliog. £1.50 pa. ISBN 0-900307-45-5

300 _______. The Magic of the Aura. Danehill, England: Academic Publications, 1974. 73p. Bibliog. £1.20 pa. ISBN 0-900307-38-2

301 _______. Negative Green (Nature's Secret Power). Dane Hill, England: Academic Publications, 1975. 52p. Illus. Bibliog. £1.50 pa. ISBN 0-900307-48-X

302 _______. Practical Pendulum (Radiesthesia). 2nd rev. ed. Danehill, England: Academic Publications, 1975. 83p. Illus. Bibliog. £2 pa. ISBN 0-900307-46-3

303 _______. Radiesthesia for Home and Garden (The Use of the Pendulum at Home and in the Garden). Haywards Heath, Academic Publications, 1974. 72p. Illus. Bibliog. £1.25 pa. ISBN 0-900307-42-0

304 Copper, Basil. The Vampire--In Legend, Fact and Art. London: Hale, 1973 (also, New York: Citadel, 1975; also, London: Corgi, 1975). 208p. Illus. Facsims. Bibliog. Index £2.50 ISBN 0-7091-3585-8
*

This is a good journalistic study of the subject, serious but not scholarly. It is divided into four parts: the vampire in legend; in literature; in film; and in the theater. Elisabeth Bathony (1610), Gilles De Rais (the French Bluebeard), and Marechal de Rais (1440), are studied, as are Haarman and Haigh, Mr. Farrant and others. One very interesting part is on vampire fiction of the 19th century. This section discusses: Dr. Polidori's "The Vampyre" (1819); Thomas Preskett Prest's "Varney the Vampire" (1847); Bram Stoker's "Dracula" (1897); Maupassant's "The Horla"; Sheridan Lefanu's "Carmilla"; and E. F. Benson's tale, "Mrs. Amworth." The art section concentrates on the stage and screen versions of Dracula, and the huge sums they have made in the 20th century.

305 Corliss, William R., comp. Strange Artifacts. Vol. M1. Glen Arm, Md.: Sourcebook Project, 1974. 262p. Illus. $6.95 LC 74-75256 ISBN 0-9600712-2-9
*

The author has sifted through old magazines searching for articles on unusual occurrences. He presents paragraph excerpts from them on the following topics: fossil footprints, Mexican Messiah, ruins at Ponape, Brittany alignments, Scottish fused forts, ancient canals in Florida and Arizona, Easter Island, Stonehenge, astronomical implications of megalithic structures.

306/7 _______, comp. Strange Phenomena; A Sourcebook of Unusual Natural Phenomena. 2 vols. Glen Arm, Md.: Sourcebook Project, 1974. Illus. $6.95 ea. vol. LC 73-91248 Vol G1, 277p. ISBN 0-9600712-1-0; vol. G2 264p. ISBN 0-9600712-5-3
*

The author has sifted through old magazines searching for articles on unusual occurrences. Volume G1 presents paragraph excerpts from the articles on the following topics: ball lightning, nocturnal lights, earthquake lights, light wheels, Barisal Guns, mistpouffers, aurora-like phenomena. Volume G2 presents paragraph excerpts on gelatinous meteors, fish falls, correlations between positions of the sun, moon, and planets and geophysical phenomena; peculiar mirages, weather oddities. The paragraphs are quoted word-for-word from Scientific American, Monthly Weather Review, Science, Nature, and other scientific journals, as well as some from popular periodicals.

308 ________, comp. Strange Planet. Glen Arm, Md.: Source-
* book Project, 1975. 282p. $7.95

309 ________, comp. Strange Universe. Glen Arm, Md.: Source-
* book Project, 1975. 279p. $7.95

The author has sifted through old magazines searching for articles on unusual occurrences concerning stars and planets. Excerpts from the articles are presented here.

310 Cornell, James C., Jr., comp. It Happened Last Year!
* Earth Events, 1973; A Report on the Planet for 1973. New York: Macmillan, 1974. 250p. Illus. Index $8.95 LC 74-8891

This report of incidents filed at the Smithsonian Institution Center for Short-lived Phenomena is similar to its parent volume, The Pulse of the Planet. The main section gives about one page each on 160 incidents of strange natural phenomena (earthquakes, volcanic eruptions, floods, oil spills, dead animals, comets and meteors). It also lists events of 1968, 1969, 1970, 1971, and 1972 in small, separate sections. There is a special 12-page report on the Tasaday Manubo Tribe Discovery. The book contains 22 pages of photos.

311 ________. Nature at Its Strangest: True Stories from the Files of the Smithsonian Institution Center for Short-lived Phenomena. New York: Sterling; London: Ward Lock, 1974. 128p. Illus. £1.50 ISBN 0-7061-2038-8

This juvenile book discusses 51 strange phenomena taken from the files of the Center (fish dying of thermal shock; boulders appearing suddenly out of the ground in a pasture). The information is sometimes given in jocular manner--"Galloping granite! Call the Sheriff" is but one example. The illustrations are cartoon-style. The book is recommended for grades 5-8.

312 ________, and John Surowiecki. The Pulse of the Planet; A
* State of the Earth Report from the Smithsonian Institution Center for Short-lived Phenomena. New York: Harmony Books [div. of Crown], 1972. 129p. Illus. $2.95 pa. LC 72-84309 ISBN 0-517-500663

This fine work reports unusual natural events on file at the Center. There are separate chapters for 1968, 1969, 1970, and 1971, with events presented in chronological order. Incidents include earthquakes, volcanic eruptions, fireballs, meteorites, animal deaths, oil spills, tidal waves, etc. Each event is treated in a long paragraph packed with information. Appendixes give selection criteria for events reported by the Center; statistical summary of events, 1968-1971; list of reporters for the Center given by country; list of Center publications; event report form.

313 Costello, Peter. In Search of Lake Monsters. St. Albans,
*** England: Panther, 1975 (also, New York: Coward, 1974; orig. pub., London: Garnstone Press, 1974). 400p. Illus. Plates Bibliog. Index £1.25 pa. ISBN 0-586-04196-6

This work is a major new contribution to occult literature. It discusses lakes all over the world, including those of Australia, the Orient, Scotland, Ireland, British Columbia, Sweden, Africa, Iceland, Italy, Japan, Patagonia, Siberia, America. The U.S. monsters mentioned include the Red Cedar Lake Monster of Wisconsin, spotted in 1891 and the 50-foot-long Slimey Slim Monster spotted in 1941 at Lake Payette, Idaho. There are three chapters on the Loch Ness Monster. He feels Nessie is an unknown species of giant seal. Other monsters mentioned include Pooka and Piast (Ireland); Ogopogo (Canada); Patagonian Plesiosaur (South America); Dragon of the Ishtar Gate (Western Asia); Waitoreke and Bunyip (Australasia); Sø-Orm and Skrimsl (Scandinavia). There are 30 photos and 40 line drawings, and also a good bibliography.

314 Courses and Other Study Opportunities in Parapsychology. New York: American Society for Psychical Research, 1973. 10p. $1

This pamphlet lists colleges and universities in the United States where one may take courses in psychic sciences.

315 Crawford, Quantz. Methods of Psychic Development. St. Paul, Minn.: Llewellyn Publications, 1973. 102p. (A Llewellyn Occult Guide) $2.95 pa.

This work outlines how to develop ESP by awakening "kundalini" through meditation and breathing exercises. Kundalini is a theory of "living electricity" or intelligent energy which believers feel may offer the only rational explanation for all the psychic phenomena now puzzling researchers. It is a high state of yoga, and requires discipline.

316 Crisp, Tony. Do You Dream? London: Spearman, 1971. 352p. £2.50 ISBN 0-85435-200-7

317 Criswell, Jeron. Criswell's Forbidden Predictions; Based on Nostradamus and the Tarot. Atlanta: Droke House/Hallux, 1972. 128p. Illus. $4.95 LC 72-83125 ISBN 0-8375-6769-6

318 Crookall, Robert. Case-book of Astral Projection, [cases
* nos.] 545-746. New Hyde Park, N.Y.: University Books, 1972. 160p. $7.95

This author is a very important figure in astral projection, and his works are classics. He is a British geologist. The 200 case histories in this volume bring the total in his personal collection to 746. The events in the cases are usually similar: floating over their own bodies; momentary blackout on leaving the body; seeing a silver cord connecting self with body. There is some discussion of drug-induced out-of-the-body experiences, such as with LSD or mescaline. Many of the cases lack real detail, and are repeated second- or third-hand (such as in discussing D. H. Lawrence). Crookall's main thesis in all his books is that man has three bodies: physical; semi-physical; double (which he calls the vehicle of vitality and the soul body). On death, the vehicle of vitality takes over and enters Hades, a cleansing state. The soul body later assumes control, and enters Paradise. Later, the soul body dies, and the entity enters Heaven, total union with God.

319 ________. Dreams of High Significance. Moradabad, India: Darshana International, 1974. 89p. $5

The author states that the dreams we occasionally have of dead people are really actual contacts we are having in our non-physical bodies with souls on the other side. These dreams usually occur a few days after the other person's death, without the dreamer's being aware of that death.

320 ________. Ecstasy: The Release of the Soul from the Body. Moradabad, India: Darshana International, 1975. 163p. $6

This work compares the trances of shamans with out-of-the-body experiences. The shamanistic practices of dancing, whirling, fasting, drugs, breathing, and so on, are all good methods to bring on astral projection. Crookall sees a parallel also in blacking out at the moment of ecstasy, leaving by the solar plexus, and the silver cord, as symbolized by branches and vines.

321 ________. The Supreme Adventure: Analyses of Psychic Communications. 2nd ed. Cambridge, England: J. Clarke, 1975 (previous ed., Cambridge, England: J. Clarke for the Churches' Fellowship for Psychical Study, 1961). xxix, 257p. Illus. Bibliog. Index £3 ISBN 0-227-67606-8

322 Crookes, William, 1832-1919. Crookes and the Spirit World. Collected by R. G. Medhurst. Introd. by K. M. Goldney. Ed. by M. R. Barrington. New York: Taplinger, 1972 (also, London: Souvenir, 1972). 250p. Illus. Bibliog. refs. $10 LC 78-185949 ISBN 0-8008-2040-1

This book is a collection of all of Crooke's writings on his psychic investigations. It also includes new material never before published: his notebook, found in the archives of the Society for Psychical Research, adds, among other things, seances with D. D. Home. This book especially studies psychokinetic phenomena. The volume has material on Florence Cook (a case on which some have questioned Crookes' integrity); sittings with Kate Fox; Crookes and his views on survival (initially, he doubted survival, but felt he had received satisfactory proof in 1916 at a sitting with William Hope). Crookes actually made his scientific reputation through inventing the cathode ray tube, and isolating the element thallium. However, while still a young man in his thirties, he had investigated spiritualism, and found the various phenomena to be genuine. His studies probably would not be scientifically acceptable today, but were excellent for that time.

323 Crossley, Alan Ernest. The Enigma of Psychic Phenomena. Elton, England: A. E. Crossley, 1974. £1.15

This work is written by a medium. It includes many pictures of spirit figures, some of them taken at a Helen Duncan materialization seance.

324 ______. The Story of Helen Duncan, Materialization Medium. Ilfracombe, England: Stockwell, 1975. 186p. Illus. Plates £2.50 ISBN 0-7223-0840-X

325 Crossley, Patricia G. Let's Learn Astrology; The First Astrology Workbook for Beginners. Rev. ed. Jericho, N.Y.: Exposition Press, 1974. 90p. Charts Bibliog. (An Exposition Banner Book) $6 LC 73-90470 ISBN 0-682-47727-3

326 Crow, William Bernard. History of Magic, Witchcraft and Occultism. London: Abacus, 1972 (orig. pub., London: Aquarian Press, 1968). 320p. Index £0.60 pa. ISBN 0-349-10640-1

327 Crowley, Aleister, 1875-1947. Aleister Crowley's Astrology: With a Study of Neptune and Uranus. Ed. and introd. by Stephen Skinner. Jersey, England: Spearman, 1974. xx, 204p. Illus. Plates (Also titled "Liber DXXVI") £2.75 ISBN 0-85978-001-5

328 ______. Book of the Law. Oceanside, Calif.: Thelema Pubns., 1973 (first printed in London, 1909). 52p. (Technically called "Liber al vel legis sub figura CCXX as delivered by XCIII-418 to DCLXVI"). LC 72-96601

This is a code of secret laws and rules, of which Crowley states, "Those who discuss the contents of this Book are to be shunned by all, as centres of pestilence. All questions of the Law are to be decided only by appeal to my writings, each for himself." This work is recommended only for serious students of magical theory or practice.

329 ________. Complete Astrological Writings. Ed. with annotations by John Symonds and Kenneth Grant. London: Duckworth, 1974. ix, 224 p. Illus. Plate Index £4.95 ISBN 0-7156-0806-1

This work contains the following sections: "Treatise on Astrology, liber 536"; "How Horoscopes Are Faked"; "Batrachophrenoboocosmomachia." It would probably be of interest only to serious students of magical lore.

330 ________. The Confessions of Aleister Crowley: An Autohagiography. Abridged ed. Ed. by John Symonds and Kenneth Grant. New York: Bantam, 1971 (orig. pub., London: Cape, 1969). xxvii, 1,058p. Illus. Plates Index (Abridged ed. means this is the text of all 6 vols., after some redundancies have been removed; first 2 vols. orig. pub. as "Spirit of Solitude," London: Mandrake, 1929) $1.95 pa. ISBN 0-552-65820-0

This is an interesting biography of the most flamboyant figure in 20th-century magic. It is called a "hagiography" since Crowley was a self-proclaimed "saint" in the Gnostic Church (and was later a "god"). Crowley discusses his early life and mountain-climbing, college study, marriage, magic ritual work, travels. Crowley tells everything in detail, yet, like so many autobiographies, totally fails to reveal himself. There is no attempt made to deeply reflect on the worth and meaning of his life. All the reader gets is "I did this" and "I did that." The 32 plates are perhaps more revealing about Crowley than the text. However, the text is a very detailed presentation of what it's like to be a life-time practitioner of the black arts.

331 ________. The Equinox of the Gods: The Official Organ of the A. A. New York: Gordon Press, 1974 (orig. pub. in 1936 as vol. 3, no. 3 of The Equinox). v, 137p. Illus. Includes bibliog. refs. (Includes author's "Book of the Law") $34.95 LC 73-21404 ISBN 0-87968-157-8

332 ________. Gems from The Equinox: Instructions by Aleister Crowley for His Own Magical Order. Ed. by Israel Regardie. St. Paul, Minn.: Llewellyn Publications, 1974. xxxiv, 1, 134p. Illus. $24.95 LC 75-305515 ISBN 0-87542-113-X

The Equinox is a periodical Crowley published from 1909 to 1914, which presents rituals, yoga, and other writings on sex and magic.

333 ________. Law Is for All. Ed. by Israel Regardie. St. Paul, Minn.: Llewellyn Pubns., 1975. 350p. $7.95 pa.

334 ________. Liber Aleph. San Francisco, Calif.: Level Press, 1975. 219p.

This work was written by Crowley for Charles Stanfeld Jones

(Frater Achad) to introduce him to his magical system. There are 208 paragraphs, each giving a major tenet of Crowley's magic.

335 ________. Magical and Philosophical Commentaries on the Book of the Law. Ed. by John Symonds and Kenneth Grant. Montreal: 93 publishing, 1975. 346p.

This work has inside it a reproduction of the original script of "Liber Legis," a reproduction of the "Stele of Revealing 718," and an unfinished 1923 essay.

336 ________. Magical Record of the Beast 666: The Diaries of Aleister Crowley, 1914-1920. Ed. by John Symonds and Kenneth Grant. London: Duckworth, 1972. xv, 326p. Index £6 ISBN 0-7156-0636-0

337 ________. Magick. Ed., annotated, and introduced by John Symonds and Kenneth Grant. London: Routledge and Kegan Paul, 1973 (part pub. privately by the author, 1911-1912; includes "Magick in Theory and Practice," orig. pub., Paris: Lecram Press for the author, 1929). xxiv, 511p. Illus. Music Index £10 ISBN 0-7100-7423-9

The Foreign Office considered Crowley a German agent in the First World War, Mussolini expelled him as an undesirable alien, and Express newspapers called him the "wickedest man in the world." This work is a collection of several different publications at various times in his career, covering the period 1911-1929. They proceed from simplistic explanations of yoga to the sexual magic which some feel drove Crowley mad. Chapters include: "Magical Theory of the Universe," "Principles of Ritual," "Formulae of the Elemental Weapons"; "Tetragrammaton"; "Alhim and Alim"; "Preparation of the Furniture of the Temple and the Instruments of the Art"; "Barbarous Names of Evocation"; "Of the Gestures"; "Of the Banishings and of the Purification"; "Of the Invocation"; "Of the Charge to the Spirit"; "Of the License to Depart"; "Of Clairvoyance"; "Of the Body of Light"; "Divinations," "Art of Alchemy." Appendices include actual rituals, the grades of the Great White Brotherhood, notes on the nature of the astral plane, and a table of correspondences of the Qabalah. This work is recommended only for serious students of magical theory or practice.

338 ________. Magick in Theory and Practice. Krishna Press, 1973 (also, Dover, 1973; orig. pub., 1929). xxvii, 436p. $34.95

This book is advertised by Dover as "the foremost book on ceremonial magic written in the 20th century." Magical theories, rites, alchemy, oaths, and divination are discussed.

339 ________. Magick Without Tears. Ed. by Israel Regardie. St. Paul, Minn.: Llewellyn Pubns., 1973. xxxv, 522p. Illus. $10 LC 73-169349

This book consists of Crowley's replies by letter to inquiries concerning many topics related to his utterances, writings, and magic techniques described in The Confessions of Aleister Crowley (entry 330). He offers advice on astrology, sexual morality, fear, death, and prophecy, and explains how to follow his system. The 83 letters are listed by subject in the table of contents. Crowley spelled magic with a "k" to distinguish ritual magic from the stage variety. One of his key laws was the Law of Thelema--"Do what thou wilt shall be the whole of the law." He believed that the highest identity of the self comes through magic communion with the masters. This work is recommended only for serious students of magical theory or practice.

340 ______. The Qabalah of Aleister Crowley: Three Texts. Introd. by Israel Regardie. New York: S. Weiser, 1973. 50, 155, 69p. $10 LC 73-80056 ISBN 0-87728-222-6

This work produces three texts, all written before Crowley had reached the age of 40: "Gematria," "Liber 777" and "Sepher Sephiroth." Much of the discussion is on gematria, a process of using names, numbers and letters. Some knowledge of Hebrew is a necessity to get the most out of the work. This book is recommended only for serious students of the occult. It is very difficult to read and comprehend.

341 ______. 777; Vel, Prolegomena Symbolica ad Systeman Sceptico-mysticae Viae Explicandae, Fundamentcem Lierogloyphicum Sanctissimorum Sciential Sunmac. New York: Gordon Press, 1974 (orig. pub., 1909). xxvii, 154p. Illus. LC 73-21397 ISBN 0-87968-105-5

342 ______. Vision and the Voice. Introd. and explanation by Israel Regardie. Dallas: Sangreal Foundation, 1972 (orig. pub., 1952). 261p. Illus. Bibliog. (At head of title, "Liber XXX Aerum vel Saeculi sub Figura CCCCXVIII, Being of the Angels of the 30 Aethyrs") LC 72-171166 ISBN 0-87913-001-6

343 ______. The Works of Aleister Crowley. 3 vols. Des Plaines, Ill.: Yogi Publication Society, 1975 (orig. pub., 1905).

This is a mixed collection of Crowley's poetry, plays, essays, and minor magical writings.

344 Crowmarsh, Preston. First Steps to Astrology. New York:
* S. Weiser, 1971 (also, London: Aquarian Press, 1971). 64p. (Paths to Inner Power) $1.25 ISBN 0-87728-089-4

This is another fine volume in the "Paths to Inner Power Series." Rather than a "first steps" book, it is really a very useful reference handbook. The first three chapters cover the signs, planets, and houses in outline form. Each entry is presented in boldface type for ease of location. There is also a chapter on

"Health from the Horoscope," giving influences on the body of each sign. The most useful part of the book is the section, "Influence of the Planets (Aspects)." This part gives the meaning of various planets in trine, sextile, opposition, and conjunction with each other. Such a simple, clear explanation is very hard to find in other astrology books. This book, and the entire series, is strongly recommended for all readers and especially for all libraries.

345 Crowther, Arnold, and Patricia Crowther. Secrets of Ancient Witchcraft with the Witches' Tarot. Introd. and notes by Leo Louis Martello. Seacaucus, N. J.: University Books, 1974. 218p. Illus. Bibliog. $7.95 LC 74-80253 ISBN 0-8216-0221-7

The Crowthers were long associated with Gerald Gardner and his witchcraft in Britain. This is a pro-witchcraft book, praising love for nature, and discussing old initiations, sex symbolism, and magic practices. A great deal of the book is devoted to presenting the "Witches' Tarot Cards." There is a great deal of witchcraft symbolism on them. Male and female figures are nude, and the symbolism is close to the original Sufi in meaning rather than the traditional Tarot pack with its Judeo-Christian influence. Cards are shown in black and white. This book was a monthly selection of the Mystic Arts Book Club (a now-defunct book club run by University Books).

346 Crowther, Patricia. Witch Blood! The Diary of a Witch High Priestess!. Introd. by Leo L. Martello. New York: House of Collectibles, 1974. 192p. $1.25 pa. LC 73-93243 ISBN 0-87637-161-6

347 _______. Witchcraft in Yorkshire. Clapham, England: Dalesman, 1973. 72p. Illus. Map £0.45 pa. ISBN 0-85206-178-1

348 Crummere, Maria Elise. Sun-Sign Revelations. New York:
* Viking Press, 1974 (also, London: Bodley Head, 1974). xi, 115p. Illus. $5.95 LC 73-19323 ISBN 0-670-68329-9

This excellent book gives its long subtitle as: "An unusual, practical, revealing, unflattering, lighthearted astrological guide to the perverse personalities of our friends, our enemies, our lovers, and ourselves." In short, it concentrates on the negative aspects of the signs, unlike most astrologers who just tell you the good parts. For each sign, the author discusses matters in general, physical appearance, personality, love, marriage, parenthood, friendship, career, rising signs. The personality and love sections are excellent. Although the author calls the book "lighthearted," it is a serious, well-done study. This bibliographer has read scores of descriptions of the signs in many books. This work by Crummere often presents new insights--apparently because of her keen mind, these insights appear unlike any encountered in normal astrological texts. One could only wish she had written much more than 115 pages.

349 Cruz, Nicky. Satan on the Loose. Old Tappan, N. J. : F. H. Revell Co., 1973 (also, London: Oliphants, 1973). 158p. $3.95 LC 73-1125

This work discusses an occult-oriented childhood the author spent in Las Piedras, Puerto Rico, where his father was a witch and his mother a medium (Cruz's dramatic conversion story is told in the best-selling The Cross and the Switchblade). Chapters include "Satan's Computer Programs"; "Beating the Devil"; "How to be Safe"; "God Can Still Work Miracles"; "5-point Program for Parents." The book is advertised as part of Nicky Cruz's "dramatic crusade against demoniac powers in America."

350 Culling, Louis T. Occult Renaissance, 1972-2008; The Great Prophecy for the Golden Age of Occultism. Epologue by Carl L. Weschcke. St. Paul, Minn. : Llewellyn Pubns., 1972. 56p. Illus. $1 pa. ISBN 0-87542-133-4

This book discusses astrological cycles, and forecasts a rise in occultism starting in 1972.

351 Cumberland, Stuart [pseud.]. Thought-Reader's Thoughts: Being the Impressions and Confessions of Stuart Cumberland. N. Y. : Arno Press, 1975 (orig. pub., London, 1888). (Perspectives in Psychical Research Series). $19 LC 75-7373 ISBN 0-405-07024-1

The author, whose real name is Charles Garner, was assistant to stage mentalist Washington Irving Bishop. Later, he performed on his own under the name of Cumberland. The book discusses his performances and travels around the world. It tells how he did various feats, who made the best subjects, and how to gather a great deal of information. He also discusses others' reactions to his work.

352/3 Cummins, Geraldine. Swan on a Black Sea. Foreword by C. D. Broad. 1974 (c1965). £2.45

This book contains mainly automatic writing messages addressed to the communicator's youngest son, Henry, by the boy's mother, Mrs. Coombe Tennant, who died several years before. There is also a 52-page foreword by a long-time psychic researcher and frequent critic of mediums, who accepts these communications as worthwhile.

354 Curtis, Robert H. On E. S. P. Englewood Cliffs, N. J. : Prentice-Hall, 1975. 85p. Illus. $5.95 LC 74-20901 ISBN 0-13-634311-2

This juvenile book discusses Kirlian photography, psychokinesis, and Sinclair experiments. Also, it mentions lots of tests the readers can try (Zener cards; photos of faces; keeping a precognition notebook). It includes discussion of mediums and faith healing. The author is skeptical, but willing to at least listen. The book is recommended for grades 3-5.

355 Dakin, H. S. High-Voltage Photography. 2nd ed. Barrington,
* N. J.: Edmund Scientific Co., 1974 (distributors). 79p. Bibliog. $5

The author is an electronics engineer with interest in biological measurement. The first part is on history, experimental results, and photographic techniques. The second and shorter part discusses three high-voltage circuits, with schematic diagrams. Dakin feels this method is of negligible value as a routine testing method, because it is not a consistent technique. However, he adds that some results indicated unexplainable luminescent effects occurring with highly bioenergetic subjects. The work is a convenient brief handbook on the phenomenon.

356 Dalton, Lynn G. Pluto in Libra. Lakemont, Ga.: CSA Press, 1972. 38p. $1 pa. ISBN 0-87707-100-4

357 Dalyell, John Graham, 1775-1851. The Darker Superstitions of Scotland. Norwood, Pa.: Norwood Editions, 1973 (reprint of orig. ed., Glasgow: printed for R. Griffin, 1835). vii, 700p. Includes bibliog. refs. $45 LC 72-7065

This reprint is a good survey of the subject matter. Chapters discuss: the evil eye, invocations, occult infection and cure of disease, amulets, propitiatory sacrifice, propitiatory charms, sorcerers, superstitions, mystical plants and animals, mystical men, prognostication and divination, imaginery beings, spectral illusions, the tongues, tests, trials, conviction and punishment of sorcery.

358 Dane, Christopher. The American Indian and the Occult. New York: Popular Library, 1973. 224p. $.95 pa.

This collection of 35 stories covers strange happenings, mythology, old and new religious traditions and legends, bits of history, medicine, archaeology, anthropology, and lore. Many of them have little or nothing to do with the occult. Typical examples of coverage are the Hopi myth of creation and the astronomical system of the Maya.

359 _______. Possession. New York: Popular Library, 1973. 174p. $.75 pa.

360 Daniel, Clarence. Ghosts of Derbyshire. 2nd ed. Clapham, England: Dalesman, 1974. 79p. Illus. £0.60 pa. ISBN 0-85206-233-8

361 _______. Haunted Derbyshire. 3rd ed. Clapham, England: Dalesman, 1975. 80p. Illus. £0.75 pa. ISBN 0-85206-291-5

362 Daniels, Cora Linn (Morrison), 1852- . The Encyclopaedia
* of Superstitions, Folklore, and the Occult Sciences of the World; A Comprehensive Library of Human Belief and Practice in the Mysteries of Life. Ed. staff, Cora Linn Daniels and C. M. Stevens. Detroit: Gale, 1971 (facsim. reprint of the 1903 ed.). 3 vols. xxiv, 1,751p. Illus. $47.50 set LC 70-141151

This interesting reference set covers: human worship, magic, witchcraft, cures, spells, astrology, strange customs, and graphology. These tidbits were extracted from many parts of the world, many times, and the writings of many languages. As with many of these old "library of knowledge" books, this set is not well-organized. More important, access to information is poor. There are no bold-faced headings and well-defined entries one has a right to expect from an encyclopedia. The work also seems more slanted towards customs and lore than toward serious occult information. However, the three volumes are a useful gathering of loose ends of knowledge.

363 Däniken, Erich von, 1935- . Chariots of the Gods?: Un-
* solved Mysteries of the Past. Trans. by Michael Heron. London: Corgi, 1971 (orig. pub., London: Souvenir, 1969; abridged ed. for younger readers, New York: Putnam, 1974). 190p. Illus. Plates Maps Bibliog. Index (Orig. pub. as "Erinnerungen an die Zukunft." Düsseldorf: Econ-Verlag, 1968) £0.35 pa. ISBN 0-552-08800-5

This work advocates the by now often heard theory that extraterrestrials visited earth a few thousand years ago and intervened with man to raise his I.Q. and teach him civilization. However, this book was the first to reach the vast masses of the public with this theory. The television program, "In Search of Ancient Astronauts," narrated by Rod Serling, was based on this book, and showed some of the same photos; it was also widely viewed and discussed. The book discusses cave paintings showing astronauts, markings on the Plain of Nazca in Peru, biblical instructions for building the Ark of the Covenant, resulting in an electric condenser. This book has become an occult classic, and should be owned by all libraries and read by all intelligent people--if only so they can ridicule it. However, in spite of all the charges against von Däniken, he deserves tremendous credit. True, others wrote of these theories years before von Däniken. Yet, he had the imagination to reach the public with these ideas.

364 ________. Gold of the Gods. Trans. by Michael Heron. Lon-
*** don: Souvenir Press, 1973 (also, London: Corgi, 1975). 216p. Illus. (some color) Map Plans Bibliog. Index (Translation of "Aussaat und Kosmos." Düsseldorf: Econ-Verlag, 1972) £2.20 ISBN 0-285-62087-8

This work is a major new contribution to occult literature. The author's two previous works, Chariots of the Gods? and Gods from Outer Space (also called Return to the Stars), have sold over three million hardcover copies total. In this work, the author covered over 76,000 miles and three continents seeking new evidence for extraterrestrial intervention in man's affairs. Von Däniken's theory is that, sometime in the past, a battle was fought in the depths of the galaxy between two highly developed civilizations. The losers escaped in spaceships and landed on earth. To evade discovery by their pursuers, they used thermal drills and electron rays, burrowed into the earth, and built underground cities. When things became safe, they began to create intelligent life on earth by mutating existing hominids. The author states that a huge system of tunnels lies beneath South America, thousands of miles in length and 750 feet deep. Those in Ecuador and Peru have already been explored. The tunnels all form right angles, the walls are smooth, sometimes polished, and the ceilings seem glazed. These areas often exhibit high radiation levels. There are huge assembly halls, ventilation shafts, and statues of pure gold written on with unknown letters. In Ecuador, a vast underground "library" has been found. The von Däniken writing style is in the first person, much of it in conversational, travel-book style. The casual ramblings jump around quite a bit, but the book is packed with good anecdotes and fascinating odd bits of information. As with all of von Däniken's work, this book is highly speculative, to say the least. Yet, it is very thought-provoking. For any occult follower, it is required reading. There are dozens of photographs, some in full color. Recently, von Däniken's works have come under heavy criticism, even in occult journals (as an example, see "Fate," July, 1976). Also, the conviction of von Däniken on fraud charges in Switzerland many years ago bothers some.

365 ________. In Search of Ancient Gods: My Pictorial Evidence
* for the Impossible. Trans. by Michael Heron. New York: Putnam, 1974 (also, London: Souvenir Press, 1974; also, London: Corgi, 1976). 249p. Illus. (part color) Bibliog. (Translation of "Meine Welt in Bildern"). $8.95 LC 73-93725 ISBN 0-399-11346-0

This book repeats many of the same theories that appear in other von Däniken books. However, this work is accompanied by 319 black-and-white photos and 57 color photos.

366 ________. Miracles of the Gods: A Hard Look at the Super-
* natural. Trans. by Michael Heron. London: Souvenir Press, 1975. 237p. Illus. Plates Bibliog. (Translation of "Erscheinungen." Düsseldorf: Econ-Verlag, 1974). £3.75 ISBN 0-285-62174-2

This work discusses interstellar thought transference, as manifested in visions people have had throughout human history. Visions (Christian miracles, mystical experiences, new ideas) are a natural phenomenon. The gods from whom these thoughts come are responsible for such things as the double helix, particle physics, and relativity (inventors will obviously not enjoy this work!). Von

Däniken feels that the extraterrestrials are expanding our consciousness. This book may bother some of the many fans von Däniken has picked up from his earlier works.

367 ______. Return to the Stars: Evidence for the Impossible.
* Trans. by Michael Heron. London: Corgi, 1972 (also pub. as "Gods from Outer Space; Return to the Stars, or Evidence for the Impossible," New York: Putnam, 1971; orig. pub., London: Souvenir Press, 1970). 190p. Illus. Bibliog. Index (Translation of "Zuruck zu den Sternen." Düsseldorf: Econ-Verlag, 1968) £0.40 pa. ISBN 0-552-09083-2

368 Darling, Harry F., 1919- , and Ruth Hale Oliver. Astro-
* psychology. Lakewood, Ga.: CSA Press, 1973 (c1972). 333p. Illus. Includes bibliogs. (First pub. as "Organum Quaterni," 1968) $11.95 LC 67-29385 ISBN 0-87707-111-X

This is an excellent, definitive work on criminal and abnormal psychology and astrology. Darling is an authority on psychiatric drugs, and has had long experience as a prison psychiatrist (especially at Bridgewater State Hospital for criminals in Massachusetts). Oliver is an experienced astrologer. With case histories, the authors discuss how mental problems can be recognized in birth charts (Senator Joe McCarthy, Hitler, Richard Speck, Jack the Ripper). There are chapters on tetradic thought, mandala, Jungian psychosocial concepts, prenatal horoscopes, Mars, Saturn, and lunar nodes; Uranus and sexual neurosis; and astrological delineation of specific disorders--homosexuals, violence, depression.

369 David-Neel, Alexandra, 1868-1969. Magic and Mystery in
* Tibet. Magnolia, Mass.: Peter Smith, 1972 (also, Dover, 1971; orig. pub., 1932). xiv, 320p. Illus. (Translation of "Mystiques et magiciens du Thibet") $5

This classic work was written by a French scholar, medical doctor, Oriental expert and practicing Buddhist, who lived and studied in Tibet for years. She discusses the Tibetan Book of the Dead, lamaistic control of the mind's experiences, psychic disciplines, necromancy, mental visualizations, physical yoga and great yogis of the past. She attempts a totally factual account of these practices.

370 Davidson, Leon, 1922- . Flying Saucers: An Analysis of the Air Force Project Blue Book Special Report No. 14. 4th ed. Clarksburg, W. Va.: Saucerian Books, 1971. Various pagings Illus. Maps $7.95 pa. LC 70-138935

371 Davies, John D. Phrenology: Fad and Science; A 19th-Century American Crusade. Hamden, Conn.: Archon, 1971 (c1955). xiii, 203p. Illus. Bibliog. note $6.50 LC 70-122405 ISBN 0-208-00952-3

372 Davies, Reginald Trevor. Four Centuries of Witch-Beliefs,

with Special Reference to the Great Rebellion. New York: B. Blom, 1972 (reprint of 1947 ed.). xii, 222p. Bibliog. $12.50 LC 74-180026

The author argues that Calvinist beliefs spurred on the witchhunts of the 16th and 17th centuries. He feels that dissident members of the Long Parliament and antiroyalist armies spread witch beliefs where they had not been before. Cromwell's permissive attitude towards the press caused such beliefs to be widely circulated. This view is a minority view not widely held by today's scholars. Experts Alan MacFarlane (who studied assize records) and Keith Thomas (who studied religious folklore) do not support Davies. Davies's work is primarily based on 17th-century English witchcraft literature and as such is a valuable work.

373 Davison, Ronald Carlyle. The Technique of Prediction: The New Complete System of Secondary Directing. Rev. ed. London: L. N. Fowler, 1971 (previous ed., 1955). 152p. Illus. Index £1.50 ISBN 0-85243-172-4

374 Davy, John, ed. Work Arising from the Life of Rudolf Steiner: Articles Published to Mark the Fiftieth Anniversary of the Death of Rudolf Steiner. London: Rudolf Steiner Press, 1975. 232p. Illus. Plates Bibliog. £3.90 ISBN 0-85440-293-4

375 Day, Harvey. Occult Illustrated Dictionary. London: Kaye and Ward, 1975. iv, 156p. Illus. Facsim. £2.50 ISBN 0-7182-1104-9

This reference work has not gotten very good reviews. The definitions are often weak or inaccurate. Little-known terms often get long explanations; well-known ones are often briefly defined. Many minor British biographies, however, are here. Day's definitions present mainly his own views--slightly pro-occult.

376 Day, James Wentworth. Essex Ghosts: The Haunting Towns and Villages of Essex. Bourne End, England: Spurbooks, 1973. 58p. Illus. £0.60 pa.

377 Day, Langston, and George de la Warr. New Worlds Beyond the Atom. Wakefield, England: EP Publishing, 1973 (orig. pub., London: Stuart, 1956). vii, 136p. Illus. Facsim. £2.25

This book reprints a survey of Oxford scientists' discoveries in the 1950's that penetrated beyond the atom into forms of radiation previously unknown.

378 De A'Morelli, Richard. Extra Sensual Perception. Chatsworth, Calif.: Books for Better Living, 1974. 174p. Illus. $1.50 pa. LC 74-80947 ISBN 0-88491-208-6

379 _______. Numerology: The Key to Your Innerself. Chatsworth, Calif. : Books for Better Living, 1972. 208p. $1.95 pa. ISBN 0-87056-285-1

380 _______. Numerology for Lovers. Chatsworth, Calif. : Books for Better Living, 1974. 192p. $1.25 pa. LC 74-76653 ISBN 0-88491-201-9

381 _______. Psychic Power; How to Develop Your ESP. Chatsworth, Calif. : Books for Better Living, 1973. 160p. $1.25 pa. LC 73-84795

This book presents a step-by-step, easy-to-follow program by which one can develop his own psychic abilities. The author discusses how to send ESP messages; how to tune in on people far away; how to find and keep a lover using ESP.

382 Dean, Douglas, and John Mihalasky. Executive ESP. Ed. by
* Sheila Ostrander and Lynn Schroeder. Englewood Cliffs, N. J. : Prentice-Hall, 1974. 284p. $7.95

The author's project was initially funded by Chester Carlson (now deceased), whose money led to creation of the Psi Communications Project of the Newark College of Engineering in New Jersey. The study put successful businessmen, especially corporation presidents, under precognition tests. Much of the work used the plethysmograph, which records changes in blood volume in certain areas of the body; the finger was used here. The rest of the work involved use of random numbers in precognition. (Dean was the main power behind getting the Parapsychological Association recognized as a branch of the American Association for the Advancement of Science). The book contains chapters on time, using psychic powers in business, and "What Enhances Psi and What Blocks Psi." There are also 80 pages of statistics in the appendix. The work asks the basic question, "Are business hunches ESP?" and answers, "Yes." One main conclusion is that psi is ever-occurring, a constant stream of information pouring into the unconscious.

383 Dearden, Harold, 1882- . Devilish but True: The Doctor Looks at Spiritualism. Wakefield, England: EP Publishing; Totowa, N. J. : Rowman and Littlefield, 1975 (orig. pub., London: Hutchinson, 1936). 282p. Illus. Index $11.50 LC 75-31550 ISBN 0-87471-618-7

384 Defoe, Daniel, 1661?-1731. History of the Life and Adventures of Mr. Duncan Campbell. Ed. by George A. Aitken. Illus. by J. B. Yeats. New York: AMS Press 1974 (orig. pub., London: Dent, 1895). (Orig. ed. issued as vol. 4 of author's "Romances and Narratives") $11 LC 74-13463 ISBN 0-404-07914-8

385 _______. A System of Magick. New introd. by Richard Landon. Wakefield, England: EP Publishing, 1973 (orig. pub.,

London: J. Roberts, 1727; dist. by Rowman and Littlefield). x, 403p. Illus. $12 LC 74-155326 ISBN 0-85409-872-0

The author discusses the devil at work in 18th-century society. He uses the Bible as a major source, studies contemporary magicians, and draws on material from earlier authors such as Sir Walter Raleigh (History of the World, 1614) and Richard Bovet (Pandaemonium, 1684). Defoe comments often on the social and political problems of his time. He believes that man no longer needs Satan, since he has taken over his place and far outstrips the devil's worst deeds.

386 De Giustino, David. Conquest of Mind: Phrenology and Victorian Social Thought. London: Croom Helm; Totowa, N. J.: Rowman and Littlefield, 1975. viii, 248p. Bibliog. Index (Croom Helm Social History Series) $18.50 LC 75-317759 ISBN 0-87471-601-2

This work is centered on George Combe, an Edinburgh lawyer who became the international leader in the field of phrenology. The author has gone through the Combe Papers, and read his over 30 books and pamphlets. Other phrenology devotees discussed are Goethe, Marx, Poe, Whitman, and Dickens. The author says the two most important areas of influence for phrenology have been in education and penology. The author sees phrenology as a "short-cut to knowledge." Because of the author's sources, his view of phrenology is Combe-centered.

387 De Jersey, Katherine, and Isabella Taves. Destiny Times Six; An Astrologer's Casebook. Greenwich, Conn.: Fawcett, 1971 (c1970). 303p. $1.25 pa.

The book contains six case histories from the files of this Chicago astrologer. All of the characters seem to be wealthy, famous, and ruled by their destinies. Love, sex, money problems, and suicide are frequent themes.

388 Delaney, Walter, 1930- . Ultra-Psychonics: How to Work Miracles with the Limitless Power of Psycho-Atomic Energy. West Nyack, N. Y.: Parker Pub. Co., 1975. 256p. $7.95 LC 74-16232 ISBN 0-13-935635-5

This book discusses: "how to create things out of thin air with ultraglyphics"; "how to multiply brainpower by a factor of 1,000"; "how to build a psychonic radar locator that can be used to locate buried treasure."

389 Delano, Kenneth J. Astrology: Fact or Fiction? Huntington, Ind.: Our Sunday Visitor, 1973. 127p. Includes bibliog. refs. $1.95 LC 73-84660 ISBN 0-87973-817-0

Written by a priest, this book is an exposé of astrology and what the author feels to be its many frauds.

390 De Louise, Joseph, and Tom Valentine. Psychic Mission. Chicago: Regnery, 1971. ix, 224p. $5.95 LC 75-143842

This Chicago hairdresser discusses predictions he has made (some on television) which have come true. He mentions: the Chappaquiddick happening of Senator Kennedy, descriptions of the Tate murderers before they were caught, train and plane crashes. The author traces his gift to a grandfather in Sicily.

391 Delphos, Omar. Psycho-Astrology. New York: Tower, 1971. $.95 pa.

392 Delsol, Paula. Chinese Horoscopes. Trans. by Peter and Tanya Leslie. London: Pan Books, 1973 (pub. as "Chinese Astrology," New York: Hippocrene, 1972). 239p. Illus. (Translation of "Horoscopes Chinois." Paris: Mercure de France, 1969). £0.40 pa. ISBN 0-330-23424-2

There are very few books out on the Chinese zodiac, and any work is welcomed. This one discusses: were you born under a good moon?; signs and their years (four to five pages each); blue moons and red moons; years and their signs (four to five pages each tells what each sign type can look forward to in each year); friendship; love and marriage; parents; business. All entries in the book are very brief. The entire work consists mostly of short sentences; it appears too superficial. The author suggests people have fun with horoscope charts without looking at them to make decisions or see their destinies.

393 Dendy, Walter Cooper, 1794-1871. The Philosophy of Mystery. Folcroft, Pa.: 1974 (orig. pub., New York: Harper, 1845). $45 LC 74-2364

394 Denning, Melita, and Osborne Phillips. The Apparel of High Magick. St. Paul, Minn.: Llewellyn Publications, 1975. (Magical Philosophy, vol. 2) $10 LC 75-2389

395 ________, and ________. Mysteria Magica. St. Paul: Llewellyn Publications, 1975. (Magical Philosophy, vol. 5) $10 LC 75-2427 ISBN 0-87542-180-6

396 ________, and ________. Robe and Ring: The Philosophy of the Magical Art, the Ethics of Western Occultism. St. Paul, Minn.: Llewellyn Publications, 1974. 192p. Illus. Includes bibliog. refs. (Magical Philosophy, vol. 1) $10 LC 75-303148 ISBN 0-85742-176-8

397 ________, and ________. The Sword and the Serpent. St. Paul, Minn.: Llewellyn Publications, 1975. (Magical Philosophy, vol. 3) $10 LC 75-2390 ISBN 0-87542-178-4

398 De Pascale, Marc. The Book of Fate. New York: St. Martin's, 1971. 78p. Illus. $3.95 LC 77-178864

399 ________. The Book of Spells. New York: Taplinger, 1971. 129p. Illus. $4.95 LC 70-163218 ISBN 0-8008-0933-5

This book presents over 30 spells to help in love and business. It is illustrated with some old woodcuts.

400 Derenberger, Woodrow W. Visitors from Lanulos. As related ... to the author, Harold W. Hubbard. New York: Vantage Press, 1971. 111p. Illus. $3.75 LC 70-24671

This book discusses visits that Derenberger had from aliens from other worlds, including Lanulos, and visits he made to that planet. The first conversation was with "Indrid Cold," an outer-space visitor who appeared on November 2, 1966. Others soon followed. The accounts are in chronological order, the last being in 1968. This is the kind of book that makes even occult believers often cringe.

401 De Rola, Stanislas Klossowski. Alchemy: The Secret Art.
* New York: Bounty Books/Crown Publishers, 1973 (orig. pub., London: Thames and Hudson, 1973). 128p. Illus. (some color) $5.95 LC 74-80670

This fine work is important mainly for its 193 illustrations (33 in full color). These plates are not usually seen in other illustrated alchemy books. The text of 30 pages discusses true and false alchemy; the four and the three; and present work in alchemy. Also included is "An Exposition upon Sir George Ripley's Vision," written by Aeyrenaeus Philalethes in 1677. De Rola's aim in the text is to show the true nature of alchemy. Its doctrine claims a hidden reality of the highest order underlying all truths and religions. Consciousness has to be transmuted from ordinary (lead-like) levels of daily perception to a subtle (gold-like) perception level, so that every element is perceived in its perfect archetypal form contained within the Absolute. De Rola's book is valuable for its beautiful illustrations; the text is a nice extra.

402 De Sabato, Mario. He Sees the Future. Trans. by Margaret Sansone Scouten. New York: Award, 1971. 153p. (Translation of "Les Confidences d'un voyant." Paris: Editions Alsatia, 1969) $.75 pa.

This tiny paperback has received virtually no reviews anywhere, yet is a fascinating and unusual work. The author, a psychic consultant in Paris, presents the usual predictions. However, he adds numerous discussions on the alienation and loneliness many of the best psychics suffer; physical and mental reactions to his gifts; inner thought processes; his state of dependence; his responsibilities towards clients. He also discusses the psychology of his clients. He states, "The seer is a detached individual who lives on the edge of society so that he may observe it better and avoid taking it for a model. His function resembles no other and always remains a mystery in life." De Sabato functions through use of psychometry, by taking hold of the client's hand and then seeing events past and future. He states that if he is making an error, an inner voice corrects him. This is a fascinating work on clairvoyance. It is not given a * only because of its lack of reviews, its shortness, and its presentation of too many case studies and not enough theory. A theoretical, 400-page study by De Sabato of his abilities would be a tremendous work.

Deusen, Wilson Van see Van Deusen, Wilson

403 Deutch, Richard. Exorcism: Possession or Obsession? Forword by Christopher Neil-Smith. London: Bachman and Turner, 1975. 144p. Illus. Bibliog. £3.95 ISBN 0-85974-042-0.

404 Devereux, George, ed. Psychoanalysis and the Occult. London: Souvenir Press, 1974 (orig. pub., New York: International Universities Press, 1953). xv, 432p. Bibliog. Index £3 ISBN 0-285-64738-5

This work consists of 31 articles by 17 authors, all psychoanalysts, taken from the last 50 years of psychoanalytic journals. Authors include: Freud (six articles); Jule Eisenbud, Nandor Fodor, and others. One chapter is titled, "Occult Processes Occurring During Psychoanalysis." Another chapter by Freud is on the occult significance of dreams. Not much in the book really sheds light on the occult, but the work does show what little attention and respect psychology has had for psychic events.

405 Devil's Prayerbook. By a witch. St. Albans, England: Mayflower, 1975 (orig. pub., London: Rigel Press, 1974). 93p. £0.50 pa. ISBN 0-583-12488-7

406 Dickinson, Alice. Salem Witchcraft Delusion, 1692: "Have
* You Made No Contact with the Devil?" F. Watts, 1974. 64p. Illus. Bibliog. Index (Focus Books) $3.95 LC 73-12085 ISBN 0-0531-01049-X

This good juvenile book discusses events before the trials (especially the Puritan Charter and fear of new ideas of science), participants, and the trial itself. It is a very factual account, with good illustrations. The author feels the girls' behavior was the result of real suffering, doctors' suggestions, play-acting, and a frightened half-believing surrender to the sweep of events. It is recommended for grades 5-9.

407 Dickinson, Peter, 1927- . Chance, Luck and Destiny. Boston: Little, Brown, 1975 (also, London: Gollancz, 1975). 254p. Illus. (Atlantic Monthly Press Book) $9.95 LC 75-28403 ISBN 0-316-18428-4

This juvenile book is a collection of anecdotes, stories, facts and activities relating to chance, odds, the laws of large numbers, coincidence, 18th-century gamblers, Tarot cards, dice, cartoons, pages from the Golden Bough, witches, magic, the Delphic oracle. It is a hodgepodge, with no real central thread organizing it.

408 Dinsdale, Tim. The Loch Ness Monster. 2nd ed. London: Routledge and K. Paul, 1972 (previous ed., 1961). xii, 160p. Illus. Maps £2.50 ISBN 0-7100-7313-5

There is a great deal of overlap in all of Dinsdale's books. This one discusses how he saw the monster in 1960 on his first visit to Loch Ness, and chronicles the many disappointments since then in trying to locate the monster.

409 _______. Monster Hunt. Foreword by Robert H. Rines. Washington, D.C.: Acropolis Books, 1972 (pub. as "Leviathans," 1966). xi, 295p. Illus. $6.95 LC 71-184717 ISBN 0-87491-325-X

The author has added 70 pages of new material to the 1966 edition. In 1960, this former British aeronautical engineer filmed a large wake on the surface of Loch Ness. Several years later, the Royal Air Force concluded it was caused by a submerged animal about 35 feet long. The new material points out the great amount of research taking place at Loch Ness. There are many problems in sighting--for one thing, the weather. From May 15 through October 1 on one year, only five days were suitable for photographing. Dinsdale reports that underwater sound equipment has detected the presence of large animals.

410 _______. Project Water Horse: The True Story of the Monster Quest at Loch Ness. London, Boston: Routledge and K.
* Paul, 1975. 213p. Illus. Plates Maps Bibliog. Index $15.50 LC 75-320936 ISBN 0-7100-8029-8

This work discusses the author's 14 years of searching for the monster, using a variety of cameras, listening and echo devices. It also mentions the use of the submarine Pisces, which found no bones of dead monsters at the bottom of the lake.

411 _______. The Story of the Loch Ness Monster. London: Target, 1973 (also, London: Wingate, 1973). 124p. Illus. Maps £0.25 pa.

The legend of a creature in this water has a long history, and the author includes the legends of St. Columba 1,400 years ago, as well as covering the fact and fiction of the modern era. He also discusses modern scientific methods and equipment being employed to solve the mystery.

412 Dione, R. L. God Drives a Flying Saucer. London: Corgi, 1973 (orig. pub., Jericho, N.Y.: Exposition Press, 1969). xi, 131p. £0.30 pa.

The author's theme is that God is not supernatural but rather "supertechnological." He created man in His own image, "for God, while humanoid, is nevertheless impartial through technology." Dione presents in his own mind not a theory but a collection of what he considers facts.

413 Dixon, Jeane, as told to Rene Noorbergen. My Life and Prophecies. London: Sphere, 1973 (also, London: Muller, 1971; also, large print ed., Boston: G. K. Hall, 1971; orig. pub., New York: Morrow, 1969). 191p. Index £0.35 pa. ISBN 0-7221-2989-0

The author lists seven different ways in which she learns of future events, distant happenings, or others' thoughts. She discusses difficulties in interpreting signs, visions, and dreams, stating that their meanings are often unclear until after the event. The first part of the book discusses the past (prophecies concerning the Kennedys and Martin Luther King). Following this are: a chapter of miscellaneous prophecy; two chapters on the anti-Christ; and two on Dixon's philosophy and theology of life. The book is basically a collection of anecdotes and reflections. Dixon feels that she functions as a channel from God to man. This may explain the great amount of preaching she does throughout this book.

414 _______. Yesterday, Today, and Forever. New York: Morrow, 1976 (c1975). 439p. \$8.95 LC 75-29145 ISBN 0-688-02984-1

This book describes her 1974 vision of the correspondence between the 12 apostles and the signs of the zodiac. The author discusses sun signs, and then makes finer distinctions within each sign based on numerology. She also includes forecasts for the future.

415 Dixon, Jeanette. Welsh Ghosts--Ysbrydion Cymru. St. Ives, England: James Pike, 1975. 32p. Illus. Maps (Viewing Wales Series) £0.30 pa. ISBN 0-85932-126-6

416 Dobbs, Betty Jo Teeter, 1930- . Foundations of Newton's
* Alchemy; or, The Hunting of the Greene Lyon. Cambridge, England and New York: Cambridge University Press, 1975. 300p. Illus. Facsims. Bibliog. Index \$22.50 LC 74-31795 ISBN 0-521-20786-X

The author shows that Newton researched alchemy deeply, and believed he had succeeded in accomplishing alchemical transformations. Dobbs went through several thousand of Newton's pages on alchemy, mostly in his own writing. They show Newton as a serious alchemist, his laboratory going constantly for six weeks in the spring and six weeks in the fall. He was devoted to laboratory alchemy, not spiritual alchemy. He believed he had found the true philosopher's mercury. Newton did have successes in toxic metal metallurgy on a small scale (the "green lion" of the book's subtitle is the ore of antimony). The author stops her research in this book in the early 1670's. She is currently taking the investigation further.

417 Doberer, Kurt Karl, 1904- . Goldmakers; 10,000 Years of Alchemy. Westport, Conn.: Greenwood Press, 1972 (c1948). 301p. Illus. Facsims. Bibliog. $12.75 LC 72-597 ISBN 0-8371-6355-2

This book discusses the history of alchemy and chemistry concerning the transmutation of metals. It moves from Atlantis to the present. The work is mostly a collection of anecdotes.

418 Donnelly, Ignatius, 1831-1901. Atlantis: The Antediluvian
* World. Rev. ed. Ed. by Egerton Sykes. 1972 (orig. pub., New York, 1882). 355p. Index $4

This book remains the classic work on Atlantis (since 1882, the literature of Atlantis has grown to over 5,000 works in 20 languages). Chapters include: "Plato's History of Atlantis"; "Was Such a Catastrophe Possible?"; "The Testimony of the Sea"; "Flora and Fauna"; "The Cross and the Pyramid"; "The Origin of Our Alphabet." A good deal of the work deals with Greek, Phoenician, Arabian, Egyptian, Turanian, and Semitic links with Atlantis. Also discussed are the deluge legends of the Bible, the Chaldeans, and the Americas.

419 ________. The Destruction of Atlantis; Ragnarök: The Age of Fire and Gravel. Introd. by Paul M. Allen. Blauvelt, N.Y.: Rudolf Steiner Pubns., 1971. 452p. Illus. (Previous eds. have title, "Ragnarök: The Age of Fire and Gravel") $2.45 pa. LC 75-175055

420 Donovan, Frank. Never on a Broomstick. London: Allen
* and Unwin, 1973 (orig. pub., Harrisburg, Pa.: Stackpole Books, 1971). 256p. Illus. Facsim. £3.25 ISBN 0-04-291010-2

This work is a good survey of witchcraft history from Neolithic times to the present. The book discusses: Eleusinian mysteries and Bacchic rites of Greece; Saturnalis of Rome; May Day celebrations of England and Europe; fertility cults with their female deities; tortures used to extract confessions; early priests; mysticism of Jewish and Christian sects; herbal lore; love potions; magic in the Dark Ages; magic spells. Most of the book covers the period when church and state tried to exterminate the cult. The author feels that many of the views most people today have concerning witchcraft are fictions invented during the Middle Ages to discredit the cult. Donovan theorizes that witchcraft has usually been the area where rebels could fight against the "status quo," and this is the case today.

421 Douce, P.M. The Incredible Alliance. New York: Dorrance, 1973. 135p.

This book is an account of the author's experiences in automatic writing with T. S. Eliot. The work begins with some poetry. There are then four main sections, and a final one. Most of the writing is Christian doctrine. There are many pages of photos of the writing.

422 Douglas, Alfred, 1942- . How to Consult the I Ching, the
* Oracle of Change. Illus. by David Sheridan. New York: Putnam, 1971 (orig. pub. as "Oracle of Change"). 251p. Illus. $6.95 LC 70-136791

In this good introduction, instructions on the I Ching are easy to grasp. The author writes primarily for those wishing to use the I Ching for divination. The first part introduces the reader to the history, meaning, and influence of the I Ching, giving three methods of consulting it. Part 2, the actual text, goes hexagram by hexagram, with statements and commentaries. The appendixes discuss mathematical aspects and European translations. This book is based on a 1715 edition of the I Ching.

423 ______. The Tarot: The Origins, Meaning and Uses of the
* Cards. Illus. by David Sheridan. Harmondsworth, England: Penguin, 1974 (orig. pub., New York: Taplinger; London: Gollancz, 1972). 249p. Illus. Plates Bibliog. Index £0.35 pa.

This is by far one of the best books written on the Tarot. It discusses the origin, history, and symbolism of the cards, touching on their mystical and psychological significance (including their possible place in Jungian theory). The major part consists of two long chapters, one on the major arcana and one on the minor. The discussion on each of the major 22 cards is especially well-done, and shows deep thought. The author suggests using the Tarot as an aid to meditation, and mentions the Italian game of torocco. There are photos of rare or curious cards, and illustrations for the body of the work provided by David Sheridan's original drawings (all in black and white).

424 Dowling, Levi H., 1844-1911. The Aquarian Gospel of Jesus the Christ. Tucson, Ariz.: Omen Press, 1972 (c1907). 260p. $2.25 pa.

This minor classic was written by a graduate of two medical schools, who was a chaplain to the end of the Civil War. Early in life as a youngster, Dowling had a vision of being told he was to build a white city. The vision was repeated three times over the years. The white city supposedly was this book, written from 2 to 6 a.m. each day. The work is written in Bible verse style. There are 22 sections, and a subject index in front. The big changes from the usual Bible text are the life and works of Jesus in India, Tibet, Persia, Assyria, and Greece.

425 Downing, Barry Howard. The Bible and Flying Saucers. Lon-

don: Sphere, 1973 (previous ed., Philadelphia: Lippincott, 1968). 175p. Bibliog. £0.35 pa.

The author is a conservative minister, who tries to relate Bible incidents to modern theories of space travel and relativity. He is fairly sure that flying saucers exist. He suggests that angels may have been visitors from space, and that the Red Sea was parted for the Hebrews by a space vehicle.

426 Doyle, Arthur Conan, 1859-1930. The Coming of the Fairies.
* New York: S. Weiser, 1972 (c1921). 196p. Illus. $2.95 LC 74-184565

This book deserves a * purely on its reputation as a classic alone. It is the standard accepted work on fairies. The case concerned two girls, Elsie and her cousin Frances, who constantly played with the fairies. Elsie one day took photos. E. L. Gardner of the Theosophical Society heard of it and got into the case. Eventually, Doyle heard of it indirectly and became interested. This work discusses: how the case started; the first published account in The Strand of 1920; observations of a clairvoyant in the area of Cottingley Glen, 1921; independent evidence for fairies; some subsequent cases; a theosophic view of fairies. This book contains reproductions of the famous Cottingley photos. Obviously, Doyle came under heavy criticism over the years for writing seriously about such a topic. The photos appear just a bit too good to be real.

427 _______. The History of Spiritualism. New York: Arno,
* 1975 (orig. pub., New York, 1926). 2 vols. in 1 (Perspectives in Psychical Research Series) $18 LC 75-7375 ISBN 0-405-07025-X

This volume is a classic, and Doyle's most comprehensive study of spiritualism. It was published shortly after he resigned his membership in the Society for Psychical Research over treatment by SPR members of several cases of apparent fraud. It is a survey of spiritualism's history and his own ideas on the field, plus some case studies.

428 Drake, Walter Raymond. Gods and Spacemen in the Ancient East. London: Sphere, 1973 (orig. pub. as "Spacemen in the Ancient East," London: Spearman, 1968). 240p. Bibliog. Index £0.35 pa. ISBN 0-7221-3044-9

The author studies the religions and history of the East in an attempt to show the influence of extraterrestrial beings in human life. Chapters include "Space Gods of India," "Space Stories in Sanskrit," "Spacemen in Tibet," "Spacemen in China," "Spacemen in Japan," "Space Kings in Egypt," "Pyramid and Sphinx," "Exodus," and "Babylon."

429 _______. Gods and Spacemen in the Ancient West. New York: New American Library, 1974 (orig. pub., London: Sphere, 1974). 230p. Bibliog. $1.50 pa.

This book is based on the by now common theory that extraterrestrials visited our planet in the past and contributed to our civilizations. Discussions include the following: origin of man; antiquity of man; Lemuria; Atlantis; Poseidon; ancient America; spacemen in ancient North America; space gods of the Aztecs and Mayas; space gods of South America; Incas, sons of the sun; lost civilizations.

430 ______. Gods and Spacemen Throughout History. Chicago: Regnery, 1975. Bibliog. $9.95 LC 74-27802 ISBN 0-8092-8279-8

This work discusses possible visits in the past from other worlds at places such as Egypt, Greece, Atlantis, Mexico, and India.

431 Driberg, Thomas. Swaff: Life and Times of Hannen Swaffer. 1974. £3.95 ISBN 0-356-04369-X

Often called the "Pope of Fleet Street," Swaffer was a theatre critic, journalist, editor, preacher, spiritualist. A hero to some, a hated figure to others, he was often drunk, constantly talking, and vain. For 30 years, he was the best-known British columnist, one of the fathers of illustrated journalism. Some critics portray him as an excellent journalist and critic. Others disliked him and his work, and ridiculed his last few years of interest in spiritualism.

432 Driesch, Hans Adolf Eduard, 1867-1941. Psychical Research: The Science of the Supernormal. Trans. by Theodore Besterman. New York: Arno Press, 1975 (orig. pub., London: G. Bell, 1933). (Perspectives in Psychical Research Series) (Translation of "Parapsychologie") $11 LC 75-7376 ISBN 0-405-07026-8

The author was professor of philosophy at Leipzig and president of the Society for Psychical Research in the mid-1900's. He viewed psychical research as a natural science.

433 Drury, Nevill. The Path of the Chameleon. Jersey, England: Neville Spearman, 1973. 160p. Illus. Plates Bibliog. Index £2.50

The title is symbolic of the mystical journey one must take to get in touch with basic truths of the universe. The first section, "Approaches," covers magic avatars (Moses, Zarathustra, and others), Gnostics, and magical symbolism (triangle, wand, cup, and others). The rest of the work discusses pantheons or systems of archetypes one may follow to reach spiritual perfection, such as the Egyptian Book of the Dead; the Graeco-Roman system, including the journey to the underworld; the Chaldean oracles; and the Hebrew Qabalah. Appendixes cover various viewpoints on reincarnation and archetypal correspondences.

434 _______, and Stephen Skinner. The Search for Abraxas. London: Spearman, 1972. xxii, 138p. Illus. Plates Bibliog. Index £2.50 ISBN 0-85435-321-6

This book discusses medieval magical literature to see if it can be applied to modern-day magic efforts to control nature. Also, it discusses some modern-day magicians. There is a good chapter on Austin Osman Spare. Also mentioned is Crowley, and some material on astral projection.

435 Duff-Masters, Susan, 1945- . The Modern Woman's Zodiac Guide to Love and Fulfillment. New York: Pilot Books, 1973. 80p. $2.50 pa. LC 72-90058

436 Duncan, Anthony Douglas. Fourth Dimension: A Christian View of Occultism. London: Mowbrays, 1975. vii, 125p. £2.75 pa. ISBN 0-264-66199-0

437 Dunninger, Joseph. Dunninger's Monument to Magic. Secaucus, N.J.: Lyle Stuart, 1974. 222p. Illus. $14.95 LC 73-76824

This book presents Dunninger in scrapbook and photo album format. Also, it is a good history of the first half of the 20th century, when stage magicians were so popular. It includes letters and documents of some of these magicians. Discussions include mystic eye, Hindu burial, demon reflection, the crystal casket mystery, a hypnotized straw, magnetic control, a spirit voice, materializations, and spirit messages.

438 _______, as told to Walter Gibson. Dunninger's Secret. Secaucus, N.J.: Lyle Stuart, 1974. $8.95 LC 73-76823

This book explains the tricks behind Dunninger's stage mind-reading demonstrations, and reveals tricks performed by other magicians.

439 Duplessis, Yvonne. The Paranormal Perception of Color.
* Trans. by Paul von Toal. New York: Parapsychology Foundation, 1975. ix, 117p. Bibliog. Index (Parapsychological Monographs, no. 16) (Translation of "Vision parapsychologique des couleurs") $4.50 pa. LC 75-19563 ISBN 0-912328-27-4

This is an excellent book on a fascinating topic. The first section contains three short chapters on "Triumph of the Statistical Method," with mention of Rhine. The second part discusses color on the psychological level. The third part discusses color on the parapsychological level. It includes Warcollier's work with cards and dominoes, Berthaux's work with blind people, and experiments on clairvoyance of colors by Perot. Also discussed here is experimental work by Rýzl and Pratt using Pavel Stepanek as a subject, and Jules Roman's studies. The fourth section, "Beyond Parapsychology," discusses detection of color without use of eyes, for example, in blind or blindfolded people. She mentions that perception of color apparently can come from the skin, usually at the top of the head or on the hands. Also mentioned is Duplessis's own research. One critic feels that Duplessis never defines the exact process by which people agree on certain colors as being real. This seems a minor criticism to a fine book.

440 Dupree, Judy. Psychic Healer. Lakemont, Ga.: CSA Press, 1972. 239p. $6.95

441 Durbin, Henry. Witchcraft at the Lamb Inn, Bristol. Introd. by Robert A. Gilbert. Leicester, England, 1971 (orig. pub. as "Narrative of Some Extraordinary Things that Happened to Mr. Richard Giles's Children, at the Lamb, without Lawford's-Gate, Bristol ...," London: R. Edwards, 1800). 59p. Unpriced ISBN 0-85544-004-X

This book discusses poltergeist activity at the Lamb Inn in 1761.

442 Dutta, Rex. Flying Saucer Message. London: Pelham, 1972. 117p. £1.75 ISBN 0-7207-0363-8

443 ______. The Reality of Occult, Yoga, Meditation, Flying Saucers. London: Pelham, 1974 (dist. in U.S. by Transatlantic Arts, Levittown, N.Y.). 199p. Illus. Bibliog. Index £3.50 ISBN 0-7207-0789-7

444 Dyall, Valentine. Unsolved Mysteries: A Collection of Weird Problems. Contributions and historical research by Larry Forrester and Peter Robinson. London: Hutchinson, 1974 (orig. pub., 1954). £2

445 Dykshoorn, Martinus Bernardus, as told to Russell H. Felton.
* My Passport Says Clairvoyant. New York: Hawthorn Books, 1974. 229p. Illus. $8.95 LC 74-2579 ISBN 0-8015-5282-6

This very interesting autobiography discusses the life of Dykshoorn, born in s'Gravenzande, July 1920. It covers later in his career when he helps police track criminals. He does not believe that ESP can be learned, or that parapsychology will ever be an exact science. In 1949, by his abilities, money buried in World War II was found. In Holland, he helped find a metal box buried 300 years before. Affidavits supporting his predictions are given in an appendix. Discussions include the years of recognition, "telefonvision" (long-distance clairvoyance), work in Australia, disappointments, the Devil's Triangle, murder cases in the U.S., and the press in America.

446 Ebertin, Elsbeth Paula (Schmidt), 1880-1944. Astrology and

Romance. Afterword by Reinhold Ebertin. Trans. by D. G. Nelson. New York: ASI Publishers, 1973 (orig. pub., Chicago: D. G. Nelson, 1936). 132p. Illus. (Translation of "Astrologie und Liebesleben") $6 LC 73-90428 ISBN 0-88231-002-X

This book is considered a classic in the field of synastry, or chart comparison. Chapters discuss the power of stars and the yearning for love; advantages and disadvantages in the character of lovers; fortune and love tragedies. The author uses over 20 horoscopes and case histories. Included are interpretations of the seventh house, related planets, and a brief description of temperament according to sun and moon signs.

447 Ebon, Martin, ed. The Amazing Uri Geller. New York:
* Signet/New American Library, 1975. 168p. $1.50 pa.

This book is a collection of 20 essays, articles, and interviews from all sides of the Geller issue. Authors include Russell Targ, Harold Puthoff, Edgar Mitchell, D. Scott Rogo, Robert Brier, Ray Stanford, Ebon, and Geller himself. They discuss scientific evidence of his abilities; the Stanford Research Institute experiments; statements of Geller. Ebon himself writes that while he feels Geller may have psychic abilities, he spends too much time dramatizing them. Many of the articles are by journalists who some may feel are not trained to decide either way.

448 ________. The Devil's Bride: Exorcism Past and Present.
*** New York: Harper, 1974 (also pub. under title, "Exorcism, Past and Present," England: Cassel, 1975). 245p. Bibliog. $6.95 LC 73-18699 ISBN 0-06-062114-1

This work is a major new contribution to occult literature. It presents the following cases of exorcism: one Ebon saw performed by Eileen Garrett and her control; 17th-century "devil neurosis"; "The Devil's Bride," a 1966 case in Zürich; a 1894 case witnessed by a missionary named Nevius; Freud's 1923 paper on an exorcism in the late 1600's; "electronic exorcism," where U.S. doctor Carl Wickland used electric currents and direct dialog with the entity; the classical "Rituale Romanum" still used by contemporary Catholic exorcists; communicating with the devil through automatic writing; an experiment by a chemistry professor on purposely developing a state of possession in oneself; how women can use it in some tribes to put their demands across to a male-dominated society; and "Jesus the Exorcist." Ebon has deliberately avoided basic questions, trying to stick to facts. He says there is hardly a civilization in the world that does not have a demonological literature. He never decides if possessions are real or not, but does feel we should be aware that often they are parts of our own personality.

449 ________, ed. Exorcism: Fact Not Fiction. New York: Sig-
* net/New American Library, 1974. 275p. $1.25 pa.

The introduction and 23 other sections cover modern examples of exorcism. There are articles by Susy Smith, D. Scott Rogo, Alson Smith, Thomas Tietze, James Hyslop, and Morton Prince. There are chapters on Titus Bull and Carl Jung (partly on Jung's personal haunting, 1913-1917). The appendix gives part of the text of the Roman Catholic Great Exorcism Rite, and instructions of the Bishop of Exeter, England, for Anglicans' use in exorcism. Ebon feels possession is hard to define, falling in the borderline between emotional sickness, group hysteria, religion, self-dramatization, and fraud.

450 ________, ed. Psychic Discoveries by the Russians. New York: Signet/New American Library, 1971. 175p. (Signet Mystic) $.95 pa.

This book reports on the great interest in parapsychology from 1960 on in Russia, Czechoslovakia, and Bulgaria. The field has gained respectability and official support, perhaps because it satisfies religious urges and is yet "scientific." This anthology includes an article on Messing written by a Polish journalist, and based on Messing's autobiography (one that some say is full of distortions and lies).

451 ________, ed. The Psychic Scene. New York: Signet/New American Library, 1974. 188p. $1.25 pa.

This selection of articles from current magazines and news accounts discusses plant ESP, reincarnation, telepathy, talking dogs, Atlantis, TM, UFO's, the I Ching, and Polynesian legends. Sources include Family Circle, Village Voice, and Flying Saucer Review.

452 ________, ed. The Riddle of the Bermuda Triangle. New
* York: Signet/New American Library, 1975. 193p. $1.50 pa.

This work contains 20 chapters on the subject, pro and con. Authors include Vincent Gaddis (who coined the phrase "Bermuda Triangle"), Joseph Goodavage, and Ivan Sanderson. The book includes the complete text of the U.S. Coast Guard report on the disappearance of the Marine Sulphur Queen; Edgar Cayce's Atlantis theory; an interview with Lawrence D. Kusche, author of The Bermuda Triangle Mystery--Solved (entry 923); texts of boards of inquiry.

453 ________, ed. Test Your ESP. New York: Signet/New Amer-
* ican Library, 1971 (orig. pub., New York: World, 1969). 153p. Illus. Charts $.75 pa.

This is a very useful how-to-do book with discussions not often found in other books. The contributors are Robert Brier, Henie Brier, Eleanore Gohdes, Joyce Jones, and Andrea Fodor Litkei. Discussions include the basics of ESP testing; tests for children; testing with photographs; testing your pet; negative ESP (scoring considerably below chance); party games with ESP; psychokinesis; investigating a haunted house; communicating drawings. The work includes examples of ESP score sheets. Anecdotes and examples of cases are sprinkled throughout the chapters.

454 ________. They Knew the Unknown. New York: New Amer-
* ican Library, 1972 (orig. pub., New York: World, 1971). 256p. Bibliog. Index $1.25 pa.

This fine book presents 23 case studies of famous authors, statesmen, philosophers, and scientists from over the ages who have had psychic experiences. Ebon feels this aspect of their lives is often a forgotten one. The famous people covered are Socrates, Swedenborg, Kant, Schopenhauer, Shakespeare, Shelley, Lincoln, Hugo, Browning, Dickens, Mark Twain, William James, Strindberg, A. R. Wallace, Conan Doyle, Thomas Edison, William McDougall, Freud, Jung, Yeats, Alexis Carrel (surgeon and biologist), Maeterlinck, W. L. Mackenzie King (a Canadian prime minister), Thomas Mann, Gilbert Murray (classicist), Aldous Huxley, Upton Sinclair, and C. J. Ducasse (philosopher).

455 ________, ed. Witchcraft Today. Signet/New American Li-
* brary, 1971. (Signet Mystic) $.75

This is a good survey of contemporary witchcraft. The work discusses Britain, America's leading witches (Sybil Leek and Louise Huebner), New York's witch explosion, the witchcraft boom in Canada, origin of the Black Mass, Lavey and Manson, Salem, Africa, Healy witches.

456 Edelson, Edward, 1932- . The Book of Prophecy. Garden
* City, N.Y.: Doubleday, 1974. 133p. Illus. $4.95 LC 73-22050 ISBN 0-385-01077-X

This juvenile book explains 10 methods of prophecy in use today: numerology, palms, dreams, crystal balls, tea leaves, dominoes, dice, cards, Tarot, and I Ching. He feels that those which promote the greatest mind-searching are the ones that have survived. When necessary, Edelson gives a table of terms. The book is recommended for grades 6-9.

457 Edelstein, Emma, and Ludwig Edelstein. Asclepius. New York: Arno Press, 1975 (orig. pub., Baltimore: Johns Hopkins Press, 1945). 2 vols. 470 and 277p. $40

This book discusses Asclepius, the first Greek physician deified as a god. His healing cult grew from centers in Thessaly to Greece, and Alexander the Great and the pan-Hellenic movement carried it throughout the world. Also, his cult competed for attention with Christianity. In the fourth century, the Roman Empire wiped out worship of the cult. The book discusses the technique of healing in the temples, particularly "incubation," a kind of initiation. The patient spends a night in the temple, hoping Asclepius will appear to him in a dream and either heal him or give a message on how to become healed. This procedure often involved drugs. The authors include all major Latin and Greek texts that mention him.

458 Eden, Jerome. Planet in Trouble; The UFO Assault on Earth. Foreword by Elsworth F. Baker. New York: Exposition Press, 1973. 214p. Bibliog. $7.50 LC 74-155362

459 Edmunds, Simeon. ESP; Extrasensory Perception. Hollywood, Calif.: Wilshire Books, 1972 (orig. pub. as "Miracles of the Mind; An Introduction to Parapsychology," 1965). 204p. Illus. Bibliog. $2 pa.

This good survey discusses the following: telepathy, clairvoyance, precognition, spiritualism, hypnotism, paranormal healing, man's survival of death, modern experimental parapsychology, psychological elements in testimony, testimony and human fallibility. The author feels the time for theorizing is not yet here. The most important thing at present is to get the facts straight.

460 Edwards, David, 1943- . Dare to Make Magic. London: Rigel Press, 1971. 94p. Illus. Music Bibliog. £1.80 ISBN 0-85528-004-2

461 Edwards, Harry, d. 1976. Guide to the Understanding and Practice of Spiritual Healing. England: Healer Pub. Co., 1973. Index £2.50

This book is aimed mainly at healers, but is also valuable to novices. It is a well-written manual on healing. The author, former president of the National Federation of Spiritual Healers (England), died in December, 1976.

462 Ehrenwald, Jan. New Dimensions of Deep Analysis: A Study of Telepathy in Interpersonal Relationships. New York: Arno Press, 1975 (orig. pub., New York, 1955). (Perspectives in Psychical Research Series) $18 LC 75-7377 ISBN 0-405-07027-6

This book presents the first extensive case material showing telepathy and precognition on the part of the patient. The author theorizes on the functioning of psi at different levels of awareness. He then mentions more case material on psi among members of the patient's family. Ehrenwald also discusses ways the therapist can use psi in treatment to the benefit of the patient.

463 Elizabeth, Anne. Half Past the Eleventh Hour. New York: Vantage Press, 1974. 79p. $3.95 ISBN 0-533-00970-7

464 Elliot, Roger. Peking Luck. London: Coronet, 1973. 219p. Illus. £0.40 pa. ISBN 0-340-16789-0

465 _______. "TV Times"'s Roger Elliot Opens the Door to Your Future. London: Independent Television Books Ltd., 1974. 12 vols. 64p. each Illus. £0.40 each

This is a set of astrology prediction books, with a different volume for each sign.

466 Ellis, Arthur Jackson, 1885- . Divining Rod; A History of Water Witching. Norwood, Pa.: Norwood Editions, 1974 (orig. pub., Washington, D.C.: U.S. Gov. Printing Office, 1917, as no. 416 of "Water-Supply Papers," U.S. Geological Survey). Bibliog. $6 LC 74-13846

467 Ellis, Keith, 1927- . Prediction and Prophecy. London: Wayland, 1973. 192p. Illus. Bibliog. Index £2.95 ISBN 0-85340-233-7

This work is a good summary of divination in the ancient world. One chapter is titled, "Prophets, Oracles and Latter-Day Saints." This is a tour of superstitious places and customs throughout the ages. There is another chapter on divinatory customs, such as onychomancy (oiled fingernails) and kephalomancy (cracked, burned donkey's head). Also, odd bits of information are presented (for example, the fact that nine-tenths of the people interviewed knew their Zodiac sign).

468 _______. Science and the Supernatural. London: Wayland, 1974. 191p. Illus. Plates Index £4.25 ISBN 0-85340-234-5

469 Ellwood, Gracia Fay. Psychic Visits to the Past; An Explor-
* ation to Retrocognition. New York: Signet/New American Library, 1971. 176p. Bibliog. $.75 pa.

The author discusses the phenomenon in which past events replay themselves spontaneously before the witness, even though he has never been part of the event. She sees three types: "walk-in" retrocognition, where the person seems physically present in the events; "former incarnation," where the person describes events of a past lifetime, and even can assume personality characteristics of another person; and psychometry. Fifteen cases are described, 12 of the walk-in variety. The cases are arranged in chronological order, the first in 1642, the last in 1963. Some of them are well-known: the Versailles case, the Dieppe Raid case, the Soul of Nyria. She points out that the 15 events are only cases where the phenomenon could have occurred. This is a useful book in a neglected area where much more research needs to be done.

470 Ellwood, Robert S., Jr. The Eagle and the Rising Sun. Philadelphia: Westminster Press, 1974. 224p. $7.95 LC 74-7317 ISBN 0-664-20707-3

This work discusses five Japanese religious cults currently

attracting converts in the U. S. among Asians and native Americans: Tenrikyo, Nichiren Shoshu, Church of World Messianity, Seicho-no-Ie, and Perfect Liberty. He tries to explain their attraction to Americans. Ellwood outlines their religious ceremonies and histories, and translates some of their documents. He also interviews Asian and native U. S. converts.

471 Elwood, Roger. Strange Things Are Happening: Satanism, Witchcraft and God. Elgin, Ill.: D. C. Cook, 1973. 127p. Bibliog. $.95 pa. LC 72-87051

This book is written in very breezy style, with many anecdotes and examples. The chapters include discussions of ghosts; when the occult motivates crime; the Manson massacres; Anton Szandor LaVey; witches of today; what God has to say about it. Needless to say, the author takes a very dim view of occultism.

472 Emenegger, Robert. UFO's, Past, Present and Future. New York: Ballantine Books, 1974. 180p. Illus. $1.50 pa. ISBN 0-345-24189-4-150

This book, at first written as an original screenplay by Emenegger for Sandler Institutional Films, Inc., highlights a dozen classic UFO cases. Mentioned are these events: Mantell Case 1947; Chiles and Whitted Case 1948; Washington, D. C., 1952; Robertson Panel 1953; Bismarck, N. D., 1953; Levelland, Texas, 1957; Intelligence Case 1959; Socorro, N. M., 1964; Dexter/Hillsdale, Mich., 1966; last Air Force Blue Book case 1969; Coyne Case. The case histories are taken from documents, and presented almost word-for-word as recorded by witnesses. Another section of this book discusses being contacted; public reaction; space probes from Earth; future scientific research. The appendices mention what Air Force Academy cadets are taught about UFO's, and give the sample nine-page report prepared by the Air Force for witnesses to fill out. There is also an interesting section of photos, some in color. Other parts discuss NASA sightings, and present newspaper clippings, 1973-1974. The book is a refreshingly different survey of UFO's.

473 Encyclopedia of Magic and Superstition: Alchemy, Charms, Dreams, Omens, Rituals, Talismans, Wishes. London: Octopus Books, 1974 (dist. in U. S. by Crescent Books, New York). 253p. Illus. (chiefly color) Index (Material taken from "Man, Myth and Magic") £3.95 ISBN 0-7064-0396-7

This attractive work contains over 350 illustrations, 194 of them in color. Topics covered include magic, exorcism, demonology, sexual rituals, strange cults, and ESP.

474 Encyclopedia of Witchcraft and Demonology: An Illustrated Encyclopedia of Witches, Demons, Sorcerers and Their Present Day Counterparts. Introd. by Hans Holzer. London: Octopus Books, 1974. 252p. Illus. (chiefly color) Map

Index (Material taken from "Man, Myth and Magic") £3.95 ISBN 0-7064-0395-9

475 Ephemeriden, 1890-1950. Zürich: Max S. Metz, 1974 (dist. in U.S. by Z.S. Mason, New York). 416p. $20.50

The main part of this reference volume consists of tables of ephemerides. The figures are very legible due to the crisp type-face used. All unnecessary details of a secondary nature are left out, due to Metz's opinion that "the ecliptic is solely to be considered as the fundamental circle of the symbolism of astrology." The appendix includes tables for Movement of the Stars, Diurnal Logarithms, and Geographical Positions (latitude, longitude, and numbers of the horizon-disks for 800 places).

476 Epstein, Perle S. The Way of Witches. Garden City, N.Y.: Doubleday, 1972. 175p. Illus. Bibliog. $4.95 LC 72-184744 ISBN 0-385-00748-5

This juvenile book consists of four main parts: "Witchcraft in History and Anthropology"; "Rituals, Practices and Tools of the Trade"; "Witchcraft vs. Church and State"; and "Salem." The work is mostly on the persecution of witches, and also descriptions of their ceremonies. It is international in coverage, including the Orient and the American Indian. The book shows some very anti-Christian bias, especially on Salem. Epstein claims some unproven things (the Church created Satan and the Sabbat; nine million accused witches were killed between the 13th and 18th centuries). The writing seems oversimplified. The book is recommended for grades 6-8.

477 Erlewine, Stephen; Michael Erlewine and Margaret Erlewine, comps. Astrological Calendar, 1976 (annual). Ann Arbor, Mich.: Circle Books, 1975. 28p. $1.75

This work gives astrological information month-by-month. Ephemerides are in traditional column form for easy reading, with the declination of both sun and moon included in the ephemeris. Also, on the opposite page to each month's calendar is writing on basic chart configurations, an introduction to radio astrology, an introduction to heliocentric astrology. Instructions for use of the calendar are on the last page.

478 Ertzbischoff, M. A. S. When a Witch Walked. New York: Vantage Press, 1973. $5.95

479 Esdaile, James. Natural and Mesmeric Clairvoyance; With the Practical Application of Mesmerism in Surgery and Medicine. New York: Arno Press, 1975 (orig. pub., London, 1852). (Perspectives in Psychical Research Series) $16 LC 75-7378 ISBN 0-405-07028-4

The author is best known for introducing hypnosis (then called mesmerism) into regular hospital practice in India in the 1840's and 1850's, for use as an anesthetic during major surgery. Much of the book is on the application of it to surgery. The work also tries to relate mesmerism to psychic phenomena. Esdaile discusses cases of clairvoyance under somnambulism, and covers other states of consciousness such as sensory modification and mesmerism accomplished over long distances.

480 Evans, Christopher Riche. Cults of Unreason. New York: Farrar, Straus and Giroux, 1974 (also, St. Albans, England: Panther, 1974; orig. pub., London: Harrap, 1973). 257p. Index $7.95 LC 73-87694 ISBN 0-374-13324-7

The author is witty and scathing in his criticism of cults. He feels that they are arising to fill the vacuum created because man's social and philosophical knowledge has not kept pace with his scientific and technological growth. Evans is an experimental psychologist with a weekly science show on British television. He is definitely anti-parapsychology. Half the book concentrates on Scientology and L. Ron Hubbard. Three chapters are given to discussing flying saucers. Also covered are radionics and the black boxes of de la Warr and Abrams, Wilhelm Reich, the Hieronymus machine, bio-feedback, Gurdjieff, Ouspensky, J. G. Bennett, T. Lobsang Rampa, theosophy, Hare Krishna, and Subud.

481 Evans, Colin, 1894- . New Waite's Compendium of Natal Astrology: With Ephemeris for 1880-1980 and Universal Table of Houses. Rev. ed. Rev. and brought up to date by Brian E. F. Gardner. London: Routledge and K. Paul, 1971 (previous ed., 1967). xiii, 252p. Illus. £2.25 ISBN 0-7100-7099-3

482 Evans, Joan, 1893- . Magical Jewels of the Middle Ages and the Renaissance, Particularly in England. Detroit: Gale Research, 1975 (orig. pub., Oxford, England: Clarendon Press, 1922). Includes bibliog. refs. Index $14 LC 75-23305 ISBN 0-8103-4181-6

483 Everything You Always Wanted to Know about Sorcery. New York: Manor Books, 1973. 190p. Bibliog. $.95 pa.

This book discusses sorcery; satanism; voodoo; hypnotism; divination; scrying; love spells; curses; hexes, powders and pills; superstitions and omens. It includes a glossary of magical gems, and a dictionary of divination. This survey includes many cases and anecdotes.

484 Eyre, Kathleen. Lancashire Ghosts. Illus. by Bruce Danz and Geraldine Rachel Hardy. Clapham, England: Dalesman, 1974. 80p. Illus. £0.65 pa ISBN 0-85206-251-6

485 ________. Witchcraft in Lancashire. Illus. by Geraldine Rachel Hardy. Clapham, England: Dalesman, 1974. 78p. Illus. £0.65 pa. ISBN 0-85206-238-9

486 Eyre, Margery. The Seeker and the Finding: A Woman's Search for Inner Truth. Wellingborough, England: Thorsons, 1974. 144p. Index £2.25 ISBN 0-7225-0261-3

Through a desire to be closer to God, the author prayed and made herself receptive to spiritual impressions. When she paused from exhaustion, she would hear a consoling, wise voice. The voice spoke over the years only in conditions of great joy or need. After a Jungian analysis, it spoke more often, until she decided to keep a record of its teaching. The voice said it was a dead being called Melchior. He and other dead entities were responsible for the lessons in this book. Eyre emphasizes companionship--of God and spiritual beings, to those who are afraid of being abandoned and lonely.

487 Fagan, Cyril, 1895- . Astrological Origins. St. Paul; Llewellyn Pubns., 1971. xii, 224p. Illus. $6.95 LC 74-30122 ISBN 0-87542-219-5

This astrological columnist states that the astrology of ancient Babylon and Egypt was based on constellations, not on the signs so often mentioned today.

488 Fairfax, Edward, d. 1635. Daemonologia; A Discourse on Witchcraft. New York: Barnes and Noble, 1971 (orig. pub., London: Herald Office/R. Ackrill Harrogate, 1882). 189p. Geneal. table (Orig. title page reads: "Daemonologia: A Discourse on Witchcraft As It Was Acted in the Family of Mr. Edward Fairfax ... in the Year 1621; Along with the Only Two Eclogues of the Same Author Known to Be in Existence, with a Biographical Introduction, and Notes Topographical and Illustrative, by William Grainge.") $6 LC 70-27712 ISBN 0-389-04141-6

Fairfax was a poet of York county. Most of the book describes the bewitching of his three daughters and one other girl by seven women, six of them known to him. The work is valuable in that it shows what people considered symptoms of witchcraft to be, and how accusations were done. The symptoms were the usual pacts with the Devil, Sabbats, spirit possessions, demons, poltergeists. His children often went into trance, and were then visited by the accused in one of three forms: human, spirit, or familiar. This book seems to be the author's condemnation and evidence, which he decided to publish after two trials had failed.

489 Falcon, Hal. How to Analyze Handwriting. Produced by Lyle and George Engel. New York: Cornerstone Library, 1974 (also, New York: Trident, 1971; orig. pub., 1964). 160p. Illus. $1.95 pa.

This work discusses these topics: how to prepare a good

handwriting specimen; are you eye-minded?; are you ear-minded?; are you action-minded?; does your handwriting limp?; what does the love arc tell?; what's your slant on life?; how do you write your name?; sex symbols in handwriting. This well-done survey is illustrated with cases and samples of handwriting throughout.

490 Farquharson-Coe, A. Devon's Ghosts. Rev. ed. St. Ives, England: James Pike, 1975 (previous ed., 1974). 40p. Illus. Map (Viewing Devon Series) £0.30 pa. ISBN 0-85932-073-1

491 ______. Devon's Witchcraft. St. Ives, England: James Pike, 1975. 32p. Illus. Map (Viewing Devon Series) £0.30 pa. ISBN 0-85932-091-X

492 ______. Hants and Dorset's Ghosts. St. Ives, England: James Pike, 1975. 32p. Illus. Map (Viewing Hants and Dorset Series) £0.30 pa. ISBN 0-85932-150-9

493 ______. Hants and Dorset's Witchcraft. St. Ives, England: James Pike, 1975. 32p. Illus. Map (Viewing Hants and Dorset Series) £0.30 pa. ISBN 0-85932-163-0

494 Farrar, Stewart. What Witches Do: The Modern Coven Revealed. London: Sphere, 1973 (also, New York: Coward, 1971; orig. pub., London: P. Davies, 1971). 204p. Illus. £0.35 pa. ISBN 0-7221-3449-5

A member of one of London's most active covens reports on what witches actually do, and how the ancient religion of Wicca is practiced today. There are photographs of actual rituals, many performed in the nude.

495 Farren, David. Living with Magic. New York: Simon and Schuster, 1974. 320p. Bibliog. Index $7.95 LC 74-4359 ISBN 0-671-21805-0

This ex-Jesuit marries a witch, and then tries to rationally understand and explain it. He discusses the historical, psychological, religious, and philosophical aspects of magic and witchcraft. It is more an analysis than the usual historical survey. This critical, scholarly work contains many original insights.

496 ______. The Return of Magic. New York: Harper, 1972. x, 118p. Bibliog. $4.95 LC 72-78054 ISBN 0-06-062333-0

The author sees the return of interest in magic as an attempt by people to recover personal relationships with the universe. He mentions his own loss of faith in established religion. His new view of reality was helped by his wife's experiences with ESP. Magic, he feels, can fill a religious need even if the person only acts as if he believes. Farren views magic as primarily a religious phenomenon (he spent 10 years as a Jesuit seminarian). He also discusses Castaneda's Don Juan, Sybil Leek, and Edgar Cayce.

497 ________. Sex and Magic. New York: Simon & Schuster, 1975. 130p. Index $6.95 ISBN 0-671-22016-0

This book discusses sex and the Bible, sex and magic, the I Ching, modern witches, symbols, the psychology of sex, vampires, spells, the alchemy of consciousness (sex and the mind, Jung and Freud), sexual mystique, and sex and evolution (Reich, D. H. Lawrence). Farren believes that sex can give a heightened view of the cosmic plan, and discusses the value of magic in enhancing sex. At times, this becomes a bit ridiculous. In the section, "Spells for Intensifying Orgasm," he says there must be a blue-eyed cat in the room, who must be fed fish, with the humans mimicking the cat's movements. Farren sees magic as "a fully legitimate category of human experience, a manner of seeing the world poetically."

498 Fate Annual. Douglas, England: Fate, 1973. 112p. Illus. £0.25 pa. ISBN 0-902341-04-9

499 Fate Magazine, Editors of, comps. Beyond the Strange. New York: Paperback Library, 1971 (c1966). 158p. $.75 pa.

500 ________. Fate's Strangest Mysteries. New York: Paperback Library, 1971 (c1966). $.75 pa.

501 Fearnley, J. R. The Way Through. London: Regency Press, 1975. 68p. £1.20 ISBN 0-7212-0389-2

The author discovered he had the gift of healing, and also felt an intelligent force close to him. Gradually, he received many impressions and answers to questions. These came to him regularly, especially in the sleep state. After two years, he developed a strong urge to compose poetry, containing messages from the beyond. Finally, he wrote this book. His purpose is to point out the way to plow through life, to show life's purpose. The work is designed to "plant seeds of awareness." Discussions include spiritualism, circles, karma, healing, pain and fear, and psychic powers. Most of the book is poetry.

502 Feola, Jose. PK: Mind over Matter. Minneapolis: Dillon
* Press, 1975. 175p. Bibliog. Index (Psychic Exploration Series) $6.95 LC 75-6515 ISBN 0-87518-078-7

This juvenile book is written by a physicist. The first six chapters are on a historical slant, discussing the nature of the problem, poltergeists and haunted houses, mediums, levitation, materializations, noises, voices and pictures. The mediums chapter covers D. D. Home, Eusapia Palladino, Rudi Schneider, and others. The last chapters are on modern research: PK in humans, PK in plants and animals, how to do your own experiments, the future of PK research. There is much discussion of test methods for PK. The appendices contain random-digit and rating tables, and a section on calculating probability figures. This is a very objective book. There is interesting information on phenomena produced by Catholic saints, and on the author's own personal experiments.

503/4 Ferguson, Robert A. Adventures in Psychic Development. London and New York: Regency Press, 1972. $6

Over the years, the author has found very few people in the psychic field who have had real talent and who could teach others how to acquire it. Therefore, the author decided to do it himself. This book is a step-by-step guide through use of colors, symbols, and vibrations. Ferguson discusses how to develop precognition, use clairvoyance, analyze auras, heal, use dreams to solve problems, and have out-of-the-body experiences.

505 Fielder, Mildred. Plant Medicine and Folklore. Illus. by Juan C. Barberis. New York: Winchester, 1975. Bibliog. Index $12.95 LC 75-9262 ISBN 0-87691-205-6

This book on folk remedies is mostly taken from early travelers' journals, which she researched for her historical studies of South Dakota. The work is arranged in eight chapters by ailment. There is also a chapter on poisonous plants. There is an index to common and scientific plant names.

506 Findhorn Foundation. Findhorn Garden. Foreword by William Irwin Thompson. New York: Harper and Row, 1975. xi, 180p. Illus. $10 LC 75-6335 ISBN 0-06-011249-2

The Findhorn community was started in 1962 by Peter and Eileen Caddy. Over the last few years, they claim to have been in contact with nature spirits, whose advice has enabled them to produce vegetables and flowers in previously barren soil. The advice comes through the "devas" (creatures) and the "Landscape Angel." Chapters include "Man Creates the Garden," "The Kingdom of Light," "Deva Consciousness," "Messages," "Nature Spirits," "The Garden Today." There are 100 photos, and quotes from the trance information that was used to build the garden.

507 Findlay, Arthur. On the Edge of the Etheric; or, Survival after Death Scientifically Explained. London: Corgi, 1971 (orig. pub., London: Psychic Press, 1931). 159p. Illus. £0.30 pa. ISBN 0-552-08677-0

This work discusses the universe of ether, mediums and seances, voices, and the author's personal evidence for survival. When the book first came out, some church papers refused to advertise it.

508 Findler, Gerald. Ghosts of the Lake Counties. Clapham, England: Dalesman, 1975 (orig. pub., 1969). 72p. Illus. £0.60 pa. ISBN 0-85206-015-7

509 Finmark, Sharon, and David Wickers. How to Make Magic.

London: Studio Vista, 1974. 68p. Illus. (some color) Index (How-to Series) £1.25 ISBN 0-289-70447-2

510 Firmicus Maternus, Julius. Ancient Astrology: Theory and Practice. Trans. by Jean Rhys Bram. Park Ridge, N.J.: Noyes Press, 1975. 336p. Illus. Bibliog. Index (Noyes Classical Studies) (Translation of "Matheseos Libri VIII," c1913, reprinted 1958) $12.50 LC 75-10865 ISBN 0-8155-5037-5

The introduction says that this work "stands as the final, as well as the most complete, work on astrology of the classical world." Bram also dismisses Ptolemy's second-century work, Tetrabiblios as a "brief theoretical background for astrology." Both comments seem incorrect. Tetrabiblios is widely regarded as the "bible" of astrology. Firmicus's work does not really appear to be a definitive work. Firmicus was a fourth century Roman literary figure and lawyer, who wrote this text for his friend Lollianus Mavortius. The author was not an expert in astrology. Besides the usual discussions, he maintains a strong criticism of all those who are anti-astrology. His philosophy is one of fatalistic determinism. The work has an index of occupations. That which occurs most is prostitute (male or female), then priest, then king.

511 Firth, Violet Mary. Psychic Self Defense: A Study in Occult Pathology and Criminality, by Dion Fortune [pseud.]. New York: S. Weiser, 1971 (c1930). 209p. $6 LC 79-27453 ISBN 0-87728-150-5

512 Fitzgerald, Donalie. Edith L. Randall's Your Place in the Cards. Los Angeles: Nash Pub., 1974. 530p. Illus. $12.50 LC 73-83528 ISBN 0-8402-1319-0

This book is based on Randall's card prophecy system. Each birthday has a corresponding card in the deck which determines that person's future and relationships. The work contains terms and diagrams that are rather difficult to understand.

513 Flammarion, Camille, 1842-1925. Haunted Houses. London: T. F. Unwin; Detroit: Tower Books/Gale, 1971 (orig. pub., 1924). 328p. (Translation of "Maisons hantées") $14 LC 76-159957

514 Flammonde, Paris. The Age of Flying Saucers; Notes on a
* Projected History of Unidentified Flying Objects. New York: Hawthorn, 1971. xiv, 288p. Illus. Bibliog. $8.95 LC 74-115903

Flammonde views flying saucer sightings as the most interesting sociopsychological phenomenon since witchcraft. He studies the events from 1947 to present. The work discusses contactees, case studies, Air Force studies, lists of organizations in the U.S.

and four other countries, lists of periodicals, motion pictures, and television shows on the saucer theme. There are 25 photos of the best-known personalities in the UFO field. Persons mentioned include Condon, Menzel, Keyhoe, Adamski, Otis T. Carr, Frank Stanges, Orfeo Angelucci, Buck Nelson, and Gabriet Breen. The book is sketchy; the author views it as a small version of a definitive book to be eventually published. His theme is that the rise of saucerism after World War II is due to man's loss of faith and fear of nuclear holocaust. Man needed new gods. He feels the saucer era is over because of man's conquest of the moon and space. Readers who are pro-saucer will not enjoy these theories.

515 _______. Living Prophets, by M. M. Delfano [pseud.]. New York: Dell Pub. Co., 1972. 220p. $.95 pa.

This book provides some good portraits of famous psychics. There is also one chapter on Flammonde's predictions, which he says are based on reason, and not on psychic abilities. The final chapter is on the history of prophecy. The main body of the work is made up of exact transcripts of tape-recorded interviews with Robert Nelson of the Central Premonitions Registry, Jeane Dixon, Daniel Logan, Edward Snedeker of Connecticut, and Joseph De Louise. Some of the interviews are most revealing, and not very flattering. Dixon says that George Patton and Douglas MacArthur were the only two great leaders of the last 100 years.

516 _______. Mystic Healers. New York: Stein and Day, 1974.
* 256p. Illus. Bibliog. Index $8.95 LC 73 01856

This work, by an author mildly skeptical of healers, discusses Mesmer, Mary Baker Eddy (Christian Science), Brinkley (of goat gland fame), Edgar Cayce, Oral Roberts, A. A. Allen, Kathryn Kuhlman, Leroy Jenkins ("Arm of God"), Tony Agpaoa, José Arigo, Ron Hubbard (Scientology), Don Stewart (Miracle Valley), Rex Humbard (Cathedral of Tomorrow). The tone of the book is mainly historical. There are interviews with John Lee Baughman (Unity), Tom Johanson (a Spiritualist), and British healer Harry Edwards. The author is anti-Scientology, but makes no judgment on psychic surgeons. Also briefly mentioned in the book are Catholic shrines and the encounter movement. In the book's last paragraph, the author states, "If you would know the value of an elixir, ask the one for whom it did not work." This comment seems grossly unfair, since every cure known to man has in some cases simply not worked.

517 Fleckles, Elliott V. Willie Speaks Out; The Psychic World of Abraham Lincoln. St. Paul, Minn.: Llewellyn Publications, 1974. 226p. Bibliog. $7.95

Lincoln's dead son Willie tells the story of his father's spiritual development on the other side, and discusses Lincoln's sittings while alive with leading mediums of his time. Willie says that the Emancipation Proclamation came with divine direction through medium Nettie Colburn Maynard. Lincoln himself was a very capable medium. There were even newspaper reports of his psychic experiences. The War Department has a report mentioning a time when Lincoln saw Confederate troops about to break through Union lines. He sent a telegram to the front. At one seance, the spirit world referred to military maps and positions of the Confederates in explaining strategy to be used. Willie died at age 11. The author does not tell how Willie's views came through. Fleckles visited libraries in the U. S. and Britain. There are 315 footnotes and a 16-page bibliography. Fleckles died shortly after writing this book.

518 Flindt, Max H., and Otto O. Binder. Mankind--Child of the Stars. Fawcett Pubns., 1974. 272p. Index $1.25 pa. ISBN 4-49-3142-125

The authors give 16 basic proofs and 138 physical reasons why humans could not possibly have evolved on earth. They theorize that earth was visited millions of years ago by extraterrestrials who created through genetic manipulation a hybrid of man and spaceman. We are under close watch by the extraterrestrials today, and function as an intentional colony. This anti-Darwinian work mentions among other things gaps in fossil records, man's high mental and physiological make-up, and the probability that life exists on other planets.

519 Flint, Leslie, and Douglas Conacher. Chapters of Experience. (Received from the spirit world by direct voice through the mediumship of Leslie Flint.) London: Muller, 1973. 143p. Index £2.10 ISBN 0-584-10068-X

Conacher has been dead 15 years, but speaks to his wife by independent direct voice communication. This book is a compilation of transcripts of actual tape recordings made with medium Leslie Flint between 1965 and 1967. Conacher discusses previous lives, the quest for truth, his lives at the time of Christ, and priesthoods in the temples of Karnak and Padua.

520 ________. Voices in the Dark: My Life As a Medium. London: Macmillan, 1971. 221p. Illus. Plates £2.25 ISBN 0-333-12201-1

Flint has been a direct voice medium from an early age. This book is a chronological account of his life; he wrote it in his late 60's. He can hear voices without even going into trance, just by sitting in darkness. He was always a film fan, and he thinks the excitement as the lights went out may have helped his development. It was at the movies that he first heard spirit voices. The work describes his childhood in England, his first psychic experiences, his sittings for famous people (such as Edison and King George V), and the tests to which he has been subjected.

521 Florescu, Radu. In Search of Frankenstein. Boston: New

York Graphic Society, 1975. 244p. Illus. Map Bibliog. Filmography $9.95 LC 74-22502 ISBN 0-8212-0614-1

This book reads like a travel book through the Alps and is loaded with anecdotes and bits of information. The author discusses visits to the original Castle Frankenstein; the career of alchemist Konrad Dippel, who lived in early 18th-century times at Castle Frankenstein on the Rhine; Mary Shelley's book; Hollywood films. The last chapter discusses the creation of an artificial man as a theme throughout literature and mythology. There are genealogies of Mary Shelley and the Frankenstein family.

Fodor, Nandor, 1895-1964. Encyclopaedia of Psychic Science. Secaucus, N.J.: Citadel Press, 1974 (also, New Hyde Park, N.Y.: University Books, 1966; orig. pub., London: Arthur, 1933). 416p. $5.95 pa. ISBN 0-8065-0429-5

This encyclopedia is a classic in the occult field. Although the work claims to represent psychic research and spiritualism terms, emphasis is on spiritualism. There are 809 entries to the encyclopedia. Main articles are on the following topics: apparitions, apports, automatic writing, clairvoyance, communication, control, double, ectoplasm, haunting, levitation, materialization, medium, movement, psychometry, spiritualism, telepathy, and xenoglossis. The longest biographical articles are on the following persons: Charles Bailey, Blavatsky, Florence Cook, Margery Crandon, William Crookes, Davenport brothers, Andrew Davis, Elizabeth d'Esperance, Hester Dowden, William Eglinton, Eva Carriere, Camille Flammarion, Fox sisters, Thomas Harris, Richard Hodgson, Daniel Dunglas Home, Oliver Lodge, William Stainton Moses, Frederick Myers, Eusapia Paladino, Leonore Piper, Charles Richet, Schneider brothers, Henry Slade, Helene Smith, Minnie Soule, William Stead, George Valiantine, and Alfred Wallace. This work shows a tremendous amount of research. It seems to rely heavily on biographical accounts, and usually accepts the account uncritically. However, it is very well done and should be owned by every individual and library even mildly interested in spiritualism.

523 Ford, Arthur, as told to Jerome Ellison. Life Beyond Death. London: Abacus, 1974 (also, London: W.H. Allen, 1972; orig. pub., New York: Putnam, 1971). 176p. £0.75 pa. ISBN 0-349-11312-2

Ford's purpose in this book was to review what he considered the best material on life after death he had read, most of it received through mediums. It is an attempt to outline belief in survival throughout history. The author discusses the Tibetan Book of the Dead, C.D. Broad, Swedenborg, William James, Stewart and Betty White, Emmet and Ruth Finley, Geraldine Cummins, Oliver Lodge, Huxley, Teilhard de Chardin, and the evolution of consciousness. Ford strongly dislikes the materialism of 20th-century America, and his purpose is to make the reader aware of the spiritual elements.

524 Ford, Brian John. The Earth Watchers. London: Frewin, 1973. 189p. Illus. £2.90 ISBN 0-85632-020-X

The author discusses theories of life on other planets, the existence of other biological systems, scientific developments far ahead of ours, and the nature of UFO's. With great scientific detail, statistics, and logical discussions, he explains why some theories have to be abandoned and some should be kept until radio telescopes and space explorations bring us more evidence.

525 Forman, Joan. Haunted East Anglia. London: Hale, 1974. 207p. Illus. Plates Map £2.80 ISBN 0-7091-4580-2

526 Fort, Charles, 1874-1932. The Book of the Damned. London: Abacus, 1973 (also, New York: Ace Books, 1972; also, New York: Garland Pub., 1975; orig. pub., New York: Boni and Liveright, 1919). 317p. £0.60 ISBN 0-349-11325-4
*

By damned, the author means all the strange data which science has excluded and ignored. The book is a collection of physical phenomena for which science has never found any explanation. The author has searched scientific and philosophical transactions and proceedings which he feels have been ignored. One hypothesis he presents is that other planets are trying to communicate with us. The author has become so important that the adjective "Fortean" is used to describe writings and phenomena similar to those he studied.

527 ________. The Complete Books of Charles Fort. New Introd. by Damon Knight. New York: Dover Publications, 1974 (republication of omnibus vol. orig. pub. for Fortean Society, New York: Henry Holt and Co., 1941). xiv, 1125p. Illus. Index $15 LC 74-79217 ISBN 0-486-23094-5
*

Fort worked 27 years full-time at the New York Public Library and the British Museum researching old journals and newspapers. Topics discussed include the following: strange noises, UFO's, falls of red snow, flat earth phenomena, poltergeists, spontaneous combustion. Fort never formed conclusions about the phenomena, but had vague ideas of an organic universe and neo-Hegelianism. His following began with literary men (Dreiser, Oliver Wendell Holmes), then science fiction writers. Now added are those who believe in extraterrestrial visits and origins. This book includes the following separately published works: The Book of the Damned, Lo, New Lands, and Wild Talents.

528 ________. Lo! New York, London: Garland Publishing Inc., 1975 (also, New York: Ace Books, 1941; orig. pub., New York: C. Kendall, 1931). 284p. (Garland Library of Science Fiction) £5.50 ISBN 0-8240-1412-X
*

This classic is full of unusual happenings mentioned in journals over the years. As usual, Fort's style of writing is very engaging--well-documented, and casually written, with wry comments and searching questions posed on every page. At times, it reads like a diary of scattered musings. Topics discussed include falls, strange animals, disappearances of human beings, strange atmospheric occurrences. The major discussion that keeps appearing again and again is of falls (unexplained materializations out of the sky).

529 ________. New Lands. New York: Garland Pub., 1975 (also,
* London: Sphere, 1974; also, New York: Ace Books, 1973; orig. pub., New York: Boni and Liveright, 1913). 222p. (Garland Library of Science Fiction) $11 LC 75-408 ISBN 0-8240-1413-8

This work by Fort is a classic. As usual, the style reads like a lively diary or notebook of incidents the author has encountered in his readings. The main thrust of the work is about astronomical phenomena. Topics discussed include planets, celestial occurrences, flying saucers, mirages in the sky, explosions.

530 ________. Wild Talents. New York: Garland Pub., 1975
* (orig. pub., New York: Ace Books, 1932). 222p. (Garland Library of Science Fiction) $11 LC 75-409 ISBN 0-8240-1414-6

This book by Fort is a classic. As with his other works it is a discussion of unusual phenomena about which he has read in scientific journals and other sources. The writing style reads like a fascinating notebook. Topics covered include mass psychology, disappearances, coincidences, vampire cases, spontaneous combustion of humans, strange raps and explosions, things invisibly acted on (paintings falling from walls, things moving by themselves through the air), and stigmatics. All the mentioned phenomena Fort considers "wild talents" that draw attention to freaks and sideshows, but fail to be properly investigated and their powers utilized. As his underlying theory, he states that his "liveliest interest is not so much in things, as in relations of things." He feels an underlying oneness of all things, and no utter absences of relations among circumstances. Some readers may be angered or confused by the series note in the above three titles: Garland Library of Science Fiction.

531 Fortune Tellers. Ed. by Yvonne Deutch; comp. by Francoise Strachan. London: Marshall Cavendish, 1974 (also, New York: Black Watch, 1974). 128p. Illus. (chiefly color) (Golden Hands Book) £1.95 ISBN 0-85685-081-0

This attractive book devotes half its pages to illustrations. Chapters include the following: "Preparation for Divination," by Francoise Strachan; "Numerology," by Richard Deutch; "I Ching," by Ashton Brown; "How to Read Hands," by Jo Sheridan; "Runes," by Athene Williams; "Crystal," by Athene Williams; "Tarot for Life," by Richard Gardner; "Tasseography," by Katherine Gray; and "Radiesthesia and Dowsing," by Katherine Gray.

532 Foster, John Galway. An Enquiry into the Practice and Effects of Scientology: Report. London: H. M. Stationery Office, 1971. vi, 192p. Bibliog. (Great Britain. Parliament, 1971-1972. House of Commons. Reports and Papers, no. 52) (Order from Pendragon, Redwood City, Calif.) $4.80 pa. LC 72-304761 ISBN 0-11-205272-7

533 Fowler, Raymond E., 1933- . UFO's: Interplanetary Visitors; A UFO Investigator Reports on the Facts, Fables, and Fantasies of the Flying Saucer Conspiracy. Foreword by J. Allen Hynek. Jericho, N. Y.: Exposition Press, 1974. xvii, 365p. Illus. (Exposition-Banner Book) $8.50 LC 74-76026 ISBN 0-682-47979-9

Fowler is chairman of the Massachusetts subcommittee of the National Investigations Committee on Aerial Phenomena (NICAP). He grew to be a believer out of investigating local reports. Most of the book is on New England reports, especially Greater Boston. He refers to similar sightings in other countries if the incidents seem parallel. The author discusses C. I. A., U. N., and U. S. Air Force concerns with what an admission of UFO existence would do. The last part is a summary of 1973 cases, including the Pascagoula kidnapping. The appendix lists an additional 150 New England sightings.

534 Frank, Joan, and the Jewellery Information Centre. Birthstones of the Month. St. Ives, England: Colourmaster International, 1973. 32p. Illus. (color) Map Index £0.30 pa. ISBN 0-85933-111-3

535 Franklyn, Julian, 1899-1970. Death by Enchantment; An Examination of Ancient and Modern Witchcraft. New York: Putnam, 1971 (also, London: Hamilton, 1971). x, 244p. Illus. Bibliog. refs. $6.95 LC 78-152769

The author is convinced that witchcraft is real. Most of his mention of contemporary witchcraft is limited to a few newspaper clippings and comments on Crowley. Discussions include the following: Daniel Dunglas Home, English witchcraft and the works of Montague Summers, Salem, the Inquisition, witchhunts, and tortures used. He recommends that we keep a constant vigilance for modern witchcraft, even to the point of watching closely one's wife or husband.

536 ________, ed. Dictionary of the Occult. New York: Causeway Books, 1973 (also, New York: Gale, 1974; orig. pub., England, 1935). 301p. $8.95 LC 72-97373 ISBN 0-88356-009-7
*

Although not quite as useful or well-done as other dictionaries and encyclopedias we have mentioned, any such gathering of information is welcomed. The work basically consists of 21 long articles. The articles are split into numbered paragraphs. The other 1,239 entries are almost entirely referrals back to these 21 sections, much as an index would function. This is exactly the kind of format many find irritating. If it is to be a dictionary, the information wanted should all be there when one looks up the word; if a writer wants to write a 21-chapter book with an extensive index at the back, that's fine also. The format we see here accomplishes nothing--except, perhaps, disguising weak definitions by burying them into a long narration. The 21 main topics covered are: alchemy, astrology, black magic, Buddhist occultism, Chinese occultism, devil worship, English literature and the occult, fairies, ghosts, history of occult ideas, illusion and hallucination, Indian occultism, literature of occultism, Moslem occultism, occultism in ancient Greece and Rome, psychotherapy and psychic phenomena, spiritualism, vampire, werewolf, white magic, and witchcraft. The longest of these are alchemy, history of occult ideas, and spiritualism. Some of the 21 chapters are very useful. The alchemy one has separate long paragraphs on 27 alchemists. Many of the sections, however, rely heavily for their information on one or two sources. This defeats the purpose of a dictionary as a gathering of information. In short, there is a lot in this work, but its organization leaves much to be desired.

537 Franz, Marie-Louise von. Number and Time: Reflections Leading Towards a Unification of Psychology and Physics. Trans. by Andrea Dykes. London: Rider, 1974 (also, Evanston, Ill.: Northwestern University Press, 1974). iii-xi, 332p. Illus. Bibliog. Index (Translation of "Zahl und Zeit." Stuttgart: Klett, 1970). £3.75 ISBN 0-09-121020-8

538 Fraser, Ronald, 1888- . Changing Consciousness. London: College of Psychic Studies, 1972. 21p. (College of Psychic Studies. Papers, no. 3) £0.25 pa. ISBN 0-903336-10-3

539 Freedland, Nat, 1936- . The Occult Explosion. New York:
* Putnam, 1972 (also, London: Joseph, 1972). 270p. $6.95 LC 74-175261

The author, a California journalist and reporter for Billboard, discusses the occult in the U.S., past, present, and future. The work covers witchcraft, ESP, astrology, magic, meditation, Rhine, Alan Watts, Linda Goodman, P.D. Ouspensky, Tarot, I Ching, experimental parapsychology, spiritualism, divination, American Indian sorcery, Dixon, Hurkos, Croiset, Cayce, and Garrett. The book also gives addresses for many organizations, mentions crimes recently committed by occult devotees, and discusses fake medium and mentalist kits. Freedland says he's a skeptic, but seems quick to believe most occult phenomena. One of his themes is the historically unique convergence of the occult with technology (occultism as big business, bookstores, mail order). Another theme is that today there is for the first time the existence of a large, well-informed audience for occult ideas.

540 French, Peter A., comp. Philosophers in Wonderland: Phil-

osophy and Psychical Research. St. Paul, Minn.: Llewellyn Publications, 1975. 376p. $10 pa. LC 75-2318 ISBN 0-87542-242-X

This scholarly work presents eight "symposia," with introductions and other papers by French. Each of the eight is titled with a one-sentence quote from Alice in Wonderland. The symposia are on dreams, spaces, times, mind-body, identity, survival, evidence for psi, theories of psychic knowledge. There is an introductory essay on "Certainty and the Real Challenge of Psychical Research." Contributors include C. D. Broad and H. H. Price. The author, philosophy professor at Northern Arizona University, became involved in current psychic affairs when his department entered the Kidd case to claim money for the state of Arizona. Some of the writing in this book is rather technical.

541 French, Peter J. John Dee: The World of an Elizabethan
* Magus. London, Boston: Routledge and K. Paul, 1972. xii, 243p. Illus. Bibliog. Index (Based on thesis) $12.50 LC 72-178131 ISBN 0-7100-7158-2

This work emphasizes the importance of Dee (born 1527) in English Renaissance intellectual life; it is really a series of essays on different parts of his career. Dee was skilled in magic, and was also a link with Renaissance currents in Europe. He was a leader in math, applied science, geography, and literature. He had the greatest library in England, and this book provides glimpses of it. This book emphasizes the nature of his hermetic philosophy, and the importance of the hermetic tradition in the Renaissance for thought, numerology, magic and alchemy. In England, under Mary he was accused of practicing sorcery against the queen's life, but was acquitted. He became Queen Elizabeth's court astrologer.

542 French, William Leslie. Graphoanalysis. Hollywood, Calif.: Newcastle Pub. Co., 1974. 226p. $2.95 pa.

This book tells how to use the analysis of one's handwriting to eliminate undesirable character traits.

543 Friedrich, Christof. UFO's: Nazi Secret Weapon? Toronto, Ontario: Samizdat Publishers, 1975. 160p. $4.95 pa.

This book discusses Germany's development of saucer-type aircraft in the last years of World War II. There are many good illustrations of German patent material and designs found in captured Nazi documents. The book discusses a secret Nazi expedition to Queen Maude Land in Antarctica in 1937-1938, and mentions claims of U-boats heading for that area in the last days of the war. The last section discusses UFO reports from 1945 to present that may be connected with the German saucers. Some contactees such as Reinhold Schmidt stated that the UFO occupants spoke German.

544 Fritscher, John. Popular Witchcraft. Secaucus, N.J.: Citadel Press, 1973 (orig. pub., Bowling Green, Ohio: Bowling Green University Popular Press, 1972; subtitle to 1972 ed., "Straight from the Witch's Mouth"). 192p. Includes biblio. refs. $6.95 LC 73-84152 ISBN 0-8065-0380-7

The author's basic thesis is that contemporary American witchcraft is a powerful force in today's pop culture, influencing our popular music, movies, television, advertisements, and marketing techniques. Much of this study is devoted to separating the different levels of witchcraft--white magic from Satanism, and true belief from commercialism. There are interviews with many practicing witches: Dr. Leo Louis Martello, Anton LaVey, Frederick de Arechaga. One of the chapters is on the legal status of witchcraft. Another covers the relationship between commercialized witchcraft and the sex interests of today.

545 Frost, Gavin, and Yvonne Frost. Witch's Bible. Los Angeles: Nash Pub., 1972. 310p. Illus. $7.95 LC 72-86673 ISBN 0-8402-1304-2

The authors conduct the School of Wicca, a worldwide correspondence school in St. Charles, Mo., with an enrollment of over 300. This well-done book discusses precepts, standard service, initiation and fertility services, tools, prayers, songs, incantations, precautions, coven, healing the sick, telepathy, clairvoyance, clairaudience, clairsentience, and prediction.

546 Fukurai, T. Clairvoyance and Thoughtography. New York: Arno, 1975 (orig. pub., London, 1931). Illus. (Perspectives in Psychical Research Series) $16 LC 75-7379 ISBN 0-405-07029-2

The book reports studies done by the author in Japan from 1910-1930. His main studies are on people who could produce images on hidden dry photographic plates. The images ranged from geometric shapes to human figures. Some were done over great distances. The work also discusses attempts to determine characters placed in sealed containers. Fukurai discusses the implications of his research in non-biological aspects of the human mind, and describes the social aspects of doing parapsychological research in Japan.

547 Full Year Zodiac for 1974 and Character Analysis (annual). Triesenberg: Datura; London: Aquarius, 1974. 12 vols. 96 pages each £0.25 pa. each

Each volume discusses the year's outlook for one of the 12 zodiac signs.

548 Fuller, John G. Arigo: Surgeon of the Rusty Knife. Afterword by Andrija K. Puharich. New York: Pocket Books, 1975
*** (orig. pub., New York: Crowell, 1974). 254p. Illus. Photos

Bibliog. Index $1.50 LC 74-3492 ISBN 0-671-78823-X

This work is a major new contribution to occult literature. Hard though it is to believe, this work has had a greater impact than Fuller's other blockbuster, Incident at Exeter. It is one of the top five most important books of the decade in the occult field. Arigo, former tavernkeeper and labor union official with only a third-grade education, became possessed by the spirit of a dead German doctor, Dr. Adolpho Fritz, who had died in 1918, the year of Arigo's birth. Arigo performed thousands of successful operations at high speed under dirty conditions, using a knife and no anesthetic. There was no pain and little bleeding. He diagnosed illnesses and wrote prescriptions, 96 per cent of which have been determined to be correct. He saw 300 patients a day, and some estimate he treated over a half million patients in his lifetime. His patients ranged from the poor to the President of Brazil. Puharich, who first visited him in 1963, brought six doctors with him in 1968 to study Arigo. Press coverage, crowds, and widespread belief in spiritualism led them to give up and leave. Arigo accepted no money, not even gifts. He was jailed occasionally, and eventually died in an auto accident brought on by a heart attack. Even in his school years, he was bothered by a bright round light he saw often, and a voice speaking in a strange language. Because of his Catholic upbringing, he resisted these spirit pressures. Finally, with headaches, blackouts, and vivid dreams, he gave in to possession by Fritz. Fuller studies newspapers, personal stories of friends, court records, church records, medical data. Fuller views the Philippine psychic surgeons as fakes, but obviously believes in Arigo's gifts. This book seems the one non-believers in the occult are most comfortable with. It has made believers out of confirmed skeptics of spiritualism.

549 Furst, Jeffrey. Edgar Cayce's Story of Attitudes and Emotions. New York: Coward, McCann and Geoghegan, 1973. 221p. $6.95

This book has been culled from 14,000 psychic readings. Chapters include "Attitude More Important than Fact," "Four Aspects of Mental/Emotional Growth," "Understanding the Past Life Experience," "Interpersonal Relationships," "Home and Family," "Balanced Living (the Problem of Extremes)," "Changing Attitudes and Emotions," "Health and Healing," "Love and Forgiveness," and "Recommended Reading." Questions mixed in with commentary is the format throughout the work. Many of the answers are to specific cases that are not very important to readers.

550/1 Galbreath, Robert, ed. The Occult: Studies and Evaluations. Bowling Green, Ohio: Bowling Green University Popular Press, 1972. 126p. (Orig. pub. in Journal of Popular Culture, vol. 5, no. 3, winter 1971) $1.50 pa.

The author as of 1974 was at the University of Wisconsin Center for 20th Century Studies. In this collection of nine essays, Galbreath starts the work off by discussing four different approaches to the occult: sociological analysis; personal evaluation; historical-literary case study; bibliographical. The other eight essays are: "Definition and Dimensions of the Occult: Towards a Sociological Perspective," by Marcello Truzzi; "Psi: Past, Present, Future," by David Techter; "New Religions: A Call for Thought," by Jacob Needleman; "Madame Blavatsky," by Russell Goldfarb; "Benjamin Lee Whorf: Transcendental Linguist," by Peter Rollins; "Esoteric Religion and Racism in the Thought of Houston Chamberlain," by Donald Thomas; "Witchcraft Studies, 1959-1971: A Bibliographical Survey," by Donald Nugent; and "History of Modern Occultism: A Bibliographical Survey," by Robert Galbreath. Nugent's witchcraft bibliography mentions Robbins's Encyclopedia with its 1,140 items, and refers to two other bibliographies put out in 1968 which contain over 500 items each. His list adds to these because it is annotated and includes newer items. Galbreath's bibliographical survey lists over 300 items, and is divided into six parts: bibliographies, reference works, general histories, occult sciences and themes, occultism from Romanticism to present, conclusions.

552 Gallant, Roy A. Astrology: Sense or Nonsense? New York:
* Doubleday, 1974. xi, 201p. Illus. Bibliog. $5.95 LC 73-15340 ISBN 0-385-07459-X

The author, who has taught at the Hayden Planetarium and at the Hackley School in Tarrytown, N.Y., has written a very well-done survey of astrology. Chapters include "The Art of Predicting the Future" (discusses case histories and using statistics in astrology); "Why do People Believe in Astrology?"; "Origins" (the first astrologers, constellations, origin of zodiac); "Setting the Stage" (Ptolemy and the Tetrabiblios, macrocosm, microcosm); "Reading the Signs"; "Putting Houses in Order"; "Astrology Through the Ages" (Romans, Arabs, Christians, alchemists, Renaissance, Copernicus, Age of Reason); "Casting a Horoscope"; "New Astrology" (marriage counseling, psychoanalysis, biological clocks). The book closes with a 15-page glossary. This excellent work would serve well as a textbook for this subject in high school or college.

553 Galloway, Donald. The Inevitable Journey. London: Muller, 1974. 170p. Illus. Plates Bibliog. Index £3.50 ISBN 0-584-10145-7

The author, a well-known British medium, tells of his early development and case histories. He mentions how much Ivy Scott helped him. Galloway also discusses the problems and pitfalls that mediums can encounter. He states that he has seen spirit people all his life, beginning when his Aunt Kate's spirit appeared to him when he was ill in bed as a youngster. The dead actor-composer Ivor Novello is mentioned often, since he is frequently in contact with author Galloway. The author emphasizes compassion and helping others throughout the book. He discusses spiritualist philosophy; guides and how they work; transfiguration; spirit world humor.

554 Galloway, Margaret. Steps from the Beyond. London: Regency Press, 1974. 113p. £1.80 ISBN 0-7212-0356-6

555 Gandee, Lee R. Strange Experience; The Autobiography of a Hexenmeister. Englewood Cliffs, N.J.: Prentice-Hall, 1971. 355p. Illus. $6.95 LC 76-157053 ISBN 0-13-850966-2

This highly personal, subjective book is written by a man who says his personality is a combination of two entities, male and female. One of his ancestors, he claims, was a Pennsylvania Hexenmeister. Raised by his grandparents, he continually had strange dreams and sexual fantasies. As a youth, he investigated many religions, including spiritualism. Also, he had a lengthy homosexual affair. He became interested in hex (Pennsylvania Dutch white magic), and later, South Carolina spells and incantations (powwow). He also spent some time in Mexico, and learned Mexican healing cults. Now settled in South Carolina, he works as a Hexenmeister. The book concentrates on Pennsylvania hex signs and symbolism, reincarnation, and lots of sex.

556 Garden, Nancy. Werewolves. Philadelphia: Lippincott, 1973.
* 127p. Illus. (Weird and Horrible Library) $4.95 LC 72-13280 ISBN 0-397-31463-9

This book discusses the origins of werewolf legends, the characteristics of werewolves, and cases of their existence in history. Discussed are these cases of people who were killed for supposedly being werewolves: Giles Garnier, Peter Stumpe, and Pierre, Georges and Antoinette Bouget. There is also a chapter on creatures which were not quite werewolves. As for a scientific basis, the author mentions cannibalism, porphyria, and rabies. This juvenile work is recommended for grades 6-9.

557 ________. Witches. Philadelphia: Lippincott, 1975. 160p. Illus. Bibliog. Index (Weird and Horrible Library) $5.95 LC 75-12621 ISBN 0-397-31564-3

This juvenile book discusses Greece and Rome, the Dark Ages, tribal witchcraft, the Inquisition, sabbats, trials in Europe and Great Britain, Salem, voodoo, and witches today. The author mentions theories that they may be either pagans or devil worshippers; the reader will have to decide for himself which theories are true about witches, she says.

558 Garfield, Patricia L. Creative Dreaming. New York: Simon
* & Schuster, 1974. $7.95

The author discusses cultures which are using "dream control" and "lucid dreaming" and tries to apply their experiences to the average U. S. dreamer of today. Tribes mentioned most are the Senoi Indians of Malaysia and the Yogis of Tibetan Buddhism. She also discusses the Tibetan Book of the Dead, Freud, Jung (who spent four years recording his dreams), Castaneda, and the latest laboratory data on dream states. The author has a Ph. D. in clinical psychology from Temple University, gives dream lectures, and travels widely to study dream cultures. She tells how to control dreams for a more productive life, free of fears and inhibitions, and for the simple fun of exciting dreams. In dreams, she feels, danger can be deliberately confronted and controlled. Also, one may meet dream friends who can help us in our waking lives. Garfield recommends keeping a dream diary, and has kept a 25-year, 10,000-entry one herself.

559 Garrett, Eileen Jeanette (Lyttle), 1893-1970. Adventures in
* the Supernormal; A Personal Memoir. Introd. by Hugh Lynn Cayce. New York: Paperback Library, 1971 (c1949; orig. pub., 1968). 175p. $.75 pa.

This fine autobiography of Eileen Garrett discusses her Irish childhood, with invisible friends she saw and played with; gradual awareness that she was different; close watching of animals in their streams and fields; the wild, hot blood in her family tree; London and marriage; the death of her two sons; bouts of delicate health and extreme sensitivity; ESP experiments. Her insights concerning her experiences are very interesting, and she tries to thoroughly explain various phenomena she heard and saw.

560 _______. My Life As a Search for the Meaning of Medium-
* ship. New York: Arno Press, 1975 (orig. pub., New York, 1939). (Perspectives in Psychical Research Series) $13 LC 75-7380 ISBN 0-405-07030-6

Written by Eileen Garrett, famed psychic and founder of the Parapsychology Foundation in New York, this book was her first autobiographical study, coming at age 45. Some consider it her best work, although she later said she didn't like it. She discusses the development and investigations of her abilities. Garrett sought out doctors and psychologists, including Jung and Rhine. The book also mentions that her early work with Rhine convinced her that her abilities were not limited to the trance state.

561 Garrison, Omar V. Medical Astrology: How the Stars Influence Your Health. New York: University Books, 1971 (also, London: Tallis Press, 1972; also, New York: Warner Paperback Library, 1973). 221p. Bibliog. Index $7.95 LC 79-118602

This work attempts to show how astrology can provide an early warning system for illness and help one to take preventive steps. It gives health information from many sources: the Rosicrucian fellowship in Oceanside, Calif., Evangeline Adams, and the Brotherhood of Light's now deceased Elbert Benjamine. The author claims that 75 per cent of laboratories surveyed could not do a simple blood chemistry test, and that more and more doctors are therefore using astrology as a diagnostic aid.

562 Gary, A. L., 1935- . The Psychic World of Doc Anderson. Atlanta: Droke House/Hallux, 1973. 176p. Illus. $5.95 LC 72-96364

R. C. Anderson of Rossville, Ga., has been the subject of an earlier biography by Robert E. Smith called The Man Who Sees Tomorrow. Gary's new work covers not only Anderson's predictions, but the human side of his life. Anderson was a boxer, strongman, and bullfighter who became a psychic. The book discusses predictions, and also Anderson's stigmata-like bleeding that occurred when he tried to locate underground oil. Also, it mentions the psychic healing the doctor occasionally has practiced.

563 Gauld, Alan. Founders of Psychical Research. New York:
* Schocken Books, 1973 (orig. pub., London: Routledge and Kegan Paul, 1968). 387p. Index $10

This fine, detailed work basically studies Henry Sidgwick, F. W. H. Myers, and Edmund Gurney, three close friends and all Fellows of Trinity College, Cambridge, in the late 19th century. Also discussed are New York State of the 1850's where spiritualism started, spiritualism in England, Arthur Balfour (later to be prime minister), Eleanor Sidgwick (Balfour's sister), William James, Richard Hodgson (who worked with James in the U. S.), Lord Rayleigh, J. J. Thomson, and Oliver Lodge. It is unusual in occult publishing to get a book packed tightly with information. This work is one of these pleasant rarities.

564 Gauquelin, Michel. Astrology and Science. Trans. by James
* Hughes. London: Mayflower, 1972 (orig. pub. as "Scientific Basis of Astrology," New York: Stein and Day, 1969; also as "Astrology and Science," London: P. Davies, 1970). 238p. Illus. Bibliog. Index (Translation of "Astrologie devant la science." Paris: Editions Planete, 1966) £0.40 pa. ISBN 0-583-12082-2

All of Gauquelin's works discuss what he considers the new science of cosmic influences. He has studied for over 20 years the relation between biological and cosmic phenomena, and works at the Psychophysiological Lab at Strasbourg University in France. The first two parts of the book discuss the history of astrology. The third part covers modern astrological findings.

565 _______. Cosmic Clocks: From Astrology to a Modern Sci-
*

ence. London: Paladin Press, 1973 (orig. pub., Chicago: Henry Regnery Co., 1967). 250p. Illus. Bibliog. Index $0.60 pa.

In this classic work, Gauquelin discusses how plants, animals, and man seem to be strongly influenced by set rhythms. He discusses the history of astrology, weather forecasting, rhythms, the unknown senses of man, season of birth, planets and heredity, effects of the universe on liquids. This fascinating, definitive work should be read by all intelligent people.

566 ______. Cosmic Influences on Human Behavior. Trans. by
*** Joyce E. Clemow. New York: Stein and Day, 1973 (also, London: Garnstone Press, 1974). 286p. Illus. Includes bibliog. refs. $7.95 LC 72-95989 ISBN 0-8128-1543-2

This work is a major new contribution to occult literature. It epitomizes the new field of statistical astrology. The author discusses the theory of planetary heredity--the mathematically demonstrable tendency of exceptionally successful professional people to be born at the exact moment when Mars, Saturn, Jupiter, or the moon is rising or has reached its meredian. He has found that a statistically significant number of politicians and actors are born under the influence of Jupiter, sports figures and soldiers under Mars, and scientists under Saturn. From this, Gauquelin comes up with "planetary personalities" (Mars is aggressive). The author used 27,000 birth records, 16,000 of them being those of famous people. Discussions include Louis XIV (the Sun King), stars and success, men of the theater, lunar temperament and writers, the baby's role in timing birth, and planetary types and modern psychology.

567 Geley, Gustave. Clairvoyance and Materialisation; A Record of Experiments. Trans. by Stanley de Brath. New York: Arno Press, 1975 (orig. pub., London, 1927). Illus. (Perspectives in Psychical Research Series) $24 LC 75-7381 ISBN 0-405-07031-4

The author, who died in 1924, was a leading French investigator of mediumship. He was careful to guard against fraud, but some claimed he was either victimized by mediums or part of the frauds himself. He accepted the evidence he saw as proof of survival, and collected extensive information on sittings.

568 Geller, Uri, 1946- . Uri Geller; My Story. New York:
*** Praeger, 1975 (also London: Robson Books, 1975). 283p. Illus. $8.95 LC 74-25462 ISBN 0-275-33170-9

This work is a major new contribution to occult literature. The author is by far the most important and visible representative of the psychic/occult field. His autobiography makes for fascinating reading. The first section, "It Happens Every Day," discusses his present life of tests, appearances, and celebrity status.

The second part of the work covers his life in war-torn Israel, including the Six Day War. Two of the many strange events surrounding his early life stand out. One occurred when he was four years old, and saw a bright silvery object hover over him, after which he lost consciousness. The other was when on maneuvers Geller was ordered to fire his machine gun. Because the gun weighed 80 pounds, he had left the barrel and other parts necessary for shooting back at camp in his bags. Certain of imprisonment, Geller stood up to shoot his worthless "fake" machine gun, when, shockingly, it fired a whole belt of ammunition. Returning back at camp, Geller unzipped his bag and found the barrel black from firing, although it had been clean when he left camp. Throughout the book, Geller takes great pains to state that he knows such stories sound totally ridiculous, but are true. The last section, "Search for Meaning," mentions the by now famous statement that Geller considers himself controlled by extraterrestrials. Again, Geller says this even knowing that his supporters are depressed he ever said it. He laments, "Why don't these intelligences reveal themselves to me? Why do they keep throwing me nothing but symbols?" This book reads with much less sensationalism than does Puharich's biography on Geller. Uri comes across as humble intelligent, mystified by his powers, but loving the limelight.

569 Gerling, Helene A. Healthy Intuitive Development; The Socratic Key for Personal Intuitive Development. New York: Exposition, 1971. 79p. (White Lotus Series) $4.50 LC 74-164862 ISBN 0-682-47337-5

570 Gervaso, Roberto. Cagliostro: A Biography. Trans. by Cormac O. Cuilleanain. London: Gollancz, 1974 (dist. in U.S. by Lawrence Verry, 1974). 272p. Illus. Plates Bibliog. Index (Translation of "Cagliostro." Milan: Rizzoli, 1972) $13.50 ISBN 0-575-01744-9

The author presents a picture of this adventurer and illusionist, examining most of the proper documents. However, the work depends on unreliable sources and conflicting findings of others.

571 Gettings, Fred. The Book of Palmistry. London: Hamlyn, 1974. 143p. Illus. (some color) Bibliog. £1.95 ISBN 0-600-37049-6

This book is a good introductory survey. The author quotes the writings of Benham, and underplays Cheiro. He does time determination by life and destiny lines, instead of by Cheiro's method. The work contains many palm prints. Gettings also tries to relate hand form and lines to astrology.

572 ______. The Book of Tarot. London: Hamlyn, 1973 (also,
* London: Triune Books, 1973). 144p. Illus. (some color) Bibliog. £1.75 ISBN 0-600-31327-1

This work is definitely one of the most attractive books out on the Tarot. Many of the color illustrations show sample cards from many packs, including those of Crowley, Marseilles, and Rider. Gettings tries to show relationships between Tarot symbolism and paintings, which are also shown in color. This is an intriguing aspect; one wishes Gettings would devote an entire book to it. Each card of the major arcana is given a thorough four-page spread of excellent text and illustrative material. In spite of the lack of book reviews on this work, we give it the * it deserves.

573 ______. The Book of the Zodiac: An Historical Anthology of Astrology. London: Ward Lock, 1972. 143p. Illus. (some color) Charts Facsims. Col. maps Bibliog. £1.75 ISBN 0-7063-1357-7

574 ______. The Hand and the Horoscope. London: Hamlyn, 1973. 203p. Illus. (some color) Facsims. Bibliog. £2.50

This is a short, clearly-written introduction to the use of astrology and palmistry in analyzing one's personality features and in making predictions. The author also tries to explain their interrelation, and show their relevance to modern reality. There are many excellent full-page illustrations.

575 Gibson, Litzka R., and Walter Brown Gibson, 1897- . Astrologers' Almanac and Occult Miscellany. Ed. by Joseph Greene. New York: Pyramid Publications, 1975. 96p. Illus. Charts (A Pyramid Book) $1 pa. LC 74-32649

576 Gibson, Walter Brown, 1897- . Witchcraft. New York: Grosset and Dunlap, 1973 (also, London: Barker, 1973). 149p. Illus. Plates $4.95 LC 72-156327

This survey covers witchcraft throughout history from the ancients and Druids to witch trials in England to modern times, with voodooism and devil worship mentioned. Included are the vampire of Croglin Grange; Gilles de Rais, who performed horrors on small children; and King James of England, who wrote Demonology in a frenzy, and had frequent witch hunts.

577 ______, and Litzka R. Gibson. The Complete Illustrated Book of Divination and Prophecy. Illus. by Murray Keshner. Garden City, N.Y.: Doubleday, 1973 (also, London: Souvenir Press, 1974). xii, 336p. Illus. $7.95 LC 71-103748

This coffee-table book covers number games, I Ching, divination by roulette, the Tarot (over 200 pages), palmistry (over 30 pages), and other topics. There are many charts, tables, and drawings. Also included is a glossary of methods of divination. This work is essentially a random collection. There is no attempt made to separate fact from fiction, amusement from divination.

578 Gillen, Jack. Jack Gillen Predicts. Hollywood, Fla.: Grand Trine Publications, 1975- . Diagrams (Vol. 1 covers through 1980) $9.95 LC 75-2887 ISBN 0-915532-00-X

579 Gitlin, Murray. Body and Mind and Their Possibilities: Especially in Occult Experience. Philadelphia: Dorrance, 1975 (c1974). 167p. Index $7.95 LC 74-15156 ISBN 0-8059-2078-1

This work explains the processes for becoming adept in use of clairvoyance, psychokinesis, and telepathy.

580 Glaskin, Gerald Marcus, 1924- . Windows of the Mind: Discovering Your Past and Future Lives through Massage and Mental Exercise. New York: Delacorte Press, 1974 (also, pub. as "Windows of the Mind: The Christos Experiment," London: Wildwood House, 1974). 268p. $7.95 LC 73-19760 ISBN 0-440-08816-X

The author, who has written 10 novels, tries to present a safe technique for astral travel. This Australian bumped into the technique in Open Mind, an occult publication issued out of Mahogony Creek, Western Australia. He tried it out himself with some friends. The process involves the massaging of ankles, feet, and the center of the forehead; there are also mental exercises to be done. Glaskin mentions the group's experiences, which astounded them in the detailed reality experienced of past lives, and as other forms of life.

581 Gleason, Judith Illsley; Awotunde Aworinde; and John Olaniyi Ogundipe. Recitation of Ifa, Oracle of the Yoruba. New York: Grossman Publishers, 1973. viii, 338p. Bibliog. $15 LC 72-90356 ISBN 0-670-59065-7

This anthropologist translates verses used in West African Ifa divination, and discusses their relevance to Yoruba mythology and religion.

582 Glut, Donald F. The Dracula Book. Metuchen, N.J.: Scarecrow Press, 1975. 388p. Illus. Index $12.50 LC 75-4917 ISBN 0-8108-0804-8

This work begins with Vlad the Impaler of 15th-century Romania, and covers the historical development of the Stoker novel. Most of the book is actually on vampire films, including those made in the 1930's and 1940's by Universal, and those of the 1950's made by British Hammer. Also mentioned is comic-book use of Dracula, with sample panels.

583 Goddard, Victor. Flight Towards Reality. London: Turnstone Books, 1975. 176p. Index £2.50 ISBN 0-85500-045-7

584 Godwin, John, 1928- . Occult America. Garden City, N.Y.:
*** Doubleday, 1972. xvii, 314p. Illus. Index $7.95 LC 79-168289

This work is a major new contribution to occult literature. Although it breaks no new ground, it is an excellent summary of occult happenings in America. Discussed are witchcraft, Cayce, Scientology and L. Ron Hubbard, ESP, astrology, prophecy, UFO's, mediums, spiritualism, cults, satanism, and psychic research. The author interviewed 300 practitioners of the occult arts, and participated in witchcraft rituals, seances, and Scientology classes. The author passes no judgment on these activities, but tries to analyze their psychological appeal. He is fair in his approach. His writing style is good, but occassionally leans toward the sensational. He believes that there is a hard core of actual phenomena around which occult beliefs are built. The book contains 47 photos and a glossary, but no bibliography, which should be a must in a survey such as this. This complete, representative, and well-researched overview is packed with information.

585 _______. Super-psychic: The Incredible Dr. Hoy. New York: Pocket Books, 1974. 239p. Illus. Plates Index $1.25 pa. LC 74-192049 ISBN 0-671-78463-3

This interesting biography discusses the life of a famous psychic. Chapters cover early life, voodoo and Hoy's missionary work in Brazil, magician act--where he discovered he didn't have to use tricks, because of his powers; ESP tests, prophecies, ESP crime work, Hoy's belief that famous people have put ESP to work for them, his campus tours, use of ESP in business by salesmen, Hoy's radio shows, power of ESP to influence other minds, answering questions by mail, home life, developing your child's ESP, healing yourself, losing weight and quitting smoking, fate and coincidences, psi and sex, hunting for treasure, which Hoy usually does underwater looking for ocean wrecks; getting jobs and raises, and coping with tragedy. Hoy's basic belief is that ESP should be completely integrated into daily life, as a natural occurrence.

586 _______. This Baffling World. Picture research by Marion
* Geisinger. Toronto, London: Bantam, 1971-1973 (orig. pub., New York: Hart, 1968). 3 vols. (orig. pub. in 1 vol.) 146, 142, 142p. Illus. Facsims. Index £0.40

This work is an excellent survey of many occult topics. Volume 2 includes the following chapters: "Flamewalkers," "Jinx Ship" (Mary Celeste), "Collins of Christ Church," "Hoodoo Sea" (Bermuda Triangle). Volume 3 has chapters on prophets, the Abominable Snowman, the boy from nowhere (Kaspar Hauser), and Houdini. All sections are excellent in their writing, research, and photographs. Particularly well-done are the chapters on Houdini and the Bermuda Triangle.

587 Godwin, William, 1756-1836. Lives of the Necromancers: or, An Account of the Most Eminent Persons in Successive Ages Who Have Claimed for Themselves, or to Whom Has Been Imputed by Others, the Exercise of Magical Power. New York: Gordon Press, 1975 (orig. pub., London: Chatto and Windus, 1876). $39.95 LC 75-31779 ISBN 0-87968-281-7

588 Goldenson, Robert M. Mysteries of the Mind. New York: Doubleday and Co., 1973. 279p. $7.95

The author takes the point of view of a scientific psychologist who feels that "tricks" on the mind are the primary causes of mysterious happenings. He discusses such psychological topics as mass hysteria, crowd behavior, split personality. Other topics covered include Patience Worth, hypnosis, dowsing, mysterious cases among primitive people, and stigmata. Goldenson feels nearly everything is explainable in terms of conventional science.

589 Gonzalez-Wippler, Migene. Kabbalah for the Modern World: How God Created the Universe. New York: Julian Press, 1974. 171p. Bibliog. $7.95 LC 74-75419

The author feels that the worth of the Old Testament and cabalistic theories of cosmogony depends on their having correlation with modern theories of creation of the universe and the evolution of man. She says that Jesus was a cabalist, and that Hermes Trismegistus was an Egyptian philosopher. The author also tries to join Jungian psychology and the cabala.

590 ________. Santería: African Magic in Latin America. New York: Julian Press, 1973. 192p. Illus. $6.50 LC 73-82439

Santería is a religion that joins elements of Yoruba myth and Christian traditions. It supposedly has 100 million followers worldwide and five million followers in large cities of the U.S. Santería means literally a cult of the saints. The Devil is the "cosmic thrust-block" of God (or gods)--it is a necessary evil based on cosmic law. The first two chapters discuss the legends and history of the Yorubas, a Nigerian people brought in great numbers to Brazil and the Caribbean. Other chapters discuss rituals of Santería, especially good and evil magic; magic spells; the seven African powers (gods). There is a list of New York "botánicas" (Santería shops), and a glossary.

591 Goodman, Felicitas D.; Jeanette H. Henney; and Esther Pressel. Trance, Healing and Hallucination; Three Field Studies in Religious Experience. New York: Wiley-Interscience, 1974. 288p. Illus. Bibliog. $12.50 LC 74-4159 ISBN 0-471-31390-4

This work is actually the Ph.D. dissertations of three students of Erika Bourguignon at Ohio State University. Henney's paper discusses two cults on the Caribbean island of St. Vincent; Pressel's paper is on the Umbanda in Brazil; Goodman's paper is on a pentecostal upheaval in Yucatan. Goodman analyzes the glossolalia and other phenomena of this peasant movement.

592 Goodman, Jerry. Powers of Mind, by Adam Smith [pseud.]. New York: Random House, 1975. 418p. $10

Goodman, the author of a best-selling work about the stock market several years ago published under the pen name Adam Smith, finds parapsychologists a financially neglected group. The field's total funding is less than the cost of a commercial break on a talk show. Goodman surveys the occult field in very breezy fashion as a "green" amateur. He took part in experiments at Maimonides Dream Laboratory, visited Stanford Research Institute while Geller was there, took a Transcendental Meditation course, and has read many books on parapsychology.

593 Goodman, Linda. Linda Goodman's Sun Signs. New York:
* Bantam, 1971 (also, London: Pan Books, 1972; also, London: Harrap, 1970; orig. pub., New York: Taplinger, 1968). xvii, 484p. $1.95 ISBN 0-553-02777-8

This work has gone through numerous printings, and Bantam's cover states there are over two million copies in print. For each sign, the author gives a 10-page general discussion; list of famous personalities of that sign; men of that sign; women of that sign; child of that sign; boss of that sign; employee of that sign. The writing is very chatty, anecdotal, and cute. Like many sign books, the author stretches out the basic information to many times the needed words with this filler material.

594 Gornick, Vivian. In Search of Ali Mahmoud: An American Woman in Egypt. New York: Saturday Review Press, 1973. 319p. $8.95 LC 72-88651 ISBN 0-8415-0242-0

This book is only partially on the occult. The author's husband was a Harvard graduate and an Arab. His family in Cairo hosted the author four months in 1971. Gornick discusses the city's atmosphere and the personal relationships of the people. She also discusses self-induced group possession and exorcism. In Cairo, women meet twice a week to participate in the "Zar," a possession experience of Africa and Arabia, especially in Ethiopia. The eight-hour ceremony has drums beating and women dancing wildly, who are being possessed and then released from many different spirits.

595/6 Gould, Rupert T. More Oddities and Enigmas. Secaucus, N.J.: University Books, 1973 (orig. pub. in 1944 as "Stargazer Talks") $5.95

This work discusses 15 true mysteries: the Indian rope trick, sea serpents, the Man in the Iron Mask, the Mary Celeste; strange ships, Jules Verne, canals of Mars, the Siberian Meteorite; Devil's hoof marks. Gould was advertised in the 1930's and early 1940's as "The Stargazer" on a radio talk show series in England.

597 Gowan, John Curtis. Trance, Art, and Creativity: A Psychological Analysis of the Relationship Between the Individual Ego and the Numinous Element in Three Modes--Prototaxic, Parataxic, and Syntaxic. Buffalo, N.Y.: Creative Education Foundation, State University College, 1975. xxvi, 448p. Bibliog. Index $5 pa. LC 75-324698

This is the third book of Gowan's trilogy (Development of the Creative Individual, c1974, and Development of the Psychedelic Individual, c1973, were the first two). This work analyzes the psychological relationship between the individual ego and the "numinous element" (soul). Loss of ego (prototaxic mode) results in schizophrenia, trance, glossolalia. Production of unclear images (parataxic mode) occurs in dreams and archetype use. In the syntaxic mode (ego-cognized symbolic meaning), creativity and ecstasy are manifest. This work is a serious study, often difficult to understand.

598 Grammary, Ann. Witch's Workbook. New York: Pocket Books, 1973. xvi, 270p. Illus. $1.25 pa.

This book includes incantations, rules, instructions, recipes, and prescriptions for witchcraft spells and rituals, from making love potions to foretelling the future.

599 Grant, Anne MacVicar, 1755-1838. Essays on the Superstitions of the Highlanders of Scotland: To Which Are Added, Translations from the Gaelic, and Letters Connected with Those Formerly Published. Norwood, Pa.: Norwood Editions, 1975 (reprinted from the orig. ed., London: printed for Longman, Hurst, Rees, Orme, and Brown, 1811). $40 LC 75-43760 ISBN 0-88305-224-5

600 Grant, James. Mysteries of All Nations. Detroit: Gale, 1971 (orig. pub., Leith, England, Reid, 1880). xxviii, 640p. $22.50 LC 79-150243

This book discusses the rise and progress of superstition, laws against and trials of witches, ancient and recent delusions, strange customs, fables and tales.

601 Grant, Joan. Far Memory. London: Corgi, 1975 (orig. pub. as "Time Out of Mind," London: Barker, 1956). 285p. Geneal. table £0.60 pa. ISBN 0-552-09853-1

602 Grant, Kenneth, 1924- . Aleister Crowley and the Hidden God. London: Muller, 1973. 245p. Illus. Facsims. Index £3.50

This work is a follow-up of the author's previous book, The Beast, the Whore and the Bastard. Grant is the present head of Crowley's Ordo Templi Orientis (O.T.O.). There are some references here to Crowley's failures and shortcomings. Grant seems to have moved from a follower role to that of revisionist. He emphasizes sexual magic even more than did Crowley.

603 ________. Cults of the Shadow. London: Muller, 1975. xi, 244p. Illus. Plates Bibliog. Index £6.50 ISBN 0-584-10158-9

This work discusses the secret sexual cults that have sprung up in the U.S. and Europe out of the practices of Crowley and his Ordo Templi Orientis. Discussed are four groups that follow the O.T.O. teachings, an Order of Thelema, the Cult of Ma-Ion, voodoo and tantric sex cults.

604 ________. Magical Revival. New York: S. Weiser, 1973 (c1972). 244p. Illus. Bibliog. $7.95 LC 72-91194

This work is a good summary of 20th-century magic. It relates Crowley's magical belief and current occultism to ancient sources which existed long before Christianity. Explained are mysteries of the Cult of Shaitan-Aiwaz; Devil-God of Sumer; Typhonian Rites of the dynasties of ancient Egypt. Magicians studied include Crowley, Dion Fortune, and Austin Osman Spare (an occult artist, some of whose works are reproduced in Man, Myth and Magic).

605 Graves, Frederick David, 1943- . The Windows of Tarot. Dobbs Ferry, N.Y.: Morgan and Morgan, 1973. 95p. Illus. Bibliog. $2.95 LC 73-85990 ISBN 0-87100-027-X

The author believes the Tarot is "a look at life," whose original purpose was to give structure to man's understanding of his daily experiences. Without such a framework, the mind can degenerate into chaos. Nearly all of this work is devoted to presenting analyses of each Tarot card for divination purposes. It is fully illustrated in black and white, using the Aquarian Tarot deck published by Morgan and Morgan. In the introduction and preface, the author accepts the usual theory of the Tarot's being an ancient book of accumulated wisdom.

606 Gray, Eden. Complete Guide to the Tarot. New York: Ban-
* tam, 1972 (c1970). 248p. Illus. Bibliog. $1.25 pa.

This work uses the Rider pack designed by Waite, and mostly discusses Tarot use in divination. Each card is discussed as to its occult symbolism and divinatory meaning. Gray also discusses methods for laying out the cards for readings, origins, symbolism, and Tarot's relation to other occult areas.

607 ________. Mastering the Tarot; Basic Lessons in an Ancient, Mystic Art. New York: New American Library, 1973 (orig. pub., New York: Crown, 1971). 221p. Illus. $1.25 pa.

Most of this book discusses the meaning of each Tarot card for divination purposes. Also included are the following discussions: diagrams for laying out cards; three quick ways to read them, as well as the Keltic method, Horoscope method, and Solar Chart method; use and misuse of Tarot; Tarot and astrology; and a glossary of terms.

608 Gray, Isa. From Materialisation to Healing. London: Regency Press, 1973. 184p. Illus. Facsims. £1.80

This is a compilation of stories and facts on materialization, spirit voices, ectoplasm, healing, and psychic surgery. In gathering it, the author made exhaustive searches in England, South Africa and Brazil. Famous mediums covered include José Arigo, Francisco Candido Xavier, and Alec Harris. One section describes an Alec Harris materialization seance where 17 spirit entities materialized before the gathered witnesses.

609 Gray, William G. The Tree of Evil. Cheltenham, England: Helios Book Service, 1974. 119p. Illus. £2.50 ISBN 0-900448-18-0

610 Gray-Cobb, Geof, 1928- . The Miracle of New Avatar Power. West Nyack, N.Y.: Parker Pub. Co., 1974. 199p. $6.95 LC 74-1316 ISBN 0-13-585372

611 Greaves, Helen. The Dissolving Veil. London: Spearman, 1975 (orig. pub., London: Churches Fellowship for Physical and Spiritual Studies, 1967). 166p. £1.95 ISBN 0-85435-003-9

612 ______. The Wheel of Eternity. London: Spearman, 1974. 152p. £2.50 ISBN 0-85435-192-2

The author moved into a small 16th-century cottage in a Sussex village. Soon she had the feeling she was being watched. She saw an old lady in an old-fashioned dress, who telepathically told her she had been a maid in the 16th century for a wealthy lady who had lived nearby. Later, the deceased retarded son of the wealthy lady appeared, along with a "brother of light." These two came to help the maid and wealthy mother realize they were dead and must leave into the next world.

613 Greeley, Andrew M. The Sociology of the Paranormal: A Reconnaissance. Beverly Hills, Calif.: Sage Publications, 1975. 88p. Diagrams Bibliog. (Sage Research Papers in the Social Sciences) (Studies in Religion and Ethnicity) $3 pa. LC 75-9046 ISBN 0-8039-0543-2

This work is a survey of psychic, mystical and survival experiences conducted by the National Opinion Research Center. The Center selected 1,460 replies from a national sample, and then sent a questionnaire which was administered by a NORC representative for one and a half hours. The author, a Catholic priest and sociologist, was senior investigator. There were five questions. The first was on "déjà vu." About 59 per cent reported having had the experience. The second asked if they had ever had the feeling of being in touch with someone far away (this question seems unclear). About 58 per cent said yes. The third question, on clairvoyance, asked if they had ever seen things happen far away as they were occurring. About 24 per cent said yes. These first three questions, after much analysis, showed that people with frequent psychical experiences have stronger feeling levels. The fourth question asked if they had ever felt in touch with someone who had died. About 27 per cent said yes. The last question asked if they ever felt close to a powerful mystical force that seemed to lift them out of themselves. About 35 per cent said yes. This scholarly study provides useful data for those writing about national opinion on psychic matters.

614 Green, Andrew Malcolm. Ghost Hunting: A Practical Guide.
* London: Garnstone Press, 1973. xi, 168p. Illus. Bibliog. £2.25

This work is a carefully done do-it-yourself guide written to assist the amateur ghost hunter in distinguishing between phony and genuine hauntings. It is not for the serious investigator or professional. The work includes these chapters: "What Is Proof of Phenomena?," "Personal Outlook and Experimentation," "Site Examination," "History of the Premises," "Description of the Phenomena," "Equipment and Its Use," "Interviewing the Witnesses," "Confirmatory Evidence." Also, there is a nine-page directory of parapsychological societies throughout the world. There is even a page giving sources for purchasing equipment.

615 _______. Haunted Houses. Aylesbury, England: Shire Publications, 1975. 32p. Illus. Bibliog. (Shire Albums) £0.35 pa. ISBN 0-85263-292-4

616 _______. Mysteries of London: Including Ghosts and Other Interesting and Unusual Aspects of London. Illus. by Montague Webb. Walton-on-Thames, England: Napier Publications, 1973. 25p. Illus. Map £0.30 pa. ISBN 0-9500570-8-8

617 _______. Mysteries of Surrey: Interesting and Unusual Aspects of the County, Including Surrey's Ghosts and Lost Villages. Illus. by Montague Webb. Walton-on-Thames, England: Napier Publications, 1972. 25p. Illus. Map £0.25 pa. ISBN 0-9500570-7-X

618 _______. Mysteries of Sussex: Including Ghosts, and Other Interesting and Unusual Aspects of Sussex. Illus. by Montague Webb. Walton-on-Thames, England: Napier Publications, 1973. 25p. Illus. Map £0.30 pa. ISBN 0-9500570-9-6

619 _______. Our Haunted Kingdom: More than 350 Authentic Hauntings or Case Histories Recorded in the United Kingdom over the Last 25 Years. London: Wolfe, 1973 (also, Fontana, 1974). 367p. Illus. Facsims. Bibliog. £4.25

This is a collection of more than 350 well-authenticated hauntings recorded in Great Britain over the last 25 years arranged in alphabetical order by county. The cases come from theaters, pubs, movie houses, hair-dressers' shops, subway stations, factories, and caravan sites. There are stories of a phantom cow, men's boots marching down a street by themselves, strange smells, ghost cars and bicycles. For all these items, the author usually first tries to give a logical explanation.

620 Green, Celia Elizabeth. Out-of-the-Body Experiences. Foreword by H. H. Price. New York: Ballantine, 1973 (c1968).
* xviii, 170p. (Institute of Psychophysical Research Proceedings, vol. 2) $1. 50 pa.

The Director of Oxford's Institute of Psychophysical Research covers the emotional and intellectual experiences of those undergoing the phenomenon. The book is based on the reports of over 300 people who have had out-of-the body experiences and replied to questionnaires sent to them. Chapter discussions include stress, parasomatic body, "bilocation," posture, muscular relaxation, paralysis, motor control, sense of time, detachment, motivation, relation to the physical body, initiation and termination of the ecsomatic state, ESP, telepathy, precognition, and psychokinesis. The book is very case-history oriented, with numerous long quotes from those undergoing the phenomenon.

621 ________, and Charles McCreery. Apparitions. London: Ham-
*** ilton, 1975 (dist. in U.S. by Transatlantic Arts). x, 218p. Bibliog. Index (Institute of Psychophysical Research Proceedings, vol. 5) £3. 75/$12. 50 ISBN 0-241-89182-5

This work is a major new contribution to occult literature. The authors are researchers at the Institute of Psychophysical Research, Oxford, England. They asked through radio and television for cases of apparitions, and received 850 accounts, to which they added others about which they had read. The ones added include reports in Phantasms of the Living and the Society for Psychical Research's Census of Hallucinations. The 200 cases they quote from are given in the participants' own words. The authors analyze various aspects of these accounts, and report general trends and variations. Discussions include collective apparitions, illumination of the environment, the sense of a presence without anything being seen, apparitions of animals and objects, the living and the dead, apparitions seen in reflecting surfaces, and similarities and differences between out-of-the-body experiences, lucid dreams, and apparitions.

622 Green, Jane Nugent, and Ethel Erkkila Tigue. You and Your Private I: Personality and the Written Self-image. St. Paul, Minn.: Llewellyn Publications, 1974. Bibliog. $3. 95 pa. LC 75-2320 ISBN 0-87542-295-0

623 Green, John. The Sasquatch File. Agassiz, B.C., Canada: Cheam Pub., 1973. 80p. $4 pa.

This work is designed as a short sourcebook. It is a gathering of short reports on Bigfoot, with bibliographies, maps of locations, and photos of tracks. The reports begin before 1900 and go to 1972, discussing California, Washington, Oregon, and British Columbia. Green considers the creature to be an ape, perhaps a direct descendant of Gigantopithecus.

624 Green, Landis Knight. Astrologer's Manual. New York: Arco Pub. Co., 1975. 255p. Illus. Bibliog. Index $11.95 LC 74-16082 ISBN 0-668-03616-8

This work gives a history and a chronological list of its development. It is a good first book to read. Discussions include astrology and occupations, personal relationships and parts of the body. There is a glossary.

625 Greenacre, David. Numerology and You. New York: Lancer, 1971. 207p. (Contempora Books) $1.25 pa.

626 Greenhouse, Herbert B. Astral Journey: Evidence for Out-
*** of-the-Body Experiences from Socrates to the ESP Laboratory. Garden City, N.Y.: Doubleday, 1975 (c1974). Bibliog. Index $8.95 LC 74-17610 ISBN 0-385-06750-X

This work is a major new contribution to occult literature. Beginning with classical times, the author discusses the experience in many cultures and periods. The work covers how it happens; forms of the astral body; techniques to induce it; scientific experiments in the 1970's (Osis through the American Society for Psychical Research with $300,000 left by James Kidd of Arizona, Tart through the University of Virginia, Targ through the Stanford Research Institute, and work conducted by the Psychical Research Foundation). Modern astral travelers Elwood Babbitt and Alex Tanous are also discussed. The author tells of his personal out-of-the-body experience (OOBE) in 1972, which led him to write the book. He mentions the double, says that astral travel may be used to help the blind to see, and feels OOBEs are good indirect proof of survival after death. Greenhouse states these OOBEs occur to many very normal people. One could perhaps criticize the author for at times making it sound too easy, with no risks.

627 ________. The Book of Psychic Knowledge; All Your Questions
* Answered. New York: Taplinger, 1973 (also, Toronto: Burns and MacEachern, 1973; London: Angus and Robertson, 1974; London: Corgi, 1975). 253p. Bibliog. $7.50 LC 72-6613 ISBN 0-8008-0932-7

This very interesting work is arranged in question-and-answer format, by chapter. Chapters cover these general topics: ESP, serious study of psychic phenomena, precognition and premonitions, psychokinesis, psychic healing, altered states of consciousness, psychic experiences in dreams, use of objects as "props" to bring on psychic experiences, automatic writing and the Ouija board, divining rod use, well-known psychics, psi ability in children, psychic abilities of animals and plants, astral projection, ghosts, mediums, evidence for survival of the soul, psychics and psychic phenomena in ancient times, witches past and present, and people throughout history who were sympathetic to the paranormal. Answers to questions are usually 40 to 100 words long. The questions are often not there as important topics, but as curiosities (example: "Whose spirit 'told' Eileen Garrett why the dirigible R-101 crashed in 1930?"). This fact, coupled with the lack of an index, makes this excellent book more for browsing than for reference use. However, this would be a fun book to give to readers who know nothing about the psychic field. The cumulative effect of all these questions is to give a great deal of information.

628 ________. Premonitions; A Leap into the Future. New York:
*** Warner Paperback Library, 1973 (also, London: Turnstone Press, 1972; London: Pan Books, 1975; orig. pub., New York: Geis, 1971). 302p. Index $1.25 pa.

This work is a major new contribution to occult literature. The book discusses premonitions on all kinds of subjects from the Greeks to the present. One purpose of this book is to make known the two centers where premonitions are now being recorded--the British Premonitions Bureau in London (begun in 1967) and the Central Premonitions Registry in New York (begun in 1968). The author states that more than 200 people had premonitions of the avalanche of slag that buried 138 Welsh schoolchildren in 1966. Had there been a premonitions registry then, this tragedy might have been avoided. Today, through such a registry, it is hoped an opportunity will occur to avert disaster--in effect, to change the future. There is also discussion of the Titanic, the 20-year cycle of presidential deaths; coincidences in the Kennedy and Lincoln assassinations. The book has no bibliography, few references given, and no real verification. However, it is a fine survey of the subject.

629 Gregor, Arthur S. Amulets, Talismans, and Fetishes: In-
* cluding a Dictionary of Amulets. Illus. by Anne Burgess. New York: Scribner's, 1975. viii, 120p. Illus. Bibliog. Index $6.95 LC 74-26002 ISBN 0-684-14460-3

This fine juvenile work discusses use of talismans from ancient times to present; signs such as the swastika, pentagram, and ankh that are used in amulets; evil eye and protection by the Bible, knots, rings, and gems; distinction between how amulets and fetishes work. There is a dictionary of amulets at the end. The author concludes that belief in amulets "reveals a false, although highly fascinating, conception of the nature of the world." Recommended for grades 6 and up.

630 ________. Witchcraft and Magic; The Supernatural World of
*

Primitive Man. Illus. by Laszlo Kubinyi. New York: Scribner's, 1972. 148p. Illus. Bibliog. $4.95 LC 72-1166 ISBN 0-684-12990-6

This well-done juvenile book covers the following topics: techniques (spells, rites), initiative magic (hair cuttings, images, true names), black magic, witchcraft, witch doctors, shaman, curing, divination, and today's magic. Discussions center on the Dobuans of Melanesia, the Mexican Indians of Chiapas, the Zulus, the Zande tribe of Africa, the Chukchee tribe of Siberia. There are very unusual black and white drawings, and also a "Magician's Dictionary" at the end. The author states that magic has played a part in bringing primitive cultures some happiness that advanced societies do not always have.

631 Gregory, William, 1803-1858. Animal Magnetism; or, Mesmerism and Its Phenomena. 5th ed. New York: Arno Press, 1975. (orig. pub., London: Nichols, 1909). (Perspectives in Psychical Research) $15 LC 75-7384 ISBN 0-405-07032-2

This book discusses clairvoyance, and apparitions seen by others of those under hypnosis. The author mentions the differences between waking suggestion and the Hypnotic trance. He feels an "odylic force," which produces emanations from the body, is the vehicle responsible for trances and the accompanying psychic phenomena.

632 Grendon, Felix, 1882-1965, comp. Anglo-Saxon Charms. Folcroft, Pa.: Folcroft Library Editions, 1974 (orig. presented as the compiler's thesis, New York, Columbia University, 1909). 133p. Includes bibliog. refs. (In English and Anglo-Saxon) $20 LC 74-3177

633 Gribben, John R., and Stephen H. Plagemann. The Jupiter Effect. New York: Vintage Books, 1975 (orig. pub., Walker, 1974). Illus. Map Bibliog. $1.95 pa.

The author theorizes that the grand alignment of the planets due in 1982 (which happens only every 179 years), in conjunction with the fact that 1982 represents the peak of the 11-year sunspot cycle, probably means a major earthquake will occur. The San Andreas Fault in California is picked as a likely target.

634 Grillot de Givry, Emile Angelo. Illustrated Anthology of Sorcery, Magic and Alchemy. Trans. by J. Courtenay Locke.
* New York, A. and W. Visual Library, 1975 (also, pub. as "Witchcraft, Magic and Alchemy," New York: Dover, 1971; available rebound in cloth from Peter Smith, Magnolia, Mass.; orig. English ed. pub. in 1931; French ed. pub. in 1929). 394p. Illus. Index $7.95 pa. LC 74-33782 ISBN 0-89104-009-9

This work is a classic in the occult field. The author took

the material for this sourcebook from ancient manuscripts, secret documents, rare books, official reports, and occult traditions. He discusses ceremonial magic, witches and the Sabbath, covens, demonology, spells, Kabbalah, astrology, talismans, and alchemy. The author includes 366 black-and-white illustrations.

635 Gross, Hugo Max. Biorhythms. 3rd ed. Albuquerque, N.M.: Motivational Development Center, 1975 (1st ed., 1966). 168p. Paperback

This book is mostly on European research on physical, emotional and intellectual cycles in human beings.

636 Grumley, Michael. There Are Giants in the Earth. London: Sidgwick and Jackson, 1975 (orig. pub., New York: Doubleday, 1974). xiv, 154p. Illus. Plates £3.50 ISBN 0-283-98284-5

The author theorizes that the Abominable Snowman, the Sasquatch, and the Mono Grande (of the Amazon and South America areas) are three strains of the prehistoric species Gigantopithecus. Most of the book is on this species (this idea was suggested 20 years ago by Bernard Heuvelmans). For evidence, Grumley discusses sightings, footprints, attacks and kidnappings.

637 Gruss, Edmond C. Ouija Board: Doorway to Occult. Chicago: Moody, 1975. 191p. $1.50 pa. ISBN 0-8024-1783-3

This work gives a view of Christian thought on use of the Ouija board and other such techniques, and attempts to present the Bible's answers to the occult. It contains discussions of the history, operation, explanation, and verification of the Ouija board; the board as a dangerous approach to psychic development; the Bible on demons, possessions, and exorcism; and "The Exorcist" (both movie and book). Appendices contain the following: Ouija board and automatic writing, an article by Bill Brinkley titled "Priest Frees Mt. Rainier Boy from Devil's Grip," and a list of selected readings. The author is against use of the Ouija board, and laments the use of such devices by unskilled amateurs. Since this is the only work out on the board, it is very useful. Hopefully, a more complete, deeper study will someday be done without the Bible/Christianity slant that appears here.

638 Guarino, Salvatore. Thermodynamic Radiation. Bellavista, Italy: Cassella P. Guarino, 1975. 271p. (In English)

The author is known mostly for his method of morphine determination, but has investigated parapsychology since 1965. The book is a collection of his papers arranged in chronological order, with connection between them not always clear. The author feels that when ATP (adenosine triphosphate--high energy chemical building blocks in the body) production exceeds consumption, psi hits occur in tests. Gradually, over a long period, production and consumption must equal each other, and individuals will stop hitting.

The author also discusses two types of radiation from an individual's nervous system. He also tests 17 drugs; three of them seem to help scores in ESP tests (vitamins B1 and B6 and ATP).

639 Gudas, Fabian, ed. Extrasensory Perception. New York: Arno Press, 1975 (orig. pub., New York, 1961). (Perspectives in Psychical Research Series) $10 LC 75-7385 ISBN 0-405-07033-0

This work is an anthology of 25 short essays on parapsychology. Some of them support the field (Rhine and Thouless), while others are opposed (Jastrow, Boring, Skinner). Also, several others are on more general philosophical issues.

640 Guirdham, Arthur. A Foot in Both Worlds: A Doctor's Autobiography of Psychic Experience. Jersey, England: Neville
* Spearman, 1973. 221p. £2.25

The author presents a study of what he calls the "labyrinth of group reincarnation." He is a practicing psychiatrist; some mediums and healers are his patients. Guirdham claims that he and many of his patients are reincarnations from the Cathars, a 13th-century people. He discusses his previous existence as a Cathar, and sees his patients' dreams as evidence that they too were part of this group. Also, he attempts to communicate the message of Catharism. He accepts the dualistic nature of life, with the presence of opposites (never pleasure without pain, or joy without sorrow), which he says are Cathar beliefs. Catharism was a form of dualism flourishing in Southern France and Northern Italy in the 12th and 13th centuries. Cathar philosophy is derived from the Manichaeans, who believed that good and evil were two coequal forces. Guirdham says that Cathars are now reincarnating all over the world and he sees a new age approaching. The writing style is almost stream-of-consciousness type.

641 _______. Obsession; Psychic Forces and Evil in the Causation of Disease. London: Neville Spearman, 1972. 186p. £2.10

The author theorizes that psychiatric disorders are not due merely to psychic impressions, but to an active, very real and evil force existing in the world. He covers various obsessions he feels are caused by inner struggles of the mind to ward off evil impressions. The author has practiced psychiatry for 40 years. Like Karl Menninger in his recent book, Guirdham deplores the fact that the concepts of evil and sin have been replaced by concepts of antisocial behavior, maladjustment, and crime, where society is to blame, not the individual.

642 _______. We Are One Another: A Record of Group Reincarnation. Jersey, England: Neville Spearman, 1974. 227p. Illus. Plates £2.95 ISBN 0-85978-010-4

The author discusses a Miss Mills and seven other people, patients of his, all of whom refer to French life in the 13th century and the Cathars. In the 20th century, all eight were educated, lived, or were born within 12 miles of Bristol, England. Mills later develops mediumistic powers. To answer the usual criticism, Guirdham says that rather than reincarnation cases' really being ones of mediumship or spirit possession, mediumship and possession are themselves processes of reincarnation. Events remembered cover the years 1242-1244, and specifically relate to the siege of the Chateau of Montsegur, the Cathar's last stronghold in the Languedoc.

643 Gunn, James Scott. You and Your ... Man. London: Mills and Boon, 1974. 12 volumes (92p. each Illus. (Mills and Boon Astral Guides) £0.35 each

This is a 12-volume set, each volume on a different sign of the zodiac.

644 Gunther, Max, 1927- . Wall Street and Witchcraft. New York: B. Geis, 1971. 256p. $6.95 LC 71-134217

A large part of the book discusses covens. In one case, a 13-member coven mentally commanded people to buy a stock, and they did. Coven members then sold at a profit. Also, the author mentions the use of astrology in predicting the market's rises and falls. Movements seem related to sunspots, and the positions of Jupiter, Saturn and Uranus. Also, one can chart a particular corporation, using the date of incorporation as the birth date. The author mentions also that spiritualists use the advice of dead acquaintances. Other discussions about tools used to analyze the market are included: Tarot, numerology, dreams, pendulums, dowsing, and magic squares.

645 Gupta, Marie, and Frances Brandon. A Treasury of Witchcraft and Devilry. Middle Village, N. Y.: Jonathan David Publishers, 1974. 179p. $8.95 LC 74-6571 ISBN 0-8246-0190-8

This work discusses witchcraft, exorcism, devil worship, gypsy lore, magic, astrology, divination, Tarot, and ghosts. It is very loosely organized, with no bibliography, no footnotes, and no index.

646 Gurney, Gene, and Clare Gurney. Unidentified Flying Objects. London, New York: Abelard-Schuman, 1971 (c1970). 144p. Illus. Bibliog. $4.50 LC 75-105262 ISBN 0-200-71677-8

This juvenile survey covers UFO's sighted over the U. S. since 1947. Discussions include two official investigations; hoaxes, identified flying objects, how scientists explain UFO's, what to do if you see one. There are three classic cases given of the 1940's, and many from the 1960's. This book is recommended for grade 4 and up.

647 Haddock, Joseph W. Somnolism and Psycheism: or, The Science of the Soul and the Phenomena of Nervation as Revealed by Vital Magnetism or Mesmerism, Considered Physiologically or Philosophically: With Notes of Mesmeric and Psychic Experience. New York: Arno Press, 1975 (orig. pub., London: J. S. Hodson, 1851). (Perspectives in Psychical Research) $14 LC 75-7386 ISBN 0-405-07034-9

The author discusses the subject from the viewpoint of an 1850's brain physiology doctor. He covers studies on clairvoyance and second sight during mesmeric states. There are many case studies given. The author also discusses homeopathic medicine, and use of clairvoyance in medical diagnosis.

648 Hagee, John C. Invasion of Demons. Old Tappan, N.J.: Revell, 1973. 158p. Bibliog. $2.95 pa. LC 72-10271

649 Haich, Elizabeth. The Wisdom of the Tarot. Trans. by D. Q. Stephenson. New York: ASI Publishers, 1975 (also, London: Allen and Unwin, 1975). Illus. (color of 22 cards) (Translation of "Tarot." Stuttgart, J. Fink, 1969) $12.95 LC 75-22379 ISBN 0-88231-018-6

650 Haining, Peter. The Anatomy of Witchcraft. New York: Tap-
* linger Pub. Co., 1972. 212p. Illus. Includes bibliog. refs. (Frontiers of the Unknown Series) $6.95 LC 72-2177 ISBN 0-8008-0201-2

This interesting survey discusses witchcraft, satanism, voodoo, witchcraft festivals and publications, Raymond Buckland, Sybil Leek, Louise Huebner, Leo Martello, black magic in California, white magic in the Eastern U.S., black magic in Britain, Europe, and Russia. Appendixes have a Gardnerian first-degree initiation ritual, a ritual for making magical instruments, and a discussion on Voudon by Madame Arboo. The book gives a good picture of contemporary 1970's witchcraft and magic.

651 ______, ed. Circle of Witches: An Anthology of Victorian Witchcraft Stories. New York: Taplinger Pub. Co., 1971 (orig. pub., London: Hale, 1971). 235p. Illus. Plates $5.95 LC 79-126286 ISBN 0-8008-1590-4

This book contains 18 tales written by women. Some are fictional, some are factual, but all are based on actual happenings. Authors include Lady Wilde, Lady Duff-Gordon, and Catherine Crowe.

652 ______. Ghosts: The Illustrated History. New York: Mac-
* millan, 1975 (also, London: Sidgwick and Jackson, 1974). 126p. Illus. $9.95 LC 74-29441

The author tries to include the best pictures of 2,000 years of ghost accounts. Included in the text and pictures are the Cock Lane Ghost, the Flying Dutchman, and the ghost of President Lincoln. The work shows how many spirit photos were faked. Also mentioned is Gambols with the Dead, a 1900's mail-order catalogue for mediums, full of apparatus. Haining also discusses the real materializations witnessed by many, and disproved by none so far. All photos are in black and white. The book ends with the sentence, "The ghosts on these pages, I venture to suggest, prove that...." Perhaps all occult works should end with the same unfinished phrase. Besides the excellent photos, the text reads very well.

653 ________, ed. An Illustrated History of Witchcraft. London: New English Library, 1975. 128p. Illus. £5.25 ISBN 0-450-02409-1

654 ________, ed. Magicians: The Occult in Fact and Fiction. New York: Taplinger, 1973 (orig. pub., London: P. Owen, 1972). 219p. $6.95

This is a collection of classic works on ceremonial magic, black masses, hypnotism, witchcraft, satanism, and necromancy. The 12 writings together cover the history of occult thought from the end of the 19th century to the present. The book includes the following stories and excerpts from writings: Huysman's 1891 novel, La Bas; Crowley's "Experiment in Necromancy"; Arthur Machen's "Strange Occurrences at Clerkenwell"; Blavatsky's fiction on mesmerism and murder written in 1875 under a pseudonym; Eliphas Levi; Dion Fortune; and W. B. Yeats. Included is an 11-page introduction by Colin Wilson.

655 ________, comp. Necromancers; The Best of Black Magic and Witchcraft. Introd. by Robert Bloch. New York: Morrow, 1972 (orig. pub., London: Hodder and Stoughton, 1971). 255p. Illus. $5.95 LC 74-166351

This collection on necromancy, the art of raising the dead, includes witchcraft, black magic, devil worship, and satanism articles, short stories, and essays. The short stories are by Crowley, Hawthorne, E. F. Benson, August Derleth, Algernon Blackwood. Essays include those by Cotton Mather, Margaret Murray, Dennis Wheatley, and Robert Graves. Articles include one by a Crowley follower; another that is a record of the sabbat reconstructed from documents; a ridicule of witchcraft by P. T. Barnum; a copy of a 17th-century pact with the devil. The book has 30 selections in all.

656 ________. The Warlock's Book: Secrets of Black Magic from the Ancient Grimoires. Illus. by George Underwood based on original woodcuts. London: W. H. Allen, 1972. 110p. Illus. Bibliog. £1.50 ISBN 0-491-00189-4

657 ________. Witchcraft and Black Magic. Illus. by Jan Parker.
* New York: Bantam Books, 1973 (also, New York: Grosset and

Dunlap, 1972; orig. pub., Feltham, England: Hamlyn Pub. Group, 1971). 159p. Illus. (all in color) Bibliog. (Bantam Knowledge through Color Series) $1.45 pa.

This work is a fine survey of the history of witchcraft and black magic. The high point of the book is the creative, intriguing color illustrations of Jan Parker. Most of these were done especially for this book; a few are embellished copies of old drawings and woodcuts. There is an illustration on every two-page spread, and the effect is excellent. The text discusses: origins of witchcraft; occult in early civilizations; beginnings of persecution; centers of devil worship; witch finders; witch in art; familiars; Sabbat; pact with the Devil; possession; divination; famous witch trials; black magic; modern witchcraft and black magic (satanists, rites of witchcraft, voodoo). This work would be an excellent first choice for teachers to use in courses. Its use of high quality, glossy paper adds to the picture quality, and gives it an exciting feel.

658 ________. Witchcraft Papers. Secaucus, N.J.: University Books, 1973. $7.95

This book discusses Essex County, England, center of witchcraft hysteria from the 1560's to 1600.

659 Haislip, Barbara. Stars, Spells, Secrets, and Sorcery: A Do-it-yourself Book of the Occult. Boston: Little, Brown, 1975. 312p. Illus. Bibliog. $7.95 LC 75-28360 ISBN 0-316-33820-6

This juvenile book discusses astrology, numerology, palmistry, cartomancy, graphology, tasseography (tea leaves), dominoes, dice, body moles, and candles. For each of these, the author gives the history and tips for use. There is a briefer mention of ESP, crystal gazing, ghosts, and dreams. The work is recommended for grades 6-9.

660 Hale, J. A Modest Enquiry into the Nature of Witchcraft. Bainbridge, N.Y.: York Mail-Print, 1973 (orig. pub., 1702).

661 Halevi, Z'ev ben Shimon. The Tree of Life: An Introduction to the Cabala. London: Rider, 1972. 200p. Illus. Index £2.75 ISBN 0-09-112260-0

662 Halifax, Charles Lindley Wood. Lord Halifax's Ghost Book: A Collection of Stories Made by Charles Lindley, Viscount Halifax. Foreword by the Earl of Halifax. London: Fontana, 1973 (also, Bath, England: Chivers, 1974; orig. pub., London: Bles, 1936). 287p. £0.35 pa. ISBN 0-00-613375-4

663 Hall, Angus. Monsters and Mythic Beasts. Garden City, N.Y.: Doubleday, 1975. 144p. Illus. (New Library of the Supernatural) $8.95 LC 75-26141

664 ________. Signs of Things to Come. Garden City, N. Y.: Doubleday, 1975. 144p. Illus. (New Library of the Supernatural, v. 1) $7.95 LC 75-16747

This is the first volume of a British-produced 20-volume series. This book contains many color illustrations, and surveys predictions from Delphi to Jeane Dixon.

665 Hall, Manley Palmer, 1901- . Astrological Keywords. 7th ed. Totowa, N. J.: Littlefield, Adams, 1975 (orig. pub., Los Angeles: Philosophical Research Society, 1958). Bibliog. Index $2.95 pa. LC 75-5706 ISBN 0-8226-0299-7

Hall, president and founder of the Philosophical Research Society, is the author of over 100 works. Sections in this book discuss the zodiac, physical characteristics, emotional characteristics, mental characteristics, anatomy, physiology, and diseases of each sign; colors; gems; cities of each sign; horoscopes, metals, plants, trees, herbs. Each section is two to three pages long, with over 100 sections. The work covers almost everything in astrology.

666 Hallam, Jack. Ghosts of London. Illus. by Chris Thornton. London: Wolfe, 1975. 303p. Illus. Maps Bibliog. £4.50 ISBN 0-7234-0460-7

667 ________. Haunted Inns of England. Illus. by Chris Thornton. London: Wolfe, 1972. 223p. Illus. Maps Bibliog. £3 ISBN 0-7234-0474-7

668 Hallowell, Alfred Irving, 1892- . The Role of Conjuring in Saulteaux Society. New York: Octagon, 1971 (c1942). xiv, 96p. Illus. Bibliog. (Publications of the Philadelphia Anthropological Society, v. 2) (Brinton Memorial Series) $6.50 LC 78-120622 ISBN 0-374-93405-3

669 Hammond, David, and David Frederick Brown. Search for Psychic Power: The Evolution of Mind. London: Hodder and Stoughton, 1975. 256p. Bibliog. Index £4.25 ISBN 0-340-20239-4

This book presents true stories of supernatural powers, such as people bending metal without using their hands, and healing cases. The authors theorize that we all may be evolving these powers gradually.

670 Hammond, Sally. We Are All Healers. New York: Harper
*** and Row, 1973 (also, New York: Ballantine, 1974). 272p. Index $5.95 LC 73-6331 ISBN 0-06-063694-7

This work is a major new contribution to occult literature. The first section discusses healing in the U. S., especially in the South and at the Association for Research and Enlightenment. The best material in the work is the section on British healing, which discusses the National Federation of Spiritual Healers, Harry Edwards, Gordon Turner, Mary Rogers, Ronald Beesley, Dr. Christopher Woodard, Gwen Murray, Brigadier Firebrace, the Spiritualist Association of Great Britain, the College of Psychic Studies, and the Quakers. The last section, called "Probing the Healing Mystery," discusses Lawrence LeShan; the Academy of Parapsychology and Medicine; four American healers (Jackson, Rolling Thunder, Schwarz, LeShan); controversial issues. The author, a New York Post reporter, has traveled a good deal to gather the information used in the book. Most of the work consists of quotes from interviews, and, as such, is a very valuable book. The author discusses measurement of the effects of psychic powers on enzymes, the growth of barley, and healing wounds in mice. Also, Hammond mentions the need for healing training centers in the U. S.

671 * Hamon, Louis, 1866-1936 [under pseud.: Cheiro]. The Cheiro Book of Fate and Fortune: Palmistry, Numerology, Astrology. New York: Arco, 1971 (also, London: Barrie and Jenkins, 1971). xii, 339p. Illus. $5.95 LC 72-164693 ISBN 0-668-02507-7

672 * _______. Cheiro's Book of Numbers. 11th ed. London: Corgi, 1975 (11th ed. orig. pub., London: Jenkins, 1935). 221p. Illus. £0.50 pa. ISBN 0-552-09585-0

This work is a classic of numerology. After a long introduction, the author discusses the numbers from one to nine (for each number, one page of text, followed by one page listing famous people born under that number); the occult symbolism of compound numbers; spiritual numbers; the importance of birth number; illustrations of names and numbers; examples of how numbers recur in lives; unfounded dread of the number 13; extraordinary example of numbers in the lives of St. Louis and Louis XVI; periodicity in numbers; lucky days; colors and numbers; music and numbers; numbers and disease; cities and towns; horse-racing; names of some Presidents of the U. S.; the Bible and numbers.

673 * _______. Cheiro's Guide to the Hand. 4th ed. London: Corgi, 1975 (also, London: Barrie and Jenkins, 1975; 4th ed. orig. pub., London: Jenkins, 1948). 126p. Illus. £0.40 ISBN 0-552-09586-9

674 * _______. Cheiro's Language of the Hand: A Complete Practical Work on the Science of Cheirognomy and Cheiromancy Containing the System and Experience of Cheiro. 28th ed. London: Corgi, 1975 (orig. pub., London: Jenkins, 1949). 238p. Illus. Plates Index £0.50 pa. ISBN 0-552-09584-2

This work is a classic on palmistry. Discussions include shapes of hands and fingers, elementary, or lowest type, square hand and its subdivisions, spatulate hand, philosophic hand, conic hand, psychic hand, mixed hand, thumb, joints of the fingers, fingers, palm, large and small hands, nails, hair on the hands, mounts, lines, life line, Mars line, head line, insanity shown by line of head, heart line, fate line, sun line, health line or hepatica, via lasciva and the line of intuition, line of marriage, children, star, cross, square, island, circle, and spot, grille, triangle, ring of Solomon, color of palm, great triangle and the quadrangle, travel and accidents, illustrative types (suicide, murder, insanity), and some interesting hands. The work is illustrated with photos of hand prints and drawings.

675 ______. Palmistry for All: A Practical Guide on the Study
* of the Lines of the Hand. Rev. [i.e., 2nd] ed. London: Corgi, 1975 (also, New York: Arco, 1964; rev. ed. orig. pub., London: Jenkins, 1951). 156p. Illus. £0.40 pa. ISBN 0-552-09587-7

This work is a classic on palmistry. It is written in much simpler style than many of Hamon's other works. Discussions include line of head, line of life, line of destiny or fate, line of sun, line of heart, line of health, minor lines of the hands, different classes of lines, how to tell time and dates, study of the shape of the hand, thumb, fingers, nails, mounts, and advice to the student. This is a good beginner's book to palmistry.

676 ______. You and Your Hand. New ed., revised by Louise
* Owen. London: Sphere, 1974 (this ed. orig. pub., London: Jarrolds, 1969). xix, 187p. Illus. Plates Index £0.50 pa. ISBN 0-7221-2262-4

677 Hansen, Chadwick. Witchcraft at Salem. London: Arrow
* Books, 1971 (also, London: Hutchinson, 1970; orig. pub., New York: Braziller, 1969). 288p. Illus. Plates Bibliog. Index £0.30 pa. ISBN 0-09-003910-6

This work is definitely a classic on Salem witchcraft. It is a revisionist view of Salem, in that it newly interprets the sources, and takes a stance contrary to the usual blaming of the government and clergy. He attacks the traditionalist view, which says that no witchcraft was practiced, that the phenomena were fake, that the clergy whipped up hysteria, that the merchants were the only ones to oppose persecution, and that the Salem executions were unique in Western civilization. Hansen says that witchcraft was widely practiced, the behavior was pathological, fear and not preaching caused panic, the merchants spoke out too late, and Salem was not unique. He mentions the spiritual humility and intelligence of Mathers and others, and discusses their measured responses although hysteria was everywhere. There is good discussion of the historiography of the Salem trials, and various historians' distortions. Some may quibble with Hansen's theory that witchcraft really existed, since he bases it on material of the period that may be suspect. However, anyone doing even a brief study of Salem must read this work.

678 Hanson, Virginia, comp. Gifts of the Lotus. Wheaton, Ill. : Theosophical Pub. House, 1974. 191p. $1.50 pa.

This is a book of daily meditations culled from various Theosophist writers.

679 ________, ed. Karma: The Universal Law of Harmony. Wheaton, Ill. : London: Theosophical Pub. House, 1975. ix, 137p. Bibliog. (Quest Book) £1.50 pa. ISBN 0-8356-0642-4

This book is a collection of articles on reincarnation and karma as the universal law of harmony, culled from the writings of theosophists.

680 ________, ed. Silent Encounter. Wheaton, Ill. : Theosophical Pub. House, 1974. 240p. (Quest Book) $2.75 pa.

This collection of writings on mysticism includes works by Geoffrey Hodson, Arthur W. Osborn, Phoebe Payne Bendit, and Stephan A. Hoeller.

681 Hapgood, Charles H. Voices of Spirit: Through the Psychic Experience of Elwood Babbitt. New York: Delacorte Press/S. Lawrence, 1975. $8.95 LC 74-22238

The author, a teacher at Keene State College in New Hampshire, discusses 60 spirits that speak through trance medium Elwood Babbitt (including his dog, Eloise). Hapgood has recorded 300 sittings taking place over eight years, which include contacts with these persons: John Kennedy, Queen Elizabeth, Socrates, Wordsworth, Bishop Pike, Twain, Einstein, Gandhi, Nostradamus, Adlai Stevenson, and Lincoln. Hapgood has an introduction about "T" and "L" fields, Hurkos, and talking to plants.

682 Hardy, Alister; Robert Harvie; and Arthur Koestler. The
*** Challenge of Chance: Experiments and Speculations. London: Hutchinson, 1973 (also, New York: Random, 1974; also, New York: Vintage Books, 1975, with new subtitle, "A Mass Experiment in Telepathy and Its Unexpected Outcome"). 280p. Illus. Includes bibliog. refs. Index £3 ISBN 0-09-116930-5

This work is a major new contribution to occult literature. In the autumn of 1967, on seven consecutive Monday nights, 200 people met at Caxton Hall, Westminster, London, to participate in a series of visual experiments arranged by Hardy, a zoologist. Coincident thoughts emerged from participants in close proximity to each other. Robert Harvie, a psychology graduate of London University, was brought in, since he had training in statistical methods. Hardy and Harvie conclude that classic ESP card guessing tests may not be examples of ESP, but of some strange property of chance and probability not yet understood. Koestler applies Jung's synchronicity theory of meaningful but not causally connected coincidences, and concludes that a mechanistic view of the world is no longer valid. Criticisms of the work have been that the design of the experiment was flawed, and that much of the discussion is a simple repeat from Koestler's earlier The Roots of Coincidence.

683 Hare, Peter H. Causing, Perceiving and Believing; An Examination of the Philosophy of C. J. Ducasse. Dordrecht, Holland/Boston: D. Reidel, 1975. 211p. Bibliog. $26 LC 75-4899

This scholarly work discusses the ideas of Ducasse, an officer of the American Society for Psychical Research in the 1960's, and professor of philosophy at Brown University for 45 years. There are 12 chapters, one of which is on paranormal phenomena. The other sections mention Ducasse's contributions to analytic philosophy (defining words and language), causation (where he criticized Hume), and perception, where he said we do not see actual things, but things as they appear to us. In the 1940's, Ducasse began studying parapsychology, with 1948 the date of his first publication in the field. From then on, one-third of his writings were on parapsychology. In this field, he is best known for his belief in survival, for which he felt there was much evidence from mediums. He felt that one was not justified in saying all this could be the result of super-ESP on the part of the living. By survival, he meant not just memories, but survival of the best capabilities of the mind. The book includes a biographical sketch of Ducasse.

684 Harper, Charles George, 1863-1943. Haunted Houses: Tales of the Supernatural, with Some Account of Heriditary Curses and Family Legends. Philadelphia: Lippincott, 1974 (dist. by Tower Books/Gale, Detroit; also pub., Wakefield, England: EP Publishing, 1974; orig. pub., London: Palmer, 1924). 288p. Illus. Index $14 LC 79-164326

685 Harper, George Mills, ed. Yeats and the Occult. Toronto: Macmillan of Canada/Maclean-Hunter Press, 1975. 332p. $24.95 LC 75-357557 ISBN 0-7705-1308-5

This collection of essays discusses Harper's own records of membership in several metaphysical societies; new views of poems seen in the light of his occult studies; biographical information; manuscripts; parallels between Yeats, alchemists, and Jung. Each essay is well-documented.

686 Harrell, David Edwin, Jr. All Things Are Possible: The
* Healing and Charismatic Revivals in Modern America. Bloomington: Indiana University, 1975. 304p. Illus. Bibliog. essay $10.95 LC 75-1937 ISBN 0-253-10090-9

This work studies the Pentecostal revival movement of 1947-1958. Discussions include history of the charismatic movement, Oral Roberts, A. A. Allen, T. L. Osborn, William Brantham, and Jack Coe. This early revival was disliked by civil authorities, the press, and organized Pentecostal churches. In the 1960's, the charismatic revival gained better acceptance, and a few independent revivalists made the adjustment and found themselves at the front of the movement.

687 Harries, John. The Ghost Hunter's Road Book. Rev. ed. London: Muller, 1974 (previous ed., 1968). 176p. Illus. Maps Index £2.50 ISBN 0-584-10106-6

688 Harris, Bertha. Traveller in Eternity. London: Regency Press, 1975. 63p. £1.20 ISBN 0-7212-0388-4

This leading British medium describes her astral projection journeys to the other side, where she has been met and accompanied by spirits of those she had known when they were alive. With each journey, she became increasingly reluctant to return to her body. Harris also describes the most important events of her life.

689 Harris, Iverson L. Mme. Blavatsky Defended. San Diego, Calif.: Point Loma Publications, 1971. 174p. $3 pa.

This work attempts to refute supposed falsehoods and misrepresentations published by NBC, Truman Capote, Walter Winchell, the John Birch Society, Time magazine, and others, concerning Blavatsky.

690 Harrison, Michael. The Roots of Witchcraft. London: Muller, 1973 (also, New York: Citadel, 1975; also, London: Tandem, 1975). 278p. Illus. Bibliog. Index £4.50 ISBN 0-584-10232-1

The author's theory is that the most ancient religion in the world was the cult of fertility--the practice of sympathetic magic. This cult was driven underground by Christianity, which has used some of the fertility symbolism (such as the vine). The cult was kept alive by witch covens, which sacrificed a divine victim every seven years. William the Conqueror invaded England to strengthen the cult. Later kings backed it, as well as Joan of Arc, Gilles de Rais, and Thomas à Becket. One of the author's claims is that Joan of Arc was a witch, and met a ritual death at Rouen, because that was a holy place of the old faith. The book is mostly theory and speculation, based on few hard facts.

691 Hart, Roger. Witchcraft. New York: Putnam, 1972 (orig.
* pub., London: Wayland Publishers, 1971). 128p. Illus. Bibliog. $4.95 LC 71-171587

This work primarily discusses witchcraft in Germany, France, Scotland, England, and Salem during the years 1484-1733. It consists of excerpts from trial records, memoirs, tracts, pamphlets, and religious treatises, plus narrative connecting it by Hart. There are over 50 illustrations from woodcuts, prints and drawings. The book is suitable for juveniles, grade 6 and up. It is a good basic documentary collection.

692 Hartford, Huntington. You Are What You Write. London: Owen, 1975 (orig. pub., New York: Macmillan, 1973). xix, 380p. Illus. Facsims. Bibliog. Index £5.25 ISBN 0-7206-0044-8

693 Hartmann, Franz. Magic: Black and White; or, The Science of Finite and Infinite Life, Containing Practical Hints for Students of Occultism. 5th ed. Hollywood, Calif.: Newcastle Pub. Co., 1971. 298p. Illus. Bibliog. $3.45 pa. ISBN 0-87877-003-8

694 Haskins, James, 1941- . Witchcraft, Mysticism, and Magic in the Black World. Garden City, N.Y.: Doubleday, 1974. 156p. Map Bibliog. Index $4.50 LC 73-11708 ISBN 0-385-02878-4
*

This very interesting book is summarized by the author's statement that "the most noticeable aspect of black life throughout the New World is the great importance of the supernatural" (some may strongly dislike that statement). Topics discussed include roots in West Africa, the era of slavery, the black world today, three legendary figures (Marie Laveau, a New Orleans voodoo queen; High John the Conquerer; and Tituba of Salem Village), and customs in South America and the Caribbean. Frequently discussed throughout the book is voodoo. The author discusses why magic flourished under slavery and oppression. He mentions that Protestantism offers African religions a more flexible theology. Haskins says blacks have not joined the occult wave of today because they have always followed witchcraft and magic. This good book could have been an excellent one with more research and deeper analysis.

695 Hawken, Paul. The Magic of Findhorn. New York: Harper and Row, 1975 (also, London: Souvenir Press, 1975). 224p. Illus. $8.95 LC 74-15831 ISBN 0-06-011787-7
***

This work is a major new contribution to occult literature. Findhorn Garden/Community has become a major and controversial topic in occult circles. Inhabitants there have converted barren soil into a lush garden where 40-pound cabbages and 60-pound broccoli grow (though not when Hawken was there). The leaders, Peter and Eileen Caddy, are helped by "devas" and the nature spirits headed by Pan, who communicate instructions to them. Also, the Caddys have been told by the guides of a time when Findhorn will be a city of light on a lost planet. Also interesting in the book is discussion of the love triangle between Peter, Eileen, and Peter's first wife, Sheena Govan. Author Hawken lived at Findhorn for a year, and has written the first study in major publishing circles. In several years, this book may be forgotten and undeserving of a readership. For now, though, it is an important work.

696 Hawley, Elizabeth, and Columbia Rossi. Bertie: The Life

After Death of H. G. Wells. London: New English Library, 1973. 283p. £2.50 ISBN 0-450-01629-3

The subject of this book is the famous writer, H. G. Wells. Supposedly he was to resume life in earth sometime in 1973, with a three-dimensionally reconstructed male body. His re-entry was supposed to dispell forever belief in the finality of death, and begin a new order where "dissonant sounds will be dispelled by the new frequency-harmonics of the atmosphere." Also, "inter-terrestrial" medicine will enable amputees to re-grow limbs. This is the kind of occult book that makes even fanatics cringe.

697 Hayes, Christine. Red Tree: Insight into Lost Continents Mu and Atlantis, as Revealed to Christine Hayes. San Antonio: Naylor, 1972. xviii, 176p. $6.95 LC 72-6829 ISBN 0-8111-0465-6

698 Hayes, James T., 1923- . Introduction to Natal Astrology. Secaucus, N.J.: University Books, 1974. iv, 238p. Illus. $7.95 LC 74-80252 ISBN 0-8216-0212-8

This book discusses casting a horoscope, step-by-step; erecting a chart; calculating the aspects; judging and interpreting the horoscope; delineation of a chart. With its clear explanations and diagrams, it could be used as a textbook.

699 Haynes, Renee, 1906- . Hidden Springs; An Enquiry into
* Extra-sensory Perception. Rev. ed. Boston: Little, Brown, 1973 (also, London: Hutchinson, 1972; orig. pub., London: Hollis and Carter, 1961). 264p. Illus. Bibliog. $7.95 LC 73-6691

This excellent work, first published in 1961, has been newly rewritten to reflect new thinking and scientific evidence in the field. It is a study of the psi-factor in all forms and various contexts (history, culture, biology, religion, psychology). Subjects covered include the following: hallucinations, divination, clairvoyance, spiritualism, magic, Christian miracles, telepathy, time displacements, poltergeists, levitation, faith healers, stigmatization, Mesmer, Cagliostro, and theories from Plutarch to those of Jung. The author is editor of the (British) Journal of the Society for Psychical Research and also of its Proceedings. She is a devout Catholic, and takes as her theme the close relationship between psi phenomena and the basic tenets of Catholicism and Christianity.

700 Heal, Jeanne. You and Your Handwriting. London: Pelham, 1973. 118p. Illus. Facsims. Index £2.50 ISBN 0-7207-0622-X

The author is a graphologist, and discusses how to judge character and personality, and how to choose careers. Many examples of handwriting are included.

701 Heaps, Willard Allison, 1908- . Birthstones and the Lore of
* Gemstones. London: Angus and Robertson, 1971 (orig. pub. as "Birthstones," New York: Meredith Press, 1969). 141p. Bibliog. Index £1.35 ISBN 0-207-95417-8

This work discusses 12 gems and their ancient lore and legends, superstitions, history, chemistry, rarity, and value. The author feels the 12 probably originated with the 12 tribes of Israel, later becoming associated with the zodiac signs, and added to the calendar year by the National Retail Jewelers Association in 1912. There are many anecdotes throughout the book, and historic tables are included.

702 ________. Psychic Phenomena. Nashville: T. Nelson, 1974.
* 160p. Bibliog. Index $5.95 LC 74-10266 ISBN 0-8407-6418-9

This basically juvenile survey discusses telepathy, clairvoyance, precognition, and psychokinesis. The author explains each and gives case histories. Later, he mentions frontiers of parapsychology, such as Kirlian photography, ESP in plants, psychic surgery, and mental healing. People covered in the work include Ted Serios, Rhine, Hurkos, Kreskin, and Edison. Appendixes give sources for materials, and addresses of organizations. The book is recommended for grade 6 and up.

703 Heather; as told to Hans Holzer. Heather: Confessions of a Witch. New York: Mason and Lipscomb, 1975. 226p. $8.95 LC 74-19447 ISBN 0-88405-096-3

Although this book has received numerous reviews, it seems improper to give it a *. There just is not enough of it that is remotely worthwhile. The work discusses how a young girl steadily moved from psychic abilities into witchcraft. At age 17, she got a pumpkin to jump off a vegetable stand and follow her. She used her skills to break up the engagement of a person she thought she loved. Then, she became initiated into a coven on Madison Avenue. In her role as high priestess, she cast the evil eye often and used her powers to seduce men to bed with her. She feels that witchcraft is an erotic religion. True witches will hate this book, for it never really discusses the religion or philosophy of witchcraft. Holzer has written nearly 40 books on the occult (see, e.g., entries 737-762) and teaches parapsychology at the New York Institute of Technology. He has his own radio program on WMCA in New York. One would think by now he had learned to write a book. Sadly, the reader must still await Holzer's first real book on the occult.

704 Helio-Arcanophus. Life Outside the Physical Body; Colour and Reincarnation: The Teachings and Lectures of Helio-Arcanophus, Founder of the Atlanteans. Cheltenham, England: Atlanteans Association, 1975. 55p. Bibliog. £0.60 pa. ISBN 0-900112-07-7

705 Heriot, John. Teaching Yourself White Magic, and How to Try It Out. South Brunswick: A. S. Barnes, 1973 (also, Newton Abbot, England: David and Charles, 1973). 122p. Illus. Bibliog. $5.95 LC 72-9070 ISBN 0-498-01270-0

706 Heron, Laurence Tunstall. ESP in the Bible. Garden City,
*** N. Y.: Doubleday, 1974. 212p. Bibliog. $5.95 LC 73-14050

This work is a major new contribution to occult literature. The author believes all men possess psychic abilities. The virtues of any faith are determined by how well its prophets and followers interpret these abilities. The work discusses over 100 Bible and religion-related incidents. Chapters discuss ESP, dreams, spirit communication, prophecy, visions, and trances. The book mentions Moses and the burning bush, Joseph and his dream, Paul on the road to Damascus, and the Pentecost. Non-biblical people discussed include Joan of Arc, Martin Luther, Joseph Smith, Pascal, Mohammed, Handel, Harriet Tubman, and Descartes. Heron states that because of the sinful nature shown by many of the people who manifested various phenomena, one can tell that telepathic sensitivity, not saintliness, was the necessary quality. The author also explains the parapsychological significances of certain Bible terms by tracing them back to their original languages.

707 Hervey, Michael. UFO's Over the Southern Hemisphere. London: Hale, 1975. 250p. Illus. Plates Index £3.50 ISBN 0-7091-4724-4

708 Heuffer, Oliver Madox, 1877-1931. The Book of Witches.
* Totowa, N. J.: Rowman and Littlefield, 1973 (also, Wakefield, England: EP Publishing, 1973; orig. pub., London: Eveleigh Nash, 1908). xi, 335p. Bibliog. $11.50 LC 73-2857

This work traces the descent of the witch from earliest times to about 1900. Topics covered include the following: witches in Greece and Rome; persecutions of the 16th and 17th centuries in Europe and New England; the medieval witch as pictured by her contemporaries; trials; general principles; the witch in fiction; witches of today; representative English witches (Mother Shipton, also Old Mother Redcap of Kentish Town and Camden Town in North London). In the excellent introduction, the author theorizes that we cannot do without the witch or magician, because they keep science from making man insignificant.

709 Heywood, Rosalind. Beyond the Reach of Sense: An Inquiry
* into Extra-sensory Perception. Introduction by J. B. Rhine. New York: Dutton 1974 (also, London: Pan Books, 1971, as 2nd ed. of "Sixth Sense"; orig. pub. as "Sixth Sense," London: Chatto and Windus, 1959). 252p. Illus. Includes bibliog. refs. $3.45 pa.

Much of this excellent work discusses survival of death as

evidenced by mediums and their communications. Topics discussed include psi, the founding of the Society for Psychical Research, Mrs. Piper, cross correspondences, the Willet scripts, Patience Worth, Mr. Leonard, qualitative experiments on psi, and quantitative experiments of psi. The appendix gives explanations and hypotheses as formulated by physical scientists (G. N. M. Tyrrell and Whately Carington), a biologist (Sir Alister Hardy), psychologists (Sigmund Freud and C. J. Jung, Gardner Murphy, R. H. Thouless), and philosophers (C. D. Broad and H. H. Price). Appendix 2 is an update of the book written by the author in 1971. Most of the book centers around work done at the Society for Psychical Research in London.

710 Hibbert-Ware, Samuel, 1782-1848. Sketches of the Philosophy of Apparitions; or, An Attempt to Trace Such Illusions to Their Physical Causes. New York: Arno Press, 1975. (orig. pub., Edinburgh: Oliver and Boyd, 1824). (Perspectives in Psychical Research) $26 LC 75-7387 ISBN 0-405-07035-7

The author was a doctor and a Fellow of the Royal Society of England. The work studies old and contemporary ideas on apparitions. He discusses the relationship of negative emotional events with apparitions, and also the role prior expectations play. He theorizes that apparitions represent recollected images or ideas that are rendered more vivid than usual impressions.

711 Higgins, Terence. The Living Zodiac. London: Marshall Cavendish, 1974 (also, New York: Black Watch, 1974). 128p. Illus. (some color) Facsims. (some color) (Golden Hands Book) £1.95 ISBN 0-85685-080-2

After a brief introduction to astrology, this well-illustrated book discusses each sun sign, giving for each the advantages and disadvantages of the group, health difficulties, physical appearance, occupation, ideal for success, and compatible signs. Each sign is introduced by original double-page color illustrations by Peter Jones and Trevor Goring. These are very interesting interpretations. The last section, "Practical Astrology," has an attractive table of aspects (conjunctions, trine).

712 Hill, Douglas Arthur, 1935- . History of Ghosts, Vampires, and Werewolves. New York: Harper and Row, 1973 (orig. pub. as "Return from the Dead," London, 1970). 119p. Illus. Photos (Man, Myth and Magic Original) $1.25 pa.

This is a good general introduction to ghosts. The writing is in summary form (few quotes), and the book is short. There are chapters on walking corpses, vampires, poltergeists, spiritualism, and inhuman phantoms (ghost lights, ghost ships, horses, dogs). The author's theme is that man has imposed an unbelievable variety of forms on those beings he believes to have risen from the dead.

713 Hill, Raymond Putnam. My Family of Souls; The Story of a Journey Through Time. Jericho, N. Y.: Exposition Press, 1974. 145p. $6 ISBN 0-682-47900-4

714 Hintze, Naomi A., and J. Gaither Pratt. The Psychic Realm: What Can You Believe? New York: Random House, 1975. 269p. Bibliog. Index $8.95 LC 75-10285 ISBN 0-394-49538-1
***

This work is a major new contribution to occult literature. Its value is not in presenting new material, but in packaging it in a new, interesting manner. In the first part of each chapter, Gothic novelist Hintze discusses one aspect of parapsychology. Parapsychologist Pratt then discusses the same topic from a scientific approach. Topics discussed are ESP, astral projection, psi in animals, possession, precognition, altered states of consciousness, psychic surgery, faith healing, ghosts, mediums, reincarnation, resurrection, and dreams. Most of the cases were chosen because they are recent and not previously discussed in books (although they may have appeared in occult periodicals).

715 Hippisley Coxe, Antony Dacres. Haunted Britain: A Guide to Supernatural Sites Frequented by Ghosts, Witches, Poltergeists and Other Mysterious Beings. Photos. by Robert Estall. London: Pan Books, 1975 (also, McGraw, 1973; orig. pub., London: Hutchinson, 1973). 201p. Illus. (some color) Plates Maps Bibliog. Index £1.50 pa. ISBN 0-330-24328-4
***

This work is a major new contribution to occult literature. It is probably the most complete collection available of ghostly phenomena by geographical location for Great Britain. The book takes England, Scotland, Wales and the Isle of Man and arranges a series of tours county-by-county. Each of the more than 1,000 sites discussed is identified by from one to seven symbols that tell the phenomena for which it is noted: apparitions, healing, witchcraft, mythical beings, strange customs, legends, or buried treasure. There are detailed maps and excellent photographs. The authors (husband and wife) traveled over 12,000 miles inspecting and selecting these sites, and the book includes their personal experiences and observations.

716 Hisey, Lehmann. Keys to Inner Space; An Open-ended Guide to Occultism, Metaphysics and the Transcendental. New York: Julian Press, 1974. xi, 250p. Illus. Bibliog. $7.95 LC 73-88235

The first part of the book discusses self hypnosis, Tarot symbology, rhythmic dreaming, color and sound, astrology, Tao and acupuncture, Gurdjieff, Zen, LSD-25, Chakras and the Seven Seals, and spirit beings. The entire second half of the book (125 pages) discusses the mediumship of the late Mark Probert and his spirit guide, E Yada di Shi'ite, who supposedly lived 500,000 years ago. Some may feel this last section detracts from the work; others may find it intriguing.

717 Hitchcock, Helyn. Helping Yourself with Numerology. West Nyack, N.Y.: Parker Pub. Co., 1972 (also, London: Wolfe, 1973). 238p. Illus. $6.95 LC 72-172406 ISBN 0-13-386771-4

The author is an Astarian and Theosophist, and has studied numerology for over 30 years. The work is an easy-to-use guide to numerology that enables one to reveal the past, study the present, and divine the future. Also, the work includes "numeroscopes" of famous people. The book's aim is to help one discover his or her true personality, goals, and hidden talents.

718 Hobana, Ian, and Julien Weverbergh. UFO's from Behind
* the Iron Curtain. London: Corgi, 1975 (also, New York: Bantam Books, 1975; orig. pub., London: Souvenir Press, 1974). ix, 308p. Illus. Facsims. Maps Bibliog. £0.65 pa. ISBN 0-552-10023-4

This well-done work discusses UFO events in Eastern Europe. Chapters include the following discussions: Tungui Mirale--Russia, 1908 (explosion); Russia UFO studiers; Robozero (1663) and Karelia (1961); Poland; Czechoslovakia; Hungary; Akademski Astronomsko Astronautiki Klub (AAAK); Rumania. The second part of the book contains 100 pages of documentation on these and other UFO happenings.

719 Hodgson, Joan. Angels and Indians. Illus. by Peter Ripper. Liss, England: White Eagle Pub. Trust, 1974. 48p. Illus. (chiefly color) £1.50 ISBN 0-85487-033-4

This juvenile book discusses the following: the Yorkshire girls who photographed fairies; closeness of North American Indians to the spirit world and natural healing; Indians working today as spirit guides; mediums; White Eagle, guide to the author's mother (Grace Cooke); guardian angels; dreams. The work is recommended for grades 4-8.

720 _______. Hullo Sun!: First Steps to Spiritual Understanding. Liss, England: White Eagle Pub. Trust, 1972. 32p. Illus. (in color) £0.75 pa. ISBN 0-85487-019-9

721 _______. Wisdom in the Stars. 3rd rev. ed. Liss, England: White Eagle Pub. Trust, 1973. (Previous ed., 1959). 124p. £0.75 pa.

722 Hodson, Geoffrey. The Brotherhood of Angels and of Men. Foreword by Annie Besant. London: Theosophical Pub. House, 1973 (orig. pub., 1927). xii, 56p. Illus. £1.50 ISBN 0-7229-5012-8

723 _______. The Hidden Wisdom of the Bible, vol. 3. Wheaton, Ill.: Theosophical Pub. House, 1974. 345p. (Quest Book) $2.75 pa.

This famous Theosophist discusses symbols and allegories in the Book of Genesis.

724 ______. The Miracle of Birth: A Clairvoyant Study of Prenatal Life. London: Theosophical Publishing House, 1972 (orig. pub., 1929). 64p. £0.50 pa. ISBN 0-7229-5022-5

725 Hoeller, Stephan A. The Royal Road: A Manual of Kabalistic
* Meditations on the Tarot. Wheaton, Ill., London: Theosophical Publishing House, 1975. xxi, 119p. Illus. (Quest Book) $2.95 pa. LC 75-4244 ISBN 0-8356-0465-9

Hoeller has composed an interesting approach to the Tarot. The introduction links Tarot with the Kabalah, and Hoeller states, "The Kabalah is not only for the learned and the pious; it is for all." The basic part of the book, titled "Road and the Journey," discusses: preparing for the journey (concentration, meditation); map for the traveler (Kabalah-Tarot combination largely through the Hebrew alphabet and Tree of Life); ten way stations (the Sephiroth of the Tree--Kingdom, Foundation, Glory, Victory, Beauty, Justice, Mercy, Understanding, Wisdom, Crown); the 22 highways; the fool's pilgrimage; the signposts (brief discussion of each card in the major arcana, giving also Kabalah path, motto taken from literature, and a paragraph for meditation). For those that are tired of the usual Tarot book which lacks much thought, Hoeller's work is packed with deep philosophical insight.

726 Holder, Robert. Handwriting Talk: How Handwriting Reveals What People Are Really Like, and How You Can Use Handwriting Analysis as a Way to Personal Power and Profit. Rockville Centre, N.Y.: Farnsworth Pub. Co., 1974. vii, 293p. Illus. $8.95 LC 74-84336 ISBN 0-87863-053-8

727 ______. Sex, Health and Your Handwriting. New York: Award, 1971. 185p. Illus. $1.25 pa.

728 Hole, Donald. Spiritualism. London: Church Literature Association, 1973 (orig. pub., London: Catholic Literature Association, 1932). 16p. Illus. £0.10 pa. ISBN 0-85191-035-1

729 Holiday, Frederick William. The Dragon and the Disc; An
*** Investigation into the Totally Fantastic. New York: Norton, 1973 (also, London: Sidwick and Jackson, 1973; also, London: Futura, 1974). 247p. Illus. Bibliog. Index $7.95 LC 73-298 ISBN 0-393-06336-4

This work is a major new contribution to occult literature. The author's earlier work was The Great Orm of Loch Ness (entry 730), and his continuing research led to the belief that other such creatures, and also flying saucers, existed in early times as well as today. The author states that the imagery found over and over in early sites, prehistoric religious myths, and Bronz Age art show that these two phenomena were present at an early age, from China to the British Isles. The dragon (symbol of evil) and the disc (symbol of good) have modern-age counterparts in today's monster and UFO reports. The book is based on research into documents, history, carvings and drawings, as well as numerous interviews with present-day witnesses of UFO and monster phenomena. Holiday offers some very creative thoughts on the occult.

730 ________. The Great Orm of Loch Ness: A Practical Inquiry into the Nature and Habits of Water-monsters. London: Faber & Faber, 1971 (orig. pub., New York: Norton, 1969). xv, 223p. Illus. Plates Maps Bibliog. Index £0.80 pa. ISBN 0-571-09703-0
*

"Great Orm" is the traditional Scandinavian name for sea serpent. The author discusses recent expeditions of photographers, observers, and sonar experts--how they were organized and what they found. Some claim the monster is a mollusc, while others believe it to be a worm, giant salmon, or giant seal. The author makes no conclusions, but mentions the many sightings over the years and interviews witnesses. He mentions the discovery in the United States of a unique fossil which closely resembles photos and descriptions of the Loch Ness monster.

731 Hollender, E. A. Humanity at the Crossroads. New York: Philosophical Library, 1972. xi, 420p. Illus. Includes bibliog. refs. $10 LC 75-16942 ISBN 0-8022-2065-7

This work is a gathering of occult lore on Atlantis, Lemuria, karma, and spiritual life.

732 Holloway, Gilbert N. This Way Up: A Psychic Autobiography and Guide to Spiritual Development. Chicago: H. Regnery, 1975. x, 278p. $9.95 LC 74-26978 ISBN 0-8092-8290-9

This strongly pro-religion book warns of terrible years ahead--wars, floods, crime, earthquakes. The author is founder of the New Age of Truth Church in Florida, a graduate of Union Theological Seminary, former follower of the Rosicrucians, and has his own radio program, "Beyond ESP." The book is designed to strengthen individuals and protect them from destructive conditions, including negative occult influences. He is a strong believer in UFO's, and believes their inhabitants may save the best humans by transporting them off earth before the final end. He hints that members of his church may be the first selected. He mentions use of the "third eye" and auras, but warns of occult evils.

733 Holmes, Ronald. Witchcraft in British History. London: Muller, 1974. 272p. Illus. Plates Facsims. Map Bibliog. Index £5.50 ISBN 0-584-10335-2

734 Holroyd, Stuart. Magic, Words, and Numbers. Garden City, N.Y.: Doubleday, 1975. (New Library of the Supernatural, vol. 7) $7.95 LC 75-26142

735 Holt, Peggy. The Lovers' Astrology Cookbook. (Formerly, The Way to a Man's Heart Is Through His Capricorn.) Los Angeles: Price/Stern/Sloan Publishers, 1974. 79p. Illus. $2 LC 74-166373 ISBN 0-8431-0088-5

736 Holy Order of Mans. Jewels of the Wise. San Francisco: Holy Order of Mans, 1974. 197p. Illus. $3.50 pa. LC 75-309845

737 Holzer, Hans W., 1920- . Alchemist: The Secret Magical Life of Rudolf von Habsburg. New York: Stein and Day, 1974. 192p. Bibliog. Index $7.95 LC 74-78542 ISBN 0-8128-1734-6

This is a biography of Rudolf II, Holy Roman Emperor in the 16th century, and his interest in alchemy and black magic. The work is partially based on a manuscript Holzer found in a tombstone in Vienna. The writing reads like a diary, and appears not very well researched.

738 _______. The Aquarian Age; Is There Intelligent Life on Earth? Indianapolis: Bobbs-Merrill, 1971. xii, 131p. Illus. $5 LC 73-163018

The author puts himself in the place of visitors from another planet coming here in a new age, and what they will find. Man will have discovered himself and realized his potential intellectually and spiritually, and will have realized interplanetary travel by individuals. There will be great changes in vocabulary, art, and clothing. Universal peace will have arrived.

739 _______. Astrology: What It Can Do for You? Chicago: H. Regnery Co., 1975. x, 160p. $10 LC 75-13224 ISBN 0-8092-9061-8

This work discusses origins, basis, systems, cosmic approach to astrology, mathematical approach to astrology, commercial astrologers, esoteric method, blessings and dangers.

740 _______. Beyond Medicine: The Facts about Unorthodox
* and Psychic Healing. Chicago: H. Regnery Co., 1973 (also, New York: Ballantine Books, 1974; also, London: Abelard-Schuman, 1974). 209p. Index $6.95 LC 73-6463 ISBN 0-8092-9059-6

Chapters discuss the following: the nature of man, what healing is, medicine men and unorthodox healers, psychic healers, religious healing, cure for cancer, nature of the body's healing of itself, hypnosis as a form of therapy, healing and the occult sciences, and how to avoid fakers and quacks. This work, unlike most of Holzer's, is a real attempt to write a book. Here, the author even occasionally abandons his case histories and quotes to think and discuss! Also, the book has very good structure. It is a bit superficial, but Holzer seems finally on the right track.

741 _______. Born Again: The Truth about Reincarnation. Folkestone, England: Bailey Bros. and Swinfen, 1975 (orig. pub., Garden City, N.Y.: Doubleday, 1970). ix, 249p. £3.75 ISBN 0-561-00217-7

Holzer investigated cases of letter-writers who had told him they felt they had lived before. He visited them, hypnotized them regressively, and had them describe their past lives in detail. All but one of them were women. They gave dates, locations, and names. One girl said she was a 16th-century noblewoman; another remembered several lives, one as an exiled Puritan in 17th-century Holland, and another in 19th-century India as the wife of a British officer. Most of the book consists of anecdotes tossed together, and long quoted conversations during interviews. Holzer feels that reincarnation occurs frequently in the world.

742 _______. Directory of the Occult. Chicago: Regnery Co.,
* 1974. 201p. $8.95 LC 74-6895 ISBN 0-8092-8377-8

This work, which has some good reference value, goes state-by-state on the following topics: scientific establishments dealing with the occult; metaphysical establishments (theosophy, Scientology); individual practitioners (mediums, readers, psychics, astrologers, and other purveyors of occult information); spontaneous phenomena (ghosts); witches and other pagans. Each entry says "recommended," "satisfactory," or "no comment." These "directory" chapters each begin with a 10-page general survey. Other chapters discuss the occult scene today, how to consult an occult practitioner, and how to be your own medium; an occult glossary is appended. Apparently the book draws on the "extensive" files of the New York Committee for the Investigation of Paranormal Occurrences. If so, one cannot think much of the files, for only about 200 persons and organizations are discussed. Method of choice seems to have been very random. Many of those discussed are people Holzer wrote about in other books, or someone he "bumped into" the other day. Information is often sketchy, and anecdotal instead of informative. The work does, however, provide a good deal of useful information. If Holzer had spent any time at all in composing the book, it might have been the definitive occult directory. Instead, it merits a "nice try."

743 _______. Ghost Hunter. Folkestone, England: Bailey Bros. and Swinfen, 1973 (also, New York: Ace Books, 1963; orig. pub., Indianapolis: Bobbs-Merrill, 1963). 160p. £1.70 ISBN 0-561-00170-7

This book contains short sections on over 20 case studies, which were investigated by Holzer through the help of medium Ethel Meyers. The author took notes or recordings of each sitting. The book is very loosely constructed, with cases chosen at random for their interest, and not necessarily their importance or authenticity. Cases include the Bank Street ghost; the Metuchen ghost; the Greenwich Village ghost; the Central Park West ghost; the Fifth Avenue ghost; the Riverside ghost; and a haunted chair.

744 ______. Ghosts That Walk in Washington. Illus. by Catherine Buxhoeveden [Mrs. Holzer]. Garden City, N.Y.: Doubleday, 1971. 232p. Illus. $5.95 LC 76-150900

To investigate these cases, Holzer used medium Ethel Johnson Meyers. He had her go to sites of hauntings, and taped her answers to questions while in trance. There are nine hauntings discussed, including those involving Woodrow Wilson's House, the Octagon House (Madison's home), Nixon, the Kennedys, Oswald, and Lincoln. The author says that the spirit world reflects the real one: "a hopelessly mixed up hodgepodge of truth, half-truths and wishful thinking."

745 ______. The Great British Ghost Hunt. Boston: G.K. Hall, 1975. (Large print ed.) $9.95 LC 75-17863 ISBN 0-8161-6307-3

The author investigates haunted homes, castles, towers, and ruins in England and Scotland, including London and Edinburgh. With the help of mediums, he "meets" Anne Boleyn, Catherine Howard, Mary Queen of Scots, and Katherine Parr. At Blanchland, near Newcastle, the medium he used reached ghosts of the 12th, 13th, and 18th centuries. Two other ghosts materialized there, and were questioned.

746 ______. The Habsburg Curse. Garden City, N.Y.: Doubleday, 1973. 147p. $5.95 LC 72-89948 ISBN 0-385-02953-5

The origin of the curse supposedly is seen in the name Habichtsburg, meaning "Hawks' Castle." Holzer took German psychic Arthur Orlop into the ancient Habsburg castle in the Aargau province of Switzerland. Near the castle, Orlop said the curse concerned a young girl and an illegitimate child. This 12th-century rape victim cursed a castle dweller friendly with the hawks that flew around the towers. This curse has come down into the 20th century. Holzer mentions Habsburgs from Guntram the Rich, A.D. 950 to Francis Joseph.

747 ______. Handbook of Parapsychology. Los Angeles: Nash Pub., 1972. 169p. $6.95 LC 72-81838 ISBN 0-8402-1217-8

The author discusses ESP testing, ghosts, apparitions, clairvoyance, reincarnation, déjà vu, witchcraft, satanism, and cults. He offers the work as a textbook, yet it lacks a bibliography and index. Also, some of the statements appear to be not fully researched.

748 ______. Hans Holzer's Haunted Houses: A Pictorial Register of the World's Most Interesting Ghost Houses. Illus. by

Catherine Buxhoeveden [Mrs. Holzer]. New York: Crown, 1971. 190p. Illus. $5.95 LC 74-168321

749 _______. Haunted Hollywood. Indianapolis: Bobbs-Merrill, 1974. xiv, 133p. Illus. $6.95 LC 73-11801 ISBN 0-672-51739-6

This book discusses among other ghosts those of Jean Harlow, Carole Lombard, Clifton Webb, and Gayle (topless dancer and mother of 8).

750 _______. Life after Death: The Challenge and the Evidence.
* London: Sidgwick and Jackson, 1971 (orig. pub., Indianapolis: Bobbs-Merrill, 1969). 175p. £1.50 ISBN 0-283-48430-6

This is a fairly good book from Holzer. He discusses ESP, ouija boards, mediums, dreams, poltergeists, hallucinatory awareness, all of which he sees as attempts of communication. Holzer feels only Spiritualism in modern times has approached a discussion of the dead with a degree of rationalism, although it sometimes uses a strange brand of evidence. The author says ghosts visit because they want one of three things: someone to know they are still alive; someone to help them with unfinished business on earth; desire to help love ones still living.

751 _______. The New Pagans. Garden City, N.Y.: Doubleday, 1972. xiii, 197p. $5.95 LC 71-173269

This book discusses among other things Alex Sanders, Psychedelic Venus Church in Berkeley, rituals.

752 _______. The Phantoms of Dixie. Indianapolis: Bobbs-Merrill, 1972. xii, 210p. Illus. $6 LC 71-188653

This book discusses among other things the many poltergeists of Texas who show themselves by using the suppressed kinetic energy of pubertal children and mentally-retarded adults.

753 _______. Possessed! Fawcett, 1973. $.95 pa.

This book is better than most of Holzer's books, but suffers from the same faults critics complain of in all his other material: sloppy writing, little thought, and no editing. In this book, the table of contents is excellent, but chapters themselves are mostly short case histories loosely tossed together. Chapters include the following: "Possession and Obsession"; "Possession Is a Two-way Street"; "How Dead Work through the Living"; "Lust for Power from the Dead (Need of the Dead to Express Themselves Further)"; "Sexual Possession (Needs of Dead Artists to Find Living Patrons)"; "Devilish Possession (Revenge, Hatred, Crimes of Evil)."

754 _______. The Prophets Speak; What the Leading Psychics Say about the World of Tomorrow. Indianapolis: Bobbs-Merrill, 1971. xvii, 201p. $5.95 LC 71-142485

This book discusses prophecies of Dr. N., a San Francisco physician mentioned in an earlier Holzer book. Others covered are mostly unheard-of prophets. Most see a holocaust in the near future, and most see a huge natural catastrophe that will damage our coasts soon.

755 _______. The Psychic World of Bishop Pike. New York: Pyramid, 1971 (c1970). 223p. $1.25 pa.

Holzer arranged to make a film on incidents of Pike's communication with his dead son. He held several interviews with Pike, and learned of several strange experiences that Pike had had earlier in life in Poughkeepsie and New York City. After Pike's death, Holzer got little help from Mrs. Pike in continuing this study of her husband. Therefore, Holzer went to several mediums, and claims he communicated with an apparition that closely resembled Pike, especially in speech. The message the apparition wished to convey is that somebody, or even several people, killed Pike.

756 _______. Psycho-ecstasy (How to Awaken the Secret Powers of Your Inner Self). New York: Lancer, 1973 (c1971). 171p. $1.25 pa.

757 _______. Reincarnation Primer: Patterns of Destiny. New York: Harper and Row, 1975 (orig. pub. as "Patterns of Destiny," Los Angeles: Nash Pub., 1974). xi, 163p. $1.75 pa. ISBN 0-06-465042-1

This book discusses karma, reincarnation, déjà vu, and hypnotic regressions. The first half is very case-study oriented. The second part gives Holzer's philosophy on reincarnation.

758 _______. The Truth about ESP; What It Is, How It Works, and How You Develop It. Garden City, N.Y.: Doubleday, 1974 (also, Folkestone, England: Bailey Bros. and Swinfen, 1974). xi, 176p. $5.95 LC 73-11709 ISBN 0-385-05253-7

This book discusses ESP, mediums, astral projection, and spontaneous phenomena. Holzer fails to mention many major researchers in the field. Yet, he discusses these minor parapsychologists: Robert Jeffries of the University of Bridgeport; Frank Anderson of Anderson Laboratories, Brookline, Mass., Harry E. Stockman of Sercolab, Arlington, Mass., and R.K. Golka of Lanston Monotype Co., Philadelphia.

759 _______. The Truth about Witchcraft. London: Jarrolds Publishers, 1971 (also, London: Arrow Books, 1971; orig. pub., New York: Doubleday, 1969). 320p. £2 ISBN 0-09-105600-4

This book discusses names involved with contemporary witchcraft, and covers the purpose of witchcraft, how it is done, and

U.S. and British covens. Also discussed are initiation ceremonies, curses, Cincinnati coven, British Druids, a goat-god worshipper, Eastern seaboard, and San Francisco.

760 ______. Victorian Ghosts. Folkestone, England: Bailey Bros. and Swinfen, 1973 (orig. pub. in U.S., 1970). ix, 182p. £1.70 ISBN 0-561-00169-3

This book is a collection of 19 tales, anecdotes, and cases. All but one of the stories concerns America.

761 ______. A Window to the Past: Exploring History through ESP. Illus. by Catherine Buxhoeveden [Mrs. Holzer]. Garden City, N.Y.: Doubleday, 1971 (c1969). 254p. Illus. $5.95

Holzer investigates eight places with a medium in order to pick up historical information. He visits a tavern south of Washington, D.C., and picks up perhaps a plan to assassinate Lincoln--a conversation of John Wilkes Booth's brother and a tavern owner, "heard" by the medium. In a London nightclub, Nell Gwyn (mistress of Charles I) speaks through the medium. At Mayerling, the medium picks up clues to the deaths of Crown Prince Rudolph of Austria and Marie Vetsera. At a cafe in Greenwich Village, Aaron Burr, with the aid of Sybil Leek as medium, nearly admits his identity.

762 ______. Witchcraft Report. New York: Ace Books, 1973. $1.25 pa.

This book discusses the following: why people want to be witches; witches of the East, North, South, Midwest, and West; occult shops; wars between witches; how to become one; spells and incantations.

763 Hone, Margaret Ethelwyn. A Modern Text-book of Astrology. Rev. ed. London: L.N. Fowler, 1972 (previous ed., 1968). 320p. Illus. Index £2.25 ISBN 0-85243-032-9

764 Hook, Diana Farington. The I Ching and Mankind. London: Routledge and Kegan Paul, 1975. 160p. Illus. Bibliog. Index $10.95 ISBN 0-7100-8058-1

This book discusses the implications of symbolism in the I Ching as they relate to the works of Confucius, Jung and others. The many diagrams are discussed not just concerning their layouts, but concerning their philosophical importance.

765 ______. The I Ching and You. London: Routledge and Kegan Paul, 1973. 149p. Illus. Bibliog. $7.50 LC 73-168455

The author presents the I Ching more as a psychological tool than as a divining device, and totally ignores occult aspects.

She teaches the practical use of the I Ching with very little theory. However, she does compare Chinese philosophy and Christian doctrine a few times.

766 Hope, Patience. Life's Purpose; and, Life Continuous! Albert Tells His Story. London: Spiritualist Press, 1971 ("Life's Purpose" orig. pub., Winnipeg, 1951; "Life Continuous" orig. pub., Winnipeg, 1956). 90, 88p. Illus. £0.75 pa. ISBN 0-85437-002-1

767 Hope-Simpson, Jacynth. Who Knows?: Twelve Unsolved Mysteries. London: Heinemann, 1974. 132p. Bibliog. £2.25 ISBN 0-434-94317-7

768 Horoscope Annual. Ed. by Edward A. Wagner. London: Atlas Pub. Co. 64p. Illus. £0.30

769 Horwitz, Elinor Lander. The Soothsayer's Handbook--a Guide to Bad Signs and Good Vibrations. Philadelphia: Lippincott, 1972. 158p. Illus. $4.82 LC 76-172143 ISBN 0-397-31215-6

This juvenile book discusses reading character and telling fortunes, using ESP, astrology, numerology, palmistry, playing cards, tea leaves, dice, dominoes, and crystal balls. The writing style is very short and direct. The work is recommended for grades 6-9.

770 Houdini, Harry, 1874-1926. Magician Among the Spirits.
* New York: Arno Press, 1972 (orig. pub., New York: Harper and Row, 1924). xix, 294p. Illus. $15 LC 71-140606 ISBN 0-405-02801-6

This classic work is an attempt by Houdini to expose the deception and fraud he felt made up all of spiritualism. Chapters discuss the following: the founders of modern spiritualism, the Davenport brothers, Daniel Dunglas Home, Palladino, Ann O'Delia Diss Debar, Dr. Slade and the spirit slates, slate writing, spirit photography, Sir Arthur Conan Doyle, ectoplasm, investigations, how mediums obtain information, what you must believe to be a spiritualist, and magicians as detectors of fraud. Houdini says he has accumulated one of the largest libraries in the world on psychic phenomena and spiritualism. Yet, "nothing I ever read concerning the so-called Spiritualistic phenomena has impressed me as being genuine." What really seals the argument for Houdini is that, of the dozen death compacts he made with friends (they would try to contact him if they ever died), not one of these people has ever come back and appeared to him. He feels, "It is not for us to prove that the mediums are dishonest, it is for them to prove that they are honest."

771 Howard, Michael. Candle Burning: Its Occult Significance.
* Wellingborough, England: Aquarian Press, 1975. 64p. (Paths to Inner Power) £0.45 pa. ISBN 0-85030-122-X

This book is another volume in a fine series, although not quite as good as others in the set. The author discusses the nature of candle burning, astral colors, spells for gain, love and happiness; candles for sickness and death, candles for protection, opening the psyche, angels and candle magic, the mystical novena. The very short appendixes give the angelic hierarchy and zodiacal colors.

772 Howe, Ellic. Astrology and Psychological Warfare During World War II. Rev. and condensed ed. London: Rider, 1972 (previous ed. pub. as "Urania's Children," London: Kimber, 1967). 208p. Illus. Facsims. Index £1.80 pa. ISBN 0-09-111561-2

773 ________. Magicians of the Golden Dawn. London: Routledge and Kegan Paul, 1972. 306p.

This book is a documentary history of the "Golden Dawn" by a researcher in underground movements. He theorizes that after Blavatsky founded the Theosophical Society in 1875, Dr. William Wynn Westcott, a Mason, liked her approach, and forged documents giving him authority from secret leaders to form the Order. Mathers helped Westcott in establishing the Golden Dawn. Howe claims that Mathers copied the Order's teachings from works in the British Museum.

774 Howe, Quincy, Jr. Reincarnation for the Christian. Philadelphia: Westminster Press, 1974. 112p. Bibliog. essay $4.95 LC 73-19758 ISBN 0-664-20996-3

This book discusses the compatibility of Christian and Hindu thoughts on reincarnation. The author believes that reincarnation can be readily brought into harmony with the main body of Christian thought. Howe finds mention of the soul's evolution through many lives to perfection in the Bhagavad-Gita, Plato, and Origen (declared heretical in A.D. 553). The opposite view of the Christian conception of one life is presented using St. Augustine's writings. The author then studies scripture, and finds references to reincarnation. Arguments for reincarnation include the continuity of special aptitudes and traits shown by young children, and the obvious justice in the laws of karma.

775 Howes, Michael. Amulets. London: Hale, 1975. 190p. Illus. Plates Index £3.25 ISBN 0-7091-4897-6

This book covers Egyptian, Sumerian, Persian, Hebrew, Gnostic, Greek, Roman, African, Indian, Chinese, and American amulets, and emphasizes ones from the early Middle East. The author mentions supernatural claims for the amulets. There is a list of birth and planetary stones.

776 Howey, Mary Oldfield. Cults of the Dog. Rochford, England: Daniel, 1972. 570p. Illus. Bibliog. (Limited ed. of 250

numbered copies) £5.25 ISBN 0-85207-004-7

777 Hoy, David. The Meaning of Tarot. Nashville/London:
* Aurora Publishers, 1971. 168p. Illus. $4.95 LC 79-128449 ISBN 0-87695-073-X

This introductory book discusses: origin of the Tarot; preliminary to the divinatory reading (when, where, who should be present, spread); methods of divination (different types of spreads, such as pyramid, three sevens, spread of 35, spread of 36, horseshoe spread, personal horoscope spread, yes or no spread, Tree of Life, Celtic, Victory Cross); major arcana (two pages for each card); minor arcana. For each card, divinatory meaning upright and reversed is given. The work gives a very simple, clear explanation of the Tarot, with very little philosophical discussion. Paper quality and type face are unusually excellent.

778 Hoyt, Olga. Demons, Devils, and Djinn. New York: Abe-
* lard-Schuman, 1974. 160p. Illus. Bibliog. $5.95 LC 73-6190 ISBN 0-200-00110-8

In this juvenile book, demons are grouped by area and era. They come mostly from the Near East and Orient, but some U.S. and European ones are also mentioned. There are anecdotes, incantations from grimoires, and a summary of the case on which the film The Exorcist was based. The book is recommended for grades 6-8.

779 Hubbard, La Fayette Ronald, 1911- . Dianetics Today. Il-
* lus. by Andre Clavel. Los Angeles: Church of Scientology of California Publications Organization, 1975. ix, 1057p. Illus. Bibliog. Index $18 LC 75-314506 ISBN 0-88404-036-4

This work merits a * not on its intrinsic worth, which may be zero, but on the book's value as a guide to Scientology. Book 1, on studying Dianetics, gives basic definitions. Book 2 covers communication, the E-Meter (a sort of biofeedback device), and dianetic auditing. Part 3 discusses the R3R procedure, drugs, and health. The entire book is really a laboratory manual workbook, mostly on the testing machine used and how to employ it. The personal cases section is 300 pages long, filled with examples of people's experiences with Scientology study courses. At the end of the book is a glossary. This book is a frightening example of the occult at its worst, and shows someone starting a cult based on thousands of meaningless words and concepts, then quoting the words and concepts to support it.

780 ______. Have You Lived Before This Life? American Saint Hill Organization, 1973. $5

This book is a study of past lives remembered through Dianetic engrams. Over 40 people recall their past lives. Hubbard feels that the hypnotism method does not lead to honesty in the person being questioned. The engrams, he feels, keep the subject alert and free from suggestion.

781 ________. Mission into Time. Los Angeles: American Saint Hill Organization, 1973. ix, 106p. Illus. (Scientology Book) $6 LC 74-151712 ISBN 0-88404-023-2

782 Huebner, Louise. Witchcraft for All. London: Tandem, 1971 (also pub. as "Power Through Witchcraft," London: Alan Wingate, 1970; orig. pub., Los Angeles: Nash Publishing, 1969). £0.25 ISBN 0-426-05995-6

783 Huggett, Richard. The Supernatural on Stage: Ghosts and
* Superstitions of the Theatre. New York: Taplinger Pub. Co., 1975. 215p. Illus. $8.95 LC 73-16966 ISBN 0-8008-7495-1

This interesting work discusses superstitions common in the theatre, opera, ballet, cinema, and has a section on theater ghosts. The final chapter is on the curse of Macbeth, and gives the over 350-year history of Macbeth. Mishaps have occurred in the production of this work possibly because Shakespeare used a true witches' spell in the play. The author, an actor himself, includes a catalog of good-luck talismans.

784 Hughes, Irene F. ESPecially Irene; A Guide to Psychic Awareness. Blauvelt, N.Y.: Steiner Publications, 1972. ix, 150p. (Steinerbooks) $1.65 pa. LC 70-189997

This famous psychic tells of foreseeing the fire that killed three astronauts; the failures of Apollo 13; the loss of two atomic submarines. She says it may be the Communist influence which keeps the government from hearing her warnings. She tells how anyone can develop ESP, and reprints some of her fan letters. Hughes includes prayers, meditations, and predictions for the future. Also mentioned are her experiments in color testing while blindfolded, and thoughtography (covered camera's picking up psychic images).

785 Hughes, Jossie Lavell. As Above, So Below. New York: Philosophical Library, 1971. 263p. $7.95 LC 76-109169 ISBN 0-8022-2317-6

The author says she lives on two levels, astral and earthly. She says she knows many people living on the other plane, and their existence is similar to the lives they led on earth.

786 Hunt, Diana. You, Your Stars and Your Partner. New York: Pocket Books, 1971 (orig. pub., Taplinger, 1970). 230p. $.95 pa.

The author states she has written the book with women in

mind, but not only for women. Under each zodiac sign, she lists best and worst qualities, especially those relevant to attracting the opposite sex. The book also helps match each sign with possible mates.

787 Hurwood, Bernhardt Jackson. Ghosts, Ghouls and Other Horrors: 50 Scarifying True Stories of the Supernatural. Illus. by Carl Keighley. London: Target Books, 1974 (orig. pub., New York: Scholastic Book Services, 1971). 124p. Illus. (Target Mystery) £0.25 pa. ISBN 0-426-10321-1

788 ______. Passport to the Supernatural; An Occult Compen-
* dium from All Ages and Many Lands. New York: Taplinger, 1972. 319p. Bibliog. $7.50 LC 78-164019 ISBN 0-8008-6261-9

This is a collection of supposedly true tales from Asia, Africa, Europe, Australia, North and South America, taken mostly from literature of the biblical period. The author provides commentary, and traces origins of a particular belief while showing how it spread. Individual countries discussed include Greece, Rome, Japan, China, India.

789 ______. Strange Talents. New York: Ace Books, 1972 (reprint). $.95 pa.

790 Huson, Paul, comp. The Coffee Table Book of Witchcraft and Demonology. New York: Putnam, 1973. 224p. Illus. Bibliog. $12.50 LC 72-87634 ISBN 0-399-11086-0

This work reprints excerpts from Margaret Murray, Gerald Gardner, McGregor Mathers, and others, with comments by Huson and numerous illustrations.

791 ______. Devil's Picturebook; The Compleat Guide to Tarot Cards: Their Origins and Their Usage. New York: Putnam, 1971. 256p. Illus. Bibliog. $6.95 LC 77-157064

This book emphasizes the relationships between Tarot and mythology, and also discusses witchcraft and casting spells. There is no detailed discussion of occult symbolism in the Tarot. The main emphasis is instead on use as an aid in divination.

792 ______. How to Test and Develop Your ESP. Briarcliff
*** Manor, N.Y.: Stein and Day, 1975. 215p. $8.75

This work is a major new contribution to occult literature. It is a gathering of methods for testing that the author has used over the last 10 years. In the beginning, there is a good discussion of what we know about ESP. Then comes the how-to-do section, on dice, Zener card guessing, and picture-drawing. Next comes a section on evaluating the picture-drawing test, and eliciting and developing ESP. Other sections discuss tracing past life memories, out-of-the-body experiences, PK, precognition, telepathy, clairvoyance, hauntings, psychometry, reincarnation, and healing. The author mentions that personality and motivation can affect ESP performance. Appendixes give Jacobson's Progressive Relaxation Exercises, a list of technical journals available, a glossary, and a list of courses one can take at colleges.

793 ________. Mastering Herbalism. New York: Stein and Day,
*** 1974. 371p. $10 LC 73-90704 ISBN 0-8128-1663-3

This work is a major new contribution to occult literature. This work discusses the history of herbs, cooking, recipes (for wine, perfumes, incense, aromatic candles, cosmetics), tips on how to grow herbs, cures, and sources for herbs. The herbs may be used as flavorings, spices, health foods, beauty aids, aphrodisiacs, incense, elixirs, or in witchcraft rituals. The appendixes list nutrient properties of herbs, astrological affinities, weights and measures, and planting and harvesting by the moon. A glossary is included.

794 Hutin, Serge. The History of Alchemy. Trans. by Ramar Alferoff. Detroit: Tower, 1971 (c1962). $.75 pa.

795 Huxley, Aldous Leonard, 1894- . The Devils of Loudun. New York: Harper, 1971 (also, Harmondsworth, England: Penguin, 1971; orig. pub., London: Chatto and Windus, 1952). 374p. Illus. $1.50 pa. ISBN 0-06-080226-X

This work discusses events in the town of Loudun, France, in the 17th century, together with the author's commentary. A group of nuns possessed by devils falsely accused a priest of sorcery. He was tortured and executed under the Inquisition. Warner Brothers made a movie based on this called The Devils.

796 Hynek, Joseph Allen, 1910- . UFO Experience: A Scien-
*** tific Enquiry. London: Corgi, 1974 (also, London: Abelard-Schuman, 1972; orig. pub., Chicago: Regnery, 1972). 336p. Illus. Plates Index £0.50 pa.

This work is a major new contribution to occult literature. The author is director of the Lindheimer Astronomical Research Center, Northwestern University, and was consultant to Project Blue Book from 1947 to 1969. This work is basically a commentary and critique on the Condon Report, which Hynek feels failed in its methods and investigations. The author also tells about the Air Force's superficial investigations. Part 1 is titled, "Innocent in UFO Land"; Part 2, "Data and the Problem"; Part 3, "Where Do We Go from Here?" He presents 80 cases in six categories or types of reports. He feels there is hard evidence of sightings not explainable in traditional terms. He believes Condon ignored the evidence, and criticizes his scientific colleagues for being unscientific. He feels we need statistical studies and experts' work, along with a global system of data-gathering.

797 ________, and Jacques Vallee. The Edge of Reality; A Progress Report on Unidentified Flying Objects. Chicago: Regnery, 1975. 288p. Index $14.95 LC 75-13226 ISBN 0-8092-8209-7
***

This work is a major new contribution to occult literature. Hynek is professor of astronomy at Northwestern University, and former consultant to the Air Force on Project Blue Book. Vallee got his doctorate in computer sciences from Northwestern University and joined the computer lab at Stanford University. The format of the book is a transcript of a long discussion between these two men. Psychologist/psychic researcher Arthur C. Hastings moderates the talk. Also included are transcripts of interviews with UFO witnesses. The style makes for relaxed reading, although with this process, some points are not as well developed as they might be. As for cases discussed, one involves a person who shot and wounded a UFO occupant. The next day, three men called on him and warned him to tell no one of it. Hynek feels UFO's are a kind of psychic phenomenon. He thinks the study of UFO's gives us an opportunity to move toward a new reality and onto the edge of knowledge. Vallee does not believe that they are extraterrestrial. Topics discussed include Soviet UFO reports, patterns of UFO sightings, future contacts, photos, statistics, and a list of 16 astronaut UFO sightings. Actually, sightings are a minor part of the book. The authors criticize both UFO nuts and scientists who ignore evidence. The book is intended for those already familiar with the phenomena.

798 I Ching! Taoist Book of Days. Calendar-Diary 1975--Year of the Rabbit. Ed. by Khigh Alx Dhiegh. Foreword by José A. Arguelles. Calligraphy by Chen Hsi. Berkeley, Calif.: Shambhala, 1974. x, 211p. Illus. $4.95 pa. LC 74-10246 ISBN 0-87773-067-9

This work gives I Ching readings for each day and week of 1975 (the Year of the Rabbit).

799 I Ching: The Sacred Books of China, the Book of Changes. 2nd ed. Trans. by James Legge. Reprint: New York: Dover, 1972. (Also, various editions pub. New York: Bantam, 1969; New York: Citadel Press, 1974; Hackensack, N.J.: Wehman, 1971; New York: Causeway, 1973; New Hyde Park, N.Y.: University Books, 1964; orig. pub. in 2nd ed. by Clarendon Press, 1899). 448p. $3.50 pa.
*

This work is a classic in occult literature. Written before 1000 B.C., it is thought to contain the key to all Chinese philosophy. Sixty-four essays discuss characteristics and significance of each hexagram. Legges' many notes explain the work to Westerners. Other translations are designed for use in divination, which this is not.

800 Ikbal Ali Shah, Sirdar. Black and White Magic: Its Theory and Practice. London: Octagon Press, 1975 (orig. pub. as "Occultism: Its Theory and Practice," London: Rider, 1952). 231p. Illus. Index £3.95 ISBN 0-900860-31-6

801 Innis, Pauline B. Astronumerology; The New Way to Tell Your Future. Foreword by Jeane Dixon. New York: McKay, 1971. 181p. Illus. $5.95 LC 72-161672

The author mentions the "birth matrix," which she claims is part of a secret tradition going back to Druid times. With this tool, she can tell personality traits and areas of conflict. The author also discusses physiognomy, sun signs, and numbers derived from a person's name and birth date. She relates that Doris Day changed her name and became famous. Also, when Jackie switched from Bouvier to Kennedy, she gained "universal influence."

802 Institoris, Henricus, d. 1508. The Malleus Maleficarum of
* Heinrich Kramer and James Sprenger. Trans., introd., bibliog., and notes by Montague Summers. New York: Dover, 1971 (also, London: Arrow Books, 1971; this ed. orig. pub., London: Rodker, 1928). xiv, 277p. (Orig. pub., Speir, P. Drach, 1485) $3.95 pa. LC 70-176355 ISBN 0-486-22802-9

This work is a classic of occult literature. For three centuries, it was the professed manual for witch hunters (the Latin title translates as "Witches' Hammer"). Under a bull of Pope Innocent VIII, the two authors exposed the heresy of those who did not believe in witches, and explained the system of devils and witches. They were two Dominican friars who traveled throughout northern Germany, looking into Inquisition records and trials, talking to accused witches. This book became the authority on witchcraft, and was kept close by at every witch trial. It explained how pacts with the devil are made, remedies, formal rules for initiating an investigation and trial, how to bring charges, and just what constituted witchcraft.

803 International Order of Kabbalists Conference, 12th October, 1974. London: Metatron Publications, 1974. 50 leaves. £1 pa. ISBN 0-9504088-0-8

804 International Order of Kabbalists Conference, 18th October, 1975. London: Metatron Publications, 1975. 82 leaves. £1.50 pa. ISBN 0-9504088-1-6

805 Iremonger, Lucille. Ghosts of Versailles; Miss Moberly and Miss Jourdain and Their Adventure: A Critical Study. London: White Lion Publishers, 1975 (orig. pub., London: Faber & Faber, 1957). 313p. Illus. Plates Facsims. Plan Bibliog. Index £4.25 ISBN 0-85617-915-9

806 Isbell, Charles D. Corpus of the Aramaic Incantation Bowls.

Missoula, Mont. : Society of Biblical Literature, 1975 (dist. by Scholars Press; orig. presented as author's thesis, Brandeis University, 1973). xiv, 200p. Bibliog. Index (In English and Aramaic) (Dissertation Series, Society of Biblical Literature, no. 17) $4.20 LC 75-15949 ISBN 0-89130-010-4

807 Ivimy, John. The Sphinx and the Megaliths. New York: Harper, 1975. 207p. Illus. Index $8.95 LC 75-4270 ISBN 0-06-012152-1

This work really deals with the construction of the great pyramids, and draws mathematical parallels between pyramid structure and megalithic sites in England. The author also tries to relate the ancient Egyptians to the mythical Hyperboreans. He theorizes that a very intelligent civilization with advanced technology built these structures.

808 Jackson, Herbert G. Spirit Rappers. Garden City N.Y.:
* Doubleday, 1972. 226p. Bibliog. $6.95 LC 71-171300

This book concentrates on the Fox sisters, who began modern spiritualism in 1848 when they used raps as a way to communicate with spirits. Later in life, Margaret and Kate confessed to fraud. Margaret later retracted the confession, and some say Kate did too (both were poor and alcoholic at the time of their confessions). The work also mentions Judge John W. Edmonds of the New York Supreme Court, and his report on spiritualism written to justify his becoming a believer, followed shortly by his resignation. Also discussed is Houdini's anti-spiritualism. The author uses letters, reports and records of the time as his source material.

809 Jacobs, David Michael, 1942- . The UFO Controversy in
*** America. Foreword by Joseph Allen Hynek. Bloomington: Indiana University Press, 1975. Bibliog. Index $10 LC 74-11886 ISBN 0-253-19006-1

This work is a major new contribution to occult literature. It is actually a collection of paraphrased newspaper clippings, covering only the U.S. sightings of 1896-1897 and 1947-1974. The author, assistant professor of history at the University of Nebraska, makes no guesses as to what they could be. He just presents the cases, along with hundreds of footnotes. The cases were taken from the files of the Aerial Phenomena Research Organization, the National Investigations Committee on Aerial Phenomena (NICAP), archives at Maxwell Air Force Base, Hynek's personal collection, newspaper clippings, other books, magazine articles, and Air Force letters. For the 1896-1897 period, the author includes the cases of Belle Plaine, Iowa, Farmerville, Texas, and Madison, Wis. He then goes to 1947, when the Mt. Rainier, Wash. sighting originated the term "flying saucer." He covers the Air Force Blue Book Project, NICAP, Condon, Adamski, Fuller, Hynek, Keyhoe, and Klass. The author feels that now with the Air Force and Keyhoe out of the controversy, and the Condon study done, more and more researchers are finally studying UFO's.

810 Jacobson, Nils Olof. Life Without Death?: On Parapsychology,
*** Mysticism and the Question of Survival. Trans. by Sheila La Farge. London: Turnstone Books, 1974 (also, New York: Dell Pub. Co., 1974; orig. pub., New York: Delacorte Press, 1973). viii, 341p. Illus. Bibliog. Index (Translation of "Liv efter Döden? Om Parapsykologin, Mystiken och Döden." Göteborg: Zinderman, 1971). £3.50 ISBN 0-85500-026-0

This work is a major new contribution to occult literature. It has been translated into eight languages. The author first discusses parapsychology, clairvoyance and psychometry, telepathy, precognition, psychokinesis, frauds, dreams, out-of-the-body experiences, ghosts, spiritualism, possession, voices from space, reincarnation, xenoglossy, and mystical experiences. Jacobson then tries to explain the phenomena in a discussion on consciousness and mystical experience. Many of the cases used as examples are new to U.S. readers, which makes the work doubly valuable. The book's discussions include both experiments and anecdotes (more of the anecdotes). Later in the work, the author discusses what life on the other side might look like (a dreamlike state where our desires, thoughts, insights, and fears can become real). The last part of the book discusses mysticism, which the author feels may hold the key to the survival question. Most of the discussion is based on the ideas of contemporary Danish mystic/author Martinus Thomsen. His ideas sound very much like the philosophies of spiritualism and occultism, although Martinus claims he has never read a book on these subjects. Some readers may consider this last part the only weak one in a fine work.

811 Jacolliot, Louis, 1837-1890. Occult Science in India and Among the Ancients, with an Account of Their Mystic Initiations and the History of Spiritism. New Foreword by Omar V. Garrison. Trans. by William L. Felt. New Hyde Park, N.Y.: University Books, 1971. xvi, 274p. (Translation of
" "Spiritisme dans le monde." Paris, 1884) $5.95 LC 73-118606

The author was a French judge who traveled throughout the East, and was appointed chief justice of the French West Indies and Tahiti. Some of his other writings were sexological studies of Eastern life, occasionally still suppressed. In this book, the first part gives initiations and magical rites of India, and compares them to the Kabbalah. The second section is on occult demonstrations witnessed by the author. He says he is just presenting facts; he does not take sides as to their nature and cause. Also, he tried to detect any fakery. However, he says he never discovered a single instance of fraud (oh, come on!). Sample discussions from the first parts of the book, which are essentially philosophical, are the doctrine of the Pitris, Brahmins, degrees of initiation, Vedas, and spiritism.

812 Jakubowsky, Frank. 1974 Diary--What Is the Word for Today? New York: Exposition Press, 1973. 124p. $6 ISBN 0-682-47887-3

813 James, Paul, 1922- . California Superquake, 1975-77?: Scientists, Cayce, Psychics Speak. Foreword by Gina Cerminara. Hicksville, N.Y.: Exposition Press, 1974. xxxviii, 294p. Illus. Plates Bibliog. Index $10 LC 75-301373 ISBN 0-682-48041-X

This book is a gathering of scientific and psychic information on a future quake. The author discusses the newest Russian and Japanese methods for predicting earthquakes, Cayce, Jeane Dixon, and Nostradamus. He gives addresses and lists of periodicals for information, and discusses the spiritual implications of a quake. The book has maps, charts, and pictures.

814 James, William, 1842-1910. William James on Psychical
* Research. Comp. and ed. by Gardner Murphy and Robert O. Ballou. Introd. and concluding remarks by Gardner Murphy. Clifton, N.J.: A.M. Kelley, 1973 (c1960). viii, 339p. Includes bibliog. refs. $12.50 LC 79-122078

This is a classic work in the field. The first section is a review of Planchette, by Epes Sargent. The second includes James's Society for Psychical Research presidential address and the essay, "What Psychical Research Has Accomplished." Other chapters discuss clairvoyance, levitation, and the astral body; James and Mrs. Piper (he was interested in her from 1885 to 1910, when he died); James and Frederic Myers; and religion and problems of the soul and immortality. The last section is titled, "Final Impressions of a Psychical Researcher."

815 Jastrow, Joseph, 1863-1944. Fact and Fable in Psychology. Freeport, N.Y.: Books for Libraries, 1971 (c1901). xvii, 375p. Illus. $14 LC 70-37347 ISBN 0-8369-6694-5

This collection of essays discusses the following topics: the occult, psychical research, mental telepathy, the psychology of deception, the psychology of spiritualism, hypnotism and its antecedents, analogy, the mind's eye, mental prepossession and inertia, involuntary movements, and dreams of the blind.

816 Jeffrey, Adi-Kent Thomas. Across the Land from Ghost to Ghost. Lahaska, Pa.: New Hope Pub. Co., 1975. 178p. $1.50 pa. LC 75-328502 ISBN 0-915460-04-1

This book recounts 24 tales of ghosts from all over the United States. It is recommended for grades 5-8.

817 ______. The Bermuda Triangle. New York: Warner Books,
* 1975 (orig. pub., Lahaska, Pa.: New Hope Pub. Co., 1973). 189p. Illus. $1.75 pa.

This short, easy-to-read book would be suitable for juveniles. The author discusses what the Bermuda Triangle is; danger-fraught passage of the Armadas; loss of ship carrying Theodosia, daughter of Aaron Burr; U.S. Navy enters the mystery; ghost ships; lost planes; the world's other triangles; is there something below?; what is happening to the people lost? The illustrations are well-done photos, ones not often seen in other Bermuda Triangle books. Included is a colorful fold-out map, which is not very detailed, but eye-catching. The book is recommended for adults, and for juveniles grade 6 and up.

818 Jennings, Gary. The Teenager's Realistic Guide to Astrology. New York: Association, 1971. 222p. Illus. $5.95 LC 73-129431 ISBN 0-8096-1803-6

This book follows the sidereal zodiac, which sets each sun sign's date three weeks from the traditional zodiac. Therefore, the author feels that most of the usual astrology is false. There are chapters on: moon signs, with charts for the years 1925-1970; sun signs; ascendant signs; natal chart; planetary aspects for June, 1970; history of astrology.

819 Jinarajadasa, Curuppumullage. The Divine Vision: Three Lectures Delivered at the Queen's Hall, London, and One Lecture Delivered at Palermo, Italy. Wheaton, London: Theosophical Publishing House, 1973 (orig. pub., London: Theosophical Publishing House, 1928). 109p. (Quest Book) £0.85 pa. ISBN 0-8356-0433-0

820 Johns, June. Black Magic Today. London: New English Library, 1971. 128p. Bibliog. £0.25 pa. ISBN 0-450-00682-4

821 ______. King of the Witches: The World of Alex Sanders. Photographs by Jack Smith. London: Pan Books, 1971 (orig. pub., London: P. Davies, 1969). 158p. Illus. Plates £0.25 ISBN 0-330-02639-9

In 1965, Sanders had 1,623 witches and 107 covens under his control, out of the 4,000 witches in England. He comes from a line of witches dating back to the 15th century. His Welsh grandmother initiated him in all the rituals, even the sexual ones. After dabbling in black witchcraft, Sanders left it for white (good) witchcraft. This interesting book has many anecdotes of Sander's experiences: being dismissed from a library dusting job when he was discovered borrowing pages from a rare copy of the Key of Solomon; helping latent witches develop their power; trying to help heal sick people; conducting rituals. The last section is an interview with Sanders.

822 Johnson, Frank Roy, 1911- . Supernaturals Among Carolina Folk and Their Neighbors. Illus. by Judy Godwin Mizelle. Murfreesboro, N. C.: Johnson Pub. Co., 1974. 256p. Illus. Bibliog. Index $8.50 LC 74-186951

823 Johnson, Kendall. The Living Aura: Radiation Field Photography and the Kirlian Effect. Foreword by Thelma Moss. New York: Hawthorn Books, 1975. 178p. Illus. (part color) $15 LC 73-19377

This book discusses the author's basic experiments with Kirlian photography, which he calls a way to photograph "unseen patterns of energies and force fields that may permeate all substances." Topics covered include astral bodies, orgone boxes, electromagnetic fields, and brain waves. He discusses also the methods: employing various types of films, temperatures, apparatus used, and composition of objects photographed. Photos show humans, animals, flowers, leaves, metals, liquids, rocks, and coins.

824 Johnson, Lilian D. Spray from an Inland Sea. Boston: Branden Press, 1974. 126p. $6.95 LC 73-83344 ISBN 0-8283-1527-2

This work is an attempt to unravel the mystery of what happens to us after we die. Through automatic writing, which the author calls "mind-to-mind manifestation," she receives the thoughts of persons that have survived death. They describe the nature of the afterlife, covering these topics: life's beginnings, human incarnation, the mind, outer space, inner space, God and religion, a pool of many thoughts, human survival, and world without end. The author is a lifelong student of psychic phenomena.

825 Johnson, Obed Simon, 1881- . A Study of Chinese Alchemy. New York: Arno Press, 1974 (reprint of the ed. pub. by Shanghai, China: Commercial Press, 1928; orig. pub. as thesis, University of California, 1925). Bibliog. $10 LC 74-352 ISBN 0-405-05914-0

826 Johnson, Raynor Carey. Imprisoned Splendour; An Approach to Reality, Based Upon the Significance of Data Drawn from the Fields of Natural Science, Physical Research and Mystical Experience. Wheaton, Ill.: Theosophical Pub. House, 1971 (orig. pub., 1953). 424p. $2.95 pa. ISBN 0-8356-0425-X

On the data of natural science, the author discusses life, patterns and purpose; macrocosm; microcosm. On the data of psychical research, he covers: telepathy; precognition; apparitions; out-of-the-body experiences; survival of death. On the data of mystical experience, he discusses reincarnation and karma. The author is an Australian physicist.

827 Johnson, Vera Scott, and Thomas Wommack. The Secrets of
* Numbers; A Numerological Guide to Your Character and Des-

tiny. New York: Dial Press, 1973. viii, 257p. $7.95 LC 72-11541

This is a fine introduction to numerology. Johnson is president and founder of Innervision, an occult school in New York that was seven years old in 1973. Chapters cover the following topics: occult numbers and cosmic vibrations; your name and birthdate; reducing numbers; history of numerology; philosophy of modern numerology; characteristics of occult numbers; finding the motivation, impression, and expression numbers; personal nine-year cycle; and personal relationships and places. Tables are included.

828 Johnston, Jean Hope. For Sceptics Also: A Collection of Writings from Philosophers of the East and West Received through the Mediumship of Jean Hope Johnston. London: Regency Press, 1971. 182p. £1.20 ISBN 0-7212-0135-0

829 Jolly, W. P. Sir Oliver Lodge, Psychical Researcher and
* Scientist. London: Constable, 1974. 256p. £3.95

This fine biography discusses Lodge's entire life. Lodge was a physicist, who worked on electromagnetics, and whose wireless work preceded Marconi's. He was also an educator (he organized the physics department at Liverpool University) and a psychic researcher. The book discusses much of his social and personal life. It also covers his book, Raymond, or Life after Death, which made medium Gladys Osborne Leonard famous overnight. It mentions Lodge's search for evidence of his son Raymond's survival after death. Author Jolly is a physicist.

830 Jones, Jessie Shaver, and Ruth Shaver. Thru Psychic Eyes. New York: Vantage, 1971. 197p. $3.95

831 Jones, Marc Edmund, 1888- . Astrology; How and Why It Works. Baltimore: Penguin, 1971 (c1969). xi, 364p. Illus. $1.95 pa. ISBN 0-14-021349-X

This book is very complete, and discusses houses, signs and planets in depth. There is an appendix on how to cast a horoscope.

832 ______. Guide to Horoscope Interpretation. Wheaton, Ill.: Theosophical Pub. House, 1974 (orig. pub., Philadelphia, 1941). xi, 195p. Illus. (Quest Book) $2.45 pa. LC 73-12102 ISBN 0-8356-0442-X

This book discusses how to recognize planetary patterns (different types, such as the "splash" or the "locomotive"), and how to organize the pattern details (planetary pairs, line of vitality, line of personality, line of efficiency, line of culture). The author discusses his "whole view" method of interpreting birth charts.

833 ______. Horary Astrology: The Technique of Immediacies,

with a Primer of Symbolism. Rev. ed. Berkeley, Calif.: Shambhala Publications; London, dist. by Routledge and Kegan Paul, 1975 (rev. ed. orig. pub. as "Problem Solving by Horary Astrology," Stanwood, Wash.: Sabian Pub. Society, 1971). 462p. Illus. Index £2.50 pa. ISBN 0-87773-071-7

According to the blurb, this book is the first major work on the divinatory aspects of astrology in 300 years. Horary astrology is the art of locating a question, and, by doing so, uncovering the answer. Discussions include phrasing the question; locating the question (over 100 pages, going house-by-house); yes and no technique; judgment chart. The 50-page appendix is titled, "Primer of Symbolism."

834 ______. How to Learn Astrology. Garden City, N.Y.:
* Doubleday, 1971 (c1941). x, 190p. Illus. $1.45 pa.

This book is a good first reading on astrology. Chapters discuss horoscopes, houses, planets, signs, meaning of the cross, meaning of the triangle, putting up the wheel and putting in the planets. The work concludes with a glossary.

835 Jung, Carl Gustav. Synchronicity: An Acausal Connecting Principle. Trans. by R. F. C. Hull. London: Routledge and Kegan Paul, 1972 (orig. pub. as part 1 of "Interpretation of Nature and the Psyche," New York: Pantheon Books, 1955). vii, 150p. Illus. Index (Translation of "Naturerklärung und Psyche." Zürich: Rascher Verlag, 1952) £1.50 ISBN 0-7100-7416-6

836 Jung, Emma, and Marie-Louis von Franz. The Grail Legend. Trans. by Andrea Dykes. London: Hodder and Stoughton, 1971. 452p. Illus. Plates Bibliog. Index (Translation of "Die Graalslegende in psychologischer Sicht." Zürich: Rascher Verlag, 1960) £3.15 ISBN 0-340-10624-7

One author is Jung's widow, and the other is one of his most famous disciples. Researching many literary sources, they highlight the archetypal themes in the legend of Perceval and the Grail, and discuss symbols such as the lance, sword, stone, and vessel. The grail legend is about a spiritual awakening to gain a clearer understanding about Christian tradition. The authors suggest it is about evil, the feminine, and one's relation to God. The index lists names, themes, and archetypes.

837 Jung, Leo, 1892- . Fallen Angels in Jewish, Christian, and Mohammedan Literature. New York: Ktav Pub. House, 1974 (reprint of 1926 ed., pub. by Dropsie College for Hebrew and Cognate Learning; orig. presented as author's thesis, University of London). Bibliog. $12.50 LC 73-22476

This work discusses sin, satanism, and eschatology. The author collects a good deal of primary material in the folklore of these areas. It is a useful work for comparative religion.

838 Kahn, David E., as told to Will Oursler. My Life with Edgar Cayce. Fawcett, 1971 (orig. pub., Garden City, N.Y.: Doubleday, 1970). 220p. $.75 pa.

Kahn, a Jewish boy from Lexington, Ky., became a very successful businessman under Cayce's guidance. He taped most of this book before his death, and made a film with Cayce's son about how much Cayce had helped his career. Kahn died late in 1968, as the book was nearing completion. His widow, Lucille, discusses the strange coincidences and strange events occurring after his death, which she feels are efforts of her husband to reach her. This book provides many interesting details not found in other Cayce books about Cayce's contacts with businessmen, some of whom wished to turn Cayce's gifts into a sideshow.

839 Kaminsky, Abraham R. Behold, the Inner Universe of Handwriting Analysis. Phoenix, Ariz.: O'Sullivan Woodside, 1974. xv, 174p. Illus. $6.95 LC 74-4909 ISBN 0-89019-002-X

840 Kaplan, Stuart R. Tarot Cards for Fun and Fortune Telling: Illustrated Guide to the Spreading and Interpretation of the Popular 78-card Tarot 1JJ Deck of Muller and Cie, Switzerland. London: Rigel Press, 1975 (orig. pub., New York: U.S. Games Systems, 1970). 96p. Illus. Bibliog. Unpriced ISBN 0-85528-015-8

This short book discusses the following: major arcana; spreading the major arcana cards; lesser arcana; spreading the 78-card deck (10-card spread; 7-card spread; name spread; 56-card horseshoe spread; 54-card royal spread; seventh card spread; gypsy card spread). For each card in the deck, the book gives description, divinatory meaning, and reverse meaning.

841 ________. The Tarot Classic. London: Hale, 1974 (orig. pub., New York: Grosset and Dunlap, 1972). xv, 240p. Illus. Bibliog. Index £3 ISBN 0-7091-4764-3

This book first presents the history and development of the Tarot. Then, each of the major arcana cards is discussed, and the four suits explained. Throughout the work, the Tarot "Classic" is used, a newly printed 18th-century deck based on original woodcuts. Kaplan also discusses spreads and gives sample readings. There are many illustrations of Tarot cards from all periods.

842 Karlin, Alma M., 1891-1950. Death-Thorn; Magic, Superstitions, and Beliefs of Urban Indians in Panama and Peru. Trans. by Bernard Miall. Detroit: Blaine Ethridge Books, 1971 (orig. pub. under title, "Death-Thorn and Other Strange Experiences in Peru and Panama," London: G. Allen and Unwin, 1934). 346p. (Translation of "Todesdorn und andere seltsame Erlebnisse aus Peru und Panama") $12 LC 73-165658 ISBN 0-87917-004-2

843 Karus, Ike. Extraterrestrial Tourist Guide. Tucson, Ariz.: Omen Communications, 1974. 192p. $5.95 pa.

This collection reprints flying saucer accounts that have appeared in popular periodicals and newspapers.

844 Kasturi, N. Sathya Sai Baba. Tustin, Calif.: Sri Sathya Sai Education Foundation, 1971.

845 Kaufman, Robert. Inside Scientology; How I Joined Scientology and Became Superhuman. New York: Olympia Press, 1972. xvi, 279p. $6.95 LC 73-189412 ISBN 0-7004-0110-5

This book was written as a way for the author to purge himself of Scientology's influence. He spent $8000 and suffered much, especially through a complete breakdown. The author discusses Scientology's appeal, hypnotic effect, inner workings and structure. It includes a glossary of Scientology terms. The author is a professional musician and began Scientology studies in April 1967.

846 Kaye, Doris. A Horoscope That Really Works. New York: Award, 1971. 190p. $.95 pa.

847 ________. How to Put the Gold in Your Horoscope. New York: Popular Library, 1971. $.75 pa.

848 ________. Pro Sports Astrology Forecasts, 1971-72. New York: Dell, 1971. $.75 pa.

849 ________. Stock Market Horoscope, 1971. New York: Pocket Books, 1971 (c1969). $.95 pa. ISBN 0-671-77351-8

850 ________; James Raymond Wolfe; and Marya Glasser. Your Prophecy; Five-year Forecast for All the Signs, 1972-1976. New York: Popular Library, 1971. $.95 pa.

851 Keel, John A. [pseud. for John Alva Kiehle, 1930-]. The Eighth Tower. New York: Saturday Review Press, 1975. 218p. Includes bibliog. refs. $8.95 LC 75-15959

This book discusses UFO's, fireballs, disappearances, alien monuments on earth, and programming of humans by extraterrestrials. The author feels that man is a biological creation once manufactured to serve a giant race he calls Titans. They were in turn ruled by the forces of the Eighth Tower. The Eighth Tower is an energy living all around us he calls the "superspectrum," which manipulates men's minds. In a few years, perhaps, all our old religious beliefs and political ones will collapse when the whole population has been reprogrammed. Even avid occult readers may have to take this one with a grain of salt.

852 ________. Jadoo. New York: Pyramid, 1972 (c1957). 283p. $1.25 pa. ISBN 0-515-02826-6

853 _______. Mothman Prophecies: An Investigation into the Mysterious American Visits of the Infamous Feathery Garuda. New York: Saturday Review Press, 1975 (dist. by Dutton). 269p. $7.95 LC 74-16272

This book claims that the many varieties of occult phenomena (from poltergeists to flying saucers) are caused by another set of beings who live on this planet and use us for strange, often evil purposes. He says they want us to believe in UFO's and gods. A good part of this book is a diary-like discussion of his investigations into occurrences of these phenomena from November 1966 to December 1967 in West Virginia. On December 15, 1967, the Silver Bridge, which crossed the Ohio River at Point Pleasant, West Virginia, collapsed. There were many strange lights, winged human-like creatures with red eyes (Mothman), and men in black, all seen by many people. Keel interviewed witnesses, and uses his own personal experiences.

854 _______. Operation Trojan Horse: An Exhaustive Study of Unidentified Flying Objects--Revealing Their Source and the Forces That Control Them. London: Souvenir Press, 1971 (orig. pub. as "UFO's: Operation Trojan Horse," New York: Putnam, 1970). 320p. Illus. Bibliog. Index £2 ISBN 0-285-62001-0

Keel, a news reporter, states that UFO's are caused by supernatural beings from another dimension, where life, matter, and energy are radically different from ours. They have been misleading us for ages, appearing as angels and spaceships.

855 _______. Our Haunted Planet. London: Futura Publications, 1975 (also, Greenwich, Conn.: Fawcett, 1971; orig. pub., London: Spearman, 1971). 191p. £0.60 pa. ISBN 0-86007-153-7

856 _______. Strange Creatures from Time and Space. London: Spearman, 1975 (orig. pub., New York: Fawcett, 1970). 288p. Index £2.95 ISBN 0-85435-372-0

The author writes a syndicated newspaper column on unusual phenomena. In this book, he discusses many stories of vampires, monsters, UFO's, giants. He suggests more research be done not just on stories, but on subjective elements of the phenomena in witchcraft, black magic, and spiritualism. He discusses a creature in 1934 rising out of South Dakota's Lake Campbell; an eight-foot, hairy creature seen in 1960 in West Virginia; sightings of the strange winged creature, Mothman, in 1967. Some of his examples seem to have been proved hoaxes. He feels we are meeting beings who are not real or physical in the usual sense.

857 Kemp, Chester. Progressions. Bournemouth, England: Astrological Association, 1972. 24p. Illus. £0.25 pa. ISBN 0-9502658-0-2

858 Kennedy, David. Venture in Immortality. Gerrards Cross, England: Smythe, 1973. 198p. £2.50

This author was voted "Spiritualist of 1973" by Psychic News and Two Worlds, two major British psychic journals. Kennedy is the first minister to win this award, and he won it principally for this book. The work is a picture of the hereafter, which some critics have found unnerving. It is basically composed of survival evidence sent back by his deceased first wife. The book caused a furor in Scotland, his native land.

859 Kennedy, Edward Stewart, 1912- , and David Pingree. Astrological History of Masha'allah. Cambridge, Mass.: Harvard Univ. Press, 1971 (also, London, dist. by Oxford University Press, 1971). xiv, 206p. Illus. Facsims. $10 LC 72-113185 ISBN 0-674-05025-8

This collection includes the following works: the Arabic text and English translation of fragments of a work by Masha'allah (A. D. 730-815); horoscopes; a note on the flood date; discussion of the prophet's birth.

860 Kennett, Frances. How to Read Your Dreams. London: Marshall Cavendish, 1975 (orig. pub. in Your Dreams and What They Mean, 1974). 64p. Illus. (chiefly color) (Golden Hands Book) £1.60 ISBN 0-85685-106-X

861 Kenton, Warren. Astrology: The Celestial Mirror. London: Thames and Hudson, 1974. 128p. Illus. (some color) Facsims. Maps £1.85 ISBN 0-500-81004-4

This beautiful book contains three main parts: narration (beginnings, gods, cosmology, ascendant, morning, zenith, eclipse, re-emergence); plates (over 60 pages of them, half in color; the total number of illustrations in the book is 146); documentary illustrations and commentaries.

862 Kerr, Howard. Mediums and Spirit-Rappers and Roaring
*** Radicals. Urbana: University of Illinois Press, 1972. 261p. $8.95

This work is a major new contribution to occult literature. It discusses American spiritualism from 1850 to 1870, especially as portrayed by literary men. Discussions include the following: Cora Hatch, the Fox sisters, James Russell Lowell, Melville, Twain, Hawthorne, William Dean Howells, F. Marion Crawford, Henry James, Judge Edmond, Poyen, and David. The book includes spiritualists' tracts, transcripts of writings of famous spirits, and other such material. Also discussed is the influence on spiritualism of free love, the women's movement, atheism, and the social reform movement. The author teaches English at the University of Illinois. Kerr says that most American writers considered spiritualism a social phenomenon.

863 Kerr, John Stevens. The Mystery and Magic of the Occult. Philadelphia: Fortress, 1971 (also, London: S. C. M. Press, 1971). 152p. Illus. Includes bibliog. refs. $3.50 pa. LC 79-154486 ISBN 0-8006-0157-2

This work is a Christian evaluation of the occult. The author studies the history and present practices of astrology, and states that he does not consider it a science. He does give a good study of it, though. Also discussed are black magic, palmistry, numerology, and ESP. He tries to understand why people have this love for the supernatural. He feels that it is good in that it has brought people back to spirituality and God.

864 Kettelkamp, Larry. Astrology: Wisdom of the Stars. New
* York: Morrow, 1973. 128p. Illus. $3.95 LC 73-4924 ISBN 0-688-20085-0

This book is a good juvenile introduction to the subject. It discusses the historical theories of astronomer/astrologers such as Ptolemy and Kepler, and famous astrologers of the past. It tells how to cast and interpret a simple horoscope. Also discussed are some scientific investigations that may soon reach the same beliefs held by astrologers for ages. This work is recommended for grades 4-6.

865 _______. Investigating UFO's: One of the World's Greatest
* Unsolved Mysteries, the Story of the Unidentified Flying Object. London: Target, 1973 (also, London: Ronald Stacy, 1972; orig. pub., New York: Morrow, 1971). 96p. Illus. £0.25 pa.

This is a well-organized, attractive juvenile book on the subject. Included is a chapter on "Illusions, Pranks and Hoaxes." There are also excellent photographs. One of the author's theories is that UFO's may be highly developed mental projections produced by superior human beings located elsewhere. Kettelkamp also implies a conspiracy of silence, and discusses the usual official reports of the government. The book is recommended for grades 4-6.

866 _______. The Sixth Sense. London: Ronald Stacy Ltd., 1973
* (orig. pub., New York: Morrow, 1970). 96p. Illus. £1.50

This book, written for juveniles, covers the following topics: telepathy, clairvoyance, precognition, psychometry, retrocognition, astral projection, mediums, possession, psychokinesis, psychic photography, healing, and phony mediums. It gives safe and easy tests and guides to developing ESP. The author cites case histories and laboratory experiments. Kettelkamp implies that some of the phenomena (retrocognition and spiritualism) may indicate survival after death and possible reincarnation.

867 Keyes, King. Master Guide to Preparing Your Natal Horoscope.

Englewood Cliffs, N. J.: Parker Pub. Co., 1974. Includes bibliog. refs. $6.95 LC 73-20022 ISBN 0-13-725721-X

868 Keyhoe, Donald Edward, 1897- . Aliens from Space; The
* Real Story of Unidentified Flying Objects. Garden City, N. Y.: Doubleday, 1973. (also, St. Albans, England: Panther, 1975). xii, 322p. Index $7.95 LC 73-83597

The author is a former Marine Corps flyer. He claims that the U. S. Air Force knows that UFO's are spacecraft from a more advanced world, and is deliberately concealing the truth from the public by censorship and the discrediting of witnesses. He states that Air Force jets are trying to down UFO's to learn the secret of their propulsion. Keyhoe was head of the respected National Investigations Committee on Aerial Phenomena. He also condemns the Condon Report, and proposes means of communication with flying saucers. He dismisses most reports of UFO occupants, including the famous Hill case.

869 _____. Flying Saucers from Outer Space. London: Tan-
* dem, 1973 (also, London: Hutchinson, 1954; orig. pub., New York: Holt, 1953). 256p. Index £0.35 ISBN 0-426-12159-7

This classic was one of the first works to discuss flying saucers seriously. The author states that the saucers are real, and come from another planet. He implies that the U. S. Air Force believes this, too, but is cloaking its knowledge in secrecy. The book cites many conversations and discussions with authorities and anonymous sources.

870 Kiej'e, Nikolas. Japanese Grotesqueries. Introd. essay by Terence Barrow. Rutland, Vt.: C. E. Tuttle Co., 1973. 260p. (chiefly illus.) $10 LC 73-75283 ISBN 0-8048-0656-X

This is a collection of ancient Japanese illustrations of ghosts, demons, monsters, and animals with magical powers. The introductory essay by ethnologist Terence Barrow, "Ghosts, Ghost-gods and Demons of Japan," studies the tradition which created these illustrations, and explains some of the stories behind them.

871 Kildahl, John P. The Psychology of Speaking in Tongues.
*** New York: Harper and Row, 1972. 110p. $4.95

This work is a major new contribution to occult literature. The well-done work is the result of a 10-year study by the author, who, together with a colleague, traveled all over the U. S. Kildahl is director of the Program in Pastoral Psychology at New York Theological Seminary, and on the faculty of the Postgraduate Center for Mental Health, New York City. He studies glossolalia in many areas of the U. S., in many socioeconomic and educational classes among several Protestant groups. The author attempts to use the methods of clinical psychology in studying the phenomenon. He feels that speaking in tongues can be learned. Certain psychological characteristics make up a glossolalist's personality, and a series of psychological events precedes and accompanies the phenomenon. Glossolalia arises from anxiety over a life crisis, psychological regression, and a magical, mechanistic view of God. The author adds that glossolalia is not a mystery or actual language, but a string of syllables from sounds the person already knows.

872 King, Bruce, 1897- . The Encyclopaedia of Ancient and
* Forbidden Knowledge, by Zolar [pseud.]. London: Abacus, 1973 (also, New York: Popular Library, 1972; also, London: Souvenir Press, 1971; orig. pub., Los Angeles: Nash, 1970). 445p. Illus. £2.50 ISBN 0-285-62020-7

This is an excellent work deserving much praise. It is a culmination of over 30 years' work in astrology by the author. The writing is highly compact, and each page is loaded with information. It is one of the best one-volume gatherings of occult tradition available anywhere. There are sections on the Kabbalah, sexual mysteries, mediumship, prophets, astrology, numerology, Tarot, and general occult tradition. The last section is a glossary of occult arts and sciences.

873 _______. Everything You Want to Know about Astrology, Numerology, How to Win, by Zolar [pseud.]. New York: Arco Pub. Co., 1973. 236p. Illus. $.95pa. LC 72-3135

874 _______. Everything You Want to Know about Fortune Telling with Cards; Karma System, Gypsy System, Professional System, Palmistry, by Zolar [pseud.]. New York: Arco Pub. Co., 1973. 222p. $.95 pa. LC 72-3138

875 _______. Everything You Want to Know about Hypnotism, Psychic Powers, Telepathy, E.S.P., Sex, and Hypnosis, by Zolar [pseud.]. New York: Arco Pub. Co., 1973. 120p. $.95 pa. LC 72-3139

876 _______. Everything You Want to Know about Nature's Mysteries, the Prophets, Nostradamus, Tea Leaf Readings, Herbs, Candle Burning, by Zolar [pseud.]. New York: Arco Pub. Co., 1973 (c1972). 203p. $.95 pa. LC 72-3137

There are chapters on the following topics: prophets (including Nostradamus); tea leaf reading (including an A to Z dictionary of symbols seen in the cup and their meanings); candles (including material on rituals and seals).

877 _______. The History of Astrology, by Zolar [pseud.]. New York: Arco, 1972. xv, 315p. Illus. Bibliog. $7.95 LC 72-173793 ISBN 0-668-02533-6

This book contains miscellaneous discussions on comets, satanism, witchcraft, alchemy, magic, Copernicus, Kepler, Newton,

Galileo, Henry Cornelius Agrippa, Claudius Ptolemaeus, Paracelsus, and Jerome Cardan. The book includes a chronology of persons and events, plus a glossary.

878 _______. The Interpretation of Dreams, by Zolar [pseud.]. London: Sphere, 1974 (orig. pub. as "Numerology Dream-book," New York: Fawcett, 1971). 191p. (Dennis Wheatley Library of the Occult, vol. 18) £0.40 pa. ISBN 0-7221-9430-7

879 _______. It's All in the Stars, by Zolar [pseud.]. London: Tandem, 1973 (orig. pub., London: Wingate, 1970). 286p. Illus. £0.40 pa. ISBN 0-426-12538-X

For each of the zodiac signs, this work gives information under the headings general, child, husband, wife, cusps, decanates, degrees, compatible and incompatible signs, and some famous persons of the sign.

880 _______. Zolar's Day-by-Day Horoscope, by Zolar [pseud.]. New York: Arco, annual. 12 volumes 88p. each volume $.75 pa. each volume

Each volume of the set includes the following: first, an introduction to the sign (general, marriage and commercial combinations, children, wife); second, the cusps of the sun section (general, month-by-month, with each month followed by a daily breakdown); third, the 12 houses' and the planets' influence; and fourth, moon tables.

881 _______. Zolar's Family Horoscope; A Complete Astrological Guide for Everyone for Each Day of the Year, by Zolar [pseud.]. New York: Arco, 1972 (c1963). 223p. $.75 pa.

882 King, Francis, 1904- , ed. Astral Projection, Ritual Magic and Alchemy: Being Hitherto Unpublished Golden Dawn Material by S. L. MacGregor Mathers and Others. London: Spearman, 1971. 254p. £2.50 ISBN 0-85435-171-X

The book consists of printed lectures given to Golden Dawn members before 1900. These short essay-type, semi-official documents were called "Flying Rolls." They include these discussions: introduction on the Golden Dawn; imagination and will power; astral projection; Rosicrucian adeptship; man, God, and the higher magic; alchemy; Christian occultism; Hermetic wisdom; mystical prayer. The three appendices contain magic documents.

883 _______. Magic: The Western Tradition. London: Thames and Hudson, 1975 (also, New York: Avon, 1975). 128p. Illus. (some color) Facsims. Bibliog. (Art and Imagination) £3.95 ISBN 0-500-80004-9

884 _______. Ritual Magic in England, 1887 to the Present Day.

London: New English Library, 1972 (also, New York: Macmillan, 1971; orig. pub. as "Rites of Modern Occult Magic," London: Spearman, 1970). 176p. Bibliog. £0.40 pa. ISBN 0-450-01346-4

885 ______. Wisdom from Afar. Garden City, N.Y.: Doubleday, 1975. 144p. Illus. (New Library of the Supernatural) $7.95 LC 75-16750

886 King, Teri. Business, Success, and Astrology. New York: St. Martin's Press, 1975 (orig. pub., London: Allison and Busby, 1974). 377p. $7.95 LC 74-83580

Each chapter discusses a sign of the zodiac, giving characteristics, proper careers, employer, employee, and how members of this sign get along in dealing with all other signs. Appendices give for each sign health tips and responses to sudden wealth or failure.

887 ______. Love, Sex and Astrology. Illus. by John Munday. London: Pan Books, 1974 (orig. pub., London: Allison and Busby, 1972). xii, 274p. Illus. £0.40 pa.

888 Klass, Philip J. UFO's Explained. New York: Random House,
*** 1975 (c1974). 369p. Illus. $8.95 LC 74-9054 ISBN 0-394-49215-3

This work is a major new contribution to occult literature. The author, avionics editor of Aviation Week and Space Technology, feels that UFO's are earth phenomena, not intelligently guided vessels. He covers 40 of the most famous UFO cases, studying them on an engineering/physics basis, with analyses of radar equipment, photographs, meteorological records, positions of astronomical bodies, the psychology of eyewitnesses. He gives his complex explanations for two famous UFO radar cases (Lakenhearth, England, 1956, and Dallas, Texas, 1957) which have been ignored by most writers. He discusses balloons, rocket boosters, airplanes, rains on a mountain, stars, ice crystals, electrified air plasma, reflecting camera lens flashes, radar "angels" (moisture, bird flocks, insects, atmospheric reflections). Klass believes that intelligent, honest persons, when suddenly seeing a strange object, may make big errors in trying to describe it. He criticizes the media for big headlines, but no follow-up on later explanations. Obviously, Klass believes UFO's are fairy tales. He feels if anyone watches the skies long enough, he will see many unusual phenomena which trained observers can easily explain. Chapters include the following discussions: hand-made UFO's, Brown Mountain UFO's, UFO's and ghosts, landing at Socorro, UFO's as brutal killers, UFO photographs, UFO's over England, UFO's over New Guinea, famous contactees, mysterious airships of the 1890's, 1973 UFO flap, abduction in Pascagoula, army helicopter incident (best case of 1973), Congress, UFO's and N-rays. This book is highly recommended to all; it balances some of the wilder UFO books.

889 Klein, Aaron E. Beyond Time and Matter; A Sensory Look
* at ESP. Garden City, New York: Doubleday, 1973. 117p. Illus. Bibliog. $4.50 LC 73-79684 ISBN 0-385-00474-5

This is a good juvenile summary on the subject. Criticizing the Society for Psychical Research and also Rhine's Duke University studies, the author goes on to try and find a basis for ESP study in the physiology of stimulus-response. Klein speculates that a unifying theory of parapsychology may emerge from current Russian research on bio-plasma. He also reports on possible connections between alpha wave production and ESP, and summarizes Ullman's research on telepathy during REM sleep. This book is recommended for grades 7-10.

890 Kleynhans, E. P. Life on Earth and Hereafter. Gerrards Cross, England: Smythe, 1974. 143p. £2.25 ISBN 0-901072-12-5

891 Knight, Damon. Charles Fort: Prophet of the Unexplained. London: Gollancz, 1971 (orig. pub., New York: Doubleday, 1969). xvi, 224p. Illus. Plates Index £2.20 ISBN 0-575-00613-7

This book is not a biography of Fort, but a discussion of his works. It contains long quotes from Fort's unpublished autobiography, and discusses his research and style. Fort took 65,000 notes on strange incidents. He theorized a new view of cosmology, presented in The Book of the Damned, of a fourth dimensional world that occasionally breaks into our world. Knight's book includes a long discussion of Velikovsky's Worlds in Collision.

892 Knight, David C. Poltergeists: Hauntings and the Haunted.
* Philadelphia: Lippincott, 1972. 160p. Illus. (Weird and Horrible Library) $4.92 LC 72-2445 ISBN 0-397-31274-1

This well-done juvenile book discusses what the author calls 12 cases of recurrent spontaneous psychokinesis (RSPK). There are chapters on the Drummer of Tideworth (1661), the Epworth Rectory Poltergeist, the Cock Lane Ghost, the Bell Witch, the Stratford Poltergeist, the Great Amherst Mystery, the Sumatra Stone Thrower, the Hauntings at Borley Rectory, the Poona Poltergeist, "Gef" the Talking Mongoose (on the Isle of Man), and the Seaford Disturbances of Long Island (1958). He discusses the theories of strange electromagnetic forces, ectoplasmic pseudopods, and the astral body's splitting off from the main one. The book is recommended for grades 6-9.

893 ______. Those Mysterious UFO's: The Story of Unidentified Flying Objects. New York: Parents' Magazine Press, 1975. 64p. Illus. $4.95 LC 74-31465 ISBN 0-8193-0820-X

This juvenile book discusses various sightings, and the U.S. Air Force's Project Blue Book. The arrangement is mostly chronological. The book is recommended for grades 4-8.

894 Knight, Gareth. The Experience of the Inner Worlds: A Course in Christian Qabalistic Magic. Cheltenham, England: Helios Book Service, 1975. xii, 254p. Illus. Bibliog. £4 ISBN 0-900448-19-9

895 _______. The Occult. London: Kahn and Averill, 1975. 103p. Illus. Bibliog. £2.50 ISBN 0-900707-37-2

896 Koch, Kurt E. Between Christ and Satan. Grand Rapids, Mich.: Kregel Pubns., 1971. 192p. (Translated from the 1962 German ed. by Evangelization Pubs.) $1.25 pa. LC 79-160690 ISBN 0-8254-3003-8

897 _______. Demonology, Past and Present. Grand Rapids, Mich.: Kregel Pubns., 1973. 161p. (Translated from the German) $1.25 pa. LC 72-93353

898 _______. The Devil's Alphabet. Grand Rapids, Mich.: Kregel Pubns., 1971. 156p. (Translated from the 4th German ed. of 1969 by Evangelization Pubs.) $1.25 pa. LC 76-160692 ISBN 0-8254-3004-6

899 _______. Occult Bondage and Deliverance; Advice for Counselling the Sick, the Troubled, and the Occultly Oppressed. Grand Rapids, Mich.: Kregel Pubns., 1971. 198p. (Translated from the 1970 German ed. by Evangelization Pubs.) $1.25 pa. LC 72-160691 ISBN 0-8254-3006-2

900 Koch, Walter Albert, 1895- , and Elizabeth Schack. Birthplace Tables of Houses for Northern Latitudes 00 to 600. New York: ASI Publishers, 1975. (Translation of "Hausertabellen des Geburtsortes für 00-600 nordliche Breite") $10 LC 75-22416 ISBN 0-88231-020-8

901 Koestler, Arthur, 1905- . The Roots of Coincidence. Postscript by Renée Haynes. New York: Vintage Books, 1973 (also, London: Pan Books, 1974; orig. pub., London: Hutchinson, 1972). 158p. Bibliog. $1.95 pa. LC 73-4446
***

This work is a major new contribution to occult literature. The author attempts to provide ESP with a foundation in quantum physics. He mentions the following: Adrian Dobb's theory of psitrons; Renaissance philosopher Pico Della Mirandola; Schopenhauer; Kammerer's "seriality"; Jung's "synchronicity," or meaningful coincidence theory. Koestler theorizes that there are acausal forces at work in the world that have nothing to do with the mechanical laws we associate with science, but work by affinity toward unity. He feels that a materialistic concept of the nature and capabilities of the human mind may be obsolete. Also, he argues that much of modern physical theory is just as "occult" as parapsychology. There is a postscript by Renée Haynes on spontaneous psi phenomena.

902 Kohn, Bernice. Out of the Cauldron; A Short History of
* Witchcraft. New York: Holt, 1972. 119p. Illus. Bibliog.
$4.95 LC 74-150030 ISBN 0-03-080229-6

This juvenile book discusses witchcraft's origins in pagan religion; witch hysteria in Europe during the 15th and 16th centuries (with many quotes from the Malleus Maleficarum); Joan of Arc; Salem; practices; covens and sabbats; famous witches; witchcraft today (including Sybil Leek); recipes and charms. The appendix has documents (excerpts from Church Canons, Papal Bulls, Civil Law) and a glossary. The book is recommended for grades 5-8.

903 Kolosimo, Peter. Not of This World. Trans. by A.D. Hills. New Hyde Park, N.Y.: University Books, 1971 (also, London: Sphere, 1971; orig. pub., London: Souvenir Press, 1970). 245p. Illus. Bibliog. refs. (Translation of "Non è terrestre." Milan: Sugar Editore, 1969) $5.95 LC 77-153999

904 ________. Timeless Earth. Trans. by Paul Stevenson. London: Garnstone Press, 1973 (also, London: Sphere, 1974; also, University Books, 1974; also, New York: Bantam, 1975). 270p. Illus. Maps Index (Translation of "Terra senza tempo." Milan: Sugar, 1964) £2.95 ISBN 0-85511-360-X

The author's theme is that man's destiny has been influenced by extraterrestrial forces, and that we really know very little about our past. Much of the work is on Mu and Atlantis, quoting James Churchward and the translation of Mayan hieroglyphics by August le Plangeon. These are not always the most reliable of sources. The author sees the destruction of Sodom and Gomorrah as caused by the thermonuclear explosion of a spaceship's fuel supply, and the dragons of Taoism as spaceships.

905 Kors, Alan C., and Edward Peters, eds. Witchcraft in
* Europe, 1100-1700: A Documentary History. London: Dent, 1973 (orig. pub., Philadelphia: University of Pennsylvania Press, 1972). viii, 382p. Illus. £5.75 ISBN 0-460-04128-2

This is a collection of documents focusing on a period when concern over witches was a major European preoccupation. The author translated many Latin documents, and provides a survey of historical and anthropological studies on witchcraft published since the 1840's. Introductions to each section place the selections in the context of the complete works from which they were taken. There are 44 documents, 13 newly translated, with 72 excellent illustrations accompanying the text. Discussions include witchcraft in Christianity, St. Augustine's treatise on evil, witchcraft and the papacy, 16th-century persecutions, and 17th-century disbelief.

906 Kresge, George, 1935- . The Amazing World of Kreskin,
*** by Kreskin [pseud.]. New York: Random House, 1973.
222p. Bibliog. $5.95

This work is a major new contribution to occult literature. One could wish, however, that the book were longer and deeper, because Kreskin has some excellent thoughts on psychic phenomena. He discusses his TV and stage shows, experiences, beliefs, mind-reading techniques, and tricks. Kreskin uses ESP, but prefers to think of his abilities as hypersensitivity (for example, he can hear a needle dropped on a hard surface in an auditorium). Whatever he calls it, he definitely is telepathic, and receives information in images. As an aid, he has also practiced automatic writing since childhood. While talking to an audience, he is constantly writing ahead of the telepathic thoughts. As he writes, certain thoughts come in clearly, and he "targets" a subject. Images then come in, sometimes accompanied by his "hearing" information. He admits that suggestion plays the biggest role in his act (over half the work is devoted to the subject of suggestion). His basic theory is that there is no such thing as hypnosis; he ridicules use of the word, and always substitutes the word "suggestion" in his shows. The author gives tips on how to tilt tables, lower the metabolic rate by autosuggestion, and do automatic writing. He also explains true psychic stories about Lincoln, Edison, and Houdini. Kreskin debunks mediums, so it is natural that spiritualists are anti-Kreskin. However, even objective spiritualists call his work "cheap magic tricks" that any serious amateur can easily perform. Such criticism seems unjustified after reading this thoughtful book. One should see this man perform. He puts on a fantastic show! As an added nugget, this book provides fascinating anecdotes on what it's like to be a psychic performer, especially one that tours and flies around as much as Kreskin does.

907 Krippner, Stanley, 1932- . The Song of the Siren: A Parapsychological Odyssey. New York: Harper and Row, 1975.
*** 311p. Bibliog. Index $12.50 LC 75-9331 ISBN 0-06-064786-8

This work is a major new contribution to occult literature. The author discusses his life and 10 years of parapsychological studies. A quarter of the book discusses his research as director of Maimonides Dream Laboratory. Most of the book is on his encounters with psychics and researchers during his many travels of recent years. He visited the USSR with Ullman to film Kulagina, traveled to São Paulo to study Brazilian spirit religions, traveled to the Philippines to see psychic surgery, went to Czechoslovakia to study psychotronics, and met Rolling Thunder, an American Indian medicine man. He mentions his boyhood on an Indiana farm, where he had some psi experiences. He also discusses the relationship of the Maimonides work to astrology, and mentions Gauquelin's findings. Krippner has since left Maimonides because of a lack of funding, and has decided to abandon the parapsychology field because he feels it will never receive adequate financial backing. He is now program planning coordinator of the Humanistic Psychology Institute in San Francisco, and editor of the Journal of Psychoenergetic Systems.

908 ________, and Daniel Rubin, eds. The Energies of Consciousness: Explorations in Acupuncture, Auras, and Kirlian Photography. New York, London: Gordon and Breach, 1975. xvi, 244p. Illus. (some color) Bibliog. (Social Change Series) £5.60 ISBN 0-677-05190-5
*

This work is a collection of articles written by scientists who attended the 2nd Western Hemisphere Conference of Kirlian Photography, Acupuncture and the Human Aura in 1973. The book also discusses the 1st International Meeting on the Problem of Bioenergetics and Related Areas held in Moscow in 1972. The subject of Kirlian photography has articles by Thelma Moss, Victor Adamenko (discussing Alla Vinogradova's ability to cause lights to move), William Tiller (on streamer phenomena), and Krippner (PK effect on Kirlian photography). Dorbin contributes an article on consciousness as an important area for study. The final article by Edgar Mitchell discusses use of a photomultiplier to detect small points of light emitted by a body in darkness.

909 ________, and ________, eds. The Kirlian Aura. Garden City, N.Y.: Doubleday, 1974. 208p. (Rev. ed. of "Galaxies of Life") $3.95 pa.
*

This collection of papers discusses historical notes, photography by means of high-frequency currents, bioplasma or corona discharges, portable Kirlian device, cold electron emission patterns, high voltage radiation photography of a healer's finger, field theory and Kirlian photography, acupuncture, skin electricity, massage in Oriental medicine, and auras. Authors of the papers include Semyon Kirlian, Thelma Moss, Krippner, and Ingo Swann.

910 Krishna, Gopi. The Awakening of Kundalini. New York: E. P. Dutton, 1975. 129p. $3.25 pa.

The author is 73 years old, and lives in Kashmir. He claims to have rediscovered kundalini, the evolutionary mechanism in man which underlies artistic and psychic powers, and also, in its negative form, causes evil and insanity. He discusses Aldous Huxley, John Lilly, Alan Watts, Puharich, Sai Baba, and proponents of TM, all of whom he criticizes for false thinking.

911 ________. Higher Consciousness. New York: Julian Press, 1974. 198p. $7.95

The author feels that higher consciousness is a new activity in the brain coming about through the opening of a normally closed chamber with the influx of a fine biochemical essence rising from the reproductive region through the spinal cord. He calls for scientists to verify his claims. The writing is in question-and-answer format. He sees kundalini as the force behind human development and evolution.

912 Krishnamurti, Jiddu. The Awakening of Intelligence. London: Gollancz, 1973. 538p. Illus. £3.20

This work is a collection of tape-recorded transcripts of extemporaneous conversations since 1967 between Krishnamurti and groups and individuals in America, Europe, and India. Some of the themes are intelligence, self-knowledge, conflict, pleasure, fear, violence, and religious experience. He feels that one must go to oneself to find the answers. He is wary of traditions, cultures, and the words and experiences of others. The author teaches a way of looking without a center.

913 _______. Beyond Violence. London: Gollancz, 1973. 175p. £1.40 ISBN 0-575-01592-6

This work is a record of talks and discussions held in 1970: four at Santa Monica, California in March 1970; three at San Diego State College in April 1970; three in London in May 1970; two at Krishnamurti's own school in Brockwood Park near London in September 1970; one in Rome in October 1970. Treated are the universal themes of violence, fear, self-awareness and the unity of all. Most lectures use his familiar technique of drawing the audience into active participation and thoughtful involvement. Each discussion goes wherever the questions take it. The author condemns a sense of the past or future, and condemns analysis. (For a devastating discussion on Krishnamurti, see Times Literary Supplement, March 2, 1973, p. 249.)

914 _______. The Second Penguin Krishnamurti Reader. Ed. by Mary Lutyens. Harmondsworth, England: Penguin, 1973 (orig. pub. as "The Only Revolution," London: Gollancz, 1970; also pub. as "The Urgency of Change," London: Gollancz, 1971). 318p. £0.40 pa.

"The Urgency of Change" is in question-and-answer format, with the themes of contemplation, meditation, aesthetic appreciation, love, and self-discipline. Krishnamurti keeps emphasizing the psychological change required to confront the harsh problems of life. In "The Only Revolution" the theme is a radical change of the human heart and mind that would put people more in touch with the world of nature, other people, and themselves. Meditation is the key to this change, and should become with little effort the center of one's daily life. His love of nature and landscape is well conveyed in his description of the book's three areas--India, California, and Europe.

915 Kriss, Marika. Werewolves, Shapeshifters, and Skinwalkers. Los Angeles: Sherbourne Press, 1972. 143p. Illus. (For the Millions Series) $2.50 pa. LC 75-183883 ISBN 0-8202-0152-9

916/7 _______. Witchcraft Past and Present, for the Millions. Award, 1971. $.75 pa.

This survey discusses the church, sadism, covens, sabbats, where witches live, healing and blighting, the evil eye, el brujo (Don

Juan and Castaneda), vestigal witchcraft and new growth, and hippie witchcraft. It is a fairly decent survey of the subject.

918 Kruger, Helen. Other Healers, Other Cures. Indianapolis: Bobbs-Merrill, 1974. 376p. $8.95

This book discusses acupuncture, folk medicine, faith healing, yoga, chiropractic doctors, homeopathy, primal therapy, and massage. It is mostly on East Coast healers. The author mentions the positive uses of the therapies, but warns of quacks. She also mentions mind-control courses. Kruger criticizes establishment medicine for failure to treat patients as a whole.

919 Kunz, George Frederick, 1856-1932. The Curious Lore of
* Precious Stones. New York: Dover, 1971 (also, London: Constable, 1971; orig. pub., Philadelphia, London: Lippincott, 1913). xiv, 406p. Illus. (some color) Facsims. Bibliog. refs. $4.50 LC 79-156815

This interesting book discusses precious stones in relation to the following topics: sentiments and folk lore, superstitions, symbolism, mysticism, use in medicine, protection, prevention, religion, divination, crystal gazing, birthstones, lucky stones, talismans, astral, zodiacal, and planetary.

920 Kurdsen, Stephen. Graphology, the New Science. Foreword by Jeane Dixon. New York: Galahad Books, 1974 (also, Washington, D.C.: Acropolis Books, 1971; also, pub. as "Reading Character from Handwriting," London, Newton Abbott: David and Charles, 1971). 157p. Illus. Bibliog. Index $4.95 LC 73-88100 ISBN 0-88365-234-X

921 Kurth, Hanns, 1904- . Glimpses of the Beyond, by Jean-
* Baptiste Delacour [pseud.]. Trans. by E.B. Garside. New York: Delacorte Press, 1974 (also, Lewes, England: Harwood-Smart Pub. Co., 1975). (Translation of "Aus dem Jenseits zurück." Düsseldorf: Econ Verlag, 1973) $5.95 LC 74-8054 ISBN 0-440-03287-3

This interesting book discusses cases of people pronounced dead and what they saw on the other side. Cases discussed include: a man who hanged himself and lived, but wanted to return to the green land he had seen; Fred Phillips, who survived the electric chair in Mexico; French ballerina Janine Charrat, who burned up on stage one night and saw her dead grandmother who accurately predicted her future marriage in the South Seas; Daniel Gelin, French film actor; Curt Jurgens, German actor; King Paul of Greece; French singer/composer/actor Charles Aznavour's auto accident; Victor Cleave, who slept for four years in the afterworld; Theresa Laffeld, who lived for three weeks with a temperature of 118 degrees, and learned of former lives. In spite of the cases he gives, the author is a bit skeptical. However, the phenomenon he describes appears to be quite common, and an increasingly important area for research.

922 Kusche, Lawrence David. Bermuda Triangle Bibliography.
* 2nd ed. Tempe: Arizona State University Library, 1974. 7p. $2

This short, unannotated bibliography presents the following sections: books (five entries), books with chapters on the Triangle (ten entries), books with chapters that discuss specific incidents (seven entries), books with brief reference to the Triangle (19 entries), general articles (18 entries), articles on specific incidents (13 entries), articles with brief reference to the Triangle (six entries), general sources, such as the Dictionary of American Naval Fighting Ships (nine entries), newspaper articles (68 entries from 14 different newspapers), reports and miscellaneous items (ten entries), films (two entries), and a supplement (two entries). This bibliography appears to be very complete, and the many sections listed above help organize the material effectively. Total of cites given is 169.

923 ______. The Bermuda Triangle Mystery--Solved. New
*** York: Harper and Row, 1975 (also, New York: Warner Books, 1975). 256p. Illus. Bibliog. Index $8.95 LC 74-1828

This work is a major new contribution to occult literature. The author's major thesis is that the legend of the Triangle came about because of bad research and even fraud. He attempts to explain each disappearance by ordinary means. He first studies the legend of the Triangle as it is usually told, and Christopher Columbus and the Sargasso Sea. The rest of the book discusses 51 specific incidents, with his comments showing the errors of logic in traditional accounts and explanations. The last three chapters discuss the Devil's Sea (an area similar to the Triangle, southeast of Japan), vortices, and magnetism. The author concludes, "There is no theory that solves the mystery." He feels it is foolish to look for one unifying theory. One does not do it with car accidents. Instead, one should look at each incident separately, as the author does here. Looked at in this way, Kusche says, the mystery of the area disappears. He states, "The Legend of the Bermuda Triangle is a manufactured mystery." The format of the book is truly excellent--clear, short sections with numerous quotes (sources given). Also, the author points up in his preface a phenomenon that is common to most occult research: "Many writers who had made the earlier attempts to solve the mystery later found themselves and their theories an integral part of it." Even those who disagree with Kusche's conclusions will want to read this book to find out how a researcher writes an excellent work.

924 Lacinio, Giano, ed. The New Pearl of Great Price; A Treatise Concerning the Treasure and Most Precious Stone of the Philosophers. Trans. and edited by A. E. Waite. New York: Arno Press, 1974 (orig. pub., London: J. Elliott, 1894). (Translation of "Pretiosa Margarita Novella de Thesauro ac Pretios-

issimo Philosophorum Lapide." 1330) (Title page adds: "Or the method and procedure of this divine art; with observations drawn from the works of Arnoldus, Raymondus, Rhasis, Albertus, and Michael Scotus, first published by Janus Lacinius, the Calabrian, with a copious index. The original Aldine edition translated into English. 'The New Pearl of Great Price ... by Peter Bonus, of Ferrara' ") $24 LC 74-349 ISBN 0-405-05911-6

925 Lady Sheba [pseud.]. Book of Shadows. St. Paul; Llewellyn Publications, 1971. 155p. $2.95 pa. LC 72-200904 ISBN 0-87542-075-3

This book is supposedly a secret book of oral tradition, published for the first time. It has three parts: laws (giving 162 of them), rituals (giving descriptions of how to do them and also the proper words), and sabbats (explaining how to celebrate them). The book has very nice-quality, light yellow paper.

926 ______. The Grimoire of Lady Sheba. 2nd rev. ed. St. Paul, Minn.: Llewellyn Publications, 1974 (1st ed., Llewellyn, 1972). 227p. Illus. Plates $10 LC 75-308391

This magical workbook is written by one who is supposedly the first witch to publish her grimoire. Discussions include the power (rules and requirements), tools (how to make and consecrate the wand, sword), language (diagrams of the lost Theban Script and Runic alphabet), rituals; recipes, herbal lore, ointments, teas, perfumes; and dances. The second part of the book contains the entire text of the Book of Shadows, the holy book of witchcraft, supposedly handed down orally through the ages.

927 ______. Witch. St. Paul, Minn.: Llewellyn Publications, 1973. Paperback

A practicing witch, the author presents the basic doctrines of witchcraft as guides for daily living in harmony with the natural order of the universe.

928 Laing, Stuart Francis James. Rayner, Lewis: An Outline of the Work of Two Spirits in Complete Harmony. London: Temple of the Trinity Lodge for Spiritual Healing, 1974. 71p. Illus. £0.40 pa. ISBN 0-9503971-0-5

This book is about medium Eva Rayner and her spirit guide, Dr. Thomas Lewis. The guide first contacted her when she visited a spiritualist church. She later gave small trance sittings, with her unknown guide in charge. One night, when her son was very ill, Dr. Lewis announced his name, and told her she could heal her son herself with Dr. Lewis's help. From that time, Rayner devoted her life to healing. She was the author's first wife, and, together with the author, founded the Temple of the Trinity Lodge for Spiritual Healing. Eva Rayner remained non-commercial, and took few fees, only enough to pay expenses.

929 Lamb, Geoffrey. Discovering Magic Charms and Talismans. Aylesbury, England: Shire Publications, 1974. 48p. Illus. Bibliog. Index £0.35 pa. ISBN 0-85263-256-8

930 Landsburg, Alan, and Sally Landsburg. In Search of Ancient
* Mysteries. Foreword by Rod Serling. London: Corgi, 1974. ix, 197p. Illus. Plates Bibliog. Index £0.50 pa. ISBN 0-552-09588-5

The book theorizes that human culture and intelligence came through extraterrestrial intervention. Chapters discuss spores and artifacts, sea in the mountains, Viracocha, colossal charts, teachers of the Egyptians, Karnak, the Bible, how man got his brain, and shortcuts in space time. The authors have traveled and interviewed a great deal in researching this theme. Alan Landsburg produced in 1972 a television special, "In Search of Ancient Astronauts."

931 ________, and ________. The Outer Space Connection. Photos by Andrew Reichline. London: Corgi, 1975. viii, 168p. Illus. Plates Bibliog. £0.50 pa. ISBN 0-552-09911-2

932 Lang, Andrew, 1844-1912. The Book of Dreams and Ghosts. New York: Causeway Books, 1974 (orig. pub., London: Longmans, Green, 1897). xxii, 301p. Includes bibliog. refs. $2.95 LC 74-77157 ISBN 0-88356-035-6

This book includes discussions of Mark Twain's apparition of a lady, and poltergeist disturbances at Wesley's Epworth Parsonage.

933 Lang, Terrye. Beginner's Astrology: For the Real Beginner. Rev. ed. Lakemont, Ga.: CSA Press, 1975 (pub. in 1974 as "Astrology, the Aquarian Age Science"). 279p. Illus. Includes bibliog. refs. $5.95 LC 74-34000 ISBN 0-87707-149-7

934 Langguth, A. J. Macumba: White and Black Magic in Brazil. New York: Harper and Row, 1975. 273p. $8.95 LC 74-1830 ISBN 0-06-012503-9

This book discusses in autobiographical/diary style this novelist's study of spirit religions in Brazil. These religions are related to Santería practiced in Cuba and Puerto Rico, and with Voodoo of Haiti and New Orleans. Macumba is really three religions--Umbanda, Quimbanda, and Candomble. The author undergoes ritualistic initiation into Macumba. At the end, he realizes it is impossible to go back to the reality of these mysteries. Three book reviews called this book fascinating and well done. This bibliographer does not agree. The book is boring and superficial. The author is so busy describing hundreds of surface details (colors, smells, what's lying on the table) that he utterly fails to think. There is no discussion of meaning, psychology, philosophy. The author asks all the wrong questions; he should not have been surprised when he left Brazil farther away from the mystery then when he arrived.

935 Larner, Saul P., 1940- . Astrological Assistance. Englewood Cliffs, N.J.: Prentice-Hall, 1974. 240p. $7.95 LC 74-11039 ISBN 0-13-049460-7

This book discusses how to supplement traditional horoscopes with amulets, talismans, color, music, yoga, and the I Ching.

936 Latchaw, Daniel S. The Book of Revelation from the Ethereal Plane. Philadelphia: Dorrance, 1971. v, 221p. $4.95 LC 70-140969 ISBN 0-8059-1526-5

937 Laubscher, Barend Jacob Frederick. Beyond Life's Curtain. Foreword by John D. Pearce-Higgins. Jersey, England: Spearman, 1975 (orig. pub., Cape Town: Timmins, 1967). 107p. Illus. Plates £2.50 ISBN 0-85978-015-5

This doctor discusses spiritualism and what it can tell us about life after death.

938 Laurence, Theodor [pseud.]. Helping Yourself with Spells, Prayers, Curses, and Chants. West Nyack, N.Y.: Parker Pub. Co., 1975. 201p. $7.95 LC 74-34237 ISBN 0-13-386714-5

939 ______. How the Tarot Speaks to Modern Man. Harrisburg, Pa.: Stackpole Books, 1972 (also, New York: Bell Pub. Co., 1973). 216p. Illus. $6.50 LC 79-179607 ISBN 0-8117-0858-6
*

The first section of this book discusses the origin, history, and use of the Tarot; also, it covers the significance of the numbering of each of the major arcana. The major body of the work discusses each card of the major arcana under three aspects--physical, psychological, and spiritual. Each of the three discussions for each card is two pages long, and philosophical in content. A chapter on the philosophical plane discusses how to divide the Tarot into three sets of the major arcana. One set represents man, another, the universe, and the third, God. A final chapter covers spreads.

940 ______. Satan, Sorcery, and Sex. West Nyack, N.Y.: Parker Pub. Co., 1974. Bibliog. $6.95 LC 74-10574 ISBN 0-13-791202-1

941 ______. A Sexual Key to the Tarot. New York: Citadel Press, 1971 (also, New York: Signet/New American Library, 1973). 121p. Illus. $5.95 LC 70-29950 ISBN 0-8065-0242-8

The main part of this book is on the major arcana. For each card, the author first discusses various sexual "keys" or symbols in the figure, then gives a one-or two-page discussion of its "sexual signification." The signification discussion covers the sexual nature of persons represented by the card, and then gives possible meaning in a spread. The next, shorter section, discusses each card of the minor arcana in a paragraph, giving meanings for regular and inverted. The last chapter discusses choosing an "agent" (card representing the person or matter in question). Needless to say, this book makes for very unusual, interesting reading. It is bound to add spice to any consultations one does for friends.

942 Laver, James. Nostradamus; or, the Future Foretold. Maidstone, England: George Mann, 1973 (orig. pub., London: Collins, 1942). 265p. Bibliog. £2.20 ISBN 0-7041-0010-X

This is a good survey on the subject. Chapters include: "Nostradamus the Physician," "Nostradamus the Prophet," "The House of the Seven," "The House of Bourbon," "Nostradamus and the History of England," "Nostradamus and the French Revolution," "Nostradamus and Napoleon I," and "The End of the World."

943 LaVey, Anton Szandor, 1930- . The Compleat Witch; or, What to Do When Virtue Fails. New York: Lancer Books, 1972 (orig. pub., New York: Dodd, 1971). 274p. Bibliog. $1.50 pa.

LaVey feels that sexual desire generates occult power. He tries to teach witches how to create lust in males. He classifies people into four types, using astrology and the somatology of Sheldon and Kretschmer. The system is shown graphically by a circle divided into 12 parts, which he calls the "LaVey Personality Synthesizer." The witch should judge a man on the synthesizer so she will know what will excite him. The book also discusses some sexual rituals.

944 ______. Satanic Rituals. New York: Avon, 1972. 220p. $1.25 pa. LC 73-154234

This book discusses rituals, original psychodrama, and satanic baptism. The entire book is one of ceremonies, giving who speaks, and the words, just as in a play.

945/7 Law, Donald. Astrology, Palmistry, and Dreams. Totowa, N.J.: Littlefield Adams, 1975 (orig. pub., Edinburgh: J. Bartholomew, 1973). 160p. Illus. $2.50 pa. LC 75-4710 ISBN 0-8226-0298-9

948 Lawrence, Edward, 1921-1936. Spiritualism Among Civilized and Savage Races; A Study in Anthropology. Freeport, N.Y.: Books for Libraries, 1971 (reprint of 1921 ed.). xii, 112p. Illus. Includes bibliog. refs. $8.50 LC 76-160980 ISBN 0-8369-5848-9

949 Lawrence, Jodi. Alpha Brain Waves. Los Angeles: Nash, 1972. ix, 237p. Illus. Bibliog. $7.95 LC 72-186923 ISBN 0-8402-1263-1

This book discusses biofeedback techniques, research, and history. The technique can help cure or control headaches, tension, epilepsy, slow reading, and incorrect thinking. The future may see its use in treatment of alcoholism, cigarette smoking, drug addiction, birth control, and cancer. There is a question-and-answer section. Also, the author mentions the dangers of homemade devices.

950 Laycock, George. Strange Monsters and Great Searches. Cover illustration by Sian Cardy; text illustrations by Mary French. London: Pan Books, 1975 (also, Boston: G. K. Hall, 1973, large print ed.; orig. pub., Garden City, N.Y.: Doubleday, 1973). 96p. Illus. (A Piccolo Book) £0.35 pa. ISBN 0-330-24624-0

This juvenile book discusses the following: the Loch Ness serpent; the yeti and its counterpart in the U.S., the Sasquatch or Bigfoot; the Komodo dragon of Japan; squid; the dodo; the supposedly extinct coelacanth (ancient fish); even an escaped python loose in Ohio. This book is really a collection of curiosities rather than monsters. It is recommended for grades 4-6.

951 Leadbeater, C.W. Chakras. Wheaton, Ill.: Theosophical Pub. House, 1972 (orig. pub., Madras, India: Theosophical Pub. House, 1927). 132p. Illus. (color) $3.25 pa.

This book is a classic of theosophical literature. Chakras--originally ancient Hindu discs representing the sun and sovereignty--now indicate supposedly subtle, psychic sense organs in the body that channel psychic energies and vital forces, and are related to glandular and nervous systems. They are wheel-like vortices appearing in vivid colors, according to some sensitives. Others have likened them to flowers with many petals. Leadbeater discusses force centers, the spine, serpent fire, glohiles, absorption of vitality (different colored rays), development of the chakras (awakened centers, astral senses, kundalini), and laya yoga (Hindu books, goal of kundalini). There are 10 color illustrations of the chakras.

952 LeBeau, Mary [pseud.]. Beyond Doubt; A Record of Psychic Experience. New York: Harper, 1971 (c1956). 179p. $1.25 LC 55-11476 ISBN 0-06-080228-6

953 Lee, Fleming. Your Hidden Horoscope. N. Hollywood, Calif.: Brandon Book, 1971. 252p. Illus. $1.95 pa. ISBN 0-87056-212-6

954 Leek, Sybil, 1924- . Astrological Guide to Beauty. New York: Popular Library, 1973. 188p. $.95 pa.

Topics discussed include hands, fingernails, figure, hair, importance of sleep, vitamins, cosmetics, dieting, and beauty shop operators. All of the above are related to one's astrological sign and ascendant planet.

955 ________. Astrological Guide to Financial Success. New York: Grosset, 1972. 216p. $6.95 LC 75-158772 ISBN 0-448-01943-4

956 ________. Astrological Guide to the Presidential Candidates. London, New York: Abelard, 1972 (also, New York: Ace, 1972). xiv, 145p. Illus. LC 79-38420 ISBN 0-200-71879-7

957 ________. The Complete Art of Witchcraft. New York: New
* American Library, 1973 (also, London: Frewin, 1975; orig. pub., New York: World, 1971). 205p. Illus. $.95 pa.

This is a well-written, intelligent discussion of the subject, concentrating on the theory and philosophy of witchcraft. Chapters include "What It's Like to Be a Witch," "Black Magic or Witchcraft," "Reincarnation," "You the Alchemist," "The Place of the Homosexual in Witchcraft," "Rituals," and "Invocations." The author emphasizes throughout, especially in the last chapter, that the main aim of witchcraft is to enable one to lead a balanced life in harmony with the universe. This is not the mediocre kind of book one often finds written by one who claims to be a practicing witch. It should be read by all those who do not realize there is a long tradition of theoretical, philosophical witchcraft. Leek has made an excellent contribution here.

958 ________. The Diary of a Witch. London: Frewin, 1975 (also, New York: New American Library, 1971). 221p. £2.75 ISBN 0-85632-148-6

959 ________. Driving out the Devils: An Exorcist's Casebook. New York: Putnam, 1975. 253p. Bibliog. $7.95 LC 74-16606 ISBN 0-399-11450-5

The first few chapters and the last two are on the author's experiences. In 1969 in Houston, she and her family were almost possessed before she did an incantation. As she wrote this book, there were winds, odors, and the like. Also mentioned are exorcisms she has performed. However, the main body of the book is a more general history of demonology and exorcism. Leek feels that evil entities exist, and can be exorcised by using a higher power, the Mother Goddess.

960 ________. ESP--The Magic Within You. New York, London: Abelard-Schuman, 1972. 192p. $6.95 LC 74-157981 ISBN 0-200-71831-2

The author believes that every person has at least some ESP ability. She discusses many cases of ESP in history, and gives tips on how to develop ESP potential. The book includes a glossary of parapsychology terms.

961 ________. Herbs, Medicine and Mysticism. Chicago: Regnery
* Co., 1975 (also, Ontario: Fitzhenry and Whiteside, 1975). 255p. $8.95 LC 74-30262 ISBN 0-8092-8431-6

The major part of this fine book is an A-to-Z herb encyclopedia. For each herb, there is a half page of the following information: botanical name, synonyms, habitat, description, action, medicinal uses, method of preparation, dosage. Other chapters include: Hopi Indians and their medicinal herbs; passionate herbs; herbs and astrology. The last chapter gives a list of addresses for herbs alphabetically by state. Leek has written a fine work that is a handy reference book to own.

962 ________. How to Succeed Through Astrology. London: Frewin, 1975. 286p. £2.75 ISBN 0-85632-147-8

963 ________. My Life in Astrology. Englewood Cliffs, N.J.:
* Prentice-Hall, 1972. 205p. $6.95 LC 72-37290 ISBN 0-13-608521-0

Much of this book is autobiographical. The author's grandmother taught her astrology, and had as clients the Sitwells, T.E. Lawrence, and H.G. Wells. Her father taught her how to draw a chart. There is discussion of Sybil's early life in England, winters on the French Riviera, and work as a nurse during World War II. She gradually developed her own clients (she predicted Ian Fleming's death, and was only eight hours off in predicting Nasser's demise). In the 1960's, Sybil came to the U.S., living, writing, and lecturing in New York, Los Angeles, Florida, Houston, and recently, Nevada. Leek discusses publishing in the U.S., and starting her astrology school in St. Louis. She includes some predictions.

964 ________. Night Voyagers: You and Your Dreams. New York: Mason and Lipscomb, 1975. $7.95 LC 74-32245

This book discusses among other things dream symbols, Freud, and what to expect from dreams. She presents cases of people learning from them, such as Robert Louis Stevenson and Bismarck. The book includes a dictionary of dream meanings.

965 ________. Reincarnation: The Second Chance. New York:
* Stein and Day, 1974 (also, New York: Bantam, 1975). 304p. Bibliog. Index $7.95 LC 73-93034

In this fine survey, the author discusses karma, reincarnation, astrology, spiritualism, Atlantis, reincarnation and animals, and religious ideas supporting reincarnation (Judaism, Christianity, Buddhism, Hinduism, China, Tibet, Japan). The last section, "Pearls of Wisdom," contains excerpts from various thinkers on the eternal life of the soul. These paragraph-long quotes include ones by Goethe, Dali, Henry Ford, Nevil Shute, Peter Ustinov, Tolstoy, Hegel, and Poe. Leek says she has lived other lives: 12th-dynasty Egypt; Rome in 30 B.C.; Yucatan, A.D. 900. She feels that the process of rebirth is speeding up.

966 ______. Star Speak: Your Body Language from the Stars.
* New York: Arbor House, 1975. xviii, 263p. Bibliog. $8.95 LC 75-11151 ISBN 0-87795-118-7

This book discusses the influence of astrology on the human body. One section discusses each zodiac sign, giving for each: ruling planet, main attributes, main faults, type of mind, vulnerable areas, physical danger signs, sports, temperament, natural movement, and ideal for success. Another chapter discusses how astrological body language is used by each zodiac sign type to express sexual interests. Other chapters discuss body language and the preschool child, body language and marriage, and body language and work. A large section on exercises gives the following for each zodiac sign: personal movement pattern, personal movement needs, exercises (breathing, balanced movement, and relief for vulnerable areas). Other chapters include signs of famous people; astrological quiz; and casting a horoscope. This is a very well-organized book.

967 ______. Sybil Leek's Astrological Guide to Successful Everyday Living. New York: New American Library, 1972 (c1970). 286p. $1.25 pa.

For each zodiac sign, this book gives advice on health, love life, family, diet, finances, sports, hobbies, general characteristics, vocations, where to live, what kind of mate to pick, and trees and shrubs.

968 ______. Sybil Leek's Book of Curses. Englewood Cliffs,
* N.J.: Prentice-Hall, 1975. 159p. $5.95 LC 74-30321 ISBN 0-13-879890-7

This well-done survey discusses the origin and history of the practice, ancient and modern rituals, voodoo rites, Catholic excommunication, Pennsylvania Dutch hexes, blood brotherhoods, secret societies, pacts with the devil, vows, curses in literature, candle power, fatal curses, and skulls working on fulfilling curses. Once again, Leek has written a fine short survey.

969 ______. Sybil Leek's Zodiac of Love. Chicago: H. Regnery, 1974 (also, London: Frewin, 1975). 201p. $7.95 LC 73-18115

970 ______. Telepathy: The Respectable Phenomenon. New York: Macmillan, 1971. 160p. $5.95 LC 71-141934

971 ______. Tomorrow's Headlines Today. Englewood Cliffs,

N. J. : 1974. $6.95 LC 74-7108 ISBN 0-13-924787-4

This book is a collection of 11 articles on astrology, discussing two types of horoscopes--genethliacal (on a person) and mundane (the fate of countries or the world). Individual horoscopes include those of Nixon, John Dean, and various assassinated world leaders. The mundane section discusses astrological ages, the effect of Neptune and Pluto on world events, the astrology of earthquakes, and the astrological evolution of countries.

972 _______. You and Your Dreams. New York: Mason and Lipscomb, 1975. 200p. $7.95

This book discusses dreams in literature and psychiatry. It also covers Leek's own prophetic dreams, and includes a dictionary of dream symbols.

973 Lefort, Rafael. The Teachers of Gurdjieff. New York: S. Weiser, 1973 (c1966). 157p. $5 LC 72-91193

This book is the story of a journey and quest that took the author to Baghdad, Damascus, Jerusalem, Istanbul, Iran, Cairo, and Afghanistan. Lefort set out to find the sources of Gurdjieff's teachings. He followed clues in Gurdjieff's writings, which suggested the origin was in the Middle East, and also began to explore Sufi tradition. He found many persons who had taught Gurdjieff.

974 Legeza, Ireneus Laszlo. Tao Magic: The Chinese Art of the Occult. New York: Pantheon Books, 1975. 125p. Illus. $4.95 pa. LC 75-10369 ISBN 0-394-73125-5

This is a pictorial book on Taoist diagrams and calligraphy, an art over 2,000 years old. These were thought to be talismans, that could cure illness and draw down blessings and good luck. The author discusses the inscriptions in Taoist thought and in terms of the lives of the people.

975 Leibel, Charlotte P. Change Your Handwriting, Change Your
* Life. New York: Stein and Day, 1972 (also, New York: Barnes and Noble, 1973). ix, 230p. $7.95 LC 72-163354 ISBN 0-8128-1416-9

The author discusses these topics: the history of graphology, form level or quality, rhythm, pressure, slant, leftward and rightward trends, base line direction, connections and disconnections, spacing, regularity and irregularity, size, speed or tempo, margins, legibility, width and narrowness, fullness and leanness, letter formations, extrovert and introvert, capital letters, small letters, numerals, beginning strokes, ending strokes, signature, and writing on envelope. The second half of the work concentrates on self-correction through handwriting.

976 Leinbach, Esther V. Degrees of the Zodiac. Richmond, Va. :

Macoy Pub. and Masonic Supply Co., 1973. xii, 206p. LC 73-161445

977 Leland, Charles Godfrey, 1824-1903. Aradia: The Gospel of the Witches. Introd. by Stewart Farrar. London: Daniel, 1974 (orig. pub., London: D. Nutt, 1899). xv, 132p. £1.75

This classic work on Italian witches was written with information the author got through friendship from 1886 on with Maddalena, a Florentine fortuneteller and hereditary witch from the Romagna Tuscana. From her, Leland got material on Diana, her daughter Aradia, and the Sabbat. Most of the collected material consists of legends.

978 ________. Gypsy Sorcery and Fortune-telling. New York: Dover, 1971 (also, Magnolia, Mass.: Peter Smith, 1972; reprint of 1931 ed.; orig. pub., 1891). xvi, 271p. Illus. $5.50

The author was president of the Gypsy Lore Society. In this book, he discusses these beliefs: curing spells, divination, talismans, amulets, charms, exorcism, warding off demons, witches, prediction of the future, love philtres, supernatural powers through heredity, and comparison of Gypsy beliefs with those of other magical traditions.

979 Leonard, Maurice. Battling Bertha: The Biography of Bertha Harris. London: Regency Press, 1975. 155p. Illus. Plates £2 ISBN 0-7212-0424-4

This book discusses Bertha's involvement in spirit photography, materializations, exorcisms, and ghosts. At the height of her powers, she has been consulted by monarchs, political leaders, generals, and scientists. She has worked with Lodge and Doyle, and been coached by Ernest Oaten in her mediumship. "Battling" refers to the fact that she has aggressively defended her skills. When her friend Helen Duncan was imprisoned for mediumship, Bertha backed her, and spent hours lobbying. This work is a well-done biography.

980 ________. Medium: The Biography of Jessie Nason. London: Regency Press, 1974. 137p. Illus. Plates £1.20 ISBN 0-7212-0332-9

This well-done biography discusses Nason's famous appearances on the David Frost show and at Royal Albert Hall, guides, what it is like to die, seances, and apports. She was clairvoyant as a child, and spoke to imaginary people. Her gifts were nurtured by her mother, who also was a medium, and worked with Jessie in circles. The author is a BBC man, who also helped on the Dictionary of International Biography.

981 Leonardi, Dell. The Reincarnation of John Wilkes Booth: A

Study in Hypnotic Regression. Old Greenwich, Conn.: Devin-Adair Co., 1975. 180p. Bibliog. $6.95 LC 74-27952 ISBN 0-8159-6716-0

In weekly sessions, one of the students in the author's hypnosis class gave the story of his life as Booth in surprising detail. In 70 taped hours of sessions, he said he was bribed by the Knights of the Golden Circle (a secret society to which Stanton, Seward, and Johnson belonged) to kill Lincoln. The student said Booth escaped to Europe, married, and died 10 years later; his double was killed. The author states that the student/Booth sometimes contradicted himself, or could not remember things he should have known easily. Later, the author saw the importance of wording the questions, and did extensive reading so as to better phrase them. After this, Booth's answers improved--a phenomenon which makes one wonder how much telepathy was involved. Leonardi draws connections between the 18 pages supposedly stolen from Booth's diary and the 18 missing minutes on the Nixon tape.

982 Le Poer Trench, Brinsley, 1911- . Flying Saucer Story. New ed. London: Tandem, 1973 (previous ed., London: Spearman, 1966). 189p. Illus. Bibliog. Index £0.35 pa. ISBN 0-426-12140-6

983 ________. Mysterious Visitors: The UFO Story. New York: Stein and Day, 1973 (also, London: Pan Books, 1975; also pub. as "The Eternal Subject," London: Souvenir Press, 1973; orig. pub., 1971). 192p. Illus. Includes bibliog. refs. $6.95 LC 72-96748 ISBN 0-8128-1535-1

The author is international chairman of Contact, a UFO-sighting organization. The work is based mostly on the Bible and examples from Flying Saucer Review. He discusses biblical passages possibly referring to UFO's. The author suggests that there is a galactic civilization that has systematically colonized all livable planets. He discusses the possible secret presence among us of the Sky People, who may have endowed the younger generation with superior intellectual powers. Also, the author believes that NASA has an operational flying saucer using some kind of anti-gravity propulsion. The appendix gives descriptions of UFO shapes.

984 ________. The Secret of the Ages: UFO's from Inside the Earth. London: Souvenir Press, 1974. 192p. Illus. Plates Map Index £2.60 ISBN 0-285-62153-X

985 ________. The Sky People. London: Tandem, 1971 (orig. pub., London: Spearman, 1960). 224p. Bibliog. Index £0.25 pa. ISBN 0-426-05346-X

986 ________. Temple of the Stars. London: Fontana, 1973 (also, New York: Ballantine Books, 1974; orig. pub. as "Men among Mankind," London: Spearman, 1963). 223p. Illus. Bibliog. Index £0.40 pa.

The author believes there is another breed of man living among the stars who once visited us. He discusses leys and dragon paths, Osiris, monotheism. He feels that through all megalithic ruins around the world there runs a thread of forgotten history.

987 LeShan, Lawrence L., 1920- . How to Meditate: A Guide
* to Self-Discovery. Boston: Little, Brown and Co., 1974. 210p. $5.95 LC 74-6210

This book gives a good discussion of how to meditate. The author discusses the traditions of Zen, yoga, Sufi, Hasidism, and Christian mysticism. LeShan says that some of meditation is hard discipline, but other parts are peaceful. Meditation gives a different, but not superior, view of reality. The author, a psychotherapist, sees both psychological and physiological benefits in it. He sees connections to ESP, but feels it is irrelevant to meditation. This book includes many practical instructions for meditation, such as breath-counting.

988 ______. The Medium, the Mystic, and the Physicist; To-
*** ward a General Theory of the Paranormal. New York: Viking Press, 1974 (also, London: Turnstone Books, 1974). xix, 299p. Includes bibliog. refs. (An Esalen Book) $8.95 LC 73-8147 ISBN 0-670-46566-6

This work is a major new contribution to occult literature. The author is a member of the Board of Trustees of the American Society for Psychical Research, a clinical psychologist, and a pioneer in the psychological study of disease and dying. Several years ago, he noticed the close similarity of statements by mediums about clairvoyant experiences with mystical experiences and with reality as seen by theoretical physics. The author tries to develop a unified theory of the paranormal and, from it, a technique to train for psychic healing. The first section of the book is called "Three Roads to One Reality"--clairvoyant, mystic, and physicist. LeShan studied clairvoyants, especially Garrett, and calls their state "clairvoyant reality." This state differs from ordinary reality in four ways: unity of all things; past, present and future are one; judgment on good or evil of event is not mentioned; information is gained by knowing one's unity to all things. The author then tries to apply these to the realities of mysticism and physics. Part 2 is called "Testing the Theory" and is on psychic healing. Part 3, titled "Next Adventure," is an area the author is currently working on. He sees five levels of healing, the top one being "transpsychic reality." Appendices include the following: non-acceptance of the paranormal; "Who Is Uvani?"--an approach to a concept of spirit controls; human survival of biological death (field theory in modern physics); physicists' and mystics' similarity in world view (a 60-question quiz with quotes, asking which group would be more likely to have said it); and an article by Ullman and Krippner on dream telepathy. The author writes in an autobiographical tone about his quest for the answers.

989 Lethbridge, Thomas Charles. ESP: Beyond Time and Distance. London: Sidgwick and Jackson, 1974 (orig. pub., London: Routledge and Kegan Paul, 1965). 156p. Illus. Index £0.45 pa. ISBN 0-283-98278-0

The author believes the Russians are wrong to see the seat of ESP in the brain. He feels the mind of man is immortal and outside both space and time. It operates the sixth sense. Much of the book is on anthropology and animal behavior, and pendulum movements.

990 _______. The Legend of the Sons of God: A Fantasy? London: Routledge and K. Paul, 1972. ix, 118p. Illus. Map £1.75 ISBN 0-7100-7159-0

The author theorizes that the Sons of God were extraterrestrials cut off from their race. He discusses the stone circle near Lamorna, England, called "Merry Maidens." The stones were electrically charged. He believes the ancient custom of dancing in a circle created bioelectricity that was then stored somehow in the stones. These stones may have been navigational beacons for the extraterrestrials.

991 Levett, Carl David. Crossings, a Transpersonal Approach. Ridgefield, Conn.: Quiet Song, 1974. 200p. $8.50 LC 74-17597 ISBN 0-915054-01-9

This psychologist discusses his use of Eastern religion and mysticism as therapy.

992 Lewis, L. M. Footprints on the Sands of Time. New York: Signet Books, 1975. $1.50 pa.

The author says that extraterrestrials arrived on earth in 6790 B.C., and were completely annihilated in 1451 B.C. Between these two dates, they ruled the world and were worshipped as gods. Chapters discuss the following: messengers of the gods, Sodom, the Great Triangle, flood, Atlantis, and were Sodom and Gomorrah destroyed by a master race using hydrogen bombs?

993 The Leyden Papyrus: An Egyptian Magical Book. Ed. by F. L. Griffith and Herbert Thompson. New York: Dover, 1974 (orig. pub. as "The Demotic Magical Papyrus of London and Leiden," 1904). xii, 207p. $2.50 pa. LC 73-90639 ISBN 0-486-22994-7

This book of practical magic probably dates from the beginning of the Christian era, and appears to be the textbook of a practicing sorcerer. It is a key document for determining the spells, incantations, and potions of ancient Egypt. It also shows influences of Gnostic beliefs and Greek magic. A transliteration of the demotic script is printed on facing pages with a fully annotated translation. Discussions include how to invoke Anubis and release the dead; how to divine with a lamp; how to have dream visions; how to make magical ointment; and how to invoke Thoth and bring good fortune.

994 Lilley, William. Introduction to Astrology. Hollywood, Calif.: Newcastle Pub. Co., 1972 (reprint of 1852 ed.; orig. pub., 1647). 346p. $3.75 pa.

The astrologer to Charles I published this work in 1647.

995 Lilly, John Cunningham. The Centre of the Cyclone: An
*** Autobiography of Inner Space. London: Calder and Boyars, 1973 (also, London: Paladin, 1973; orig. pub., New York: Julian Press, 1972). 220p. Illus. Bibliog. (Open Forum) £2.50 ISBN 0-7145-0961-2

This work is a major new contribution to occult literature, though it falls more under the area of psychology. The book is the exciting, fascinating account of a scientist who has spent his life searching for the truth anywhere it leads him, even into himself. Lilly worked in many fields of science--biophysics, neurophysiology, electronics, and neuroanatomy. He wrote many studies on solitude and loneliness. He spent 12 years on dolphin-human relationships, two years as an Esalen Institute group leader, and eight months in Arica, Chile, under the sage Oscar Ichazo. The work discusses various "trips" Lilly has taken--with and without the use of LSD, a solitude-isolation-confinement tank, hypnosis, Gestalt therapy, and group encounter. Chapters include: "My First Two Trips"; "LSD Spaces and Projections"; "A Guided Tour of Hell"; "The Human Biocomputer"; "Work at Kairos." This book is required reading for any searching human being.

996 Lilly, William, 1602-1681. The Last of the Astrologers: Mr. William Lilly's History of His Life and Times from the Year 1602 to 1681. Introd. by Katherine M. Briggs. London: Folklore Society, 1975 (2nd ed. orig. pub. as "Mr. William Lilly's History of His Life and Times from the Year 1602 to 1681," London: J. Roberts, 1715). xvii, 108p. Illus. Bibliog. (Dist. in U.S. by Rowman and Littlefield) $9 LC 74-181741

The author discusses his self-education, patrons, important people who consulted him, and writings. He supported Parliament in the Civil War. The work shows the strong belief in astrology in 17th-century England.

997 Lindsay, Jack, 1900- . The Origins of Astrology. New
* York: Barnes and Noble, 1971 (also, London: Muller, 1971). xii, 480p. Illus. Bibliog. $12.75 LC 73-28190 ISBN 0-389-04118-1

This book was written as a companion to go with the author's The Origins of Alchemy in Graeco-Roman Egypt. It covers the

Babylonians, Greeks, Romans, and Egyptians. The author feels that the current view of astrology as held by historians is a distortion that does not admit the tremendous influence it had on ancient life. This study was written to correct that view. The ancients held the idea that earth and the heavens were two closely related halves of a whole. Astrology revealed their relationship on even the smallest matters in endless correspondences. This concept was deeply imbedded in all thinking, and gave astrology vast power. The author has written over 60 books, and has a degree in classics from Queensland University. This book is loaded with data and footnotes.

998 Lindsey, Hal. Satan Is Alive and Well on Planet Earth. Grand Rapids, Mich.: Zondervan Pub. Co., 1972. 255p. $2.25 pa.

This book has chapters on the other side (Pike and Ford, Tarot, spiritualism, Russia), "thought bombs" (Kant, Hegel, Kierkegaard, Marx), "angels of light" (mostly on Jeane Dixon), signs and wonders (speaking in tongues), and demon possession. In theory, this should be a good survey, but the author puts the devil everywhere in history. The Bible is quoted throughout.

999 Linhares, Margaret. I Married a Witch's Love. New York: Vantage Press, 1974. 113p. $4.50 ISBN 0-533-01025-X

1000 Links with Space. Forres, Scotland: Findhorn Foundation, 1975. 24p. £0.40 pa. ISBN 0-905249-03-8

1001 Linton, Elizabeth (Lynn), 1822-1898, comp. Witch Stories. New York: Barnes and Noble Books, 1972 (also, Detroit: Grand River Books, 1972, dist. by Gale Pub. Co.; London: Muller, 1972; orig. pub., London: Champman and Hall, 1861). iv, 428p. Index $12.50 LC 73-155608

This collection covers cases of alleged witchcraft in Scotland and England, from earliest times to the mob murder of Ruth Osborne, the Witch of Tring, in 1751. Gathered from manuscripts, the cases include many not found in the usual anthologies. The author presents them without any philosophical analysis, except to call them a "landmark of the excesses to which a blind belief may hurry and impel humanity." The index is newly added.

1002 Lippman, Deborah, and Paul Colin. Amulets, Charms and Talismans: What They Mean and How to Use Them. New York: M. Evans and Co., 1974. 208p. $8.95

This is actually a craft book, giving detailed diagrams and instructions for making pentagrams, ankhs, voodoo love charms, thighbands, and marriage pomanders. Appendices give the following lists: suppliers, tools, processes, herbs, stones, and symbols.

1003 Litvag, Irving. Singer in the Shadows; The Strange Story
* of Patience Worth. New York: Popular Library, 1973 (orig. pub., New York: Macmillan, 1972). 319p. Includes bibliog. refs. $.95 pa.

This is the first complete account of the Patience Worth case. The author is director of special events at Washington University in St. Louis. The book concerns a St. Louis housewife, Mrs. Pearl Curran, who, beginning in 1913 and lasting through 1937, received seven full-length books through her Ouija board, as well as hundreds of stories, poems, and thousands of pages of conversation. The total output was over four million words. Four of the books were published by reputable firms, and some literary experts wrote book reviews in high praise of her writing. Mrs. Curran claimed that all of the material was written by a 17th-century Englishwoman, Patience Worth. Most of this work is devoted to a study of Patience Worth, and not Mrs. Curran.

1004 Liu, Da. I Ching Coin Prediction. New York: Harper and Row, 1975 (c1974). $6.95 LC 73-18695 ISBN 0-06-061664-9

This book is written by a noted authority on traditional Chinese culture. It explains the hexagrams, and gives instructions for predicting the future using coins and yarrow stalks.

1005 Livingston, Peter. On Astrology. Illus. by Rick Schneider. Englewood Cliffs, N.J.: Prentice-Hall, 1974. 143p. Bibliog. Index $5.95 LC 74-8164 ISBN 0-13-638825-6

This book discusses the usual sun signs, houses, ruling planets, horoscopes for juveniles. On each sign, the author gives the typical personality, famous people born under the sign, and how one born under the sign would take to mountain climbing. In a chapter, "The Future of Astrology," he discusses views of scientists, psychiatrists, and researchers. The book is recommended for grades 5-8.

1006 Lobsang Rampa, Tuesday. Twilight. London: Corgi, 1975. 204p. £0.50 pa. ISBN 0-552-09767-5

1007 The Loch Morar Survey. Annual Report. 1970, 1971, and 1972. London: Loch Morar Survey, 1970-1972. 3 vols. 39, 12, 8p. Illus. Maps £0.25 pa. each

1008 Lockhart, John Gilbert, 1891- . Curses, Lucks and Talismans. Detroit: Singing Tree Press, 1971 (orig. pub., London: Geoffrey Bles, 1938). viii, 184p. Illus. $12.50 LC 70-132016

1009 Loeper, John J. Understanding Your Child through Astrology. New York: Paperback Library, 1971 (orig. pub., New York: McKay, 1970). 220p. $1.25 pa.

The author is an educator and school administrator. He goes sign-by-sign, and gives good and bad characteristics, study habits, behavior patterns, and personality traits. He also mentions astrological signs most compatible with the child's.

1010 Logan, Daniel, 1936- . America Bewitched; The Rise of Black Magic and Spiritism. New York: Morrow, 1974 (c1973). 187p. Bibliog. $5.95 LC 73-12734 ISBN 0-688-00221-8

The author's theme is that organized evil is taking over America at a frightening pace. He writes of evil groups in lower California, the Manson cult, on-campus black magic, and Anton LaVey and the Process church. He even sees Alice Cooper (a rock star) and the Vietnam War as influences of the powers of evil. The book also includes Ouija-board messages concerning his previous life as a warlock.

1011 ________. The Anatomy of Prophecy. Englewood Cliffs, N.J.: Prentice-Hall, 1975. 192p. Bibliog. Index $6.95 LC 74-23151 ISBN 0-13-035188-1

The first few chapters of this book give incidents from Logan's own life. He discusses predictions, how they occur and how to make sense of them; Shakespeare; Sam Clemens; J.B. Priestley; Lincoln; the Kennedys; Logan's warnings about Bishop Pike; the state of Jane Fonda's soul delivered by spirit entity Dr. Stanley Padulsky, who works through Logan; Padulsky's comment that Blatty was possessed while writing The Exorcist; and the work of Jane Roberts and her contact Seth. The last part of the book contains transcripts of trance sessions under control of Dr. Padulsky, who gives lectures on the state of the world.

1012 ________. Your Eastern Star; Oriental Astrology, Reincarnation and the Future. New York: Morrow, 1972. 240p. Illus. $5.95 LC 75-166354

The first 60 pages of this book discuss the author's experiences while researching the topic in Japan. The rest of the work then goes year-by-year (the 12 animal years) and month-by-month within the year, giving personality traits and qualities.

1013 Loman, Eve. You Are What You Dream. Greenwich, Conn.: Fawcett, 1972. 208p. $.75 pa.

1014 Long, Mary. Our Son Moves Among You: A Revelation. London: Bachman and Turner, 1974. x, 252p. £3.30 ISBN 0-85974-003-X

1015 Lowell, Laurel. Pluto. St. Paul, Minn.: Llewellyn, 1973. $2.95 pa.

This is a fine, thorough work on a relatively new aspect

of astrology. It was formerly believed that Pluto had no influence on astrology; the planet was thus ignored in constructing horoscopes. Lowell does not agree with this view, and with good cause. She is a cousin of Percival Lowell, who discovered Pluto. The author has been practicing astrology for 25 years, giving her added credentials. Chapters include: "Mythological Background," "Pluto's Rulership," "Pluto's Correspondences," "Pluto in Houses," "Pluto in Signs," "Aspects Arranged by Planets," "Transits," "General Aspects," and "Ephemeris from 1851-2000."

1016 _______. Secondary Progressions, Using the Adjusted Calculating Date. Richmond: Macoy Pub. Co., 1973. 91p. $4.75 LC 73-76620

This work is a quick and accurate reference to locating the ACD (adjusted calculating date) and to interpreting its use in relation to prediction work with secondary progressions. Such progressions operate on the theory that the progressed position of planets on a given day of a given year after birth present a correct evaluation of events culminating during that year. Why the system works is unknown. Astrologers have found it an expedient method (especially in the old days, since ephemerides were not readily available until 1767). This is a difficult text for serious students only.

1017 Lowengard, Manfred. How to Analyze Your Handwriting. London: Marshall Cavendish, 1975 (first pub. as "Handwriting: What It Reveals about You," 1974, and "Come Alive," 1975). 64p. Illus. (chiefly color) (Golden Hands Books) £1.60 ISBN 0-85685-105-1

1018 Luce, Gay Gaer. Biological Rhythms in Human and Animal Physiology. New York: Dover, 1971 (also, Peter Smith, 1972; orig. pub. as "Biological Rhythms in Psychiatry and Medicine," Washington, D.C.: U.S. Dept. of Health, Education and Welfare, 1970). 183p. Bibliog. $3 LC 76-169785

This book, originally published as a government document, discusses research on rhythms in human and animal life, such as menstruation, disease susceptibility, emotions, and sleep. It covers the importance of these rhythms in work-rest schedules and health care, and mentions the work of many noted scientists.

1019 Lucis Trust. Library. Lucis Trust Library Catalogue, 1973. New York: Lucis Trust, 1975. ii, 79p. $1 pa. (donation)

This work lists by author and title over 2,000 books held by this library. Since Lucis Trust through its Arcane School emphasizes world goodwill, prayer, and peace based on the writings of Alice Bailey, its holdings reflect an acquisitions policy similar to the Theosophical Society. There are many books on cosmic consciousness, religion, meditation, mythology, the philosophy of occultism, mysticism. Books may be borrowed by individuals only upon filling out an application. Organizational borrowing requests are not honored.

1020 Lunan, Duncan. Interstellar Contact; Communication with
* Other Intelligence in the Universe. Chicago: Henry Regnery Co., 1975 (orig. pub. as "Man and the Stars," London: Souvenir Press, 1974). x, 324p. Illus. Bibliog. $9.95 LC 74-30199 ISBN 0-8092-8258-5

The first half of this very interesting book discusses these topics: will there be suitable planets?; will there be suitable ships?; life, as we know it; is your journey really necessary?; who will go to the stars, and why; colonization program; second phase, an interstellar civilization; are we mentally prepared?; contact on our terms; first contact after landing; they find us. The second part of the book discusses applications of the preceding discussion, presenting specific incidents. The major one covered is the 1973 discovery by Lunan, an eminent Scottish scientist, that radio signals that had puzzled scientists since the 1920's were actually a series of star maps apparently transmitted by a space-probe circling earth. The messages seemed to have originated in the constellation Bootes 13,000 years ago. Lunan then discusses other similar cases from the past as discovered in old myths, old maps, and early records.

1021 Lusson, M., 1938- , and D. Lusson, 1938- . The Beginning or the End: Where Are We Going? By the Lusson Twins. Virginia Beach: Donning, 1975. 123p. Illus. Maps $5.95 LC 75-22487 ISBN 0-915442-02-7

This book discusses events through six cycles of seven years each, beginning in 1958, and ending in the year 2000. The predictions emphasize land changes and economics. The author states that we can change potential catastrophes if we act soon. Also discussed is the world after 2000, covering social, political, religious, scientific, and human changes.

1022 Lutyens, Mary. Krishnamurti: The Years of Awakening. New York: Farrar, 1975. 326p. Illus. $8.95 LC 75-17840

This book discusses Krishnamurti's early years as proclaimed Messiah of the Theosophical Society, and ends with his leaving the Society (1911-1929). It mentions his close relationships with Annie Besant, president of the Theosophical Society from 1907 to 1933, and with C. W. Leadbeater, who first discovered him. Lutyen's mother was one of Krishnamurti's disciples. The work discusses many meetings and travels through use of letters and the memories of participants. This is the first of a projected two-volume study.

1023 Lynch, John, 1904- , comp. The Coffee Table Book of Astrology. Rev. ed. New York: Viking Press, 1975 (c1967). Illus. $12.95 LC 75-17707 ISBN 0-670-00596-7

This book discusses the history of astrology in the West; the planets; a full-color supplement of the Book of Hours of the Duc de Berry; the 12 signs of the zodiac (200 pages worth, going sign-by-sign, giving characteristics); spiritual astrology; Shakespeare's use of astrology; the game of the spheres; how to make a horoscope; palmistry and astrology; table of ascendants; ephemerides of moon, 1900-1974. Except for the full-color supplement mentioned above, all illustrations are black and white or two tones of various colors. The book is fine for browsing, but loosely organized.

1024 Lyons, Arthur. Satan Wants You: The Cult of Devil Worship. London: Hart-David, 1971 (also, London: Mayflower, 1972; orig. pub. as "Second Coming; Satanism in America," New York: Dodd, Mead, 1970). 211p. Illus. Plates Bibliog. Index £1.75 ISBN 0-246-64050-2

The first part of this book discusses the history of satanism, covering Persia in the 6th century B. C. and satanism as a reaction to the Inquisition. Then, the author tries to determine psychological reasons for the resurgence of demonology, discussing hippies, drug-takers in covens, Anton LaVey and the Church of Satan, San Francisco, and London's "Process." He collected his information on these groups through many interviews and personal attendance at classes and rites. Lyons also quotes various people on how things are falling apart today: R. D. Laing, Ortega y Gasset, Erich Fromm, Eric Hoffer, William James, Santayana, Dewey. For each period of history mentioned, the author gives differing reasons for satanism's appeal. He sees today's appeal as being due to alienation of the individual from the contemporary system of values.

1025 McArthur, Margaret. Scottish Ghosts. St. Ives, England: James Pike, 1975. 32p. Illus. Map (Viewing Scotland Series) £0.30 pa. ISBN 0-85932-103-7

1026 McCaffery, Ellen Conroy. Astrological Key to Biblical Symbolism. Wellingborough, England: Thorsons, 1975. 192p. £3.50 ISBN 0-7225-0272-9

This book emphasizes the signs and symbols of the four elements, air, water, fire, and earth. It also discusses the 12 zodiac signs. In all the discussions, the sign is studied for its relation to the Bible, with numerous Bible quotes given. The work ends with meditative exercises on each sign. Old Testament, New Testament, Hindu, and Roman influences are among those covered.

1027 McCampbell, J. M. UFOlogy. Belmont, Calif.: Jaymac Co., 1973. 153p. $10

This is a serious, technical study of UFO phenomena, attempting to break new ground. The author is an engineer and scientist, with some experience in nuclear power stations. He divides UFO cases by the type of phenomena they have exhibited, treating the phenomena chapter-by-chapter. Under each, he attempts to relate what we know scientifically about that phenomenon. Chapters discuss flight and propulsion, electrical interferences, activities on earth, and composition and luminosity. The author proposes a study program to analyze their technology. This highly technical book will be difficult for some to read.

1028 McCarroll, Tolbert. Exploring the Inner World: A Guidebook for Personal Growth and Renewal. New York: Julian Press, 1974. 223p. Bibliog. $7.95 LC 73-92174

The author is director of the Humanist Institute in San Francisco. He discusses techniques of meditation, the I Ching, the Tarot, keeping a journal of dreams and fantasies, and doodling. The book includes many examples of each.

1029 McConnell, Robert A. ESP Curriculum Guide. New York:
* Simon & Schuster, 1971. 128p. Illus. Bibliog. $5.95 LC 75-159134 ISBN 0-671-21007-6

This book is designed for secondary school and college teachers of psychology, biology, and general science who want to teach ESP and related topics, and need a guide to doing it. Sections include the following: important ideas of science illustrated by ESP; books and articles recommended for the school library (15 items covered by a one- to three-page annotation); syllabus (outline of topics to cover); a lecture to introductory psychology classes at Carnegie-Mellon University entitled "ESP and Credibility in Science"; an article, "Sale of Occult Books," being a study for the American Society for Psychical Research of occult book sales at the University of Pittsburgh; how to conduct an ESP picture-drawing experiment; how to conduct a card-guessing experiment; building a PK placement apparatus; and conducting the experiment. The author is a biophysics professor at the University of Pittsburgh.

1030 McCormack, Kathleen. Fortune-telling. London: Fontana, 1972. 128p. Illus. £0.25 pa. ISBN 0-00-613117-4

1031 ________. The Tarot. London: Fontana, 1973. 127p. Bibliog. £0.35 pa. ISBN 0-00-613398-3

1032 ________. White Magic for Lovers. London: Fontana, 1973. 160p. Illus. £0.35 pa. ISBN 0-00-613351-7

1033 McCreery, Charles. Psychical Phenomena and the Physical
* World. Foreword by Sir George Joy. London: Hamilton,

1973 (also, New York: Ballantine Books, 1973). 138p. Index (Institute of Psychophysical Research Proceedings, vol. 4) £2.30 ISBN 0-241-02340-8

In the first part of this book, the author discusses philosophical questions concerning these phenomena: lucid dreams, out-of-the-body experiences, apparitions, materializations, and psychokinesis. The second part is empirical, studying results of the Institute of Psychophysical Research's experiments in the area of birth order and ESP abilities, Marquis d'Hervey de Saint-Denys and his book on dreams, the out-of-the-body and lucid dream experiences of an exceptional case at the Institute, and ESP and alpha-rhythm. The author's philosophical theory is that only the self is real; all else is either an illusion or simply does not exist.

1034 McDonnell, Kilian, ed. The Holy Spirit and Power. Garden City, N.Y.: Doubleday, 1974. 192p. $2.95 pa.

This book is a collection of essays by theologians participating in the Catholic charismatic movement. It discusses healing, prayer, and speaking in tongues.

1035 McGarey, William A. Acupuncture and Body Energies. Phoenix, Ariz.: Gabriel Press, 1974. 160p. $6.95

The author is Director of the Association for Research and Enlightenment Clinic. He discusses the relationship of acupuncture to Chinese medicine, Western medicine, and parapsychology.

1036 ________. There Will Your Heart Be Also; Edgar Cayce's Readings about Home and Marriage. Englewood Cliffs, N.J.: Prentice-Hall, 1975. 252p. $7.95

The authors are a husband and wife who head the Association for Research and Enlightenment Clinic in Phoenix. Their basic theme is that God has given man physical desires and appetites to be used properly. The authors wrote the chapters separately. There are many quotes from Cayce's readings, the authors' interpretations, and their personal experiences. Chapters discuss sexual energy and choice, pregnancy and birth, homosexuality, karma, pre-marital chastity, marriage vows, birth control and abortion, parenthood, divorce and separation, and the ideal home.

1037 McGarry, Jim, ed. Irish Tales of Terror. London: Fontana, 1971. 158p. £0.25 pa. ISBN 0-00-612537-9

1038 McGill, Ormond. The Secret World of Witchcraft. South Brunswick, England, New York: Barnes, 1973 (also, London: Yoseloff, 1973, dist. by W.H. Allen). 202p. Illus. Index $8.95 LC 72-9836

This work discusses witchcraft in Asia and Africa. Topics include: New Guinea sorcery, witches in Melanesia, Borneo, and Macao; animal and devil worship of Taiwan, magic and witchcraft in Thailand, Burma, Cambodia, and Vietnam; magic of India; witchcraft in Tibet, Zaïre, and the Belgian Congo, and poltergeists in Brazil. The author is a magician and hypnotist who has toured many parts of the world for years displaying his talents. Much of the work is on personal experiences, anecdotes, and case studies.

1039 McHargue, Georgess. Facts, Frauds, and Phantasms; A Survey of the Spiritualist Movement. Garden City, N.Y.: Doubleday, 1972. viii, 296p. Illus. Bibliog. $4.95 LC 73-180090
***

This work is a major new contribution to occult literature. It discusses the following topics in its survey of spiritualism: ancient and primitive beginnings, the Catholic Church's stance against spiritualism, Mesmer, the Fox sisters, Andrew Jackson Davis and his spirit system, Daniel Dunglas Home, Florence Cook, Sir William Crookes, the Davenport brothers, Eusapia Palladino, the founding of spiritualist associations, the decline of mediumship primarily because of fraudulent mediums, cross-correspondences, spiritualism in the 20th century, Houdini, Garrett, and Bishop Pike's communication with his dead son. The work concludes with a glossary. The author seems to lean more against spiritualism than for it.

1040 MacHovek, Frank J. Exorcism. Mt. Vernon, N.Y.: Peter Pauper Press, 1974. 60p. $1.95

This book gives English translations of official exorcism rites from the Roman Ritual of 1614.

1041 McIntosh, Christopher, 1943- . Astrologers and Their Creed: An Historical Outline. Foreword by Agehananda Bharati. London: Arrow Books, 1971 (also, New York: Praeger, 1969; orig. pub., London: Hutchinson, 1969). 191p. Illus. Plates Chart Facsims. Index £0.30 pa. ISBN 0-09-905510-4

The author discusses the history of astrology including the Babylonians and Greeks, horoscopes, and the pros and cons of astrology. McIntosh, who went to school at Oxford University, and has studied folklore, magic, and comparative religion, is not really a believer.

1042 ________. Astrology; The Stars and Human Life: A Modern Guide. New York: Harper and Row, 1973 (c1970). 124p. Illus. Plates Chart Facsims. (Man, Myth and Magic Original) $1.25 pa. ISBN 0-06-087041-9

This survey has chapters on the planets, the signs of the zodiac, the houses, applying the principles, a short history, the growth of mass astrology, science and astrology, astrology and magic, the Chinese zodiac, astrology as symbolic truth, and anecdotes from the astrological scrapbook. A short glossary is included.

1043 _______. Eliphas Levi and the French Occult Revival. London: Rider, 1975 (orig. pub., 1972). 238p. Illus. Plates Bibliog. Index £2.50 pa. ISBN 0-09-112271-6

1044 McKenna, Dennis J., 1950- , and Terence K. McKenna. The Invisible Landscape: Mind, Hallucinogens, and the I Ching. New York: Seabury Press, 1975. 242p. Bibliog. Index (Continuum Book) $10.95 LC 75-12675 ISBN 0-8164-9249-2

The authors had a visionary experience after eating mushrooms in the Amazon River jungle. It led them to study the effects hallucinogens have on the mind. The book discusses shamanism as a technique for attaining ecstasy, and mentions the holographic theory of the mind. There are many diagrams of the molecular structure of hallucinogenic drugs, discussions of theoretical physics, and thoughts on the nature of time as perfected in the I Ching. This book is a very difficult and highly technical work.

1045 MacKenzie, Andrew. Apparitions and Ghosts. Foreword
* by G. W. Lambert. New York: Popular Library, 1971 (also, London: Barker, 1971). 207p. $.75 pa.

The author, a member of the Council of the (British) Society for Psychical Research, attempts to see if there are any well-documented cases of apparitions today, as there were in the 19th century as studied by the Society (Myers, Podmore, Gurney). He finds some, mostly reports which he himself investigated. He believes apparitions have no objective reality, existing only in the minds of people. He also studies two old cases--the Versailles Case (1901-1902) and the Morton Ghost of Cheltenham (19th century).

1046 _______. A Gallery of Ghosts; An Anthology of Reported
* Experience. Introductory dialogue with Rosalind Heywood. New York: Taplinger Pub. Co., 1973 (c1972). 160p. $5.95 LC 73-2019 ISBN 0-8008-3122-5

This book is a collection of 20 little-known stories of famous writers involving phantoms, footsteps, reflections in mirrors, poltergeists, precognition, and astral projection. Also, there are some classic cases from the files of the (British) Society for Psychical Research (such as the Samuel Bull haunting reported in 1932). Cases involve the following persons: Pamela Frankau, Jung, Margaret Murray, John Masters, Osbert Sitwell, Wilt Hudson, Ngaio Marsh, George Russell (known as A. E.), and criminologist Cesare Lombroso. The author reflects that fictional stories have a beginning, middle, and end, while true ghost stories are fragmentary and often meaningless.

1047 ________. The Riddle of the Future: A Modern Study of
*** Precognition. Preface by Robert H. Thouless. New York: Taplinger Pub. Co., 1975 (orig. pub., London: Barker, 1974). 172p. Bibliog. Index $8.50 LC 75-8199 ISBN 0-8008-6795-5

This work is a major new contribution to occult literature. The author discusses recent cases of prophetic dreams and visions, most of them reported in the Journal and Proceedings of the (British) Society for Psychical Research. Much of it is on methodology--how cases are researched and validated. It is pointed out that often the information is symbolic and thus hard to interpret correctly. Also mentioned is long-range prediction (many years in advance of an actual event). MacKenzie states that precognition is one of the hardest phenomena to understand. Chapters discuss the Drem Airfield Case of 1935, when Wing Commander Victor Goddard got a view of the airfield as it was to look five years later; Eva Hellstrom, one of the founders of the Swedish Society for Psychical Research (her two published casebooks have 239 cases she experienced between 1947 and 1964); the British Premonitions Bureau; and the sinking of the Titanic. The author concludes that "precognition cannot be considered as an isolated phenomenon, but as a manifestation of one aspect of ESP." He states that he does not have his own theory on precognition, but likes research in two areas: quantum physics (which is the only field that has little difficulty in accepting the precognition corollary that the effect can precede the cause) and consciousness studies.

1048 ________. Unexplained; Some Strange Cases in Psychical
* Research. Introd. by H. H. Price. New York: Popular Library, 1971 (also, Abelard, 1970; orig. pub., 1966). 180p. Index $.75 pa.

The author is a member of the (British) Society for Psychical Research, and author of several mystery books. He discusses 13 ghost cases, including the case of 1901 at Versailles when Moberly and Jourdain traveled in time to the 1700's. He discusses the reasonableness of the various stories. The cases are taken from the Society's Journal and Proceedings.

1049 McKenzie, Paige. Heavens Help the Working Girl. New York: Franconia Pub., 1972. 268p. Illus. $4.95 LC 74-188276 ISBN 0-912390-02-6

This is an astrology guide for the working girl, for use at work and in social life. The author writes humorously and includes her own experiences.

1050 McKinnie, Ian. Fun in a Teacup; Your Complete Guide to Tea Leaf Reading. Illus. by Dian de Wolf. Photos by Sonoma Classics, Martin L. Nelson. Millbrae, Calif.: Celestial Arts, 1974 (orig. pub. as "The Art of Reading Tea Leaves." Santa Rosa, Calif.: India House, 1972). 61p.

Illus. $2.95 pa. LC 74-5159 ISBN 0-912310-61-8

1051 Mackintosh, William Hunter. The Essence of Spiritualism. Gerrards Cross, England: Smythe (for the Spiritualist Association of Great Britain), 1973. 61p. £0.75 pa. ISBN 0-900675-96-9

1052 Macklin, John. Brotherhood of the Strange. New York: Ace Books, 1972. 190p. $.95 pa.

1053 ______. Other Dimensions. New York: Ace Books, 1972. 190p. $.75 pa.

1054 ______. Out of This World. New York: Ace Books, 1972. 190p. $.75 pa.

1055 Maclagan, Robert Craig, 1839- . The Evil Eye in the Western Highlands. Wakefield, England: E. P. Publishing, 1972 (also, Norwood, Pa.: Norwood Editions, 1973; orig. pub., London: Nutt, 1902). vii, 232p. Index £2.50 ISBN 0-85409-811-9

This is a good study of this superstition of Gaelic-speaking peoples of Scotland. In Gaelic, the evil eye is termed "eolas a chronachaidh." Chapters cover the following topics: possessors of the evil eye, the symptoms of victims, the disadvantages to owners of the evil eye, avoiding the look, the forms of payment, preventing by blessing, rowan and juniper, horse nails and shoes, a small gift, spitting, churning, peculiarity in clothes, tar, nicking the ear, urine, chains, the use of water to cure (called "uisge a chronachaidh" or "water of injury"), and odd cures (cats, honeysuckle, whisky, lead dropping). The writer is a believer only in so far as it is a term applied to the natural selfishness of the human being which finds expression inevitably in our habits.

1056 Maclean, Dorothy. Wisdoms, by Divina [pseud.]. Forres, Scotland: Findhorn Foundation, 1975. 60p. £0.75 pa. ISBN 0-905249-10-0

1057 MacLeod, Charlotte. Astrology for Sceptics. London: Turnstone Books, 1973 (orig. pub., New York: Macmillan, 1972). ix, 308p. Illus. Bibliog. Index £2.50 ISBN 0-85500-011-2

The author feels that astrology is a "technique for visualizing and understanding our personal relationships to the cosmic laws by which the Life Force operates." She discusses the concepts of energy and order, balance and growth, and astrological common sense. MacLeod then has chapters on each planet, describing the science and astrological function of each. She then discusses the characteristics of each zodiac sign. The chapters on the planets often ramble on philosophically about nothing, while the zodiac sections are filled with too much cute writing and humorous comment. At one point, she states, "let's overlook the rhetoric for the moment." One could only wish she had done it more often.

1058 MacLeod, Nicholas A. Scottish Witchcraft. St. Ives, England: James Pike, 1975. 32p. Illus. Map (Viewing Scotland Series) £0.30 pa. ISBN 0-85932-115-0

1059 * McNally, Raymond T., 1931- , comp. A Clutch of Vampires: These Being Among the Best from History and Literature. Greenwich, Conn.: New York Graphic Society, 1974. 255p. Illus. $6.95 LC 73-89955 ISBN 0-8212-0594-3

This collection includes stories by J. S. Le Fanu ("Carmilla"), R. Matheson ("Drink My Red Blood"), and B. Stoker ("Dracula's Guest"). There are also essays by Blavatsky, Montague Summers, and William Seabrook. Historical discussions cover ancient Greece, 12th-century England, 18th-century France, and a modern case in Romania. There are 25 selections in all from fiction and non-fiction.

1060 *** ________, and Radu Florescu. In Search of Dracula: A True History of Dracula and Vampire Legends. London: New English Library, 1973 (orig. pub., Greenwich, Conn.: New York Graphic Society, 1972). 223p. Illus. Facsim. Geneal. Table Map Plan Bibliog. £3

This work is a major new contribution to occult literature. The book is probably the definitive study on Dracula. McNally is a Russian history scholar at Boston College; Florescu is a former colleague. Both have spent 10 years in intensive research on this topic. They have traced nearly everything concerning the 15th-century entity from Transylvania. They found his grave in a monastery on the island of Snagov, and also discovered his castle. They have searched monasteries, documents, maps, and archives. There are 60 illustrations, photos, woodcuts and paintings from the 15th to the 17th centuries, some of them rare.

1061 MacNutt, Francis. Healing. Notre Dame, Ind.: Ave Maria Press, 1974. 333p. $3.50 pa.

The author, a priest, is a leading Catholic pentecostal spokesman. He discusses the role of faith in healing, four basic kinds of healing, why some healings fail, exorcism, and miracles. He feels that healing is not a miracle, but part of normal church life, and a sign of continuity with the apostles. At a 1974 pentecostal gathering at Notre Dame, his healing service was very successful.

1062 Macrae, Norman, ed. Highland Second-Sight; With Prophecies of Coinneach Odhar and the Seer of Petty. Introductory study by William Morrison. Ed. by Norman Macrae. Norwood, Pa.: Norwood Editions, 1972 (orig. pub., 1908). 202p. LC 72-7291

1063 Madame Fabia [pseud.]. The Book of Fortune-telling. London: Coronet, 1974 (also, New York: Arco, 1975; orig. pub. in 1 vol., Folkestone, England: Bailey Bros. and Swinfen, 1972). 2 vols. 244, 244p. Illus. £0.50 pa. each volume

This two-volume work discusses dreams, card readings, phrenology, crystal-gazing, teacup fortune-telling, fire reading, and numerology.

1064 Maeterlinck, Maurice, 1862-1949. The Light Beyond. Trans. by Alexander Teixeira de Mattos. Freeport, N.Y.: Books for Libraries, 1972 (orig. pub., 1917). vii, 299p. (Essay Index Reprint Series) $12 LC 70-37844 ISBN 0-8369-2607-2

1065 ________. The Unknown Guest. Foreword by Leslie Shepard. Secaucus, N.J.: University Books, 1975 (orig. pub., New York: Dodd, Mead, 1914). xiv, 339p. $7.95 LC 75-317565 ISBN 0-8216-0220-9

This classic work discusses apparitions, precognition, psychometry, and the Elberfeld horses.

1066 Mafteah Shelomo. English. The Key of Solomon the King. Trans. and ed. by S. Liddell MacGregor Mathers. Foreword by Richard Cavendish. London: Routledge and K. Paul, 1972 (reprint of 1909 ed., London: Kegan Paul, Trench, Trubner; orig. pub., London: G. Redway, 1888). xi, 126, xv p. Illus. LC 72-196871 ISBN 0-7100-7324-0

A note in the reprint of this classic work, Clavicula Salomonis, originally published about 1456, states, "there is no reason to join Mathers, who prepared this edition from seven manuscripts in the British museum, in accepting the traditional authorship of King Solomon."

1067 Magre, Maurice. The Return of the Magi. Trans. by Reginald Merton. London: Sphere, 1975 (orig. pub., London: P. Allan, 1931). 224p. (Dennis Wheatley Library of the Occult) (Translation of "Magiciens et illuminés." Paris: Fasquelle, 1930) £0.65 pa. ISBN 0-7221-5845-9

1068 Mahony, Patrick. Escape into the Psychic Kingdom. Los Angeles: House of Words, 1975. 162p. $2.95 pa.

The author, who has written five previous psychic books, discusses karma, exorcism, astral projection, auras, retrocognition, prophecy, Luther Burbank, getting to know the subconscious better, and "The Magic of Serendipity." He includes anecdotes about famous people's psychic experiences.

1069 Malchus, Marius. Secret Grimoire of Turiel; The Rites of Ceremonial Magick. New York: S. Weiser, 1971 (c1960).

42p. Illus. $3.50 LC 71-31558 ISBN 0-87728-113-0

This work purports to be a rewritten English translation of a Latin manuscript dated 1518.

1070 *** Man, Myth, and Magic; An Illustrated Encyclopedia of the Supernatural. Ed. by Richard Cavendish. New York: Marshall Cavendish Corp., 1970 (dist. in U.S. by Purnell; orig. pub., London: BPC Publishing, 1970). 24 vols. 3376p. Illus. (chiefly color) Bibliog. Index (Previously pub. in 112 weekly parts as "Man, Myth and Magic") $169.50 LC 70-141143

This work has to be the occult publishing event of the century, and the best occult set ever produced. The set contains 1,404 total items, 917 of them true entries (over one paragraph in length and containing substantial information). Of these, 707 are long (over one page in length). The set contains the following very long articles (over five pages): Africa, alchemy, animals (as symbols), arts of the moderns, Arthur the once and future king, astrology, Atlantis, Australia, automatic art, Aztecs, Basque witchcraft, birds, Blake, Book of the Dead (Egyptian), Buddhism, bull, burial, Cabala, Camelot, cards, cave art, Celts, China, Christianity, Congo, costume, creation myths, Crowley, cult of the dead, dance, death, John Dee, devil, Dionysus, disease, divination, double, dragon, dreams, drugs, Druids, dying god, East Anglian and Essex witches, ecstasy, Egypt, end of the world, Ethiopia, European witch persecutions, evil, extrasensory perception, eye, fairies, Faust, fertility, films, Finland, fire, Freemasonry, games, ghosts, Grail, Greece, gypsies, haunted houses, head, Hell, hero, Hinduism, horns, house, iconography, imitative magic, initiation, Islam, Japan, Jesus, Judaism, judgment of the dead, king, landscape symbolism, light, magic, man, masks, mediums, Mesopotamia, messianic movements, Mexico and Central America, mysticism, palmistry, psychokinesis, race myths, religion, Rosicrucians, saints, spontaneous psi experiences, sword, time, voodoo, woman, Zen. As can be seen from these long articles, the set covers the occult, parapsychology, mythology, anthropology, spiritualism, mysticism, and symbolism. The work was under supervision of this excellent editorial advisory board: C.A. Burland, Glyn Daniel, E.R. Dodds, Mircea Eliade, William Sargant, John Symonds, R.J. Zwi Werblosky, and R.C. Zaehner. The articles are scholarly and many of them will be definitive for years to come. This set should reach the same level of authority in the occult that Macmillan's two sets, Encyclopedia of Philosophy and International Encyclopedia of the Social Sciences have in their areas. Most of volume 23 and part of volume 24 contain supplementary articles referred to as "Frontiers of Belief." Volume 24 contains an excellent, 43-page index to the entire set. Besides the well-done text, the many color illustrations are excellent and imaginative. This is easy to understand, because Marshall Cavendish Corp. excels at layout, organization, and illustration in all their sets. One error was made in planning--the covers usually have the most frightening pictures possible (skulls, mirror-distorted figures, faces with red eyes). This idea has hurt sales to schools and colleges, and does not adequately convey the scholarly nature of the set. Many of the witchcraft pictures show nude figures; some libraries may want to watch this. However, every library in the U. S. should definitely buy this set, which is a relative bargain in price. Individuals also may wish to buy this set. One hopes that Cavendish will produce another set in the future covering the many topics not covered here. Buy this one before it goes out of print.

1071 Mandel, Henry A., 1894- . Banners of Light; The First Time the Truth Has Been Given from the Spirit World. New York: Vantage, 1973. 528p. $6.95

This book consists of tape recordings made of ghosts talking through mediums.

1072 Manning, Al G. Helping Yourself with ESP. New York: Award, 1971. $.75 pa.

1073 ______. Helping Yourself with White Witchcraft. West Nyack, N. Y.: Parker Pub. Co., 1972. 226p. Illus. $6.95 LC 72-8115 ISBN 0-13-386565-7

This book discusses using rituals to attract money, rituals to hold a lover, how to make love potions, rituals in health matters, herbs and herb teas, warding off the evil eye, protecting the home, gaining power over others, calming angry persons, obtaining favor in court, keeping your husband or wife at home, sex magic, astral travel, and group witchcraft. The author received a summa cum laude B. S. degree from the University of California. He was a C. P. A., and later, the leader of several large companies in aerospace and electronics. After the Korean War, a personal tragedy led him into ESP and religion. He is founder of the E. S. P. Lab in Los Angeles, of which he is also president.

1074 ______. The Miracle of Universal Psychic Power: How to Pyramid Your Way to Prosperity. West Nyack, N. Y.: Parker Pub. Co., 1974. 228p. $6.95 LC 73-13512 ISBN 0-13-585729-5

1075 ______. Miracle Spiritology. West Nyack, N. Y.: Parker Pub. Co., 1975. $7.95 LC 75-19350 ISBN 0-13-585745-7

1076 Manning, Matthew. The Link: Matthew Manning's Own Story of
*** His Extraordinary Psychic Gifts. Introd. by Peter Bander. New York: Holt, Rinehart and Winston, 1975 (also, London: Corgi, 1975; orig. pub. as "Link: The Extraordinary Gifts of a Teenage Psychic," Gerrards Cross, England: Smythe, 1974). 176p. Illus. $7.95 LC 74-25202 ISBN 0-03-014486-8

This work is a major new contribution to occult literature. It is written by an 18-year-old who some consider one of the most gifted psychics in the Western world. Manning has had experiences of apports, poltergeists, and apparitions, and has especially the gift of automatic writing and art (signed by famous masters, such as Dürer, Picasso, and Beardsley, each done in the artist's style). His messages come in all sorts of languages, including Arabic. The sheer magnitude of the phenomena (walls at home covered with thousands of signatures and drawings) seems to argue against fraud. The book won the National Listening Library Talking Books nonfiction award for 1974-1975, and publication rights to it have already been bought in over 20 countries.

1077 * Maple, Eric. Incantations and Words of Power. New York: S. Weiser, 1974 (orig. pub., Wellingborough, England: Aquarian Press, 1974). 62p. (Paths to Inner Power) $1.25 ISBN 0-87728-234-X

This survey volume in the fine "Paths to Inner Power" series discusses the following topics: words of power, the genesis of the incantation, its hallucinatory effect, sacred songs, love incantations, healing words, "Whispers of Nature" (talking to flowers, incantations for rainfall, oracles), power of evil (witches' sabbat, voodoo), white magic, communication with the dead, and prayer. This is a good survey, although the subject is more nebulous than others discussed in the series.

1078 * ______. The Magic of Perfume: Aromatics and Their Esoteric Significance. New York: S. Weiser, 1973 (orig. pub., Wellingborough, England: Aquarian Press, 1973). 64p. (Paths to Inner Power) $1.25

The author has written an excellent short introduction to the subject. There are chapters on incense burners, sacred salves, the ancient world, magicians, flowers, and history. A short glossary of aromatics ends the work. The book is another excellent contribution to the "Paths to Inner Power" series.

1079 * Mar, Timothy T. Face Reading; The Chinese Art of Physiognomy. New York: Dodd, Mead, 1974. ix, 150p. Illus. $6.95 LC 74-6806 ISBN 0-396-06981-9

This is designed as a how-to-do-it book that supposedly enables the reader to use face-reading on a scientific basis as developed by tens of thousands of cases over the centuries. Chapters discuss the following topics: zones and shapes, position system, five vital features, eyebrows, eyes (glitter, shapes, irises, and eyelids), nose, mouth, ears, forehead; groove, wrinkles, cheeklines, moles, and beards; cheekbones, jawbones, chin; long life, short life; problems of application; and photo analysis, presenting analysis plus a full-page picture of Abraham Lincoln, Li Hung-Chang, Clare Boothe Luce, Min Yong-Ik, William McKinley, Ellen Smith, James Forrestal, Adolf Hitler, George Marshall, Madame

Chiang Kai-Shek, Martin Luther King, Dwight Eisenhower, a Japanese warrior, Franz Kafka, Andy Warhol, Robert McNamara, Henry Kissinger. The information in this work is not well-covered elsewhere, so this book is very useful. Nearly every page has three or four small drawings of feature types.

1080 Marie-Simone [pseud.]. Astrology: What Your Stars Foretell. Large print ed. Litton, England: Magna Print Books, 1975 (orig. pub., London: Foyle, 1967). 117p. Illus. £3 ISBN 0-86009-033-7

1081 Martello, Leo Louis. Black Magic, Satanism, Voodoo. New York: HC Publishers, 1972. 192p. $1 pa.

This book discusses the following topics: satanism in the 1970's, sex and satanism, homosexuality, bi-sexuality, the Church of Satan, an interview with Anton LaVey, and voodoo. Martello emphasizes the differences between black magic, satanism and voodoo, and tells how they differ from the Old Religion (witchcraft). The work gives a good insider's view of current occult practices.

1082 ________. Understanding the Tarot. New York: HC Publishers, 1972. 192p. $1 pa.

This book goes card by card using the Waite deck, giving for each: description, meaning, rhymed message (very short), and combinations for each card. There is a lot of white space on each page.

1083 ________. Witchcraft: The Old Religion. Secaucus, N.J.:
* University Books, 1974. 287p. $7.95 LC 73-80369

The first part of this book is autobiographical, discussing Martello's ancestors who were witches, and covering his battles through the Witches Liberation Movement, Witches International Craft Associates (WICA), and the Witches Anti-Defamation League. Martello states that witchcraft was the Old Religion, based on happiness and reverence, having no sense of evil and no avenging god. The author discusses use by modern religions of ancient witchcraft rites, the Horned God, Halos, Mediterranean and Sicilian witchcraft (he calls himself a Sicilian witch), Mother Shipton, Welsh witchcraft, the healing power of plants and herbs, and the magic Sator square.

1084 Martin, Kevin [pseud.]. The Complete Gypsy Fortune Teller. London: Arlington Books, 1973 (also, St. Albans, England: Mayflower, 1975; orig. pub., New York: Putnam, 1970). 315p. Illus. Bibliog. £1.95 ISBN 0-85140-220-8

This book discusses Gypsy use of dice, dominos, phrenology, cards, Tarot, hands, crystal balls, creams, handwriting, flowers, and tea leaves. The author's name is a pseudonym which the publisher has supposedly sworn to keep secret to protect the author from the anger of the Gypsies. The Gypsies are descendants of a special caste of Hindus driven out of the East over 500 years ago.

1085 Martin, Margaret Rhett. Charleston Ghosts. Columbus: University of South Carolina Press, 1972 (c1963). x, 105p. Illus. $2.25 pa. ISBN 0-87249-286-9

1086 Martin, Renee C. Renee Martin's Secrets of Handwriting. New York: Bantam, 1972. 208p. Illus. $1.25 pa.

1087 ________. Scriptease. Lahaska, Pa.: New Hope Pub. Co., 1975. $1.50 pa. LC 75-43908 ISBN 0-915460-10-6

This book is an introduction to handwriting analysis alphabetically arranged by traits and by letters. The author includes suggestions for parlor games and a chapter on doodling.

1088 Maruyama, Magoroh, and Arthur Harkins. Cultures Beyond the Earth. New York: Random House, 1975. 203p. $2.95 pa. LC 75-12681 ISBN 0-394-71602-7

This work consists of eight stories and essays which won a contest held at the 1974 American Anthropological Association Annual Symposium. The topic was "extraterrestrial communities," with the purpose being to get the reader out of a human-centered view of the universe.

1089 Marwick, Max, comp. Witchcraft and Sorcery; Selected Readings. Magnolia, Mass.: Peter Smith, 1971 (orig. pub. by Penguin, 1970). 416p. Bibliog. (Penguin Modern Sociology Readings [rebound]) $4

1090 Mason, Herbert Molloy. Secrets of the Supernatural. New York: Four Winds Press, 1975. 216p. Illus. Bibliog. Index $6.95 LC 75-9729 ISBN 0-590-17304-9

This book discusses the following topics: witchcraft, voodoo, classic tales of hauntings, poltergeists, communication with the dead, astral projection, vampires, werewolves, ESP research, and witchcraft today.

1091 Mason, Peggy. New Age Companion. Crowborough, England: the author, 1975. vi, 166p. £2 pa. ISBN 0-905512-00-6

1092 ________. Tales of Two Worlds: A Bedside Book for the New Age. Crowborough, England: the author, 1975 (orig. pub., 1972). 194p. £1.50 pa.

1093 Masters, Anthony, 1940- . Natural History of the Vampire.
* New York: Putnam, 1972 (orig. pub., London: Hart-Davis, 1972). xii, 258p. Illus. Bibliog. $7.95 LC 70-175268 ISBN 0-399-10931-5

This well-done book has chapters on the following topics: human vampire or psychic sponge--origins, vampire traits and practice, pagan vampires, the vampire in Christianity, the vampire in literature, the vampire as entertainer, and the vampire today. The author relied a great deal in the book on the works of Montague Summers.

1094 Masters, R. E. L. Eros and Evil; The Sexual Psychopathology of Witchcraft. Baltimore: Penguin Books, 1974 (c1962).
* xxviii, 254p. Bibliog. $2.50 pa.

This book is a classic study on the sex psychology and pathology of witchcraft.

1095 Mathes, Joseph H., 1928- , and Lenora Huett. The Amnesia Factor: Extraterrestrial Communications Breakthrough. Millbrae, Calif.: Celestial Arts, 1975. Index $4.95 pa. LC 75-9446 ISBN 0-89087-023-3

Most of this work is a dialogue the authors conducted through automatic writing with an alien intelligence (printed in bold-faced dark print where the alien speaks). Most of the answers from the alien are general, and concern UFO contacts, kidnappings, and alien goals. Joseph Mathes has had 25 years experience as an airline pilot, and therefore provides a nice complement to Huett, who works through her automatic writing ability. There are chapters on four fundamental questions (what am I? what am I for? why? is someone else out there?), amnesia island, space missions, communications with a legend (Akashic Records), and experiments with control.

1096 Matson, Archie. The Waiting World; or, What Happens at Death. London: Turnstone Books, 1975 (also, New York: Harper, 1975). v, 151p. Bibliog. £2.95 ISBN 0-85500-042-2

The author is a minister whose own mystical experiences inspired him to write the book. He discusses out-of-the-body experiences, deathbed observations, communication with the dead through mediums, the Bible, ghosts, and the thrill of dying. Matson says that the Mosiac law forbidding contact with the dead was disobeyed by Jesus and the early Church, and has no validity today.

1097 Maxwell, Joseph. The Tarot. Trans., introd. and notes by Ivor Powell. London: Spearman, 1975. 223p. (Translation of "Tarot," Paris: Presses Universitaires de France, 1933) £2.95 ISBN 0-85435-292-9

This book discusses numerology, symbolism, and astrological significance of the Tarot.

1098 May, Antoinette. Haunted Ladies. San Francisco: Chronicle Books, 1975. Bibliog. $7.95 LC 75-26670

This book discusses six women who have studied psychic phenomena--four mediums, a physician, and a parapsychologist. Three of the mediums are Eileen Caddy (Findhorn), Rosemary Brown (spirit music), and Betty Bethards (out-of-the-body experiences). The physician is Irene Hickman, who specializes in psychosomatic medicine, and who regresses patients hypnotically to see what in their past lives is causing problems. The other medium is Anne Armstrong, one of Hickman's former patients and now a psychic who searches for karmic causes to patients' present problems. The parapsychologist is Thelma Moss, Kirlian photography researcher.

1099 Mayne, William, ed. Ghosts: An Anthology. London: Hamilton, 1971. viii, 188p. £1.50 ISBN 0-241-01939-7

This is a juvenile collection of seven stories, 11 true tales, and eight poems, with the editor's comments before each. The book includes Kipling's "The Return of Imray," Robert Louis Stevenson's "Waif Woman," and T. H. White's "The Troll." There is verse by Walter De La Mare and Thomas Beddoes, among others. The book is recommended for grade 6 and up.

1100 Mayo, Jeff. The Planets and Human Behaviour. London: L. N. Fowler, 1972. 176p. Index (Astrologer's Handbook Series, no. 4) £1.50 ISBN 0-85243-268-2

1101 Meares, Ainslie. Strange Places, Simple Truths. London: Fontana, 1973 (orig. pub., London: Souvenir Press, 1969). 192p. £0.35 pa. ISBN 0-00-613209-X

This Australian psychiatrist investigates Eastern mystical practice in 21 countries to see if any can be adapted to modern medicine. He discusses Zen, yoga, voodoo, and other such cults.

1102 Meek, George W. From Enigma to Science. New York: Samuel Weiser, Inc., 1974. 199p. Index $6.95 ISBN 0-87728-242-0

The author discusses the need for an interdisciplinary study of parapsychology that would join ideas about "energy field" forces. His purpose is to tell other scientists about parapsychology and tell parapsychologists about other scientific developments. Meek has excerpts from research papers in parapsychology. He discusses some neglected areas, such as suggesting re-evaluation of the mathematics of basic wave equations.

1103/4 ________, and Bertha Harris. From Seance to Science. 2nd ed. London: Regency Press, 1973 (previous ed., 1973). viii, 194p. Illus. (some color) Bibliog. Index (Life's Energy Fields, vol. 1)

The authors discuss clairvoyance, clairaudience, telepathy, psychometry, psychokinesis, and precognition. He attempts to bridge spiritualism and science, and promote understanding between them.

1105 * Mendelssohn, Kurt. The Riddle of the Pyramids. New York: Praeger Publishers, 1974. 224p. Illus. (some color) Bibliog. $12.95 LC 73-18485

The author, a physicist, strongly emphasizes building and construction techniques throughout this book. He studies the actual construction of Mexican and Egyptian pyramids, and theorizes that they were built out of political needs for unity and strong, centralized government. The building of the pyramids, not the structures themselves, was the important thing. He includes many plans, charts, and photographs.

1106 Merrell-Wolff, Franklin. Pathways Through to Space; A Personal Record of Transformation in Consciousness. Introd. by John C. Lilly. 2nd ed. New York: Julian Press, 1973. xvi, 288p. $7.50 LC 73-75897

The author discusses transcendent consciousness and how to achieve it. It is a diary of the author's transformation in cosmic consciousness during a 101-day "trip," including his thoughts, emotions, problems, joys, and even spontaneous poetry. The events took place in 1936, after much previous yoga training. Chapters discuss meditative technique, cosmic consciousness, Jesus, bliss, different levels, being born again, triune man, omniscience, beauty, karma, sleep and death, and many other areas. The author concludes that there is not one path to perfect consciousness, but many, since each person is at a different point in spiritual development. There is a glossary at the end. This is a very difficult book to read and understand, since so much of it is personal.

1107 Mes, G. M. Faith Healing and Religion. New York: Philosophical Library, 1975. $8.75

The author is a general practitioner and surgeon. He discusses faith healing and what it requires and three types of religions (those believing in God the Father, those believing in God the King, and those believing in the Eternal Mystery).

1108 Metaphysical Research Group. Aura Research: Aura Goggles and Colour Filters. Hastings, England: Metaphysical Research Group, 1975. 11p. Illus. (A Borderline Science Instruction Booklet) £0.35 pa. ISBN 0-900684-21-6

1109 Métraux, Alfred. Voodoo. Trans. by Hugo Charteris. 2nd ed. New introd. by Sidney W. Mintz. London: Sphere, 1974 (2nd ed. orig. pub. as "Voodoo in Haiti," New York: Schocken; London: Deutsch, 1972; orig. ed. pub., New York: Oxford Univ. Press; London: Deutsch, 1959). 368p. Illus. Map Bibliog. (Dennis Wheatley Library of the Occult, vol. 19) £0.75 pa. ISBN 0-7221-6060-7

This book gives the history, practices and beliefs of voodoo in detailed discussions. It includes many anecdotes, and a glossary of terms.

1110 Metzner, Ralph. Maps of Consciousness: I Ching, Tantra, Tarot, Alchemy, Astrology, Actualism. New York: Collier Books; London: Collier Macmillan, 1974 (orig. pub., New York: Macmillan; London: Collier Macmillan, 1971). xiii, 161p. Illus. £2.25 pa. ISBN 0-02-077400-1

In 1961, the author started taking psychedelic drugs and studying the occult. The many discussions are short, well-documented and interesting to read.

1111 Meyer, Michael R. The Astrology of Change: Horary Astrology and Its Humanistic Applications. Garden City, N.Y.: Anchor Press, 1975. 183p. Illus. Bibliog. $3.50 pa. LC 74-31518 ISBN 0-385-04009-1

This book puts horary astrology (the ancient divinatory type of astrology) into humanistic psychology concepts. Horary charts help individuals evaluate deeply the inner meaning of crucial decision points. Discussions include why and when to use horary astrology, posing the inquiry, initial consideration, the whole chart (whole patterns, focal points, lunation cycle), Sabian symbols, natal and progressed factors, and bringing it all together--a case study. Appendices include a horary view of astrological symbols (60 pages long), how to cast a horoscope (40 pages), and various tables (65 pages).

1112 ________. Handbook for the Humanistic Astrologer. Garden City, N.Y.: Anchor Press, 1974. xv, 362p. Illus. Bibliog. $5.95 pa. LC 73-83657 ISBN 0-384-05729-6

This book covers Dane Rudhyar's contributions to astrology in studying character instead of prediction, drawing parallels to Jung. Discussions include numbers, midpoints, and cycles. Meyer says that the basic chart is a seed indicating one's potential, not a fixed thing.

1113 Michel, Aimé. Humanoids. Ed. by Charles Bowen. London: Futura Pubns., 1974 (orig. pub., London: Spearman, 1969). 256p. Illus. Map £0.45 pa. ISBN 0-86007-057-3
*

This book is a collection of eight articles written by scientists and astronomers, discussing the most famous recent visits from UFO's. Cases include the Antonio Villas Boas case in Brazil, the Villa Scantina case in Italy, and the Socorro, N.M., case. The authors are Charles Bowen, Vallee, Antonio Ribera, Gordon Creighton, W.T. Powers, Coral Lorenzen, Donald Hanlon, and Aimé Michel.

1114 Michelet, Jules, 1798-1874. Satanism and Witchcraft; A
*

Study in Medieval Superstition. New York: Dell, 1971 (also, Secaucus, N.J.: Citadel Press, 1973). xx, 331p. Bibliog. $1.95 pa.

This is a classic work by a famous French historian known for his ability to get inside his subject and discuss it with the emotional feeling of the original participants. Chapters discuss the following topics: death of the gods, what drove the Middle Ages to despair, the little demon of the hearth and home, temptations, diabolical possession, a pact with Satan, the king of the dead, the prince of nature, Satan the healer, charms and love potions, communion of revolt, witches' sabbaths, the black mass, persecutions, 100 years of toleration in France, Basque witches in 1609, Gauffridi 1610, the nuns of Loudun--Urbain Grandier, 1633, 1634; the nuns of Louviers and satanic possession--Madeleine Bavent, 1640-1647; satan triumphant in the 17th century, Father Girard and Charlotte Cadiere, Charlotte Cadiere at the Convent of Ollioules, trial of Charlotte Cadiere, 1730, 1731.

1115 Michell, John F. City of Revelation; On the Proportions
*** and Symbolic Numbers of the Cosmic Temple. New York: D. McKay Co., 1972 (also, Abacus, 1973; orig. pub., London: Garnstone Press, 1972). 176p. Illus. Index $5.95 LC 72-88116

This work is a major new contribution to occult literature. The author theorizes that, over 2,000 years ago, man was highly civilized and completely understood the natural laws controlling seasons, human behavior, and the most subtle mathematical relationships between the whole of the universe and its parts. This relationship was preserved in the great temples of man--Chartres, Stonehenge, St. Mary's Chapel at Glastonbury, the Great Pyramid, and the Temple of Jerusalem. The author gets clues ranging from the Book of Revelation to Plato's works on measurements of ancient buildings ("cosmic" temples) which embody perfect proportions. The title is from the Holy City in the Book of Revelation. Chapters include: Number 666"; "Number 1080"; "Gnostic Numbers"; "3168 (perimeter of fusion)"; and "1746 (number of fusion)".

1116 ________. Flying Saucer Vision: The Holy Grail Restored. London: Abacus, 1974 (orig. pub., London: Sidgwick and Jackson, 1967). 170p. Illus. Plates Bibliog. Index £0.60 pa. ISBN 0-349-12319-5

1117 ________. The View Over Atlantis. Rev. ed. London:
* Garnstone Press, 1972 (also, London: Abacus, 1973; also, New York: Ballantine Books, 1972; original ed., 1969). 211, xxxiiip. Illus. Plan Bibliog. Index £2.50 ISBN 0-85511-020-1

This book was an important publishing event when it came out in 1969. Especially in paperback form, it has been read by millions in the U.S. The author theorizes that we all live within the ruins of an ancient structure, whose vast size has up to now made it invisible. The entire surface of the earth is marked with the remains of a gigantic work of prehistoric engineering, which was once a system of magic. It involved use of polar magnetism and solar energy forces. The first part of the book discusses how old and new religious sites in Britain are in a series of straight lines hundreds of miles long. The second part discusses ancient works and their mathematical proportions (Stonehenge, Woodhenge, the Great Pyramid, alchemy, and astrology). The third section brings all parts of the book together in a discussion of sacred engineering--design for a religious, magical purpose of universal scope. The Ballantine paperback edition is printed in an interesting bold-faced type.

1118 Miller, Carey. Dictionary of Monsters and Mysterious Beasts. Illus. by Mary I. French. London: Pan Books, 1974. 175p. Illus. Index (Piccolo Original) £0.35 pa. ISBN 0-330-24074-9

1119 Milner, Dennis, and Edward Smart. The Loom of Creation: A Study of the Purpose and the Forces that Weave the Patterns of Existence. London: Spearman, 1975. 319p. Illus. (some color) Bibliog. Index £4.95 ISBN 0-85435-182-5

1120 Minor, Marz Nono. Astrology's Lucky Twelve. New York: Popular Library, 1971. $.95 pa.

This book discusses each sign of the zodiac. It explains how to increase, protect, and change luck, how to separate yin (negative personality elements) from yang (positive elements), and using yang to one's benefit.

1121 ________. Be Your Own Fortune Teller. New York: Popular Library, 1971. 381p. Illus. $.95 pa.

This book has numbered and lettered diagrams and mystical symbols to use with a pointer. The work discusses cards, dice, charms, and stars.

1122 Mishlove, Jeffrey, 1946- . The Roots of Consciousness: Psychic Liberation Through History, Science, and Experience. New York: Random House, 1975. 350p. Illus. Includes bibliog. refs. Index $9.95 pa. LC 75-10311 ISBN 0-394-73115-8
*

This book is a survey of consciousness exploration. The first section is historical, and discusses Mesopotamia, Egypt, India, China, Greece, Rome, the Hebrews, the Christians, Hermeticism, alchemy, Kabalah, medieval times, the Renaissance, the Age of Reason, the 19th century, the (British) Society for Psychical Research, and William James. The second part, a review of parapsychological findings, discusses ESP, out-of-the-body experiences, healing, firewalking, PK, spiritualism, UFO's and aura.

The third section, titled "People, Places, and Theories," discusses consciousness, practical applications of ESP, dowsing and behavior modification. The work includes a list of research organizations. This study is based on the author's Ph. D. dissertation. The book has 66 color illustrations, and many black and white photographs.

1123 Mishra, Madho Prasad. Panjika; The Hindu Astrological Almanac, 1971-1972. Trans. and adapted by Savitri Dutt. Ed. by Ashoka Kumar Dutt. New York: Winter House, 1971. 235p. Illus. $3.95 pa. LC 79-152761 ISBN 0-87806-013-8

1124 Mitchell, John V. Ghosts of an Ancient City. Illus. by John Brown. Photographs by Brian Jackson. Cartoons by Robert Nield. York, England: Cerialis Press, dist. by Herald Printers, 1974. 58p. Illus. £0.75 pa. ISBN 0-9502631-2-5

1125 Mitchell, Margaret Claire. Message to Mankind. London: Regency Press, 1975. 275p. £3.20 ISBN 0-7212-0429-5

1126 Mitchell, William Reginald. Yorkshire Ghosts. New ed. Clapham, England: Dalesman, 1973 (previous ed., pub. as "Haunted Yorkshire," 1969). 72p. Illus. £0.50 pa.

1127 Molinaro, Ursule. Life by the Numbers; A Basic Guide to Learning Your Life Through Numerology. New York: Morrow, 1971. 158p. $5.95 LC 72-151907

1128 Monahan, Evelyn, and Terry Bakken. Put Your Psychic Powers to Work; A Practical Guide to Parapsychology. Chicago: Nelson-Hall Co., 1973. x, 138p. $6.95 LC 73-84208

This book is a very short survey of various psychic phenomena by a teacher at Georgia State University.

1129 Monroe, Robert A. Journeys Out of the Body. London:
* Souvenir Press, 1972 (also, London: Corgi, 1974; also, Garden City, N.Y.: Anchor Press, 1973; orig. pub., New York: Doubleday, 1971). 280p. £2.50 ISBN 0-285-62049-5

The author, a journalist who can have out-of-the-body experiences apparently at will, began doing it in 1958. He discusses how he developed this ability, experiments he has done with it (including lab work), and experiences that have occurred in his travels. He tells how to induce the state, and gives his theories on the meaning of the phenomena. Monroe claims to have contacted a parallel universe, and communicated on a very elemental level with those he met on the "trips." He is sometimes projected to earth, or to an ugly world, or to a beautiful one. He has helpers in the other dimension, including the dead. Charles Tart's introduction surveys scientific thought on the subject.

1130 Montandon, Pat. The Intruders. New York: Coward, McCann and Geoghegan, 1975. 286p. $8.95 LC 74-16638 ISBN 0-698-10636-9

This San Francisco television star, famous hostess, and author of How to Be a Party Girl was cursed together with her house by an angry Tarot card reader in 1967. Soon after, strange phenomena began occurring. Her apartment was very cold at times; her dog became frightened and ill. She nearly died from an overdose of sleeping pills, and her career deteriorated. Her secretary, Mary Lou, was visiting her for a week, when a fire started in the bedroom. Mary Lou was found dead in bed, and a coroner said she had died of unknown causes before she burned. Another secretary and her cousin both committed suicide. The appendix gives details, and includes the report of two psychics who visited the apartment five years later at Montandon's request, using cameras and tape recorders. The author feels that the malevolent forces were present in the house all the time, and the Tarot reader just put them in motion. A further fact was that the lot on which the house was built had been a cemetery at one time.

1131 Montgomery, John Warwick. Principalities and Powers; The World of the Occult, Including a Ghost Story by the Author, a Reformation-Era Letter on Demon Possession, and Hitherto Unpublished Cartoons on the Occult by C. S. Lewis. Minneapolis: Bethany Fellowship, 1973 (also, new ed., New York: Pyramid Publications, 1975). 224p. Illus. Includes bibliog. refs. $4.95 LC 73-3206

The author is professor of church history at Trinity Evangelical Divinity School in Deerfield, Ill. The book is meant as a reply to Hal Lindsey's Satan Is Alive and Well ... (entry 998). Montgomery studies Rosicrucianism, Masons, Kaballah, C. S. Lewis and Owen Barfield. The author presents a strict biblical interpretation, and advocates censorship.

1132 Montgomery, Ruth Schick, 1912- . Born to Heal: The Astonishing Story of Mr. A. and the Ancient Art of Healing with Life Energies. New York: Coward, McCann and Geoghegan, 1973. 224p. $6.95 LC 72-87588 ISBN 0-698-10493-5

This book discusses healer "Mr. A," who since 1941 has worked full-time at healing. He usually puts his ear to the patient's chest to "hear" by vibrations what is wrong. He then sends his own energy into the body to cure the ailment. His power comes by tuning into the "Universal Ring," the earth's magnetic field. The Ring also tells him how to use his powers. Until 1941, he was an electrician, salesman, and developer of land. He then did healing work, first in Nevada and later in California. Montgomery writes in an interesting style, giving many quotes, anecdotes, and cases. Perhaps the most interesting chapter is on Mr. A's trial for "practicing medicine without a proper license," urged by the California

Medical Association. He was acquitted in 20 minutes by the jury, after numerous testimonies as to the great good he has done. Mr. A is now 81 years old, and works with Dr. Dana L. Smith's Life Energies Research Foundation in Burbank. Mr. A. says that each person has his own energy frequency that delivers energy to his body. When the energy field misfunctions, illness comes.

1133 _______. Companions Along the Way. New York: Coward, McCann and Geoghegan, 1974. 256p. $6.95 LC 74-79680 ISBN 0-698-10619-9

All the material in this book was received through the author's automatic typewriter from a circle of spirits that included Arthur Ford, Montgomery's main theory is of group karma--Ford Cayce, her husband, and her friends have been together for many lifetimes. A major part of the book discusses her Palestine incarnation, where she was the sister of Lazarus and a disciple of Jesus. She discusses Jesus's unknown years, and quotes him. She also discusses other lives, in the Moab, Egypt, Persia, Greece, Tibet, Italy, and France. In one of her incarnations, she claims she was Elizabeth Barrett Browning.

1134 _______. The World Beyond; A Startling Message from
* the Eminent Psychic, Arthur Ford, from Beyond the Grave. New York: Coward, McCann and Geoghegan, 1971 (also, Greenwich, Conn.: Fawcett, 1973; London: Souvenir Press, 1973; London: Futura Pubns., 1974; Boston: G. K. Hall, 1972). 220p. $5.95 LC 77-154779

This book is a description of the afterlife delivered in a series of messages through automatic typewriting from the deceased medium Arthur Ford to Montgomery. It contains views of the afterlife by John F. Kennedy, Martin Luther King, Franklin D. Roosevelt, Ernest Hemingway, and other famous people. It also discusses Ford's book, Nothing So Strange. Chapters discuss these topics: thoughts are things, what happens after death, Ford's discussion of specific cases and stories (which seem more like parables), proper preparation, conquering bad habits, between earth lives, examples of reincarnation, higher planes and other planets, and prophecy. In its rambling way, the book provides a good view of what most Spiritualists feel the other side is like.

1135 Moon, Margaret, and Maurine Moon. Wedge: The Extraordinary Communications of an Earthbound Spirit. St. Paul, Minn.: Llewellyn Publications, 1975. 113p. Illus. Plates $3.95 pa. LC 75-309094 ISBN 0-87542-497-X

For 30 years, the author had done spirit communications the old way, using the ouija board and other such devices. In 1971, her husband made an electrically circuited board and connected it to an electric typewriter (Wilcoxon Psi-Writer). The author feels it allows a broader scope for interplane communications, with increased accuracy and automatic recording of material. Through this device, Jude Wedge describes his life in 17th-century England.

1136 * Mooney, Richard Edwin. Colony--Earth. New York: Stein and Day, 1974 (also, London: Souvenir Press, 1974; St. Albans, England: Panther, 1975). 251p. Index $7.95 LC 73-90698 ISBN 0-8128-1658-7

This interesting work theorizes that not merely was man tampered with, but that we actually were colonized by aliens from space. Chapters discuss the following: was there life before earth? is there life elsewhere? did we come from the stars? was earth colonized? the evolution hoax, the myth of ape man, Ice Age or catastrophe, Atlantis, the Great Flood, the destroyer God, the re-emergence of civilization, the riddle of great stones, Stonehenge, computers of stone, prehistoric fallout shelter, pyramids, the New World, and culture bearers. This is a good theoretical book, full of creative ideas to provoke thought.

1137 ______. Gods of Air and Darkness: The Possibility of a Nuclear War in the Past. New York: Stein and Day, 1975 (also, London: Souvenir Press, 1975). 203p. $8.95 LC 75-8926 ISBN 0-8128-1815-6

The author says we are the remains of a colony of extraterrestrials put on earth thousands of years ago to live better in a new environment. Instead, thanks to a prehistoric nuclear explosion, we are doing poorly, evolution-wise. The holocaust shifted Earth's position, moving us farther from the Sun. It also may have destroyed three other inhabited planets within our solar system.

1138 * Moore, Gerun. Numbers Will Tell. New York: Grosset and Dunlap, 1973 (also, London: Barker, 1973). xii, 178p. Illus. $5.95 LC 72-81246

The author, a famed numerologist, has written perhaps the best and most complete work available on the topic. Chapters discuss the following topics: numerology alphabets, your zodiac number, the numbers one through nine, lucky days, dates, months; important years in your life, compatible numbers, compound numbers and their meanings, Jesus and his numbers, changing your birthdate, the awesome number 13, the magnetic power of four and eight, a name number chart and its use, name changing--serious business, matching name to birthdate, selecting a home address, United States and its four, numerology and the Presidents, place names and their numbers, your telephone number and you, banking by number, selecting your automobile and license number, numerology and colors, flowers by number, numbers and music, gems--their legends, use and numbers; sex and numerology, and predictions, past and future.

1139 Moore, Marcia, and Mark Douglas. Astrology, the Divine Science. York Harbor, Maine: Arcane Pubns., 1971. xiii,

850p. Illus. Bibliog. $19.95 LC 77-82609 ISBN 0-912240-04-0

This book covers definitions used in astrology, houses, planets, casting horoscopes, and reading charts. Eastern and Western astrology is covered.

1140 Morgan, Glyn. Essex Witches: The Witches, Enchantments, Charms and Sorcerers of Essex. Bourne End, England: Spurbooks, 1973. 64p. Illus. £0.60 pa.

1141 Morienus, d. 700? The Testament of Alchemy; Being the Revelations of Morienus, Ancient Adept and Hermit of Jerusalem, to Khalid ibn Yazid ibn Mu'awiyya, King of the Arabs, of the Divine Secrets of the Magisterium and Accomplishment of the Alchemical Art. Ed. and trans. with commentary by Lee Stavenhagen. Hanover, N.H.: University Press of New England for the Brandeis University Press, 1974. 76p. Facsims. Latin and English Includes bibliog. refs. $7.50 LC 73-91752 ISBN 0-87451-095-3

This primary text on Western alchemy has Latin and English on facing pages. The book is the teaching of Morienus, a Christian monk, to a Umayyad prince, who died in A.D. 704. Stavenhagen also writes a critical essay on the text.

1142 Morrison, Sarah Lyddon. The Modern Witch's Spellbook. New York: McKay, 1971. vii, 246p. Illus. Bibliog. Index $6.95 LC 71-135588

This book is the result of the author's own experiments with witchcraft, and also research. She discusses love magic (spells, aphrodisiacs, lotions), hate magic, amulets and talismans; how to catch men, excite them, release them, get even with them; and divination (who the man will be).

1143 Moss, Thelma. The Probability of the Impossible: Scien-
*** tific Discoveries and Explorations in the Psychic World. Los Angeles: J. P. Tarcher; New York: dist. by Hawthorn Books, 1974. 410p. Illus. Bibliog. Index $10 LC 73-92094 ISBN 0-87477-025-4

This work is a major new contribution to occult literature. The author is a medical psychologist at UCLA's Neuropsychiatric Institute, and has traveled throughout the Western world, including the Soviet Union and Czechoslovakia. She discusses the International Conference on Psychotronics in 1973 at Prague, where scientists from 20 countries met. A major part of the book is on "Bioenergy," covering especially Moss's Kirlian photography research, but including also: psychic healing, dowsing, skin vision, acupuncture. Part 2 is on "Biocommunication," a survey of parapsychology that discusses ESP, mediumship, trance states, and possession. The last section tries to offer evidence that there is a second body inhabiting the physical body that can occasionally leave it. Topics discussed in this part include apparitions, ghosts, reincarnation, and astral projection. The evidence the author uses to back up her discussion is sometimes incomplete, but the work is an excellent survey on parapsychology.

1144 Moyer, Ernest P. Day of Celestial Visitation. 2nd ed. Hicksville, N. Y.: Exposition Press, 1975 (orig. ed. pub. as "God, Man, and the UFO's," 1970). 304p. Illus. Includes bibliog. refs. $12.50 LC 75-308060 ISBN 0-682-48071-1

1145 Mulholland, John, 1898- . Beware Familiar Spirits. New York: Arno Press, 1975 (orig. pub., New York: Scribner's, 1938). (Perspectives in Psychical Research) $20 LC 75-7388 ISBN 0-405-07036-5

The author, a professional magician, writes on how to detect fraudulent psychic phenomena, especially spiritualism and mediumship. He also discusses other psychic stage acts, and mentions experimental research. He mentions a statistical experiment he did that may give an alternate explanation for card-guessing tests.

1146 Mumford, John. Sexual Occultism: The Sorcery of Love. St. Paul, Minn.: Llewellyn Publications, 1975. Bibliog. $10 LC 75-2303 ISBN 0-87542-491-0

This book discusses sexual magic in Egyptian, Greek, and Hebrew traditions, where the sex act was viewed as symbolic of the highest union, oneness with God. The work also covers "Sex Magic in Mass of the Holy Spirit," reprinted from Israel Regardie's Tree of Life. Modern lovers are shown how to find the divinity in each other.

1147 Murchison, Carl, ed. The Case For and Against Psychical Belief. New York: Arno Press, 1975 (orig. pub., Worcester, Mass., 1927). (Perspectives in Psychical Research) $22 LC 75-7389 ISBN 0-405-07037-3

This work is a collection of papers submitted during a 1926 psychical research symposium at Clark University, including papers sent too late for presentation, and reprints of the authors' best comments published elsewhere. There are four sections, representing those who are convinced of the multiplicity of psychical phenomena; convinced of the rarity of psychical phenomena; unconvinced as yet; antagonistic to claims that the phenomena occur. The work gives a good idea of opinions prior to the beginning of Rhine's work at Duke.

1148 Murphet, Howard. Hammer on the Mountain. Wheaton, Ill.: Theosophical Pub. House, 1972. 339p. Illus. $7.95

1149 ________. Sai Baba, Man of Miracles. Levittown, N. Y.: Transatlantic Arts, 1972. 208p. $8.50

This book discusses a 46-year-old man living in Puttaparti Village in southern India. He heals by touch and thought, and uses telepathy and astral projection. He multiplies food, transforms matter, and produces materializations. He preaches that we must seek God through self-surrender.

1150 ______. When Daylight Comes; A Biography of Helena Petrovna Blavatsky. Wheaton, Ill.: Theosophical Pub. House, 1975. 277p. Bibliog. $3.50 pa. ISBN 0-8356-0459-4

This pro-Blavatsky biography by an Australian journalist portrays her as a great mystic. Murphet discusses all of her life, and says she was a very bad judge of character. She was very blunt, and made many enemies.

1151 Murphy, Joseph, 1898- . Cosmic Energizer: Miracle Power of the Universe. West Nyack, N.Y.: Parker Pub. Co., 1974. $7.95 LC 74-11089 ISBN 0-13-170036-6

1152 ______. Psychic Perception: The Magic of Extrasensory Power. West Nyack, N.Y.: Parker Pub. Co., 1971. 242p. Includes bibliog. refs. $6.95 LC 71-150580 ISBN 0-13-732073-6

1153 ______. Secrets of the I Ching. New York: Tower, 1971 (c1970). 251p. $.95 pa.

1154 Murray, Richard D., 1921- . The Key to Nostradamus. Cleveland: Scorcap Pub. Co., 1975. xiii, 523p. Illus. $15.95 LC 75-319955

1155 My Lucky Birthday Book. London: Nelson Young World, 1974. 61p. Illus. (chiefly color) £1.50 ISBN 0-7238-1022-2

1156 Myers, Frederic William Henry. Human Personality and
* Its Survival of Bodily Death. Introd. by Gardner Murphy. New York: Arno Press, 1975 (reprint of ed. pub. London and New York, 1954; orig. pub. 1901). 2 volumes (Perspectives in Psychical Research) $80 (set) LC 75-7391 ISBN 0-405-07038-1

This book is a classic in psychical research and psychology. The author discusses psychological experiences and altered states of consciousness. He develops the concept of the subliminal self as responsible for psychical abilities, as opposed to spiritualist beliefs that they are produced by departed spirits. The appendices have a great deal of case material.

1157 Napier, John Russell. Bigfoot; The Yeti and Sasquatch in
*** Myth and Reality. New York: Dutton, 1973 (also, London:

Cape, 1972). 240p. Illus. Includes bibliog. refs. $8.95 LC 71-179857 ISBN 0-525-06658-6

This work is a major new contribution to occult literature. The author is a well-known anthropologist and professor of primate biology at the University of London. He adopts a fairly skeptical outlook on almost all evidence on the subject. He tries to separate the myth of the Abominable Snowman and other such monsters from the real facts. He begins with a chronological account of yeti sightings in the Himalayas--the first in 1832, the latest during the Annapurna expedition of 1970. Napier then discusses the Sasquatch of the Northwest coast. In 1924, a lumberjack was kidnapped by one. In more recent times, there is the case of the Minnesota Iceman, a man-ape frozen in a block of ice. The chief problem is that no remains have ever been found. The author discusses proof from sightings, photographs, footprints, ecology, and fossils. He concludes that Bigfoot probably is a species of bear known already to science, or an unknown ape or protohuman. After all, the gorilla was known only through legends until the first white man saw him in the 19th century.

1158/9 Navarra, Fernand. Noah's Ark: I Have Touched It. Plainfield, N.J.: Logos International, 1974. 137p. Illus. (some color) $5.95

The 1955 discovery by this French industrialist and explorer of hand-hewn wood on Mt. Ararat led to over 20 expeditions. The wood was carbon-dated at 4,484 years old. The book contains many excellent color photographs of Mt. Ararat.

1160 Needham, Joseph. Refiner's Fire: The Enigma of Alchemy in East and West; The Second J.D. Bernal Lecture, Delivered at Birkbeck College, London, 4th February 1971. London: Birkbeck College, 1971. 31p. (Bernal Lectures, 2) £0.17 pa. ISBN 0-900975-12-1

1161 Neff, H. Richard, 1933- . Psychic Phenomena and Religion: ESP, Prayer, Healing, Survival. Philadelphia: Westminster Press, 1971. 176p. Includes bibliog. refs. $3.50 pa. LC 70-158122 ISBN 0-664-24931-0

The author, a Presbyterian minister, discusses the effect parapsychology may have on various tenets of Christianity, especially prayer, healing, and survival after death. The author tries to argue scientifically; he uses statistics.

1162 Nemec, Jaroslav. Witchcraft and Medicine, 1484-1793. Washington, D.C.: U.S. Gov. Printing Office (National Institutes of Health, Dept. of Health, Education and Welfare, Bethesda, Md.), 1974. 10p. Illus. Bibliog. (Pub. in conjunction with an exhibit at the National Library of Medicine, March 25 to July 19, 1974)

This pamphlet is a brief survey of the witch hunt craze, and the opposition of some physicians to the harshness of the Church's attitude against witchcraft. The author discusses the Malleus Malificarum, and states that physicians were often called upon to diagnose illnesses of the accused. If they could identify the disease, the case was often dropped. Also physicians had to examine the witch's physical and mental state, to determine her ability to undergo torture, and also to look for telltale marks.

1163 Nevins, Winfield S. Witchcraft in Salem Village in 1692; Together with a Review of the Opinions of Modern Writers and Psychologists in Regard to Outbreak of the Evil in America. New York: Burt Franklin, 1971 (orig. pub., 1916). 273p. Illus. Includes bibliog. refs. (Burt Franklin Research and Source Works Series, 886. American Classics in History and Social Science, 222) $20 LC 79-161383 ISBN 0-8337-4300-7

1164 *** Newall, Venetia. Encyclopedia of Witchcraft and Magic. Introd. by Richard M. Dorson. London: Hamlyn, 1974 (also, New York: Dial Press, 1974). 192p. Illus. (some color) Facsims. Bibliog. Index £3.25 ISBN 0-600-33077-X

This work is a major new contribution to occult literature. It contains 142 articles, most of them a half page in length. The author is an English folklorist, and emphasis is on historical development. There are also over 200 illustrations, 32 of them in color. Sample topics include abracadabra, Agrippa, ankou, burning of witches, cabala, cannibalism, dice, healing, Hecate, heresy, Lilith, May Day, Medea, Merlin, nudity, Tarot, toads, voodoo, zombie. The author writes as an outsider to the occult, which gives rise to an occasional error. However, the work is a very useful reference tool.

1165 Newport, John P., 1923- . Demons, Demons, Demons; A Christian Guide Through the Murky Maze of the Occult. Nashville, Broadman, 1972. 159p. Includes bibliog. refs. $4.95 LC 78-189503 ISBN 0-8054-5518-3

1166 Nic Leodhas, Sorche. Scottish Ghosts. Cover illus. by Terry Moesker. Text illus. by Nonny Hogrogian. London: Pan Books, 1974 (orig. pub. as "Gaelic Ghosts," London: Bodley Head, 1966). xii, 180p. Illus. £0.30 pa. ISBN 0-330-24069-2

1167/8 Nicola, John J. Diabolical Possession and Exorcism. Rockford, Ill.: Tan Books, 1974. 172p. $5.95

Nicola, a Roman Catholic priest, was technical advisor to the movie The Exorcist and is also an expert on stage magic. He has worked with Rhine on experiments. Nicola disliked some of the more vivid scenes in the movie, but feels that the film will bring men to face their own consciences, and will spotlight the current crisis of faith. The author discusses the Rituale Romanum, and mentions exorcism by Taoist priests in China. He feels poltergeist cases show many similarities to exorcism. He says there are many in mental institutions who could profit more from exorcism than from psychiatric therapy.

1169 Nolen, William A. Healing: A Doctor in Search of a Miracle. New York: Random House, 1975. 308p. $8.95 LC 74-9084
***

This work is a major new contribution to occult literature. The author, a physician, studies the Pentecostalism of Kathryn Kuhlman, the healing of Norbu Chen, and the Philippine psychic surgery phenomenon. He interviewed the healers, and says they all put on good dramatic effects during their performances. He failed to find any cure of a major illness (cancer or heart conditions), and says cures work only on psychosomatic cases. For Kuhlman, he studied 23 of her "cures," and found that none of the people were any better shortly after the service. However, Nolen says that there are many mysteries of how we all heal ourselves. Some will criticize this book as superficial, taking only the flashiest, least respectable healers. Nolen chastises the medical profession, saying that some healers show more warmth and caring than doctors do.

1170 Noorbergen, Rene, and Bubar, David Noble. You Are Psychic; The Incredible Story of David N. Bubar. New York: Morrow, 1971. xiv, 171p. $5.95 LC 74-142416

Bubar, former Baptist minister and self-proclaimed psychic, makes prophecies through the year 2000, and gives many anecdotes about predictions that have come true (he claims he foretold Senator Dirksen's death). He operates the S. O. S. Foundation, which uses radio and television and publishes the newspaper Psychic Adventurer. The book is written in the first person. Actually, few facts are given. Bubar claims that by following 17 steps, we all can develop psychic ability. Bubar dislikes most areas of the occult, such as reincarnation, witchcraft, and ouija board use. The book assumes worth only when one realizes this is the same David Bubar who has been implicated in the biggest arson case in U. S. history--the burning of the Goodyear Sponge Rubber Plant in Shelton, Conn., several years ago. Bubar, who predicted the fire, was convicted along with six other men of conspiracy to commit arson. The U. S. District Court sentenced him to 20 years, and the conviction was upheld by the U. S. Court of Appeals in June 1977. The burning appears to have been done to get insurance money for Bubar's long-time friend, the owner of the company. The book's publisher considers Noorbergen the "author" but it is clear that in substance it is written by Bubar.

1171 Norling, Rita, 1936- . Rituals and Magic for Perfect Living. West Nyack, N. Y.: Parker Pub. Co., 1974. $7.95 LC 74-10631 ISBN 0-13-781328-7

1172 Norman, Eric. Gods and Devils from Outer Space. New York: Lancer, 1973. 175p. $1.25 pa.

This work theorizes the by-now familiar thought that earth is a vast project of cosmic beings. Chapters include: "Legends of the Sky People," "Flying Saucer Gospel," "Sky People, Sea Saucers and Soviet UFO's," "There Were Giants in Those Days," and "The Enigma of Ancient Culture." The author sees Osiris and Isis as space travelers, and believes spaceships and atomic energy are cited in Genesis. Napoleon was visited by a flaming "red man" and Jefferson saw a dark-skinned man in a hooded cloak appear. Malcolm X was visited inside his prison cell by a strange figure.

1173 Norris, David, and Jacquemine Charrott-Lodwidge. The Book of Spells. Illus. by Scott Russell. London: Lorrimer, 1974. 139p. Illus. £1.50 pa. ISBN 0-85647-035-X

1174 Northage, Ivy. The Mechanics of Mediumship. London: Spiritualist Association of Great Britain, 1973. 89p. £0.95 pa. ISBN 0-900697-15-6

1175 Norton, Thomas, d. 1477. Thomas Norton's Ordinal of Alchemy. Ed. by John Reidy. London: Oxford University Press for the Early English Text Society, 1975. lxxv, 125p. Illus. Plates Facsims. Index (Early English Text Society, Original Series, no. 272) £3 ISBN 0-19-722274-9

1176 Norvell, Anthony [pseud. for Anthony Trupo, 1908-]. Astrology: Romance, You and the Stars. Wilshire, 1971. (Wilshire Self-improvement Library) $2

This book is a star-guide to happiness, explaining how astrology can help the reader get love, wealth and fame.

1177 ______. Astrology: Your Wheel of Fortune. New York: Barnes and Noble Books, 1974. v, 166p. (Barnes and Noble Occult Book) $2.50 pa. LC 74-9258 ISBN 0-06-464008-6

This book contains the following discussions: 12 signs, career, love and marriage, your children, using astrology to become rich, using it to make you a social success, health and length of life, for women only, for men only, peace of mind, artistic and creative talent, and your ultimate destiny according to your birthsign.

1178 ______. Exorcism: Overcome Black Magic with White Magic. West Nyack, N.Y.: Parker Pub. Co., 1974. $7.95 LC 74-10630 ISBN 0-13-294991-1

This book contains chapters on the following topics: putting powers of exorcism to work for a new life (20 things you can do with exorcism), overcoming negative forces in your life, breaking spells of black magic, stopping bad luck, developing psychic abilities, breaking evil spells of obsessing entities, seven mystical money mantras, spells to win true love, exorcising mental and physical sickness, how to control masters, karma, and rites from the Temple of Isis in ancient Egypt. This is actually an interesting book, more psychological than occult in tone.

________ see also Trupo, Anthony

1179 Nostredame [Nostradamus], Michel de, 1503-1566. The Prophecies of Nostradamus. Trans., ed., and introd. by Erika Cheetham. London: Corgi, 1975 (also, London: Spearman, 1974; orig. pub., 1973). 426p. (Parallel Middle French text and English translation) £0.75 pa. ISBN 0-552-09828-0

1180 Notestein, Wallace, 1878- . The History of Witchcraft in England from 1558 to 1718. Magnolia, Mass.: Peter Smith, 1971 (orig. pub., 1912). xiv, 442p. Bibliog. $5

1181 The Occult and the Supernatural. London: Octopus/Phoebus, 1975. 124p. Illus. (many color) Facsims. Index £2.50 ISBN 0-7064-0431-9

This attractive work contains 145 illustrations, 74 of them in color. Topics include spiritualism, mediums, ghosts, demonology, exorcism, the occult, and mysticism. The material is taken from Man, Myth and Magic (item 1070).

1182 O'Clery, Helen. The Pegasus Story of Atlantis. Illus. by Ann O'Clery. London: Dobson, 1971. 192p. Illus. Maps Bibliog. Index (Pegasus Books, no. 29) £0.95 ISBN 0-234-77358-8

1183 O'Connell, Margaret F., 1935- . The Magic Cauldron:
* Witchcraft for Good and Evil. New York: S. G. Phillips, 1975. 256p. Illus. Photos. Bibliog. $8.95 LC 75-26757 ISBN 0-87599-187-4

This juvenile book discusses the etymology and definition of witch, Babylon, Greece, medieval Europe, the Church, the Inquisition, Loudun, Salem, and the Moon Goddess/Earth Mother concept. The author, an editor of the New York Times Book Review, also covers larger political, social and religious issues. She gives spells and recipes, a witch's calendar, and a sabbat guide. There are excerpts from ancient incantations, cures, and chants. The role of women is stressed in the book. It is recommended for grades 6-9.

1184 O'Donnell, Elliott, 1867- . Elliott O'Donnell's Casebook of Ghosts. Ed. by Harry Ludlam. London: New English Library, 1971 (orig. pub. in 1 vol., New York: Taplinger, 1969). 2 vols., 112p. each £0.25 pa. each

This is another collection of O'Donnell's ghost stories. The present work gives 30 tales and is more autobiographical than the other books. He was physically attacked by a ghost in his youth, and decided to make ghost hunting his career. The tales, which are not verified, discuss banshees, apparitions, strange noises, and the ghosts of dogs and cats.

1185 _______. Elliott O'Donnell's Ghost Hunters. Slough, England: Foulsham, 1971. 175p. Illus. £1.90 ISBN 0-572-00793-0

1186 _______. The Hag of the Dribble and Other True Ghosts, from the Files of Elliott O'Donnell. Ed. by Bernhardt J. Hurwood. London: Hale, 1971 (orig. pub., New York: Taplinger, 1971). x, 166p. £1.80 ISBN 0-7091-2336-1

This book is a collection of supposedly true ghost stories by an Irish ghost hunter and psychic investigator. Discussed are phantoms, haunted trees and forests, werewolves, and evil forces. The tales are not authenticated.

1187 _______. Scottish Ghost Stories. Illus. by Tim Hunt. Norwich: Jarrold and Sons, 1975 (orig. pub., London: Kegan, Paul, 1911). 179p. Illus. £0.95 pa. ISBN 0-85306-458-X

1188 Oesterreich, Traugott Konstantin, 1880-1949. Possession
* and Exorcism: Among Primitive Races, in Antiquity, the Middle Ages, and Modern Times. Trans. by D. Ibberson. New York: Causeway Books, 1974 (orig. pub. 1921 as "Possession: Demoniacal and Other"). viii, 400p. Includes bibliog. refs. Index (Translation of "Die Besessenheit") $12.50 LC 74-76824 ISBN 0-88356-035-6

In his novel, The Exorcist, William Blatty calls this book the definitive study of possession, and admits his great debt to it. The author discusses the following topics: the constant nature of possession throughout the ages, external signs of possession, the somnambulistic form of possession, the lucid form of possession, the genesis and extinction of possession by exorcism, spontaneous possession among primitive races, spontaneous possession in the higher civilizations (Egypt, Greece, Christians, Jews, ancient India, Middle Ages, modern times), shamanism, and artificial and voluntary possession among higher civilizations (priests, temples, oracles, automatic writing). There is an appendix on parapsychological phenomena occurring during states of possession. The work continues many very lengthy quotes. Oesterreich's discussions are very psychological in tone, mentioning split personalities and neurological abnormalities, guilt problems and sexual repressions. He states, "possession begins to disappear amongst civilized races as soon as belief in spirits loses its power." The necessary autosuggestion is then lacking.

1189 * Oken, Alan. As Above, So Below: A Primary Guide to Astrological Awareness. New York: Bantam, 1973. viii, 344p. Illus. Bibliog. Index $1.95 pa.

There are two main parts to this fine survey. Part 1 gives for each zodiac sign the following information: drawing of the symbol and star chart showing which stars make up the sign, discussion of that sign in the sky, symbolism, the sign in mythology and history, the sign in nature's yearly cycle, the sign in mundane astrology, physiognomy and temperament, the sign in human experience, and keyword concepts for the sign (positive natural tendencies and misuse or exaggeration of traits). Part 2 gives for the sun and each planet: anatomy (scientific discussion); symbolism, mythology, and history; place in the natal horoscope, astrological rulership, and keyword concepts. Other chapters in the book discuss astrology and its place in the universe of man, the astrological tree of knowledge and its branches, the horoscope and natal astrology, the earth and its movements through the heavens; earth, elements, and triplicities; and earth, seasons, sexes, and quadruplicities. The title comes from the author's belief that in all of creation "there is a repetition of the same pattern in all structures from the tiniest atom to the greatest unit of the cosmos. Astrology points the way to a greater understanding of man's place in this repeating universe."

1190 ______. Astrological Guide to Living in the Age of Aquarius. New York: Popular Library, 1971. $.95 pa.

1191 ______. The Horoscope, the Road and Its Travelers. Toronto, London: Bantam, 1974. xi, 402p. Illus. Bibliog. Index £0.50 pa. ISBN 0-552-68372-8

The author tries to present astrology as both a spiritual path toward the expansion of one's understanding of universal law, and as a practical tool for helping others through use and interpretation of the horoscope. Part 1 discusses the horoscope. Part 2, titled "The Road," covers chart erection and interpretation (time, wheel of life, interplanetary relationships, interpretation, and prognostication). Part 3, titled "The Travelers," discusses Jung, Isadora Duncan, Joseph Stalin, Angela Davis, Harry Houdini, Greta Garbo, and Edgar Cayce. For each, the author gives charts, and then discusses them. Question-and-answer sections follow the chapters.

1192 * Olcott, Henry Steel, 1832-1907. Inside the Occult: The True Story of Madame H. P. Blavatsky. Introd. by Daniel Grotto-Kurska. Philadelphia: Running Press, 1975 (orig. pub. as "Old Diary Leaves," New York: Putnam, 1895). 491p. Index $9.80 LC 75-17044 ISBN 0-914294-31-8

This classic contains, among others, the following chapters: the first meeting of the founders, Madame Blavatsky in America, Philadelphia phenomena, Madame Blavatsky's second marriage, Spiritualism, Dr. Slade, the Theosophical Society proposed and formed, Baron de Palm, Isis Unveiled, reincarnation, the New York headquarters, Swami Dyanand, a character sketch of Madame Blavatsky, Blavatsky becomes an American citizen, the foundation of the British Theosophical Society, last days in New York, the founder sails for India, the founder dies.

1193 ________. People from the Other World. Illus. by Alfred Kappes and T. W. Williams. Introd. to new ed. by Terence Barrow. Rutland, Vt.: Tuttle, 1972 (orig. pub., 1875). xii, 492p. Illus. Bibliog. $8.25 LC 74-152114 ISBN 0-8048-0979-8

This book discusses spirit occurrences at the Eddy Brothers' farm in Chittenden, Vt., in 1874. Olcott witnessed the events, and published a series on them in the New York Daily Graphic. He discusses also attempts to detect any fakery, and mentions Blavatsky's mediumship abilities.

1194 Old, Walter Gorn, 1864-1930. The Book of Charms and Talismans, by Sepharial [pseud.]. New York: Arco, 1971. Illus. $3.50

This book discusses the potency of numbers; precious stones and the zodiac; symbols of fish, owl, horseshoe, and acorn; metal charms; and the meaning of the swastika, scarab, moon, and eye. The work includes illustrations of amulets, talismans, and seals, some of them rare. There is also a section on how to make lucky talismans.

1195 ________. The Kabala of Numbers, by Sepharial [pseud.]. Hollywood, Calif.: Newcastle Pub. Co., 1974 (reprint of 1928 ed., pub. Philadelphia: D. McKay Co., orig. pub., 1913). 204, 215p. $3.95 pa. LC 74-6128 ISBN 0-87877-027-5

This book, originally published in two volumes, discusses the relationship between astrology, numerology, and phenomena existing in nature.

1196 ________. The Manual of Occultism, by Sepharial [pseud.]. London: Rider, 1972 (orig. pub., 1910). xiii, 356p. £2.75 ISBN 0-09-110910-8

1197 ________. Sepharial's New Dictionary of Astrology, by Sepharial [pseud.]. New York: Arco, 1972 (orig. pub., 1963). 158p. $.95 pa. ISBN 0-668-02589-1

This book discusses hundreds of terms. There is new material on the influence of Pluto, which governs transformation and annihilation. There is a table to show the difference between a country's standard time and Greenwich Mean Time, and many charts. The book has an appendix on the mathematics of astrology, and gives a biography of notable contributors to astrological literature.

1198 Oliver, Frederick S., comp. Dweller on Two Planets. Blauvelt, N.Y.: Steinerbooks, 1974 (orig. pub., 1894). 424p. $2.95 pa.

This is a reprint of a classic discussion of Atlantis received from "Phylos the Thibetan" by Frederick Oliver through automatic writing.

1199 Oliver, George, 1772-1867. The Pythagorean Triangle; or, The Science of Numbers. Minneapolis: Wizards Book Shelf, 1975 (orig. pub., Edinburgh: Ballantyne, 1875). xxiv, 237p. Includes bibliog. refs. (Secret Doctrine Reference Series) $8 LC 75-16015 ISBN 0-913510-17-3

1200 * Olson, Alan M., ed. Disguises of the Demonic; Contemporary Perspectives on the Power of Evil. New York: Association Press, 1975. 159p. $6.95 LC 74-31321 ISBN 0-8096-1896-6

This book consists of 11 articles, four of which were originally delivered as Lowell Lectures in the Boston University School of Theology. They discuss the following topics: the devil in folklore and literature, especially American, African, and Romanian; Luther's theology; The Exorcist film; demonic manifestations in history; religions of the East, Islam, and Protestant views of the gospel; and Jung's psychology. The author feels that current occult interest is due to a longing for experimental immediacy. He feels that the demonic should be dealt with seriously as real and not as myth. This is a scholarly book, with many footnotes.

1201 Olyanova, Nadya. The Psychology of Handwriting. North Hollywood, Calif.: Wilshire, 1972 (orig. pub., 1969). 371p. Illus. $3 pa.

1202 Omarr, Sydney. Astrology and You; Personal Guide to Your Potential, Money, and Love. New York: Pyramid, 1972. 206p. $.95 pa.

1203 _______. Sydney Omarr's Astrological Guide for 1972. New York: New American Library, 1971. $1 pa.

1204 _______. Sydney Omarr's Astrological Guide for 1974. New York: New American Library, 1973. 274p. $1.25 pa.

For each sign, there is a general introduction. The following discussions are then given for each month of the year: key numbers, significant days, answer to probable question, high cycle days, low cycle days, and special notes. Special articles for this year include "You and the World of Finance in 1974," by Dale Richardson, "Memories and Reflections: A Survey of Modern Astrology," by Carl Payne Tobey, and "Planetary Picture in 1974," by Sydney Omarr.

1205 * ______. Sydney Omarr's Astrological Revelations About You. New York: New American Library, 1973. 239p. $1.25 pa.

For each sign in the zodiac, the author gives a discussion on these topics: your character and life (including a paragraph of special material for those born at every two-hour stage within the sign), careers, hand, secrets, and special associations (chart-form information on birthstone, flower, numbers, color, cities, countries, part of body). The text provides a good deal of information. The writing is clever; the author lectures the person under each sign as "you," often saying things like "Listen, Taurus," or, "Am I being too harsh?"

1206 ______. Sydney Omarr's Weekly Astrological Guide. New York: New American Library, annual. 12 vols. 128p. each $1 pa. each

After briefly discussing the closing months of the previous year (October, November, and December), the author discusses the coming year week by week. First, he gives the high-cycle days and low-cycle days for the month. He then divides the month up into segments of six, seven, or eight days each. For each segment of the month, Omarr usually gives key numbers, answer to a probable question, whom you may be attracted to, most significant day, special notes and warnings, and general tone. Each year, different short articles appear in the front and back of the book.

1207 ______. The Thought Dial Way to a Healthy and Successful Life. Introd. by Carl Payne Tobey. New York: New American Library, 1973 (c1969). 174p. (Signet Mystic) (A Stuart L. Daniels Book) (Parts of this book appeared in author's previous work, "Thought Dial") $.95 pa.

According to the author, this book heralds a new dimension in the mantic sciences. It combines ancient concepts of planet and number symbols with modern Jungian psychology. The operation of the dial is as follows: the forefinger is placed on the arrow and the arrow is moved to indicate three different digits which are then added and reduced to a single number (only 11 and 22 double numbers stay unadded).

1208 O'Neil, Barbara, and Richard Phillips. Biorhythms: How to Live with Your Life Cycles. Pasadena, Calif.: Ward Ritchie Press, 1975. 128p. $7.95

This book shows the effects of biorhythms on the lives of

politicians, entertainers and sports figures. The most important dates in their lives are taken, and then biorhythm charts are drawn for these dates. The results usually coincide well. The authors tell how the reader can chart his or her own physical, emotional and intellectual cycles.

1209 Opheil [pseud.]. The Oracle of Fortuna. St. Paul, Minn.: Llewellyn, 1971. ix, 127p. Illus. $2 pa. LC 72-181228 ISBN 0-87542-589-5

The author gives a system of divination which does not tell the fortunes of people, but gives them a feel for the future. After discussing oracles of the past, the author discusses the symbolism of the four elements and the planets. Opheil then discusses working the oracle, with element cards and planet cards. The cards themselves are in the appendix. They are very simple in design, with several bold colors and simple symbols such as circles, squares, and lines. Brief information is given, to be stuck to the back of each card. Basically, the system involves these cards' being set down in a certain spread.

1210 Ordo Templi Orientis. Secret Rituals of the O. T. O. Ed. and introd. by Francis King. London: Daniel, 1973. 240p. £3.15 ISBN 0-85207-111-6

1211 Osborn, Arthur Walter, 1891- . Superphysical: A Review of the Evidence for Continued Existence, Reincarnation, and Mystical States of Consciousness. Rev. ed. New York: Barnes and Noble, 1974 (also, London: Muller, 1974; orig. pub., London: Nicholson and Watson, 1937). xviii, 350p. Includes bibliog. refs. Index $13 LC 74-2674 ISBN 0-06-495304-1

This book reviews telepathy, precognition, telekinesis, ghosts, and many other areas, and mentions James, Huxley, Wells, McDougall.

1212 Ostrander, Sheila, and Lynn Schroeder. Astrological Birth Control. Englewood Cliffs, N. J.: Prentice-Hall, 1972. vii, 243p. Bibliog. $6.95 LC 75-180550 ISBN 0-13-049411-9

This book is an expansion of a section in the authors' Psychic Discoveries Behind the Iron Curtain (entry 1214) on Dr. Eugen Jonas, who set up an astrological birth control clinic in Czechoslovakia. Parallels are drawn to other reports.

1213 ________, and ________. Handbook of Psi Discoveries. New
*** York: Berkley Pub. Corp., dist. by Putnam, 1974. 342p. Illus. Plates Bibliog. Index $8.95 LC 73-88532 ISBN 0-399-11288-X

This work is a major new contribution to occult literature. The first third discusses parapsychology around the world. The rest of the work gives many suggestions for amateur experiments, techniques, and devices that can be built. Most devices are cheap and easily constructed. Areas covered are dowsing, Kirlian photography, pyramids, voice recordings, plants, PK, and auras. The book also mentions games for developing telepathy. Some of the devices are for serious research, some are quite whimsical. In effect, this is a book of experiments and is also a Whole Earth Catalog-type book.

1214 ________, and ________. Psychic Discoveries Behind the
* Iron Curtain. Introd. by Ivan T. Sanderson. New York: Bantam, 1971 (also pub. as "Psi: Psychic Discoveries Behind the Iron Curtain," orig. pub., Englewood Cliffs, N.J.: Prentice-Hall, 1970). 457p. Illus. Bibliog. Index $1.25 pa.

This book made a sensation in the U.S. when it was published. It is definitely an occult classic already. It broke new ground in considering Soviet research in psychical sciences. Discussions include the following: psychics Karl Nikolaiev, Vanga Dimitrova of Bulgaria, and Pavel Stepanek; Rosa Kuleshova and eyeless sight; Dr. Nikolai Kozyrev, an astrophysicist who is working on time research; and Nelya Mikhailova, psychokinesis medium. One of the book's highlights is an excellent discussion of telepathist Wolf Messing of the 1940's. Although some critics complain of grossly overstated and exaggerated facts, this work is a major contribution to the serious literature of parapsychology. It ends with an excellent bibliography containing mostly Russian citations.

1215 The Other World: Experiences and Messages Received Telepathically from [the late] Albert Pauchard, ex-President of the Society for Psychical Studies in Geneva, written down by M.J. London: College of Psychic Studies, 1973. 74p. £0.75 pa.

These messages were transmitted between 1935 and 1937. Pauchard (1878-1935) was a Swiss spiritualist who studied the occult and developed the gift of magnetic healing. The book contains 42 short discussions devoted to various aspects of life on the other side. His purpose is to comfort those afraid of death.

1216 Ouellette, Raymond. Psychic Magic: A Creative Approach for the Expansion of Inner Consciousness; An Oracular Study of Geomancy, I Ching, Astrology. Fall River, Mass.: Aero Press, 1974. 343p. Illus. $8.95 LC 74-78491

Over, Raymond Van see Van Over, Raymond

1217 Owen, Alan. Psychic Mysteries of the North; Discoveries
*** from the Maritime Provinces and Beyond. New York: Harper and Row, 1975. 243p. $8.95 LC 74-15845

This work is a major new contribution to occult literature.

A large part of it discusses current research in Canada previously available only in the Canadian psychic journal, New Horizons. Owen is director of the New Horizons Research Foundation in Toronto. The following research is covered: PK tests with Jan Murta, Professor Emerson's use of a psychic in trying psychometry with archaeological artifacts, experiments by Bernard Grad and Sister Justa Smith with healer Oskar Estabany, telepathy, physics, poltergeists, ghosts, reincarnation, haunted houses, mysticism, dowsing, auras, astral projection, psychic photography (thoughtography), PK, Geller, plants and psi, pyramid experiments (they found it had no effect on razor blades and food decomposition), and spiritualistic beliefs and practices of Indian tribes of Canada. One of the most interesting sections describes the "Philip" research, where a circle attempted to create a ghost who would manifest himself by PK, and succeeded in getting raps and table-liftings. Owen also covers brain states, and Bucke and his "cosmic consciousness" (see entry 163).

1218 Owen, Alan Robert George, and Victor Sims. Science and the Spook: Eight Strange Cases of Haunting. New York: Garrett Pubns., 1971 (also, London: Dobson, 1971). 218p. Includes bibliog. refs. $4.50 LC 71-88054 ISBN 0-912326-26-3

Owen, a biologist and mathematician, wrote the first seven chapters; the rest were done by British newsman Sims. The two visited eight haunted places, each a different type of haunting, each recent, and each witnessed by more than one person. Cases include a haunted pub, a gray lady in a hospital, exploding clocks, an apparition of two Afghan hounds and their owner; a 98-room mansion where a floating arm rattled windows from outside and 30 feet above the ground, and the Northfleet municipal housing area (noises, disappearing objects). The authors felt that one case was not paranormal.

1219 Oxley, Cyril Thomas. Haunted North Country. Photos by J. Leach. Harrogate, England: C. T. Oxley, 1973. 68p. Illus. £0.25 pa.

1220 Oyle, Irving. The Healing Mind. Millbrae, Calif.: Celestial Arts, 1974. 128p. $7.95

The author is a California physician and now head of Bolinas Headlands Healing Service, which combines ordinary medicine with massage, positive thinking, mental imagery, hypnosis, and sonapuncture (using ultrasound at acupuncture points). Oyle discusses Kirlian photography, body cycles, Teilhard de Chardin, biofeedback, meditation, yin and yang. He feels all of these show the mind as the most effective healing force.

1221 Pagan, Isabelle Mary. The Astrological Key to Character

Birthday Book: The 12 Zodiacal Types. Adyar, London: Theosophical Pub. House, 1973. 70p. Illus. £0.70 pa.

1222 Paine, Lauran. A Gaggle of Ghosts. London: Hale, 1971. 191p. Bibliog. Index £1.50 ISBN 0-7091-1769-8

1223 ________. Sex in Witchcraft. New York: Taplinger, 1972. 186p. Illus. Bibliog. $6.50 LC 72-76258 ISBN 0-8008-7151-0

The author discusses the sex practices of witches as seen by the medieval church clergy. He argues that celibacy has harmful effects in the church and says that witchcraft was practiced by Catholic and later Protestant clergymen. Paine discusses the following: witchcraft persecutions, metamorphosis--especially into werewolves, Marie Catherine, a 17th-century mother superior who seduced her nuns, Major Weir and his incestuous sister, Gilles de Rais, who had sex with beautiful children and then tortured them to death, the Inquisition, and copulation with incubi, succubi, and the devil. The work is illustrated with woodcuts and engravings of various periods.

1224 ________. Witchcraft and the Mysteries. New York: Tap-
* linger Pub. Co., 1975 (orig. pub., London: Hale, 1975). 192p. Illus. Plates Bibliog. Index $8.50 LC 73-16636 ISBN 0-8008-8377-2

The author begins by discussing ancient mysteries and philosophies of pagan worship, their vulgarization by followers, and suppression by the church. The rest of the work goes subject by subject, presenting what the past historical lore and documents of witches have to say. In discussing these past practices, the work could really function as a grimoire or handbook for witches of today. Topics covered are simple spells, transvection, conjuration, the function of trance, the forces of color, numerology, demons, the night-watch, and implements. The author believes in the existence of Satan and the reality of witchcraft. This book is a fine survey, packed with information not usually found in other witchcraft works. There is a tremendous amount of excellent philosophical discussion as well.

1225 ________. Witches in Fact and Fantasy. New York: Taplinger, 1972 (c1971). 188p. Illus. Bibliog. $6.50 LC 74-185625 ISBN 0-8008-8374-8

The author calls witchcraft a Christian heresy, and lumps together witchcraft and satanism. Using largely primary sources, the author discusses the history and folklore of witchcraft. Some reviewers feel that his material is sometimes incorrect.

1226/7 Palmer, Geoffrey, 1912- , and Noel Lloyd. Ghosts Go Haunting. Illus. by Sara Silcock. London: Pan Books, 1975 (orig. pub., London: Odhams, 1963). 157p. Illus. (Piccolo Book) £0.40 pa. ISBN 0-330-24560-0

1228 *** Panati, Charles, 1943- . Supersenses; Our Potential for Parasensory Experience. New York: Quadrangle/New York Times Book Co., 1974 (dist. by Harper; also, London: Cape, 1975). 301p. Illus. Bibliog. Index $8.95 LC 74-77937 ISBN 0-8129-0472-9

This work is a major new contribution to occult literature. The author is a physicist, science broadcaster, lecturer, and writes the science column for Newsweek. The book is a survey of modern experiments in telepathy, precognition, clairvoyance, psychokinesis, psychic healing, dream ESP, astral projection, hypnosis and ESP, and mysticism and psi. He sees three stages in the history of parapsychology: field work, the qualitative phase, and the statistical phase. Panati feels there has been a change in research methodology, with great use today of devices and increasing emphasis on altered states of consciousness. He says that "the question today is no longer whether parasensory perception is real or imaginary, but under what conditions it manifests itself."

1229 Paracelsus, 1493-1541. The Archidoxes of Magic. Trans. by Robert Turner. 2nd ed. London: Askin Publishers; New York: Samuel Weiser, 1975 (orig. pub. London: printed by J.C. for N. Brook and H. Harison, 1656). 162p. Illus. (Translation of "De Spiritibus Metallorum," "De Occulta Philosophia" and "Archidoxis Magica") $25 LC 76-372352 ISBN 0-87728-282-X

This classic work discusses the following topics: magic, the mysteries of nature, the spirits of the planets, the secrets of alchemy, occult philosophy, the mysteries of the 12 signs of the zodiac, the magical cure of diseases, and celestial medicines.

1230 ________. The Prophecies of Paracelsus: Magic Figures and Prognostications Made by Theophrastus Paracelsus about Four Hundred Years Ago. London: Rider, 1974 (orig. pub., 1915). 115p. Illus. (Translation of "Prognostication auff xxiiii Jar Zukunfftig." Germany, 1530). £2 ISBN 0-09-120260-4

1231 ________. The Prophecies of Paracelsus; Occult Symbols and Magic Figures with Esoteric Explanations. With The Life and Teachings of Paracelsus, by Franz Hartmann. Introd. by Paul M. Allen. Blauvelt, N.Y.: Rudolf Steiner Publications, 1973. ("The Life and Teachings of Paracelsus" is a reprint of ed. pub. as "Life of Philippus Theophrastus, Bombast of Hohenheim Known by the Name Paracelsus," London: G. Redway, 1887) 86, xiii, 220p. Illus. ("The Prophecies of Paracelsus" is a translation of "Prognosticatio Eximii Doctoris Theophrasti Paracelsi"). $2.45 pa. LC 72-81591

1232 * Parapsychology and Anthropology: Proceedings of an International Conference Held in London, England, August 29-31,

1973. Ed. by Allan Angoff and Diana Barth. New York: Parapsychology Foundation, 1974. xviii, 328p. Illus. Includes bibliog. refs. (Proceedings of the 22nd International Conference of the Parapsychology Foundation) $9 LC 74-82959 ISBN 0-912328-24-X

There are 18 papers in all. Bob Brier, now philosophy professor at C. W. Post, presents the paper, "Parapsychological Principles from Anthropological Studies" (on I Ching, Tarot, astrology, and a practice no longer used, Egyptian magic). Hans and Shulamith Kreitler, now at Harvard, report on "Implications of ESP Experiments for Anthropological ESP Research." Marcel Martiny has a paper on "Some Reflections on Anthropology and Parapsychology." Jamuna Prasad discusses "Occultism in Sakt Religion" (on Tantra). Emilio Servadio reports on "Peasant-Healers and the Paranormal," with Jeffry Smith of Stanford University covering "The Occult and the Intellectual." Robert L. Van de Castle, professor of clinical psychology at the University of Virginia School of Medicine, presents an " Investigation of Psi Abilities Among the Cuna Indians of Panama." Herbert Weiner, a New Jersey rabbi, discusses "Folk Use of the Dream in Religious Societies." Then, the anthropologists take over. Agehananda Bharati, chairman of the Department of Anthropology at Syracuse University, reports on "The Ontological Status of Psychic Phenomenon in Hinduism and Buddhism." Devereux gives a paper on "Trance and Orgasm in 'Euripides'." Dingwall's presentation, titled "End of a Legend: A Note on the Magical Flight," keys on the Ascension of Christ and the Indian Rope Trick. Ioan Lewis discusses "An Anthropologist's Encounter with the Supernatural" (he concludes that the anthropologist does not encounter the paranormal, even in possession). Adrian Boshier's paper, "African Apprenticeship--Study of the 'Sangoma' Witch Doctor in Southern Africa," covers his interesting years as a witch doctor/investigator. Gerda Grober-Gluck reports on "Second Sight in Northern Germany: Traditional Popular Belief and Precognition." Joan Halifax-Grof, medical anthropologist at Maryland Psychiatric Research Center, discusses "Hex Death." Elliott Skinner, chairman of the Department of Anthropology at Columbia University, presents a paper on "African Beliefs in the Psychic Manipulation of Material Phenomena: The Tengsoba in Mossi Society." Robert and Linda Sussman, anthropology professors at Washington University, discuss "A Description of Divination Among the Sakalava of Madagascar." Alister Hardy, director of the Religious Experience Research Unit at Manchester College, covers "Anthropology, Parapsychology and Religion."

1233 Parapsychology and the Sciences; Proceedings of an International Conference Held in Amsterdam, the Netherlands, August 23-25, 1972. Ed. by Allan Angoff and Betty Shapin.
* New York: Parapsychology Foundation, 1974. xiii, 289p. Illus. Includes bibliog. refs. (Proceedings of the 21st International Conference of the Parapsychology Foundation) $7 LC 73-92492 ISBN 0-912328-23-1

There are papers by D. J. West (psychology), Emilio Servadio (psychoanalysis), Solco Trump (meteorology), John C. Boynton (biology), George Zorab (genetics), Arthur Koestler (physics), and John R. Smythies (neurology). Bob Brier discusses why parapsychology should be considered a science. Harold Cahn, professor at Northern Arizona University, felt that investigators had to get "existentially involved" in psychic states. John Beloff of Edinburgh University felt that we should not talk about other forms of reality, when what we mean is only psychological subjective experience. Dr. Smythies of Edinburgh University, in his paper, "The Mind-Brain Problem," said that the universe consisted not only of one physical world, but of "many image (private, mental, sensible, perceptual) worlds as well." Other contributors include D. Scott Rogo, Edgar Mitchell, Eric Dingwall, Helmut Schmidt, John Cutten, and Russell Targ (on precognition).

1234 <u>Parapsychology in South Africa.</u> Ed. by J. C. Poynton.
* Johannesburg: South African Society for Psychical Research, 1975. 163p. (Proceedings of the 1st Conference, 1973)

This conference was jointly sponsored by the South African Society for Psychical Research and the South African Institute for Parapsychological Research. Contributors of the 17 papers are all South African, except for two guest speakers, J. G. Pratt and John Cutten. Psychiatrist B. J. F. Laubscher presents a paper, "Psi in Traditional Bantu Culture." A. K. Boshier, an anthropologist, discusses his becoming a witch doctor in the Soweto tribe. A. E. H. Bleksley reports on his investigation of W. van Vuurde over the period 1960-1970. L. H. van Loon, a civil engineer, presents the paper, "Some Unusual Phenomena Associated with the Recovery of Lost Objects"; it concerns his wife, who finds things by teleportation. Basil Shackleton discusses Soal's integrity and his earlier life in South Africa. J. C. Poynton writes about a questionnaire he circulated on out-of-the-body experiences. J. H. M. Whiteman, who can astrally project at will, discusses how to evaluate the authenticity of reports. He also presents the paper, "Three-Tier Ontology for Parapsychology and Physics." J. G. Pratt writes on "Some Notes for a Future Einstein of Parapsychology."

1235 <u>Parapsychology Today: A Geographic View; Proceedings of</u>
*** <u>an International Conference, Held at Le Piol, St. Paul de Vence, France, August 25-27, 1971.</u> Ed. by Allan Angoff and Betty Shapin. New York: Parapsychology Foundation, 1973. xiii, 258p. Illus. Includes bibliog. refs. (Proceedings of the 20th International Conference of the Parapsychology Foundation) $6.50 LC 72-94940

This work is a major new contribution to occult literature. This is a collection of 19 papers presented at the conference. The purpose of the conference was to hear representatives of different geographical areas give a history of parapsychology in their area and a survey of current parapsychological activity there. Areas covered were the United Kingdom, Japan, California, India, Turkey, Israel, Germany, Eastern Europe, South Africa (two papers), the Nordic countries, Italy, France, Switzerland, Argentina, Canada, and the Netherlands. Contributors included J. M. O. Wheatley, Joseph Rush, Hans Bender, Jarl Fahler, Emilio Servadio, and D. J. West. There are two other papers besides the 17 area reports. Milan Rýzl presents an excellent paper entitled, "Parapsychology's Century of Progress." This survey also mentions traps into which parapsychology researchers can fall. The last paper is Andrija Puharich's "Protocommunication Progress in Parapsychology," in which the author states that parapsychology's continued growth and success is dependent on solving these basic problems: origin of life, replication of life process, sensory perception, artificial perception and intelligence, memory in the brain, direct brain perception, direct brain action, memory in nature, and precognition.

1236 Park, Duncan. Occultism. London: S. C. M. Press for the Christian Education Movement, 1974. 32p. Illus. Bibliog. (Probe, no. 19) ISBN 0-334-01172-8

1237 *** Parker, Adrian. States of Mind: ESP and Altered States of Consciousness. London: Malaby Press, 1975 (also, New York: Taplinger, 1975). 198p. Bibliog. Index £3.95

This work is a major new contribution to occult literature. This study of ESP research literature concludes that ESP phenomena occur most often when a person shifts from one state to another (waking to dreaming, for example). The author is a British clinical psychologist who has studied lab data and anecdotal materials. There is much discussion of altered states of consciousness: hypnotic, psychological, pharmacological, religious, and psychic (such as a medium's trance states). Parker also discusses the brain, central nervous system, synapses, nerve bundles and fibers.

1238 Parker, Derek. Familiar to All: William Lilly and Astrology in the Seventeenth Century. London: Cape, 1975. 272p. Illus. Plates Bibliog. Index £5.50 ISBN 0-224-01112-X

1239 ________, and Julia Parker. The Compleat Astrologer: The Practical Encyclopaedia of Astrological Science. London: Mitchell Beazley, 1975 (also, London: Mitchell Beazley, 1971; New York: Bantam, 1975; orig. pub., New York: McGraw-Hill, 1971). 256p. Illus. (some color) Charts (chiefly color) Maps Index £3.50 pa. ISBN 0-85533-064-3

This encyclopedic survey of the history of astrology includes a section, "Atlas of Astrology," which gives a guide to the astronomy behind astrology. The work also gives brief biographies of famous astrologers. The author used hundreds of sources in compiling this work. It is illustrated with 400 illustrations, 64 of them in color. A table of planetary positions from 1900-1975 is included.

1240 ________, and ________. The Compleat Astrologer's Sun-
* Signs Guide. New York: Crown Publishers, 1973 (also, London: Mitchell Beazley Pub. Ltd., 1973). 224p. Illus. (some color) Index $10. LC 73-79846

This book is excellent graphically. There are many illustrations, some in color, the rest, black and white or brown-tone drawings of unusual, striking creativity. For each sign, the following is discussed: general, in action, emotional relationships, parents and children, career and pastimes, at home, dinner, and recipes.

1241 ________, and ________. Love Signs. London: Mitchell
* Beazley, 1973. 12 vols. 48p. each Illus. (some color) Index £1.35 pa. each

The Parkers have contributed another excellent graphic work to astrological literature. Each volume is on one sign of the zodiac. The paper is glossy, with many small, striking illustrations. Discussions for each sign include the following: love with a partner from each of the 12 signs, making the most of your sign, planets of love, gods of love, herbs of love, synastry (charting the chances of love), Venus chart, and Mars chart. The set is excellent for browsing or giving one creative ideas.

1242 ________, and ________. The Zodiac Library. London: Mitchell Beazley; St. Albans, England: Mayflower, 1972. 12 vols. 48p. each Illus. (chiefly color) Index £0.75 pa. each volume

1243 Parker, Faye W. ESP, Your Latent Talent. Santa Monica, Calif.: DeVorss, 1974. 112p. Illus. LC 74-75031 ISBN 0-87516-182-0

One section of this book discusses techniques: breathing exercises, psychic centers, meditations, astral projection, and health and healing. A second part covers philosophic foundations (soul, spirit, reincarnation and karma, death, suicide). The third section is a guide to psychic reading (palmistry, signs of the zodiac, lucky numbers, automatic writing).

1244/5 Parrott, Wanda Sue. Automatic Writing. Los Angeles: Sherbourne Press, 1974. 123p. $2.50 pa.

This book discusses how to become most receptive to receiving automatic writing, and how to transcribe the messages correctly.

1246 Past, Present, Future: How to Read and Interpret Dreams, Handwriting, Palms, Cards, Tea Leaves, Dice, Doodles, Numbers. Indianapolis: Bobbs-Merrill, 1975. 192p. Illus. $9.95 LC 74-29205 ISBN 0-672-52130-X

1247 Pasteur, George. The Healing Germ. Broadstone, England: The Sanctuary, 1975. 68p. £0.50 pa.

This British healer discusses how he does absent healing.

1248 Paulsen, Kathryn, comp. Witches' Potions and Spells. Illus. by Maggie Jarvis. Mount Vernon, N.Y.: Peter Pauper Press, 1971. 62p. Illus. (color) $1.25 pa. LC 70-25332

1249 Pauwels, Louis, and Jacques Bergier. Morning of the Ma-
* gicians. Trans. by Rollo Myers. London: Mayflower, 1971 (also, New York: Avon Books, 1968; orig. pub. as "Dawn of Magic," London: Gibbs and Phillips, 1963). 304p. Illus. Plates (Orig. pub. as "Matin des magiciens." Paris: Gallimard, 1960) £0.50 pa. ISBN 0-583-11970-0

This is a strange, fascinating book, with few hard facts but thousands of exciting speculations. The book is the result of five years of thought and quest by the authors. Bergier helped Pauwels organize the work by giving him articles, newspaper clippings, books, and reports of all sorts of events and creative ideas. In this work, "legend and fact, conjecture and accurate observation intermingle." The first two sections discuss the 19th-century narrow scientific thinking that all knowledge had been achieved (a feeling that is sometimes expressed today). The author feels that science erects barriers of impossibilities, with the magician and the technician both breaking through these barriers. Pauwels claims that we are forgetful of past knowledge. Europe possesses treasures which he feels are hardly exploited at all--ancient documents stored in the great libraries. He recommends a systematic probing of all past learning. The third section is on alchemy, and includes a discussion of exactly what takes place in an alchemist's laboratory. Again, he says over 100,000 alchemy books and manuscripts exist, and yet are not read today. The fourth section is on vanished civilizations, and emphasizes the ideas of Charles Fort. The fifth part is entitled "A Few Years in the Absolute Elsewhere." It discusses coincidence, chance encounters, flashbacks and tie-ins to the past as making up the true, "invisible history" of man. He also has some very interesting discussions about the Nazis and their connection with magic, pseudo-sciences, and the hollow earth theory. The last section in the book discusses man's nature, covering the brain, language, and mutations among humans. The work is excellent for provoking creative thinking, and violent disagreement.

1250 Pavitt, William Thomas, and Kate Pavitt. The Book of Talismans, Amulets, and Zodiacal Gems. North Hollywood, Calif.: Wilshire, 1972 (also, Detroit: Tower Books, 1971, dist. by Gale; orig. pub., London: W. Rider, 1914). 292p. Illus. $3 pa. ISBN 0-85030-042-8

1251 Pearce, Joseph Chilton. The Crack in the Cosmic Egg: Challenging Constructs of Mind and Reality. New York: Pocket Books, 1973 (also, London: Lyrebird Press, 1973; orig. pub., New York: Julian Press, 1971). 219p. Bibliog. $1.50 pa. ISBN 0-671-78901-5
***

This work is a major new contribution to occult literature. It relates the observations of a college teacher on his personal search for reality and creativity, with particular attention on the men who have influenced him most--William Blake, Teilhard de Chardin, Carlos Castaneda, and Carl Jung. The "cosmic egg" is the sum total of our ideas of what the world is, which in effect defines what reality can be to us. The crack is the insight by which man escapes this shell and creates a new world view for our time. Emphasis is placed on the values of "autistic thinking," a dream-world type of thinking, non-logical (but not illogical), and creative. In effect, the book is an indictment of our educational system, which screens out fantasies. The work contains an excellent bibliography. The book was not designed as an occult work, but contributes much to occult thought.

1252 ______. Exploring the Crack in the Cosmic Egg; Split Minds and Meta-Realities. New York: Pocket Books, 1975 (orig. pub., New York: Julian Press, 1974). 239p. Bibliog. $1.95 pa. ISBN 0-671-80638-6
***

This work is a major new contribution to occult literature. It is an expansion of the author's ideas first presented in The Crack in the Cosmic Egg (entry 1251; where he says that what we call reality is a semantic construction). In this work, he says that our culture gives us hopes and dreams which have no validity today, and we must empty our heads of them and start again. Pearce focuses on the role of fear in maintaining reality constructs of society, and man's lack of faith in his autonomic nervous system. He also discusses how fear of death affects many parts of our lives. He covers the nature of "body knowing," and mentions the left and right hemispheres of the brain. Pearce dislikes new consciousness, "quickie-enlightenment" techniques, and also doubts psychic phenomena. He believes the solution to our problems lies in "irreversibility thinking." Sample chapters are: "Sensory-Mediant Perception," "Prediction and Control," "Feeding and Feedback," "Lying," "Will to Power," "Double-Mindedness," "Mind Engineering," and "Embracing Despair." The book was not written as an occult work, but contributes a great deal to occult thought.

1253 Pearce, William John. The Hidden Truth. London: Regency Press, 1974. 238p. £3 ISBN 0-7212-0338-8

1254 Pearce-Higgins, D., Canon, and the Rev. G. S. Whitby, eds. Life, Death, and Psychical Research. London: Rider and Co., 1973. 272p. £4

This work discusses the implications for religion of facts revealed by psychical research. The parapsychology part presents these essays: a condensation of a Society for Psychical Research pamphlet by Rosalind Heywood and Renée Haynes on ESP, Brigadier Spedding on psychical phenomena, Colin Brookes-Smith on the PK work of Batcheldor, Canon Pearce-Higgins on trance mediumship, Crookall on OOBE's (out-of-the-body experiences), and the Rev. K. G. Cumins on healing. The rest of the book, on the religious implications of psychical research, presents these discussions: the Rev. Donald Bretherton on prohibitions of psychic practices in Deuteronomy, Canon Pearce-Higgins on Biblical miracles, Pearce-Higgins on poltergeists, hauntings, and possession, based on his personal experiences, Allan Barham on life after death, and Martin Israel on the nearness of God.

1255 Pearsall, Ronald. Table-Rappers. New York: St. Martin's
*** Press, 1973 (orig. pub., London: Joseph, 1972). 258p. Illus. Bibliog. Index $6.95 LC 72-92008

This work is a major new contribution to occult literature. The author, a journalist, social historian, and member of the Society for Psychical Research, surveys 19th-century spiritualism, with its many oddities and frauds. The book gives many facts and details. Chapters discuss the following: mesmerism, the birth of spiritualism, table-rapping, seances, D. D. Home, seance phenomena, materializations, spirit writing and drawing, spirit photography, clairvoyance, hallucinations, collective hallucinations, hauntings, poltergeists, and Theosophy. The author remains skeptical and rational throughout the book. He asks, "if one had been in the midst of it all, would one have been objective?" He states that its impact on everyday life in Victorian England was very small. Pearsall feels that much of the clairvoyance was genuine, as was table-rapping. The evidence for spirit drawing and painting, spirit photography, apports, and materializations is thin, however.

1256 Pearson, Margaret Mary. The Complete Zodiac Entertainer. Aylesbury, England: Cadbury Lamb, 1973. 96p. Illus. Bibliog. Index £1.50 ISBN 0-85994-000-4

1257 Pell, Florence West. Death Has No Sting: The Story of a Quest. London: Churches' Fellowship for Psychical and Spiritual Studies, 1972. xii, 100p. £1.40 ISBN 0-902666-15-0

1258 Pelton, Robert W., 1934- . Ancient Secrets of Fortune-Telling. South Brunswick, N.J.: A. S. Barnes, 1975. Bibliog. Index $9.95 LC 74-9293 ISBN 0-498-01487-8

1259 ______. The Complete Book of Voodoo. New York: G. P. Putnam's Sons, 1972. 254p. Illus. Bibliog. $6.95 LC 72-181864

This is a how-to-do-it book on making voodoo dolls, talismans, and vever. It also tells how to use candles, powders, oils, and incense.

1260 ________. Lost Secrets of Astrology. Nash Pub. Co., 1973. $7.95

Part of this book is on astrology and astrology-related areas such as astrological anatomy (what does a typical Aries body look like). The rest of the work is on phrenology, precious stones, herbs, moles, the Golden Wheel (from the Middle Ages), and the Mystical Oracle of Destiny.

1261 ________. Voodoo Charms and Talismans. New York:
* Drake Publishers, 1973. 220p. Illus. Bibliog. $6.95 LC 73-4346

This is a very interesting, even charming book, perfect for browsing. The chapters, which are short, include: "How to Place a Curse," "How to Control a Person Sexually," "How to Cast Love Spells," "How to Influence Others," "How to Overcome Legal Problems," "How to Influence Fate," "How to Bring Financial Gain," "How to Ward Off Evil Spirits," "How to Change Your Personality," even "How to Keep a Place Rented." Each chapter gives about five different formulas for mixing ingredients, and tells what to do with the concoction. The formulas are named for whoever originated them, and their brief histories are given. Also given are sources of free catalogs for ordering supplies, and a few pages advertising voodoo dolls and various lotions. Although a few critics have ridiculed this book as just another weak hodgepodge, the formula names and the biographies on their originators would seem to make this book fairly important and very worthwhile.

1262 ________. Voodoo Secrets from A to Z. South Brunswick, N.J.: A.S. Barnes, 1973. 138p. Illus. Bibliog. $6.95 LC 72-9063

This work is an illustrated glossary of voodoo terminology, concentrating on Haitian Creole, and giving 600 definitions. At times, it appears to be more a dictionary of pidgin French than a dictionary of secret voodoo ritual words. Included are brief biographies of famous practitioners.

1263 ________. Voodoo Signs and Omens. South Brunswick, N.J.: A.S. Barnes, 1974 (also, London: Yoseloff, 1974). 284p. Illus. Bibliog. $8.95 LC 73-113 ISBN 0-498-01213-1

Most of the book (the first 223 pages) is on omens, giving 3,000 entries on the following topics: animals, weather, sneezing, snakes, lightning, sex, birthmarks, bodies of water, and so on. Pelton also covers these areas: voodoo rituals, methods of casting hexes and curses, love sorcery that works, illness cures, making charms and conjuring others. In the preface, the author mentions the importance of the Bible to voodoo, and the great part luck plays in the lives of voodoo believers.

1264 ______. Your Future, Your Fortune. Greenwich, Conn.: Fawcett, 1973. 176p. $.95 pa.

This book discusses various methods of divination. The first three chapters are the major ones of the book. They cover: geomancy (done with a combination of dots or points), the Oracle of Love (done with the aid of a diagram), and the Divining Wheel. Other chapters include fingernails, postage stamps, sealing wax, the art of onychomancy (oil or wax on nails), the art of spodanomancy (ashes), coffee grounds, and astrology.

1265 Penfield, Marc. Astrological Who's Who. York Harbor, Me.: Arcane Pubn., 1972. xxv, 543p. Illus. Bibliog. $10 LC 74-188580 ISBN 0-912240-08-3

1266 Pennick, Nigel. Geomancy. Cambridge, England: Cokaygne Publishing, 1973. 67p. Illus. Facsims. Maps Bibliog. £0.60 pa. ISBN 0-904063-00-3

1267 Pentecost, Martin. Sex and the Stars: A Zodiacal Study of Sexual Profiles. Toronto; London: Bantam, 1973 (also, Toronto: Kakabeka Pub. Co., 1973). 192p. £0.35 pa. ISBN 0-552-68245-4

1268 Pepper, Elizabeth, and John Wilcock. Witches' Almanac (annual). New York: Grosset, 1971-1975. 90p. Illus. $1.50 pa. LC 73-29853

For a sample, we looked at the volume, Aries 1975-Pisces 1976. The book begins with a section "Today and Tomorrow," a three-page year in brief. There is a short article on the Magic Stones of Rollright. Then comes the moon calendar. For each sign, it has the month's calendar, with about 15 brief messages of warning and guidance. On the opposite page to the calendar sheets are various short articles on assorted topics. Then follows the major section, which gives for each zodiac sign the month in general, a paragraph discussion under fire, earth, air, and water, and a brief paragraph on the jewel of the sign. After this come mixed articles: the Sphinx, Pythagoras, Diana of Ephesus, poison plants, Old Irish, occult fare on television, Atlantis, and three pages of book reviews. It is a nice browsing type of almanac.

1269 Perkins, James S. Through Death to Rebirth. Wheaton, Ill.: Theosophical Pub. House, 1974. 124p. (Quest Book) $1.95 pa.

This theosophist discusses the movement of the soul through the cycles of death and rebirth.

1270 Persinger, Michael A. The Paranormal. New York: MSS Information Corp., 1974. Includes bibliog. refs. $11 LC 74-19227

1271 Petersen, William J. Those Curious New Cults. New Canaan, Conn.: Keats, 1973. vii, 214p. Bibliog. $4.95 LC 72-93700

The author, editor of an evangelical magazine, Eternity, discusses satanism, witchcraft, astrology, Scientology, spiritualism, and the Black Muslims. He sees them as the work of the Devil, as well as clever money-making schemes. The author also attacks Eastern religions. There are numerous Bible quotes in the book.

1272 Pettit, Florence E. Shrines of Psychic Power: A Spiritual Pilgrimage. Wellingborough, England: Thorsons, 1974. 192p. Illus. Bibliog. £3.50 ISBN 0-7225-0278-8

The author discusses visits to Iona, Kingley Vale, Glastonbury, the Camargue, and White Lodge (where Ronald Beesley influences her development greatly). The writing moves haphazardly from subject to subject about experiences that affected her spiritual consciousness.

1273 Pettiward, Cynthia. The Case for Possession. Foreword by G. S. Whitby. Gerards Cross, England: Smythe, 1975. 129p. Bibliog. £2.50 ISBN 0-901072-18-4

The author believes that misguided human spirits are responsible for obsession and possession. She does not believe in demons. Pettiward discusses the work of Carl Wickland and Brazilian physician Inacio Ferreira. She also discusses multiple personality and other states confused with true possession.

1274 Petulengro, Leon. Romany Remedies and Recipes. Hollywood, Calif.: Newcastle Pub. Co., 1972. 150p. (unnumbered) $2.25 pa.

This book discusses gypsy lore and folk remedies. It is illustrated by old woodcuts.

1275 ______. Secrets of Romany Astrology and Palmistry. London: Pan Books, 1971 (orig. pub., London: Souvenir Press, 1969). 158p. Illus. £0.20 pa. ISBN 0-330-02749-2

1276 Phillips, P. L., and W. L. Macleod. Here and There: More Psychic Experiences. London: Corgi, 1975. 208p. (Corgi Library of Psychic Exploration) £0.50 pa. ISBN 0-552-09775-6

1277 Phillips, Philip, and S. Phillips. Is Death the End? An Authentic Record of Twenty-Five Years' Investigation into the Many Claims that There Is a Life After Death. London: Corgi, 1972. 222p. £0.35 pa. ISBN 0-552-08927-3

1278 Phillips, Ted. Physical Traces Associated with UFO Sightings. Northfield, Ill.: Center for UFO Studies, 1975. 144p. Illus. Paperback

1279 Philpott, Kent. Manual of Demonology and the Occult.
* Grand Rapids, Mich.: Zondervan Pub. House, 1973. 191p. Bibliog. $2.95 pa. LC 73-8363

This is a good survey on the topic. It includes sections on understanding the demoniac (animalistic, psychological, dualistic, and biblical approaches), theological problems of demonology (problems of disease, the Bible, and popular world views), and principles of demonology (contemporary occultism and demon possession, Christianity versus the occult). Philpott is an ordained minister who feels that the Bible is the only truly reliable source of information on demonology. The bibliography is very good, and a well-done glossary is an added feature.

1280 Pilgrim of the Night [pseud.]. Death and the Afterlife. New ed. London: Regency Press, 1975 (previous ed., 1971). 165p. £1.80 ISBN 0-7212-0416-3

1281 Piper, Raymond, and Lila Piper. Cosmic Art. Ed. by Ingo Swann. New York: Hawthorn, 1975. Illus. $16.50

This work presents a collection of paintings, sculpture, and graphics gathered by the Pipers over a 40-year period on the theme "infinity." These works, done from 1907-1967, are by 69 unknown artists from Italy, India, France, Great Britain, Uruguay, Bolivia, and Iceland. Most were painted in the 1930's and 1940's. Raymond Piper was professor of philosophy at Syracuse University. He died in 1962; his wife continued his collecting work. This book contains over 100 reproductions, with 16 pages in color.

1282 Place, Marian Templeton. On the Track of Bigfoot. New York: Dodd, Mead, 1974. 156p. Illus. Bibliog. $4.25 LC 73-15375 ISBN 0-396-06883-9

This book discusses these cases: the kidnapping of a prospector in 1924; the 1884 news account of the capture of a gorilla-like monster; the many sightings since 1958; the alleged filming of Bigfoot in 1967. The author draws comparisons to "Beowulf" and "The Epic of Gilgamesh." This book is recommended for grades 4-6.

1283 Plant, Ruth. Journey into Light: An Account of Forty Years' Communication with a Brother in the After Life. London: Cassell, 1972. xiii, 181p. £2.80 ISBN 0-304-93864-5

The author's brother Ralph, who died 40 years ago at the young age of 13, communicates through Mrs. Osborne Leonard (who herself died in 1968).

1284 Platnick, Kenneth B. Great Mysteries of History. Harrisburg, Pa.: Stackpole, 1971. 224p. Illus. Includes bibliog. refs. $6.95 LC 72-162444 ISBN 0-8117-0754-7

This book discusses in short chapters 16 mysteries, including Jack the Ripper, the Man in the Iron Mask, the Loch Ness Monster, the Abominable Snowman, Dag Hammarskjold, Sir Edmund Godfrey, Louis XVII, Grand Dutchess Anastasia, Czar Alexander, Atlantis, Stonehenge, Judge Crater, and Roanoke Island.

1285 Playfair, Guy Lyon. Flying Cow: Research into Paranormal Phenomena in the World's Most Psychic Country. London: Souvenir Press, 1975 (also, Ontario: Dent, 1975). 320p.
* Illus. Plates Index £3.50 ISBN 0-285-62160-2

The author, who has lived in Brazil since 1961, discusses a variety of topics linked to that country. He considers Carmine Mirabelli, a medium who died 20 years ago, very gifted. Mirabelli did automatic writing in over 30 languages, and spoke in many tongues, as well as transporting objects and levitating himself. Playfair also discusses Brazilian psychic surgeons Lourival de Freitas, Maria (who operated with her eyes closed), and Edivaldo (who operated on the author). Other topics discussed are D. D. Home, Eusapia Palladino, communications with E. J. Dingwall about healing (Dingwall wrote back that most of psychic surgery was nonsense), and poltergeists (Playfair feels they are "bad spirits").

1286 Podmore, Frank, 1856-1910. The Newer Spiritualism. New
* York: Arno Press, 1975 (orig. pub., London: T. F. Unwin, 1910). (Perspectives in Psychical Research) $18 LC 75-7392 ISBN 0-405-07041-1

Although he initially accepted spiritualism, the author became one of the harshest critics of mediumship. This was due to frequent frauds and his study of little-known capabilities such as cryptomnesia, which could provide alternate explanations to spiritualism. He does say that his later work with mediums, especially cross-correspondence data, gave him more optimism for spiritualism.

1287 ________. Studies in Psychical Research. New York: Arno Press, 1975 (orig. pub., New York: Putnam, 1897). (Perspectives in Psychical Research) $26 LC 75-7393 ISBN 0-405-07042-X

The author worked as a postal clerk while writing this book. He discusses ghosts, poltergeists, hauntings, mediumship, possession, physical phenomena, telepathy, clairvoyance, and precognition. He also covers some of the early experimental work of the Society for Psychical Research in London. Podmore mentions problems of interpreting the phenomena, and attempts to provide guidelines.

1288 Pollock, W. C., 1902- . Character-Analysis from Fingerprints and Hands. New York: Exposition Press, 1972. 95p. Illus. $5 LC 75-164865 ISBN 0-682-47315-4

1289 Polonsky, Jane Keane, and Joan McFarland Drum. Ghosts of Fort Monroe. Fort Monroe, Va.: Polyndrum Pubns., 1972. 42p. Illus. $3.25 pa.

1290 Ponce, Charles. The Game of Wizards: Psyche, Science, and Symbol in the Occult. Harmondsworth, England; Baltimore: Penguin Books, 1975. 240p. Illus. Includes bibliog. refs. $2.50 pa. LC 73-90932 ISBN 0-14-003864-7

The author tries to show the relation between the studies of occultists and empirical sciences in the area of cycles in nature. Ponce discusses polarities and seasonal variations as influencing man and the world. He uses the I Ching, Tarot, Kabbalah, and astrology in his discussion.

1291 ________. The Kabbalah: An Introduction and Illumination
* for the World Today. London: Garnstone Press, 1974. 300p. Illus. Bibliog. Index £3.95 ISBN 0-85511-161-5

The author discusses background, literature and history of the Kabbalah, outline of mystical significations of the Hebrew alphabet, doctrine of the four worlds, and the similarities of Kabbalah to Yoga, Buddhism and Gnosticism. On some points, Ponce's coverage seems a bit superficial. There are many diagrams and marginal notes in the work.

1292 Porter, Jean. Psychic Development. New York: Random House, 1974. $5.95 LC 74-8133 ISBN 0-394-49357-5

This book discusses these topics: how to reach inner regions of the mind, psychometry, telepathy, precognition, and healing.

1293 Potts, A. Middleton. Popular Handbook for ESP. St. Petersburg, Fla.: Harbour Pub. Co., 1974. 160p. $3.95 pa. LC 74-83652

1294 Potts, Thomas, d. 1620? Trial of the Lancaster Witches, 1612. Ed. and introd. by G. B. Harrison. New York: Barnes and Noble, 1971 (also, London: Muller, 1971; reprint of 1929 ed.; orig. pub., London: by W. Stansby for John Barnes, 1613). xlvi, 188p. $6.50 LC 75-27610 ISBN 0-389-04140-8

This work discusses the discovery of witches in the county of Lancaster, and covers the arraignment and trial of Jennet Preston in 1612.

1295 Powell, Arthur Edward. The Astral Body and Other Astral

Phenomena. London: Theosophical Pub. House, 1972 (orig. pub., London: Theosophical Pub. House, 1926). xiv, 265p. Index £2 ISBN 0-7229-5013-6

1296 ________. The Casual Body and the Ego. London: Theosophical Pub. House, 1972 (orig. pub., London: Theosophical Pub. House, 1928). xiv, 355p. Illus. Index £2 ISBN 0-7229-5003-9

1297 Powell, Jemma. The Stars in Your Hand. New York: Macfadden, 1971. 272p. $.95 pa.

This work is a study of hand shapes in conjunction with the natal horoscope. There are four main sections: earth hand; air hand; fire hand; water hand. Each of these four then matches up with the signs (earth hand to air; earth hand to fire). Then, the author gives a brief discussion of each sign.

1298 Pratt, Joseph Gaither, 1910- . ESP Research Today: A
*** Study of Developments in Parapsychology Since 1960. Metuchen, N.J.: Scarecrow Press, 1973. 195p. Bibliog. $7 LC 73-3098

This work is a major new contribution to occult literature. The author has been president of the Psychical Research Foundation, Inc., which publishes the journal Theta. Introductory chapters try to show how parapsychology is grounded in everyday psychical experiences, and give a summary of current research. Then come chapters on ESP research in Russia (a serious, authoritative summary), the Van Vuurde "alarm clock experiment" in South Africa, Ted Serios and his psychic photography, poltergeists, reincarnation, the author's own work with Pavel Stepanek of Czechoslovakia, and an evaluation of parapsychology as an emerging scientific field. This work covers the field's outstanding events, literature, and organizations. It is written in a serious, well-informed style, with the author relying quite frequently on his own research.

1299 Prediction Annual: Your Occult Guide to the Year Ahead. Croydon, England: Link House Publications, annual. 97p. Illus. £0.35 pa.

1300 Price, Harry, 1881-1948. Confessions of a Ghost-hunter. Introd. by Michael Lord. New York: Causeway Books, 1974. vi, 396p. Illus. Plates Includes bibliog. refs. Index $10 LC 74-34225 ISBN 0-88356-031-3

1301 ________. The End of Borley Rectory. Bath, England: Chivers, 1975 (orig. pub., London: Harrap, 1946). 358p. Illus. Plates Facsims. Maps Plans Bibliog. Index £5 ISBN 0-85594-074-3

1302 ________. Fifty Years of Psychical Research: A Critical
* Survey. New York: Arno Press, 1975 (orig. pub., London:

Longmans, Green, 1939). (Perspectives in Psychical Research) $23 LC 75-7394 ISBN 0-405-07043-8

This classic work was intended to update Frank Podmore's Modern Spiritualism. The author discusses the origins of psychical research, drawing largely on his lectures at the University of London. Much of the book is on research by Price and others of mediumship. He explains techniques for collecting data under lab and field conditions. There are also chapters on legal problems of mediumship and physiological factors responsible for firewalking.

1303 ______. "The Most Haunted House in England": Ten Years' Investigation of Borley Rectory. Bath, England: Chivers, 1975 (orig. pub., London: Longmans, 1940). xii, 255p. Illus. Plates Facsims. Map Plans Index £4.40 ISBN 0-85594-075-1

1304 ______. Stella C.: An Account of Some Original Experiments in Psychical Research. Foreword by C. R. Haines.
* Ed. by James Turner. London: Souvenir Press, 1973 (orig. pub., 1925). ix, 182p. Illus. £2.50

This study consists of the verbatim reports of 13 sittings. Added are further sittings of 1926, 1927 and 1928. During the sittings, blue sparks, rappings, the moving of small objects, and gusts of cold air occurred around her. They occurred with greater intensity at the carefully controlled seances she was persuaded to undergo. Thermometer readings showed a drop at these tests. Stella C. did not want to be a professional medium, and felt her powers more strange than important. This is a very factual work, with good pictures of the mechanical devices used for testing.

1305 ______, and Eric J. Dingwall. Revelations of a Spirit Medium. New York: Arno Press, 1975 (orig. pub., London, 1922). Bibliog. Index (Perspectives in Psychical Research) $22 LC 75-7395 ISBN 0-405-07044-6

The book is basically a reproduction of an anonymous work by a self-proclaimed fraudulent medium, giving details and procedures he used. Price and Dingwall add their own notes.

1306 Prieditis, Arthur A., 1909- . Fate of the Nations. St. Paul, Minn.: Llewellyn Publications, 1973. 422p. $12.95 LC 73-20450 ISBN 0-87542-624-7

This work discusses the prophecies of Nostradamus. Although the prophecies came to Nostradamus in visions, he used astrological symbolism and planetary conjunctions and aspects to time many of the predictions. He wrote in obscure form because he was afraid his works would not be preserved if he used ordinary language. Prieditis gives biographical information on Nostradamus, and then analyzes some of his fulfilled prophecies. Then, he mentions quatrains that are difficult to interpret or have not yet occurred. He summarizes the conflicting views of three other authors who have discussed the predictions. Prieditis lists prophecies made by famous saints and by some modern psychics such as Jeane Dixon.

1307 Prince, Walter Franklin. The Enchanted Boundary: Being
* a Survey of Negative Reactions to Claims of Psychic Phenomena, 1820-1930. New York: Arno Press, 1975 (orig. pub., Boston, 1930). (Perspectives in Psychical Research) $20 LC 75-7396 ISBN 0-405-07045-4

In the first part of this work, Prince gives excerpts from writings against psychical research by 40 major scientists and writers, including Thomas Huxley, Michael Faraday, T.B. Macaulay, G. Stanley Hall, Hugo Muensterberg. He discusses also the long controversy between Arthur Conan Doyle and Harry Houdini. Prince appraises the negative opinions and debates them. In the second part, Prince presents correspondence from 70 individuals to whom he wrote and posed questions about their willingness to accept a well-done study as evidence for psychic phenomena. He concludes the doubters do not have a case, but admits he is biased. This book was written just before Rhine's Duke work began.

1308 ________. They Saw Beyond; Distinguished Witnesses to
* Psychic Phenomena. New York: Olympia Press, 1972 (orig. pub., Boston: Boston Society for Psychical Research, 1928). 151p. Bibliog. $1.45 pa.

This very useful work presents psychical experiences in the lives of famous people from all walks of life. There are sections on men of science, men of the army and navy, statesmen, diplomats and publicists, poets and playwrights, novelists, miscellaneous writers, artists, sculptors, actors, composers and musicians, clergymen, theologians, evangelists, persons of title, financiers, teachers, travelers and magicians. People covered include Susan B. Anthony, Twain, Dickens, Hugo, Socrates, Shelley, and Luther Burbank.

1309 Progoff, Ira. Jung, Synchronicity, and Human Destiny. New
* York: Julian Press, 1973. 192p. $6.50

This book discusses Jung's theory of meaningful coincidences. Progoff's ideas were discussed with Jung personally, and the book includes handwritten comments from Jung. The main part of the work was done in 1955. Chapters discuss the following: I Ching, philosophical foundations of synchronicity, archetypes, patterning of time, paraphysic events, man's views of the universe, Teilhard de Chardin and "noosphere," astrology, alchemy, and theoretical physics. Jung did not feel the latter three were literally true, but saw them as symbolic of the interior landscape.

1310 Progress in Parapsychology. Ed. by J.B. Rhine. Durham,
* N.C.: Parapsychology Press, 1971. xv, 313p. Illus. Bibliog.

(Contains papers and addresses presented at the review meetings of the Institute for Parapsychology during 1968-1969) $7 LC 76-140922

Most of the 25 papers in this work are adapted from complete reports published in the Journal of Parapsychology. The volume is dedicated to William McDougall (1871-1938) on the centenary of his birth, and begins with a summary of his contributions to parapsychology. There are discussions on tests with mice, electronic equipment, psi, and sex differences affecting ability. There is a glossary at the end of the book.

1311 Proskauer, Julien J., 1893-1958. Spook Crooks! Exposing the Secrets of the Prophet-eers Who Conduct Our Wickedest Industry. Illus. by James and Howard Savage. New York: A. L. Burt Co.; Ann Arbor, Mich.: Gryphon Books, 1971 (orig. pub., 1932). 300p. Illus. $14 LC 70-162517

1312 * Psychiatry and Mysticism. Ed. by Stanley R. Dean. Chicago: Nelson-Hall Co., 1975. 424p. Illus. Tables Bibliog. Index $12.95 LC 75-8771 ISBN 0-88229-189-0

This is a collection of 31 papers, most presented at symposia during three conventions of the American Psychiatric Association. There are four main sections: metapsychiatry, mysticism and ESP; biological and physical energy fields, and Kirlian photography (including work by Moss, Hubacher, and Saba); psychic healing (including work by LeShan); and health and mind control (shamanism, transcendental experiences). Many of the discussions present methodology that might be used in future research. This work is recommended for advanced readers only.

1313 *** Psychic Exploration: A Challenge for Science. Edgar D. Mitchell. Ed. by John White. New York: Putnam, 1974. 708p. Illus. Plates Graphs Bibliogs. Index $17.50 LC 73-93737 ISBN 0-399-11342-8

This work is a major new contribution to occult literature. It is a very important reference handbook in the field--in fact, the only real "handbook" in parapsychology we have. Mitchell provided fine leadership in the project, and John White did an excellent job of editing. Mitchell flew the Apollo 14 mission, and was the sixth person on the moon. He is director of the Institute of Noetic Sciences in Palo Alto, California. John White worked as Educational Director of the Institute of Noetic Sciences, and is currently working as a writer and frequent book reviewer. This work consists of 29 articles, most 20-25 pages long. Each article has a brief biography of the writer, a half-page summary of the contents, and a one-page introduction. Also, each article ends with a bibliography of 25-50 items. White is to be congratulated for keeping these four features constant throughout the book (more editors should do it). Topics and their authors are: "History of Parapsychology" (Martin Ebon); "Famous Western Sensitives" (Alan Vaughan); "Psychic Personality" (Gertrude Schmeidler); "Telepathy" (Stanley Krippner);

"Clairvoyance" (Rex G. Stanford); "Precognition and Retrocognition" (E. Douglas Dean); Psychokinesis" (Helmut Schmidt); "Parapsychology Today" (Rhea A. White); "Psychobiology of Psi" (Robert L. Morris); "Psi and Psychiatry" (Montague Ullman); "Anthropology and Psychic Research" (Robert L. Van de Castle); "Man-Plant Communication" (Marcel Vogel); "Psychic Photography and Thoughtography" (Jule Eisenbud); "Psychic Research and the Healing Process" (Henry K. Puharich); "Out-of-the-Body Experiences" (Charles T. Tart); "Apparitions, Hauntings, and Poltergeists" (D. Scott Rogo); "Survival Research: Problems and Possibilities" (William G. Roll); "Emergence of Paraphysics: Research and Applications (James B. Beal); "Emergence of Paraphysics: Theoretical Foundations" (Brendan O'Regan); "Psychic Research in the Soviet Union" (Thelma Moss); "Devices for Monitoring Nonphysical Energies" (William A. Tiller); "Psychic Research and Modern Physics" (Harold Puthoff and Russell Targ); "Consciousness and Quantum Theory" (Evan Harris Walker); "Psychic Phenomena and Mystical Experience" (Lawrence L. LeShan); "Myth, Consciousness, and Psychic Research" (Jean Houston); "Consciousness and Extraordinary Phenomena" (Robert Masters); "Psi-Conducive States of Awareness (Charles Honorton); "Social Implications of Psychic Research (Willis W. Harman). These articles are organized in four main sections: "Parapsychology: Foundations of a New Science," "Expanding Range of Psychic Research," "Emergence of a New Natural Science," and "Convergence with Transpersonal Psychology." The book has a glossary, and a short article on Geller. Some reviewers of this excellent work were a bit bothered by Mitchell's essays at the beginning and end, where he sets the tone of the handbook by preaching "noetics" and a "new awakening of consciousness." These reviewers felt the tone carried over into the transpersonal psychology section, and stated that a reference work was a poor place to be pushing over a particular theology or philosophy. The point is a good one to note. However, this bibliographer feels that an editor has a right, even duty, to set a tone for his work provided that it does not interfere with the work's objectivity. Mitchell's comments about "noetics" in his two essays are used as specific insights and contributions of the author. They are used sparingly, and in no way impede his fine general discussions of psychical research. All reviewers agree, however, that this book is an excellent job. One can only hope Mitchell and White keep this handbook going with new editions, more and different articles, and the same fine craftsmanship and intelligence.

1314 <u>Psychics; In-depth Interviews by the Editors of "Psychic" Magazine.</u> London: Turnstone Press, 1973 (orig. pub., New York: Harper, 1972). x, 148p. £1.95 ISBN 0-85500-009-0
*

This book is a collection of nine interviews which originally appeared in Psychic magazine. There are interviews of Arthur Ford, Eileen Garrett, Irene F. Hughes, Peter Hurkos, Douglas Johnson, Kreskin, Sybil Leek, James A. Pike, and Jeane Dixon. The interviewers knew their subjects and asked relevant--sometimes embarrassing or difficult--questions.

1315 Puharich, Andrija. Beyond Telepathy. Introd. by Ira Einhorn. Garden City, N. Y.: Anchor Press, 1973 (also, London: Pan Books, 1975; London: Souvenir Press, 1974; orig. pub., 1962). xv, 340p. Illus. Bibliog. Index $2.50 pa. LC 72-84967
*

Puharich wrote this book as a doctor of medicine specializing in neurology. The work has a great deal of technical information in it. Puharich discusses field theory and the possible existence of "psi plasma." He mentions two psychosomatic conditions, cholinergia (state of relaxation) and adrenergia (state of tension). Relaxation helps in receiving telepathic messages; tension helps send them. Mentioned also are the techniques of shamans and yogis used to attain ecstasy.

1316 ______. The Sacred Mushroom. Garden City, N. Y.: Anchor Books, 1974. 220p. $2.95 pa.

This is a classic study of the Amanita muscaria and its hallucinatory effects.

1317 ______. Uri: A Journal of the Mystery of Uri Geller. Garden City, N. Y.: Anchor Press, 1974 (also as "Uri: The Original and Authorized Biography of Uri Geller, the Man Who Baffles the Scientists," London: W. H. Allen, 1974; also, London: Futura Pubns., 1974). 285p. $7.95 LC 73-17770 ISBN 0-385-00992-5
***

This work is a major new contribution to occult literature. It is also a highly controversial book. In the introduction, Puharich tells of work done with Hurkos and Arigo. The first part of the book is a straightforward account of the author's meeting and testing Geller in Israel. From then on, the book becomes wilder and wilder in its allegations, while Puharich keeps a deadpan "this is the simple truth" attitude throughout. The author claims he and Geller were contacted by "Spectra," a voice they believed to represent an extraterrestrial intelligence called "Hoova." This intelligence explained the source of Geller's powers and the relationship between Hoova and the inhabitants of earth. The messages come on self-destructing tape recordings, and are often accompanied by large objects that vanish and reappear in other rooms, spelled-out messages on desks, and other phenomena. At the end of the book, Puharich discusses the Stanford Research Institute experiments, and includes the text of a film made there during five weeks of study on Geller. Given Puharich's fine credentials (scientific researcher, with 58 U. S. and foreign patents to his name for various inventions), this book makes for very strange, disturbing reading. Some of the material is just too absurdly incredible to believe.

1318 Quantum Physics and Parapsychology: Proceedings of an In-
*

ternational Conference Held in Geneva, Switzerland, August 26-27, 1974. Ed. by Laura Oteri. New York: Parapsychology Foundation, 1975. 283p. Illus. Includes bibliog. refs. (Proceedings of 23rd Annual International Conference of Parapsychology Foundation) $12 LC 75-14867 ISBN 0-912328-26-6

This work contains 12 papers, discussing such topics as quantum theory, information theory, and entropy. Russell Targ and Harold Puthoff present a paper on remote viewing of natural objects (precognition), together with a transcript of a sample session.

1319 Quigley, Joan. Astrology for Adults. New York: Paperback Library, 1971 (orig. pub., New York: Holt, 1969). 245p. $1.25 pa.

This is a do-it-yourself guide, discussing the sun (influencing individuality), the moon (influencing personality), and constellations in the ascendant (physical body and temperament). The rest is on the planets, with chapters such as "Pluto and Your Group Involvement." The book includes an ephemeris to determine the moon's position at birth.

1320 ________. Astrology for Parents of Children and Teenagers. Englewood Cliffs, N.J.: Prentice-Hall, 1971. 678p. $10.95 LC 76-154768 ISBN 0-13-049767-3

1321 Quinn, Daniel. Land and Sea Monsters. Illus. by George Suyeoka and Don Meighan. Northbrook, Ill.: Hubbard Press, 1971. 64p. Illus. $3.95 LC 73-163507 ISBN 0-8331-0002-7

This book discusses the following topics: sphinx, centaur, unicorn, mermaid, Great Sea Serpent, Loch Ness Monster, Abominable Snowman, the Sasquatch.

1322 Rachleff, Owen S. The Magic of Love. Illus. by Roland Rodegast. Norwalk, Conn.: C.R. Gibson Co., 1974. 56p. Illus. $3.95 LC 73-88089 ISBN 0-8378-1752-8

This short book is a gathering of miscellaneous tidbits of fascinating lore on love. Each chapter is about six pages long, and consists of many short paragraphs. The work contains these chapters: ancient formulas and incantations of love, divination of love (palmistry, cartomancy, astrology, powers of Venus and the moon), amulets and talismans of love (including discussions on gems and colors), love potions and perfumes, oracles and omens, games for lovers, and the magic of marriage.

1323 ________. The Occult Conceit; A New Look at Astrology,
*

Witchcraft and Sorcery. Chicago: Cowles, 1971 (also, New York: Bell Pub. Co., 1971). xvii, 235p. Bibliog. Index $6.95 LC 77-143489

In this book, Rachleff criticizes the occult as "a clear and present danger." Besides the foolish dependency of believers and the possibility of backlash against them (as happened in the witch-hunts), what the author really fears is the spread of ignorance, which may halt the growth of scientific knowledge if a whole generation grows to despise science and deny its need. He discusses fallacies of thinking in these areas: astrology, numerology, palmistry, phrenology, physiognomy, Tarot, omens, magic (black and white), spiritualism, precognition, and ESP. The author emphasizes the high cost of this occult deception. Rachleff sees science as the "true magic." He quotes Oscar Wilde, "The mystery of the world is in the visible, not the invisible." Since there are few critical books out on the occult, this would be a good one to have. The author writes in scathing tone.

1324 ________. Sky Diamonds; The New Astrology. Illus. by
*** Robert Rappaport. New York: Hawthorn Books, 1973. ix, 266p. Illus. $7.95 LC 73-346

This work is a major new contribution to occult literature. It could be so labeled based on its controversial nature alone. The author is associate professor of humanities at New York University and a television and radio personality. The author's controversial claim is that the zodiac constellations no longer govern the periods usually ascribed to them. He states that the earth has shifted 30 degrees to the west in the last 2,000 years. A major part of the book goes sign by sign, presenting detailed descriptions of the new signs (Sagittarius used to rule the dates November 23 to December 21; under Rachleff's system, Sagittarius now rules December 18 to January 21). Most of the signs are shifted a month. As a corollary, the author states that each of the 12 zodiac constellations occupies a diamond-shaped area in the sky. All stars in this diamond influence you, including many formerly neglected stars. The book is largely contrary to traditional theories of astrology and the beliefs of most practicing astrologers. The work is based largely on ancient Greek mythology, mixed with a material view of astrology (he believes radiation from stars and planets is the real governing force). He joins the sidereal astrologers who base the divisions upon the constellations themselves. Also, the author feels that the time and place of birth are unimportant; only the birth date and year matter. He thus ignores the ascendant. In another minor point, Rachleff claims the importance of moons of planets. For each sign, the author gives a drawing of the diamond with animal and mythological figures representing the stars; the zodiacal influence, the primary superordinate, the secondary superordinates, the primary subordinate, the secondary subordinates (the last four are at north and south tips of the diamond), the chief planets and moons, relatedness to other diamonds, a general charting for planets and moons, and the typical person born under that sign. All astrology followers will want to read this work, if only to keep their blood pressure up.

1325 Rakoczi, Basil Ivan. Foreseeing the Future. New York: Harper and Row, 1973 (first pub. as "Fortune Telling: A Guide to Foreseeing the Future." London: Macdonald, 1970). 128p. Illus. Bibliog. $1.25 pa.

This work includes the following topics: fortune-telling with cards, the Tarot, the Tarot of the Bohemians, trance meditation, palmistry, numerology, the casting of lots, crystal-gazing, and the planchette.

1326 Ramsay, Raymond H. No Longer on the Map; Discovering
* Places That Never Were. New York: Ballantine, 1973 (orig. pub., New York: Viking, 1972). xii, 244p. Illus. Includes bibliog. refs. $1.65 pa.

This is a fascinating discussion of an unusual phenomenon. The author's main concern is with the evolution and influence of legends whose mythological presence was enough to get them placed on maps. The work combines history, myth, philosophy, anthropology, and cartography. The author is the former "Rat Fink" columnist for the Berkeley Barb. Discussed in the work are Greenland, the Northwest Passage, Terra Incognita (which originated from the logical calculations of Greek and Roman geographers), El Dorado, Norumbega, St. Brendan's Isle, Terra Australis Incognita, Mayda, and Daculi. Fictional places are not discussed, and Atlantis is left out because it supposedly sank too early to appear on classical maps. The author mentions the histories of these places, how and when they first appeared on maps, and when and why they disappeared from them. Ramsay theorizes that there are still perhaps a few islands in the ocean waiting to be discovered or rediscovered.

1327 Randall, John L. Parapsychology and the Nature of Life.
*** New York: Harper and Row, 1975 (also, Don Mills, Canada: J.M. Dent and Sons, 1975; orig. pub., London: Souvenir Press, 1975). 256p. Includes bibliog. refs. Index $8.95 LC 75-30341 ISBN 0-06-013509-3

This work is a major new contribution to occult literature. The author, a British biologist, discusses biology and its mechanistic ideas, emphasizing Darwinism and evolution. He argues against the mechanistic theories, saying that there are facts in parapsychology that do not fit them. He feels that parapsychology alone can challenge this view on empirical grounds, and presents experimental evidence from psychical research. Besides attacking mechanistic theories, the book functions as a fine survey of parapsychology. The author talks of his own work on PK in wood lice, and ESP in schoolboys. He feels that Helmut Schmidt's work is very important, in that it has complete automation of recording. Much of the book is a philosophical discussion. Randall sees a need for adopting a dualistic theory of mind and body, and studying their interaction. This would bring man back to a spiritual view of life, and end man's present inner emptiness. Randall also adds that he personally has had successful parapsychology experiments, and he knows that he doesn't cheat!

1328 Randall, Neville. Life After Death. London: Hale, 1974. 181p. £3 ISBN 0-7091-4861-5

The author and Mrs. Betty Greene recorded voices that have spoken to them during twenty years of sittings with medium Leslie Flint. After two years of evaluating this library of 500 voices on tape, Randall has written this book. He has an Oxford honors degree in English, was in the Burma Campaign in World War II, and attained the rank of major. He writes the documentary cartoon strip "Focus on Fact" in the Daily Mail. Most of the discussion in this book is about what life is like on the other side. Famous dead people supposedly recorded include Oscar Wilde, Queen Victoria's servant John Brown, and pilot Amy Johnson.

1329 Randi, James. The Magic of Uri Geller. New York: Ballantine Books, 1975. 320p. $1.75 pa.
***

This work is a major new contribution to occult literature. It is a scathing ridicule of Uri Geller. The first half is by Randi; the second is comprised of pro and con articles about Geller, annotated by Randi. He discusses semi-controlled experiments, confessions from accomplices, interviews with witnesses. He mentions that Shipi, a quiet young companion of Geller's, is always around during experiments, and feels Shipi helped Geller in the Stanford Research Institute tests. The psychologists at SRI ran a double-blind test. Geller, claims Randi, did not attempt a specific guess on any of their 100 sealed envelopes. As for Geller's famous ability to start stopped watches, Randi claims merely picking up an old watch will jar it into briefly moving, and also heat the oil in it. One critic of Randi's book says that Randi made 24 errors just in summarizing the SRI tests. This book has an Ambrose Bierce-type humorous glossary of parapsychology terms at the end.

1330 Rao, K. Ramakrishna. Mystic Awareness: Four Lectures on the Paranormal. Mysore, India: University of Mysore, 1972. 107p. $2

These lectures were given by Rao at the University of Mysore in March 1969 as an introduction to experimental parapsychology. The first sees four levels of human experience: survival, ego and emotion, fulfillment in others, and mystical experience (psi occurs here). The second is on lab attempts to study ESP quantitatively. The third discusses use of hypnosis, psychedelic drugs, meditation, and yoga. Rao likes yoga best for controlling the paranormal. The fourth lecture discusses whether ESP leads one to accept theories of rebirth and survival of death.

1331 Raphael, Edwin. Raphael's Astrological and Herbal Almanac. Annual. Slough, England: Foulsham, 96p. Illus. (Title changed as of 1975 from "Raphael's Astrological Almanac and Yearbook") £0.45 pa.

This annual publication gives astrological predictions concerning rulers of nations and politicians, with many of these predictions in horoscope form. Also, there are personal horoscope readings for everybody, a daily guide for all, a weather guide for each day of the year, herb information, tables, and articles.

1332 * ______. Raphael's Astronomical Ephemeris of the Planets' Places; With Tables of Houses for London, Liverpool and New York. Slough, England: Foulsham, annual. 48p. £0.75 pa.

This work gives longitudes of the planets and sidereal time for noon of each day of the year; declination of the sun, moon, Mercury, Venus and Mars for each day of the year, and of the other planets for every alternate day. It contains all information necessary to cast horoscopes for all places of the world, both north and south of the equator. The work is supported by a team of mathematicians, so that every calculation is double-checked. This annual is a basic working manual for any serious astrologer.

1333 Raskin, Joseph, and Edith Raskin. Ghosts and Witches Aplenty; More Tales Our Settlers Told. Illus. by William Sauts Bock. New York: Lothrop, Lee and Shepard Co., 1973. 128p. Illus. $4.50 LC 73-4949

This is a collection of old American lore found in early American diaries, documents and records. It is the second such gathering by these authors. The 13 tales include girls accused of witchcraft, poltergeists, disembodied voices, and a woman who wills her mill to the devil.

1334 *** Raudive, Konstantin, 1909-1974. Breakthrough; An Amazing Experiment in Electronic Communication with the Dead. Trans. by Nadia Fowler. Ed. by Joyce Morton. Preface by Peter Bander. New York: Lancer Books, 1973 (also, New York: Taplinger, 1971; orig. pub., Gerrards Cross, England: Smythe, 1971). xxxi, 391p. (Translation of the German "Unhörbares wird hörbar." Remagen: Otto Reichl, 1968) (Taplinger ed. accompanied by phonodisc) $1.75 pa.

This work is a major new contribution to occult literature. It is a pioneering work of research into the new field of tape-recorded voice phenomena. Rösterna från Rymden (Voices from Space) was published by Friedrich Jurgenson in Sweden in 1964, and it discussed his work in recording spirit voices. Raudive met him in 1965, began his own work, and published a shorter version of the present work in 1968 in German. The added material in this edition includes reports by experts in electronics, engineering, physics, and parapsychology who have heard the 16,000 recordings in Raudive's collection.

1335 Rauscher, William V., and Allen Spraggett. Spiritual Frontier. Garden City, N.Y.: Doubleday, 1975. 312p. Bibliog.
*** $7.95 LC 73-15361 ISBN 0-385-07189-2

This work is a major new contribution to occult literature. The author is rector of Christ (Episcopal) Church of Woodbury, N.J., former president of the Spiritual Frontiers Fellowship, and magician. In this book, he reports his experiences with parapsychology and spiritualism over the last 20 years. His interest in this area grew gradually as he noticed the phenomena in the lives of his parishioners. He discusses ESP, healing, spiritualism, mediumship, ghosts, poltergeists, ESP in the Bible, the parapsychology of prayer, possession, automatic writing, and reincarnation. He criticizes the fraud of Arthur Ford. Many of Ford's papers came to Rauscher on Ford's death, and he found newspaper obituaries and an information notebook on persons Ford had sittings for. This was quite a shock to the author, who still feels Ford had some genuine talent. The appendix, "Houdini Mystery Solved," discusses Ford's 1928 sitting, when Ford claimed to have guessed Houdini's secret message known only by Houdini's widow. Rauscher mentions evidence that Mrs. Houdini was in love with Ford. Mention is also made of the fact that Ford cheated during the 1967 televised seance with Bishop Pike. The appendix also lists organizations and publications devoted to psychic phenomena. Rauscher feels that parapsychological phenomena "support, strengthen and inform" Christian faith. "Parapsychology is not an enemy of faith, but the best friend faith has."

1336 Ravenscroft, Trevor, 1921- . Spear of Destiny; The Occult Power Behind the Spear Which Pierced the Side of
*** Christ. New York: Putnam, 1973 (also, London: Corgi, 1974; orig. pub., London: Spearman, 1972). xxii, 362p. Illus. Bibliog. $8.95 LC 73-75239

This work is a major new contribution to occult literature. It traces the history of a spear which may have pierced Christ's side. The spear is now on display in a Vienna museum. Men who have possessed it include Herod the Great, St. Mauritius, Constantine the Great, Charles Martel, King Athelstan, Barbarossa, Frederick II, the Hapsburg dynasty, and, finally, Hitler. He asserts that the spear was the central force behind Hitler's lust for power. Most of the book is in fact an occult interpretation of the satanic faculties of Hitler and Nazi Germany. Ravenscroft also refers to Atlantis, reincarnation, and the Holy Grail (an alleged form of Christianity which is really a mystical awakening of consciousness). The book is largely based on conversations with Walter Johannes Stein, who was an advisor to Churchill, an associate of Rudolf Steiner, and Ravenscroft's former teacher.

1337 Ravensdale, Tom, and James Morgan. The Psychology of
*

Witchcraft; An Account of Witchcraft, Black Magic and the Occult. Foreword by Sir Alec Kirkbride. New York: Arco, 1974 (also, Edinburgh: J. Bartholomew, 1974). 200p. Illus. $10 LC 74-77592 ISBN 0-668-03501-3

This book adds anthropological evidence from non-European countries to the usual survey of witchcraft. The authors' thesis is that witches have been scapegoats throughout history. There are a few problems with the work. The foreword states that witchcraft is on decline in the West, which seems very wrong. The authors also say that witches worship satan, and give directions for a black mass, including the "Lord's Prayer" in reverse. Some readers will object to this slant. There are discussions of witch persecutions, psychedelic drugs, and the magic of women, animals, trees, numbers, and metals. The 70 pages of photographs and illustrations are very useful.

1338 Rawcliffe, D. H. Occult and Supernatural Phenomena. Foreword by Julian Huxley. New York: Dover, 1973 (orig. pub. as "The Psychology of the Occult," 1952). $4 pa. ISBN 0-486-20503-7

This book discusses the following topics: collective hallucinations, lycanthropy, black magic, fire-walking, levitation, clairvoyance, stigmata, somnambulism, multiple personalities, vampires, faith healing, ghosts and apparitions, dowsing, ESP and telepathy, auras, hallucinogenic drugs, PK, and demons.

1339 Rawsthorne, John. How to Interpret Your Dreams. London: Hale, 1973 (orig. pub., Adelaide, England: Rigby, 1970). 64p. Illus. (Hale Instant Book) £0.17 pa. ISBN 0-85179-071-2

1340 Records of Salem Witchcraft, Copied from the Original Documents. Comp. by W. E. Woodward. New York: Burt Franklin, 1972 (orig. pub., 1864). 2 vols. in 1 (Burt Franklin Research and Source Works Series) (American Classics in History and Social Science, no. 236) (Orig. issued as nos. 1 and 2 of Woodward's Historical Series) $26.50 LC 76-178940 ISBN 0-8337-2916-0

1341 Redgrove, Herbert Stanley, 1887-1943. Alchemy: Ancient and Modern. 2nd rev. ed. Introd. by H. J. Sheppard. New York: Barnes and Noble, 1973 (orig. pub., 1922). xx, 141p. Illus. $9 ISBN 0-06-495809-4

Redgrove was one of the first modern researchers to see the relationship between alchemy and modern science, and also to recognize that alchemy is basically a philosophical search. His theme was the then new discovery of radioactivity, which he calls "modern alchemy." His chapters on the meaning of alchemy and the alchemists are excellent.

1342 _______. Magic and Mysticism: Studies in Bygone Beliefs. Foreword by Leslie Shepard. New Hyde Park, N. Y.: University Books, 1971 (orig. pub. as "Bygone Beliefs"). xx, 205p. Illus. Includes bibliog. refs. $7.95 LC 71-118600

1343 Regardie, Israel. The Golden Dawn: An Account of the Teachings, Rites, and Ceremonies of the Order of the Golden Dawn. 4th ed., rev. and enlarged. St. Paul, Minn.: Llewellyn Publications, 1971. 4 vols. in 1 Illus. (A reissue in one binding of vols. 1 and 2 of 4th ed. (1971), rev., corr., and enl., and of vols. 3 and 4 of 2nd ed. (1969), rev. and enl.) $24.95 LC 75-310780 ISBN 0-87542-664-6

1344 _______. How to Make and Use Talismans. New York:
* Samuel Weiser, 1972 (orig. pub., London: Aquarian Press, 1972). 63p. Illus. Bibliog. (Paths to Inner Power) $1.25 ISBN 0-87728-169-6

This is another well-done volume in the Paths to Inner Power series. There are discussions of these topics: origin of talismans (magic squares, Qabalah of Nine Chambers), how to overcome unfavorable aspects, words of power, talismans of the five elements, a practical example, how to charge the talisman, appendices giving the Hebrew alphabet, Tarot meanings, and other charts. The work has many illustrations.

1345 _______. My Rosicrucian Adventure; A Contribution to a Recent Phase of the History of Magic, and a Study in the Technique of Theurgy. 2nd ed., rev. and enl. St. Paul, Minn.: Llewellyn Pubns., 1971 (1st ed. pub., 1936). 168p. $2 pa. ISBN 0-87542-660-3

This book discusses the history of the Order of the Golden Dawn, the true nature of its rituals, the reasons for its decline (failure to live by its original teachings and grabbing for degrees and titles by members). It defends Regardie's decision to publish secret information on its practices and ceremonies. For the 2nd edition, the author adds a brief introduction, a long postscript giving the text of the Ritual of the Ring and the Disc, and comments on three books on the Order (Virginia Moore's Unicorn, 1954, Francis King's Ritual Magic in England, 1970 [entry 884], and Torrens's Golden Dawn, 1973). He likes the first two, and dislikes Torrens's book.

1346 Regush, June, and Nicholas M. Regush, eds. Psi; The Other
* World Catalogue. New York: Putnam's Sons, 1974. 320p. Illus. $5 pa. LC 74-16613 ISBN 0-399-11475-0

This book looks like the Whole Earth Catalog. It is a graphically pleasing book for browsers, and has many drawings, prints, ads, addresses, book titles and prices. It is arranged in five parts: societies, journals, books and bookstores; methods of psychic and spiritual development (divination, mediums, psychics, altered states of consciousness, personal paths); healing; mysteries of time and space (mysteries, UFO's, multi-dimensional self); and energies (aura, plants and pyramids, fields of life and cosmic influences). Actually, the chapters lose their identities among all the ads. The work has a good deal of scattered, miscellaneous information.

1347 Regush, Nicholas M., and Jan Merta. Exploring the Human Aura; A New Way of Viewing and Investigating Psychic Phenomena. Englewood Cliffs, N.J.: Prentice-Hall, 1975. 224p. Illus. Bibliog. $7.95

The author feels the human aura receives and transmits information between the mind and the outside world. ESP can be explained by watching the aura. The author discusses PK and Jan Merta, Mesmer, the space-time enigma, Cayce, Kirlian photography, yoga, the Bermuda Triangle, Atlantis, Velikovsky, Gurdjieff, crib deaths, cancer, Mothman, Loch Ness Monster, Uri Geller, UFO's, possession, and poltergeists. He feels all of these can be explained as terrestrial manifestations of cosmic configurations in harmony with the universe.

1348 Rehn, K. Gosta. UFO's Here and Now. Trans. by Patricia Crampton. London: Abelard-Schuman, 1974 (dist. in U.S. by Transatlantic Arts). 198p. Illus. Plates Bibliog. (Translation of "Tefaten är här." Sweden: Zindermans, 1974) £2.95 ISBN 0-200-72195-X

The author, a Swedish lawyer 86 years of age, has studied UFO's for over 20 years. This is probably his first book translated into English. He discusses the Condon Report, claims the U.S. Air Force is spreading secrecy over the knowledge it has, discusses the search for extraterrestrial life, shows photos of UFO's, and concludes the UFO's have an extraterrestrial origin. He disagrees with John Keel, Jacques Vallee, and others for their belief that the saucers do not come from outer space.

1349 Reich, Peter. Book of Dreams. Fawcett World, 1974
* (orig. pub., 1973). $1.50 pa.

The author is the son of psychiatrist Wilhelm Reich, and this book discusses their relationship in intimate terms. After being labeled a quack, in 1957 his father was imprisoned for contempt of court. The boy was then 13 years old. The father later died in Lewisburg Federal Penitentiary. Peter discusses orgone accumulators, sexual liberation, Wilhelm's other ideas, his hounding by the Food and Drug Administration, the burning of his books, and the destroying of his apparatus.

1350 Reichel, Willy. An Occultist's Travels. Philadelphia: Running Press, 1975 (orig. pub., 1908). 244p. $3.95 pa. LC 74-31539 ISBN 0-914294-10-5

This book discusses the travels of a German professor from New York to Japan, and the healing he did.

1351 Reichenbach, Karl Ludwig Friedrich, Freiherr von, 1788-1869. Researches on Magnetism, Electricity, Heat, Light, Crystallization, and Chemical Attraction in Their Relations to the Vital Force. Trans. and ed. by William Gregory. Foreword by Leslie Shepard. Secaucus, N.J.: University Books, 1974 (orig. pub., London: Taylor, Walton, and Maberly, 1850). xlv, 463p. Illus. Plates (Translation of vol. 1 of "Physikalisch-physiologische Untersuchungen über die Dynamide des Magnetismus, der Elektrizität, der Wärme, des Lichtes, der Kristallisation, des Chemismus in ihren Beziehungen zur Lebenskraft") $10 LC 74-75173 ISBN 0-8216-0216-0

This book discusses the existence of a non-physical vital energy force--odic energy (odyle). It covers the author's experiments. Reichenbach was an expert on meteorites, chemicals, technology, metallurgy, and the discoverer of kerosene.

1352 Reid, Vera W. Towards Aquarius. Rev. ed. New York: Arc, 1971. 124p. Bibliog. $1.45 pa. LC 75-145662 ISBN 0-668-02413-5

1353 Reifler, Sam. The I Ching: A New Interpretation for Modern Times. New York: Bantam Books, 1974. 279p. $1.50 pa.

1354 Reilly, Harold J. Edgar Cayce Handbook for Health Through
* Drugless Therapy. New York: Macmillan Pub. Co., 1975. 337p. $10.95 LC 74-30015 ISBN 0-02-601960-4

The author, now 81 years old, ran for years the Reilly Health Institute at Rockefeller Center, where celebrities such as Nelson Rockefeller and the Dutchess of Windsor were treated. He studied under Cayce in the 1930's. Cayce referred over 1,000 patients to Reilly for treatment. The author discusses osteopathy, electrotherapy, diet, nutrition, hydrotherapy, massage, internal cleansing, and skin care. He has studied the 15,000 Cayce trance readings for 6,000 people with over 8,000 diagnoses, and applied them at his clinic. Reilly says Cayce readings and Reilly's work try to produce a healthy body that will heal itself. The four basic goals of Cayce are emphasized--improvement and normalization of the functions of assimilation, elimination, circulation, and relaxation.

1355 Rejaunier, Jeanne, and Lu Ann Horstman. Astrology for Lovers. New York: Pocket Books, 1971 (also, London: New English Library, 1972). 246p. Tables $1.25 ISBN 0-671-78047-6

This guide to sex life at first goes sign-by-sign, giving for each a general discussion and the famous people born under that sign. Other sections discuss the moon in each sign, the ascendant, Mercury in each sign, Venus in each sign, Mars in each sign, Jupiter in each sign, Saturn in each sign, Uranus in each sign, Neptune in each sign, Pluto, the sun, the planets in various houses, yoga exercises, and beauty tips. Much of the work is actually a primer on astrology, explaining what various things mean and how to calculate them. The book is loaded with tables of such things as moon placement at time of reader's birth (1890-1970), and positions of each planet at time of reader's birth.

1356 Remi, Nicolas, 1530-1612. Demonolatry. Trans. by E. A. Ashwin. Ed. with introd. and notes by Montague Summers. Preface by Leslie Shepard. Secaucus, N. J.: University Books, 1974 (also, London: J. Rodker, 1929-30). (Vol. 1 is a reprint of 1930 ed. of Remi's "Demonolatry," a translation of his "Daemonolatreiae Libri Tres"; vol. 2 is a reprint of 1929 ed. of F. M. Guazzo's "Compendium Maleficarum") $25 LC 74-80540 ISBN 0-8216-0215-2

1357 * Research in Parapsychology, 1972: Abstracts and Papers from the 15th Annual Convention of the Parapsychological Association [Held at the University of Edinburgh], 1972. Ed. by W. G. Roll, R. L. Morris, and J. D. Morris. Metuchen, N. J.: Scarecrow Press, 1973. 249p. $7.50 LC 66-28580

In this collection, Association President John Beloff criticizes parapsychologists who feel there is no more use for experiments to reinforce proof of ESP. Arthur Koestler was the after-dinner speaker. Among the papers, three special subjects are mentioned: Pavel Stepanek, Lalsingh Harribance, and Bill Delmore. Also discussed is a PK machine built by W. E. Cox. Helmut Schmidt has gotten good results with it. K. R. Rao and H. Dukhan report that they got good results with meditation in an ashram. Russell Targ covers the directionality of time. There was also a symposium on survival, with participants asked what evidence would convince them of survival. Martin Johnson presents the paper, "Scientific Method and Social Issues in Parapsychology." James McHarg discusses his work in "Enquiry into the Ostensibly Synchronistic Basis of a Paranoid Psychosis."

1358 * ________, 1973: ... 16th Annual Convention ... [Held at the University of Virginia, Charlottesville], 1973. Ed. by W. G. Roll, R. L. Morris and J. D. Morris. Metuchen, N. J.: Scarecrow Press, 1974. vi, 249p. $8 ISBN 0-8108-0708-4

There were 59 participants at this convention. Association President Rex Stanford discussed "psi-mediated instrumental response," a species of unintentional psi, in a paper called "Concept and Psi." He says that contemporary parapsychology has a failing in that there are no hypothetical constructs, no processes to converge on conclusions. Tart's address, "On the Nature of Altered States of Consciousness," had very little on parapsychology. It stressed the importance of the individual's perceptions and differences. Pratt and Keil report on first-hand observations of Nina Kulagina (PK). Ullman compares her to Alla Vinogradova. There are reports by Charles Honorton and G. and A. Watkins on the PK of Felicia Parise, a medical technician at Maimonides Hospital. Targ and Puthoff of Stanford Research Institute report on Geller's tests.

1359 _______, 1974: ... 17th Annual Convention ... [Held at
* St. John's University, Jamaica, N.Y.], 1974. Ed. by J.D. Morris, W.G. Roll, and R.L. Morris. Metuchen, N.J.: Scarecrow Press, 1975. 265p. $9 ISBN 0-8108-0850-1

This work gives long abstracts on 31 research briefs and 24 papers. Robert Morris's presidential address, "Tacit Communication and Experimental Theology," discusses the difficulty in distinguishing different types of psi in experiments (telepathy, clairvoyance). He asks for a simple terminology. Gary E. Schwartz gave the invited address on biofeedback and its relation to parapsychology. He suggested that the term ESP be replaced by "extra-sensitive perception." A. Parker feels that ESP scores depend on the degree of acceptance of ESP by those doing the testing. J.G. Craig shows that the psi performances of rats are sensitive to experimenter differences. Helmut Schmidt says that mechanical parts of apparatus may be subject to PK influences. There are also some papers on out-of-the-body experiences. Hartwell, Janis and Harary report on the physiological state during self-induced out-of-the-body experiences (OOBE's). Otis discusses how to discriminate between success by ESP and by OOBE perception. Palmer and Lieberman report on the relation between ESP scores and OOBE's. Palmer and Dennis survey psychic experiences. Roll discusses poltergeists and focusing effect. Wells and Watkins report on the awakening of anesthetized mice.

1360 Reyner, John Hereward. The Age of Miracles. London: Spearman, 1975. 200p. Illus. Bibliog. Index £3.25 ISBN 0-85435-322-4

This book discusses telepathy, ESP, hypnosis, homeopathy and psionic medicine, talking to plants and animals, dowsing and radiesthesia, cosmic rhythms, body fields and auras, and reincarnation. The author works from the theories of Steiner and Gurdjieff in postulating the existence of the unmanifest world he calls the "Super World." Once this is understood, Reyner feels the above things will be seen as very natural phenomena.

1361 _______. Diary of a Modern Alchemist. London: Spearman, 1974. 155p. Illus. Index £2.50 ISBN 0-85435-172-8

This work by a student of Maurice Nicoll's discusses the philosophy of Gurdjieff and the beliefs of Sufism. The author feels men exist like robots, responding to conditioning. Only through effort can man awaken and reach higher consciousness levels. He believes alchemists were searching for a spiritual alchemy, but disguised it under tedious lab procedures. Reyner discusses Gurdjieff's "Law of Seven," with energy feeding the seven cosmic levels. To tap the energy, man must emphasize communication with cells and plants.

1362 Rhine, Joseph Banks, 1895- . New Frontiers of the Mind; The Story of the Duke Experiments. Westport, Conn.: Greenwood Press, 1972 (orig. pub., 1937). 275p. Illus. $13 LC 71-178080 ISBN 0-8371-6279-3

1363 Rhine, Louisa Ella, 1891- . Mind Over Matter: Psychokinesis. New York: Collier Books; London: Collier-Macmillan, 1972 (orig. pub., New York: Macmillan, 1970). 410p. Illus. Index £0.70 pa. ISBN 0-02-077690-X

The author tells the story of research on PK at Duke University by her husband, beginning in 1934. She covers the contributions of associates Laura Dale, Karlis Osis, and J.G. Pratt. Much of the book presents data on coin spinning, and dice throwing.

1364 ______. Psi, What Is It? New York: Harper and Row,
*** 1975. 256p. Includes bibliog. refs. Index $10 LC 74-25697 ISBN 0-06-066826-1

This work is a major new contribution to occult literature. Although technically an adult book, it is really designed for teenagers. Since it attempts to be an authoritative introduction, the tone is very conservative in its judgments. Part 1 is on psi. Rhine dislikes the occult, which she feels tends to pull these phenomena away from science. Part 2 is historical and autobiographical, discussing the Duke work and its excitement. She downplays other parapsychology history a bit. She covers precognition, telepathy, clairvoyance, and psychokinesis. Part 3 discusses the advances of the last 30 years, including psi in the schoolroom, in dreams, and in other mental states. She explains laboratory techniques, including those for testing animal psi and healing. Part 4 is on psi in everyday life. Part 5 discusses survival. Rhine says that it would be wishful thinking to believe that science can prove the soul's survival. Part 6 discusses the meaning of psi--that mechanistic or physical views of man are incomplete pictures of the human condition. As for college courses, she recommends getting a related scientific degree, saying, "Today, as in the past, each person must acquire his own knowledge of the field mainly by his own reading and individual study." At the end, she gives some simple tests for use by readers in testing for ESP and PK. The work is excellent for teenagers, since it is free of the usual jargon, has many anecdotes, and includes excerpts of letters Rhine has received from young people. This fine work is recommended for adults, and juveniles from grade 9 up.

1365 Rhodes, Henry Taylor Fowkes. The Satanic Mass. London:
*

Arrow Books, 1973 (orig. pub., London: Rider, 1954). 254p. Bibliog. Index £0.45 pa. ISBN 0-09-906960-1

This work is an excellent historical, sociological, and criminological study of the subject. The writing is factual and serious. Chapters discuss origins, theoreticians, legists, prelude to the Mass, the Sabbat of the Goat, the Black Turnip Mass of Black Priests, the Children of Satan, overturned chalices, the Mass of the Holy Ghost, the 17-century background, La Reynie and his police, the Gibourg Mass, White Mass priests, Gabriel Jogand, and the devil in the 20th century. The author divides the history of the satanic mass into five stages: origins, middle years ("Revolution: Sources and Evidence"), later phase (crime), final stage ("Burlesque and Farce"), 20th century ("Indefinite Conclusion").

1366 Rich, Stella. Sunday Afternoon Astrologer. St. Paul, Minn.: Llewellyn Pubns., 1971. v, 195p. Illus. $2.95 pa. ISBN 0-87542-632-8

1367 Richardson, Alan. Introduction to the Mystical Qabalah. Wellingborough, England: Aquarian Pub. Co., 1974. 64p. Illus. (Paths to Inner Power) £0.40 pa. ISBN 0-85030-115-7

1368 Richelieu, Peter. The Soul's Journey. London: Turnstone Press, 1972 (orig. pub. as "From the Turret," Durban, England: Graphic Stationers and Publishers, 1958). vii, 192p. £1.75 ISBN 0-85500-000-7

The author, in despair over the death of his younger brother Charles (a RAF pilot just killed in battle), is repeatedly visited by an Indian in turban and sandals named Acharya. The author keeps a diary of these visits. He is told of the laws of karma, evolution, and reincarnation, and is taught how to achieve astral projection.

1369 Richet, Charles. Thirty Years of Psychical Research: Being a Treatise on Metaphysics. Trans. by Stanley de Brath. New York: Arno Press, 1975 (orig. pub., New York, 1923). Illus. (Perspectives in Psychical Research) $37 LC 75-7397 ISBN 0-405-07046-2

The author was a French psychiatrist and the first major French psychical researcher. He discusses early European research, especially work with which he himself was involved. He uses the term "metaphysics" to cover all psychical phenomena. Richet discusses three areas: cryptesthesia (ESP), including research on mediums, sensitives, hypnotized normals, and normals; telekinesis (including table-tipping); and ectoplasm (including levitation, bilocation, and hauntings).

1370 Richmond, Kenneth. Unpublished F. W. H. Myers Scripts; Selected from the Richmond Material. Ed. by Elizabeth Gaythorpe. Note by Zoe Richmond. London: College of Psychic Studies, 1972. 27p. (College of Psychic Studies. Papers, no. 4) £0.25 pa. ISBN 0-903336-15-4

1371 Rieder, Thomas. Astrological Warnings and the Stock Market; A Study of Astrology and the Startling Correlation Between Planetary Cycles, Investor Confidence, and Stock Market Patterns. Toronto: Pagurian Press, 1972 (dist. in U.S. by Stephen Greene, Brattleboro, Vt., 1972, and Arco, New York, 1974). 116p. Illus. Includes bibliog. refs. $7.95 LC 75-187961 ISBN 0-919364-17-9

The author attempts to present proof that there is a neat correlation between stocks and certain planetary patterns. He takes the historical performance of the Dow Jones Industrial Average back to 1899. He discusses these topics: Saturn and money signs, pinpointing sell signals, extrapolating to 1980, 4½-year Martian cycle.

1372 Rigaud, Milo. Secrets of Voodoo. Trans. by Robert B. Cross. New York: Pocket Books, 1971 (orig. pub., New York: Arco, 1970). 219p. Illus. Photos. Index $.95 pa.

The author is a Frenchman who has lived in Haiti for 30 years, and extensively studied the subject of voodoo. He discusses the symbolism of ceremonies and costumes, voodoo priesthood, the tracing of rites back to traditional African and other sources, voodoo pantheon, midnight ceremonies, drums, dances, prayers, chants, blood and human sacrifices, magic lamps, vengeance, foods, amulets and talismans, and Joukoujou. The work includes a glossary and calendar of voodoo ceremonies.

1373 Righter, Carroll. Dollar Signs; How to Increase Your Personal Worth by Astrological Forecasting. New York: Putnam, 1971. 191p. Illus. $6.95 LC 71-136794

1374 Rinaldi, Peter M. The Man in the Shroud: This Is the Face of Christ. London: Sidgwick and Jackson, 1974 (orig. pub. as "It Is the Lord: A Study of the Shroud of Christ," New York: Vantage Press, 1972). 115p. Illus. Bibliog. £2.60

1375 Riotte, Louise. Planetary Planting. New York: Simon and Schuster, 1975. 352p. $9.95 LC 74-32481

This book tells how to garden by the signs of the zodiac. Chapters include "Vines by Virgo" and "Luna Lore for Lawns"; information on when and how to take cuttings is also given.

1376 Riva, Anna. Modern Herbal Spellbook. Toluca Lake, Calif.: International Imports, 1974. 64p. $2 pa.

This book discusses use of herbs for magic in business, health, and to improve psychic abilities.

1377 ________. Secrets of Magical Seals. Toluca Lake, Calif.: International Imports, 1975. 64p. $2.50 pa.

1378 Roberts, Anthony. Atlantean Traditions in Ancient Britain. Llanfynydd, Wales: Unicorn Bookshop, 1975. xv, 121p. Illus. Plans Bibliog. Index £2.40 pa. ISBN 0-85659-019-3

1379 * Roberts, Estelle, 1889- . Fifty Years a Medium. Introd. by Hannen Swaffer. New ed. London: Corgi, 1975 (also, Avon, 1972; this ed. orig. pub., 1969; 1st ed. pub. as "Forty Years a Medium," London: Herbert Jenkins, 1959). 222p. Illus. Plates (Corgi Library of Psychic Exploration) £0.60 pa. ISBN 0-552-09908-2

This book is an autobiography of one of Great Britain's most famous mediums. She and her spirit guide, Red Cloud, are well known, and have done many public performances, including ones at Royal Albert Hall. Chapters discuss the coming of Red Cloud, healing, psychometry, haunting, murder and suicide clairvoyance (public and private), materialization and apports, direct voice, speaking in many tongues, and war. Even as a child, Roberts often heard spirit voices, and conversed with them. From age 14 on, they started to warn her of future events. As with all biographies of truly sincere, committed spiritualists, this one is fascinating. As for her general philosophy, she states that the universe is ordered by divine law, with the first law being that of love, especially as manifested in service to others.

1380 * Roberts, Jane, 1929- . Adventures in Consciousness: An Introduction to Aspect Psychology. Englewood Cliffs, N.J.: Prentice-Hall, 1975. ix, 288p. Illus. Index $7.95 LC 75-8610 ISBN 0-13-013953-X

In 1963, the author and her husband had their first experience with a Ouija board. Seth began coming through. The author soon started going into trance, and Seth spoke with his voice through her. In 1972, she discovered many other levels of awareness (Seth I, II, and III--she's hit III only three times in her life). She and her students studied psychic events, and taped Seth's voice. Aspect psychology began with the idea that man's consciousness is mobile. Part 1 of this book (the fifth of the Seth books) discusses adventures with the class that went too far, Seth and alterations of consciousness, reincarnational dreams, spirit guides, and Sumari development in 1972. Part 2 gives an introduction to aspect psychology (source self, focal personality) and discusses apprentice gods, God, and earth experience as a white hole. This is a very interesting book. It functions as an autobiography and a work full of creative, original thoughts by Roberts.

1381 * ________. The Nature of Personal Reality: A Seth Book. Notes by Robert F. Butts. Englewood Cliffs, N.J.: Prentice-Hall, 1974. xxiv, 510p. $3.95 pa. LC 74-7356 ISBN 0-13-610576-9

This fourth Seth book is dictated by Seth, who was once a minor pope in the fourth century, according to his testimony. He communicates through Jane's voice, and her husband Robert tapes it or makes notes. This book is a change in the Seth series, because Jane now feels she is an active participant in producing the material. Before, Seth dictated all the material. Seth says that our beliefs shape our personal reality, and that the present is the point of power. The work discusses reality and personal beliefs, the health of body and mind, illumination, the conscious mind, grace, good and evil, natural hypnosis and healing, inner and outer storms, concentration of energy, the dream landscape, telepathy, drugs, insanity, prisons, and reincarnation. The Seth series is not only interesting, but destined to go down as a classic set in the occult tradition.

1382 ________. Seth Speaks; The Eternal Validity of the Soul.
* Notes by Robert F. Butts. Englewood Cliffs, N. J.: Prentice-Hall, 1972. . xxiv, 505p. $7.95 LC 78-38925 ISBN 0-13-807206-X

This book consists of recorded sessions with the spirit voice Seth. These sessions have been recorded by her husband since 1963, and number over 600. The work discusses Atlantis and earlier civilizations, the nature of Christ, and spirits that have appeared over the centuries to keep truths alive and guide man to spiritual growth.

1383 Roberts, John Morris. Mythology of the Secret Societies. St. Albans, England: Paladin, 1974 (orig. pub., London: Secker and Warburg, 1972). 478p. Index £1.50 pa.

1384 Roberts, Susan. Witches U. S. A. Rev. ed. Hollywood, Calif.: Phoenix House, 1974 (1st ed. orig. pub., New York: Dell, 1971). 318p. $3.95 pa. LC 74-75805

The author got much of his information for this work from direct contact with witches. He discusses the philosophy of witchcraft and happenings in the U. S., describing the types of people engaged in it. One chapter discusses an alleged curse used by a union to get control of a factory. A self-blessing ritual and sample coven ritual are given, but rituals are not emphasized in the work. An epilogue lists names and addresses of witchcraft publications and organizations.

1385 Roberts, Ursula. Colour Healing for the New Age. 1974. 30p.

Ramadahn, the spirit guide for Ursula Roberts, says that spirit healing is done by color radiations that bring a response from the patient's soul. These colors appear much more vividly to the medium than in normal seeing, and vibrate intensely.

1386 ________. I Knew Moses. London: Psychic Press, 1973. 191p. Bibliog. £2

This material was dictated from the other side through Roberts, a medium, with help from her famous Egyptian guide Ramadahn, who began coming through to her in 1967. Moses is presented as a man with superior physical, mental, and spiritual powers. Much of this work is about Moses and his closest friend, a royal Egyptian scribe named Tek-sek.

1387 Robertson, Olivia. The Call of Isis. Clonegal, Ireland: Cesara Publications, 1975. vii, 126p. Illus. £1 pa. ISBN 0-9503871-0-X

1388 Robinson, Lytle. Cayce's Story of the Origin and Destiny of Man. New York: Coward, McCann and Geoghegan, 1972. 209p. $5.95

The author presents Cayce's claims that after the fall of Atlantis, the survivors established civilizations in Egypt and Peru, but among them were Sons of Belial, whose depravity caused their homeland to sink. A large part of the book discusses the role of reincarnated Atlanteans in today's society. The large influx of such souls should result in a utopian civilization by the year 2000. The author also mentions measurement of the Great Pyramid and reincarnation in general. Cayce predicted that the world will have dire things happen by 1998, unless man changes.

1389 Robinson, Stearn, and Tom Corbett. The Dreamer's Dictionary. London: Coronet, 1975 (orig. pub., New York: Taplinger; London: Souvenir Press, 1974). 256p. £0.75 pa. ISBN 0-340-20002-2

This book has more than 3,000 entries and over 500 cross-references. The authors are a British journalist and a psychic. It is a browsing book, non-Freudian, and a synthesis of ancient and modern interpretations.

1390 Robson, Arthur. Man and His Seven Principles. London: Theosophical Publishing House, 1973. viii, 186p. Illus. £1.50 ISBN 0-7229-7309-8

1391 Robson, Vivian Erwood. Astrology and Sex: An Infallible Guide to Happiness in Love-life and Marriage as Determined by the Stars in Their Courses. London: Foulsham, 1973 (orig. pub. as "Astrology and Human Sex Life," 1963). 142p. Illus. £1.50

1392 Rogo, D. Scott, 1952- . An Experience of Phantoms.
*** New York: Taplinger Pub. Co., 1974. 214p. Illus. Bibliog. Index $7.95 LC 73-18793 ISBN 0-8008-2470-9

This work is a major new contribution to occult literature. Rogo wrote his first book, Nad, at age 18. In this work, he discusses poltergeists, apparitions, animal ghosts, out-of-the-body experiences (OOBE's), mediumship, materialization, phantom faces appearing on walls and floors, photographs of spirit faces, phantom voices, fiery phantoms, and haunted houses. He says that the psychic literature before Rhine is a great source that has been poorly investigated by statistically-minded researchers. He discusses experiments with Los Angeles medium Attila von Szalay in making tapes of paranormal voices. Rogo warns to prepare carefully for OOBE's; he has experimented with them himself. He feels there may be several different explanations for all these psychic phenomena. Rogo states, "Apparitions, as no other phenomenon, bring to the fore that man is a spiritual being." He feels that lab tests can never take the place of personal psychic experiences.

1393 _______. Methods and Models for Education in Parapsychology. New York: Parapsychology Foundation, 1973. 71p. Bibliog. (Parapsychological Monographs, no. 14) $2 LC 73-75209

The author is the book review editor for Psychic magazine. The book is concerned with university-level teaching. He presents three models for organizing a course, each using an annotated survey outline giving selected references--"Historical Approach," "Survey of Psychical Phenomena," and "Parapsychology as an Experimental Science." Rogo sees psychical research as the perfect course to use in developing the self-directed, creative student.

1394 _______. Nad, Volume 2: A Psychic Study of the "Music
* of the Spheres." Secaucus, N.J.: University Books, 1973. 176p. $6.95

Nad is a Sanskrit term meaning paranormal or transcendental music. The author here adds 58 new cases to the 100 already covered in his original volume, Nad: A Study of Some Unusual "Other World Experiences." He emphasizes the connection between music and out-of-the-body experiences. The music is heard either for a short time (1 to 5 minutes) or a long time (15 minutes or longer). The longer music has definite pitch, rhythm and melody; the short version does not. The music starts faintly, increases to fairly loud, and then fades awy. His information sources are the magazines Light, Fate, and Psychic News; the American Society for Psychical Research and the Society for Psychical Research in London; Crookall's collections, and historical accounts. Rogo feels that only in its connection to death and survival does the music have any meaning.

1395 _______. Parapsychology: A Century of Inquiry. New
*** York: Taplinger Pub. Co., 1975. 319p. Bibliog. Index $12.50 LC 74-22890 ISBN 0-8008-6236-8

This work is a major new contribution to occult literature. It is a good attempt to write a basic textbook for parapsychology, using data in an unbiased manner and mentioning the classic cases and theories. Chapters discuss the following areas: parapsychology and the ESP controversy, foundations of psychical research, ESP--the search and the evidence, ESP in the laboratory, spontaneous ESP, gifted subjects, telekinesis, PK in the laboratory, new horizons in ESP research, and psi, death, and survival. The work is packed with material and very thorough in attempts to include all trends. Famous psychic researcher J. G. Pratt, in a review of this book in the Journal of the American Society for Psychical Research, writes a harsh review. He criticizes Rogo for inaccuracies, misquotes, careless writing, and the lack of a uniform method for citing sources. This angry review seems unfair. It is true that, at times, the writing style makes it unclear what Rogo is trying to say. There is a uniform citation style, although a few minor inconsistencies can be found; there are not many, and most readers would never notice them. Pratt says that he fears this work will become a textbook, with all its distortions. He says further that the ASPR may not review the next of Rogo's books unless it is better researched. We do not know exactly how this "feud" started, but Pratt's review is very biased and cruel. There are valid criticisms to be made of Rogo's book. It is an embarrassment for any reviewer to see them so badly made by Pratt. In sum, Rogo has done a fine job of summarizing the field, especially in the vast amount of material he has digested for the reader. He bends over backward to completely explain everything he says. This desire to summarize all thought on a subject may be the real cause of his occasionally cloudy sentences, and also, his errors. Sometimes, you can say too much, and get caught.

1396 ________. Welcoming Silence; A Study of Psychical Phenomena and Survival of Death. Secaucus, N. J.: University
* Books, 1973. 191p. $7.95

This book discusses out-of-the-body experiences (OOBE's), experiments on the phenomena and visions surrounding the moment of death, haunted houses, and mediumship. Rogo says that, besides corroborative evidence, there is content analysis evidence, where a large body of data is searched for recurring patterns. If many independent witnesses agree on the same phenomena, this is strong evidence that the events are real. He feels that the crux of the survival evidence is in the OOBE, and, yet, it has been largely ignored by parapsychologists. He ends the book with a discussion of the super-ESP theory (which states that the medium's success is not due to contact with spirits, but to unusually strong ESP that can fathom all a person did while alive). Rogo feels this theory is false, saying that even one of the main proponents of it, E. R. Dodds, admits there is no factual basis for it.

1397 Rolfe, Mona. Man--Physical and Spiritual. London: Spearman, 1971. 285p. £2.10 ISBN 0-85435-380-1

1398 Roll, William G. The Poltergeist. Foreword by J. B. Rhine.
*** Garden City, N. Y.: Doubleday, 1972 (also, New York: New American Library, 1972). xx, 234p.

This work is a major new contribution to occult literature. The 15 chapters discuss six main cases and many minor ones. Roll discusses the famous poltergeist cases in Seaford, Long Island; Newark, N. J.; Indianapolis, and Miami. He covers also two lesser known ones, one in Olive Hill, Ky. (1968), and the other in Clayton, N. C. The author is one of the leading authorities on poltergeists (the other is Dr. Hans Bender of Freiburg University). He worked in Rhine's lab at Duke, and is now project director of the Psychical Research Foundation at Durham, N. C. He discusses earlier events as well, surveying 47 poltergeists mentioned in serious literature from 1859 to 1957, and covering 29 of them here. He includes in his book mention of European poltergeist cases and Bender's work. This book has a good deal of autobiographical material in it on Roll. He and Gaither Pratt investigated the case at Seaford. There is also a great deal of discussion on the Miami case, where the author actually brought the subject to Durham for testing. There is a good deal of theoretical discussion in this work, centering around this Miami case. Roll theorizes that poltergeists are involuntary PK effects acting as outlets for repressed aggression. The PK effect moves in a clockwise force field or vortex outward from the person. The author says that massive PK may someday be used for helpful purposes.

1399 ________. Theory and Experiment in Psychical Research. Foreword and index added by author. New York: Arno Press, 1975 (orig. pub. as B. Litt. thesis, St. Catherine's College, Oxford University, 1959). Illus. (Perspectives in Psychical Research) $29 LC 75-7398 ISBN 0-405-07047-0

This work discusses ESP, PK, English mediums, and Dutch "paragnosts." Roll discusses how ESP and PK are transmitted from one person to another person or object. Included are Roll's experiments at Oxford on the relationship between ESP and personality traits, hypnosis, and memory.

1400 Rolph, C. H. Believe What You Like: What Happened Between the Scientologists and the National Association for Mental Health. London: Deutsch, 1973. 172p. £2.25

This work discusses litigation brought by, and occasionally against, the Church of Scientology or its members. Half the book is devoted to the action of Scientologists against the National Association for Mental Health for expelling them. Also covered is the unsuccessful action for libel brought against radio figure Geoffrey Johnson Smith for his criticism of the movement. The work mentions that Scientologists had, at one time or another, 36 writs against British newspapers. All were later withdrawn.

1401 Ronay, Gabriel. The Dracula Myth. London: Pan Books, 1975 (orig. pub., London: W. H. Allen, 1972). 190p. Illus. Plates Map Index £0.50 pa. ISBN 0-330-24246-6

1402 ________. The Truth About Dracula. New York: Stein and
* Day, 1974 (c1972). 180p. Illus. Includes bibliog. refs. $1.95 pa. ISBN 0-8128-1750-8

Although covering Vlad the Impaler, Ronay concentrates on the life of Countess Elizabeth Bathory as the origin of the vampire information in Stoker's novel (this disagrees with McNally's work, which presents Vlad as the model). Bathory killed 650 young women. The author also discusses how vampire belief was exploited by religion and the state for their own purposes. Ronay uses classical printed sources of Europe as his evidence.

1403 Roquemore, Kathleen. It's All in Your Numbers: The Secrets of Numerology. New York: Harper, 1975. 312p. $10.95

The author discusses vocations, dieting, behavior patterns, naming children; how to learn the major numbers, including outer self, inner self, destiny, and heart numbers; how to chart them, colors, gems, musical notes, and the planets. She believes the coming of Christ is near, and that numerology will help us identify some of the many master souls now incarnating on earth.

1404 Rose, Karen. In the Land of the Mind. New York: Athen-
*** eum, 1975. 267p. Illus. Photos. Charts $7.95 LC 74-19195 ISBN 0-689-30456-0

This work is a major new contribution to occult literature. The author approaches parapsychology through psychology and psychobiology, covering the brain and altered states of consciousness, extrasensory people, psi in the lab and outside, and "Doors into the More Than Incredible." The first part covers neurophysiology, Freud, biofeedback, sleep, hypnosis, yoga, and meditation. Some errors are made here. The part on extrasensory people gives short chapters on Garrett, Cayce, Gerard Croiset, Ted Serios, and Jack Schwartz. The third part is very good, discussing: telepathy versus clairvoyance, PK in the lab, PK and poltergeists, PK and plants, and healing. The fourth part is on Sai Baba, precognition, and the author's views. This excellent juvenile survey is recommended for grade 7 and up.

1405 Rosen, Barbara, comp. Witchcraft. New York: Taplinger,
* 1972 (c1969). xii, 407p. Illus. Bibliog. (Stratford-upon-Avon Library, no. 6) $9.95 LC 74-179662 ISBN 0-8008-8372-1

This is a selection of 25 widely distributed pamphlets of Elizabethan and Jacobean England that greatly influenced trial judges and the public. Sample ones discuss the Witches of Warboys, and the Chelmsford Trial (1566). Not even Cornell University's White collection has all the facsimiles. The works are printed with modern spelling and punctuation. However, Rosen omits long passages. This will hurt the scholar, since he will then have to go to the originals. For the average reader, though, it is a very useful work. Rosen's good 50-page introduction differentiates between English and Continental witchcraft. There is a glossary, and separate indexes for familiars, persons, and places.

1406 Rosenblum, Arthur. Unpopular Science: An Unnatural Book about Natural Phenomena. Philadelphia: Running Press, 1974. 111p. Illus. Index $3.95 LC 74-84855 ISBN 0-914294-19-9

The author, head of the Aquarian Research Foundation from 1969-1974, published newsletters on parapsychological developments. This book collects them in a Whole Earth Catalog format. They discuss auras, acupuncture, astrological birth control, plant ESP, out-of-the-body experiences (OOBE's), and pyramid power.

1407 Ross, Judy, 1936- , and L. Strom. Cats Around the Zodiac. Pictures by Judy Ross. Words by M. Strom. Englewood Cliffs, N.J.: Prentice-Hall, 1975. $2.95 LC 74-28186 ISBN 0-13-120782-2

This book is based on sun-sign astrology, with cats acting just as humans would born under that sign. It is illustrated with black-and-white photographs.

1408 Roszak, Theodore. The Unfinished Animal. New York:
* Harper and Row, 1975. 271p. $10 ISBN 0-06-067016-9

The author feels we have lost touch with spiritual power, but are in a good dialogue between modern experience and sacred tradition. He discusses the sociological meaning of the current occult revival, viewing it himself with skepticism. Roszak says that this revival parallels other such periods in history. He feels the occult is misdirecting the true spiritual quest of the Aquarian Age.

1409 Royal, Margaret, and Ian Girvan, comps. True Stories of the Ghosts of Bath. Bath, England: the author, 1974. 25p. Illus. £0.30 ISBN 0-9503499-0-9

1410 Rudhyar, Dane, 1895- . Astrological Houses; The Spec-
* trum of Individual Experience. Garden City, N.Y.: Doubleday, 1972. vi, 208p. Includes bibliog. refs. $6.95 LC 74-180105

This is an attempt by the author to develop a theory of humanistic astrology by applying to it Oriental and Western philosophy as well as Jungian psychology. He defines the houses as archetypal categories of experience through which an individual passes during his life. His system is progressive, moving up in consciousness from a sense of self (first house) to a sense of ownership (second house), and so on. Other chapters discuss these topics:

houses as the basic astrological frame of reference, houses as fields of experience, the three-level cycle of individual experiences, the four angles and their zodiacal polarities, and the planets in the houses.

1411 ________. Astrological Mandala: The Cycle of Transformations and Its 360 Symbolic Phases. New York: Random
* House, 1973. xi, 392p. $10 LC 72-12954

The author has written a creative contribution to astrological literature. Three decades ago, in an attempt to produce symbols more relevant to today's times, Marc Edmund Jones and a clairvoyant friend created these symbols. Rudhyar interprets them, emphasizing their character as a structured, cyclic series which codifies and reveals the archetypal meaning of 360 basic phases of human life. The author also shows how these symbols can be used for divination. In essence, the work is a reinterpretation of the Sabian symbols, presenting them as a contemporary American I Ching.

1412 ________. Astrological Timing; The Transition to the New
* Age. New York and London: Harper, 1972 (orig. pub. as "Birth Patterns for a New Humanity," 1969). 246p. $2.95 pa. LC 78-184653 ISBN 0-06-090260-4

The work is on astrological cycles, ages, and periods. Part 1 of this book discusses three centuries of crisis (18th, 19th, and 20th), planetary cycles, the 10,000 year period, the cycle of Uranus, the cycle of Neptune, the cycle of Pluto, and cycles of relationship linking the above three. Part 2 discusses stars, constellations, and signs for three periods: from Buddha to Christ, the Piscean Age, and the Aquarian-Leo Age. Part 3 discusses the zodiacal earth-field (the Sphinx, the Great Pyramid, the earth as an organic whole, and the Oceanic Age.)

1413 ________. The Astrology of America's Destiny. New York: Random House, 1974 (also, New York: Vintage Books, 1975). 211p. Illus. Includes bibliog. refs. $6.95 LC 74-8786 ISBN 0-394-49061-4

This book discusses the birth of the U.S. as a collective "person," the roots of the American nation, America's place in the cosmic process, the birth chart of the U.S.A., 200 years of growth through crisis, a chart for the beginning of the federal government, America at a crossroad, and the prospect for the last quarter of the century. It mentions that the rising sign of the American people is Sagittarius. Also, every American president since 1842 who took office under the conjunction of Jupiter and Saturn has died in office. The work contains many other tidbits such as these.

1414 ________. The Lunation Cycle: A Key to the Understanding of Personality. Rev. and enl. ed. Berkeley: Shambala; London: dist. by Routledge and K. Paul, 1971 (this ed. orig. pub., The Hague: Servire, 1967; previous ed. pub. as "Moon, the Cycles and Fortunes of Life," New York: David McKay Co., 1946). ix, 138p. Illus. £1.20 pa. ISBN 0-87773-029-6

This work discusses astrology, time, and cycles; the lunation cycle as a dynamic pattern of relationship, the eight lunation types of personality, the part of fortune, the part of spirit, and the planets in relation to the lunation cycle.

1415 ________. Occult Preparations for a New Age. Wheaton, Ill.: Theosophical Pub. House, 1975. 275p. Illus. Includes bibliog. refs. (Quest Book) $3.25 pa. LC 74-19054 ISBN 0-8356-0460-8

This book has a long discussion on the Secret Doctrine, by Madame Blavatsky, and calls itself "a planetary approach to occultism and its source."

1416 ________. Person Centered Astrology. Lakemont, Ga.: CSA Press, 1972. 375p. Illus. $8.95 LC 72-93586 ISBN 0-87707-097-0

In 1969, the author began a new movement: the International Committee for a Humanistic Astrology. This book is a series of essays written after that 1969 date. Topics discussed are the study of birth charts, planetary and lunar nodes, and interpreting the birth chart as a whole (the holistic, or Gestalt approach to charts).

1417 ________. The Sun Is Also a Star; The Galactic Dimension of Astrology. New York: E. P. Dutton, 1975. 209p. Includes bibliog. refs. $3.95 pa. LC 75-11852 ISBN 0-525-47404-8

This work is on the influence of the non-classical outer planets (Saturn, Uranus, Neptune, and Pluto). The author stresses the need for astrologers to move into a galactic instead of a planetary frame of reference. Much of the book is theoretical.

1418 Rudwin, Maximilian Josef, 1885- . The Devil in Legend and Literature. La Salle, Ill.: Open Court Pub. Co., 1973 (c1971). xi, 354p. Illus. Includes bibliog. refs. $3.95 LC 73-85284

The author discusses the impact legends and biblical accounts have had on literature. One chapter is devoted to the concept of pacts between the devil and human beings. The book refers to English, French, and German sources.

1419 Runeberg, Arne. Witches, Demons and Fertility Magic; Analysis of Their Significance and Mutual Relations in West-European Folk Religion. Norwood, Pa.: Norwood Editions, 1974 (orig. pub., Helsinki: Societas Scientiarum Fennica, 1947). Bibliog. (Issued as no. 14/4 of the "Commentationes Humanarum Litterarum") $17.50 LC 74-3091

1420 Rush, John A. Witchcraft and Sorcery; An Anthropological Perspective of the Occult. Springfield, Ill.: Thomas, 1974 (c1973). Bibliog. $10.50 LC 73-16066 ISBN 0-398-02981-4

1421 Russell, Edward Wriothesley. Design for Destiny; Science
* Reveals the Soul. New York: Ballantine, 1973 (c1971). x, 213p. Bibliog. $1.25 pa.

This is a highly original, intriguing and serious contribution to occult thought, based on new scientific research into electromagnetic fields. The author theorizes that our bodies and brains are maintained by permanent such fields which mold the constantly changing cellular material. These fields of life (L-fields) can be measured with sensitive voltmeters. Also, the author presents the theory that thought is independent of the physical brain, and is actually another kind of field, the T-field. Russell feels that this gives a rational explanation for the existence and immortality of the soul.

1422 Russell, Eric. The History of Astrology and Prediction. London: New English Library, 1974 (orig. pub. as "Astrology and Prediction," London: Batsford, 1972; also, New York: Drake Publishers, 1973). 144p. Illus. Bibliog. £0.50 pa. ISBN 0-450-02006-1

This book discusses these topics: the classical world, the challenge of Christianity, the Renaissance, astrology in England, the 19th century, the modern world, the grammar of astrology (actually a brief textbook on the usual material of houses, signs), "The Book of the Prophets" (Nostradamus), and apocalyptic societies. He feels that one great virtue of astrology over other systems of prediction is that one can check a chart after events and see how accurate it was.

1423 Russell, George William. Candle of Vision; The Autobiography of a Mystic. Introd. by Leslie Shepard. Wheaton, Ill., London: Theosophical Pub. House, 1974 (orig. pub. London: Macmillan, 1918). xv, 175p. Bibliog. $2.25 pa.

This book, written under the pseudonym A. E., is by a leading figure of the Irish literary renaissance of the late 19th and early 20th centuries. Yale University gave him a Litt. D. degree. He writes on meditation, imagination, dreams, intuition, Celtic cosmogony, and Celtic imagination, in a series of 20 essays. Russell began his life of meditation with glimpses of ESP in dreams as a youth. He pictured and drew mystical symbols, and saw all nature as moving and breathing.

1424 Russell, Jeffrey Burton. Witchcraft in the Middle Ages.
* Ithaca, N. Y.: Cornell University Press, 1972. xi, 394p. Bibliog. Index £7.15 ISBN 0-8014-0697-8

The author's thesis is that Christian witchcraft of the 15th century was the result of a long process of assimilation of pagan beliefs into Christianity. A key part of the process was the linking of witchcraft with heretical movements. He emphasizes the period from St. Augustine to 1427, and summarizes more briefly the literature of 1427-1486 (the year Malleus Malificarum was published). Russell disagrees with those who say the Middle Ages were skeptical of witchcraft, and that witchcraft was invented by Scholastics and the Inquisition. He shows instead that the Middle Ages believed in it. He suggests that once criteria of witch theory were formed (marks and so on), the witch frenzy of the 16th and 17th centuries was bound to follow. He says that witchcraft was a form of dissent against church and society, and feels it should be differentiated from sorcery as magic.

1425 Rutherford, Adam. Pyramidology. 2nd ed. Harpenden, England: Institute of Pyramidology, 1975 (first ed., 1966). 5 vols. Illus. Plates Maps Plans £7 ea.

1426/7 Ryall, Edward W., 1902- . Born Twice; Total Recall of
* a Seventeenth-Century Life. Introd. by Ian Stevenson. New York: Harper and Row, 1975 (orig. pub. as "The Second Time Round," St. Helier, England: Neville Spearman, 1974). 214p. Illus. Plates Map Bibliog. Index $7.95 LC 74-20412 ISBN 0-06-013713-4

In 1910, at the age of eight, Ryall saw Halley's Comet and told his father he had seen a similar sight before. This incident and many others led to an almost total recall of a past life as a farmer, John Fletcher, who lived in England 1645-1683. Everything Stevenson could check out on Ryall's story was correct. Unfortunately, there is no proof that Ryall had these memories as a young boy; he told no one until much later in life. The real value of this book is the excellent introduction by Stevenson. He cautiously states that the Ryall case appears to be one of reincarnation, after rejecting theories of hoax or cryptomnesia (unconscious memory).

1428 Ryan, Charles J. H. P. Blavatsky and the Theosophical Movement. San Diego, Calif.: Point Loma Pubns., 1975. 441p. $7 pa.

This biography emphasizes Blavatsky's problems in organizing and maintaining the Theosophical Society.

1429 Ryan, Peter, 1939- . UFO's and Other Worlds. Illus. by Ludek Pesek. Harmondsworth, England: Kestrel Books, 1975 (also, Baltimore: Penguin Books, 1975). 48p. Illus. (some color) Index £1.30 ISBN 0-7226-6804-X

This juvenile book discusses UFO sightings, and explains away most of them as natural events. The author gives reasonable hypotheses for those cases not explainable by natural phenomena.

1430 Rýzl, Milan. Biblical Miracles; Jesus and ESP. San Jose,
* Calif.: Milan Rýzl, 1972. 150p. $6 pa.

This book discusses the applications of reincarnation and hypnosis to ESP historical research. Rýzl covers experiments in hypnotic retrocognition he did 25 years ago while living in Czechoslovakia. He asked his subjects to go back to biblical times and tell what occurred. Jesus, John the Baptist, Elijah, Elisha, Moses, and Abraham are mentioned. The subjects also were able, through telepathy, to communicate with Jesus and answer questions. The subjects, three female Catholics working independently, came up with similar answers. These answers were quite different from traditional Catholic teaching. The book heralds the possible use of ESP to get knowledge of history (for example, he got a description of the physical appearance of Jesus). Rýzl gave Pavel Stepanek his start, and has worked at Rhine's Foundation for Research on the Nature of Man.

1431 ________. ESP in the Modern World. San Jose, Calif.: Milan Rýzl, 1972. 167p. $8.50

In 1968, the author moved to California, and has taught courses in the state university and college system, and at the University of California. He is now director of parapsychological research for the Silva Mind Control organization. In this book, he spends half his discussion on the occult and its relationship to parapsychology. He tells how occult experiences can be explained in terms of psychology, physiology and physics. Rýzl also discusses stage telepathy, dowsing, fortune-telling, the Ouija board and automatic writing, trance states, and possession. Part 2 of this work is autobiographical, telling of his early interest in parapsychology as a student at Prague, and of the communist government's attempts to use him. He attacks both gullible believers and blind scientists in this book.

1432 ________. How to Develop ESP in Yourself and Others. San Jose, Calif.: Milan Rýzl, 1973. 94p. (Includes 2 long-playing cassettes)

The author says that only with dedication and persistence, plus adjustment to his method, will a student develop ESP. The cassettes are furnished to put the mind in a proper state of consciousness to perform ESP. At the end, the book gives tests to measure improvement. There are also background chapters on ESP theory, hypnosis, the nature of ESP, and the future of ESP in geology, police work, marriage, medicine, industry, and business. He feels that ESP is no mystery, but a natural phenomenon.

1433 ________. Parapsychology: A Scientific Approach. New York: Hawthorn, 1971.

This book discusses ESP, clairvoyance, telepathy, and precognition. It gives the history, experimental work, and future of each area. Many cases are given from the author's own files. He says that many individuals have or can be trained to have ESP.

1434 Sabin, Katharine Cover, 1910- . ESP and Dream Analysis.
* Chicago: H. Regnery Co., 1974. 205p. Illus. $6.95 LC 74-7072 ISBN 0-8092-8397-2

In this book, the author gives easy exercises to program one's subconscious so that dreams may be remembered and become more precognitive. She discusses how the dreamer can choose symbols and their meanings for use in his or her dreams. She differentiates between Jungian and Freudian dream interpretation. Sabin mentions black and white dream symbol methods, to be used when a choice must be made at once between two alternatives, and techniques for multiple choice situations. She recommends a dream diary to increase one's ability to shape his destiny. She also covers free will, man's divine nature, automatic writing and possession. Sabin is an amateur parapsychologist, with no degrees or laboratory work. She made headlines in 1971 with her accurate predictions concerning the Apollo 14 mission.

1435 Sadoul, Jacques. Alchemists and Gold. Trans. by Olga
* Sieveking. New York: Putnam, 1972 (orig. pub., London: Spearman, 1972). 284p. Illus. Index (Translation of "Le Trésor des alchimistes." Paris: Editions Publications Premières, 1970) $7.95 LC 72-85243 ISBN 0-399-10990-0

This book is about the search for the philosopher's stone. The first part discusses the history of alchemical philosophy and principles. Part 2 covers the lives of those the author feels were the most nearly genuine alchemists--those that claimed they possessed the philosopher's stone. The third part discusses materials and methods for making the philosopher's stone. Sadoul believes it can be made, and tries to prove its material reality. The work concludes with a glossary. This book contains a great deal of material, and could serve well as a sourcebook.

1436 Sailaja, P., and K. Ramakrishna Rao. Experimental Studies of the Differential Effect in Life Setting. New York: Parapsychology Foundation, 1973 (based on Sailaja's thesis, Andhra University, Waltair, India). viii, 78p. Includes bibliog. refs. (Parapsychological Monographs, no. 13) $3 pa. LC 72-84013

One of the key problems in ESP experimentation is that results are usually so weak that they could be explained as having been caused by an improperly designed experiment or as simply due to the margin of error and chance. These authors explore ways of strengthening the results of ESP experiments. The best readings occur in real-life settings and situations, presumably because of the subject's motivation. Thus, one experiment of the authors made correct guessing in tests a requirement for admission into college. The authors feel their experiments prove their theory, and should be applied to laboratory work. Rao was director of the Department of Library Science at Andhra University, India, where the experiments were done.

1437 St. Clair, David. Drum and Candle. Garden City, N. Y.:
* Doubleday, 1971 (also, New York: Bell Pub. Co., 1971; London: Macdonald and Co., 1971, with subtitle, "First-hand Experiences and Accounts of Voodoo and Spiritism"). 304p. Illus. $6.95 LC 79-131103

In this interesting book, the author studies spiritism and magic in Brazil as he travels around the country. He discusses Condomble, which he claims began with Allen Kardek (Hippolyte Leon Denizard Rivail). He also covers Umbanda, including its magical symbols and midnight gatherings at Copacabana beach. Healing done by the laying-on of hands is mentioned, as is the work of Arigo. There is a section on the Catholic Church and Brazilian spiritism. By the close of the book, St. Clair comes to realize he has been hexed, and finds a reverse hex very successful. He admits that he believes Brazilian spiritism works in ways we do not yet understand. St. Clair is a free-lance writer who also wrote part of Fodor's Guide to South America. As a youth, he had an interest in the occult, and sent away for the Rosicrucian teaching materials.

1438 ________. How Your Psychic Powers Can Make You Rich. Toronto, London: Bantam Books, 1975. xiii, 237p. £0.50 pa. ISBN 0-552-68894-0

1439 ________. Psychic Healers. Garden City, N. Y.: Doubleday,
* 1974. 336p. Illus. $8.95 LC 74-2833 ISBN 0-385-04797-5

This very interesting book consists of chapters on largely unknown healers. Most of the material was gathered by interviews and is presented as conversations with the author. Most of the material is not sensational, but tries to present the healer's background, personal beliefs in the paranormal, source of powers used in healing, and techniques. Persons covered are Dorie D'Angelo of Carmel, Calif.; Charles Cassidy of Los Angeles; Rosita Rodriguez of Chicago, who practices the healing style of Tony Agpaoa of the Philippines (a very controversial psychic surgeon); Harold Plume of Monterey, Calif., another psychic surgeon; Ethel de Loach of Morristown, N. J. (on whom E. Douglas Dean has done research, particularly with Kirlian photography); Willard Fuller and Amelia Fuller (religious healing); Betty Bethards of Novato, Calif.; Bob Hoffman of Oakland, Calif. (psychiatric healing through the help of spirit guide and ex-psychiatrist Dr. Sigfried Fischer); Dorothy Vurnovas of San Jose, Calif.; William Brown and his psychic surgery, with the aid of 28 specialists who use his body and never physically touch the patient; William McGarey and his use of the Cayce techniques at the A.R.E. Clinic in Phoenix, Ariz. In between the chapters, the author gives short accounts of unusual cures. There is a list of healers and their addresses at the end.

1440 ________. The Psychic World of California. Garden City,
* N.Y.: Doubleday, 1972. x, 323p. Bibliog. $7.95 LC 75-178834

The first chapter of this book is an historical survey of occultism in California. The rest of the work is geographically arranged, with sections on north, central, and southern California. Entries discuss the psychic's start, philosophy of life, his gift, and views on the occult revival. Entries cover, for example, Patricia Diegel of Sacramento; Nola Van Valer of Mt. Shasta; Monterey's Harold G. Plume (healer); Carroll Righter (astrology); Ernesto Montgomery (who says he predicted the Tate murders, and also predicted California would be destroyed by earthquake and fire on April 22, 1972). The work has an index by city.

1441 St. Elmo Nauman, ed. Exorcism Through the Ages. New
* York: Philosophical Library, 1974. 311p. Illus. $10 LC 74-80275

This collection includes the following works: "Erichtho," by Wade Baskin (about a witch of ancient Greece); "The Devils of Loudun," by Wade Baskin; "Exorcism and the Bible," by Charles Buck; "Exorcism and the Catholic Faith," by Patrick J. Toner; "Exorcism and the Greek Orthodox Church," by George C. Papademetriou; "Exorcisms or Prayers of Deliverance for General Use," by St. John Chrysostom, A.D. 344-407 (as found in the Orthodox Book of Divine Offices); "Exorcism and Satanism in Medieval Germany," by St. Elmo Nauman; "Concepts of Possession and Obsession," by Gougenot des Mousseaux; "Concept of the 'Dybbuk' (Demon) in Hebrew Literature and Thought," by Leo Lieberman; "Legend of the Golem," by Leo Lieberman; "Genesis and Extinction of Possession," by T.K. Oesterreich; "Demonic Encounters," by Caesar of Heisterbach; "Elizabeth Knapp of Groton," by Samuel Willard (on the possession of Knapp in 1671); "The Nuns of Aix-en-Provence," by Wade Baskin; "Exorcism," by Rossell Hope Robbins (reprint of the "Exorcism" article in Robbins's Encyclopedia of Witchcraft and Demonology); "History of the Devil," by Albert Reville; and "Glimpses of Exorcism in Religion," by Edmund B. Keller. This collection pacts a great deal of information into a small book.

1442 St. George, E.A. Casebook of a Working Occultist. London: Rigel Press, 1972. xi, 148p. £1.80 ISBN 0-85528-005-0

1443 St. Leger-Gordon, Ruth Eleanor. Witchcraft and Folklore of

Dartmoor. 2nd rev. ed. Wakefield, England: E. P. Publishing, 1973 (also, New York: Bell Pub. Co., 1973; previous ed., London: Hale, 1965). 196p. Illus. Bibliog. Index £2.50 ISBN 0-85409-868-2

This collection of folktales includes the following: pixies, wish hounds, black dogs and other livestock, Lady Howard and Cranmere Binjy, Childe the Hunter, stories about stones, old river gods, haunts, the White Bird of Oxenham, the Legend of Chaw Gully, hairy hands, witchcraft, magic circles, evil eye, warts and ringworm, cures, charms, and adder (snake) lore. The author states that many of the old, discredited tales have modern postscripts that seem to link together past and present. To her, this linking is often more interesting than some of the tales themselves. The stories fall into three categories: those not originating in the area, being variations of a type found in many other places; standard ghost stories into which local color and people have been inserted; and stories originating in the district.

1444 Sakai, Sueko. Mysteries of Life. New York: Vantage, 1972. 89p. $3.75 ISBN 0-533-00558-2

1445 Sakoian, Frances, and Louis S. Acker. Astrologer's Handbook. New York: Harper and Row, 1973 (also, London: P. Davies, 1974). xiv, 461p. Illus. $9.95 LC 78-160647

This work claims to be a professional's guide to horoscope interpretation. It not only covers sun signs, but also studies important planetary aspects--trines, squares, oppositions, conjunctions, and sextiles. It lists every planet, in every sign, in every house, in every major aspect to every other planet.

1446 Salisbury, Frank B. Utah UFO Display: A Biologist's Report. With data from the files of Joseph Junior Hicks. Foreword by J. Allen Hynek. Old Greenwich, Conn.: Devin-Adair Co., 1974. xxiv, 286p. Illus. Plates Bibliog. Index $7.95 LC 74-75389 ISBN 0-8159-7000-5
*

The author, a biologist at Utah State University, studies 80 sightings in Uintah Basin of northeastern Utah. Actually, the hard work was done by junior high science teacher Joseph Hicks, who collected newspaper clippings from 1956 to 1972. Salisbury believes the UFO's come from outer space, and feels that many of the reports have not been adequately explained. He also discusses 12 other sightings outside Utah. Appendices give a table of the 80 sightings, and astronomical data on the moon and planets.

1447 Salter, W. H. Zoar; or, The Evidence of Psychical Research Concerning Survival. New York: Arno Press, 1975 (orig. pub., London, 1961). (Perspectives in Psychical Research) $13 LC 75-7399 ISBN 0-405-07048-9

For many years, the author was honorary secretary of the

Society for Psychical Research in London. This work includes discussion of cross correspondence work, with which he was personally involved. Also covered is evidence for survival and problems in the field.

1448 Saltmarsh, Herbert Francis, 1881- . Evidence of Personal Survival from Cross Correspondences. New York: Arno Press, 1975 (orig. pub., London: G. Bell, 1938). Bibliog. (Perspectives in Psychical Research) $9 LC 75-7400 ISBN 0-405-07049-7

This book discusses cross correspondences in general, emphasizing work done by a group associated with the Society for Psychical Research in the early 1900's, involving several languages and complex metaphors. There is an explanation of the logic of the research plan that was set up. The author gives arguments pro and con on evidence these cases give for survival.

1449 _______. Foreknowledge. New York: Arno Press, 1975 (orig. pub., London: G. Bell, 1938, in Psychical Experiences series). (Perspectives in Psychical Research) $8 LC 75-7401 ISBN 0-405-06990-1

This book discusses evidence for precognition, especially as revealed by spontaneous cases. Saltmarsh set up criteria for evidential cases, then selected 281 reports from the (British) Society for Psychical Research's files that met the criteria. He discusses parts of these cases in this volume. He also discusses logical alternatives to precognition as seen in the cases, mentions theories on precognition advanced by other thinkers, and gives the implications of precognition.

1450 Samarin, William J. The Tongues of Men and Angels. New York: Macmillan, 1972. 277p. $7.95

The author, an anthropologist and linguist at the University of Toronto, concentrates on comparing glossolalia to other forms of language. He sees it as similar to baby talk and pig Latin. It is not an actual language. He does not see any paranormal element in it, unless it were xenoglossy (speaking in actual languages totally unknown to the speaker). However, he disagrees with those who take a purely psychological view of the phenomenon.

1451 Sampson, Charles. Ghosts of the Broads. Norwich, England: Jarrold and Sons, 1973 (orig. pub., London: Yachtsman Pub. Co., 1931). 174p. Illus. Maps Bibliog.

1452 Sampson, Walter Harold. The Zodiac: A Life Epitome, Being a Comparison of the Zodiacal Elements with Life-principles, Cosmic, Anthropologic, and Psychologic. New York: ASI Publishers, 1975 (orig. pub., London: Blackfriar Press, 1928). $12.50 LC 75-25826 ISBN 0-88231-019-4

1453 Samuels, Mike. Seeing with the Mind's Eye: The History, Techniques and Uses of Visualization. New York: Bookworks/Random, 1975. 331p. Illus. (some color) Index $9.95 ISBN 0-394-73113-1

The author, a medical doctor, discusses the creation of images inside the mind in dreams and thought. He covers parapsychology, ESP, psychology, medicine, creativity, archetypes, healing, and religious experience. Samuels and his wife Nancy feel that the process can be used to increase creativity and spirituality, as well as improve the health of the physical body. The work contains many illustrations.

1454 ________, and Hal Bennett. Spirit Guides: Access to Secret Worlds. Illus. by Linda Bennett. New York: Random House, 1974. 55p. Illus. $5.95 LC 73-20584 ISBN 0-394-49194-7

This book basically tells "how to use body relaxation, together with a directed program of fantasy techniques for developing your inner voice." Chapters discuss imagination, going inside, how it feels, visions, dreams, using spirit guides for health, tools for access to inner worlds, the many faces of spirit guides, talking with them, listening for answers, demons (imagined or real), and the inner world of harmony.

1455 *** Sanderson, Ivan Terrance, d. 1973. Investigating the Unexplained: A Compendium of Disquieting Mysteries of the Natural World. Englewood Cliffs, N.J.: Prentice-Hall, 1972. 339p. Illus. Photos. Maps Bibliog. Index $7.95

This work is a major new contribution to occult literature. The author was a famous naturalist and scientist, and founder of the Society for the Investigation of the Unexplained. He discusses unusual events and things: sea monsters, giant bats, rainmakers, spontaneous human combustion, strange objects falling from the sky ("falls"), origin of the zodiac as map symbols for early travelers, Baghdad batteries of 200 B.C. drawn in Egyptian temples, and looking very similar to today's, a 1000-year-old model of a modern bulldozer found in southern Panama, and a 1000-year-old airplane model found in Colombia. Appendix A gives a four-page list of spontaneous combustion cases from 1600 to 1969. Appendix B is a 23-page partial list of falls, 1948-1968 (he calls them "fafrotskies"). Sanderson's theories are controversial and sometimes far-fetched, but become important due to his excellent reputation.

1456 * ________. Invisible Residents; A Disquisition upon Certain Matters Maritime, and the Possibility of Intelligent Life Under the Waters of This Earth. London: Tandem, 1974 (orig. pub., New York: World Publishing, 1970). 254p. Illus. Includes bibliog. refs. Index £0.40 pa. ISBN 0-426-13880-5

The author discusses reports of historical and recent sightings of lighted objects that have risen from, descended into, and maneuvered over reservoirs, rivers, lakes, and oceans. He mentions ancient art objects that may represent air-to-water craft, wheels of light in the Indian Ocean, time-speed warps experienced by flyers, and the disappearances of air and water craft and passengers in certain "lozenge-shaped" areas around the world. He theorizes that there may be an underwater civilization that has been here a very long time, either evolving here or coming from outer space. Sanderson covers OINT's (other intelligences), UAO's (unidentified aquatic objects), and UFO's. He includes a four-page appendix listing the sightings from 1948 to 1968. The first part of the book portrays the problems Sanderson had in dealing with the U. S. Navy bureaucracy.

1457 Sandys, Cynthia Hill. Letters from Our Daughters. London: College of Psychic Studies, 1972. 2 vols. 27p. ea. (College of Psychic Studies. Papers nos. 1 & 2) £0. 25 pa. ea.

These two volumes discuss messages received through the mediumship of Sandys by Rosamond Lehmann from her late daughter Sally Kavanagh, and by Sandys from her late daughter-in-law Patricia Hill.

1458 Sargant, William. The Mind Possessed: A Physiology of
*** Possession, Mysticism and Faith Healing. Philadelphia: J. B. Lippincott Co. , 1974 (orig. pub. , London: Heinemann, 1973). xii, 212p. Illus. Bibliog. Index $7. 95 LC 73-15627 ISBN 0-397-01011-7

This work is a major new contribution to occult literature. The author is an expert on altered states of consciousness, a British psychiatrist, and, for many years, director of Psychological Medicine at St. Thomas Hospital, London. Part 1 studies the effects of stress, and reviews the literature of hysteria and hypnosis as it relates to possession. Sargant includes discussions of sex, magic, and drugs. Part 2 describes the author's experiences among members of primitive and modern religious cults throughout different parts of the world. He discusses African experiences, tribal Sudan, expelling spirits, experiences in Zambia, Zar possession, casting out devils, Nigeria and Dahomey, Macumba in Brazil, experiences in Trinidad, experiences in Jamaica and Barbados, voodoo in Haiti, and revivals in the U. S. He feels that stress, hysteria, hypnosis, and any strong emotional experience all contain common elements that can lead to hypersuggestibility. He theorizes that possession can sometimes cause beneficial changes in behavior. He states that an obsessive personality is more resistant to possession than a normal one. The work contains photographs of possessed individuals in tribal rituals and revival meetings.

1459 Sato San. Juneeshee: An Oriental System of Fortune Telling; The Legend of the Twelve Spirits, and the Year of the Animals. Los Angeles: Sato San Press, 1971. 60p. Illus. $2. 95 pa.

1460 Saunders, Michael William. Destiny Mars. Postscript by Duncan Lunan. Caterham, England: Downs Books, 1975. 65p. plus separately issued supplement. Illus. Charts Index £1 pa. ISBN 0-9502260-2-5

1461 Saunders, Nicholas, and Georganne Downes. Self Exploration: A Guide to Groups Involved. London: the author, 1975. 128p. Illus. Map Index (Extracted from "Alternative England and Wales" with minor revisions) £0.85 pa. ISBN 0-9501628-7-6

1462 Saxon, Kurt. Keeping Score on Our Modern Prophets. Eureka, Calif.: Atlan Formularies, 1974. 136p. $2 pa.

The main part of this book is a "box score" on various prophets. At times, he is very strong in his ridicule and scorn. His strong feelings sometimes lead him to call a prophecy a miss when it is really only vague. He strongly dislikes Jeane Dixon. He has written to the FBI and the White House to try and verify Dixon's claimed visits to Franklin D. Roosevelt. He reports Dixon's claim that the gypsy Madame Pierce discovered her, and gives pictures of Pierce.

1463 Scharfstein, Ben-Ami. Mystical Experience. Indianapolis: Bobbs-Merrill, 1973 (also, Oxford, England: Blackwell, 1973). 195p. Bibliog. Index $6.95 LC 72-14014

The author studies Eastern and Western mysticism in a rational manner, investigating types, methods and claims. He calls mysticism "a name for our infinite appetites." The work is really a series of essays. The first is on superlative states of mysticism, and presents three modes of mystical experience--passionate, passionless, or a combination of the two. Then come two chapters of East-West comparisons, one comparing Al-Ghazali with William James, the other contrasting Freud with Patanjali. The last chapter is on the 11 quintessences of the mystic state: sameness, separation, uniqueness, familiar, strangeness, depletion, aggression, conscience, mirror-reversal, humor, and reality. Discussions also consider mysticism in art and science, psychoanalytic theories of Freud, healthy and psychotic mysticism, Einstein, Sartre, Van Gogh, Rodin, and Aristotle.

1464 Schmeidler, Gertrude Raffel, and Robert A. McConnell. ESP and Personality Patterns. Introd. by Gardner Murphy. Westport, Conn.: Greenwood Press, 1973 (orig. pub., New Haven, Conn.: Yale University Press, 1958). xiii, 136p. Bibliog. $9 LC 73-9258

This work discusses the sheep-goat experiments carried out for nine years, presenting major findings and work done by eight other researchers to test the hypothesis (six confirm the ESP success results). Also, there are chapters on the Rorschach test, cerebral concussion patients, and frustration in relation to ESP. The authors discuss the question of how many people have ESP, and suggest avenues for possible future research.

1465 Schmidt, Steven. Astrology 14: Your New Sun Sign. New York: Pyramid Books, 1971 (orig. pub., Indianapolis: Bobbs-Merrill, 1970). 160p. Illus. Bibliog. $.95 pa.

The author radically changes the dates traditionally given to each sign, and introduces two constellations into the zodiac--Cetus the whale (between Aries and Taurus) and Ophiuchus, the dragon slayer (between Scorpio and Sagittarius). This makes a total zodiac of 14 signs. Schmidt's research is based on the procession of the equinoxes.

1466 ________. Astrology 14 Horoscope; How to Cast and Interpret It. Illus. by Mitzi Schmidt. Indianapolis: Bobbs-Merrill, 1974. xviii, 394p. Illus. Bibliog. $12.95 LC 73-1743 ISBN 0-672-51647-0

1467 Schoenholtz, Larry. New Directions in the I Ching. Secaucus, N.J.: University Books, 1975. 157p. $7.95

This book discusses not just divination, but mathematics, geometry, and higher philosophy in the I Ching.

1468 Scholem, Gershom. The Kabbalah. New York: Quadrangle,
* 1974 (dist. by Harper). 492p. Illus. Bibliog. Index (New York Times Library of Jewish Knowledge) $9.95 LC 73-77035 ISBN 0-8129-0352-8

This work is made up of articles the author originally did for the Encyclopedia Judaica and rewrote for this volume. The author, from Hebrew University, is one of the great scholars of the century on Jewish mysticism. The first part discusses history and basic doctrines. The second part covers eschatology, demonology, providence, and other such concepts with an essay on each. The third part gives biographies of minor figures of Jewish mysticism, such as Azriel of Gerona, Moses de Leon, Isaac Luria, and Nathan of Gaza. The material is a bit difficult to read in spots.

1469 Schrenck von Notzing, Albert Philibert Franz, Freiherr von, 1862- . The Phenomena of Materialisation. New York: Arno Press, 1975 (orig. pub., London: K. Paul, Trench, Trubner, 1920). (Perspectives in Psychical Research) (Translation of "Materialisationsphänomene." Includes not only orig. vol. but also more important parts of supplementary work, "Kampf um die Materialisations-Phänomene," 1914, as well as certain subsidiary material accumulated since these researches were first made public) $34 LC 75-7408 ISBN 0-405-06995-2

This book discusses methods used with physical mediums to produce materializations, and to exclude frauds. The author includes many photos of supposed ectoplasmic manifestations; this was an area of frequent fraud. The work is interesting, since physical mediums have largely faded to the background in spiritualism.

1470 Schul, Bill, and Ed Pettit. The Secret Power of Pyramids. Greenwich, Conn.: Fawcett Publications, 1975. 223p. Illus. Plates Bibliog. Index $1.75 pa. LC 75-323049

This book discusses the ancient and modern miracles of the pyramid (an introduction), the Great Pyramid, mysterious energy fields, pyramids and plant power, effects on liquids, effects on solids, healing powers, rejuvenation, voice of the pyramid (pyramid acting as a sound resonator and producing beneficial vibrations), the pyramid and altered states of consciousness, esoteric geometry and energy grids, home experiments the reader can try, and the pyramid as microcosm of the universe.

1471 Schulman, Arnold. Baba. New York: Viking Press, 1971. 192p. Illus. Photos. $5.95 LC 77-151261

Baba can supposedly materialize objects (including valuable jewels and sacred ash), heal the sick, tell the future, read minds, and see visions. The author (a playwright and screenwriter who for instance did Goodbye, Columbus) traveled to Puttaparthi, India, and spent time with Baba in his ashram. When the author had a high fever, a vision of Baba appeared to him at night. The next day, the author was well. Sathya Baba was born in 1926, and began materializing objects at age eight or nine. At puberty, he went into trances, finally announcing he was Sai Baba, the incarnation of a Baba who had died in 1918. On October 20, 1940, a bright halo supposedly appeared about him. He announced he was the incarnation of the god Vishnu, and must leave his family and do his work. The book discusses Baba's various claimed powers.

1472 Schwarz, Berthold Eric, 1924- . Parent-Child Telepathy: Five Hundred and Five Possible Episodes in a Family; A Study of the Telepathy of Everyday Life. New York: Garrett Pubns., 1971. xii, 241p. Includes bibliog. refs. $7.95 LC 70-155052 ISBN 0-912326-24-7

The author is father of a family, a New Jersey psychiatrist, and student of parapsychology. He records cases of telepathy occurring in his family over eight years. As of November, 1970, 1,520 such events were recorded. However, he only reports here on 505 of them, occurring 1957-1965. Some of the cases may appear to the reader to be simple coincidence.

1473 Scot, Reginald, 1538?-1599. The Discoverie of Witchcraft.
* Ed. and introd. by Brinsley Nicholson. Totowa, N.J.: Rowman and Littlefield, 1973 (also, New York: Dover Pubns., 1972, a reprint of 1886 ed.; orig. pub., 1584). xlvii, xxxviii, 589p. Illus. $16 LC 72-79958

The author's thesis is that witchcraft and magic should be rejected by all reasonable men. Most of the stories given are taken from the Inquisition, about the supposed powers of witches (pacts with the devil, causing storms, succubi and incubi, how witches flew). He also gives the opinions of medical men and transcripts of interviews with those convicted of witchcraft. Later, he studies those black arts that were not purely imaginary. These he felt depended for success on tricks and skill. The sources Scot used are excellent, many being rare or forgotten texts. There are many detailed formulas for magic and the raising of spirits, as well as stories, anecdotes (some very humorous), and tales of spells and potions. The frequent margin references list the sources Scot used. In spite of Scot's thesis, the work is, in effect, an encyclopedia of 16th-century occultism.

1474 Scott-Elliot, W. The Story of Atlantis, and the Lost Lemuria. London: Theosophical Pub. House; Wheaton, Ill.: Theosophical Press, 1972 ("The Lost Lemuria" orig. pub., 1962). xi, 108p. Illus. LC 72-212453

1475 Seabrook, William. Witchcraft--Its Power in the World Today. London: White Lion Publishers, 1972 (orig. pub., New York: Harcourt, Brace, 1940). 351p. Illus. £2.50 ISBN 0-85617-782-2

Formerly a disbeliever, the author went to conviction that witchcraft is deadly, dangerous, and real. The book discusses the witch and her doll, the vampire and the werewolf, white magic, and the supernormal. The writing is very anecdotal and case-study orientated.

1476 Seear [pseud.?], and Jammal [pseud.?]. How to Run a Home Circle [by Seear; and] Steps upon the Road of Progress [by Jammal]. Leeds, England: Fellowship of the Star, 1971. 12p. £0.15 pa. ISBN 0-9502010-0-6

Two pamphlets bound together.

1477 Seed. New York: Crown, 1973. $6.39 pa.

This is basically an audiovisual source book. There are many photos, which are perforated so that they may be ripped apart and used for I Ching cards, Tarot cards, or anything. There is also a section with many quotes printed in large green letters. The book is essentially trying to take Eastern religion and Westernize, particularly Americanize, it. The resource was originally conceived as a box of cards whose purpose was to break down perceptual habits, and present the user with many combinations of visual images contrary to conventional thought patterns. The box idea was too expensive, causing the publisher to issue the concept in book form.

1478 Self Discovery: Know Your Inner Self Through Analysis of

Your Fortune, Handwriting and Dreams. London: Marshall Cavendish, 1975. 64, 64, 64p. Illus. (chiefly color) (Golden Hands Books) £2.99 ISBN 0-85685-107-8

This book actually contains three works in one: "How to Tell Your Fortune," by Peter Brent (1975); "How to Analyze Your Handwriting," by Manfred Lowengard (1975); and "How to Read Your Dreams," by Frances Kennett.

1479 * Seligmann, Kurt, 1900-1962. Magic, Supernaturalism, and Religion. New York: Pantheon Books, 1973 (also, London: Allen Lane, 1971; St. Albans, England: Paladin, 1975; orig. pub. as "Mirror of Magic," New York: Pantheon Books, 1948; also, as "History of Magic," New York: Pantheon, 1948). 342p. Illus. Bibliog. Index $12 LC 74-39720

This classic work attempts to show the great influence magic has had on Western civilization. It conveys a great deal of information in its 79 short articles, and actually serves as a reference book. Its use might have been enhanced with an A-to-Z arrangement, but instead uses that of a textbook survey, roughly chronological. These topics are discussed: Mesopotamia (divinatory arts, Tower of Babel), Persia (Zoroaster), the Hebrews, Egypt (Sphinx, mortuary magic, journey to the underworld, Isis); Greece (dreams, omens, oracles, mysteries of Eleusis); Gnosticism, the Roman Empire, alchemy (Hermes Trismegistus, hermetic enigmas, famous transmutations), the Middle Ages (Arabs, Albertus Magnus, Roger Bacon), the Devil, witchcraft, diabolic rites, portraits (Pico Della Mirandola, Trithemius, Agrippa von Nettesheim, Theophrastus Paracelsus, Nostradamus, Guillaume Postel, Giambattista della Porta), Cabala, the magical arts (astrology, chiromancy, Tarot), reformers (Rosicrucians, secret societies, the classical ideal), and the 18th century (vampires, Masonic lodges, the Count of Saint-Germain). The author concludes that "magic upheld the great civilizations of the ancient world.... It freed man from fears, endowed him with a feeling of his power to control the world, sharpened his capacity to imagine, and kept alive his dreams of higher achievement."

1480 Sergeant, Philip Walsingham. Historic British Ghosts. Wakefield, England: EP Publishing, 1974 (orig. pub., London: Hutchinson, 1936). 288p. Illus. Plates Index £3.25 ISBN 0-85409-996-4

1481 ________. Witches and Warlocks. Introd. by Arthur Machen. Wakefield, England: EP Publishing, 1974 (also, New York: B. Blom, 1972; orig. pub., London: Hutchinson, 1936). 290p. Illus. Plates Index £4 ISBN 0-7158-1028-6

1482 Sevarg, Luba. Do-It-Yourself Witchcraft Guide. New York: Award, 1971. 153p. Illus. $.75 pa.

1483 Seymour, St. John Drelincourt. Irish Witchcraft and Demonology. Wakefield, England: EP Publishing, 1972 (orig. pub., Dublin: Hodges, Figgis; London: Humphrey Milford, 1913). vii, 256p. Index £3 ISBN 0-85409-927-1

This book discusses the following topics: Dame Alice Kyteler, sorceress of Kilkenny in A.D. 1324; James I and the Irish Prophetess; witchcraft trials in the 16th century; possession; apparitions of murdered people at Portadown; visions; Florence Newton, the witch of Youghal; a haunted house in Dublin; an Irish witch in America, Mrs. Goodwin, hanged for witchcraft in Boston in 1688; Dr. Francis Hutchinson; Mary Butters, the Carnmoney witch; and a witch in 1911.

1484 Shah, Idries. Oriental Magic. St. Albans, England: Paladin, 1973 (orig. pub., London: Rider, 1956). xv, 238p. Illus. Bibliog. Index £0.50 pa. ISBN 0-586-08145-3

This work contains chapters on Jewish magic, Solomon, Babylonia, Egypt, India, Ju-Ju, Fakirs, Persians, Arabs, China, Tibet, Japan, legends of the sorcerers, calling the spirits, Iranian magic, Brahmins, Indian alchemy today, love magic, and spells. It is mainly historical, but also presents information which the author has collected on his trips to the Orient.

1485 Sharma, I.C. Cayce, Karma and Reincarnation. Introd. by Hugh Lynn Cayce. New York: Harper and Row, 1975. 192p. $3.95 pa.

The author is chairman of the Philosophy Department at the University of Udaipur, and a visiting professor in the U.S. He discusses Edgar Cayce, man's search for eternal truth, the nature of the soul, reincarnation, karma, and the Avataravada (nature and purpose of Divine Descent).

1486 Sharpe, Charles Kirkpatrick. An Historical Account of the Belief in Witchcraft in Scotland. Foreword by Raymond Lamont Brown. Wakefield, England: S.R. Publishers, 1972 (orig. pub., London: Hamilton, Adams, 1884). x, 268p. Bibliog. Index £3.15 ISBN 0-85409-747-3

1487 * Shealy, C. Norman, and Arthur S. Freese. Occult Medicine Can Save Your Life; A Modern Doctor Looks at Unconventional Healing. New York: Dial Press, 1975. 256p. $7.95

The author is a neurosurgeon and an expert on pain. He does his work at the Pain Rehabilitation Center in LaCrosse, Wis. He feels that faith healing can be used as a supplement to, but not a substitute for, regular medical treatment. He covers Olga Worrall, LeShan, Katherine Kuhlman, Anton Mesmer, Mary Baker Eddy, and Lourdes. He got results himself from Chicago healer Henry Rucker and his associates of the Psychic Research Foundation, whom he used to diagnose illnesses. The choice of title for this book is a poor one, in view of the serious discussion it contains. Added to his other credentials is that of the author's invention of a "dorsal column stimulator" which places electrodes over the spinal column to shut off acute pain.

1488 Shealy, Julian B., 1902- . The Heavens Speak in Astrology Marvelous Things. Jericho, N.Y.: Exposition, 1974. 207p. $7.50 ISBN 0-682-47827-X

1489 Sheargold, Richard K. Hints on Receiving the Voice Phenomenon. Maidenhead, England: Richard K. Sheargold; Gerrards Cross, England, 1973 (dist. by Smythe). 12p.

1490 Sheed, Francis Joseph, 1897- , comp. Soundings in Satanism. Introd. by John Updike. New York: Sheed and
* Ward, 1972. xii, 236p. (Includes 11 articles from an earlier volume pub. as "Satan," 1951) $6.95 LC 72-6688

This is a fine collection on the subject. Chapters cover the Devils of Loudun, dream demons, pseudo-possession, exorcism, demons in the gospels, the devil in Dante, the devil in art, the devil in Gogol and Dostoevsky, the Black Mass in Paris, and Balzac, Bosch, and Brueghel the Elder. The author has interesting thoughts on the topic. He theorizes that Satan actually loathes the human victims who are with him in hell, and goes after them only because they represent victories over God, who for some strange reason continues to love man.

1491 Sheridan, Jo. What Your Hands Reveal. London: Mayflower, 1972 (orig. pub., London: Arco, 1963). 143p. Illus. £0.35 pa. ISBN 0-583-12144-6

1492 _______. The Wheel of Fortune, Which Never Fails to Answer Your Questions. New York: Popular Library, 1972 (c1971). 221p. Illus. $.75 pa.

1493 Sherman, Harold Morrow, 1898- . Harold Sherman ESP Manual. Little Rock, Ark.: Human Development Associates, 1972. 88p. $7.50 pa.

1494 _______. You Live After Death. Rev. ed. Greenwich, Conn.: Fawcett, 1972 (orig. pub., 1949). 175p. $.75 pa.

This book discusses these topics: is there a personal God? do you possess a soul? evidences of a spirit body, the afterlife, a way of communication, how to prepare for the future life, and how to face death.

1495 _______. Your Power to Heal. New York: Harper and Row, 1972. 246p. $6.95

This work is mostly on healers Olga and the late Ambrose Worrall, plus the author's own personal experiences. There are short discussions on Oral Roberts, Kathryn Kuhlman, and Tony Agpaoa of the Philippines. Other topics covered include psychic photography, spiritualism, and precognition. Sherman feels the key is to visualize the diseased part as healthy. He has some interesting insights on the healer-patient relationship. Sherman and Worrall find belief in reincarnation harmful, saying that it is almost impossible to heal anyone who believes in it. The book includes brief passages to be used as aids to meditation and self-healing.

1496 ________, and Hubert Wilkins, 1888- . Thoughts Through
* Space. Greenwich, Conn.: Fawcett, 1973 (authors' names in reverse order in earlier ed., London: Muller, 1971; orig. ed.--also in reverse order--pub. as "Thoughts Through Space; A Remarkable Adventure in the Realm of Mind," Hollywood, Calif.: House-Warren, 1951). 352p. $.95 pa.

This work discusses the Sherman-Wilkins experiment in excellent fashion. It began when a group of Russian fliers crashed on the Alaskan side of the North Pole. The Russian government commissioned Sir Hubert Wilkins, famed arctic explorer, to find and rescue them. Just before leaving, he met Harold Sherman, telepathist. They agreed to try mind contact during the rescue mission. This contact was kept up three nights a week for six months over a 3,400-mile distance. This work recreates the adventure, and also tells the reader how to develop telepathy through such chapters as: "The Part Emotions Play," "How Thoughts Are Received," "Keeping One's Mental and Physical Balance," and "Practical Aspects of Telepathy."

1497 Shiels, Tony "Doc." Entertaining with ESP. Newton Abbey, England: David and Charles, 1974. 109p. £2.95

Shields says that ESP is a fact of life, and mentalism, which tries to imitate it, sometimes produces the real thing by accident. He also discusses party games to use with ESP. Most of the book, however, is on pseudo-telepathy, miracle memory work, mediums and ghost tricks, and precognition and teleportation acts to do on stage.

1498 Shirley, Ralph. The Mystery of the Human Double: A Case for Astral Projection. London: Olympia Press, 1972 (orig. pub., London: Rider, 1938). 189p. £0.50 pa. ISBN 0-7004-1281-6

1499 Showers, Paul. Fortune Telling for Fun. Hollywood, Calif.: Newcastle Pub. Co., 1971. xii, 349p. Illus. $2.95 pa. ISBN 0-87877-007-0

This survey discusses divinatory techniques, including palmistry, astrology, numerology, and cartomancy.

1500 Shumaker, Wayne. Occult Sciences in the Renaissance; A
*** Study in Intellectual Patterns. Berkeley: Univ. of California Press, 1972. xxi, 284p. Illus. Bibliog. $15 LC 70-153552 ISBN 0-520-02021-9

This work is a major new contribution to occult literature. It consists of five sections: astrology, white magic, witchcraft, alchemy, and the ideas of Hermes Trismegistus. The author is a literature scholar, who is worried that young people have revolted strongly against reason and science. He finished his study much more appreciative of our modern culture and especially of the physical sciences. His study showed that Renaissance scholars had an unquestioned faith in the wisdom of the ancients, which supposedly came from supernatural sources. He gives many long citations from Renaissance sources in Latin and Greek. Shumaker writes a strongly worded refutation of astrology, on the usual grounds that the signs have moved.

1501 Shuttlewood, Arthur. UFO's, Key to the New Age. London: Regency Press, 1971. 216p. Illus. £1.80 ISBN 0-7212-0120-2

1502 ________. Warminster Mystery. London: Tandem, 1973 (orig. pub., London: Spearman, 1967). 205p. Illus. £0.35 pa. ISBN 0-426-12730-7

1503 Sibley, Mulford Quickert. Life After Death? Minneapolis: Dillon Press, 1975. 159p. Bibliog. Index (Psychic Explorations) $6.95 LC 75-26949 ISBN 0-87518-079-5

This juvenile book discusses ghosts, apparitions, dreams, out-of-the-body experiences, materializations, automatic writing mediums, direct voice and mental mediums, cross-correspondences, and Raudive's taped voices. The appendix has quotes on survival from Plato, St. John, St. Paul, Charles Drayton Thomas, and others.

1504 Sidgwick, Eleanor Mildred Balfour, 1845-1936, ed. Phantasms of the Living: Cases of Telepathy Printed in the "Journal of the [British] Society for Psychical Research" During Thirty-Five Years. New York: Arno Press, 1975 (orig. pub., New Hyde Park, N.Y.: University Books, 1962). (Perspectives in Psychical Research) (Includes book, "Phantasms of the Living," by Edmund Gurney, Frederick W. H. Myers, and Frank Podmore, abridged and ed. by Sidgwick; book orig. pub., 1886, and reprinted, Delmar, N.Y.: Scholar's Facsimile and Reprints, 1972) $56 LC 75-7403 ISBN 0-405-06991-X

This book has two parts: an abridgment by Sidgwick of the two-volume classic by Gurney, Myers and Podmore, originally published in 1886, plus two of her own journal articles on telepathy.

1505 Silberer, Herbert, 1882-1922. The Hidden Symbolism of Alchemy and the Occult Arts. Trans. by Smith Ely Jelliffe. New York: Dover, 1971 (also, Magnolia, Mass.: Peter Smith, 1972; orig. pub. as "Problems of Mysticism and Its Symbolism," 1917). v, 451p. Bibliog. (Translation of "Probleme der Mystik und ihrer Symbolik") $3 pa. LC 74-176356 ISBN 0-486-20972-5

The author stumbled on a document called "Geheime Figuren der Rosenkreutzer," which was a symbolic narrative in terms of alchemy. The narrator pursues a quest, meeting symbolic persons, animals, and localities, which ends in the death of a bride and groom and their rebirth as a king and queen with magical powers. This began Silberer's study of hidden symbolism among alchemists and occultists, such as Hermes Trismegistus, Michael Meier, Paracelsus, Boheme, the Rosicrucians and Christian Rosenkreutz, and the Masons. To these, he added his own psychoanalytic study of alchemy. He concludes that both mystical and psychoanalytic approaches to alchemy stem from introversion, a withdrawal from the world.

1506 Simester, Peter. Astrological Book of Time. London: Croom Helm, 1975. 411p. Illus. £3.50 ISBN 0-85664-297-5

1507 Simmonds, L. Welsh Witchcraft--Ofergoeliaeth Cymru. St. Ives, England: James Pike, 1975. 32p. Illus. Map (Viewing Wales Series) £0.30 ISBN 0-85932-139-8

1508 Simmonite, William Joseph. W. J. Simmonite's the Complete Arcana of Astral Philosophy; or, The Celestial Philosopher. Hollywood, Calif.: Newcastle Pub. Co., 1974 (orig. pub., London: W. Foulsham, 1890). 420p. $3.95 pa. LC 74-6220 ISBN 0-87877-026-7

This book gives a step-by-step discussion of the basics of astrology, with questions and problems to help readers teach themselves.

1509 Simmons, Marc. Witchcraft in the Southwest; Spanish and Indian Supernaturalism on the Rio Grande. Flagstaff, Ariz.: Northland Press, 1974. xiii, 184p. Illus. Bibliog. $8.50 LC 74-76085 ISBN 0-87358-125-3

The author, an historian, says that witchcraft among the Navajos of the Rio Grande Valley is still very active. He discusses their fear of the dead, herbalism, and healing.

1510 Simone [pseud.]. Eyeless Sight: A How to Manual. Stanton, Calif., 1974. 48p. Paperback

The author discusses her studies at the True Sight Church, and gives exercises based on those created by William A. Foos.

1511 Simons, Geoffrey Leslie. Witchcraft World. New York: Barnes and Noble Books, 1974 (also, London: Abelard-Schuman, 1974). 231p. Bibliog. $10.75 LC 74-186958 ISBN 0-06-496265-2

This book discusses the sources of witchcraft, including studies of mythology and anthropology.

1512/4 Sinclair, John Rollo. The Other Universe. London: Rider, 1973. 128p. Bibliog. £2.35 ISBN 0-09-113890-6

1515 Sinistrari, Luigi Maria, 1622-1701. Demoniality. Trans. with introd. and notes by Montague Summers. New York: B. Blom, 1972 (orig. pub., 1927). xliii, 127p. Includes bibliog. refs. $12.75 LC 72-83751

1516 Sinnett, Alfred Percy. Esoteric Buddhism. New ed. London: Theosophical Pub. House, 1972 (orig. pub., London: Trubner, 1883). xxiv, 181p. £2 ISBN 0-7229-5230-9

This early disciple of Blavatsky's discusses a system of theology predating Gautama.

1517 Skinner, J. Ralston. Key to the Hebrew-Egyptian Mystery in the Source of Measures. Savage, Minn.: Wizard's Bookshelf, 1972 (orig. pub., 1875). 394p. $15

The author discusses hidden meanings in the mathematics of the Great Pyramid and Solomon's Temple.

1518 Skultans, Vieda. Intimacy and Ritual; A Study of Spiritual-
* ism, Mediums and Groups. London, Boston: Routledge and K. Paul, 1974. vii, 106p. Bibliog. Index $8.25 LC 73-87318 ISBN 0-7100-7760-2

The author, a social anthropologist and lecturer at the Department of Mental Health at the University of Bristol, worked in the field for three years as a participant in spiritualism groups in southern Wales, and studied the personalities of 400 other participants. The sittings usually take place under semi-darkness in circles, under the guidance of a medium. She discusses colors of the aura. Also mentioned is the Bishop of Exeter's 1972 report on exorcism, which the author feels shows the importance Anglican and Roman Catholic clergy place on spiritualism. Skultans concludes that spiritualism is therapeutic to participants, and usually is used to cure "sociosomatic" illnesses (illnesses due to difficulties in social roles, especially the role of women).

1519 Sladek, John. The New Apocrypha: A Guide to Strange Sci-
* ence and Occult Beliefs. New York: Stein and Day, 1974 (orig. pub., London: Hart-Davis MacGibbon, 1973). 376p. Illus. Bibliog. Index $8.95 LC 74-79418 ISBN 0-8128-1712-5

This book debunks Atlantis, Mu, perpetual motion machines, Root-Races, Dragon Roads, lost tribes, flying saucers, divine astronauts, healers, astrologers, mediums, occultists, and prophets (such as Mother Shipton). He also covers minor groups (Koreshanity, vegotherapy, and promoters of trepanation), individuals (the Nun of Kent), and concepts (sanpaku). At times, the author seems unfair in his demands for total verification.

1520 * Smith, Richard Furnald. Prelude to Science; An Exploration of Magic and Divination. New York: Scribner's, 1975. 129p. Illus. Includes bibliog. refs. Index $8.95 LC 75-17959 ISBN 0-684-14370-4

This book grew out of a course the author taught at the University of California Extension at Berkeley (he is a biochemist in his regular role). The author discusses astrology, the I Ching, Kabbalah, magic, oracles, the Tarot, and divination. These are precursors to modern science that still exist in some form today. His major section (50 pages long) is on astrology. He discusses the zodiac, the usual definitions, and synchronicity. He does not agree with the usual views of astrologers. He claims that the zodiac has shifted over the centuries, and says it was invented not by the Babylonians, but by Macedonian Greeks living in Alexandria, and was codified in the A.D. 100's by Claudius Ptolemy. He states that astrology was nothing secret, but merely a tool to tell farmers when to plant. He says that astrology is unreliable in prophecy. The work is a good introductory text, light in tone and well documented.

1521 Smith, Robert E. Doc Anderson: We Live Many Lives. New York: Paperback Library, 1971. $.75 pa.

1522 Smith, Robert Tighe, 1926- . Cult and Occult. Minneapolis, Minn.: Winston Press, 1973. 142p. $2.95 pa. LC 72-93590

The author is a newspaper reporter, which may explain why his writing is direct, clear, and factual. The work treats ESP, exorcism, messages from the dead, dreams that foretell the future, and other occult topics of current interest.

1523 Smith, Susy. The Book of James. New York: Putnam, 1974. 212p. Bibliog. $6.95 LC 74-79667 ISBN 0-399-11392-4

This book was received through automatic typewriting, supposedly sent through Smith by William James. Topics discussed include the following: God, the closed mind and where it gets you, how to use thoughts effectively, the sad state of the earthbound, sex between the spheres, angels and gods are real, babies, reincarnation, exorcism, mediums are a necessity, children are to be cherished, animals are forever, suicide is not recommended, out-of-the-body travel, questions and answers. James denies reincarnation, and believes in the immortality of each unique individual. The entire book was dictated to Smith in one week in February 1967. James's narration is often interrupted by short "commentary" sections by Smith, usually discussing supportive books, cases, and research. The book makes for very interesting reading.

1524 ________. Confessions of a Psychic. New York: Macmillan, 1971 (also, London: Collier-Macmillan, 1971). 315p. Illus. $7.95 LC 78-156993

This is an autobiography of Smith's life of research into spiritualism and parapsychology. She started with automatic writing, and believes she has reached her dead mother and possibly William James. Then, she began going to seances. After years, she concluded she was mediumistic. Her work includes a discussion of frauds.

1525 ________. ESP and Hypnosis. New York: Macmillan, 1973. x, 253p. Bibliog. $5.95 LC 72-90990

This is a layman's survey attempting to show the close connection between parapsychology and hypnosis throughout history. The author discusses the history and practice of hypnosis, the psychic use of hypnosis, Mesmer, the researches of Osty, Pagenstecher, and Rýzl, Wolf Messing, and Olof Jonsson. The book omits some modern laboratory evidence on the subject.

1526 ________. ESP and You. New York: Macfadden, 1972. 160p. Bibliog. $.95 pa.

1527 ________. Ghosts Around the House. New York: Pocket Books, 1971 (orig. pub., New York: World Pub. Co., 1970). 222p. Illus. Photos. Bibliog. $.95 pa.

Designed as a sequel to Prominent American Ghosts (1967), this book is an undocumented account of famous haunted houses. Places discussed are the Audubon House of Key West, Fla. (haunted by bird painter John James Audubon, whom this book claims may have been the lost dauphin, Louis XVII), Mackenzie House in Toronto (haunted by ancestors of Canadian Prime Minister William Mackenzie King), the Dakota Apartments in New York City (inspiration for the setting of Rosemary's Baby), the San Marcos Bridge in Texas, a haunted house inhabited by a doctor in Gulfport, Miss., the governor's mansion in Delaware (the home is named "Woodburn"), a Miami poltergeist (continued from her Prominent American Ghosts discussion), San Antonio's Brooks House (a house of tragedy), Careby Hall in Fork Union, Va., a haunted house in Murray, Utah; Fort Sam Houston's Service Club # 2 and its ghost Harvey; Machias, Me., where the author went to investigate by trance state a ghost case of 1799, only to be, with a companion, haunted by a view of a woman who murdered her three children that very day, a haunted house in Miami, the Bell Witch case of Tennessee (a continuation of the discussion in Prominent American Ghosts), and the "Bradmar" house in Denver.

1528 ________. How to Develop Your ESP. New York: Putnam,
* 1972. 284p. Bibliog. $6.95 LC 72-79516 ISBN 0-399-11025-9

This book contains 28 chapters, discussing the alpha state, Patience Worth, slate writing, healing, meditation, trances, seances, out-of-the-body experiences, psychic games, and mediumistic children. There is a chapter on pitfalls to avoid, such as sensitive persons being where tragedies have occurred, taking psychedelic drugs as preventing proper development of ESP, experiences of people who have done things without adequate preparation. The suggestions on developing ESP are mostly general.

1529 ________. Life Is Forever; Evidence for Survival After
* Death. New York: Putnam, 1974. 256p. Bibliog. $7.95
LC 73-78598 ISBN 0-399-11201-4

This excellent survey conveys a great deal of information, discussing these topics: out-of-the-body experiences, visions of the other world seen during astral travel; ghosts, apparitions, and phantoms; ghosts with a goal, deathbed visions, deathbed visions of relatives on the other side when the dying are not aware they have died (the "Peak in Darien" phenomenon), guardian angels, spirit music (discussing Rosemary Brown, Shirley Waklyn, Jesse Shepard, and many psychic episodes of famous musicians), cross correspondences, Ouija boards, automatic writing, the study of automatic writing by handwriting experts, possession, unknown communicants who suddenly interrupt sitters and mediums at seances while they are working on other spirits they do know (called "drop-ins"), experiences of amateurs, professional mediums, book tests where the deceased spirit refers to a passage in a book that means nothing to the medium, but a great deal to the sitter, direct voice mediums, and the tape recorded "voice phenomena" of Jurgenson and Raudive. The work is a fine study that would be excellent as a high school or college introductory text. There is no real discussion of experimental laboratory work, but coverage of the issues present in the survival field is reward enough.

1530 ________. The Power of the Mind. Radnor, Pa.: Chilton
* Book Co., 1975. 294p. Includes bibliog. refs. Index
$7.50 LC 75-15652 ISBN 0-8019-6137-8

Smith, the author of 24 other books on the psychic field, discusses these topics in the book's 29 chapters: mediums, experiments, object-moving, psychic surgery, gambling, healing, fire-immunity, stigmata, hypnosis, biofeedback, dowsing, Kirlian and psychic photography, ghosts, voices on tape, Geller, prayer, ghosts, and poltergeists (especially the Miami case, which she was instrumental in investigating). The author has done a great deal of research in gathering her information, and, as usual, includes many anecdotal cases reported to her by readers of previous books.

1531 ________. She Spoke to the Dead. New York: Award Books,
1972. 156p. Bibliog. $.75 pa.

This is a biography of English trance medium Gladys Osborne Leonard.

1532 ________. Susy Smith's Supernatural World. New York: Macfadden, 1971. 192p. $.95 pa.

This is a collection of her magazine articles, most of them published in Fate. They concern the following topics: the search for a talking cat, violent ghosts of Amherst, Nova Scotia, appearances of the "Bhagwan" (chief village spirit of Nepal), Gladys Leonard, a prophetic dream of Walter Franklin Prince in 1917, Alfred Russel Wallace and his spiritualism investigations (Wallace came up with idea of natural selection at same time Darwin did), an out-of-the-body experience in England in the early 1900's, Katie Fox, a clairvoyant's finding a missing girl in Enfield, N. H., in 1898; the Yorkshire Museum ghost (in York, England), Frederick W. H. Myers--the scholar who was ahead of his time; a crystal ball vision in 1892, the spirit of ballet dancer Vaslav Nijinsky speaking through a medium two days after he died in 1950; Sundar Singh--man of miracles and visions--who taught Christianity to the Tibetans; a poltergeist in Newark, N. J., 1961; Charles Drayton Thomas--pioneer psychic researcher; "Mr. ESP"--Ronald Edwin Cockersell--who confessed at one time to being a fraudulent medium; a climber experiencing the "sleep of the snows" in the Alps (death by freezing), which caused him to leave his body and psychically see events; reincarnation; and psychic Renee Dubonnet and a haunted portrait.

1533 ________. Today's Witches. New York: Award Books, 1971 (c1970). 186p. Bibliog. $.95 pa.

The author says that there are 60,000 witches in the U. S. today. She discusses the U. S., Mexico, Canada, Haiti, and Great Britain. Smith covers these topics, among others: Lewis van Dercar of Miami, founder and head of the Royal Order of Warlocks and Witches; black witches Billie and Rohn, charms, spells, potions, herbs, and incantations.

1534 Smith, Warren. Strange Hexes, Fully Documented. New York: Popular Library, 1971. $.60 pa.

1535 Smyth, Frank. Modern Witchcraft; The Fascinating Story of the Rebirth of Paganism and Magic. New York: Harper and Row, 1973 (orig. pub., 1970). 125p. Illus. Photos. (Man, Myth and Magic Original) $1.25 pa.

This book discusses the following topics: witchcraft today, witchcraft in Britain, Gerald Gardner, early witchcraft, persecution, witchcraft in America, witch healing, "King of the Witches" Alex Sanders, and other chief witches of the modern era.

1536 Snow, Edward Rowe. Supernatural Mysteries and Other Tales: New England to the Bermuda Triangle. New York: Dodd, Mead, 1974. xiv, 268p. Illus. Plates Includes bibliog. refs. Index $7.95 LC 74-25671 ISBN 0-396-07013-2

This is a collection of true stories from the 17th to the 20th centuries, only partly on the supernatural. Topics discussed include the following: witchcraft, the rescue at sea of the crew of the submarine Squalus, salvage and pirates, sea monsters (the last sighted in Massachusetts Bay in 1970), Boston Tea Party, and search for a lost H-bomb at Palomares, Spain.

1537 Snyder, Al. Satan's Sauna and the Devil's Triangle. Redondo Beach, Calif.: Snyder Institute of Research, 1974. $3.95 pa.

The author discusses the two "agonic lines" on earth (where the compass points to zero), and says that one of these lines passes right through the Devil's Triangle. He covers the phenomena of the Triangle--"white water," the spinning of reliable compasses, sudden radio failure, and the stopping of motor electrical systems.

1538 Soal, Samuel George, and F. Bateman. Modern Experiments in Telepathy. Introd. by G. E. Hutchinson. Westport, Conn.: Greenwood Press, 1975 (orig. pub., New Haven, Conn.: Yale University Press, 1954). Bibliog. Index $22 LC 75-18403 ISBN 0-8371-8336-7

1539 Solomon, Shirl. How to Really Know Yourself Through Your Handwriting. London: Coronet, 1975 (also, New York: Taplinger Pub. Co., 1974; orig. pub., Newton Abbot, England: David and Charles, 1974). 189p. Illus. Bibliog. Index £0.75 pa. ISBN 0-340-20184-3

Written by a Florida graphologist, this book is a combination of graphology and psychology. She says there are four motivational symbols that can be traced in handwriting. She discusses self-help by the elimination of undesirable traits in handwriting, and the formation of new, more useful habits.

1540 Somerlott, Robert. "Here, Mr. Splitfoot"; An Informal Exploration into Modern Occultism. New York: Viking, 1971. 311p. Illus. Bibliog. $7.50 LC 75-132185 ISBN 0-670 36876-8

The title is taken from the phrase Katie Fox called out in March, 1848, at age 12. The work studies mediums of the past. Somerlott says that, while frauds exist, many mediums seem to be genuine. He also discusses poltergeists, crystal gazing, precognition, divination, parapsychology and ESP, John Dee, Jeane Dixon, and Edgar Cayce.

1541 Song, Kim Hai. Chinese Zodiac Book; The Secret Astrology of the Orient. Hollywood, Calif.: Biplane Productions, 1973. 61p. Illus. $3 LC 72-93014

1542 Sontheil, Ursula, 1512-1561. Life and Prophecies of Ursula

Sontheil. New ed. [orig. written under pseud., Mother Shipton]. Knaresborough, England: Dropping Well Estate, 1975 (previous ed., 1967). 31p. Illus. £0.15 pa. ISBN 0-9505152-0-5

1543 Spangler, David. Festivals in the New Age. Ed. by Roy McVicar. Calligraphy by Anne Zontine. Forres, Scotland: Findhorn Foundation, 1975. 92p. Illus. £1.25 pa. ISBN 0-905249-12-7

1544 _______. The Laws of Manifestation. Forres, Scotland: Findhorn Foundation, 1975. 90p. Illus. £1 pa. ISBN 0-905249-16-X

1545 _______. Manifestation. Forres, Scotland: Findhorn Foundation, 1975. 15p. ISBN 0-905249-02-X

1546 _______. New Age Vision. Forres, Scotland: Findhorn Foundation, 1974 (orig. pub., 1970). 109p. ISBN 0-905249-14-3

1547 _______. Revelation: The Birth of a New Age. Forres, Scotland: Findhorn Foundation, 1974 (orig. pub., 1971). £1.50 pa. ISBN 0-905249-09-7

1548 _______. Synergy. Forres, Scotland: Findhorn Foundation, 1975. 16p. ISBN 0-905249-01-1

1549 _______. The Vision of Findhorn in World Transformation. Forres, Scotland: Findhorn Foundation, 1971. 8p. ISBN 0-905249-06-2

1550 _______; R. Ogilvie Crombie; and Dorothy Maclean. Man, Nature and the New Age. Forres, Scotland: Findhorn Foundation, 1974. 57p. £0.60 pa. ISBN 0-905249-00-3

1551 Spano, Ann. Lib and Let Lib for Women in Orbit. London: Schlesinger, 1975. 82p. Illus. £1 pa. ISBN 0-85093-249-1

This book is a guide to astrology written specifically for women.

1552 Spence, Lewis, 1874-1955. Arcane Secrets and Occult Lore of Mexico and Mayan Central America; A Treasury of Magic, Astrology, Witchcraft, Demonology, and Symbolism. Detroit: B. Ethridge Books, 1973 (orig. pub. as "Magic and Mysteries of Mexico; or, The Arcane Secrets and Occult Lore of the Ancient Mexicans and Mayas," London: Rider, 1930). 288p. Illus. $12.50 LC 73-78358

This work includes chapters on Mexican magic, witchcraft, astrology, demonology and the mystical books of the Aztecs, as well as on the religion, magic, and mysticism of the Maya people of Yucatan. In effect, the book, a result of 35 years of research in archaeology and ethnology, supplements Sir James Frazer's The Golden Bough.

1553 ______. Atlantis in America. Detroit: Singing Tree Press,
* 1972 (orig. pub., 1925). 213p. Illus. Plates $11 LC 76-167196

This classic work is a fine discussion of the tradition of Atlantis. Chapters discuss Atlantis and Antillia, Cro-Magnons of America, Quetzalcoatl the Atlantean, Atlantis in American tradition, Atlantean tradition in American religion, evidence from the mummy, evidence from witchcraft, ethnological evidence, evidence from art and architecture, folk-memories of an Atlantic continent, the analogy of Lemuria, the Sargasso Sea, and Atlantis in America. A chronological table is included. In the preface, the author states, "The time has for ever departed when a farrago of myths collected at random, interspersed with wild etymologies and witnessed by dogmatic assertions passed for a justification of the Atlantean hypothesis."

1554 Spencer, John Wallace, 1934- . No Earthly Explanation: Mankind, a Space Experiment. Springfield, Mass.: Phillips Pub. Co., 1974 (also, Toronto, London: Bantam, 1975). 240p. Illus. Plates $5.95 LC 75-302450

This book on the UFO phenomenon discusses these topics: 1973, year of the UFO resurrection (going month-by-month and state-by-state for 1973, and giving brief information on the history of UFO sightings in the U.S.), where did we aliens originate? (discusses important dates in evolution of life on earth, and also dating techniques), early civilizations and how they may have had instructors, strange structures possibly left behind by visitors (Stonehenge, Easter Island), the Bermuda Triangle (based on his highly successful book Limbo of the Lost), astronomy and the planets, and extraterrestrial life. The author believes we are a combination of earth and outer space beings. Through interbreeding, our evolutionary time table was deliberately pushed ahead for experimental purposes. He feels we are part of a gigantic galactic experiment. The book has bold-faced headings every page or so, to make it attractive. More authors should use this technique.

1555 Spiritual Community Guide, 1975-1976. San Rafael, Calif.: Spiritual Community Publications, 1974. 192p. $3.50 pa.

Part 1 of this work gives one-page discussions on spiritual leaders (Bubba Free John, Mehr Baba). Part 2 discusses about 100 spiritual groups. Part 3 discusses spiritual centers, communities, bookstores, foodstores, and restaurants in the U.S. and Canada. A glossary lists publishers, publications, and films.

1556 Spraggett, Allen. The Case for Immortality. New York:
*

New American Library, 1974 (dist. by W. W. Norton). 154p. Index $6.95 LC 73-91365

The author, who has written six previous books on parapsychology, discusses cases of those medically dead who lived to tell of their experiences. He also discusses communication with the dead through mediums such as Arthur Ford as being good proof for survival. The second part of the book discusses how we carry memories of our past lives with us. He says that some modern researchers have proven that reincarnation is a fact, and that this is the ultimate test of immortality. He also mentions Kirlian photography, Olga Worrall, Upton Sinclair, Swedenborg, Jung, and the Chaffin Will case. The author says that mediums' messages may come not by spirit possession, but from mediums' communicating telepathically with the deceased and the sitter. Also, he sees the next world as neither material nor immaterial, but between them, and formed by our mental states. He feels a "theta" body may pass on after the death of the physical body; this body is only slightly material.

1557 ________. Probing the Unexplained. New York: World,
* 1971. 256p. $6.95 LC 79-160481

This book discusses these topics: Atlantis, Cayce's predictions, Sydney Omarr (Hollywood astrologer), ESP and plants, the power of suggestion, healing (especially the Rev. Fuller's dental healing), Ian Stevenson (reincarnation), precognition, Irene Hughes, and Rosemary Brown and spirit music. Most of the chapters are built around interviews with astrologers, clairvoyants, faith healers, and parapsychologists.

1558 ________, and William V. Rauscher. Arthur Ford, the Man
*** Who Talked with the Dead. New York: New American Library, 1973 (dist. by W. W. Norton). xii, 301p. Illus. Bibliog. Index $7.95 LC 72-9600

This work is a major new contribution to occult literature. Spraggett is the psychic investigator who brought together Ford and Bishop Pike on network television. Rauscher is the person who was given custody of Ford's papers. The authors give details of how Ford broke the Houdini coded message and supposedly proved to Beatrice Houdini that her husband had communicated from the other side. Also, there is a new evaluation of the Pike affair. The authors discovered that Ford had thoroughly researched some incidents concerning Pike in advance of the televised seance. Ford kept files on thousands of people going back for years. The book discusses Ford's alcoholism and possible frauds. The authors did not see all of Ford's papers, for a secretary, on Ford's instructions, destroyed an unknown amount of them. However, the authors did have a large amount of letters, diaries, and scrapbooks for source material. Spraggett and Rauscher conclude that Ford was genuine, but often fell back on tricks if he felt it necessary.

1559 Sri Ram, Nilakanta. The Nature of Our Seeking. London: Theosophical Pub. House, 1973. 282p. £1

The author, president for over twenty years of the world-wide Theosophical Society, died April 8, 1973. These are articles he selected for inclusion himself, from papers contributed to The Theosophist during the period 1966 to 1972. They summarize theosophical thought over the last 60 years. Blavatsky is quoted often, and Sri Ram was close to Annie Besant for many years. Chapters include "The True Nature of Man," "Receptivity to Truth," "The Dynamics of Brotherhood," "The Lotus Symbol," "The Other India," and "To Be a Lamp unto Oneself."

1560 ______. Thoughts for Aspirants, Compiled from Notes and Writings of N. Sri Ram. 4th enl. ed. Wheaton, Ill., London: Theosophical Pub. House, 1972 (previous ed., 2nd enl. ed., 1956). vi, 145p. (Quest Book) $1 pa. ISBN 0-8356-0431-4

1561 Sri Rama Murthi, Govindu. Hindu Horary Astrology. Jyotishacharya, India: Srikakulam, 1974. 100p. $4.50

1562 Stacey, David. Fire in My Bones: Prophets and Prophecy, Then and Now. Illus. by Laszlo Acs. Oxford, England: Religious Education Press, 1975. 127p. Illus. Bibliog. (Man and Religion series, part 4, the Old Testament Scene) £1 pa. ISBN 0-08-018054-X

1563 Staff, V. S. Remembered on Waking; Concerning Psychic and Spiritual Dreams and Theories of Dreaming. Crowborough, England: V. S. Staff, 1975. 148p. £1.25

This work was published under the sponsorship of the Mysticism Committee of the Churches' Fellowship of Psychical and Spiritual Studies in Great Britain. It discusses various dream types, using sources from biblical times to the present day dreams of members of the Fellowship. Discussions include the modern study of dreams, books on dreaming, and psychic dreams in literature (such as those of De Quincey, and the discovery of the lost 13 cantos of the Divine Comedy by Dante's son, who had seen the location revealed by his dead father in a dream). The author feels evidence will grow that other intelligences besides ours are at work in our dreams.

1564 Stancil, Carol F. The Bermuda Triangle; An Annotated Bibliography. Los Angeles: University of California at Los Angeles College Library Reference Section, 1973. 10p.

This bibliography lists 44 sources under the following headings: books (16 citations), periodical articles (8), newspaper articles (9), correspondence (7), and government publications (4).

1565 Stanford, Ray. Speak, Shining Stranger; An Outstanding Collection of Psychic Readings. Austin: Association for the Understanding of Man, 1975. xvi, 239p. (Selections from author's psychic readings, orig. appearing in first 7 issues of "Journal of the Association for the Understanding of Man") $8.95 LC 75-22512 ISBN 0-915908-02-6

These readings by the author discuss meditation, prayer, healing, dreams, psychedelic drugs, and other psychic areas.

1566 * Starkey, Marion Lena. A Tall Man from Boston. Illus. by Charles Mikolaycak. New York: Crown Publishers, 1975. 46p. Illus. $5.95 LC 75-9970 ISBN 0-517-52187-3

This juvenile book emphasizes the role of John Alden (son of John and Priscilla) in the Salem witchcraft controversy. Fortune-teller and slave Tituba stirred up trouble by telling the fortunes of minister Samuel Parris's daughter and his niece, Abigail. The two girls then supposedly began to act hysterically because of guilt feelings about having fooled with fortune-telling and the occult. Tituba compounded the hysteria by claiming she had seen in visions a mysterious tall man from Boston. She claimed this man was John Alden, and caused so much ill feeling against him that he had to flee to Plymouth until the Salem trials were over. The book contains some interesting pencil drawings. It is recommended for grades 4-6.

1567 * ________. Visionary Girls: Witchcraft in Salem Village. Boston: Little, Brown, 1973. ix, 176p. $5.50 LC 72-13940

This is a good juvenile treatment of the subject of Salem Village in 1692. It views the social, political, and psychological make-up of the town, and tells the story of the madness that struck it. The story is told in a fictionalized form to make it more dramatic, especially in regard to courtroom scenes, the girls' personalities, and the terror in the village. A brief author's note tells which details are officially recorded and which are fictitious. The story of Ann Putnam is central to her narration. Starkey is the author of The Devil in Massachusetts (1949). This latest work, Visionary Girls, is recommended for grades 7-10.

1568 Staves, Marjorie. One Sense Ahead: The Story of a Clairvoyant. London: Barker, 1971. 157p. £2 ISBN 0-213-99350-3

1569 Stearn, Jess. Adventures into the Psychic. London: Muller, 1971 (also, New York: New American Library, 1971; orig. pub., New York: Coward-McCann, 1969). 259p. Index £2.20 ISBN 0-584-10001-9

This book presents additional material on Edgar Cayce besides what the author already wrote in his The Sleeping Prophet. Stearn also discusses these persons: Helen Stalls, who predicted

Jackie's marriage to Onassis, an Air Force major assigned to find persons with telepathy for possible use in communicating with other planets, and Peter Hurkos, and gives an astrological analysis of Mia and Frank's love affair. These are some predictions given in the book: the second coming of Christ, Nixon's return of the country to the path of morality (well, nobody's perfect), and the sinking into the sea of Manhattan and Los Angeles after 1978.

1570 _______. The Miracle Workers: America's Psychic Consultants. Garden City, N. Y.: Doubleday, 1972. 280p. $6.95 LC 73-175399

Most of this book is on California psychics Doug Johnson and Bill Corrado. Other California psychics are also covered, as well as a few in New York and Maryland. Chapters discuss Corrado and his predictions, Johnson and his healing, help in business life, healing work, fate and free will, researchers' use of psychics in experiments, connections between spiritualism and psychic work, public service and predictions (performances, prediction of historical events, political predictions), and reincarnation.

1571 _______. The Power of Alpha-thinking: Miracle of the Mind. Introd. by John Balog. New York: Morrow, 1975. Index $8.95 LC 75-23120 ISBN 0-688-02978-7

Stearn took a four-day course in California on reaching one's various levels--a Mind Dynamics program. He says anyone can diagnose illnesses in strangers, lose weight without dieting, cure psychosomatic illnesses. The method works on the same levels as biofeedback and love of Jesus.

1572 _______. Prophet in His Own Country; The Story of the Young Edgar Cayce. New York: Morrow, 1974 (also, Boston: G. K. Hall, 1974, large print ed.). 301p. Illus. $7.95 LC 74-700 ISBN 0-688-00258-7

This book discusses Cayce's early years, 1904-1910, covering his psychic abilities, learning how to use them, finding his wife, and getting the attention of the medical profession through Dr. Wesley Ketchum. The story is told largely in dialogue. The work closes with an epilogue by Hugh Lynn Cayce.

1573 _______. Search for a Soul: Taylor Caldwell's Psychic
* Lives. Garden City, N. Y.: Doubleday, 1973 (also, New York: Fawcett World, 1974). 309p.

This book discusses the 37 previous incarnations of Taylor Caldwell using the usual breezy style of Stearn with its numerous dialogs. Among the incarnations covered are in Atlantis, the Incas, China before Genghis Khan, Victorian England, George Eliot's maid, a nun in the Renaissance Florence of Savanarola--which helped explain a recurring nightmare, Mary Magdalen's mother, and Helena--a doctor in Periclean Greece. Caldwell's past lives were searched with the use of hypnosis; seances and astrological readings were supplemental aids. She said she had spent the time between incarnations living on the planet Melina. At the end, Stearn is skeptical concerning reincarnation, although he admits that at the time of the recorded sessions, he was made a believer. Caldwell also remains skeptical, although it was she herself who proposed the regression sessions. In the epilogue to this book, she says she initiated the experiment to prove once and for all that "reincarnation is the desire of trivial people who have never suffered." Now, after the sessions, she still feels that reincarnation, if it does exist, is a gigantic curse, and not a hope. No god could be so cruel to keep inflicting life on humanity when so few of us enjoy it.

1574 _______. Time for Astrology. New York: New American Library, 1972 (orig. pub., New York: Coward-McCann, 1971). 435p. Illus. $1.50 pa.

This book surveys astrology in 16 chapters, discussing these topics: history, planets, health, sickness, birth control, love, marriage, homosexuality, work, nations, investing, gambling, Nixon, to everything there is a time and a season, Zipporah Dobyns and his attempts to integrate psychology and astrology, and Eugen Jonas and his astrological birth control work in Czechoslovakia. There are many cases, charts of famous people, and anecdotes from the author's travels. He says that after the year 2007 life will improve. There is an appendix showing how to set up a birth chart, and giving ephemeris tables. There is also a glossary.

1575 Stearne, John. The Confirmation and Discovery of Witchcraft. Exeter, England: "The Rota" at University of Exeter, 1973 (orig. pub., London: William Wilson, 1648). 61p. Bibliog. £1.50 pa. ISBN 0-9501950-3-0

1576 Steiger, Brad, ed. Aquarian Revelations. New York: Dell, 1971. $.75 pa.

1577 _______. Atlantis Rising. New York: Dell, 1973. 220p. Bibliog. $.95 pa.

This is a collection of legend and supposition on Atlantis: whether it sank in historical times, is still in existence under the water, inside the earth, or in outer space. The author also mentions the Incas, Edgar Cayce theories, and the Shaver mystery hoax in this wide-ranging work. Some of the topics discussed include Edgar Cayce's vision of a dying nation, prehistoric scientists and hero-gods, angels and demons from other dimensions, and the question, does the rising of Atlantis herald Armageddon? Some readers may find the evidence used and discussions a bit weak at times.

1578 _______. Haunted Lovers. New York: Dell, 1971. 214p. $.75 pa.

1579 ________. Irene Hughes on Psychic Safari. New York: Paperback Library, 1972. 174p. $.95 pa.

The author had Hughes visit nine haunted places to get her impressions. Steiger discusses the psychological atmospheres of the places as well, and the reactions of witnesses to the disturbances. Some of Hughes's impressions could have been due to information picked up telepathically from witnesses.

1580 ________. Medicine Power. Garden City, N.Y.: Doubleday, 1974. 226p. $6.95

The author discusses herbs, altered states of consciousness, drug use, healing, clairvoyance, precognition, prophecy, and the control of weather through the rain dance. Included are interviews with medicine men (Sun Bear of the Chippewa, Rolling Thunder of the Shoshone, and others). Steiger sees the Indian religion not as primitive superstition, but as a system of deep spiritual thought. Most of the book is in question-and-answer format.

1581 ________. Medicine Talk; A Guide to Walking in Balance and Surviving on the Earth Mother. Garden City, N.Y.: Doubleday, 1975. 320p. Illus. $7.95 LC 74-1774

This book discusses Seneca, communing with nature, the symbolism of four, seven worlds, the pathway of peace, the Sioux, the legend of White Buffalo, the Bear Tribe, practicing medicine power, and the coming great purification and the emerging new age. There are three main interviews, with Twylah Nitsch (Seneca), Dallas Chief Eagle (Sioux), and Sun Bear (Chippewa). Many Indian legends and songs are given.

1582 ________. Mysteries of Time and Space. Special ar-
* chaeological research by Ron Calais. Englewood Cliffs, N.J.: Prentice-Hall, 1974. 240p. Illus. $7.95 LC 74-7288 ISBN 0-13-609040-0

This very thought-provoking book includes these chapters: death of a world before our own, Atlantis, physical evidence of visitors from other realities, our cosmic tutors--their mysterious manuscripts and some of their pupils, UFO's, men dressed in black, the rules of physics are there to be broken, you are what you think; winning at the reality game. Steiger feels that, based on all the evidence of early technological achievements equal to or beyond our own, there are four alternate explanations: intelligent, tool-making man is millions of years older than previously thought; an as-yet unknown physical law has distributed artifacts of the present throughout time; other space-time levels may occasionally intrude on our reality to teach us new techniques of manipulating our mental and physical world; our opponents in the reality game are trying to confuse and frighten us. This is a good work, mixing theory with quotes from Hesse, Lilly, and others. Steiger has written over 40 books on the occult. He says that solutions to many problems lie not in the gods, but in ourselves. The best otherworld leaders can do is give us a fragment or two of the answer.

1583 ________. Psychic City: Chicago. Garden City, N.Y.: Doubleday, 1975. 160p. $6.95

This book includes discussions on the Illinois Center for Parapsychological Research, the Institute for Human Sciences (led by Norman Don), the Ancient Astronaut Society, Irene Hughes, Olof Jonsson, and Fate magazine. Most of the book is a hodgepodge written in very light style. The appendix, compiled by J. Gordon Melton, is a directory of Chicago's psychic and occult organizations and leaders.

1584 ________. The Psychic Feats of Olof Jonsson. Introd. by David Techter. Englewood Cliffs, N.J.: Prentice-Hall, 1971 (also, New York: Popular Library, 1973). x, 221p. $6.95 LC 75-157724 ISBN 0-13-732016-7

The author discusses the phenomena Olof Jonsson has experienced: out-of-the-body trips, radiesthesia, healing, materializing and dematerializing objects and ghosts, levitating objects, solving mysteries clairvoyantly through retrocognition, and card tricks. Jonsson was the man who experimented telepathically with astronaut Mitchell of Apollo 14. The book also discusses the author's personal theories on how psychic mechanisms work (Jonsson sees meditation as basic to his method), and states that anybody can develop ESP and prediction abilities.

1585 ________. Revelation, the Divine Fire. Englewood Cliffs,
*** N.J.: Prentice-Hall, 1973. 309p. Bibliog. Index $7.95 LC 72-10243 ISBN 0-13-779322-7

This work is a major new contribution to occult literature. The interesting book is an investigation of people who have claimed to be in spiritual communication with a higher intelligence. Chapters discuss the following topics: revelation as not respectable in the eyes of traditional church leaders; new gospels (basically on two new religions--the Church of Essential Science in Scottsdale, Ariz., led by Kingdon Brown, and the Church of the New Birth in Washington, D.C., led by John Paul Gibson), the new self (on sudden personality changes after being struck by revelation), blinding light from heaven, tuning in on primal sounds and cosmic vibrations (on music), anima and aumakua--contacting the high self (on repressed female attributes, called anima by Jung, and on a godlike level of consciousness above our usual one, called aumakua by the Hawaiians); angels, guides, and other messengers; communications from outer space, prophecy and the coming spiritual age, the ageless message of revelation which is remarkably consistent in the world's great religions; Judgment Day; ego-traps, possession, and parasites of the soul; testing the divine fire, and the questions should we seek the revelatory experience and if so, how? Most cases discussed concern messages from outer space aliens and spirit guides speaking through humans. There is a great deal of theoretical discussion, along with numerous quotes from interviews with occult devotees and religious experts. This work shows Steiger in his usual form--excellent writing, a bit too gullible, but very creative. Unlike his other works, this one shows fine organization and more scholarship.

1586 ________. Strange Disappearances. New York: Lancer Books, 1972. 159p. $.95 pa.

1587 ________. Strange Encounters with Ghosts. New York: Popular Library, 1972. 144p. $.75 pa.

This book discusses ghosts, poltergeists and hauntings, and is based mostly on newspaper accounts.

1588 ________, and Louis Gittner, comps. Words from the Source. Englewood Cliffs, N.J.: Prentice-Hall, 1975. 176p. Index $6.95 LC 74-25571 ISBN 0-13-963348-0

Louis Gittner lives in an old inn on Orcas Island off the coast of Washington. When he goes into a trance state, the Source answers questions through him on: God, psychic abilities, the soul, reincarnation, Jesus, health, sex, diet, astral travel, cosmic colors, auras, meditation, and Lemuria. Gittner's mission is to establish Light Centers to charge our spiritual batteries. He has already set up a Louis Foundation.

1589 ________, and Warren Smith. Satan's Assassins. New York: Lancer, 1971. 206p. $1.25 pa.

1590 ________, and Ron Warmeth. Tarot. New York: Award Books, 1973 (orig. pub., 1969). 168p. $.95 pa.

The first part of this book is a discussion of Ron Warmeth and his Tarot-reading abilities, which he began developing in 1965. Most of this section is a collection of case histories of people for whom Warmeth has read, including "Murph the Surf." Part 2 is a historical survey of divination, discussing the Bible, the Oracle of Delphi, astrology in Rome, Christianity, alchemy, Tarot card origins, Tarot and the Cabala, Tarot in the Renaissance, and Tarot mysteries. The rest of the book is a study of each card in the Tarot deck.

1591 ________, and John White, eds. and comps. Other Worlds,
* Other Universes: Playing the Reality Game. Garden City, N.Y.: Doubleday, 1975. xvii, 245p. Bibliog. $7.95 LC 74-18835 ISBN 0-385-06448-9

This work is a collection of 16 articles from philosophy, religion, and psychology. The aim of the book is to expand the reader's consciousness, enlarge his concept of the universe, deepen his understanding of his intimate relationship to it, and teach him how to play the reality game. The book presents these thinkers: Timothy Leary discussing his plan to launch into space a replica of earth in the year 2000, Luis Navia, David Spangler, D. Scott Rogo on out-of-the-body experiences, Ivan Sanderson, Gerald Massey on prehistoric Egypt and Africa, Trevor James Constable--who theorizes that UFO's may be living organisms, Jacques Vallee on UFO occupants and their possible relationship to fairies, angels, and demons; Yogi Ramacharaka, a 19th-century spiritual leader, on the nature of astral existence; and Arthur Ford on communications from the deceased Frederic Myers. There is also a section from Steiner's Knowledge of the Higher Worlds and Its Attainment. The book concludes with a science fiction classic, Olaf Stapledon's Star Maker.

1592 _______, and Loring G. Williams. Minds Through Space and Time. New York: Award, 1971. $.75 pa.

1593 Steinbach, Marten. Medical Palmistry: Health and Character in the Hand. Secaucus, N.J.: University Books, 1975. 192p. Illus. Bibliog. $8.95 LC 74-31756 ISBN 0-8216-0222-5

This book is basically on palmistry, with not that much on medical aspects. The author includes quotes from Fromm and Jung, among others. He includes rules for determining character and personality.

1594 Steiner, Rudolf, 1861-1925. Anthroposophical Leading Thoughts; Anthroposophy as a Path of Knowledge: The Michael Mystery. Trans. by George and Mary Adams. London: Rudolf Steiner Press, 1973. 220p. (Translation of vol., in complete ed. of Steiner's works, entitled "Anthroposophische Leitsätze. Der Erkenntnisweg der Anthroposophie; Das Michael Mysterium") £2.25 ISBN 0-85440-268-3

1595 _______. Between Death and Rebirth: Ten Lectures Given in Berlin between 5th November 1912 and 1st April 1913. Trans. by E.H. Goddard and D.S. Osmond. London: Rudolf Steiner Press, 1975. 186p. (Translated from shorthand reports unrevised by lecturer; in complete ed. of works of Steiner, vol. containing orig. German texts is entitled "Leben zwischen dem Tode und der neuen Geburt in Verhaltnis zu den kosmischen Tätschen") £3.25 ISBN 0-85440-287-X

1596 _______. The Bridge over the River. Spring Valley, N.Y.: Anthroposophic Press, 1974. 99p. $2.95 pa.

This book discusses communications received through automatic writing from a German soldier killed in World War II.

1597 _______. Building Stones for an Understanding of the Mystery of Golgotha: Lectures Given in Berlin from 27th March to 8th May, 1917. 2nd ed. Trans. by A. H. Parker, with two additional lectures. London: Rudolf Steiner Press, 1972 (previous ed., London: H. Collison, 1930). 240p. (This ed. trans. from shorthand reports unrevised by lecturer; orig. text is included as 2nd section in vol. of complete ed. of works of Steiner, entitled "Bausteine zu einer Erkenntnis des Mysteriums von Golgotha") £2.15 ISBN 0-85440-263-2

1598 ______. The Dead Are with Us: Lecture Given in Nuremburg, 10th February 1918. Trans. by D. S. Osmond. 2nd ed. London: Rudolf Steiner Press, 1973 (previous ed., 1964). 29p. (Translated from shorthand report unrevised by lecturer; orig. text is included in vol., of complete ed. in German of works of Steiner, entitled "Tod als Lebenswandlung") £0.25 pa. ISBN 0-85440-274-8

1599 ______. The Etherisation of the Blood: The Entry of the Etheric Christ into the Evolution of the Earth; A Lecture Given in Basle, 1st October, 1911. Trans. by Arnold Freeman and D. S. Osmond. 4th ed. London: Rudolf Steiner Press, 1971 (3rd ed., 1955). 42p. Illus. £0.32 pa. ISBN 0-85440-248-9

1600 ______. Guidance in Esoteric Training. Trans. revised by Charles Davy and Owen Barfield. London: Rudolf Steiner Press, 1972. 109p. (Revised translation of extracts from vol., in complete ed. in German of works of Steiner, entitled "Aus dem Inhalt der 'esoterische Schule' ") £1.30 ISBN 0-85440-258-6

1601 ______. Karmic Relationships: Esoteric Studies, vol. 6: Nine Lectures Given in Berne, Zurich, Stuttgart and Arnhem, between 25th January and 20th July, 1924. Trans. and revision of lectures 1 to 6 by D. S. Osmond and E. H. Goddard, and of lectures 7 to 9 by D. S. Osmond and M. K. London: Rudolf Steiner Press, 1971. 183p. Bibliog. (Translated from shorthand reports unrevised by lecturer) £1.40 ISBN 0-85440-242-X

1602 ______. Karmic Relationships: Esoteric Studies, vol. 7: Nine Lectures Given in Breslau from June 7th to June 15th, 1924. Trans. by D. S. Osmond. London: Rudolf Steiner Press, 1973. 139p. (Translated from shorthand reports unrevised by lecturer) £1.40

1603 ______. Karmic Relationships: Esoteric Studies, vol. 8: Six Lectures Given in Torquay and London to Members of the Anthroposophical Society between 12th and 27th August, during Rudolf Steiner's Last Visit to England in 1924; With an Appendix. Trans. by D. S. Osmond. London: Rudolf Steiner Press, 1975 (orig. pub. as "Cosmic Christianity and the Impulse of Michael," London: Anthroposophical Pub. Co.,

1953). 101p. Illus. (Translated from shorthand reports unrevised by lecturer; orig. texts of lectures are included in vol. VI of series in complete ed. in German of works of Steiner entitled "Esoterische Betrachtungen karmischer Zusammenhange") £1.75 ISBN 0-85440-018-4

1604 _______. Love and Its Meaning in the World: Lecture Given in Zurich, 17th December 1912. Trans. by D. S. Osmond, E. F. and S. Derry. 2nd ed. London: Rudolf Steiner Press, 1972 (orig. pub., London: Anthroposophical Publishing Co., 1960). 27p. (Translated from shorthand report unrevised by lecturer; orig. text is contained in vol., of complete ed. in German of works of Steiner, entitled "Erfahrungen der Übersinnlichen. Die Wege der Seele zu Christus") £0.25 pa. ISBN 0-85440-254-3

1605 _______. Man as a Picture of the Living Spirit: Lecture Given in London, 2nd September 1923 on the Day of the Foundation of the Anthroposophical Society in Great Britain. Trans. by George Adams. 2nd ed. London: Rudolf Steiner Press, 1972 (orig. pub., London: Anthroposophical Publishing Co., 1952). 30p. (Translated from shorthand report unrevised by lecturer; orig. text is included in vol., of complete ed. in German of works of Steiner, entitled "Initiationswissenschaft und Sternenerkenntnis") £0.25 pa. ISBN 0-85440-253-5

1606 _______. Man--Hieroglyph of the Universe: Sixteen Lectures Given in Dornach, Switzerland, between 9th April and 16th May 1920. Trans. by George and Mary Adams. London: Rudolf Steiner Press, 1972. 221p. Illus. Bibliog. (Translated from shorthand notes unrevised by lecturer; in complete ed. in German of works of Steiner, orig. text published with title "Entsprechungen zwischen Mikrokosmos und Makrokosmos. Der Mensch--eine Hieroglyphe des Weltenalls") £1.75 ISBN 0-85440-251-9

1607 _______. The Meditative Year; An English Version by A. C. Harwood of the "Calendar of the Soul" by Rudolf Steiner. London: Rudolf Steiner Press, 1972. 52p. (Translation of "Anthroposophischer Seelenkalender." Berlin, 1912). £0.75 ISBN 0-85440-257-8

1608 _______. Mysteries of the East and of Christianity: Four Lectures Given in Berlin, 3rd-7th February 1913. Trans. revised by Charles Davy. 2nd ed. London: Rudolf Steiner Press, 1972 (orig. pub., 1943). 78p. Bibliog. (In complete ed. in German of works of Steiner, orig. text published with title "Mysterien des Morgenlandes und des Christentums") £0.60 pa. ISBN 0-85440-259-4

1609 _______. Mystery Knowledge and Mystery Centres: Fourteen Lectures Given in Dornach, 23rd November to 23rd December, 1923. Trans. and revised by E. H. Goddard and D. S. Osmond. 2nd ed. (new translation). London: Rudolf Steiner Press, 1973 (orig. pub., 1943). 208p. Illus. (Translation of "Mysteriengestaltungen." Dornach: Philosophisch-anthroposophischer Verlag am Goetheanum, 1931) £1.80 ISBN 0-85440-265-9

1610 _______. The Occult Movement in the Nineteenth Century and Its Relation to Modern Culture; Ten Lectures Given in Dornach, 10th to 25th October, 1915. Trans. by D. S. Osmond. London: Rudolf Steiner Press, 1973. 190p. Illus. (Translated from shorthand reports unrevised by lecturer; in complete ed. in German of works of Steiner, vol. containing the German texts of the 10 lectures entitled "Okkulte Bewegung zur Weltkultur") £2

1611 _______. Occult Signs and Symbols; Four Lectures Given in Stuttgart, September 13-16, 1907. Trans. by Sarah Kurland, with emendations by Gilbert Church. New York: Anthroposophic Press, 1972. 60p. Illus. (Translated from German shorthand reports unrevised by lecturer) $2.25 pa. LC 72-76474

1612 _______. Theosophy: An Introduction to the Supersensible Knowledge of the World and the Destination of Man. 4th ed. London: Rudolf Steiner Press, 1973 (previous ed., 1965). 158p. (Translation of "Theosophie; Einfuhrung in übersinnliche Welterkenntnis und Menschenbestimmung." Dornach: Rudolf Steiner-Nachlassverwaltung, 1961) £1.65 ISBN 0-85440-269-1

1613 _______. The Work of the Angels in Man's Astral Body: Lecture Given in Zurich, 9th October 1918. Trans. by D. S. Osmond with the help of Owen Barfield. 2nd ed. London: Rudolf Steiner Press, 1972 (orig. pub., London: Anthroposophical Publishing Co., 1960). 38p. (Translated from shorthand report unrevised by lecturer; orig. text is included in vol., of complete ed. in German of works of Steiner, entitled "Tod als Lebenswandlung") £0.30 pa. ISBN 0-85440-255-1

1614 Steinerbooks Dictionary of the Psychic, Mystic, Occult. Blau-
*** velt, N. Y.: Rudolf Steiner Publications, 1973. 235p. Illus. $1.95 pa. LC 72-86344

This work is a major new contribution to occult literature. It is an excellent dictionary, with over 1,300 entries. The definitions are short (most are one to four sentences long, with a few half a page in length), but cover the entry well. The work attempts to also cover related areas to the occult, such as psychology, sociology, literature, philosophy, and religion. Several hundred of the entries are biographical.

1615 Stemman, Roy, 1942- . Medium Rare: The Psychic Life of Ena Twigg. Preface by Mervyn Stockwood. London: Spiritualist Association of Great Britain, 1971. 130p. £0.50 pa. ISBN 0-900697-02-4

1616 ________. One Hundred Years of Spiritualism: The Story of the Spiritualist Association of Great Britain, 1872-1972. London: Spiritualist Association of Great Britain, 1972. 73p. Illus. £0.75 pa. ISBN 0-900697-14-8

1617 ________. Spirits and Spirit Worlds. Garden City, N.Y.:
* Doubleday, 1975 (orig. pub., London: Aldus Books, dist. by Jupiter Books, 1975). 142p. Illus. (some color) (New Library of the Supernatural) $7.95 LC 75-16751

This well-done survey discusses the Fox sisters, Daniel Dunglas Home, Abraham Lincoln, Alfred Russel Wallace (19th-century British naturalist), William Crookes and his investigation of Florence Cook, Harry Houdini and Boston medium Margery Crandon, concepts of life after death, Kirlian photography, the taped voices of Friedrich Jurgenson, Eileen Garrett's speaking in a seance with the voice of the commander of the R-101--a British dirigible that had recently crashed, and Lenore Piper--who was investigated by William James and Richard Hodgson. The book has many illustrations, line drawings, and photographs, often in color.

1618 Stern, Henry L., 1899- . Help from Beyond. New York: Walker, 1974. 177p. $7.95 LC 73-90380 ISBN 0-8027-0444-1

This autobiography tells of the author's introduction to spiritualism at seances after the death of his nephew in 1930. He decided to do experiments on his own, and gradually developed clairvoyance and automatic writing skills, as well as improving his spiritual life and solving personal problems. He and his wife Lillian developed the ability to heal, and do it on weekends. He claims an 80 percent success rate. The book discusses how to achieve a relaxed state of mind for receiving psychic gifts and spirit communications. The author believes we all have these latent abilities, but can only develop them by exercises and certain mental attitudes. Stern is a certified public accountant, and now lives in Bridgeport, Conn.

1619 Stern, Madeleine Bettina, 1912- . Heads and Headlines; The Phrenological Fowlers. Norman: University of Oklahoma Press, 1971. xx, 348p. Illus. Bibliog. $8.95 LC 77-160506 ISBN 0-8061-0978-5

Shortly after phrenology was introduced in the U.S. in 1832, brothers Orson and Lorenzo Fowler spread its techniques. They published a monthly, Phrenological Journal, which came out for over 70 years, and also many books. Lorenzo's wife, Lydia, became the second accredited woman M.D. in the U.S., and the first female professor of medicine. Her daughter, Jessie, tried to keep phrenology alive, but failed. The Journal ceased publication in 1911. In the Journal's heyday, famous people were associated with it. Walt Whitman had an edition of his Leaves of Grass published by the firm, and also had his head read by them. Edward Fowler, half-brother of Orson and Lorenzo, was a trance medium.

1620 Stevens, Austin N., comp. Mysterious New England. Dublin, N. H.: Yankee, Inc., 1971. 319p. Illus. $7.50 LC 74-172976

1621 * Stevenson, Ian. Cases of the Reincarnation Type. Vol. 1: Ten Cases from India. Charlottesville, Va.: University Press of Virginia, 1975. 374p. $20

This volume is the first in a series, each one on a particular geographical area. The introduction discusses problems of validating such cases, and covers special problems of working in India. Stevenson has 1,300 reincarnation cases on file, with a recent increase of cases reported in the United States. There are 150 cases on India, of which 105 are considered "well investigated" by Stevenson. For each case reported in this book is given the case in outline form, a list of persons interviewed and their connection with the case, the possibility of the two families having made normal communication; life, death and personality of previous entity; statement made by subject, attempts at verification, subject's attempts to recognize people he knew in the previous life, birthmarks, subsequent history of the person to the present, and evaluation of the importance of the case for reincarnation and parapsychology. Most of the cases are spontaneous ones of children two to four years of age suddenly discussing past lives with their parents.

1622 * ________. Twenty Cases Suggestive of Reincarnation. 2nd ed., rev. and enl. Charlottesville: University Press of Virginia, 1974 (orig. pub. as vol. 26 of "Proceedings of the American Society for Psychical Research," 1966). xvi, 396p. $15 LC 73-93627 ISBN 0-8139-0546-X

The new material in this edition is a follow-up consisting of investigations on 18 of the 20 original cases. The cases come from India, Ceylon, Brazil, Alaska, and Lebanon. Stevenson discusses the possibility that the phenomenon could be ESP, mediumship, or possession. Strong evidence for reincarnation is seen in birthmark phenomena, such as the case of Corliss Chotkin, who had marks exactly where the former personality had a scar. The author's conclusions are that cases of reincarnation usually occur in cultures believing in rebirth; reincarnation often occurs in neighboring villages or even within the same family; sex changes are very rare.

1623 ________. Xenoglossy: A Review and Report of a Case.

Charlottesville: University Press of Virginia, 1974 (orig. pub. as "Proceedings of the American Society for Psychical Research," v. 31, Feb. 1974). vii, 268p. Bibliog. $8.50 LC 73-77947 ISBN 0-8139-0443-9

Xenoglossy means speaking in a real language one has never studied. Stevenson differentiates between "recitative xenoglossy," where the subject babbles in a foreign language, and "responsive xenoglossy," where the subject can carry on a conversation in the strange language. The work studies one case, that of a woman living in Philadelphia. Her husband, a physician, sent his wife back under deep hypnosis, and hit a period where she was a Swedish male named Jensen. She spoke in Swedish to people sitting in the room. There were eight sessions in the years 1956 and 1957. No replies by "Jensen" were longer than three or four words. Fearing possession, her husband experimented in mediumship with her. During these sessions, she often gave scientific information. One day, notes were discovered in her handbag, probably copied from books at the public library. Some readers may feel this casts doubts on her xenoglossy experience.

1624 Still, Henry. Of Time, Tides and Inner Clocks. Harrisburg, Pa.: Stackpole Books, 1972. 218p. $8.50

The author discusses sunspots, tides and marine life, flower openings and closings, and human cyclic changes in sleep, arousal, temperature, mood, and work ability. Charts are provided to help the reader determine his cycles: a sleep chart to find the hour at which sleep comes most easily, a mood chart, and a medication effectiveness chart.

1625 Stirling, William. Canon: An Exposition of the Pagan Mystery Perpetuated in the Cabala as the Rule of All the Arts. Foreword by John Michell. Preface by R. B. Cunninghame Graham. London: Garnstone Press, 1974. xvi, 404p. Illus. Plans Index (Prehistoric and Ancient Science Library) £6.50 ISBN 0-85511-251-4

1626 Stobart, Mabel Annie (Boulton), 1862-1954. Torchbearers of Spiritualism. Port Washington, N.Y.: Kennikat, 1971 (orig. pub., 1925). 231p. Bibliog. $9.25 LC 70-118550 ISBN 0-8046-1175-0

1627 Storms, Godfrid. Anglo-Saxon Magic. Folcroft, Pa.: Folcroft Library Editions, 1975 (orig. pub., The Hague: M. Nijhoff, 1948). ix, 336p. Bibliog. Index $35 LC 75-11736 ISBN 0-8414-7842-2

1628 Story, Francis, and Nyanaponika Thera. Rebirth as Doctrine and Experience. Kandy, Ceylon: Buddhist Publication Society, 1975. 286p. (Also contains pamphlet "The Case for Rebirth")

This book gathers articles published at different times, and includes a pamphlet. It discusses Buddhist doctrines on rebirth and specific cases are included. Accounts are given on what happens during the wait between births.

1629 Strachan, Francoise. Casting Out the Devils. Wellingborough, England: Aquarian Press, 1972. 127p. Illus. Bibliog. £1.75 ISBN 0-85030-085-1

1630 ______. Natural Magic. London: Marshall Cavendish, 1974 (also, New York: Black Watch, 1974--pub. by Black Watch under arrangement with Ottenheimer Publishers, Baltimore). 128p. Illus. (some color) Facsims. (some color) £1.95 ISBN 0-85685-082-9

The author attempts to "expose and define the fraudulent side of magic, while at the same time pointing to its enduring sources in the natural world." The book includes the following discussions: the history of magic, the current status of magic, the world of natural magic (merging with nature, embracing trees, Mother of Earth, angels, the power of trees), nature's power house (mostly on hair, but with some mention of teeth and bones), stones and birthstones, taking magical precautions (auras, avoiding drugs, vampires, the hazards of sex), and bringing out the magical you (your roots of power, your body as a temple, spirit guides, consecration, daily purification). The author's statements and theories are usually not backed up with sources or evidence. However, Strachan has written a very creative, refreshing work. The illustrative paintings and pictures are unusual and very interesting. The book was printed by Henri Proost, Turnhout, Belgium.

1631 Street, Noel. Reincarnation. Miami, Fla.: Lotus Ashram, 1974. 71p. $2.95 pa.

1632 Stresau, Marion. Tomorrows Unlimited. Boston: Branden Press, 1973. 143p. Illus. $5.95 pa. LC 72-91222

The author writes of her search for proof that her deceased daughter lives on the other side. Included are details of her sittings with Arthur Ford, and a discussion of her membership in the Spiritual Frontiers Fellowship.

1633 Stringer, Edward Trevor. The Secret of the Gods: An Outline of Tellurianism. London: Spearman, 1974. 264p. Illus. Plates Map Bibliog. Index £4.25 ISBN 0-85435-461-1

This book discusses astrology, UFO's, ghosts, telepathy, clairvoyance, dowsing, and claims that they are tied together by one basic concept.

1634 Sturzaker, Doreen, and James Sturzaker. Colour and the Kabbalah. Wellingborough, England: Tjorsons, 1975. 287p. £3.95 ISBN 0-7225-0283-4

1635 Sturzaker, James. Kabbalistic Aphorisms. London: Theosophical Pub. House, 1971. x, 118p. Illus. £1.50 ISBN 0-7229-5226-0

1636 Suares, Carlo. The Resurrection of the Word. Trans. by Vincent and Micheline Stuart. Berkeley, Calif: Shambhala, 1975 (dist. in U. S. by Random House; in Britain by Routledge and Kegan Paul). 152p. (Translation of "Clês du sacre." Geneva: Editions du Mont-Blanc, 1974) £4 ISBN 0-87773-066-0

This book is a spiritual autobiography and scholarly treatment of the Old Testament by a Cabalist. He says that the idea of Israel and the idea of a state are incompatible. To him, Israel is a spiritual reality, not a geographical area. He says that this is clearly understood by a study of the Cabala.

1637 Sullivan, Eileen. Arthur Ford Speaks from Beyond. Chicago: J. P. O'Hara, 1975. 186p. $6.95 LC 74-25385 ISBN 0-87955-317-0

This book discusses messages by Arthur Ford from the other side. There are also messages through the Rev. Moon of Korea, who says that all souls must work their way to God.

1638 Summers, Montague, 1880-1948. The History of Witchcraft and Demonology. London: Routledge and Kegan Paul, 1973 (orig. pub., London: Routledge, Kegan Paul, Trench and Trubner, 1926). 353p. Illus. Facsims. Bibliog. Index £2.50 pa.

This work is the result of 30 years of intensive research, during which the author consulted monographs, judicial records, legal codes, and the work of demonologists. There are chapters on possession, the witch in scripture, the Sabbat, and the doctrine of witchcraft, and a final discussion on the stage, especially in respect to English theater.

1639 ________. Witchcraft and Black Magic. London: Arrow
* Books, 1974 (also, New York: Causeway Books, 1974; Detroit: Grand River Books, 1971; orig. pub., London: Rider, 1946). 320p. Index £0.45 pa. ISBN 0-09-909420-7

This book discusses the following topics: what witchcraft is, how one becomes a witch, pacts, familiars, witchcraft at Cambridge and Oxford, Manichee sorcerers, witchcraft of the Templars, origins of witchcraft, Assyrian and Egyptian witchcraft, library of the witches, Sibylline Books and grimoires, Witches' Bible, The Magus (1801) of Francis Barrett, ceremonial magic, ranks of demons, satanism today, sympathetic magic, wax images, the Sabbat, and the Black Mass. Summers felt that witchcraft and black magic were a threat to society, and he supported the great persecutions throughout history. He felt that modern magic and witchcraft should be wiped out.

1640 Sun, Ruth Quinlan. Asian Animal Zodiac. Illus. by Norman Sun. Rutland, Vt.: Tuttle, 1974 (dist. in Britain by Prentice-Hall). 218p. Illus. Bibliog. £4.70 ISBN 0-8048-1128-8

The author uses folktales of Asia in this book to illustrate the 12 animal types contained in the Oriental zodiac.

1641 Super Horoscope (annual.) New York: Grosset and Dunlap. 12 vols. 208p. ea. vol. $1.95 pa. ea. vol.

In reviewing this set, we are using the "1977 edition" (published in 1976). Each volume includes the following discussions: note to the cusp-born, the history and uses of astrology (horoscopes, problem of love, history of astrology, influences on personality), moon (briefly discussed in each sign, with moon tables); the signs (discussing dominent characteristics of each, with a short section on famous personalities); and the one main sign to which the volume is devoted. The main section gives character analysis (general, health, occupation, home and family, social relationships), love and marriage (matching a woman or man born under the sign with an opposite mate from all other signs), yearly forecast, daily forecast, and daily forecast for the last two months of the previous year.

1642 Swain, Jasper. On the Death of My Son. Ed. by Noel Langley. London: Turnstone Books, 1974. 101p. (privately pub. in South Africa as "Mike?") £1.95 ISBN 0-85500-028-7

The author, a South African lawyer, lost his son in a car crash in 1967. The next day, medium Nina Merrington offered to help, since the father had once helped her. Swain became convinced she had contact with his son, and brought his wife and younger son to a session. When he tried to bring the parents of the girl who also had died in the crash, they refused. Mike appeared to the father of this girl four days after the refusal and convinced him that he still existed. These parents then went back to the medium with Swain, and communicated with their daughter. As time went on, Mike began to discuss life on the other side. The last section of the book is on automatic writing between Mike and his father. Mike asked Swain to write this book to take away the terror of death from readers.

1643 Swann, Ingo, 1933- . To Kiss Earth Good-bye. Foreword
*** by Gertrude Schmeidler. New York: Hawthorn Books, 1975. xix, 217p. Illus. Plates Bibliog. Index $10 LC 73-21321 ISBN 0-8015-7774-8

This work is a major new contribution to occult literature. Swann has been a frequent ESP and PK subject in laboratory experiments. He discusses what it's like to be psychic, and his experiences as a subject (some of the experiences are mystical ones).

Swann, also a gifted painter, understands his experiments not just as a subject, but as a scientific researcher. He discusses 18 months of experiments on out-of-the-body experiences at the American Society for Psychical Research in New York City. He did well, but got bored, and disliked the experimenter. He also did experiments at City College of New York under Dr. Gertrude Schmeidler, where he was successful paranormally causing objects to undergo changes in temperature. He worked with Targ and Puthoff at the Stanford Research Institute. Psychic probe experiments were also done, with Harold Sherman, in which both men tried to focus on Jupiter and Mercury to see if the information they got compared favorably with data received by NASA's Pioneer 10 and Mariner 10 (it did). Swann says he did all these things simply by deciding they were possible to do. He refused to let barriers of culture limit him, and says the reader can do the same.

1644 * Swedenborg, Emanuel, 1688-1772. Heaven and Its Wonders and Hell. Introd. to this ed. by Helen Keller. New York: Swedenborg Foundation, 1971 (orig. pub. in Latin, London, 1758). 496p. Index of subjects $1 pa. ISBN 0-87785-068-2

A reading of this classic would give one a very clear picture of the basic tenets of some spiritualists. The author claimed to have seen and heard the other side in visions. His discussions include the kingdoms of Heaven, heavens and societies, all Heaven in the aggregate reflecting a single man, the correspondence of all things in Heaven with all things of man; sun, light, and heat in Heaven; the four quarters of Heaven, angels, space in Heaven, divine worship in Heaven, children and marriage in Heaven, the world of spirits, man after death, the three states of man on the other side, man after death being in same state or level he had been while alive, casting into Hell done by the spirit itself, and not by God, Hell-fire and the gnashing of teeth; the appearance, situation, and number of the hells; the equilibrium between Heaven and Hell, and this equilibrium's giving man freedom. Swedenborg's discussion of the soul's finding its own level on the other side is very interesting. He says that a tainted soul would not enjoy the company of good souls, and thus he "longs to get away from the good." Eventually, the soul finds those it is in harmony with, and then "leads a life like that which he led in the world."

1645 Sylvester, Arline. Who, Me? Yes, You! Boston: Branden Press, 1975. 153p. $4.95 LC 74-82230 ISBN 0-8283-1581-7

The author claims that everyone can communicate with the spirit world, and gives a study plan for learning how to do it. She discusses how she learned her own mediumship, and the nature of her communications.

1646 Symonds, John. The Great Beast: The Life and Magick of Aleister Crowley. Unabridged, revised and updated ed. St.

Albans, England: Mayflower, 1973 (also, London: Macdonald and Co., 1971; orig. pub., London: Rider, 1951). 464p. Illus. Index (Contains relevant chapters from "The Magic of Aleister Crowley." London: Muller, 1958) £0.60 pa. ISBN 0-583-12195-0

Crowley was a poet, mountaineer, and drug addict, expelled from Italy and France because of his black masses and sexual orgies. He gathered a devoted following of disciples who believed him to possess great powers. Symonds has relied largely on Crowley's own accounts of himself, and has written a journalistic-style survey.

1647 * Tabori, Paul, 1908-1974. Crime and the Occult; How ESP and Parapsychology Help Detection. New York: Taplinger, 1974 (also, London: David and Charles, 1974). 260p. Bibliog. Index $8.95 LC 74-5812 ISBN 0-8008-2028-2

Tabori, the author of more than 100 books, presents cases mostly from Europe, since he was at one time a crime reporter in Budapest before moving to England. The book contains the following discussions: the use of hypnotism and trance mediums in criminal investigations (Alfred Pethes, Georg Mittelmann, medical and legal views); graphology, covering Raphael Schermann, handwriting expert and clairvoyant, as well as Michael Fischl and Luce Vidi; second sight, covering spontaneous clairvoyance, clairvoyant detection of crime, and contemporary clairvoyants (Marinus Bernardus Dykshoorn, Irene Hughes, Reverent Gwen, Beverly Jaegers, Olof Jonsson, Alex Tanous); pendulum, rod and board, which covers dowsers and their skeptics, psychic diviners such as Jeanne Couret, and use of the Ouija board; "Macbeth prophecies," a term the author uses in covering prophecies, usually malignant, which cause to happen what they foretell (such as in witchcraft, voodoo, satanism); witchcraft in California; and parapsychological elements in crime (behavior of witnesses, future of forensic occultism, elements of psychology in crime work). This work is on a topic rarely given serious consideration in occult books. Tabori presents a vast amount of careful thought on the subject.

1648 ________. Harry Price: The Biography of a Ghost Hunter. Introd. by Dennis Wheatley. London: Sphere, 1974 (orig. pub., London: Athenaeum Press, 1950). 303p. Illus. Plates Bibliog. Index £0.60 pa. ISBN 0-7221-8326-7

1649 * ________. Pioneers of the Unseen. New York: Taplinger, 1972 (also, London: Souvenir Press, 1972; Toronto: J. M. Dent and Sons, 1972). 243p. Illus. $6.50 LC 74-185948 ISBN 0-8008-6310-0

The author has written this book as a study of the psychology of the psychical researcher. He first presents an ideal picture of the perfect researcher, and then gives six cases of geniuses who have worked in this field. The six are Hereward Carrington, Sir Oliver Lodge, Charles Richet, Baron von Schrenck-Notzing, Cesare Lombroso, and Raphael Schermann. Much of the information on von Schrenck and Schermann had not before been translated into English.

1650 ________, and Phyllis Raphael. Beyond the Senses; A Report of Psychical Research in the Sixties. New York: Taplinger, 1972 (orig. pub., London: Souvenir, 1971). 218p. (Frontiers of the Unknown Series) $6.50 LC 70-185482 ISBN 0-8008-0735-9

The author discusses faith healers and psychic surgeons, precognition, and reincarnation, among other topics. Most of the material is British, since Tabori is Vice President of the London Ghost Club. The author presents the pros and cons on each topic. The last chapter is on Rosalie, a supposed materialization of a spirit child which researcher Harry Price observed in 1937.

1651 Taimni, I. K., 1898- . Man, God and the Universe. Wheaton, Ill. and London: Theosophical Pub. House, 1974 (orig. pub., Madras and Wheaton, Ill.: Theosophical Pub. House, 1969). 447p. Illus. (Quest Book) $3.45 pa. LC 71-906172 ISBN 0-8356-0447-0

1652 Talamonti, Leo. Forbidden Universe: Mysteries of the Psy-
*** chic World. Preface by William Mackenzie. Trans. by Paul Stevenson. London: Garnstone Press, 1974 (also, New York: Stein and Day, 1975). 230p. Illus. Plates Includes bibliog. refs. (Prehistory and Ancient Science Library) (Translation of "Universo proibito." Milan: Sugar Editore, 1974) £3.50 ISBN 0-85511-311-1

This work is a major new contribution to occult literature. The following topics are discussed: dreams, clairvoyance, precognition, telepathy, psychokinesis, retrocognition, out-of-the-body experiences, magic, mediums and spiritualism, and psi in animals. Most of the book covers these phenomena in everyday life or with mediums. There are many cases presented, most of them taken from European, especially Italian, French, and German sources. These include psychometry by Sandra Bajetto of Rome, clairvoyant medical diagnosis by Pasqualina Pezzola, PK disturbances in Treviso, and the PK work of Gustavo Adolfo Rol of Turin. Talamonti theorizes that psychic events are due to every person present at the scene, not just a "psychic" person. Much of the material in the book is based on old sources and theories, such as the discussion of out-of-the-body experiences. The author says that parapsychology must advance boldly and not let itself be trammelled by official methods that cannot solve its problems.

1653 Tarree, Kathy O. Earthseeds. Meriden, Conn.: Earthseeds, 1975. 44p. $2 pa.

The author discusses her training at the Psychic Research Institute in New Haven, Conn., and the dreams and regressions that followed it.

1654 Tart, Charles T., 1937- . The Application of Learning Theory to ESP Performance. New York: Parapsychology Foundation, 1975. ix, 149p. Illus. Bibliog. Index (Parapsychological Monographs, no. 15) $5 pa. LC 75-14709 ISBN 0-912328-25-8

In 1966, Tart wrote a paper which proposed that the usual card-guessing procedure was really an extinction paradigm, since the subject got no feedback on his performance trial-by-trial, and thus could not learn to respond to internal clues. This paper, "Card Guessing Tests: Learning Paradigm or Extinction Paradigm," is chapter 1 of this book. Chapter 2 further explains this theory and reviews over 10 studies using feedback over the period 1964-1974. Then comes the main part of the work. Chapter 4 is titled "Three-Stage Study in Training ESP Ability." It discusses the process whereby Tart selected first 138 and finally 25 subjects from 1500 tested initially. Chapter 5 has Tart's best experimenter, Gaines Thomas, explain his role in getting psi from his subjects. Tart states that repeated testing without feedback, even with high-scoring subjects, can decline to chance.

1655 _______. States of Consciousness. New York: Dutton, 1975. 224p. Bibliog. Index $12.50 LC 75-5940 ISBN 0-525-20970-0

In this book, Tart tries to provide a framework for organizing the consciousness field. He divides mental life into ten systems, such as body awareness, external sense perception, emotion, judgment, and so on. Each performs in a different fashion and role. The author covers d-SOC ("discrete state of consciousness") and d-ASC ("discrete altered state of consciousness"). He discusses William also, a subject used in experiments who was very susceptible to hypnosis.

1656 _______. Transpersonal Psychologies. New York: Harper
*** and Row, 1975. 502p. $16.50

This work is a major new contribution to occult literature. Tart has been a researcher in altered states of consciousness, ESP, and marijuana intoxication. He contributes three papers, and has selected eight others. His papers discuss his conception of state-specific sciences, assumptions of orthodox Western psychology, and paranormal phenomena and their relation to transpersonal psychology (methods, phenomena, psychology of psi, altered states of consciousness, healing, animal psi, survival). The other papers are these: Claire M. Owens on Zen Buddhism, Daniel Goldman on Buddhistic meditation and states of consciousness, Haridas Chaudhuri on yoga, Kathleen Riordan on Gurdjieff, John Lilly and Joseph Hart on Arica training, Robert Ornstein on contemporary Sufism, William McNamara on Christian mysticism, and William Gray on Western magic.

1657 Taylor, Alfred. A Human Heritage: The Wisdom in Science and Experience. Wheaton, Ill.: Theosophical Pub. House, 1975. 146p. £1.50 pa. ISBN 0-8356-0455-1

1658 Taylor, Frank Sherwood, 1897-1956. The Alchemists. New York: Arno Press, 1974 (orig. pub., New York: H. Schuman, 1949). x, 246p. Illus. Bibliog. $14 LC 74-361 ISBN 0-405-05922-1

1659 Taylor, John Gerald, 1931- . Superminds; A Scientist
*** Looks at the Paranormal. New York: Viking Press, 1975 (also, New York: Warner Books, 1975; London: Macmillan, 1975). 183p. Illus. Bibliog. Index $10.95 LC 75-19231 ISBN 0-670-68470-8

This work is a major new contribution to occult literature. Taylor is head of the Department of Applied Mathematics at King's College, London University, and a theoretical physicist. In this book, he discusses thirty-eight "mini-Gellers," those who discovered their abilities by watching Geller perform, and tries to determine the cause of the "Geller effect." He theorizes that ESP and PK phenomena associated with Geller are the result of very low frequency electromagnetic waves sent by the brain or nervous system. Taylor admits that he was skeptical until he appeared on a BBC broadcast with Geller. Then, he suddenly realized that science had to somehow explain the phenomenon or else Taylor's whole view of the universe would have to be dismantled. He feels an "intentionality field" connects the PK subject and the object he moves. Included in the book is a brief history of parapsychological research.

1660 Taylor, John Metcalf, 1845-1918. Witchcraft Delusion in Colonial Connecticut, 1647-1697. New York: Burt Franklin, 1971 (orig. pub., 1908). xv, 172p. Facsim. Bibliog. (Burt Franklin Research and Source Works Series, 412) (American Classics in History and Social Science, 196) $15 LC 73-165414 ISBN 0-8337-4445-2

The first section of the book, four chapters in length, offers a general survey, a survey of major works in the field, legislation against witchcraft in history, New England laws (Massachusetts, Connecticut, and New Haven), and the Salem trials. The second section discusses these Connecticut cases: the first execution for witchcraft in New England, that of Mary Johnson, who was put to death for witchcraft in Windsor in 1647; Goodwife Bassett of Stratford in 1651; Goodwife Knapp of Fairfield in 1653; the trial of John Carrington and his wife of Wethersfield in 1662. The last section, the major part of the book, consists of word-for-word quotes of depositions used in these cases: Katherine Harrison of Wethersfield in 1669; Thomas Bracy and Joseph Dickinson of Northampton in 1668; Nathaniel and Rebecca Greensmith in 1661; Elizabeth Clawson of Stamford; Hugh Crohsaw; Knapp of Fairfield in 1653; Mercy Disborough; Elizabeth Seager, 1662; and Elizabeth Godman, 1653. The witchcraft craze reached its peak in Connecticut in 1692, the same year as the Salem trials. It was largely centered in Fairfield. The author closes with a complete list of Connecticut witchcraft cases. He says that the alleged witches "were victims of delusion, not dishonor, of a perverted theology fed by moral aberrations."

1661 Tchernine, Odette. In Pursuit of the Abominable Snowman.
* New York: Taplinger, 1971 (orig. pub. as "Yeti," 1970). viii, 184p. Illus. Maps $6.95 LC 75-147809 ISBN 0-8008-4187-5

This work discusses the following topics: the probable hoax case of a mysterious hairy creature encased in a block of ice which was exhibited by showman Frank Hansen for several months in the spring of 1969, and investigated by Bernard Heuvelmans and Ivan Sanderson; reassessing Snowman history, little-known Russian research, former incidents, Mongolian cases, Himalayan cases, fringe reports, Borneo, California, Chinese links and legends, past legends, the work of Doctor B. Porshnev, assessing the candidates, and feuds and labels. The last chapter provides a list of names and terms identified throughout the world as possibly denoting various types of "remnant hominids." The author has written an interesting survey, leaning heavily on the records of Dr. Boris Porshnev, Russian historian and scientist, and Dr. Rinchen of the Mongolian Academy of Science.

1662 Tegner, Henry. Ghosts of the North Country: Being an Account of Some of the Folklore and Ghost Stories of the Northern Counties of Northumberland and Durham and Their Adjacent Lands. Newcastle upon Tyne, England: Graham, 1974. 79p. Illus. £0.75 ISBN 0-85983-080-2

1663 Teltscher, Herry O. Handwriting--Revelation of Self: A Source Book of Psychographology. New York: Hawthorn Books, 1971 (1st-4th eds. pub. under title "Handwriting, the Key to Successful Living"). xiii, 338p. Illus. Bibliog. $6.95 LC 72-115908

1664 Temple, Robert Kyle Grenville. The Sirius Mystery. New
* York: St. Martin's Press, 1975. 244p. Illus. Plates Diagrams Bibliog. Index $7.95 LC 74-83583

The author shows that knowledge about the star system Sirius has been preserved by an African tribe, the Dogon of the Sudan, while the modern world has only recently learned of this knowledge. The mystery centers on an invisible white dwarf star, Sirius B., orbiting Sirius. The tribe knew it was there, and made it a key part of their rituals. The dwarf star can be seen only by strong telescopes. Temple theorizes the knowledge came from the Sumerians, who were taught it by "Oannes," an amphibious creature. The author says that we once may have been visited by beings with a "magical technology" who locked certain knowledge in Eastern mystical religions. This book is very scholarly, and fairly difficult to read. There are summaries at the end of each chapter.

1665 Tenhaeff, Wilhelm Heinrich Carl. Telepathy and Clairvoyance; Views of Some Little Investigated Capabilities of Man. Trans. by Cora Matteson-Lauta van Aysma. Foreword by Berthold Eric Schwarz. Springfield, Ill.: Thomas, 1972. xii, 161p. Illus. Bibliog. (Translation of "Telepathie en Helderzienheid." 1965) $12.50 LC 77-187679
***

This work is a major new contribution to occult literature. It was originally published in 1965; the present edition is the first translation of the author's ten Dutch language books. Tenhaeff, now over 85, taught parapsychology for credit as early as 1951 and was the first to be granted a university chair of parapsychology. A pioneer in Dutch parapsychology, the author helped found the Institute for Parapsychology at the University of Utrecht. Most of his research has been case study work on psychics, especially of their personality structures. This book is not one of his best works, but still is excellent. In it, Tenhaeff discusses how psychic impressions are related to laws of memory. Also, he concludes that impressions cover themes usually psychologically important to the psychic. Chapters include discussions on memory, telepathy, proscopy (future memory), possession, ghosts, reincarnation, and quantitative method. The best of his work is still to come in the other nine volumes, which key on the personality structure of Gerard Croiset. This book is a serious, deep study involving basic research.

1666 Thierens, A. E. Astrology and the Tarot. Introd. by A. E. Waite. Hollywood, Calif.: Newcastle Pub. Co., 1975 (orig. pub. as "General Book of the Tarot," Philadelphia: D. McKay Co., 1930). 159p. $2.95 pa. LC 74-31486 ISBN 0-87877-031-3

1667 Thiering, Barry, and Edgar Castle, eds. Some Trust in Chariots: Sixteen Views on Erich von Däniken's "Chariots of the Gods?" Folkestone, England: Bailey Bros. and Swinfen, 1973 (orig. pub., Australia, 1972). 128p. Illus. Plates £1.75

1668 Thomas, Chan. Body 2; The Incredible World of ESP. Los Angeles: Emerson House, 1972. 201p. $5.95 LC 72-93805

The author is an engineer who taught ESP at UCLA's experimental college in 1972. He says that "Body 2" is the astral body, made up of subatomic particles. He mentions a device he has constructed to communicate with Body 2's, both living and dead. It seems to be similar to a Ouija board. The book has brief discussions on mediums, deathbed period, afterlife, UFO's. The appendix has a 20-page vocabulary test, so that the reader can communicate well with spirits and all others. The appendix also has 50 pages giving wild theories concerning gravitation and its use in ESP, and the technology of spaceships.

1669 Thomas, John Frederick, 1874-1940. Beyond Normal Cognition; An Evaluative and Methodological Study of the Mental Content of Certain Trance Phenomena. New York: Arno Press, 1975 (orig. pub., Boston: Boston Society for Psychic Research, 1973; orig. presented as author's thesis at Duke University). (Perspectives in Psychical Research) $19 LC 75-7405 ISBN 0-405-06992-8

The author discusses how to evaluate verbal material from mediums. Chapters discuss experiments in person and in absentia, experiments with Mrs. Leonard, theories of fraudulent action, and the Leonard records. The 100-page appendix gives procedures, outlines of methodology, various theories and hypotheses. The book is mostly charts, records, and quotes from written transcripts.

1670 Thomas, Keith Vivian. Religion and the Decline of Magic:
*** Studies in Popular Beliefs in Sixteenth- and Seventeenth-Century England. Harmondsworth, England: Penguin, 1973 (also, New York: Scribner's, 1971; New York: Scribner's, 1973; orig. pub., London: Weidenfeld and Nicolson, 1971). xxi, 853p. Bibliog. Index £3 pa.

This work is a major new contribution to occult literature. It is a scholarly, definitive book, built on solid primary research, and has an anthropological approach. The author especially discusses the social significance of the beliefs he is examining. This is noticeable in his post-Reformation pictures of social life, particularly of the lower classes of 16th- and 17th-century England. There are discussions on the following topics: astrology, witchcraft, magic, ghosts, ancient prophecies, astrologer William Lilly, fairies, and the royal touch (King Charles II supposedly practiced his skills on 90,798 people in 19 years). The author's thesis is that the decline in the belief of magic is central to the development of a modern technological society.

1671 Thompson, Charles John Samuel, 1862-1943. The Lure and Romance of Alchemy. London: G. G. Harrap; Detroit: Gale Research Co., 1974 (orig. pub. as part of the Simple Guide Series in 1932). 248p. $12 LC 76-167224 ISBN 0-8103-4000-3

1672 ________. Mysteries and Secrets of Magic. New York:
* Causeway Books, 1973 (also, New York: Olympia Press, 1972; orig. pub., 1927). 320p. Bibliog. Index $8.95 LC 72-97386 ISBN 0-88356-005-4

This work discusses the genesis of magic--magic and religion, supernatural beings, the cult of magic--the Magi and their mysteries, Babylonian and Assyrian magic, magic in ancient Egypt, ancient Jewish magic--the Kabbala, Greek and Roman magic, Celtic, Arab, Slav and Teutonic magic, Hindu, Chinese and Japanese magic, necromancy, sorcery, and pacts with the devil; witchcraft and demonology, witches' ointments, the Black Mass and Mass of

St. Secaire, divination, crystal gazing, how magic circles and pentacles were made, perfumes used in magic, magical numbers, magical talismans, magical rings, magic in jewels, love and magic, records of magic from the fourth to the 15th century, "The Clavicle or Key of Solomon" rites and ceremonies; "The Nine Tomes of Magic," "The Booke of Hidden Philosophy," "The Booke of the Seven Images", grimoires or handbooks of magic, magical manuscripts on spells and curses, Elizabethan magicians--John Dee and Edward Kelly, magic in Shakespeare's plays, herbs of mystery and the witch's broom, and the survival of witchcraft and magic in modern times. The author states that there is no proof that practitioners of magic ever produced any phenomena that could not be produced by natural means. He feels the manifestations of the magicians of the Middle Ages seem ridiculous to us today and says that the things modern science has done "are more extraordinary than anything ever attributed to magic."

1673 Thompson, Francis, 1931- . Ghosts, Spirits and Spectres of Scotland. Aberdeen, Scotland: Impulse Books, 1973. 179p. Illus. Bibliog. £2.50 ISBN 0-901311-31-6

The author, a schoolteacher, attempts to depict the Scottish ghost as a spirit manifestation with its own nationalistic, independent, and distinctive nature. He includes first-hand accounts, and also legends and folklore. The book is printed on special green "Spectrum" paper from the Culter Guardbridge paper mills in Scotland, with a silver foil jacket which gives a ghostly appearance and supposedly a cold, clammy feel.

1674 Thompson, Reginald Campbell, 1876-1941. Semitic Magic; Its Origins and Development. New York: Ktav, 1971 (orig. pub. as vol. 3 of Luzac's Oriental Religions series, 1908). lxviii, 286p. $16.95 LC 76-160684 ISBN 0-87068-172-9

1675 Thomson, Mary. To Elsie with Love: An Adventure into the Unknown. London: Regency Press, 1975. 160p. Illus. Plate £2.40 ISBN 0-7212-0395-7

1676 Thouless, Robert Henry, 1894- . From Anecdote to Experiment in Psychical Research. London: Routledge and K. Paul, 1972. x, 198p. Illus. Bibliog. Index $10 LC 72-189404 ISBN 0-7100-7285-6
***

This work is a major new contribution to occult literature. The book is directed at those already acquainted with other scientific fields, with the main goal being to convince them important things are happening in the psychical research field. The 17 chapters discuss the following topics: Rýzl's dual target design, Fisk's clock cards, Tyrrell's lighted boxes, Thouless's picture-construction test, the use of machines in testing (by Kahn and Schmidt, among others), ESP done by stage performers, experimental precautions--listing errors a researcher might make, experiments of Schmidt, Warner, Rhine, Pratt and Pearce, and Soal and Goldney,

ESP testing by transmission of drawings--particularly the experiments of Whately Carington, parapsychology critics--especially G. R. Price and E. M. Hansel, precognition, PK, the pattern of ESP, survival problems (a fine chapter), and spontaneous cases--which he feels are not strong enough to be used as evidence of psi but which can give suggestions for researchers. There are four appendices: variance in ESP, measuring psi, British stage performer Marion, and internal controls. This book was originally intended as a revision of Thouless's Experimental Psychical Research and ended up as a new book.

1677 Tietze, Thomas R. Margery. New York: Harper and Row,
*** 1973. xxii, 201p. Bibliog. $6.95 LC 72-11364

This work is a major new contribution to occult literature. It is a well-written, detailed study of mediumship using one of the 20th century's most controversial mediums. Margery Case (Mrs. Mina Crandon) was the wife of a Boston surgeon; she attempted to win a $5000 award offered by Scientific American to any medium who could convince a select committee that she was genuine. Investigators included W. Franklin Prince, J. B. and Louisa Rhine, William MacDougall, Dr. Comstock, and Houdini. Herewood Carrington, expert investigator, remained convinced she was genuine all his life. The peak of the case was during the years 1925 to 1931 and it led to a split in the American Society for Psychical Research. The author sees the case as a turning point in psychic research, and the peak of interest in physical mediumship. Hereafter, the trend turned to experimental methods. Tietze's conclusion is that Margery was probably a fraud. However, other writers have mentioned a close associate of Houdini's who, 10 years after the case, admitted that Houdini planted the much-publicized ruler in the cabinet where Crandon was seated.

1678 Timbs, John, 1801-1875. Predictions Realized in Modern Times. New ed., rev. and corr. Ann Arbor, Mich.: Gryphon Books, 1971 (orig. pub., London: C. Lockwood, 1880). xii, 276p. Includes bibliog. refs. (Things Not Generally Known) $12 LC 73-159861

1679 Tiryakian, Edward A., ed. On the Margin of the Visible; Sociology, the Esoteric, and the Occult. New York: Wiley-
*** Interscience, 1974. 364p. Bibliog. (Contemporary Religious Movements) $9.95 LC 73-21981 ISBN 0-471-87435-3

This work is a major new contribution to occult literature. Part 1 of this book, on representative esoteric doctrines, gathers 17 occult texts: Ouspensky on esoterism and modern thought, Jung and Paracelsus on alchemy, Papus on the Tarot, Blavatsky's essay "Occultism versus the Occult Arts," Carbonari and Masonic initiation ceremonies, Max Heindel on the Rosicrucians, Rudolf Steiner on supersensible realms of experience, a section from Bacon's The New Atlantis, Yeats on Irish fairies, sociologist Simmel's study on secrecy and secret societies, sociologist Abner Cohen's study of the political implications of Freemasonry in Sierra Leone, Maurice Bouisson on Gnosticism, Eric Voegelin on the Gnosticism of mass movements, two sections from Pauwel's and Bergier's Morning of the Magicians (entry 1249), one of them on Nazism and Theosophy. Part 2, on the social setting of the occult, presents historian Jeffrey Russell on medieval witchcraft and heresy, Marcello Truzzi surveying modern witchcraft, Renaissance witchcraft, Salem, and Edward Moody on the First Church of Satan. Part 3, on sociological perspectives and research on the esoteric and the occult, gives these papers: Trent Eglin on alchemy, Hubert and Mauss on magic, Marcello Truzzi on occult dimensions and definitions, Andrew Greeley and William McCready on the sociology of mystical states, Tiryakian on the sociology of esoteric cultures, Greeley on youth culture and the occult with implications for religion, and Claude Fischler on astrology and French society. Tiryakian, who teaches at Duke University, feels that the occult has been a catalyst for modernization in Western civilization. This work has received numerous reviews.

1680 Toben, Robert; Jack Sarfatti; and Fred Wolf. Space-time and Beyond; Toward an Explanation of the Unexplainable. New York: E. P. Dutton, 1975. 174p. $5.95 pa.

This book discusses: black holes, time-space dislocations, PK, astral travel, reincarnation, UFO's, levitation, modern physics, and ancient magic. Toben is an artist-inventor. The other two participants are physicists. They try to put complex ideas into simple drawings, and discuss energy and consciousness. They feel that possibly we live on several levels of reality at once, which "interpenetrate" each other, causing illusions that are actually real.

1681 Tobey, Carl Payne. Astrology of Inner Space. Illus. by Barbara Brandel. Tucson, Ariz.: Omen Press, 1972. vi, 440p. Illus. $4.95 LC 72-90286

The author attempts to correct the materialistic distortion of astrology by Ptolemy and the Greeks. The book spends 200 pages linking sign and house (Leo and the first house, Cancer and the second house). He attempts to correct what he feels are basic errors in the interpretation of signs. He also discusses the Age of Aquarius and mathematical coincidence. There are 24 figures in the back of the book, most done in red and black, with a few multicolored ones.

1682 Todd, Helen. Psychic Powers. London: Theosophical Publishing House, 1975. vii, 77p. (Theosophical Study, no. 11) £1.20 pa. ISBN 0-7229-5044-6

1683 Toler, Ben. Fortune Fingerprints; On Characteristics, Personality Traits and Fortunes According to an Individual's Fingerprints. Vienna, Va.: Relot, Inc., 1972. 59p. Illus. $1.25 pa.

1684 Tomas, Andrew. Atlantis: From Legend to Discovery. London: Sphere, 1973 (orig. pub., London: Hale, 1972). 155p. Illus. Map Plan Index £0.35 pa. ISBN 0-7221-8542-1

1685 ________. Beyond the Time Barrier. Salisbury, England: Compton Russell Ltd., 1974 (also, London: Sphere, 1974). 160p. Illus. Plates £2.25 ISBN 0-85955-010-9

This book discusses the problem of time (atom, tricks of Cronus, clocks and the soul, time travel) and those who broke the time barrier (Nostradamus, Count Louis de Hamon, Jeane Dixon, Edgar Cayce).

1686 Tompkins, Peter, and Christopher Bird. The Secret Life
*** of Plants. New York: Harper and Row, 1973. 402p. Illus. Bibliog. $8.95 LC 72-9160 ISBN 0-06-014326-6

This work is a major new contribution to occult literature. The 1975 World Almanac lists this book among the top 25 non-fiction bestsellers of 1973-1974. It was the occult publishing event of 1973. The work has five main sections: the animal-like properties of plants, pioneers of plant research, the effects of music and electromagnetic energy, organic gardening, and alchemy (changes of one element into another). The work discusses how, beginning in 1966, Cleve Backster, a New York polygraph (lie-detector) expert, wired plants in his office to a polygraph. The plants showed distinct emotional reactions to events and thoughts around them (the term "Backster effect" has since come to be used in some circles in discussing emotional reactions in plants). Others began to do similar work, among them Marcel Vogel (a research chemist at IBM). Then, Pierre Paul Sauvin (former electronics specialist at ITT) tried to communicate with them. The book reports on other such experiments now underway, especially the work of Russian professor Ivan I. Gunar, head of the Department of Plant Physiology at the Timiryazev Academy of Agricultural Sciences. The authors mention Sir Jagadis Chandra Bose, an Indian researcher publishing around 1900. Also treated is Russian researcher Semyon D. Kirlian, who developed a technique of photographing a luminous fringe around the leaves of plants. One section discusses the life of a community in Scotland on the North Sea (Findhorn), where people are trying to meditate with and talk to plants, expressing their appreciation and love to individual plants. Even though the soil is bad, the plants have done very well. An 18-page bibliography ends the work. Recently, this book has come under criticism from some quarters. The complaints are those most frequently leveled at parapsychological research--poorly designed experiments, lack of controlled environments, and inability to repeat results. Some critics state that when temperature and humidity are carefully watched and kept constant, no plant reactions occur. In spite of this criticism, Tompkins and Bird deserve praise for breaking new ground, and also for writing the most important occult book of the year--one destined to become a classic.

1687 Torrens, Robert George. Secret Rituals of the Golden Dawn. Wellingborough, England: Aquarian Press, 1973. 304p. Illus. Bibliog. Index £2.50 ISBN 0-85030-097-5

This work includes texts of some of the rituals, edited from original manuscripts.

1688 Toth, Max, and Greg Nielsen. Pyramid Power. New York: Freeway Press, 1974. 235p. $1.75 pa.

This book studies pyramids in both Egypt and South America, and theorizes on the secret powers of pyramids.

1689 Tralins, Robert. Clairvoyant Women. New York: Popular Library, 1972. 175p. $.75 pa.

1690 Travers, Peter, and Stephanie Reiff. The Story Behind "The Exorcist." New York: Crown, 1974. 245p. Illus. Photos. Index $6.95 LC 74-80297 ISBN 0-517-51656-X

This book discusses production data, writing the script, casting, shooting, public and critical reaction to the film. However, it does not really go into a detailed discussion of special effects work, which may disappoint some readers. The appendix gives the complete Roman Catholic exorcism rite.

1691 Travis, Peter. In Search of the Supernatural. London: Wolfe, 1975. 128p. £2.50 ISBN 0-7234-0630-8

1692 Trigg, Elwood B. Gypsy Demons and Divinities; The Magic and Religion of the Gypsies. Preface by Edward Evans-Pritchard. Secaucus, N.J.: Citadel Press, 1974. 238p. $7.95 LC 73-84146 ISBN 0-8065-0379-3

The author, an Episcopal priest, did a great deal of research and talked personally with gypsies. The book gathers together material from many sources. Topics discussed include cults of the dead, vampires; taboos about death, mourning and sexuality; folklore, recipes, charms, cures, and philters. Trigg portrays them as religious, but with no real liturgy, depth, or historical content to their religion. In the Preface, Evans-Pritchard says that Gypsy society is very difficult to penetrate.

1693 Trowbridge, William Rutherford Hayes, 1866-1938. Cagliostro: Savant or Scoundrel? The True Role of This Splendid, Tragic Figure. New York: Gordon Press, 1975. xxiii, 311p. Illus. Bibliog. Index $34.95 LC 74-180 ISBN 0-87968-106-3

1694 Trupo, Anthony, 1908- . Occult Sciences: How to Get What You Want through Your Occult Powers. By Anthony Norvell [pseud.]. West Nyack, N.Y.: Parker Pub., 1971. 220p. $6.95 LC 76-133414 ISBN 0-13-627877-9

1695 Tucker, Cyril. Research on Survival. Rochester, N. Y.: 1974. 212p. $3.50 pa.

The author, a member of the Spiritual Frontiers Fellowship, discusses eight years he has spent studying survival after death.

1696 Tucker, William Joseph. Genetics and Astrology. Sidcup, England: Pythagorean Publications, 1971. 127p. Illus. Index £2.75 ISBN 0-85387-037-3

1697 Turner, Gordon, 1925- . A Time to Heal; The Autobiography of an Extraordinary Healer. Talmy, England: Franklin, 1974. £2.75

The author healed the publisher's wife, leading to this book. He has also had good success in healing animals. Turner says that if he is not carefully attuned to the subject, or if he becomes personally involved, then his own body energy is taken, rather than the usual process of energy flowing through him from an inexhaustible source. Such a mistake happened in 1966. After treating a stroke victim, Turner had a stroke himself that paralyzed one side of his body. The author does absent healing for people all over the world. He criticizes healer Harry Edwards and his "form letters," with standard replies changed twice a week. He also describes a materialization seance with Alec Harris. Turner mentions Healers' Federation work he did, where hospital patients at 500 hospitals now have a right to ask for a healer just as they would request a priest.

1698 Turner, James, 1909- . Ghosts in the South West. Newton Abbot, England: David and Charles, 1973 (dist. in U. S. by David and Charles, Vt.). $8.95 LC 73-179657 ISBN 0-7153-6263-1

Most of these 17 cases emphasize the setting--history, landscape, or architecture. Stories in this work include appearances of Dorothy Dingley at Petherwin; hauntings by a dog, horse, cleric, two old ladies and a Moorish servant, all seen between 1970 and 1972 at Manor House, Sanford Orcas; and ghosts at Bodmin Moor, Wadebridge, Launceston, Okehampton, Puddleton, Totnes, and Watchet. The author has visited these places, and comes to his own conclusions concerning the stories.

1699 Tweddell, Margaret Flavell. Witness from Beyond: New Cosmic Concepts on Death and Survival Received from the Late A. D. Mattson, S. T. D., Through the Clairvoyant, Margaret Flavell Tweddell. Transcribed and edited by Ruth Mattson Taylor. New York: Hawthorn Books, 1975. xii, 152p. Bibliog. $6.95 LC 75-5033 ISBN 0-8015-8776-X

1700 Twigg, Ena, and Ruth Hagy Brod. Ena Twigg, Medium.
* Introd. by Mervyn Stockwood. London: W. H. Allen, 1973. xix, 295p. Index £3 ISBN 0-491-00903-8

The first half of the book is an autobiography, with a long section on the Bishop Pike affair. On September 4, 1969, Mrs. Twigg and her husband and a canon sat in the Twigg living room, when a voice commanded Mrs. Twigg to turn on the tape recorder. It was the voice of Bishop Pike that then came through her, although Pike had been dead for 24 hours. The entire transcript of that tape is here, plus other experiences Twigg has had as psychic and medium. The second half of the book concerns case studies of famous people she has held sittings for, including Bert Lahr and author Rosamund Lehmann. Ena Twigg has lectured in Europe and the United States, and was the 1967 winner of the "Spiritualist of the Year" award sponsored by Psychic News, an English weekly newspaper.

1701 Tyl, Noel, 1936- . Astrological Counsel. St. Paul, Minn.: Llewellyn Publications, 1974. (Llewellyn Syllabus for Home Study and College Curriculum) (Principles and Practice of Astrology, vol. 10) $3.95 pa. LC 73-19927 ISBN 0-87542-809-6

This volume in Tyl's series discusses the psychodynamics of the astrologer/client relationship. His view is that the horoscope should be shared with the client, and not be a one-sided affair. The astrologer should use the client's judgment and experience. The book gives many diagnostic and counseling techniques, and covers role-playing. Tyl feels that the chief value of astrology is that of "objectification"--bringing an analytical light to the inner recesses of the personality.

1702 * ______. Astrology: Astral, Mundane, Occult. St. Paul, Minn.: Llewellyn Publications, 1974. (Llewellyn Syllabus for Home Study and College Curriculum) (Principles and Practice of Astrology, vol. 11) $3.95 pa. LC 73-19926

In this volume of his series, the author shows how analyzing a country's horoscope is an extension of analyzing a person's horoscope. He discusses using the horoscope of leaders, parties, subcultures, and other nations. Tyl uses Israel as an example of a chart, and compares it with the Arabs' and Kissinger's. He also discusses Crowley, Manson, Nixon, and Ford.

1703 * ______. The Expanded Present. St. Paul, Minn.: Llewellyn Publications, 1974. (Llewellyn Syllabus for Home Study and College Curriculum) (Principles and Practice of Astrology, vol. 6) $3.95 pa. LC 73-19923

The author discusses how to extend the birth horoscope into time, with the aim at finding the person's place in the inexorable flow of time. The book contains these discussions: radix methods, rapport measurement, secondary progressions, Tyl's own discovery--factor 7 time span, man's identity, free will, causality, awareness of potentials. The many examples given include Truman, Nixon, actresses, and executives. (Although no reviews on Tyl's works were found, they are very well done and some have been in this bibliography given a * on their own merits.

1704 ________. Horoscope Construction. St. Paul, Minn. : Llewellyn Publications, 1973. (Llewellyn Syllabus for Home Study and College Curriculum) (Principles and Practice of Astrology, vol. 1) $3.95 pa. LC 73-19904 ISBN 0-87542-800-2

1705 ________. The Houses: Their Signs and Planets. St. Paul, Minn. : Llewellyn Publications, 1974. ix, 135p. Illus. (Llewellyn Syllabus for Home Study and College Curriculum) (Principles and Practice of Astrology, vol. 2) $3.95 pa. LC 73-19909 ISBN 0-87542-801-0

1706 ________. Integrated Transits. St. Paul, Minn. : Llewellyn
* Publications, 1974. (Llewellyn Syllabus for Home Study and College Curriculum) (Principles and Practice of Astrology, vol. 7) $3.95 pa. LC 73-19933 ISBN 0-87542-806-1

In this volume of the series, Tyl interprets the "press of environment" through secondary progressions. These topics are discussed: fate and will, Saturn (architecture of advance), Nixon, LBJ, JFK, Eisenhower, FDR, and Jackie Onassis; Uranus (architecture of change)--covering Uranus with every other planet, Neptune (architecture of the unknown), Pluto (press of perspective), and Jupiter (architecture of opportunity). The book also discusses transits and accidents.

1707 ________. Planets: Their Signs and Aspects. St. Paul, Minn. : Llewellyn Publications, 1974. 175p. (Llewellyn Syllabus for Home Study and College Curriculum) (Principles and Practice of Astrology, vol. 3) $3.95 pa. LC 73-19910 ISBN 0-87542-802-9

1708 ________. Prediction Techniques Synthesized. St. Paul,
* Minn. : Llewellyn Publications, 1974 (also pub. as "Analysis and Prediction"). (Llewellyn Syllabus for Home Study and College Curriculum) (Principles and Practice of Astrology, vol. 8) $3.95 pa. LC 73-19928 ISBN 0-87542-807-X

The author tries to gather information presented in his previous seven volumes and focus it on full-life portraiture. Section 1 discusses many cases. Section 2, on horary astrology, discusses three cases: should I take a teaching job?; the missing necklace; and who took the money? Section 3, on electoral astrology, discusses Ford and Reagan, and also covers cases on a silver purchase, a motion picture premiere, and an aborted take-off.

1709 ________. Special Horoscope Dimensions. St. Paul, Minn. :
* Llewellyn Publications, 1974. (Llewellyn Syllabus for Home Study and College Curriculum) (Principles and Practice of Astrology, vol. 9) $3.95 pa. LC 73-19924

This work is really three separate books on success, sex, and illness. It serves as an introduction to vocational and medical astrology, as well as covering the often neglected sexual principle in horoscope interpretation. Synastry is also discussed. The work gives and interprets 49 detailed case charts.

1710 _______. Times to Come. St. Paul, Minn.: Llewellyn Publications, 1974. (Llewellyn Syllabus for Home Study and College Curriculum) (Principles and Practice of Astrology, vol. 12) $3.95 pa. LC 73-19932 ISBN 0-87542-811-8

1711 Tyrrell, G. N. M. Science and Psychical Phenomena. New York: Arno Press, 1975 (orig. pub., New York, 1938). (Perspectives in Psychical Research) $22 LC 75-7406 ISBN 0-405-06993-6

This book discusses spontaneous cases, early experimental research, the theoretical significance of the studies, mediumistic research, mathematical evaluation of mediumistic material, quantitative studies of trance personalities, cross-correspondences, and book tests.

1712 UFO's--A Scientific Debate. Ed. by Carl Sagan and Thornton Page. Ithaca, N.Y.: Cornell University Press, 1972 (also, New York: Norton, 1974). xxxi, 310p. Illus. Bibliog. Index (Papers presented at symposium sponsored by American Association for the Advancement of Science, Boston, Dec. 26-27, 1969) $12.50 LC 72-4572 ISBN 0-8014-0740-0
***

This work is a major new contribution to occult literature. The following papers are presented: "Education and the UFO Phenomenon" by Thornton Page, "Historical Perspectives: Photos of UFO's" by William K. Hartmann, "Astronomers' Views on UFO's" by Franklin Roach, "Twenty-one Years of UFO Reports" by J. Allen Hynek, "Science in Default: Twenty-Two Years of Inadequate UFO Investigations" by James E. McDonald (including in an appendix summaries of four cases--south central U.S. on July 17, 1957, Lakenheath and Bentwaters, England, on August 13-14, 1956, Haneda AFB, Tokyo, Japan, on August 5-6, 1952, and Kirtland AFB, N.M., on November 4, 1957); "UFO's--The Modern Myth" by Donald H. Menzel (including an appendix containing seven discussions--Papua case of June, July, and August, 1959, Clearwater, Fla. on July 4, 1964, UFO's of March 3, 1968, phantom plane at Colorado Springs on May 13, 1967, whether flying saucers move in straight lines, UFO's in art, and flying saucers of the Bible); "Unusual Radar Echoes" by Kenneth R. Hardy, "Motion Pictures of UFO's" by R. M. L. Baker, Jr., "Sociological Perspectives on UFO Reports" by Robert L. Hall, "Psychology and Epistemology of UFO Interpretations" by Douglass R. Price-Williams, "Psychiatry and UFO Reports" by Lester Grinspoon and Alan D. Persky, "On the Abilities and Limitations of Witnesses of UFO's and Similar Phenomena" by Frank D. Drake, "Influence of the Press and Other Mass Media" by Walter Sullivan, "UFO's: The Extraterrestrial and Other Hypotheses" by Carl Sagan, and "Nature of Scientific Evidence: A Summary" by Philip Morrison. The book takes no stand on the issue of UFO reality, but the editors feel that all unanswered questions should be confronted through scientific investigation.

1713 Ullman, Montague; Stanley Krippner; and Alan Vaughan.
*** Dream Telepathy. London: Turnstone Books, 1973 (also Baltimore: Penguin, 1974; orig. pub., New York: Macmillan, 1973). xv, 300p. Illus. Plates Includes bibliog. refs. Index £2.95 ISBN 0-85500-012-0

This work is a major new contribution to occult literature. The author was director of the William C. Menninger Dream Lab at Maimonides Medical Center in Brooklyn, N.Y., at the time he wrote this book. The first section consists of four chapters on spontaneous telepathic dreams, from biblical times to the present. The second section discusses experimental studies at the dream lab, the third discusses implications of the research, and the fourth has three appendices. One appendix is composed of comments by psychologists and parapsychologists on Ullman's work, some favorable and some not. A second appendix is the complete transcript of one night of subject William Erwin's dreams. The third appendix gives statistics from experiments. The book discusses Ullman's background, subjects William Erwin, Robert Van de Castle, Alan Vaughan, and Malcolm Bessent, and basic methodology (they use EEG to monitor dream state while the person has an agent beam target material to him during his REM periods; the person is awakened, and tells his experience).

1714 Umland, Craig, and Eric Umland. Mysteries of the Ancients: Early Spacemen and the Mayas. London: Souvenir Press, 1975 (orig. pub., New York: Walker, 1974). 186p. Illus. Map Bibliog. Index £3.25 ISBN 0-285-62162-9

The authors claim that the Mayas came from another solar system to mine minerals after cleaning out the moon's core. Their main base was destroyed, and they became stranded on Earth. Their race may be planning a rescue mission soon to Earth, with disastrous effects for us. Chapters discuss the mysterious Mayan numbers, cracking the code, the pyramid cult, the mystery of the wheel, asteroids as pieces of the puzzle, Antarctica as the first Mayan base, Atlantis, Mu, and Lemuria as Ice Age islands, Earth as a cosmic treasure chest, and the Mayan menace.

1715 Understanding Astrology: The Influence of the Stars on You and Others. London: Octopus Books, 1973. 176p. Illus. (some color) Facsims. Index

There are over 200 illustrations in this work, many of them in full color. It is an introduction to the principles and history of astrology, and includes information on how to cast a horoscope and how the stars influence our careers, health, and loves. The chief value of the work is in its many illustrations, some of them modern graphic charts and symbols.

1716 Underwood, Peter, 1923- . Deeper into the Occult. London: Harrap, 1975. 200p. Bibliog. Index £4.30 ISBN 0-245-52565-3

1717 ________. Gazetteer of British Ghosts. New York: Walker
*** and Company, 1975 (also, London: Fontana, 1974; London: Pan Books, 1973; orig. pub., London: Souvenir Press, 1971). 256p. Illus. Photos. Bibliog. Index $7.95 LC 74-81613 ISBN 0-8027-0470-0

This work is a major new contribution to occult literature. The fine book is an illustrated guide to 236 haunted sites in Great Britain. The entries are arranged alphabetically by name of house; if there is no name, the entry is that of the location. The author includes both famous and lesser known sites. Entries about which Underwood has personal knowledge (from interviewing the witnesses, investigating the case, or visiting the site himself) are marked with an asterisk. As to whether he believes in ghosts, Underwood says that the question of belief does not enter into his work. However, he is impressed by "the wealth of evidence for ghosts and hauntings." The author has been president of the Ghost Club (founded by Harry Price) for over 10 years. Sites mentioned include Borley Rectory, Marshwood (with its screaming skull), Meopham (the headless monk), Number 50 Berkeley Square (the site used by Lytton in The Haunters and the Haunted). Tales range from authentic to legendary. There are 32 plates included. The index is only by county. Sites include 11 Scottish and five Irish.

1718 ________. Gazetteer of Scottish and Irish Ghosts. New York:
* Walter and Company, 1975 (orig. pub., London: Souvenir Press, 1973). 251p. Illus. Plates Index $7.95 LC 74-81614 ISBN 0-8027-0471-9

This work is an illustrated guide to 130 sites, 103 in Scotland and 27 in Ireland. It is not as important as his Gazetteer of British Ghosts (entry 1717) because this book leans more toward folklore and legend. This can be seen in the fact that most entries in the present work are by place, not on a specific house where specific phenomena took place. However, the work is still very useful and well done. Underwood states, "I do not claim that all the entries included are factual accounts in the literal sense." He has tried to present a representative selection of traditional tales, famous and little known. There are 32 plates included. The index is very well done, 10 pages in length, and a great improvement over the index in the British Gazetteer.

1719 ________. Haunted London. Photos. by Chris Underwood. London: Harrap, 1973 (also, London: Fontana, 1975). 200p. Illus. Plates Bibliog. Index £3.10

1720 _______. A Host of Hauntings: A Shuddersome Book of Ghosts and Ghostly Adventures. London: Frewin, 1973. 258p. Illus. Plates Bibliog. Index £2.95

1721 _______. Into the Occult. London: Harrap, 1972. 158p. Illus. Bibliog. Index £1.75 ISBN 0-245-50673-X

1722 _______. The Vampire's Bedside Companion: The Amazing World of Vampires in Fact and Fiction. Illus. by Geoffrey Bourne-Taylor. London: Frewin, 1975. 248p. Illus. Plates Bibliog. £3.50 ISBN 0-85632-101-X

1723 _______, and Paul Tabori. The Ghosts of Borley; Annals
* of the Haunted Rectory. Newton Abbot, England: David and Charles, 1973 (dist. by David and Charles, Vt.). 240p. Illus. Bibliog. $9.95 LC 73-179653 ISBN 0-7153-6118-X

This is probably the best survey on this topic, and the definitive work for years to come. It includes a great deal of hitherto unpublished material. Paul Tabori is literary executor to the Harry Price estate, and has access to all relevant materials. The authors say that there is reasonable evidence that strange events have occurred and still take place there. The hauntings are not just at the rectory and garden, but across the road to the church. They occur especially in periods when the moon is full or on the wane. This fact leads to a possible geophysical explanation, such as small shifts in the earth. This may be supported by reports of panic by animals and the ringing of house bells in the area. The rectory is close to the line where clay beds end and chalk ones begin. It is also at the foot of an escarpment in the Cotswold Hills.

1724 _______, and Leonard Wilder. Lives to Remember: A Case Book on Reincarnation. Foreword by Bernard Finch. London: Hale, 1975. 224p. Bibliog. Index £3.60 ISBN 0-7091-5224-8

1725 Unger, Merrill Frederick, 1909- . The Haunting of Bishop Pike; A Christian View of "The Other Side." Wheaton, Ill.: Tyndale House Pubs., 1971. 115p. Includes bibliog. refs. $2.95 pa. LC 76-144329 ISBN 0-8423-1340-0

The author says that Pike was deluded by evil spirits into thinking he was contacting his dead son, since many of the messages from Jim do not conform to the Bible. In fact, Unger claims that all spiritualism and non-Christian religions may also have a demoniac origin. Only 40 pages are actually on the Pike case. The rest of the book applies Bible quotes to Pike's book, The Other Side. Unger was professor of Old Testament studies at Dallas Theological Seminary from 1948 to 1967, and has a Ph.D. from Johns Hopkins University. He has written many books on the Old Testament and archaeology in the Bible.

1726 Uphoff, Walter, and Mary Jo Uphoff. New Psychic Frontiers: Your Key to New Worlds. Foreword by Harold Sherman. Gerrards Cross, England: Smythe, 1975 (dist. by M. J. Uphoff, Oregon, Wisc. and by DeVorss and Co., Santa Monica, Calif.). xvii, 278p. Illus. Bibliog. Index $9.50 LC 74-32517 ISBN 0-901072-17-6

This book was written as a textbook for parapsychology courses. Topics discussed include psychic surgery, Kirlian photography, Backster's plant research, spirit photography, and taping spirit voices. A 30-page chapter quotes many sensitives and psychic researchers. Another chapter (30 pages) gives an international list of colleges offering courses in parapsychology and research organizations. Addresses are included. Many of the topics chosen in this book are in the less widely accepted areas of parapsychology.

1727 Valcourt-Vermont, Edgar de. Practical Astrology, by Comte C. de Saint-Germain [pseud.]. Hollywood, Calif.: Newcastle Pub. Co., 1973 (orig. pub., 1901). 257p. $2.95 pa. ISBN 0-87877-018-6

This book discusses the use of astrology in judging character and in divination. The author also gives a discussion of astrology and its relationship to the Tarot.

1728 _______. The Practice of Palmistry for Professional Purposes, by Comte C. de Saint-Germain [pseud.]. Introd. by Adolphe Desbarroles. Hollywood, Calif.: Newcastle Pub. Co., 1973 (orig. pub. in 2 vols., 1897). 416p. Illus. $3.95 pa. ISBN 0-87877-019-4

This work is a complete palmistry dictionary, and contains over 1,250 original illustrations.

1729 Valentine, Tom. The Great Pyramid: Man's Monument to Man. New York: Pinnacle Books, 1975. 176p. $1.50 pa.

The author feels that the Hyksos built the Pyramid. They were a civilization who coexisted with Cro-Magnon man. They educated the tribes and organized a volunteer labor force to build the Great Pyramid as a symbol of man's perfectibility. It was also built to give scientific information and to predict the future. The author is a Chicago journalist. He states at the book's close, "The Great Pyramid is not one thing, it is many things."

1730 _______. Psychic Surgery. Introd. by Harold Sherman.
* Chicago, Ill.: Henry Regnery, 1973. 160p. Illus. Photos. $6.95 LC 72-11190 ISBN 0-8092-9090-1

This book discusses Antonio C. Agpaoa and other psychic surgeons of the Philippines. Valentine covers operations by Agpaoa, and investigations of him under laboratory conditions. Valentine claims to take a middle-of-the-road stance on whether Agpaoa is gifted or the perpetrator of a hoax. Although the author seems to have been convinced the phenomena were genuine, after interviewing people and seeing the movies, even before he visited Agpaoa himself, the tone of the book is objective. Valentine discusses cases where fraud was claimed, and says that only one fraud has been proven. The author also discusses Arigo, Oscar Estabany, and Kathryn Kuhlman. The introduction is by Harold Sherman, who wrote the pioneer work on Agpaoa, Wonder Healers of the Philippines.

1731 Valentine, William Alexander, 1905- . ESP at Work. Philadelphia: Franklin Pub. Co., 1974. 149p. Includes bibliog. refs. $6.95 LC 74-81562 ISBN 0-87133-019-9

The author, a psychic, discusses the development of his abilities since youth, including experiences with dreams, predictions, and visions. He says that the reader can go through the same development as he did.

1732 Valiente, Doreen. ABC of Witchcraft Past and Present.
* London: Hale, 1973 (also, New York: St. Martin's Press, 1974). xvii, 377p. Illus. Index £3.50 ISBN 0-7091-3164-X

This work is a good encyclopedia of witchcraft, especially concerning English practices. There are over 125 entries in this book by a practicing English witch. To her, witchcraft means the the Old Religion. Therefore, satanism is excluded, while the occult and magic are included. Topics covered include magical alphabets, amulets, the Book of Shadows, Druids, evocation, herbs, incense, pentagram, stone circles, astral plane, astrology, Atlantis, vampires, werewolves, and biographies of the most famous witches.

1733 ________. Natural Magic. New York: St. Martin's Press, 1975 (also, London: Hale, 1975). 184p. Illus. $6.95 LC 75-4210 ISBN 0-7091-4916-6

This book discusses flora, fauna, weather, dreams, and how each influences occult practices, the history of each, and uses in rituals and divination. The author mentions major persons who practice each type. She also covers how to improve sex, the properties of colors, and removing evil spirits from the garden. Valiente is a British gardening columnist.

1734 Vallee, Jacques. The Invisible College: An Investigation of
* the Reality Behind the UFO Phenomenon. New York: Dutton, 1975. 223p. Bibliog. Index $8.95 LC 75-12843 ISBN 0-525-13470-0

The author is one of the foremost authorities and theorists

on the UFO phenomenon. He says that "unidentified flying objects are neither objects nor flying." He feels that no theory of UFO's is acceptable if it does not account for the psychic effect produced by these objects. This book therefore discusses the psychic component, the winged disk, the morphology of miracles (Fatima, Guadalupe, Mormons), Uri Geller, control systems, the physics of the Blessed Virgin Mary, confrontation, and ESP with saucer occupants. He concludes that the UFO phenomenon is a control system, forcing us through a learning process including experimentation, which is based on some kind of mythological process we do not understand. Needless to say, the book is very thought-provoking.

1735 Vance, Charles Bruce, and Clyde Beauregarde Vance. International Astrological Register, 1974-1975. Fresno, Calif.: Fresno Astrology Book Center, 1974. 129p. $5.95 pa.

This work is an international list of astrologers, astrological organizations, and bookstores.

1736 Vance, Clyde Beauregarde. The Astrologer's Electronic Calculator Manual. Fresno, Calif.: Fresno Astrology Book Center, 1974. 254p. $8.95 spiralbound.

1737 Vandenberg, Philipp. The Curse of the Pharaohs. Trans.
* by Thomas Weyr. Philadelphia: J. P. Lippincott Co., 1975 (also, London: Hodder and Stoughton, 1975). 221p. Illus. Map Plan Bibliog. Index (Translation of "Fluch der Pharaonen." Bern: Scherz, 1973) $8.95

This work summarizes information on the deaths of archaeologists, curators, and others involved with digging up the tombs of Egypt. Vandenberg claims that over 30 untimely deaths have occurred since 1900. He discovered three principal causes of death: fever with delusions, strokes accompanied by circulatory collapse, and sudden cancers that were quickly terminal. He rules out coincidence, and studies alternatives such as poisons, bacteria, radioactivity, and energy fields. He discusses Egyptian medicine, astronomy, methods of embalming, tombs, and pyramid power. The book makes for fascinating reading, although some of the deaths could well be coincidence. The author is writer-editor of the German "Playboy" magazine, and lives in Munich.

1738 Van Deusen, Wilson. The Presence of Other Worlds. New York: Harper and Row, 1974. 240p. $6.95

The author is a clinical psychologist and member of the Swedenborg Foundation. He has spent a great deal of time studying Swedenborg, because of his own religious visions that seem to confirm Swedenborg's experiences. Van Deusen admits that there was madness along Swedenborg's path because of the tremendous forces he released within himself. He feels that possibly Swedenborg discovered too much, causing his works to seem puzzling and mad.

1739 Van Over, Raymond, ed. Psychology and Extrasensory Perception. New York: New American Library, 1972. 416p.
* Illus. Bibliog. $1.95 pa. LC 72-88856

This work is a collection of 18 articles published in books and journals from 1897 to 1972, arranged in three parts. Part 1, "Early Roots," has seven papers: "What Psychical Research Has Accomplished," by William James (1897), "Psychology and Psychical Research" by F. C. S. Schiller (1898), "Frederic Myers's Service to Psychology" by William James (1901), William McDougall's 1921 Society for Psychical Research address, "Psychoanalysis and Telepathy" by Freud (1921), "The Psychological Foundations of Belief in Spirits" by Jung (1919), and "Occult Processes Occurring During Psychoanalysis" by Helen Deutsch (1926). Part 2, "Beginning Science: Observations and Overviews," presents these papers: "Psi and Psychology: Conflict and Solution" by J. B. Rhine (1967), "Psychology and Psychical Research" by Gardner Murphy (1953), "ESP Breakthroughs: Paranormal Effects in Real Life" by Gertrude Schmeidler (1967), "The Establishment of Basic Concepts and Terminology in Parapsychology" by Louisa Rhine (1971), "Personality and ESP" by H. J. Eysenck (1966), and "The Problem of Repeatability in Psychical Research" by Gardner Murphy (1969). Part 3, "Implications," presents these papers: "The Role of Parapsychology in Modern Thinking" by Ira Progoff (1959), "The Telepathy Hypothesis and Doctrinal Compliance with Psychotherapy" by Jan Ehrenwald (1957), "Implications of Parapsychology for General Psychology" by Cyril Burt (1967), "Sympathy and Telepathy: A Model for Psycho dynamic Research in Parapsychology" by Joost A. M. Meerloo (1968), and "The Place of Theory in Parapsychology" by John Beloff (1972). The appendix contains the paper, "Psychical Research as a University Study" by William McDougall (1926).

1740 ________. Unfinished Man. New York: World Publishing
* Co., 1972. xiii, 210p. $6.95 LC 73-183084 ISBN 0-529-04556-7

The author feels that all psychology and physiology research is wrong. A mechanistic approach will never give man an understanding of himself. Thus, man is still not finished. The book discusses these topics: man in general (with many quotations given), man as a unique being, the unconsciousness, trance states (hypnotic, mediumistic, and paranormal), dreams, ESP, psychedelic drugs, the source of art, language, religion, philosophy, and aspiration, behaviorism and reductionism, and sense perception. The appendix discusses experimentation in ESP.

1741 Varahamihira, d. 587? The Brihajjatakam of Varaha Mihira. Trans. by Swami Vijnanananda, alias Hari Prasanna Chatterjee. New York: AMS Press, 1974 (orig. pub., Allahabad, Panini Office, 1912; orig. ed. issued as vol. 12 of "Sacred Books of the Hindus. English and Sanskrit; foreword and notes in English). $32.50 LC 73-3800 ISBN 0-404-57812-8

This book of Hindu astrology contains the commentary of Bhattotpala (A. D. 950), the Jagaccandrika, and three lesser-known commentaries, the Subodhini, the Mudraksari, and the Sripatiyam. Translator Vijnanananda's dates are 1868-1938.

1742 *** Vaughan, Alan. Patterns of Prophecy. New York: Hawthorn Books, 1973 (also, London: Turnstone Books, 1974). xii, 244p. Includes bibliog. refs. Index $7.95 LC 72-11219

This work is a major new contribution to occult literature. The author is articles editor of Psychic magazine. The book grew out of his trying to understand prophecy and the turmoils it created in his own life. The eight chapters discuss prophecy and his experiences in learning how to do it, which started with a ouija board. The work covers the Central Premonitions Registry in New York, the Maimonides Dream Lab in Brooklyn, precognition, prophecy, Jung's theory of synchronicity or meaningful coincidences, and archetypes. There are also chapters about Atlantis, the great San Francisco earthquake (which never happened), the end of the world, and the Apollo moon trip. Vaughan tries to answer several basic questions, for example, why are only certain events forseen? and can predictions alter the future? The author postulates his "blueprint theory"--each person is born with a psychic blueprint containing the basic patterns of his future, and based on building block-type patterns of life from the past called archetypes. At its best, prophecy can show what possibilities these archetypal roles might offer, if given proper expression in one's life. Meeting these patterns would not only fulfill the individual's basic needs, but would make him a co-creator with God.

1743 Vaughan, Richard Blackmore, 1916- . Astrology in Modern Language; How to Read Your Character and Destiny Through the Stars. Illus. by John Sarando. New York: Putnam, 1972. 351p. Illus. $8.95 LC 70-171475

The author says that astrology plays a major role in shaping one's life. He includes a sample reading on Nixon.

1744 Veer, M. H. J. Th. van der, and P. Moerman. Hidden Worlds: Fresh Clues to the Past; Did Columbus, Magellan and Piri Reis Know the Glareanus Maps? Trans. by A. D. Hills. London: Corgi, 1975 (orig. pub., London: Souvenir Press, 1974). xiii, 207p. Maps Index (Translation of "Nieuwe Sporen Naar het Verleden." Deventer, the Netherlands: Ankh-Hermes, 1972) £0.60 pa. ISBN 0-552-10041-2

1745 * Vesco, Renato. Intercept--But Don't Shoot; The True Story of the Flying Saucers. Trans. by D. D. Paige. New York: Grove, 1971. xi, 338p. Includes bibliog. refs. (Translation of "Intercettateli senza sparare") $8.50 LC 76-125004

Although this book discusses UFO sightings and Project

Blue Book, much of it is on German World War II devices that could possibly have been developed into flying saucers. Vesco feels that Britain and Canada have jointly developed them, and built them in large underground Canadian factories. These craft have caused the UFO sightings since 1947. The author does not give the locations of these saucer bases. He does not believe in the concept of extraterrestrial UFO's. Vesco is a former Italian Air Force pilot, and now works as an aircraft designer. The book is interesting in its discussions of German research during World War II.

1746 Vice, Diana. Stainton-Moses Communications through Diana Vice. Taunton, England: Martigan Publications, 1973. 34p. £0.24 pa. ISBN 0-902801-07-4

This work contains shortened versions of more elaborate dissertations, purporting to be communications received by the South African medium, Diana Vice, from alleged spirit entities, under the control of one presumed to be the late Reverend William Stainton-Moses.

1747 Views from the Real World: Early Talks [of Gurdjieff] in Moscow, Essentuki, Tiflis, Berlin, London, Paris, New York and Chicago as Recollected by His Pupils. Foreword by Jeanne de Salzmann. London: Routledge and Kegan Paul, 1973 (orig. pub., New York: Triangle Editions, 1973). xiii, 284p. Illus. £4.25 ISBN 0-7100-7811-0

This work is about Gurdjieff. It contains what some of his pupils remember about his early discussions, lectures and conversations. These are not directly transcribed, for he did not allow students to take notes. Gurdjieff felt that students should only be given a rough idea, which they would develop to perfection through hard work.

1748 Vignon, Paul. The Shroud of Christ. Secaucus, N.J.: University Books, 1974 (orig. pub., 1902). 171p. $10

The shroud was displayed in 1898, and photographed by Secondo Pia. The negatives gave a positive image of a face and body, meaning that the shroud acted like a photographic negative. Vignon, a Catholic artist and scientist, made a serious study of these photos. He claimed that sweat reacted with the spices with which the shroud had been anointed. Mention is made of a confession in medieval times that it was a hoax.

1749 Villiers, Elizabeth. The Book of Charms. Illus. by Victoria Hayatt. New ed. London: Lorrimer, 1973 (also, New
* York: Simon & Schuster, 1974; previous ed. pub. as "The Mascot Book," London: Laurie, 1923). 144p. Illus. Index £1.50 pa. ISBN 0-85647-025-2

This work is a well-done introduction to the subject. The

author presents discussions on these topics: the origins and mythology of charms (cross, wheel of fortune, and swastika); signs, sigils, and talismans; stones, jewels, and beads (moonstone, lapis lazuli); days, numbers, and colors; animals and plants (lotus, mandrake, stork, bat); and metals and miscellaneous charms. There are over 50 full-page, black-and-white drawings.

1750 Voldben, A. After Nostradamus. Trans. by Gavin Gibbons. Secaucus, N.J.: Citadel Press, 1974 (also, St. Albans, England: Mayflower, 1975; orig. pub., London: Spearman, 1973). xiii, 183p. Bibliog. (Translation of "Dopo Nostradamus." Rome: Edizioni Mediterranee, 1972) $6.95 LC 74-80821 ISBN 0-8065-0431-5

The author has studied the prophecies of Nostradamus, and theorizes that wars and confusion will come in the transition from the Piscean to the Aquarian Age.

1751 Volguine, Alexandre. Lunar Astrology: An Attempt at a Reconstruction of the Ancient Astrological System. Trans. by John Broglio. New York: ASI Publishers, 1974. 128p. Illus. Bibliog. (Translation of "Astrologie lunaire") $7.95 LC 74-75523 ISBN 0-88231-004-6

1752 Vollman, Herbert. Concerning Grail Activities on Earth. Stuttgart, The Grail Message Foundation Pub. Co., 1971 (also, London: The Grail Foundation, 1971). 27p. Illus. £0.40 pa. ISBN 0-902307-07-X

von Buttlar, Johannes see Buttlar, Johannes von

von Däniken, Erich see Däniken, Erich von

von Franz, Marie-Louise see Franz, Marie-Louise von

1753 Von Ifft, Rebecca. Astrology for Men, as Interpreted by.... Woodbridge, Conn.: Apollo Books, 1971. xiii, 507p. Charts $1.25 pa.

1754 ______. Astrology for Women, as Interpreted by.... Woodbridge, Conn.: Apollo Books, 1971. xiii, 465p. Charts $1.25 pa.

1755 ______. Everyone's Complete Astrology and Horoscope, as Interpreted by.... New Haven, Conn.: Apollo Books, 1971. ix, 438p. Charts $1.50 pa.

1756 Vosper, Cyril. The Mind Benders. St. Albans, England: Mayflower, 1973 (orig. pub., London: Spearman, 1971). 175p. Illus. Facsims. £0.40 pa. ISBN 0-583-12249-3

This book is a good summary of Scientology teachings and organization. In it is strong criticism of the group by one who was an officer in it for 14 years. An important responsibility for all top Scientology officials is to produce in their sections a large number of successful, paying students. If the official fails in this production, he is classed into various levels: Non-existence, Liability, Doubt, Enemy, Treason. An Enemy can be deprived of property, injured or destroyed, according to the author. A chapter on Scientology ethics is included.

1757 Wagman, Naomi. Sun and Daughter Signs: An Astrological Guide to Child Care. Ed. and introd. by Sylvia Sherman. New York: M. Padell, 1974. xvii, 275p. Illus. $12.95 LC 73-87928 ISBN 0-87538-000-X

This book goes sign-by-sign, giving mother, child, mother and child together, star guide, and famous personalities of that sign. Appendices give meaning of planets, emotions and characteristics controlled by each planet, and girls' and boys' names and meanings. A full-page color picture of each sign starts each chapter.

1758 Waite, Arthur Edward, 1857-1942. A Pictorial Key to the
* Tarot; Being Fragments of a Secret Tradition under the Veil of Divination. Illus. by Pamela Colman Smith. Introd. by Paul M. Allen. Blauvelt, N. Y.: Rudolf Steiner Pubns., 1971 (also, New York: Causeway Books, 1973 [color plate ed.]; New Hyde Park, N. Y.: University Books, 1959; orig. pub., London, 1910). xii, 340p. Illus. Bibliog. $1.95 pa. LC 79-175056

This classic work features a redesign of the Tarot deck by psychic artist Pamela Colman Smith, working with Waite. In his discussions, Waite feels that the Tarot has no history prior to the 14th century. However, this by no means prevents it from being the carrier of secret doctrine. Instead of bearing Egyptian knowledge, though, it carries Western insights. After a discussion of the history and symbolism of the Tarot, Waite concentrates on the major trumps as the bearers of mystical tradition. He then covers the minor arcana, discussing its difference from the major. Besides giving the symbolic meanings, he also later gives the divinatory meaning for major and minor arcana. Other smaller sections discuss the recurrence of cards in dealing and various methods of divination; an annotated bibliography of the chief Tarot books is included. Discussion of each of the 78 cards is accompanied by an illustration of the card, done in the "Waite deck" style.

1759 Waite, Margaret. The Mystic Sciences. Woodbridge, Conn.: Apollo Books, 1971. xi, 217p. $1 pa. ISBN 0-524-00105-1

1760 Wake, C. Staniland. The Origin and Significance of the Great Pyramid. Savage, Minn.: Wizard's Bookshelf, 1975 (orig. pub., 1882). 131p. $6.50

1761 Waldo-Schwartz, Paul. Art and the Occult. New York: Braziller, 1975. 168p. Illus. Bibliog. $17.50 LC 75-7655 ISBN 0-8076-0784-3

The author discusses the use of the occult in interpreting art objects, and in understanding the role of artists. There are many small black-and-white illustrations, with quotes, definitions, and comments. Artists and writers are mostly from the 19th and 20th centuries. The book is very scholarly in style. An appendix discusses the Tarot.

1762 Walker, Charlotte (Abell), 1863- . Astrology Interpreted; Your Complete Guide to the Stars. Northbrook, Ill.: Hubbard Press, 1973. 189p. Illus. $1.50 pa. LC 73-83188 ISBN 0-8331-1102-7

1763 Walker, Daniel Pickering. Spiritual and Demonic Magic: From Ficino to Campanella. Notre Dame, Ind.: University of Notre Dame Press, 1975 (reprint of 1969 ed. pub. by Kraus Reprint; orig. pub., London: Warburg Institute, 1958). vi, 244p. Includes bibliog. refs. Index (Issued as vol. 22 of Studies of the Warburg Institute) $4.95 pa. LC 74-34547 ISBN 0-268-01670-4

1764 Walker, George Benjamin, 1913- . Beyond the Body; The Human Double and the Astral Planes. London, Boston: Routledge and K. Paul, 1974. viii, 224p. Bibliog. Index $9.25 LC 74-174785 ISBN 0-7100-7808-0

This book discusses the astral body, out-of-the-body experiences, life and consciousness, physiology, transcendental states of awareness, the nature of other planes and inhabitants, traditional lore on the etheric double, and the soul.

1765 Walker, Jeanne, 1924- . Always, Karen. Foreword by George Daisley. New York: Hawthorn Books, 1975. 137p. Illus. Plates Bibliog. $6.95 LC 74-20288 ISBN 0-8015-2840-2

The author discusses communications received through medium George Daisley from her daughter, Karen, who died of leukemia. The phrase, "Always, Karen," is the way she signed her last letter from up above to the man she had planned to marry. In her messages, Karen was very specific in mentioning traits of her family members. She also discussed life on the other side.

1766 Walker, Kenneth Macfarlane, 1882- . Extra-Sensory Mind. New York: Harper, 1972 (c1961). 256p. $1.25 pa. ISBN 0-06-080248-0

1767 Walker, Sheila S. Ceremonial Spirit Possession in Africa and Afro-America; Forms, Meanings, and Functional Significance for Individuals and Social Groups. Leiden: Brill,

1972, (dist. in U. S. by Humanities Press, New York). xii, 179p. Bibliog. (Dissertationes ad Historiam Religionum Pertinentes, vol. 4) $19.95 LC 73-168738

This work reviews sociological and anthropological literature on spirit possession, relying mainly on examples from Brazil, Haiti, and West Africa. It centers on the neurophysiology of possession. The author begins by studying the physiological basis of possession, and then discusses how each culture super-imposes a different context over this base. Walker argues that we cannot call possession normal or abnormal without studying it in its cultural context.

1768 Wallace, Alfred Russel. Miracles and Modern Spiritualism. Rev. ed. New York: Arno Press, 1975 (orig. pub., London, 1896). (Perspectives in Psychical Research) $14 LC 75-7409 ISBN 0-405-06996-0

This book is based in part on an 1874 paper, "Defense of Modern Spiritualism." The author argues that the supernatural should be studied with the tools of science, and its phenomena studied as natural events. Wallace discusses animal magnetism, od-force, clairvoyance, apparitions, phantasms, and spiritualism.

1769 Walton, Alan Hull. The Open Grave. New York: Taplinger, 1971 (c1969). 233p. Includes bibliog. refs. $5.95 LC 76-143494 ISBN 0-8008-5835-2

1770 Warcollier, René, 1876- . Experimental Telepathy. Ed. by Gardner Murphy. Trans. by Josephine B. Gridley and Maud King Murphy. New York: Arno Press, 1975 (orig. pub., Boston: Boston Society for Psychic Research, 1938). (Ed. and abridged by Murphy from Télépathie, articles in La Revue Métapsychique, and recent unpub. studies) (Perspectives in Psychical Research) $17 LC 75-7411 ISBN 0-405-06997-9

This book is a collection of Warcollier's best papers. It includes six chapters from his 1921 book Télépathie, eight articles published in the journal La Revue Métapsychique, and two unpublished articles covering later work done under the auspices of the Boston Society for Psychical Research. The work includes a mixture of experimental details, philosophical speculations, and mention of the psychological conditions most conducive to successful telepathy.

1771 Warner, Rebecca Micca. Tarot; An Illustrated Guide. London: Academy Editions, 1974 (also, New York: St. Martin's Press, 1974, same ed.). 87p. Illus. Bibliog. $10 LC 72-85555 ISBN 0-902620-18-5

1772 Warren, Doug. Demonic Possession. New York: Pyramid Books, 1975. 190p. $1.50 pa.

This book includes interviews with exorcists, and case histories.

1773 Waters, Frank. Mexico Mystique; The Coming Sixth World
* of Consciousness. Chicago: Swallow, 1975. 326p. $10
LC 74-18579

The author discusses pre-Columbian cultures, which he feels show a level of consciousness different from the Western European mind. Waters discusses pre-Columbian mythology, Edgar Cayce, Atlantis, astrology, anthropology, Jungian psychology, pyramids, and UFO's. He attempts to join astrology, mythology and Jungian psychology. He draws parallels between Mesoamerican myths and those of Indians in the southwestern U. S. He feels that Mesoamerican cultures had the correct view of reality as dualistic, cyclical and redemptive. Cyclical periods of spiritual development are linked to the rise and fall of civilizations under control of astral forces. He predicts the end of our era on December 24th, 2011, in catastrophe, when the Age of Aquarius (the sixth world of consciousness) begins. The book shows a vast amount of research.

1774 Waters, Thomas A. The Art of Using Your Mind; or, The Science of Psychologistics. London: Allen and Unwin, 1973 (orig. pub., New York: Random House, 1971). xiii, 236p. Illus. £2.95 ISBN 0-04-130017-3

The author is a writer and investigator of fraudulent psychic phenomena. He tells how to improve one's personality and mental efficiency, and how to interpret the unconscious through accidental clues obtained through the ouija board and other occult tools that catch the unconscious unaware.

1775 Watson, Lyall. The Romeo Error: A Matter of Life and
*** Death. London: Hodder and Stoughton, 1974 (also, New York: Anchor/Doubleday, 1974). 254p. Bibliog. Index £3.25
ISBN 0-340-19136-8

This work is a major new contribution to occult literature. The author discusses our knowledge and ideas on death, which, he suggests, may be indistinguishable from life. The title comes from Shakespeare's Romeo and Juliet, in which Romeo thinks Juliet is dead, although she is only in a deep sleep, and kills himself. The author wonders how often we, too, have mistaken life for death. He discusses an invisible, magnetic, possibly immortal life force surrounding all living things. This force may be the source of ESP, PK, and OOBE's. It may also explain ghosts, UFO's, and the Loch Ness Monster. These topics are discussed: death regarded as a disease, death as part of a cycle, the mind, personality and the body, enlightenment as a biological process, dissociation between body and mind, the soul, survival without the body, possession within other bodies, and miracles and other realities. Much of the discussion in the book is scientific and biological. This is because the author served for a time as apprentice to Desmond Morris at the London Zoo, and is presently director of Biologic of London, a consulting firm in the life sciences. Watson makes the point in closing that there is a definite barrier in investigating psychic phenomena, not put there by frauds afraid of exposure, but existing independently of anyone. The author feels the barrier may be set up deliberately by something, perhaps by our unconscious minds, to keep us from traveling too far too fast. Watson says he will try to go through this unexpected barrier, "but I must admit that right now on the edge of this unexpected chasm, I am a little afraid."

1776 ________. Supernature; The Natural History of the Supernatural. Garden City, N.Y.: Anchor/Doubleday, 1973 (also, London: Hodder and Stoughton, 1973; also, London: Coronet, 1974). xiv, 344p. Bibliog. Index $7.95 LC 72-92399
***

This work is a major new contribution to occult literature. There are four large sections in it: matter, mind, cosmos, and time. The author claims that there is a measurable, natural mechanism in all living things which connects them to the cosmos. Man responds to earth tremors, air tides, and cosmic rays through the principle of resonance. The author discusses pyramid shapes, brain waves, life fields, cosmic law, alchemy, auras, psychokinesis, palmistry, graphology, hypnosis, and mysteries. He theorizes that there is a free dialogue of influence and information among all types of creation which makes all life part of one large organism. Watson visualizes man as sitting at the helm of "supernature." The work is a popular survey, not a scholarly or original work, but it is very thought-provoking.

1777 Watters, Barbara H., 1907- . Horary Astrology and the Judgment of Events. Washington, D.C.: Valhalla, 1973. 220p. Illus. LC 73-78387

1778 ________. Sex and the Outer Planets. Washington, D.C.: Valhalla Paperbacks, 1971. vii, 222p. Illus. $3.95 pa. LC 75-159422 ISBN 0-912356-03-0

1779 Waylen, Barbara. The Story of Frances Banks: The Great Seeker. London: Regency Press, 1972. 121p. Illus. Facsim. Plan £1.20 ISBN 0-7212-0268-3

1780 Webb, James, 1946- . The Occult Establishment. La Salle, Ill.: Open Court Pub. Co., 1975. $12.50 LC 75-22157 ISBN 0-912050-56-X
***

This work is a major new contribution to occult literature and is a companion book to the author's The Occult Underground [entry 1781]. It discusses how that underground emerged to install itself in even the most traditional 20th-century social/political institutions. Webb says that supposedly scientific or rationalist theories of man and the universe which appear to have nothing to do with irrational ideas, actually use many occult concepts. Webb is advisory editor of "The Occult," a 33-book series, and has contributed to the set, Man, Myth and Magic. The present work started out as an attempt to study the connection between Nazism and the occult. It eventually led the author into a much wider view, but much of this book retains Nazism as its focal point. Chapters discuss the following topics: the struggle for the irrational (the occult as rejected knowledge, World War I and the failure of rationalism); occultism in the 1920's (Prague, Vienna, Munich, Rudolf Steiner); the rise of youth movements and utopian groups in England during the 1920's and 1930's; the occult revival in Russia; Protocols of the Elders of Zion and anti-Semitism; the underground in power--Hitler; discovery of the unconscious (Freud, Jung, Wilhelm Fliess, Eranos Conferences); occultism in society and politics (Timothy Leary, Ken Kesey, drugs, Haight-Ashbury, Reich, Marcuse, R. D. Laing); and rationalists and irrationalists (fantastic literature, flying saucers, creative imagination). Webb concludes that most occultists "become trapped in their private worlds and produce sadly little evidence of the power of imagination." He says that while it is possible that the flight from reason will eventually expand the limits of human life, it is more likely that it will "shipwreck man on a desert island separated from all that is humanly satisfying by an ocean of illusion. Unreason exists to be made reasonable." Most chapters end with a bibliography of 100-150 citations (with occasional notes). This excellent work reflects a great deal of research and careful thought by Webb. It is a great pleasure to read an exciting, creative work that rests on such solid foundation.

1781 ________. The Occult Underground. La Salle, Ill.: Open
*** Court Pub. Co., 1974. (Rev. of author's "Flight from Reason." London: Macdonald and Co., 1971) 387p. Illus. Bibliog. Index $8.95 LC 73-22458 ISBN 0-912050-46-2

This work is a major new contribution to occult literature, and is an excellent study of 19th-century occultism. It is a companion volume to the author's The Occult Establishment [entry 1780]. The author discusses the general crisis of 19th century thought, and sees its most important aspect as the occult revival. More basically, the work attempts to discover what "the occult" in fact is. The following topics are discussed: Blavatsky, the Fox Sisters, the Parliament of Religions, Polish Messianism, Yeats, Theosophy, Annie Besant, Krishnamurti, Swami Vivekananda, the Paris Bohemians, Marquis Stanislas de Guaita, the Rosicrucians, the Mithraic cults, and the historical origin of secret traditions. The author concludes that failure to properly study this revival before has led to a partial view of the 19th century. Study of this period today will make it easier to understand the occult revival of the 1960's and 1970's. The work includes 56 pages of notes.

1782 Webb, Richard, 1915- . These Came Back. Introd. by Freda Morris. New York: Hawthorn Books, 1974. xix, 188p. Bibliog. Index $8.95 LC 73-21324 ISBN 0-8015-7580-X

The author, who was "Captain Midnight" on television, discusses 16 people whose behavior in this life he feels is due to previous lives. Hollywood psychic Gregg Tiffin told Webb that his, Webb's, career has been influenced by previous incarnations as a friend or relative of Genghis Khan, Marco Polo, Pope Leo I, and Leonardo da Vinci. He discusses these cases: a woman painter in Texas who recalled a life as a slave on a plantation near New Orleans; a minister's traveling to Tibet to confirm his previous life; a Roman Catholic priest's discussing memories of a period of persecution of his order in Italy; a man dreaming and getting information on the new incarnation of his dead daughter; actor Robert Middleton, who had a vision at the ruins of the city of Ephesus, where he saw himself near the Virgin Mary; an apartment house manager's memory of life 250,000 years ago as a cannibal in the Great Indian Desert. Webb also mentions events in 1954 on his CBS series "Captain Midnight," when the death of a stunt man began his interest in survival. The cases mentioned are not well researched or verified.

1783 ________. Voices from Another World; True Tales of the Occult. New York: Manor Books, 1973 (first pub. as "Great Ghosts of the West," Los Angeles: Nash, 1971). x, 278p. $.95 pa.

The author discusses psychic phenomena that have occurred in southern California. Topics discussed include a haunted house in Los Angeles investigated by Raymond Bayless, Attila von Szalay, and other ghosts and haunted houses. The information seems largely unverified, and there are some errors of fact. This is a very casual hodgepodge of cases. The author was "Captain Midnight" on television.

1784 Webre, Alfred L., 1942- , and Phillip H. Liss. The Age of Cataclysm. New York: Berkley Pub. Corp., 1974 (dist. by Putnam). xii, 303p. Illus. Includes bibliog. refs. Index $7.95 LC 74-79671 ISBN 0-399-11307-X

In the first part of this book, the authors say that the earth is entering a period of earthquakes, floods, and volcanoes, all due to the movement of the earth's tectonic plates. They discuss how to plot future plate movements. Also, they offer suggestions for coping with these events, saying a new, better global society will result. They propose a new Federal Party, abolishing Congress, and replacing the president with a committee of great minds. The second part of the book discusses predictions by psychics as to when disaster will strike. Webre is an environmentalist-lawyer; Liss is a Rutgers University professor of psychology.

1785 Webster, Hutton, 1875-1955. Magic: A Sociological Study. New York: Octagon Books, 1973 (orig. pub., Stanford, Calif.: Stanford University Press, 1948). xv, 524p. Includes bibliog. refs. $17 LC 73-4250

This work studies magic among preliterate peoples, stressing the operation of occult powers, magic, witches, divination, and the evil eye. Webster has used primary sources exclusively. His aim is to develop principles of magic with universal applicability. For four decades, he has tried to study and compare preliterate cultures in an objective fashion and his research must therefore be seriously considered.

1786 Wedeck, Harry Ezekiel, 1894- . Dictionary of Astrology. Secaucus, N. J. : Citadel Press, 1973 (also, London: Owen, 1973; New York: Philosophical Library, 1973). 189p. Illus. $3.95 LC 74-155465 ISBN 0-8065-0371-8

This work consists of over 1,000 entries, most of them very short. The book appears very similar in print and format to other occult dictionaries published by the Philosophical Library. The work includes astrological terms, biographies, and principles.

1787 ________, and Wade Baskin. Dictionary of Spiritualism. New York: Philosophical Library, 1971 (also London: Owen, 1971; also, New York: Bonanza Books, 1971). vi, 390p. $10 LC 73-104365 ISBN 0-8022-2039-8

This useful dictionary contains approximately 1,925 entries, covering biographies, sects, and terms. The same problems appear in this dictionary as with others put out by the same publisher. First, the definitions are short. This in itself is not bad, so long as the content is tightly packed with information. Sadly, such packing is very absent here. One can skim entry after entry and see very few dates, names, places or proper nouns. Also, all the Philosophical Library dictionaries are interchangeable in scope, regardless of their title. This one on "spiritualism" covers astrology, psychical research, religion, legends and mythology, and divination. As for the area the dictionary supposedly is covering, "spiritualism," many important names and terms are simply absent. Perhaps Wedeck would have done better to take all these dictionaries (spiritualism, astrology, satanism, mysticism, occult, and witchcraft), and combine them. As it is now, all the hard work of Wedeck and collaborator Wade Baskin in this dictionary will merely cause disappointment, or worse, anger.

1788 Wedel, Theodore Otto, 1892-1970. The Mediaeval Attitude Toward Astrology, Particularly in England. Folcroft, Pa.: Folcroft Library Editions, 1974 (reprint of New Haven: Yale University Press, 1920, ed.). Bibliog. Index (Orig. was author's thesis, Yale University, 1918) (Issued as vol. 60 of Yale Studies in English) $4.45 LC 74-30404 ISBN 0-8414-9593-9

1789 Weed, Joseph J. The Complete Guide to Oracle and Prophecy Methods. West Nyack, N. Y. : Parker Pub., 1971. 222p. $6.95 LC 74-164925 ISBN 0-13-160325-6

The author, a member of the Rosicrucian Order, discusses methods used by world-famous seers in history and present. He discusses the Delphic Oracle, the Gnostics, the Magi, the Lamas of Tibet, the Druids, training methods in the Eleusinian mysteries, the prophet schools of biblical times, Nostradamus, Roger Bacon, Mother Shipton, Merlin, Blavatsky, Cayce, Cheiro, Peter Hurkos, Jeane Dixon, Maurice Woodruff, Wolf Messing, techniques for reading the Akashic Record, the third eye, and the silver cord exercise.

1790 Weingarten, Henry. A Modern Introduction to Astrology: With the Most Frequent Questions about the Science Answered. New York: ASI Publishers, 1974. 85p. Illus. Bibliog. $1.95 pa. LC 74-15939 ISBN 0-88231-014-3

This is a very easy-to-read basic introduction to astrology. It is done in large print, with lots of space for the margins. Much of it consists of questions (one per page). These are especially questions a person not familar with astrology would ask, which are sometimes the toughest to answer.

1791 Welch, William Addams. Talks with the Dead. New York: Pinnacle Books, 1975. 176p. $1.50 pa.

The author discusses his experiences in recording spirit voices on tape, and covers the history of spirit recording. He mentions each of the many rational explanations for the voices, and gives a chapter on techniques for the reader to use in doing it himself.

1792 Wellard, James. The Search for Lost Worlds; An Exploration of the Lands of Myth and Legend Including Atlantis, Sheba and Avalon. London: Pan Books, 1975. 176p. Illus. Bibliog. £0.50 pa. ISBN 0-330-24253-9

1793 Wellesley, Gordon. Sex and the Occult. London: Souvenir
* Press, 1973. 224p. Illus. Bibliog. Index £2.60 ISBN 0-285-62095-9

In this work, the author attempts to give a picture of the sensual, cruel and sometimes terrifying beliefs and practices that have resulted from the attraction of sex and the occult for each other. These topics are discussed: the pagan heritage of sex in Egypt, India, and Greece, the werewolf, possession, incubi and succubi, drugs and sex, sex and the ecstasies, sex, occultism, and the quest and a global report of present-day cases of sex and occultism. The author has written a serious, reasoned book on the subject. He sees the sex-occultism interest as a desire for transcendence, a search for God, and says that wherever man's journey towards new thresholds leads, "sex and occultism will share the trip."

1794 Wells, Samuel Roberts, 1820-1875. How to Read Character;

A New Illustrated Handbook of Phrenology and Physiognomy for Students and Examiners with a Descriptive Chart. Rutland, Vt.: Tuttle, 1971 (also, Hemel Hempstead, England: Prentice-Hall, 1971; orig. pub., New York: Samuel R. Wells, 1871). 191p. Illus. $1.65 pa. LC 75-142766 ISBN 0-8048-0964-X

1795 Werner, Elizabeth M., ed. California Directory, Psychic Arts and Sciences, 1975-1976. Burbank, Calif.: Inner-Space Interpreters Services, 1975. 36p. $2 pa.

This work lists 66 organizations in California specializing in the occult. Each entry gives the following information: president, founder, executive director, or minister, the organization's aim, membership (open or closed, fees), public meetings, classes, services, and publications. Werner has sprinkled a few quotes and mention of selected recommended readings throughout the work at the bottom of the pages. This directory is useful, since California is the seed-bed for such groups. Arrangement is A to Z.

1796 * ________. Guide to Occult Periodicals, 1976. Burbank, Calif.: Inner-Space Interpreters Services, 1975. 48p. $2 pa.

This work lists 187 periodicals on the occult published in the United States and other English-speaking countries. Arrangement is A to Z. Each entry gives the following information: address, editor, frequency and price, and a short three- or four-line description of the magazine.

1797 ________. Guide to Occult Tape Recordings, 1976. Burbank, Calif.: Inner-Space Interpreters Services, 1975. 48p. $2 pa.

This work lists 568 tapes available on occult topics from 15 major distributors. There are nine other sources given, but none of their tapes are listed. Some of the entries have a brief annotation. Many of the 15 organizations' tapes record mediums used as channels for communications from outer space and beyond. There are also many yoga tapes. The Association for Research and Enlightenment's tapes are listed, as are those of Big Sur Recordings, the official recorder for the Esalen Institute and the Association for Humanistic Psychology. The tapes cover all psychic areas, as well as the occult.

1798 Weslager, C. A. Magic Medicines of the Indians. New York: Signet Books, 1974 (orig. pub., Somerset, N.J.: Middle Atlantic Press, 1973). 161p. Illus. Bibliog. Index $1.50 pa.

This book discusses the rituals, beliefs, medical folklore, use of herbs, potions and witchcraft, of the Delaware or Lenape Indians, who no longer exist. The author uses literary sources and a few survivors' accounts for sources. Weslager says that most of their practices were based on sound observation.

1799 West, John Anthony, and Jan Gerhard Toonder. The Case
* for Astrology. Harmondsworth, England: Penguin, 1973 (also, New York: Coward-McCann, 1970; orig. pub., London: Macdonald and Co., 1970). x, 310p. Illus. Bibliog. Index £0.50 pa. ISBN 0-14-003546-X

This book is a defense of astrology as a scientific study. These topics are discussed: origins (horoscope, evolution of astrology, symbolist interpretations of Egypt, oral tradition), Babylonian astrology's being accepted by the Greeks and Romans, Islam and the early Middle Ages, the period from de Cusa to Kepler, astrology in disgrace, the 19th- and 20th-century awakening of interest in astrology, objections to astrology by scientists and scholars, the evidence for astrology (statistical evidence, Michel Gauquelin, John M. Addey, cosmic influences upon living organisms, Frank A. Brown, Leonard J. Ravitz, Eugen Jonas, experiments of the Anthroposophists, celestial phenomena affecting radios, inorganic chemistry, cycles and sunspots, cymatics and wave forms, and the testing of astrologers), pop astrology (which the author strongly dislikes), the potential of astrology (medicine, criminology, economics, education, psychology, science), astrology and the press, the battle against ignorance and superstition, free will or no free will--the eternal question, and the Age of Aquarius. This is a very well-done survey with a pro-astrology slant.

1800 West, Mae. Mae West on Sex, Health and ESP. London: W.H. Allen, 1975. vi, 237p. Illus. Plates £3.50 ISBN 0-491-01613-1

After years of feeling that her career had been helped by outside forces, Mae West spent time developing psychic abilities. She gradually became clairvoyant and clairaudient. She discusses her psychic experiences, her philosophy of life, and her career.

1801 Westcott, William Wynn. Numbers--Their Occult Power and Mystic Virtues. 4th ed. London: Theosophical Publishing House, 1974 (previous ed., 1911). 131p. £1.50 ISBN 0-7229-5027-6

1802 Western Hemisphere Conference on Kirlian Photography, Acupuncture, and the Human Aura, 1st, N.Y., 1972: Galaxies of Life; The Human Aura in Acupuncture and Kirlian Photography. Ed. by Stanley Krippner and Daniel Rubin. New York: Gordon & Breach, 1973. xxviii, 182p. Illus. Bibliog. (Social Change Series) $12.50 LC 72-96759

This conference was sponsored by the Center for the Study of Social Change and the Foundation for Parasensory Investigation. Discussions center around Kirlian photography, the aura, acupuncture, and a measuring device called the biometer. Much of the conference involved the reading of papers written by Soviet scientists, even though these scientists were not in attendance. One can conclude from the papers that, as yet, no paranormal aspect to Kirlian photography can be proved. Yet, there are many possible theories that may link its effects to aura or astral body phenomena. The work is unevenly assembled and edited.

1803 * Wheatley, Dennis. The Devil and All His Works. London: Arrow Books, 1973 (also, New York: American Heritage Press, 1971; orig. pub., London: Hutchinson, 1971). 302p. Illus. (some color) Facsims. Maps Index £2.50 pa.

This work discusses mesmerism, faith healing, telepathy, divination, religions of the East and West, and esoteric movements (such as Rosicrucianism and theosophy). The main feature of the work is that it has 48 color and 167 black-and-white plates. This collection of examples of art, artifacts and folklore dealing with the devil is definitely designed for the coffee table. It is a highly readable work, suitable for browsing or use as a survey. However, much of the book is on magic and religion, not about the devil. Wheatley gathered his knowledge for this work from the 4,000 books in his library.

1804 ________, ed. Satanism and Witches: Essays and Stories. London: Sphere, 1974. 190p. Illus. (Dennis Wheatley Library of the Occult, vol. 21). £0.45 pa. ISBN 0-7221-9038-7

1805 White, Fraser. Handwriting Secrets. London: Everest Books Ltd., 1974. 160p. Facsims. £0.40 pa. ISBN 0-903925-05-2

1806 * White, John, ed. Frontiers of Consciousness: The Meeting Ground between Inner and Outer Reality. New York: Julian Press, 1974. 366p. Includes bibliog. refs. $8.95 LC 73-92173

The author has been director of education for the Institute of Noetic Sciences, and associate editor of Psychic magazine. He gives two papers on each of these 11 areas: transpersonal psychology, madness, biofeedback, meditation research, paraphysics, biotechnology, neurosciences, ecological consciousness, space travel and extraterrestrial life, death as an altered state of consciousness and psychical research. Most papers have a two-page introduction to the topic by White (giving associations dealing with the area, books to read, and a summary of the field's status), and include a bibliography at the end of the paper. Papers presented include: "The Ultraconscious Mind" by Stanley R. Dean, "Final Integration in the Adult Personality" by A. Reza Arasteh, "Visions, Voyages and New Interpretations of Madness" by Elsa First, "Hallucinations as the World of Spirits" by Wilson van Dusen, "Yogi in the Lab" by John White, "EEG Alpha Feedback and Subjective States of Consciousness" by Durand Kiefer, "Meditation Research: Its Personal and Social Implications" by Fred F. Griffith, "Intermeditation Notes: Reports from Inner Space" by Durand Kiefer, "Tracing ESP through Altered States of Consciousness" by Charles Honorton, "Unexplored

Areas of Parapsychology" by Charles W. Johnson, "Plants, Polygraphs and Paraphysics" by John White, "Messages to and from the Galaxy" by Oliver L. Reiser, "The New Biotechnology" by James B. Beal, "Energy Fields and the Human Body" by William Tiller, "Life, Death and Antimatter" by Henry Conway, "Of Time and Mind: From Paradox to Paradigm" by Keith Floyd, "Our Passport to Evolutionary Awareness" by Robert A. Smith, "Synergy and Social Pollution in the Communal Imagery of Mankind" by A. H. Esser, "Global Consciousness and the View from Space" by Edgar Mitchell, "Exobiology--Where Science Fiction Meets Science Fact" by John White, "Some Perspectives on Survival" by Thomas R. Tietze, and "Dying and Mystical Consciousness" by Russell Noyes. There is a three-page "About the Authors" section at the end of the book.

1807 White, Rhea A., and Laura A. Dale. Parapsychology: Sources of Information. Compiled under the auspices of the American Society for Psychical Research. Metuchen, N. J.: Scarecrow Press, 1973. 302p. Bibliogs. Index $8.50 LC 73-4853 ISBN 0-8108-0617-7
***

This work is a major new contribution to occult literature. The main section is an annotated bibliography arranged by subject, listing 282 books. The cut-off date is basically 1971, with only 10 titles listed that were published in 1972. There are also other sections, which complement the bibliographical section nicely. These sections discuss coverage of parapsychology in the general encyclopedias, list major psychical research centers, and cover the various parapsychology journals available. The section, "Scientific Recognition of Parapsychology," lists masters' theses and Ph. D. dissertations in the field, and mentions opportunities for graduate research. Appendices at the back of the work help locate books with glossaries or illustrations. Very helpful is an important list titled, "Books with over 100 Bibliographical References." This is an excellent work, reflecting hard, intelligent labor by White and Dale. The authors' credentials are ideal: White is director of information of the American Society for Psychical Research (ASPR) and a frequent, superior book reviewer for psychic journals and library periodicals; Dale is editor of the American Society for Psychical Research's Journal and Proceedings. Every student of the occult, every library and research organization, and any intelligent human of whatever avocation should definitely have this bibliography in his or her collection.

1808 White, Ruth, and Mary Swainson. Gildas Communicates: The Story and the Scripts. London: Spearman, 1971. 222p. £2.10 ISBN 0-85435-141-8

This is a record of over 13 years of mediumistic work, with help from a psychologist and later help of a supportive group. Chapters discuss the following topics: who is Gildas? the training of Ruth and Mary from 1962 to 1964, teaching, karma, reincarnation, groups and centers, and preparing for the new age.

1809 ________, and ________. Seven Inner Journeys. London: Spearman, 1974. 216p. £2.95 ISBN 0-85435-312-7

This book is an account of the emergence of Gildas in Ruth White's consciousness, covering the years 1957-1968. Gildas supposedly was a soul whose final incarnation was in the 14th century.

1810 Whyte, H. A. Maxwell. Dominion over Demons. Monroeville, Pa.: Banner Pub., 1973. 96p. $.95 pa. LC 73-81102 ISBN 0-88368-020-3

1811 Wickland, Carl A. Thirty Years among the Dead. Hollywood, Calif.: Newcastle Pub. Co., 1974 (orig. pub., 1924). 390p. $3.95 pa.

This work covers three decades of spirit communication, recording verbatim a large body of it. Messages from the other side discuss auras, spirits and crime, spirits and narcotics, suicide, life after death, Christian Science, and theosophy.

1812 Wickwar, John Williams, 1874- . Witchcraft and the Black Art; A Book Dealing with the Psychology and Folklore of the Witches. Detroit: Gale Research Co., 1973 (also, Ann Arbor, Mich.: Gryphon Books, 1971; orig. pub., London: H. Jenkins, 1925). 320p. $15 LC 71-151817

This work is a popular history written in a lively tone. The work describes the ceremony of initiation, casting spells, witch-hunting, and trials. It concentrates on witchcraft in England, with an outline of its history on the continent and in America.

1813 Wigglesworth, Harold. Astrology of Towns and Cities: The Municipal Corporation of England. Bournemouth, England: Astrological Association, 1973. 38p. Bibliog. £1 pa. ISBN 0-9502658-1-0

1814 Wilburn, Gary. Fortune Sellers. London: Scripture Union, 1973 (orig. pub., Glendale, Calif.: G/L Publications, 1972). 223p. £0.45 pa. ISBN 0-85421-346-5

1815 Wilkie, James H. P. The Gift Within: Experiences of a Spiritual Medium. Rev. ed. Introd. by Allen Spraggett. New York: New American Library, 1971 (orig. pub., 1967). $.75 pa.

1816 * Williams, Thomas Andrew, 1931- . Eliphas Levi, Master of Occultism. University of Alabama Press, 1975. x, 174p. Illus. Plates Bibliog. Index $9 LC 74-493 ISBN 0-8173-7061-7

This book discusses the great influence Levi had on Hugo, Baudelaire, Yeats, and Blavatsky, among others. He was an authority on Cabalistic numerology, which he studied as to its abstract meaning. Levi also studied angelology, metempsychosis (transmigration of souls), telepathy, déjà vu, and astrology. He saw the universe as One. His key work, The Dogma and Ritual of High Magic, came after years of solitary study. He also did interesting studies of the Tarot. One of the chapters in this book by Williams discusses Levi as poet.

1817 Wilson, Clifford A. Chariots Still Crash. New York: New American Library, 1975. 182p. Bibliog. $1.50 pa. LC 76-353863

The author, director of the Australian Institute of Archaeology, discusses von Däniken's Chariots of the Gods? and its theory that extraterrestrials influenced early civilizations. Wilson presents evidence that only men built the pyramids and Stonehenge. He says that von Däniken's airstrip in the Andes and golden library in Ecuador are imaginary. This book is a sequel to the author's Crash Go the Chariots. This time, Wilson does not just criticize von Däniken's theories, but gives solutions of his own to the mysteries of man's origin. Besides discussing various ancient structures, the author presents a very interesting chapter on methods used to date rocks and artifacts.

1818 ______. UFO's and Their Mission Impossible. New York: New American Library, 1975. x, 225p. Bibliog. $1.50 pa. LC 75-312250

The author talks of extradimensional beings who move into and out of our space and time levels through energy conversion. It is done by drawing blood and body fluids from animals, and electric energy from automobiles. Wilson says that most humans are in a posthypnotic state, waiting for a word from the humanoids to take over the earth.

1819 Wilson, Colin, 1931- . Mysterious Powers. London: Aldus Books, 1975 (dist. by Jupiter Books). 144p. Illus. (some color) Facsims. £3.95 ISBN 0-490-00332-X

This book was chiefly designed as a colorful pictorial work. The brief, survey-type text gives short information on a variety of topics, including wild talents, the will to power, wonder makers, magic at work, great magical revival, and three modern magicians (Dion Fortune, Rasputin, Gurdjieff).

1820 ______. The Occult; A History. New York: Vintage Books,
*** 1973 (also, St. Albans, England: Mayflower, 1973; New York: Random House, 1971; orig. pub., London: Hodder and Stoughton, 1971). 601p. Illus. Bibliog. Index $10 LC 72-7474

This work is a major new contribution to occult literature. The author feels that magic is the science of the future. He discusses magic, adepts, occultists, spiritualism, telepathy, clairvoyance, witchcraft, wolfmen, flying saucers, and mystics. The conclusions of the work are drawn after an intelligent consideration of the entire field of the occult. Wilson postulates the existence of a subconscious power or sixth sense in man which he calls "faculty X." He considers it the "latent power that human beings possess to reach beyond the present." Critics claim that this definition could apply to all creative persons, including poets and artists. They also claim the book is not well researched, and is written by a man not knowledgeable in the occult and psychic fields. The work is full of anecdotes and personal experiences the author has accumulated over a lifetime. In effect, the book is one man's intelligent, highly personal confrontation with a field which has always puzzled and intrigued him. The author has written nearly 30 books--novels, detective and spy stories, scholarly literary studies, and philosophical works.

1821 ______. Strange Powers. New York: Random House,
* 1973 (orig. pub., London: Latimer New Dimensions, 1973). 146p. Illus. Plates $6.95 LC 74-17353 ISBN 0-394-49585-3

This work is a sequel to The Occult (entry 1820). The book basically consists of three profiles: Robert Leftwich of Crowborough, Sussex, a dowser; Eunice Beattie, an expert in automatic writing; and Arthur Guirdham, who believes he is the reincarnation of a 13th-century Cathar. Also, Wilson discusses coincidence as being very important, since science consists of observing events that are repeated (such as the return of a comet). Wilson's introduction contains interesting material on his years of occult reading and gradual involvement in the field.

1822 ______. They Had Strange Powers. Garden City, N.Y.: Doubleday, 1975. (New Library of the Supernatural, vol. 2) $7.95 LC 75-16748

This work, part of the 20-volume series under the editorship of Christopher Evans, discusses Geller, Rasputin, and Gurdjieff, among others.

1823 Wilson, Joyce. The Complete Book of Palmistry. New York; London: Bantam, 1971. 192p. Illus. £0.35 pa. ISBN 0-552-65689-5

1824 Wiltshire, Kathleen. Ghosts and Legends of the Wiltshire Countryside. Ed. by Patricia M. C. Carrott. Illus. by Hilary Williams. Salisbury, England: Compton Russell Ltd., 1973. 126p. Illus. Col. map £1.50

1825 Windham, Kathryn Tucker. Jeffrey Introduces Thirteen More Southern Ghosts. Huntsville, Ala.: Strode Publishers, 1971. 128p. Illus. $5.95 LC 70-170663 ISBN 0-87397-016-0

1826 ________. Thirteen Georgia Ghosts and Jeffrey. Illus. by Frances Lanier. Huntsville, Ala.: Strode Publishers, 1973. ix, 154p. Illus. $5.95 LC 73-87004 ISBN 0-87397-041-1

This work is an interesting juvenile ghost collection. These stories cover from pre-Revolutionary War times ("Eternal Dinner Party") to this century ("Chanting Friars"). All are associated with real people, traditions, events, and places (for which photographs are provided). The author discusses the ghosts' activities and the situations that provoke them. Recommended for grades 5-9.

1827 ________. Thirteen Mississippi Ghosts and Jeffrey. Illus. by H. R. Russell. Huntsville, Ala.: Strode Publishers, 1974. 147p. Illus. $5.95 LC 74-15509 ISBN 0-87397-047-0

1828 Winer, Richard. The Devil's Triangle. New York: Bantam
* Books, 1975. 223p. Illus. Photos. Maps Bibliog. Index $1.50 pa. ISBN 0-553-08445-150

The author, a documentary filmmaker, recently made a film narrated by Vincent Price with the same title as this book. He claims to have researched the book for four years, sailing in his own sailboat to the perimeters of the region, flying over the area, and even visiting the sea floor 1,200 feet down. This journalistic survey covers these topics: the famous December 5, 1945, Flight 19, Columbus, other airplane disappearances, ship disappearances, the disappearance of the ship Cyclops in 1918, loss of the yawl Spray sailed alone by Joshua Slocum, the loss of sulphur ships, Christmastime hex, boat and plane crashes near Florida's beaches, ghost ships, and strange phenomena in the Triangle, some of it witnessed underwater by the author.

1829 Witch Figure; Folklore Essays by a Group of Scholars in England Honouring the 75th Birthday of Katharine M. Briggs. Ed. by Venetia Newall. London; Boston: Routledge and Kegan Paul, 1973. xiii, 239p. Illus. Includes bibliog. refs. LC 73-83077

This is a collection of 11 essays by British scholars in honor of folklorist Katharine Briggs. Discussions include the following: hostile magic, possession, witchcraft in Japan, Scandinavia, and Iceland, and witchcraft among primitive peoples. Two of the best studies are one on the Jew as a witch figure and another on Celtic fears of female divinities.

1830 Witch, Spirit, Devil. Comp. by A. F. Scott. London: White Lion Publishers, 1975. 189p. Illus. Plates Facsims. Bibliog. Index £3.75 ISBN 0-7274-0050-9

1831 Witchcraft, Magic and the Supernatural: The Weird World of the Unknown. London: Octopus Books, 1974. 176p. Illus. (chiefly color) Facsims. Bibliog. Index £1.95 ISBN 0-7064-0351-7

This work is of interest chiefly for its illustrations and graphics. In this day of cheap, bland covers, it is also a nice surprise to see a very attractive blue and white cover with an old print forming the back and front of the outside cover. This is perhaps the nicest cover design of all the books studied in the present bibliography. This book was printed in Hong Kong. The following essays appear in this work: "The Supernatural at Work" by Douglas Hill, "Devils, Demons and Evil Spirits" by Tessa Clark, "The Practice of Magic and Witchcraft" by Pat Williams, "The Forces of Nature" by Tessa Clark, "Ritual and Ceremony" by Frank Smyth, and "Magic in the Modern World" by Frank Smyth. This book contains some nude photographs.

1832 Witchell, Nicholas. Loch Ness and the Monster. Newport, England: Dixon, 1975 (orig. pub., Newport, England: Dixon, 1971). 31p. Illus. (chiefly color) Map £0.39 pa.

1833 ________. The Loch Ness Story. Rev. ed. Harmondsworth, England: Penguin, 1975 (previous ed., Lavenham, England: Dalton, 1974). 156p. Illus. Plates Facsim. Map $2.25 pa. LC 76-363224

This book discusses the Loch, the towns and people around it, the oldest account of the monster (A.D. 565, when St. Columba saved a victim from the creature), and also the wave of sightings after 1933 when a new road opened. One interesting addition to the usual accounts is reports of sightings of the monster on land. Witchell also covers use of underwater cameras and sonar.

1834 * Witches and Witchhunters: A Reprint of "Treatise of Witchcraft" by Alexander Roberts (1616), "Discovery of Witches" by Mathew Hopkins (1647), and "Scottish Witchcraft Trials" by J.W. Brodie (1891). Foreword by A.E. Green. Norwood, Pa.: Norwood Editions, 1973 (reprint of 3 works; 1st orig. printed by N.O. for S. Man, London; 2nd orig. printed for R. Royston, London; 3rd orig. printed at Chiswick Press, London). $9 LC 73-14633 ISBN 0-88305-000-5

This work covers the great witch hunts of the late medieval and early modern period, beginning in southern Europe in the 15th century and spreading gradually north and west across the Atlantic until they died out at the beginning of the 18th century. The writer of the foreword, Green, states that these persecutions show how a popular belief can develop into a coherent and systematic ideology shared by king and peasant alike. The work provides a good basis for comparing witch trials and belief in Scotland and England, and the selections are also interesting for psychological and social reasons. Roberts reports an outbreak of witchcraft in the parish of King's Lynn, resulting in the killing of Mary Smith in 1616. The first section discusses the theology of witchcraft; the second part is an account of Mary's evils against her victims. Hopkins reports a 1645 trial, where three people were condemned to death in Essex. Then, he studied Suffolk and other areas. He was accompanied on his journeys by Calvinist lawyer John Sterne and a woman called Phillips, who searched the bodies of the accused for witches' marks. Brodie reports on Elizabeth (or Bessie) Dunlop (1576), Lady Munro and Mr. Hector Munro (1590), and Agnes Sampson (1591).

1835 * Wolf, Leonard. A Dream of Dracula; In Search of the Living Dead. Boston: Little, Brown and Co., 1972. 352p. Illus. Photos. Bibliog. $8.95 LC 72-7337

The author discusses literary history, criticism, and philosophy of the vampire in the past and today. These topics are discussed: symbolism, Gilles de Rais, Christopher Lee, Whitby Harbor, Vlad IV, Bram Stoker, Bela Lugosi, John Caradine, Transylvania, the modern scene, and Dracula films. The author stretches his points a bit sometimes. For example, his chapter on the modern scene even sees Mick Jagger as a sort of modern vampire.

1836 Wood, John Maxwell. Witchcraft and Superstitious Record in the South-Western District of Scotland: Witchcraft, Witch Trials, Fairy Lore, Brownie Lore, Wraiths, Warnings, Death Customs, Funeral Ceremony, Ghost Lore, Haunted Houses. Illus. by John Copland. Wakefield, England: EP Publishing, 1975 (orig. pub., Dumfries, England: J. Maxwell, 1911). 355p. xvii p. Illus. Index £4.95 ISBN 0-7158-1139-8

1837 Woodruff, Maurice, 1916- . Probing the Unknown; The Personal Experiences of a Psychic. New York: Cowles, 1971. 198p. Illus. $5.95 LC 79-118897 ISBN 0-402-12631-9

The author is the son of a well-known British sensitive. Some of the book is autobiographical, but most discusses his predictions concerning well-known people, including Peter Sellers. The author discusses various methods for telling fortunes--cards, palmistry, telepathy, phrenology, and dice. He also discusses astrology. The book does not delve very deeply into any of these topics.

1838 _______. The Secret of Foretelling Your Own Future. London: Pan Books, 1971 (also, New York: New American Library/World, 1969; orig. pub., London: Cassell, 1969). 141p. Illus. £0.20 pa. ISBN 0-330-02735-2

This book discusses cards, dice, palmistry, tea leaves, astrology, Napoleon's Prediction Spinner, and phrenology. Woodruff feels that by using these the reader can predict his own future.

1839 Woods, Richard. The Devil. Chicago: Thomas More Press, 1973. 142p. $5.95

The author is a Dominican priest who lectures on the occult in Chicago. One 50-page section reviews recent books on demonology published in the United States. Other topics discussed include these: the church and the devil, exorcism, the philosophy of evil, and theories of Teilhard de Chardin.

1840 _______. The Occult Revolution; A Christian Meditation New York: Seabury Press, 1974 (orig. pub., New York: Herder and Herder, 1971). $2.50 pa. LC 73-21568 ISBN 0-8164-2584-1

The author, a Catholic priest, takes a scholarly, theoretical approach to the occult, discussing witchcraft, astrology, and occult orders. He discusses the effects of the occult on the life of the Christian, and tries to understand how the failure of the Church has turned young Americans to the occult. He feels the occult has possibilities for opening new areas of mental and spiritual progress, areas which have been hidden by the Church's exaggerated attack against the occult. Woods also emphasizes the dangers of the occult, saying it becomes just another ideology, and can take over one's personality.

1841 Woods, William Howard, 1916- , comp. Casebook of Witchcraft: Reports, Depositions, Confessions, Trials, and Executions for Witchcraft During a Period of Three Hundred Years. New York: Putnam, 1974. 216p. $6.95 LC 74-79672 ISBN 0-399-11403-3

1842 _______. History of the Devil. London: W. H. Allen, 1973 (also, New York: Putnam, 1974; also, St. Albans, England: Panther, 1975). 251p. Illus. Bibliog. Index £3.50

This book has no table of contents, and seems rambling and not well organized. However, it has a very scholarly tone. The author sees the devil as the remains of an old folk religion, where, as a god of nature, he was neither good nor bad. He blames Christianity for distorting the nature of the devil, persecuting heresies, and suffering some of its own priests to practice sorcery. The illustrations trace the historical development of pictorial work on the devil.

1843/4 Worth, Valerie. The Crone's Book of Words. St. Paul, Minn.: Llewellyn Pubns., 1971. 155p. Illus. $2 pa. ISBN 0-87542-891-6

The author is a graduate of Swarthmore College, and has published poetry in various magazines. This book contains spells, charms, talismans, rites, inscriptions, incantations, and magical verses for various occasions and purposes. There are four parts to the work: spirit, world, conjuror, and cosmos. This is one of those "cute" books with each page almost all white throughout the work; there are very few words per page.

1845 Wright, John Stafford. Christianity and the Occult. Chicago:

Moody Press, 1972 (orig. pub., London: Scripture Union, 1971). 160p. Illus. $.75 pa.

This book is aimed at the reader who has discovered he is psychic, often against his will. Wright considers psychic ability only a small part of human nature. He discusses the relationship of the psychic and the occult, spirits, and the responsibility of the psychic; he mentions cases of current psychic phenomena. He says that the Bible is an up-to-date source to use in understanding psychic matters, even though it is often distorted by ministers. Wright recommends ways in which to reconcile any conflict the reader may have between his Christian teaching and his psychic experiences.

1846 Wright, Leoline L. Reincarnation; A Lost Chord in Modern Thought. Additional chapters by Helen Todd and Steele O'Hara. Wheaton, Ill.: for Point Loma Publications by Theosophical Pub. House, 1975. viii, 113p. (Theosophical Manual, no. 2) $2.25 pa. LC 74-18350 ISBN 0-8356-0453-5

This book discusses the views of theosophy with respect to reincarnation, and answers criticisms of the reincarnation concept.

1847 Wright, Theon. The Open Door; A Case History of Automatic Writing. New York; Ballantine, 1973 (orig. pub., New York: John Day, 1970). 373p. Illus. Facsims. Includes bibliog. refs. $1.50 pa.

This book presents the work of three generations. Seances were run first under Theon Wright's mother Adelle; then under his grandmother; and then throughout the long marriage of George and Nella Wright. Automatic writings came, which were recorded as messages from the "Voice of the Master." Theon Wright calls it the "New Dispensation," which deals with the philosophy of the self or cosmic consciousness. He begins and ends his book with discussions of psychology, new theology, and existentialism in relation to his parents' work. The book also mentions various life after death theories and surveys the early history of spiritualism.

1848 Wright, Thomas, 1810-1877. Narratives of Sorcery and Magic, from the Most Authentic Sources. 2nd ed. Detroit: Gale Research Co., 1974 (also, Grand River Books, 1971; orig. pub., London: R. Bentley, 1851). 2 vols. $24 (set) LC 73-19779

1849 Wulff, Wilhelm Theodor H., 1912-1945. Zodiac and Swastika; How Astrology Guided Hitler's Germany. Foreword
* by Walter Laqueur. New York: Coward, McCann and Geoghegan, 1973 (orig. pub., London: Arthur Barker, 1973).

192p. (Translation of "Tierkreis und Hakenkreus") $5. 95
LC 73-78733 ISBN 0-698-10547-8

The subtitle of the book can be misleading, since Hitler never really is discussed. Wulff's contacts were through Heinrich Himmler, for whom he became personal astrologer. He was introduced to Kersten, Himmler's personal masseur and close friend. Kersten put him in touch with high S. S. men such as Nebe and Schellenberg, and even with Hitler. Himmler asked him questions--how long would the Führer live? how would he die? Also, Himmler asked for astrological profiles of himself, Hitler, Eisenhower, Churchill, and Montgomery. One of the author's aims in writing this was to show that he was not pro-Nazi. There is no real documentation in this book, and not one horoscope is illustrated. Chapters discuss the following topics: I become an astrologer, Herbert Volck, Captain Lohmann, in the hands of the Gestapo, Felix Kersten, find Mussolini, my first meeting with Walter Schellenberg, lunch with Heinrich Himmler, counterespionage headquarters in Berlin; Himmler and July 20, 1944, Count Bernadotte's mission, the end approaches, and Heinrich Himmler's final orders.

1850 Wyckoff, James. Franz Anton Mesmer: Between God and
* Devil. Englewood Cliffs, N. J. : Prentice-Hall, 1975. 176p. Illus. Index $8. 95 LC 75-11759

This book discusses Mesmer's life and work, his predecessors, the Mesmerist movement, and his medical and spiritual disciples, many of whom Mesmer himself disclaimed. The author is decidedly pro-Mesmer. Medical disciples mentioned include John Elliotson and James Esdaile. Mesmer's chief idea supposedly was to transfer animal magnetism to cure nervous disorders that were not psychotic. However, Wyckoff claims that Western rationalism is wrong in limiting him to this. He says that Mesmer discussed a unique psychic phenomenon--the vibrational character of natural processes. Wilhelm Reich is mentioned as a descendant of Mesmer, as are theosophy and Christian Science.

1851 Wynne, Barry. Behind the Mask of Tutankhamen. New York: Taplinger Pub. Co., 1973. 201p. $7. 50 LC 72-7716 ISBN 0-8008-0719-7

The author is a reporter for the BBC television network. He uses contemporary dispatches to the London Times, reconstructed dialogues, and interviews to write his story about Howard Carter's expedition to Egypt. Carter's sponsor, Lord Carnarvon, was very interested in the occult, and visited seers Cheiro and Velma, who predicted danger if the tomb was entered. Carnarvon died five weeks after the tomb was opened from a mosquito bite (in exactly the same place on his face where the Pharaoh had a mark). The journalists then went wild about a curse. The author describes the tomb well and covers the deaths of those associated with Carnarvon.

1852 Yates, Frances Amelia. The Rosicrucian Enlightenment.
*** St. Albans, England: Paladin, 1975 (orig. pub., London; Boston: Routledge and Kegan Paul, 1972). 315p. Illus. Plates Facsims. Map Index £1.50 pa. ISBN 0-586-08221-2

This work is a major new contribution to occult literature. The author sees the Rosicrucian movement as the chief aspect of European culture between the Renaissance and the scientific revolution in the 17th century. The Rosicrucian goals of spiritual enlightenment and intellectual knowledge influenced Bacon, Newton, Comenius, Descartes, and the Royal Society of England. Yates discusses the "Rosicrucian Manifestos," which most scholars find ridiculous. He sees them as important, and links them to major political movements in the early 17th century. This is especially seen in the move to place Elector Palatine Frederick V and his English princess on the Bohemian throne. The scheme failed in 1620, and Rosicrucian literature disappears after 1620.

1853 Your Day-by-day Zodiac International Horoscope (annual). New York: Essandess Special Edition (a div. of Simon & Schuster). 12 vols. 143p. ea. $.95 pa. ea.

Each volume of this set is on a different sign of the zodiac, and gives the following information: character analysis, compatibility guide, general forecast for the year, monthly and day-by-day forecast (major section), moon charts, and rising sign charts.

1854 Your Solar Horoscope (annual). New York: Dell. 223p. $.95 pa.

For each of the 12 signs, the author gives the following information: general features of the sign (personal initiative, finances, home and family, love and recreation, work and health, partnership, tax and estate matters, philosophy and religion, ambitions and prestige, friendship, private affairs), the year's prospects in general for the signs, and month-by-month forecasts for the signs.

1855 Zarchy, Harry, and Roger Lewis. Color and the Edgar Cayce Readings. Virginia Beach, Va.: A.R.E. Press, 1973. 48p. Bibliog. $1.25 LC 73-175202 ISBN 0-87604-068-7

1856 Zaretsky, Irving I., and Mark P. Leone, eds. Religious
* Movements in Contemporary America. Princeton, N.J.: Princeton University Press, 1975. xxxvi, 837p. Bibliog. $25

Zaretsky, a professor at Yale Law School, and Leone, an anthropology professor at Princeton, have included 27 papers, each by a different author. The papers were taken from conferences in 1970 and 1971. The work serves as an excellent study of marginal religion in the United States. In an introductory essay, the editors mention features found most often in the minor religions by the 26 other authors. They view these religions as translations of "the individual's enthusiasm for change into a change that can be tolerated." Papers presented in the book include these: Raymond Price discussing mystical experiences as easing youth into adult roles, J. Stillson Judah discussing Hare Krishna, Dick Anthony and Thomas Robbins discussing Meher Baba, Edward Moody on modern satanism, June Macklin on New England spiritualism and Mexican spiritism, Marcello Truzzi's "Toward a Sociology of the Occult," Harriet Whitehead on Scientology, Vivian Garrison on Puerto Rican Catholics and Pentecostals, Zaretsky on language and social organization in spiritualist churches, E. Mansell Pattison on personality, glossolalia, and faith healing, Janet Dolgin and Mark Leone on Mormons, John A. Wilson on a historical study of marginal religious movements, and Roger Lauer's "Medium for Mental Health" (on medium Dave Johnson and his control, Dr. Wagner, a former psychiatrist, who gave mediumship training to six psychiatrists including Lauer). The work closes with a 43-page bibliography.

AUTHOR INDEX

(includes authors, joint authors, editors, illustrators, translators, and writers of introductions, prefaces, forewords, afterwords)

TITLE INDEX

(all initial articles have been dropped)

SUBJECT INDEX